Special Edition
Using
Groove®
2.0

Bill Pitzer

CONTENTS AT A GLANCE

que®

800 East 96th Street
Indianapolis, Indiana 46240

SPECIAL EDITION USING GROOVE® 2.0

Copyright © 2002 by Que Publishing

International Standard Book Number: 0-7897-2677-7

Library of Congress Catalog Card Number: 2002100462

Printed in the United States of America

First Printing: July 2002

This product is printed digitally on demand.

Trademarks

Warning and Disclaimer

Publisher
David Culverwell

Acquisitions Editor
Loretta Yates

Development Editor
Sean Dixon

Managing Editor
Thomas Hayes

Project Editor
Carol Bowers

Copy Editor
Kate Givens

Indexer
Rebecca Salerno

Proofreader
Linda Seifert

Technical Editor
Anonymous

Team Coordinator
Cindy Teeters

Interior Designer
Anne Jones

Cover Designer
Anne Jones

Page Layout
Brad Lenser

Graphics
Stephen Adams
Tammy Graham
Oliver L. Jackson, Jr.
Laura Robbins

TABLE OF CONTENTS

III Creating Your Own Custom Tools

10 The Foundation for Development: the Groove Development Kit (GDK) 305

ABOUT THE AUTHOR

Bill Pitzer earned his MBA from Xavier University and his Bachelor of Science degree in Computer Science from Westminster College. Cutting his teeth on the AS/400 in the early 1990s he migrated to the PC platform a short time later. Starting Web development in 1995, he's rounded himself out by obtaining both his MCSD and MCSE+I certifications. Currently residing in Cincinnati, Ohio, Bill spends his spare time teaching his son Liam advanced C++ development.

DEDICATION

Dedicated to my wife, Rose, my son Liam, and to all the people out there making great strides in the peer-to-peer technology arena.

ACKNOWLEDGMENTS

A special thanks goes out to all those who made this possible. First and foremost, I'd like to thank my wife for her patience with my severe mood swings and helping me get the figures organized. More thanks go to Ashok Hingorani, whose upbeat personality and extensive Groove knowledge helped immensely. For more technical proofing, a big thanks goes out to Pat Pesch and the excellent Groove support staff including Colleen, Lance, and Greg. Last but not least, a big debt of gratitude goes out to all the other Groove Networks employees who helped me on a moment's notice in my time of need including: Richard Eckles, the marketing guru who pulled a few strings for me; Jill Guardi, who offers excellent training courses; Alex Harwitz, the "Network Services guy"; and finally Ryan Hoppe, who responded to my desperate pleas for help. For helping make this all possible, I also must not forget Rich Wallace, whose vision helped make this all possible. The Groove community is getting larger everyday and it's the direct result of the hard work put in by all the Groove Networks employees and the entire Groove community.

WE WANT TO HEAR FROM YOU!

As the reader of this book, *you* are our most important critic and commentator. We value your opinion and want to know what we're doing right, what we could do better, what areas you'd like to see us publish in, and any other words of wisdom you're willing to pass our way.

As an associate publisher for Que Publishing, I welcome your comments. You can email or write me directly to let me know what you did or didn't like about this book—as well as what we can do to make our books better.

Please note that I cannot help you with technical problems related to the *topic* of this book. We do have a User Services group, however, where I will forward specific technical questions related to the book.

When you write, please be sure to include this book's title and author as well as your name, email address, and phone number. I will carefully review your comments and share them with the author and editors who worked on the book.

Email: feedback@quepublishing.com
Mail: Associate Publisher
          Que Publishing
          800 East 96th Street
          Indianapolis, IN 46240 USA

For more information about this book or another Que title, visit our Web site at www.quepublishing.com. Type the ISBN (excluding hyphens) or the title of a book in the Search field to find the page you're looking for.

INTRODUCTION

WHO THIS BOOK IS FOR

Groove is a new collaborative software package from Groove Networks, Inc. It leverages the power of the Internet and peer-to-peer technology to create the perfect collaborative environment for businesses and individuals. The Internet enables people to make connections regardless of geographic location. At the same time, the peer-to-peer network structure Groove uses enables communication between participants without the need to pass through a central server. Combining these two enables communication regardless of the distance between participants and in a dynamic fashion without centralized control, which mimics how human beings naturally interact.

The Groove application is built using peer-to-peer technology, the same technology used to power many of the popular instant messaging software applications. Groove has taken the technology from its role in personal consumer applications and geared it toward business applications. Groove offers participants the capability to collaborate in real-time with text chat, shared resources, and shared applications. It would be unfair to classify Groove as just another software application. Groove is an entire framework designed to provide a secure environment for participants using the many tools provided. Using the Groove Development Toolkit, businesses can extend the application further by creating their own custom applications that will share the security and other features the framework provides.

This book is targeted at power users and developers who want to truly leverage the power of the Groove application. Most users can easily grasp the materials in Chapters 1 through 8 with little or no development knowledge. These chapters demonstrate how to take full advantage of the Groove Workspace features provided "out of the box" from an end-user's perspective. System administrators who plan on using the Groove Management Server locally or hosted by Groove will find the overview given in Chapter 9 useful. In Chapters 10 through 13, you'll need some experience with XML and JavaScript to fully understand these chapters that deal with custom tool development. However, these chapters present a hands-on approach using tools provided with the Groove Development Kit, so even programming novices can begin developing custom tools right away. These chapters show how to develop a simple tool step-by-step and also provide more in-depth information to guide those striving to learn more about advanced development topics.

HOW THIS BOOK IS ORGANIZED

This book is divided into three parts. Part I, "Understanding, Installing, and Configuring Groove," explains the concepts that are the underpinnings of the Groove framework. In Chapter 1, we'll give you some of the history behind peer-to-peer technology and the Groove application. In Chapter 2, we'll explain how to install Groove and create your first account.

In Part II, "Using Groove to Collaborate," we demonstrate how you can used shared spaces and the tools provided to communicate with groups of other members. Chapter 3 gives you an understanding of how to set up your shared space and other tasks needed to start communicating with others. Chapter 4 gives an in-depth look at what shared spaces are in Groove while Chapters 5 through 8 describe the tools available for use in these shared spaces. Taking the administrative tasks a step farther, in Chapter 9 we detail Groove's Enterprise Network Services and how to use them to manage your own Groove domains.

In Part III, "Creating Your Own Custom Tools," we begin discussing how you can tailor Groove by creating your own custom tools. This begins in Chapter 10 when we introduce you to the Groove Development Kit. In Chapter 11 we'll use the utilities provided with the GDK to create a sample tool used in small focus groups. Chapter 12 introduces you to several more advanced tool concepts that you may want to leverage in your own tool. Finally, in Chapter 13 we'll show you how to share your tools with others by demonstrating how to publish your tools for others to download and install.

CONVENTIONS USED IN THIS BOOK

This book uses various stylistic and typographic conventions to make it easier to use:

Convention	Meaning
Italic	New terms and phrases when initially defined
`Monospace`	Parts of code, Web addresses, and filenames
`Bold Monospace`	Information that you type
➡	Indicates the continuation of a long code line from the previous line

NOTE

A Note indicates additional information beyond the principal discussion that will give you a larger understanding of the current topic.

TIP

Tips suggest easier or alternative methods of executing a given procedure. Tips introduce techniques to simplify potentially complicated tasks or bypass needless effort.

CAUTION

Cautions warn you against hazardous activities that could potentially cause you to lose part or all of your work, or even damage the system itself. Always read each Caution carefully.

At the end of several chapters, you'll find projects to further enhance your knowledge of Groove Workspace. In Chapter 2 you'll see how to configure your firewall software to allow Groove to work most efficiently. At the end of Chapter 3, you'll see how to clone and modify one of the existing Groove skins. At the end of Chapter 10, you'll learn how to debug your tool code using Microsoft Visual InterDev to add a breakpoint. Finally, at the end of Chapter 13, you'll configure Microsoft Internet Information Server to work correctly when publishing your own Groove tools.

To download the code files for the example focus group tool demonstrated in the last part of the book, go to http://www.quepublishing.com. Type the book's ISBN (0789726777) into the Search field to go to this book's Web page. There you will find a link to download the source code.

UNDERSTANDING, INSTALLING, AND CONFIGURING GROOVE

CHAPTER 1

What Is Groove?

In this chapter

A Successful Industry Veteran's Vision for Peer-to-Peer Technology

An introduction to Groove would not be complete without an introduction to its creator, Ray Ozzie. Many refer to Ozzie, who is credited with the initial creation of Lotus Notes, as the "Father of Groupware." When Lotus Notes hit the market in 1989, it was not greeted with open arms because many business leaders considered it to be overpriced. "Overpriced" is a relative term in this context, but many organizations still thought its actual return on investment was questionable. Its collaborative capabilities were too unorganized for them. Many wondered where value could be found in a collection of unstructured data created and organized in a free-form fashion by users. They believed that relational databases and the hierarchical records stored in mainframes held the truly valuable information and countless resources were expended to keep it that way.

Despite this cool reception, Ozzie believed his product would revolutionize the way businesses worked. Ray knew that his software could enable companies to communicate more efficiently than they had ever done in the past. His perseverance eventually paid off; Lotus Notes has become one of the most successful software packages ever released.

Now Ozzie has a new vision, one he calls Groove. Given his previous success with Lotus Notes, his claims that Groove will revolutionize the way people communicate are not surprising. Ozzie believes that Groove and its capability to allow "innovation at the edge of the network" will fill the gap left by traditional groupware applications, which generally fall short of providing the real-time communication capabilities that are often necessary for efficient collaboration. In addition, these groupware applications often do not provide truly dynamic facilities to encourage ad hoc communication. Using something called *peer-to-peer* technology, he hopes Groove will enable the real-time, ad hoc communications that many businesses desperately need. In this chapter, you'll get the background on Groove and the technology behind it that's essential for understanding what the product is truly intended to accomplish.

"Innovation at the Edge of the Network"

"The advantage, proponents say, is that communication within the network is like a board meeting without the presence of an overbearing and rules-obsessed chairman."

—"The Great Leveler, Part Two" by Art Jahnke

Advocates of peer-to-peer computing often point to the technology's capability to provide "innovation at the edge of the network." So what exactly does this mean? Where is the edge? Let's start by looking again at one of the most mainstream peer-to-peer applications, Napster.

Napster is a music-swapping service that allows individuals to share music files, primarily in the MP3 format. The file-sharing technology it uses is far from revolutionary, but its quick adoption was nothing short of extraordinary. After its introduction to the public in August 1999, its membership rolls quickly swelled to several million users. File-sharing technology is nothing new. You've probably used it at your office, at work, or perhaps even at home. The technology has enjoyed such rapid growth because it utilizes "innovation at the edge of the network." No new network had to be constructed for Napster to function; it utilized consumer's already established Internet connections. Additionally, it really did not depend on monstrous servers storing millions of music files. It used the existing capacity already established on individual's home (and yes, in many cases, work) desktop machines. These are the machines at the "edge of the network."

These machines at the edge of the network are where Ray Ozzie sees so much potential. Desktop computers at home and work represent to him *high-function endpoints* with under-utilized capabilities. A high-function endpoint in this case is the peer computer with its processing and storage capabilities. Contrast this to an endpoint with a limited amount of processing or storage capability, such as a simple router. Napster was able to leverage the tremendous amount of storage individuals had on their desktop machines. Because they were already storing all these music files out there already, why not use the storage capacity of these individual machines? These client machines had already connected to the Internet, so why not use some of their bandwidth? Just about any class of desktop machine has the processing power to run a Napster client, a simple application responsible for cataloging available music files. Again, why not utilize the programmatic and processing capability on each individual machine?

At the edge of the network, users can realize efficiencies not possible in traditional server-based systems. By tapping into previously underutilized resources, this system can theoretically continue to grow without new storage, processing, or networking requirements. This can make peer-to-peer applications cost effective, but not without some of the disadvantages mentioned before. Although the advantages of a peer-to-peer structure rely on a relatively simple concept, that is, "Use what is already there," this is easier said than done. Ray Ozzie hopes Groove becomes the enabler that helps companies create their own "innovation at the edge of the network."

Groove's Groupware Roots

To understand where Groove is coming from, an understanding of Ray Ozzie's early experience with software creation is helpful. Ray Ozzie's first exposure to a collaboration tool was with his work on a mainframe system called PLATO Group Notes in the late '70s. A rather basic system, it provided some rudimentary messaging features. As the name suggests, it enabled the basic posting of notes to other users in a secure manner. The features of this software left quite an impression on Ozzie, so much that he began to work further on a similar system during his subsequent employment at Digital Equipment Corporation. He took this idea and began planning his own PC-based version of the system. Later, under contact from Lotus Development Corporation, Ray took the PLATO Group Notes concept to the PC and bolstered it with additional features. It soon came to be known as Lotus Notes and the category of software known as *groupware* was born.

1

By creating a new category of software, Lotus Notes revolutionized the industry. Not only did others try to copy Lotus Notes, but they also rushed to develop products for integration with it. In addition to Lotus Notes' worldwide success, it has spawned a multibillion dollar market for complementary products. It is tough to find many other products today that have been so inextricably linked to one individual. Regardless of the label attached to this type of software, groupware or otherwise, Ray Ozzie's initial purpose was to find a way to build and foster relationships within and across an organization. He didn't need a fancy term like groupware to describe it; he just knew it was valuable. Now, Ozzie wants to take the collaborative possibilities inherent in the concept of groupware and fully realize them in a new product, Groove.

THE UNVEILING OF GROOVE

After three years of top-secret development in Beverly, Massachusetts, Groove has been released as the first product of Ray Ozzie's newest company, Groove Networks. The Groove product and services are supposed to enable direct business and personal interaction over the Internet. So what's new about this? Email and instant messaging already enable this type of interaction. Perhaps the collaborative functionality Groove provides isn't so revolutionary, but what's really important is "how" Groove does it.

Groove's architecture is built on the concept of peer-to-peer (P2P) networking. This is quite a departure from the Lotus Notes client/server architecture that depended on a central store of documents. Peer-to-peer applications, the most popular of these being file-sharing applications such as Gnutella or Napster, have come under fire for many different reasons. Most recently, the media attention highlighting the illegal trading of copyrighted materials over peer-to-peer networks has cast the technology in a bad light. In addition, the lack of centralized control mechanisms in peer-to-peer applications means that they tend to have an unorganized structure, in stark contrast to the precisely designed, tightly controlled applications corporate systems require to maintain effective security. So in effect, Groove Networks already has had to combat these two widely held arguments against peer-to-peer technology before Groove was even shipped. Whether the negative connotations attached to peer-to-peer technology are deserved or not, they are definitely an obstacle Groove will have to overcome.

Realizing there might be misunderstandings about what peer-to-peer technology is about, Groove Networks is fast becoming the most outspoken advocate of the value of peer-to-peer technology for use within the corporate space. Groove Networks is not only very much involved in producing their own software, but also actively working on augmenting current peer-to-peer technology standards to support Groove's own software needs. A case in point involves Groove's use of the Device Presence Protocol (DPP). Groove needed a way to efficiently discover other Groove users. Groove helped formulate this specialized network protocol exclusively for their Groove client's needs. Aside from some of Groove Network's groundbreaking technical work, Ray Ozzie truly epitomizes someone who believes in the product his company creates. Ray wholeheartedly believes that current collaborative software does not do enough to enable the types of ad hoc, real-time communications that many businesses desperately need. This excerpt from the *Fortune* magazine article "Software's Humble Wizard Does it Again" shows how Ozzie's venture has gained more than just an inquisitive passing interest in the business community:

> "[Ozzie's] creation is Groove, software that enables small ad hoc groups of workers to get together quickly online to collaborate on projects. Three years in the making, Groove is emerging just in time to supercharge the trend toward peer-to-peer computing, the first great evolution of software beyond the Web."

So why do we need to go beyond the Web? The Web challenges the ways companies do business, and this challenges businesses to rethink the way things are done. Definitely a revolution in itself, the World Wide Web still lacks the real-time interaction necessary for certain types of business functions. Many businesses using the Web only utilize the technology as a place for static, unchanging content to be presented. Even using Web-based discussion groups for posts by business personnel often ends up being no more, or even less, effective than a standard email would be for encouraging communication. The Web has not turned out to be the answer for every business need. Given the intense competitive environment, collaboration in many industries needs to be in real time. Peer-to-peer is the technology that can help software solutions overcome the Web's own limitations.

PEER-TO-PEER TECHNOLOGY: THE CORE OF GROOVE

Groove's use of peer-to-peer technology has definitely set it apart from the rest of the groupware applications available. These applications typically rely on a central source of data, whereas Groove's decentralized structure puts it in a class of its own. In order to efficiently use Groove the way it's intended to work, you should first understand a little about peer-to-peer technology, the core of Groove. However, settling on the "correct" definition of peer-to-peer technology is a rather formidable task. A pretty basic definition states that a peer-to-peer network consists of "peers" that are joined in a free-form fashion. So what exactly is a peer? The term usually describes our co-workers or those at the same level as ourselves in our place of employment. When used in the context of a computer network, "peer" carries much the same meaning. The notion here is that each entity in a network has an equivalent role or responsibility. This means that each node in the network is treated as an equal to all the others. From a technical perspective, this means that each entity in the network is treated equally.

It might be easiest to begin to define peer-to-peer by explaining what it is not. A network with clearly defined and delineated roles, as is the case with a client/server configuration, would not be considered a peer-to-peer network. For example, Figure 1.1 shows a typical client/server system. In this particular application, the application server and database reside on a central "server." Requests come from each client for a resource from the central server. This could be a report, a document, a single record—just about any kind of data that a server can "serve" up. As you can see by the connections, there is never a link between the clients, meaning that a request from one client will never be served by another client.

Figure 1.1
This typical
client/server system
shows the server and
the clients accessing
the system.

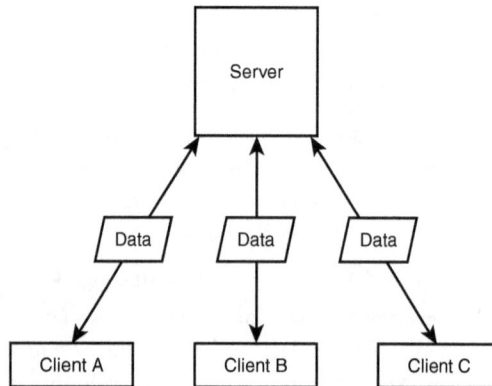

The term peer-to-peer technology means different things to different people. However, most of the definitions fall into one of two camps: the purists and those who believe in a less strict definition of the term. Although both camps agree that peers make up the network, there are different views as to whether any type of centralized control disqualifies an application from truly being considered a peer-to-peer application. Purists believe that peer-to-peer applications should demonstrate no centralized control whatsoever. On the other hand, some argue that even applications with a limited amount of centralized control, but with certain peer-to-peer characteristics, can still wear this label. Any application that exhibits some peer-to-peer characteristics is usually labeled as a peer-to-peer application because "pure" peer-to-peer applications are often unfeasible for most systems.

In the end, it's not the classification of the system that is important, but the suitability of the design for your particular application. For example, the "thin client" and "fat client" debates have gone on for some time. Whether or not most of an application was stored on the client (desktop) machine became a heated argument within many organizations. Many thought that they had to take a side and implement either a full "fat client" or a full "thin client" solution. For fat clients, a majority of processing is done on each client machine, resulting in larger software installations and the need for adequate processing power on the client. For thin clients, a minimal amount of software is installed and the lion's share of the processing takes place on the server. In the end, people have discovered that different applications functioned better by choosing one or the other. More often than not, a combination or hybrid of the two is necessary. This is where Groove comes in.

Groove does not fall into a purist's definition of a strictly peer-to-peer system because the application exhibits both decentralized and centralized characteristics. There are definitely portions of the application that are peer-to-peer in the truest sense, but there are also certain functions that seem to lean more toward a system with centralized control. Certain Groove functions had to be centralized (such as license management or relay services), so deviance from a pure peer-to-peer system was inevitable. This isn't to say that you don't have some degree of control over how your Groove application ultimately functions. If

1

you're a developer using the Groove framework, you can control whether applications exhibit more centralized or decentralized properties. For decentralized applications, Groove gives each client machine their own local database that can be used to store and synchronize data between participants. In addition, Groove also offers additional services that can be added to perform centralized functions, such as the Groove Relay Server or the Groove Management Server.

The file-sharing application Gnutella is probably the most popular example of a completely decentralized peer-to-peer network. This application allows networks of individuals to share any type of file, from music to movies to applications. A Gnutella network is an ever-changing mass of peers, shaping and reshaping itself dynamically as peers enter and leave the network. Figure 1.2 illustrates what a Gnutella network could conceivably look like at a given point in time. At any time it is possible for users to drop out of the network, possibly dividing groups of participants. If Liam and Sarah become disconnected for some reason, this would actually alienate the two groups shown in the figure until a common participant joins the groups again. Conceptually, you could envision this as the way an amoeba can split and become two entirely new organisms. As a user searches for a file, the request travels from peer to peer and is not guaranteed to take the same route each time. For many purists, this is how a true peer-to-peer network would be structured. But most of these types of systems usually do not recover well when clients leave the network. For critical business communications, this lack of data integrity does not suffice. For most Groove users, a centralized Groove relay server would augment the true peer-to-peer structure demonstrated by Gnutella. This server's primary goal is to "store and forward" data for users when they become disconnected or other network conditions interrupt data transmissions.

In a sort of organized chaos, the Gnutella system actually works for what it is intended to do. Users connecting to a Gnutella network can easily find thousands of files for downloading. Speed has been a major factor so far with the network because certain operations can congest the network significantly. Not that this is bound to change eventually. Gnutella operates using its own protocol and specifications with source code that has been publicly available for some time now. This has resulted in many different working groups constantly tweaking the clients and developing slight variations, which might actually signal a move toward some centralized control. However, in the original spirit of the application Gnutella still remains arguably one of the "purest" peer-to-peer applications widely distributed today.

The darling of the media, Napster, has single-handedly introduced more people to a peer-to-peer application than any other in history. (If, that is, you discount the Internet and its clearly original peer-to-peer design.) This consumer file-sharing application undoubtedly deserves a place in history not only for the technology it so visibly demonstrates, but also for the firestorm it created in the intellectual property community. Although many consider it one of the most popular examples of a peer-to-peer application, some believe is better labeled a *hybrid* application and is not truly peer-to-peer.

Figure 1.2
This Gnutella peer-to-peer network demonstrates the connections that bind each user, or peer, together.

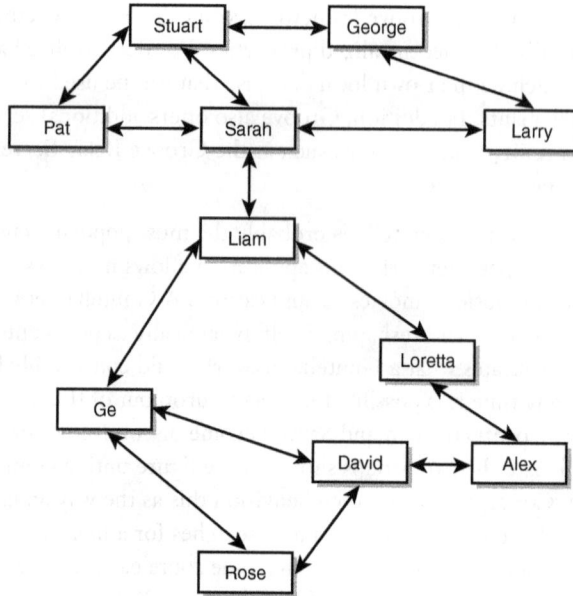

Napster has earned this categorization because it does in fact have a centralized server. Although the music files shared actually reside on each consumer's personal computer, the indexing and searching capabilities are provided by one of the Napster servers. Figure 1.3 is a simple illustration of what a Napster network looks like with a few users actively connected. Groove would also best be characterized as a *hybrid* peer-to-peer application because a centralized server, such as groove.net or the Groove Management server hosted internally, is often found in most configurations. Similar to the Napster structure, a centralized server often allows Groove to perform more efficiently. For Napster, the central index server allows quick searches of music files. For Groove, the centralized server can be used for offline queuing, navigating through firewalls, and other tasks to allow Groove to perform as efficiently and seamlessly as possible.

Figure 1.3
All searches pass through Napster's own server. The dotted lines show that files themselves pass directly between Napster users without passing through this server.

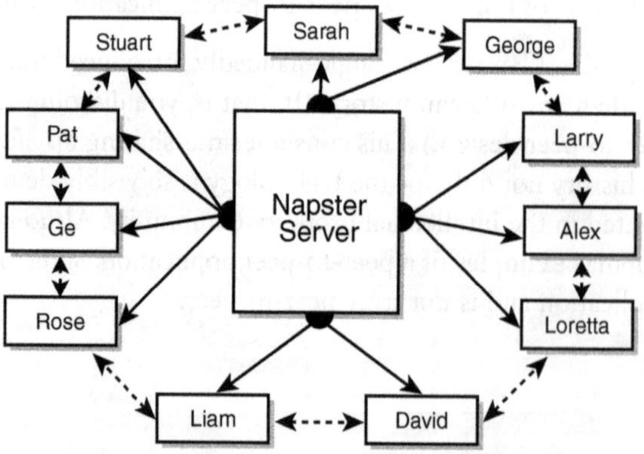

While the theoretical debate over what constitutes a true peer-to-peer network rages on, there are more than a few legal debates surrounding the technology as well. Used for the distribution of copyrighted materials, a peer-to-peer structure that owes nothing to a central "source" has paved the way for some legal precedents. To put it into perspective, let's look at Gnutella and Napster. To the average user, they may have a little different look and feel, but in the end they are both file-sharing applications. To the user there may be no discernable difference, but to those attempting to thwart copyright infringement, they are two totally different animals.

Whereas the Gnutella architecture requires no central server to function, queries for a particular piece of music in the Napster architecture require a trip through one of these central servers. Unlike the way Gnutella functions, loss of a client only affects the availability of the resources that the client shared. Remaining clients are still bound together due to the central server to which they are all connected. It's hard to argue that file sharing would be possible without the functions provided by the servers that Napster maintained. This is probably part of the reason that the recording industry chose to pursue legal action against Napster—Napster as a company had direct involvement with keeping the service running. On the other hand, given the truly non-centralized nature of Gnutella, it's much harder to find a central figure responsible in the dispute.

The peer-to-peer model not only includes file-sharing applications like Gnutella and Napster, but also can include applications that share other resources as well. There are some other intriguing uses of the technology, such as SETI@home's search for extraterrestrial life, which is a good example of using peer-to-peer to take advantage of free computing cycles on consumer computers. Basically, while a SETI screensaver runs, it crunches packets of information about radio signals in search of ET-like beings. Although peer-to-peer may be hard to define, it's a concept that will produce some interesting developments as individuals use a little imagination and take advantage of the "innovation at the edge of the network."

THE HISTORY OF PEER-TO-PEER TECHNOLOGY PRIOR TO GROOVE

In the 1960s ARPAnet, the precursor to the Internet as we know it today, was developed to allow different classes of machines and networks to communicate. Each element in the network was intended to receive equal treatment, meaning each endpoint in the network could alternate between being a client receiving information and a server distributing information. This equal treatment among participants in the network fits in very well with the traditional view of how peer-to-peer networks operate. Most Internet users don't really understand that the Internet itself is really a very large peer-to-peer network. Most consumer users are probably much more familiar with the concept behind file-sharing applications such as Napster or Gnutella; these are probably the tools that most openly exposed people to the technology.

Although these products are good examples of the consumer use of peer-to-peer technology, many business professionals were likely introduced to the technology many years earlier.

Early adopters of Microsoft's Windows for Workgroups were probably exposed to the technology without ever really knowing it. Workers discovered they could now share resources with their colleagues and Windows for Workgroups became a great tool for collaboration, especially in smaller offices without the benefit of a central network server. It is hard to find a business today in which the employees aren't doing some sort of sharing of files, printers, CD-ROM drives, and so on using Windows or some other operating system.

In the next few years, you should see peer-to-peer technology and its capability to forge effective relationships for the exchange of information being used in new, dynamic ways. Its capability to foster ad hoc group discussions in the corporate setting may be the only way some companies will experience growth in this rapidly changing age. Like any new technology, it has its detractors and benefactors, as you will shortly see.

BENEFITS PROVIDED BY THE PEER-TO-PEER STRUCTURE OF GROOVE

Just as with any other new technology, there are going to be arguments on both sides of the fence. Similar to the heated arguments about Linux versus Windows, both sides seem to have valid points. It would be unrealistic to assume peer-to-peer technology is an ideal fit for every application. Let's not concentrate here on the use of peer-to-peer technology for personal use because a lot of it boils down to personal preference. However, Groove's current battle is to prove that peer-to-peer is a valuable tool for businesses. Even Ray Ozzie understands that Groove is not going to be an ideal fit for every application, but wants to ensure that Groove is given proper consideration within businesses where it may very well be an ideal fit.

MORE OPEN COLLABORATION

First of all, the dynamic nature of a peer-to-peer network lends itself well to the ad-hoc groups that are very much a part of a business. Even the most proactive organizations find themselves having to react to the issues at hand as things change. A peer-to-peer network, by its very nature, allows a more dynamic creation of these groups to take place. This is not saying that other solutions based on the concept of a central server can't provide this same sort of collaboration, but they generally place more restrictions on the types of collaboration that can occur. Internet Relay Chat over all the publicly available IRC servers is an excellent example of a collaboration tool that is centrally based. In a sort of anarchistic fashion, users have the capability in a P2P-based tool to set up their own meetings with participants they decide to include without the need to involve some sort of central authority. For example, a Groove user can determine when a new virtual meeting is supposed to take place and what tools the participants can use, such as a calendar, a whiteboard, shared documents, and so on. Most systems around today would require someone from the IS department to create such an environment on a shared server. Groove allows users to do this without additional

IS support. Technically this type of collaboration is not such a unique aspect of peer-to-peer, but the rather free-form way in which it occurs is the differentiating factor. Many see this as an advantage because it fosters true dynamic interaction between participants.

DISTRIBUTED STORAGE

Distribution of storage is another highly touted benefit of peer-to-peer technology. Using Napster as an obvious example, countless terabytes of music files could be stored without the need for a server with that type of capacity. Within Groove, documents on each user's desktop hard drive can be shared with other users. In the past, documents would all be stored on network servers, leaving much of the space on each individual PC attached to the networks unused. The reduction of necessary central storage space is the most obvious advantage of the distributed storage mechanism that peer-to-peer employs. However, the benefit is two-fold. Not only are central storage requirements minimized, but also the data is often much closer to the consumers who need it. This can often result in faster access to the information, as it no longer has to hop through some central server to the individual requesting it. Although many variables affect whether this "shortest path" scenario actually results in any tangible benefit, with the capability of data in P2P applications to generally take the shortest path, in this case from one peer directly to another, one can only assume that overall for most data distributions that some efficiency will be realized.

AN ALTERNATIVE TO THE PROBLEM OF SCALABILITY

High-volume transaction-based systems on traditional platforms are often designed to scale using many different techniques. Data and applications are generally separated and distributed to maximize transaction processing. In this way, bottlenecks are alleviated and processing distributed accordingly. Peer-to-peer applications, by their very design, do have limited options when it comes to trying to scale them to handle increased loads.

However, peer-to-peer applications like Groove are intended for small groups of people and generally aren't serving up millions of transactions. There have been several academic pursuits trying to gauge the scalability of peer-to-peer networks, but it really is a difficult equation to work out, and so far only rather limited studies have been done on real-world situations where peer-to-peer applications have received widespread usage. Processing power that would typically be required of a central server is now distributed among client machines, which can have a broad array of different configurations. Network traffic can be variable depending on the types of interaction taking place, online/offline usage, and so on.

From the earliest beta release, Groove Networks has been constantly tweaking Groove to reduce the network traffic each client generates to transmit data for synchronization between users. There are several questions you must answer before you can begin to determine how your particular application of peer-to-peer technology will scale in relation to its server-based counterpart, including the following:

■ Is redundancy a problem for storage, or is it a benefit because it provides better access to data?

Peer-to-peer applications generally contain redundant data that is stored on everyone's machine. For example, a document in a peer-to-peer application would need to be stored locally in each client machine in a peer-to-peer network for all the clients to share it. For a client/server application, a single copy of this document could reside on the server and be accessed by each client on the server itself.

■ Do you need to upgrade your network to handle the additional traffic?

In peer-to-peer applications such as Groove, a lot of network traffic is necessary to keep each peer's view of the data constant. Without examining a specific application, the amount of data transferred is hard to quantify. However, depending on the synchronization mechanism used, the amount of data transferred by a peer-to-peer application is generally greater than the data transferred by the application's client/server counterpart. Initially, Groove consumes more than its fair share of bandwidth but great strides have been made to decrease the amount of network traffic demands dramatically.

■ Do you require connections to external data stores "outside" the peer-to-peer network?

If an application requires access to data outside the current network, configuring each peer in a peer-to-peer network can be very difficult. Typically, a client/server application can use a single iterative or batch process to gather this data through a single connection. In a peer-to-peer application, each individual peer could require its own independent connection. Groove's answer to this is the Enterprise Integration Server, which provides a mechanism using automated bots to capture data needed for individual Groove clients.

REDUCED ADMINISTRATIVE OVERHEAD

When determining the return on investment for any new software application, whether developed in-house or purchased from an external vendor, you would be foolhardy not to incorporate the cost of administrative overhead into your equation. This can be a significant drain on resources and exists during the entire life of the application. P2P's departure from the traditional paradigm of client/server applications affords some benefits by reducing the burden placed on administrators. The end users, who tailor and design their own peer-to-peer space, begin consuming some of this overhead. They decide what data is available to other users and moderate the interactions occurring in the spaces in which they participate. This moderation includes the administration of user permissions to resources available, which is something that usually consumes a majority of an administrator's time. Also, incorrect permission assignments by overtaxed administrators can greatly reduce the efficiency of the participants involved in a given task. As long as groups remain small, resolution of permission problems can often be handled in a much quicker fashion in a peer-to-peer environment.

CRITICAL RESPONSES TO GROOVE'S PEER-TO-PEER STRUCTURE

A balanced review of the peer-to-peer structure of Groove would not be complete without presenting some of the detractors' viewpoints and why they feel that a peer-to-peer application is not always the right fit for every situation. There are definitely some aspects of P2P that make corporations a little uneasy about the technology. Many of these organizations' concerns are rooted in the flexibility of the technology, which is the very thing others consider to be a definite benefit. Lack of centralized management is a primary concern for many businesses. Others point to scalability and security issues that are paramount concerns that Groove and other prime movers in the market have tried very hard to address.

RESOURCE MANAGEMENT

Knowledge and resource management are great concerns for many corporations. By allowing individuals to share resources freely, companies lose their ability to centrally manage this flow of information. Any sort of digital asset has some value attached to it and in the wrong hands it could prove disastrous. Without all information passing through one centralized server, the security of these resources comes into question. Also, because in a true peer-to-peer environment storage of resources is decentralized, it is very possible for redundant copies of this information to propagate. If an unused resource is taking up space on an individual's machine, it should be that person's responsibility to adequately "clean it up," but many worry that out-of-date and invalid information could propagate because individuals will not accept this responsibility. This is a valid point, but many seem to forget that Groove and other platforms stress that groups within the corporate peer-to-peer environment should remain intimately small. This, in theory, should nullify many of their concerns.

SECURITY CONCERNS

As I lightly touched on when talking about resource management, security is a huge hurdle that peer-to-peer technology must overcome. In a true peer-to-peer environment, who's to say that someone will not impersonate someone else to gain access to confidential information? Most corporate networks use a firewall to block access from outside. Peer-to-peer, especially in situations that cross the traditional enterprise firewall boundaries, could open "holes" for accessing data behind the firewall. For peer-to-peer applications residing completely inside the firewall, this is usually not a concern. The increasing popularity of Instant Messaging software has brought attention to the security issues that can arise when software is used that may be difficult for security administrators to "police" adequately. Groove, however, provides very strong security, as you will see in the next section.

GROOVE'S COMPLETE ENVIRONMENT FOR GROUP INTERACTION

Up to this point, we've discussed peer-to-peer in a very generic sense. Painting Groove with a broad peer-to-peer brush would not be fitting. Although Groove exhibits decentralized characteristics that make it peer-to-peer, it is much more. The Groove product is intended to revolutionize the way people interact. Groove accomplishes this through a sophisticated mix of software and services. The Groove client interface is just one piece of the equation; the interactions within it are all supported by the underpinnings of a next-generation relationship management system. The rest of this chapter takes a closer look at all the different components that make Groove what it is. Some are straightforward software components, like the graphical Transceiver that is used as the primary Groove interface. Others are not so clear-cut, like the Management Services, which are designed to evolve and change as the Groove community's needs change. You'll notice constant references to *open standards* in this chapter and the rest of the book. Everything within Groove either adheres to a currently existing standard or is an area where Groove has attempted to pioneer standards where previous attempts were lacking. At the end of this chapter you will look at a few of the organizations actively developing open standards for peer-to-peer technology.

Groove should not be confused with a simple standalone utility that runs on your desktop. It's a dynamic platform on which applications enabling direct communication and interaction can be built. At the topmost level, its capabilities are enabled by the user interface and the tools provided with it. By inviting other participants to a *shared space*, members of this space can collaborate in the environment originally designed by the person initiating the collaboration. The space itself can be tailored depending on what is required for effective collaboration and can be further molded as needs change. There is the capability for direct dialogues among participants, content sharing, and other activities that members can perform simultaneously. I'm describing them briefly here because we examine the capabilities enabled by Groove tools in Chapter 9, "Groove Enterprise Network Services."

Many of us have found Instant Messaging tools such as ICQ and AOL Instant Messenger to be invaluable to our daily personal and business lives. Groove provides Instant Messaging capability so that text and voice messages can be distributed instantly to other individuals in a very personal one-on-one manner. Although the text option is most common, Groove enables voice communication in an almost real-time fashion. For offline users, the option to save voice messages for later retrieval by recipients is also provided in a very similar fashion to voicemail and home answering machines. Threaded discussion is provided so that messages can be posted and replied to in a fashion similar to the bulletin board systems that became popular just a few years ago. These communication tools are common threads that run throughout just about any implementation of Groove.

Although communication is obviously a primary driver of effective group collaboration, there are many other types of content in addition to dialogue that make dynamic group interaction valuable. Groove allows participants to share different types of content. In a business setting, this can include documents, graphics, and any other type of files for business communication. Although Instant Messaging and other dialogues are the informal communication that is valuable within the workplace, this type of content represents the structured dialogue that is a huge part of any business. In a personal setting, families and other small groups can share personal documents, graphics, music files, and anything else that lets them connect with other members in the group. But content sharing is not limited to file-based objects. Groove enables sharing of each individual's contact information. This is what allows a user to establish contact with other Groove members, but this contact information can also include offline information, such as addresses and phone numbers, thus extending Groove's value past the online interactions that take place.

In addition to Groove's support for communication and content sharing, there are other tasks that can be labeled joint activities. This type of activity includes anything that a group performs together in a sort of shared environment. Participants can surf the Web together as if everyone is sharing the same computer. A Sketchpad tool provides a group with a virtual whiteboard where ideas can be expressed visually just as they might be in a meeting room with a whiteboard. A shared calendar can be used for tracking project milestones or monitoring the vacation schedules of everyone involved in the shared space.

SYSTEM-LEVEL SERVICES

We've discussed at a high level what the Groove environment facilitates. Perhaps we've painted a too simplistic view of what Groove really does in this summation. Groove allows users to interact with other trusted users in an environment that is updated in real time. Enabling this real-time interaction takes a complex array of supporting services that work behind the scenes. Because most of these services work seamlessly and transparently, most users aren't even aware of the rich, complex inner workings that make all this possible. Developers have access to rich system-level services that can be leveraged as they are or extended as needed. As part of the platform, system-level services are woven throughout a Groove application, thus their rich functionality is provided without explicitly making calls to the services. The following are the Groove system-level services provided:

- Security
- Storage
- Synchronization
- Peer Connection
- Device Presence

The following sections describe each of these services separately, but all of these services must work together to provide Groove's environment for real-time interaction.

SECURITY SERVICES

Groove handles its own security services, including the creation, distribution, and maintenance of public and private keys. In this way, no outside authority is needed. Data packets transmitted by Groove are all secured via 192-bit encryption. This service ensures data is received by only the proper authenticated recipients. Groove not only guarantees that transmitted data is encrypted, but also it ensures that all data stored on disk is never in the clear (unencrypted).

STORAGE SERVICES

Every instance of Groove has its own local XML store where Groove maintains all information, including all content stored in shared spaces and any other activity information that requires persistence. This is also the mechanism that ensures activity in a shared space is stored in the local XML store. This enables users to switch between online and offline mode while still keeping their changes to shared spaces synchronized.

SYNCHRONIZATION SERVICES

Because Groove implements the peer-to-peer model, it is important that everyone within a space sees the same information. Groove's Synchronization Services ensure all information is kept up-to-date in the local store on each participant's machine. These services have quite a difficult task given the ability of members in a space to function in both an online and offline mode. After setting up your own shared spaces in Chapter 4, "Understanding Shared Spaces," you'll see how shared spaces synchronize as you collaborate with other participants within the space.

PEER CONNECTION SERVICES

Groove is designed to work properly under many different network configurations. This service takes care of such tasks as determining the IP address, optimizing itself depending on available bandwidth, and dealing with issues introduced by firewalls separating participants. Chapter 2, "Installing and Configuring Groove," outlines some of the different network configurations Groove may have to deal with and some details to help you understand how Groove functions in the different scenarios.

DEVICE PRESENCE SERVICES

Groove alerts you when others are online and ready to send and receive data. This process of discovering the status of other users happens regularly and is handled by the Device Presence Services. This service allows your Groove client to not only tell the current device status of other Groove users but to enable you to discover new participants on the local area network and across any wide area networks you may have access to.

MANAGEMENT SERVICES

Although some see it as a departure from being a pure peer-to-peer architecture, Groove provides some centralized management services that allow administrators to exert some control over a corporate Groove installation. Although Groove does decentralize many of the administration tasks associated once it is installed, there is a certain level of control that many enterprise installations will undoubtedly require. Currently, Groove Networks and its Web-based Groove Enterprise Network services provide most of these features. In 2002,

Groove plans to roll out a server-based version of this service that can be run internally. The following services fall under the Groove Management Services area:

- License Management
- Component Management
- groove.net

These three services are provided to allow some degree of centralized control that will be required by many enterprise installations.

→ To learn more about how Groove handles security issues, **see** "Groove Security," **p.426**

LICENSE MANAGEMENT

This service manages licenses for a Groove installation. In addition to getting accurate counts regarding license usage, there are other options that can be set to determine how licenses are distributed. This can include automatic verification of new accounts, or a more controlled environment in which all new users must be explicitly approved before being granted access.

COMPONENT MANAGEMENT

Groove's component-based architecture requires a way for administrators to consistently manage component deployment. On-the-fly component upgrades are provided by Groove to ensure end-users are always using the most up-to-date software. However, this may not always be desirable depending on the environment in which they are functioning. Using the Centralized Management services, administrators can manage component updates by blocking, limiting, or scheduling these downloads.

GROOVE.NET

Although not strictly falling under the "Management Services" umbrella, Groove Networks also offers a service named groove.net. Currently, groove.net provides a directory service for Groove users who have chosen to be listed. The groove.net directory is in addition to the local network directory, which I describe in more detail in Chapter 4, "Understanding Shared Spaces." In addition, groove.net provides temporary storage for account information for users wanting to use their Groove account on multiple computers. Look for the services offered by groove.net to grow as the Groove application and user community expands.

→ To learn more about Directory options, **see** "Listing Your Name in the Directory," **p.63**
→ To learn how to use the same Groove account on multiple computers, including how you can use groove.net, **see** "Running Groove on Multiple Computers," **p.47**

BANDWIDTH EFFICIENCY AND FIREWALL TRANSPARENCY

In situations where direct peer-to-peer communication is not possible or practical, Groove offers relay services that essentially transmit data to a central store for retransmission to the intended recipient. When a user is behind a firewall, these services are used to package data into http packets so that they can be transferred across a firewall to the relay server. This is also the service used to "queue" data for transfer when one or more members of a space are offline so no data is lost.

DEVELOPMENT WITHIN THE GROOVE ARCHITECTURE

Now that you've seen some of the rich services that Groove provides, let's discuss how developers begin constructing applications within Groove. As a secure and extensible platform, developers can easily leverage the core Groove services. Anyone with some basic scripting language skills and an understanding of XML can quickly begin developing applications around the framework. The Groove Development Kit (GDK) is provided, offering all the samples, documentation, and utilities an aspiring Groove developer will need to get started. In Chapter 10, "The Groove SDK," we'll introduce you to the GDK and the components that make it up. Taking your knowledge of the GDK, we'll then give you a step-by-step example of developing a tool within Groove in Chapter 11, "Creating a Tool." Some of the highlights of the Groove development environment are described in the following sections.

SERVICE-LEVEL COM SUPPORT

Groove's usage of Microsoft's Component Object Model (COM) provides a standard way for developers to exploit the Groove system-level services. With this in place, service calls can be made from popular languages such as JavaScript, Visual Basic, C++, and the new C# language.

A FLEXIBLE TOOL-DEVELOPMENT FRAMEWORK

With its flexible framework, developers can integrate existing COM objects into Groove, where they will automatically inherit all the standard services. Developers have the flexibility to include only the components required by their application requirements. If additional functionality is needed beyond that exposed by the objects provided, development at a lower level is supported by allowing developers to make direct API calls. At a lower level, developers can get at the core Groove functions while shedding some of the restrictions that higher level components may impose.

BUILT UPON OPEN STANDARDS AND PROTOCOLS

In addition to the COM standards mentioned earlier, just about every part of Groove has been constructed on open standards. For communications, Groove uses the standard TCP/IP, UDP, and HTTP protocols. For data encoding and storage, XML is used. The Open Software Description (OSD) standard is used for publishing components. Even contact information is stored in the W3C vCard format. Groove has stated on several occasions that its component-based system is an advantage because it can continually adapt as new standards emerge.

USER INTERFACE COMPONENTS

Groove provides a standard user interface that can be modified by the user through the use of skins. *Skins* are a collection of colors and graphics that give the Groove client, or Transceiver, its look and feel. Developers have access to all elements provided by the primary interface. If the elements provided by the Transceiver are not sufficient, developers can further modify the user interface to meet their specific needs.

INTEGRATING GROOVE WITH OTHER EXTERNAL SYSTEMS

Groove Networks has consistently reiterated that it does not consider Groove itself to be an island—that integration with an organization's existing business systems is critical for the customer, and for the overall success of Groove. Their recent involvement with Microsoft's My Services project (formerly codenamed "Hailstorm") is a great example of the work in this area. My Services, which is part of Microsoft's .NET initiative, is a set of user-centric and XML Web services. Microsoft's goal for My Services is to bring together the islands of information that belong to an individual, but may exist in many different places. This user-centric, rather than device-centric, approach is one that Groove has been trying to pioneer. The Microsoft Messenger and Groove integration demo at the My Services announcement earlier this year was an early glimpse of the possibilities for Web and peer services integration, and should make for some exciting developments in the future. This early demonstration might also help forge some interoperability standards that are desperately needed in this area.

NOTE

> The Microsoft initiative, previously codenamed Hailstorm, was quietly launched as part of Microsoft's .NET rollout. Now called My Services, it offers a suite of XML services that provide new ways to customize applications based on select personal data. You can find out the latest developments on Microsoft's site at `http://www.microsoft.com/myservices/`.

Currently, Groove Networks offers its Groove Enterprise Integration Server for access to legacy data. Groove users can gain access to data residing in other business systems through automated processes called *bots* and client-side agent technology. The bots reside on server-based systems and can push or pull information from centralized business systems to Groove users. With the Groove Enterprise Integration server, authorized members of Groove shared spaces can securely access, share, and work with data residing in centralized server-based systems, such as customer relationship management or sales force automation systems. An attractive feature of the Groove Enterprise Integration Server is its single point of integration to a business system, which allows secure access to firewall-protected systems and provides a rich set of APIs that allow enterprise developers to build integration solutions. As Groove becomes more popular, you'll undoubtedly see interesting developments in this area as external vendors develop system-specific implementations of the Groove Enterprise Integration Server.

1

BUILD IT AND THEY WILL COME?

The popularity of other peer-to-peer tools such as Napster and Instant Message software arose because they were easy to use even for the most inexperienced computer user. Napster kept the interface simple with very few configuration options and only a few screens to navigate, and made searching a simple process. Instant Messaging software such as AOL Instant Messenger used many of the same strategies along with pretty icons to entertain users. As with any new technology and application, its true success will lie in the adoption of the technology. Although the underlying technical architecture could be sound, its complex architecture is not going to do much good if users don't open it and communicate with others.

Although it is tough to do a real scientific evaluation, by all accounts it appears the initial response to the tool's interface has been very positive. Groove has kept the interfaces simple and configuration tasks to a minimum. Users invited to shared spaces are greeted with very familiar tabs and other controls that are standard to any Windows-based applications. Groove has continually reworked the interface, incorporating external suggestions and weighing internal debates on its usability.

WHERE GROOVE IS HEADING

Groove Networks is one company that is sticking to its guns. The company still maintains that Groove and its peer-to-peer framework have great potential for many organizations. It has been able to constantly tweak the platform due to its flexible component-based structure. The company has listened to suggestions from business leaders and consumers and taken action by incorporating them in their next release. The best indication of Groove Network's unchanging vision is summed up by Ray Ozzie's comments in one of the first press releases by the company in October 2000:

> "We've developed Groove with one core purpose in mind: to strengthen the online connections among people who need to interact closely with one another across all boundaries such as time, place, or organizational affiliation. Groove is a powerful peer computing platform that will dynamically bring together the right people, the right information, and the right tools, at the right time. Just as the Web browser has become the means by which people interact with Web sites, Groove will increasingly become the means by which people interact directly with one another. Over time, we believe that most everyone who uses a PC or network appliance to communicate over the Net will have three primary tools: email, a browser, and Groove."

PEER-TO-PEER TECHNOLOGY STANDARDS

> "One of the reasons that the Internet and the Web moved rapidly from being research experiments to widespread public infrastructure was the adoption of standards—basic agreements on how certain things are to be done. Much along the same lines as 'everyone drive on the right side of the street,' standards provide freedom to create

specific products in such a way that they can interoperate with other products in a given space, but without having to develop a soup-to-nuts solution."

—Charlie Catlett, Chair of the Global Grid Forum

Groove Networks is committed to adopting new popular standards as they emerge. However, the area of peer-to-peer technology is relatively new and thus there are many emerging and evolving practices and methods. In addition to the established Internet-related standards groups such as the Internet Engineering Task Force (IETF, www.ietf.org) and World Wide Web Consortium (W3C, www.w3c.org), several new groups are attempting to create an environment in the industry where widespread adoption of the best approaches and standards is possible. Not meant as an endorsement of any particular group, the following two sections describe a couple of them that have been doing some notable work in this area.

PEER-TO-PEER WORKING GROUP

With a little political thrashing here and there, the Peer-to-Peer Working Group (http://www.peer-to-peerwg.org/) has made some significant progress in getting people to come together and realize we need to start developing some semblance of standards for the technology. As with any attempt to nail down specifics of any technology, there's a firestorm of debate and opinions about where the group should be heading. However, with their impressive list of corporate members, including Groove Networks, they are well on their way to making significant strides for the peer-to-peer community.

GLOBAL GRID FORUM

Many of the experimental Internet and distributed computing technologies developed and used in the academic and high performance computing worlds over the past several decades have been inherently "peer to peer" or, as they refer to them, "grids." As a community of industry professionals and those from the academic realms, the Global Grid Forum (http://www.gridforum.org/), or GGF, is a set of technical working groups that began in the U.S. in 1999 and has spread to Europe and Asia-Pacific. GGF participants come from more than 30 countries and 200 organizations, with sponsorship from multiple U.S. Federal agencies and more than a dozen companies ranging from software (such as Microsoft and Sun Microsystems) to communications (such as Level(3) and Qwest.) They are actively working toward the development of "best practices," implementation guidelines, and standards for distributed computing.

CHAPTER **2**

INSTALLING AND CONFIGURING GROOVE

In this chapter

PREPARING FOR THE GROOVE WORKSPACE INSTALLATION

This chapter details the installation and configuration of Groove's Workspace product. Groove has been designed to work in a variety of environments, from a casual home user's system with a dial-up connection to a corporate environment behind a firewall or proxy. Hopefully, after you've downloaded the install program, you'll be up and running in just a few minutes. In case you have problems, I outline the different network scenarios you might encounter and give you some troubleshooting tips to avoid typical problems.

If you're a current user of Groove, you can use this chapter to learn how to upgrade your system properly or transfer accounts from one computer to another. Given the security measures used by Groove, this can often be trickier than it sounds. I'll take the mystery out of the process and at the same time provide you with valuable insight into how Groove handles your identities. Lastly, you'll learn how to completely uninstall Groove. With the information in this chapter, you'll not only be well-practiced in installing your personal version of Groove but also be on your way to understanding some of the essential administrative tasks required for deployment in a corporate setting.

The Groove documentation specifies the following minimum system requirements. Remember that these hardware requirements are the bare minimum and may be underpowered depending on your exact system configuration:

- Pentium 233Mhz processor or higher
- 64MB System RAM (with 32MB available for Groove)
- 100MB of free disk space for Groove itself with 60MB additional space for data
- Video card capable of 800×600 resolution with at least 15-bit color
- Sound card and microphone to enable voice-messaging and audio features (a full-duplex sound card is required for some voice chat features)

NOTE

> Most sound cards manufactured in the past few years are full duplex. A full-duplex sound card (versus one that operates in half-duplex mode) allows you to listen to audio and use a microphone at the same time. Think of half-duplex mode as being roughly analogous to how a CB radio works (in other words, one-way), whereas full-duplex mode is similar to how your home telephone works. Some sound cards may need different software to enable full-duplex operation even if the hardware itself is capable of such operation. Consult your sound card specifications and documentation if you encounter problems with Groove audio features.

TIP

> Don't skimp on RAM. These are minimum requirements. If you plan on running other applications simultaneously with Groove a configuration with 256MB is more appropriate. If not, you may find yourself waiting more than working.

OPERATING SYSTEMS SUPPORTED

Groove runs on a variety of different platforms, the following operating systems are currently supported:

- Microsoft Windows 98
- Microsoft Windows NT (Service Pack 5 or greater must be applied)
- Microsoft Windows Me
- Microsoft Windows 2000
- Microsoft Windows XP

Running Groove on Linux

Officially, Groove has not yet been ported to Linux. However, you can run Groove on Linux using Windows emulation software. Emulation software allows Windows-based applications to run on top of a Linux installation by mapping Windows system calls to their appropriate Linux counterparts. Many require some tweaking to work properly but have become easier to use since the more widespread adoption of Linux.

Some of the Windows emulators for Linux include the following:

- VMWare: A very powerful emulator that many consider a "hardware" emulator because it creates a functioning Windows virtual machine that runs separately from Linux. VMWare's Workstation product allows different operating systems to coexist peacefully. For example, a Groove user running Red Hat Linux could install a Windows 98 virtual machine that can be accessed within the same session without needing to reboot the machine. Groove Networks has stated that this is one option when trying to run Groove on the Linux platform. More information can be found at http://www.vmware.com.

- WINE: This stands for WINdows Emulation software. Proud of its 100% Microsoft-free code, WINE can use Microsoft native system libraries if needed. Offering a Windows compatibility layer, WINE is an implementation of the Windows 3.1 and Win32 APIs on top of the X Window and Linux platforms. Considered by many not to be as stable as VMWare, it does offer a freely distributable alternative. There may be new developments in this area as Groove Networks has completed some demos using WINE. The case study detailing the Groove porting project can be found at http://www.macadamian.com/services/clients.html. Complete documentation along with source and other tools can be found at http://www.winehq.com.

- Win4Lin: Offered by a company called neTraverse, which claims its Win4Lin product is one of the fastest Windows 95/98 emulators for Linux. The list of popular applications supported is impressive and it comes with an installer for incremental enhancements to the software. For more information refer to http://www.netraverse.com.

Keep in mind that emulators do not necessarily guarantee 100% compatibility with current and future releases of Groove. Groove has hinted that they may port Groove to the Linux platform in the future. Because Groove continuously enhances its product, it is possible that these changes could cause compatibility issues with some emulators.

SOFTWARE REQUIREMENTS

Groove Workspace uses several of the components installed with Internet Explorer 4.x or later so you must have a copy of an appropriate version of this browser installed on your machine. Users of Netscape Navigator and other browsers such as Opera can still use these as their default Web browser. Because it has been a reputed source of connection problems in the past, you should also ensure Internet Explorer has Internet connectivity even if you aren't using it as your default browser.

INTERNET CONNECTION

A 56Kbps connection is the minimum required for dial-up usage. Otherwise, a LAN connection with an Internet or broadband (DSL, cable, T1) connection is suggested. Keep in mind that it's not only your connection that is important, but also the connections of others with whom you will be collaborating. You should always keep in mind that synchronization can consume significant amounts of bandwidth. Although not a requirement, Groove runs optimally when all participants have a broadband connection.

THE DIFFERENT VERSIONS OF GROOVE WORKSPACE OFFERED

Recently, Groove has begun offering Groove Workspace in a few different versions. Previously, most personal users of Groove utilized the standard free Preview Edition that has been offered since the product's introduction. Versions now offered include the following:

- Preview Edition: This version is offered on Groove Network's Web site for free download. This edition is restricted, so it might not be the best choice for business use but provides all the functionality more casual personal users could need. Most noticeably, there are limitations on the number of shared spaces that can be created.

- Standard: For small businesses, this provides most of the features, including interoperability with Microsoft Word. The only noticeable limitation involves the Form Builder tool that will be discussed in more detail in Chapter 4, "Understanding Shared Spaces."

- Professional: This is the premium version of Groove that has all the available features.

INSTALLING GROOVE

Groove Workspace is usually installed from the Web or from an installation CD. A Preview Edition is available on the Groove Networks Web site with limited features. Fully licensed versions for Enterprise users are usually contained on an installation CD, but can also be deployed using an intranet site.

INSTALLING GROOVE WORKSPACE PREVIEW EDITION FROM THE WEB

Groove currently offers a free Preview Edition of Groove Workspace for personal use that's available on its Web site. Users of the Standard and Professional versions of the software can also download the software from the Groove Network's site. Using an activation key, licensed users can unlock all the features not available in the Preview Edition. Groove users participating in an environment with Groove Management server installed may be directed to a link to download Groove Workspace from an intranet site. For most users, this will likely be the preferred method of installation. To do this, follow these steps:

1. Close down any applications that are currently running.

2. If you want to use the free Preview Edition of Groove Workspace, you should establish your connection to the Internet and open your browser. Navigate to the Groove Installation page at `http://www.groove.net/downloads/groove`, where you'll find the Groove installer as shown in Figure 2.1.

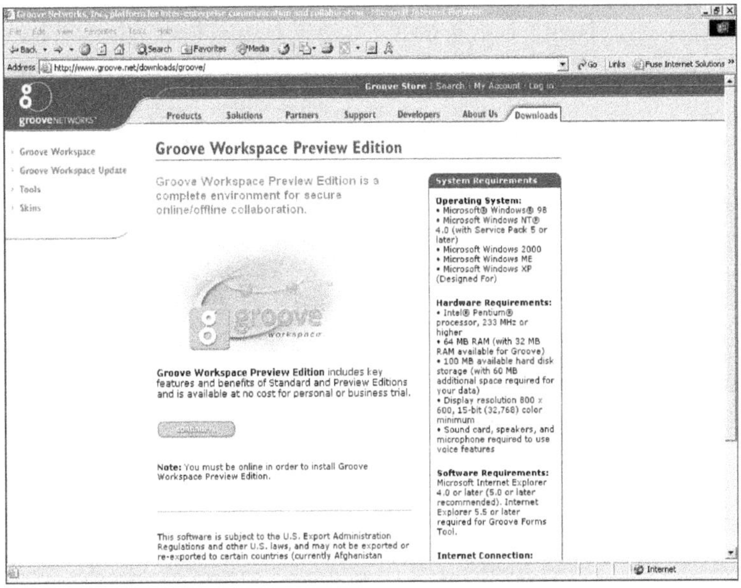

Figure 2.1
You can download Groove Workspace from the Groove Networks Web site.

If you are an Enterprise user, you should ask your administrator for the address to the Groove installer.

TIP

> Inspect the readme file provided with Groove before any installation. You have the option of viewing it after the installation is complete, but unfortunately this may be too late. The readme file often contains not only information about new enhancements, but also information pertaining to backward-compatibility problems. Some newer versions of Groove may have specific instructions you might need to follow to ensure any data relating to current Groove usage is maintained after the upgrade. Once installed, you can view the readme by pointing your browser to `<groove installation root>\Groove\ReadMe\readme.html`.

3. Click the link leading to the Groove workspace installer. For Preview Edition users this will be the Continue button shown in Figure 2.1. After filling out a short survey and clicking the Download Groove button, you'll be asked if you want to run or save the installation file. Choose Save This Program to Disk and then click OK.

4. You'll be asked to specify a location on your computer to save the Groove Preview Edition installer file. Navigate to the desired location and click Save.

5. When the download has completed, execute (double-click) the Groove Workspace installer program you've just received. The Groove installer will examine your system and determine the installation needed. When it is ready, it will begin the download process.

6. When the download has completed, the installer program begins. Click the Next button to continue.

If you're a Windows NT/2000/XP user and are receiving errors launching the installer, see "User Permission Problems During Installation" in the Troubleshooting section at the end of this chapter.

NOTE

> As previously mentioned in this chapter, a proper Internet Explorer installation is required. If there are problems with the install, you may receive a message from the installer saying `"Bad Command Line"`. This may indicate a problem with the Internet Explorer installation. Reinstalling Internet Explorer and trying again can often remedy this. You can always ensure you have the latest version by visiting Microsoft's Internet Explorer site at `http://www.microsoft.com/windows/ie/default.htm`. Try to steer clear of beta or preview versions of the browser software as they can cause unpredictable results.

If Groove was already installed on the target computer, you may receive errors about files being in use that will end the installation. Consult "Installation Stops Because File Is in Use" in the Troubleshooting section at the end of this chapter.

7. Decide where the application will be installed. To change the destination location from the default, click the Browse button and choose a new location. Click Next when you are satisfied with the location.

8. Choose the location where the user data used by Groove Workspace will be installed. To change the destination location from the default, click the Browse button and choose a new location. Click Next.

9. Specify where the system data used by Groove Workspace will be installed. To change the destination location from the default, click the Browse button to choose a new location. Click Next.

10. You will be asked to select from one of the following installation options as shown in Figure 2.2:

    - Install for All Groove Users—If this is checked, Groove is installed for all user accounts on the machine. Otherwise, Groove is only installed for the current active user account.

    - Add Groove to Startup Folder—If this is checked, Groove is added to the Windows Startup folder.

    - Add Groove to Desktop—If this is checked, a shortcut to Groove is added to the Windows Desktop.

Figure 2.2
Tailor your Groove installation.

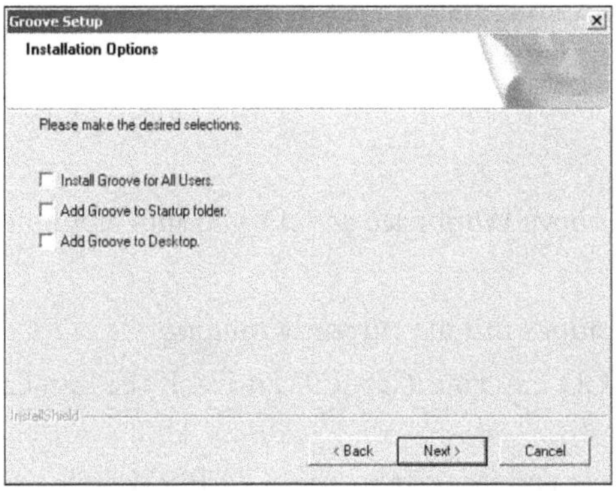

11. Next you will be asked where you would like the program icon to be located. The default location is shown in Figure 2.3.

Figure 2.3
Choose where the Groove program icon will be located.

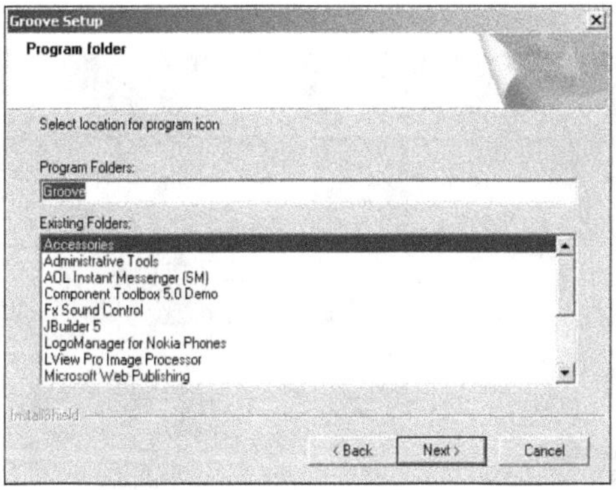

12. Verify the location of the Groove installation. Figure 2.4 shows the screen if the default installation directory was chosen. If you are unhappy with the current selection, you may click the Back button and change it. Otherwise, click Next.

Figure 2.4
Double-check your Groove installation location and click Next.

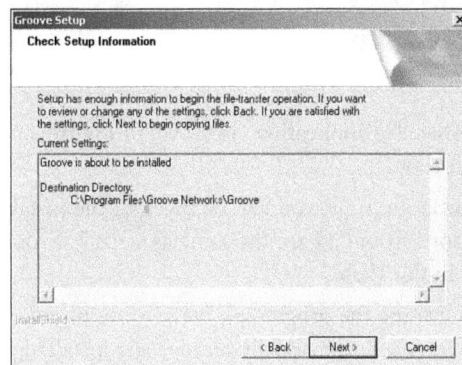

13. A status bar displays indicating the progress of the Groove installer. If at any point this process is interrupted, you need to manually remove any installed portions and reinstall.

INSTALLING GROOVE WORKSPACE FROM CD

If you received a copy of Groove Workspace on CD, you should follow these steps to install Groove:

1. Close down any applications that are currently running.

2. Insert the installation CD into your CD-ROM drive. If the installation application opens, proceed to step 5.

3. Open Windows Explorer and navigate to your CD-ROM drive.

4. Double-click the Start (or `Start.exe`) application file to open the Groove Workspace installation application.

5. You should now be greeted with the Groove Workspace installer as shown in Figure 2.5. Click the Install link to begin.

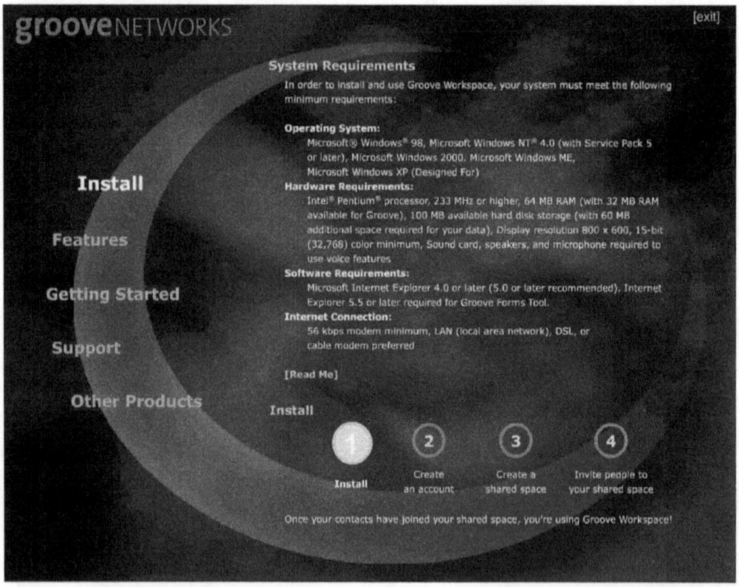

Figure 2.5
Begin installing
Groove Workspace.

6. This should run the SETUP.EXE application, as shown in Figure 2.6. Choose the Open option to run the application.

7. When the SETUP.EXE program runs, you will be taken to the installation screen. The steps for installing Groove from CD are the same as steps 7 through 12 for installing Groove Workspace from the Web.

8. A status bar displays indicating the progress of the Groove installer. If at any point this process is interrupted, you need to manually remove any installed portions and reinstall.

Figure 2.6
When prompted, click the Open button to run the SETUP.EXE application from the Groove Workspace CD.

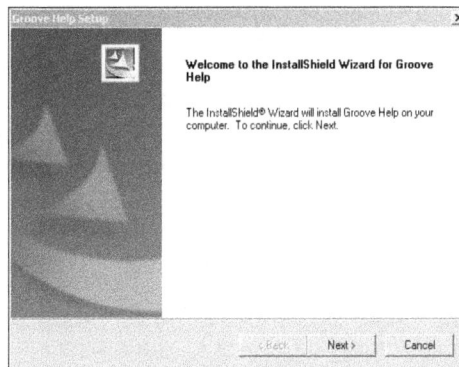

9. Before the Groove Workspace installation is complete, you will have the option of installing the Groove help files. When the installation status bar reaches 100%, the Groove help installer should be started, as shown in Figure 2.7. Click the Next button to begin the installation.

Figure 2.7
The Groove help installer will start automatically.

> NOTE
>
> At this point, you can click the Cancel button if you don't want to install the help files. You should install them from the CD if possible; otherwise, they will be downloaded from the Web. The entire help file is several megabytes in size so installation from the CD can save you time, especially if your Internet connection isn't very fast.

10. After all the files have been installed, you can click Finish to complete the help files installation.

11. When the Groove Workspace help installer has finished, you will return to the Groove Workspace application installer. From the screen shown in Figure 2.8, you now have the option of viewing the readme file and launching Groove automatically. Make your selection(s) and then click Finish. Depending on whether needed components already existed on your machine, you may be asked to reboot your computer when the installation completes.

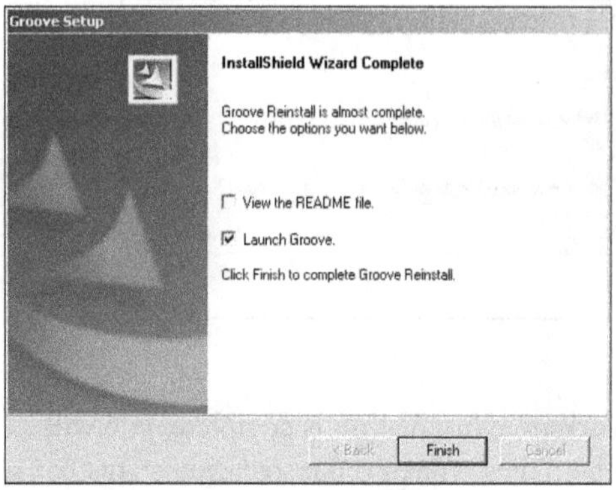

Figure 2.8
Click Finish and the
Groove Workspace
installation is
complete.

GETTING GROOVE STARTED

Whether you're a Preview Edition user or you've purchased a licensed copy of Groove, there are a few steps you'll need to take when you first launch Groove Workspace. All users will need to perform the steps in the following section, "Running Groove Workspace for the First Time." If you are a licensed user, you'll also need to follow the steps in the next section, "Activating Your Copy of Groove Workspace," in order to unlock the features available to licensed users only.

RUNNING GROOVE WORKSPACE FOR THE FIRST TIME

When Groove Workspace is run for the first time, you need to follow these few steps to begin using the product:

1. Review and accept the license agreement for Groove Workspace, as shown in Figure 2.9. Click Next.

Figure 2.9
Review the license
agreement thorough-
ly, select the check
box, and click the
Next button when
you've completed this
step.

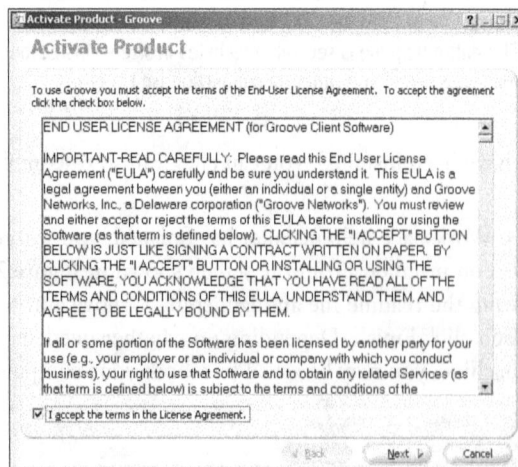

2. Now you must fill out a form with some user information, as shown in Figure 2.10. When you have completed the required fields, click the Submit button.

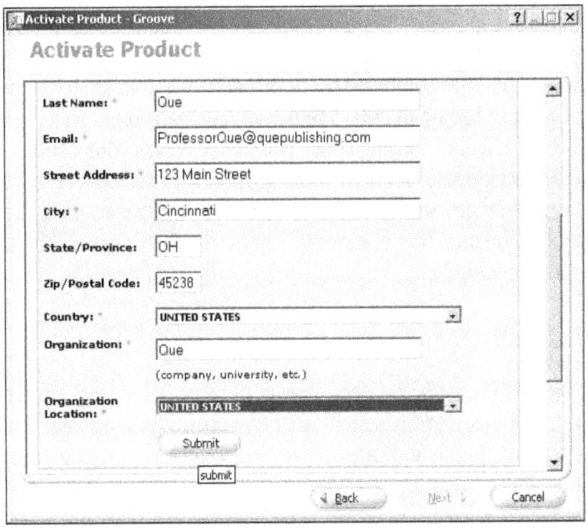

Figure 2.10
Before running the Preview Edition of Groove Workspace for the first time, you must complete this short user profile and click the Submit button.

3. Create a Groove account to use with the application. First of all, you must create a username for your account and enter it into the Name box provided, as shown in Figure 2.11. It's important to choose a username for your Groove account that will make you recognizable to your other Groove contacts.

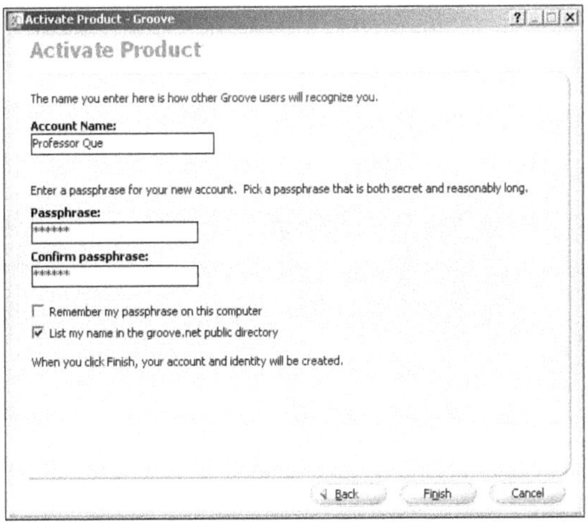

Figure 2.11
You must specify a username and password to use for your account.

4. After you've entered an account name, you must decide on a passphrase and enter it into the Passphrase and Confirm Passphrase boxes. This will not display onscreen as you type it to ensure confidentiality. Your passphrase should be easy to remember yet difficult for anyone else to guess. For instance, a single word can be easily guessed, such as a pet's name. However, choosing several words can make guessing the passphrase

much more difficult. For instance, instead of using "Angel" as a passphrase you may want to try something like "Angel is a good dog" instead.

NOTE

> You'll also see in Figure 2.11 that there are two additional options provided in the check boxes at the bottom of the screen. Although not recommended, checking the Remember My Passphrase on This Computer check box allows you to launch Groove on this particular device without having to enter the passphrase each time. This is unwise because anyone with access to your machine could potentially access your Groove account. By default, the option to include your identity in the groove.net directory is checked. This selection lists your identity in groove.net, which allows other Groove users to search for your identity in the public directory. If you leave this checked, other users will be able to search for and find your Groove identity.

NOTE

> I use the term *passphrase* here instead of what you would more commonly expect as *password*. A password is usually a string consisting of one word like "redhat," whereas a passphrase generally indicates something longer than a single word. Many "brute force" hacking attempts can find passwords by simply looping through a dictionary of words until a match is found. However, a passphrase like "give me 52 balloons" is harder to hack using unsophisticated techniques.

CAUTION

> Keep your passphrase in a safe place. If it is lost, there is no way to reset or recover it.

5. After you have satisfactorily completed the fields in step 4, click the Finish button and your account will be created. Groove Workspace will automatically open to the Welcome Page, as shown in Figure 2.12.

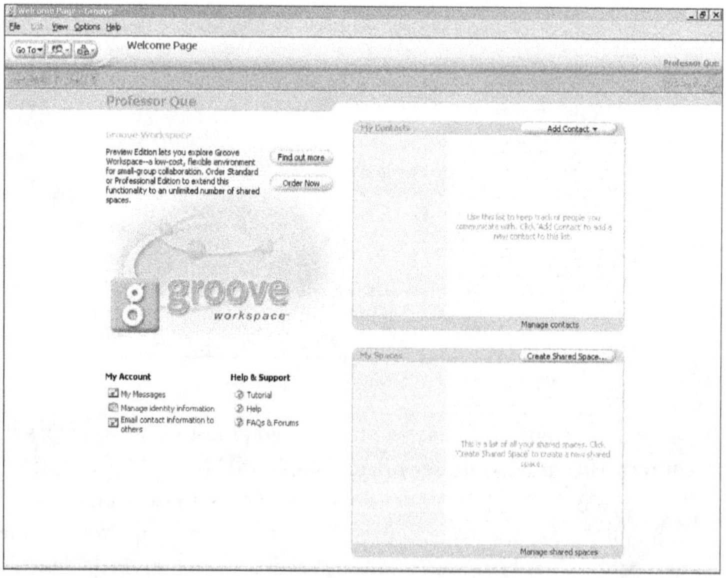

Figure 2.12
When you click the Finish button, Groove Workspace opens to the Welcome Page automatically.

ACTIVATING YOUR COPY OF GROOVE WORKSPACE

To unlock all the features of Groove, you need to purchase a license. By purchasing a license, you will receive an activation key that can be used for your copy of Groove Workspace. If you purchased Groove on the Groove Networks Web site, you should have received an activation code via email. If you are a managed user working with an Enterprise Edition of Groove, the system administrator should provide the activation key number. If you installed the product from CD, there should be an activation code on the CD case. Preview Edition users will not need an activation code when using the product. When you have obtained a copy of the activation key, follow these steps to activate your installation:

1. After starting Groove Workspace, choose Help, Activate Product.

2. You should now be prompted to enter the activation code, as shown in Figure 2.13. For existing Preview Edition users, you can enter your activation key when Groove is started by choosing Help, Activate Product from the main menu. Enter the activation code in the space provided. Standard users will leave the Activation provided by field as is. However, Enterprise users may be activated using an internal Groove Management Server. If this is the case, your system administrator will provide you with the necessary server address. When you have completed both fields, click Next to activate this instance of Groove Workspace.

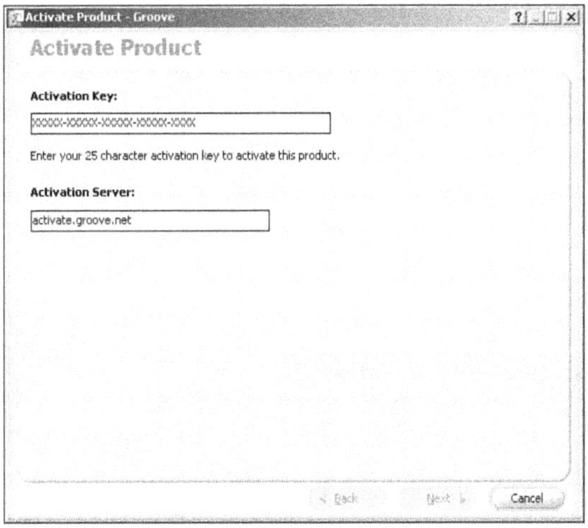

Figure 2.13
For product activation to occur, you need to provide the activation code and the Groove Management Server to use.

3. After clicking the Next button, there will be a pause while Groove verifies the activation code. Once completed, a message will be displayed showing that the product has been activated for the account, as shown in Figure 2.14. Click the Finish button to complete the product activation process.

Now that the product has been activated, you can enjoy all the features available in your edition of Groove Workspace. If you want to review the licenses added to an account at any time, you can choose Help, About from the main menu within Groove Workspace and click the Licenses button.

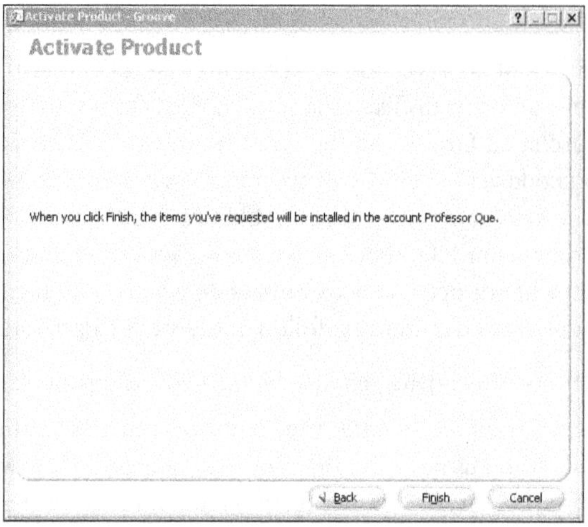

Figure 2.14
When the activation code is verified, you will receive a message like this one.

When you click Finish, the items you've requested will be installed in the account Professor Que.

GROOVE ACCOUNTS

A Groove user has an associated Groove account. The Groove account is a container of unique Groove identities, which allow the user to have multiple personas. Each Groove identity has a name that is displayed in the Groove user interface.

However, it is not the display name representing your identity that makes you unique; in fact it is possible for two identities to have the same name. For example, it is entirely possible that two identities with the name "John Smith" exist. So it is more than the identity name itself that makes secure and confidential communication in Groove possible.

When you create a Groove identity, two keypairs are generated: one for signing and the other for encryption. The public half of each keypair is stored in your vCard, whereas the private key itself is stored in the encrypted portion of the Groove account protected by the account's passphrase. Each identity has its own personal *digital fingerprint*, which is calculated with an algorithm that uses the identity's public key.

The concept of generating a keypair with a public and private key falls under the branch of cryptography called *public key cryptography*. Introduced in 1976, public key cryptography depends on the generation of a public key and related private keys. Any material encoded with the known public key can only be easily decrypted by someone who has been given a copy of the private key that is part of the public/private key pair. The benefit of this type of cryptography is that the public key can be transmitted using an unsecured method; in this case it is within the body of a user's unencrypted vCard.

To get a better understanding of the process, let's look at what happens when our Groove user, Professor Que, creates a new identity, Volunteer Que:

1. Professor Que creates the identity Volunteer Que, which will be contained in his Professor Que account.

2. For this identity, a public and private key pair is created using an algorithm. The public half of the key pair is stored in Volunteer Que's vCard. The private half of the keypair is stored in Professor Que's encrypted account (see Figure 2.15).

Figure 2.15
When an identity is added to an account, a public and private key is generated.

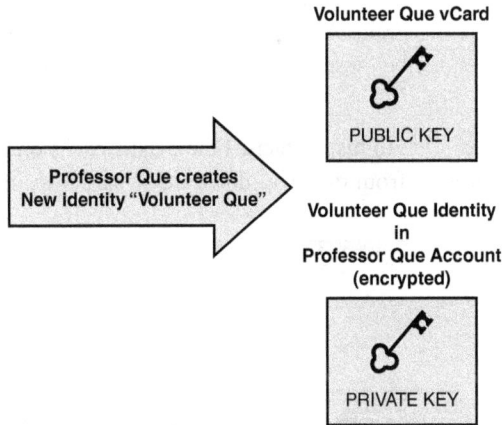

3. Volunteer Que sends his colleague, Frank, his vCard. The vCard contains Volunteer Que's public key. Frank decides to view Volunteer Que's digital fingerprint. Using the public key contained in the vCard, Frank's Groove client locally computes the digital fingerprint and displays it, as shown in Figure 2.16. The digital fingerprint itself is a string of characters; this same value will always be generated for Volunteer Que's identity. It is deterministically generated using a standard message digest mathematical algorithm called SHA1.

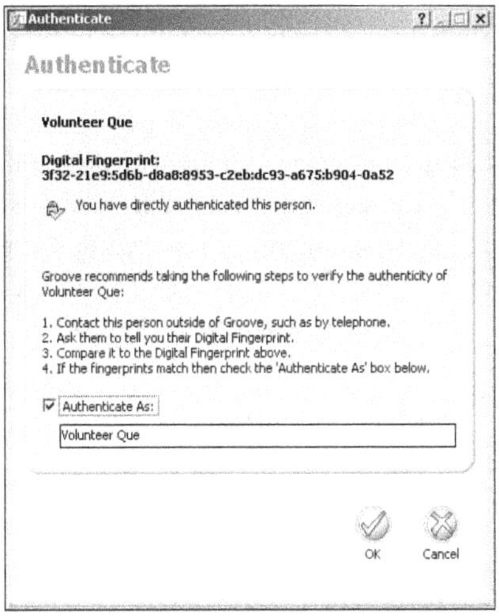

Figure 2.16
Frank views Volunteer Que's digital fingerprint, which has been calculated using the public key.

GROOVE'S UNSPOOFABLE IDENTITIES

With Volunteer Que's vCard, and subsequently his digital fingerprint, Frank can now verify that all communications are coming from "Volunteer Que." As long as Frank initially authenticates Volunteer Que, he can be assured that all messages come from Frank and not from someone impersonating Frank. You can see how Groove ensures the integrity and security of an instant message being sent from Volunteer Que to Frank in the following steps:

1. Frank adds Volunteer Que to his contacts. Frank right-clicks on Volunteer Que's name and chooses Authenticate from the drop-down menu as shown in Figure 2.17.

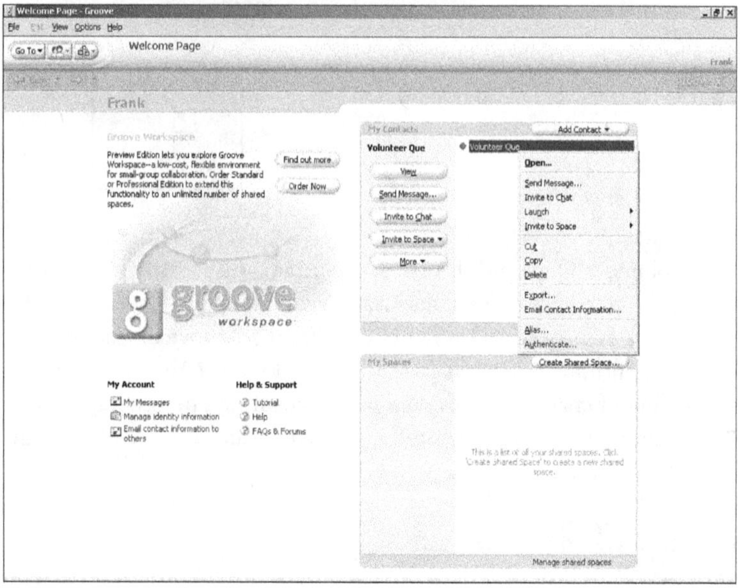

Figure 2.17
The Groove Workspace user Frank prepares to authenticate Volunteer Que by right-clicking his name in the contacts listing and choosing Authenticate.

2. Franks calls Volunteer Que on the phone and checks the digital fingerprint shown in Figure 2.18 with the one that Volunteer Que sees when looking at his own account vCard. When they match up, Frank selects the Authenticate As check box and clicks the OK button to add Volunteer Que as a trusted identity. The Volunteer Que contacts entry will now be displayed with a green check mark and padlock in the Contacts listing.

3. Volunteer Que composes a Groove instant message to Frank, as shown in Figure 2.19.

Figure 2.18
You can authenticate
users by comparing
the digital fingerprint
shown onscreen with
the one contained
in the target's
installation.

Figure 2.19
Professor Que creates
an instant message
and sends it to anoth-
er Groove user named
Frank.

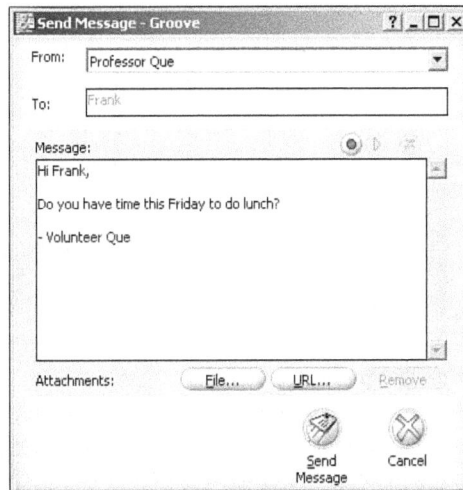

4. Groove packages the message into an encrypted package that uses a one-time *symmetric key*. In contrast to the public/private keypairs attached to an identity, a symmetric key is a single key that is known and used by both the sender and recipient of the encrypted message. Using this method, the key must be sent confidentially, so Groove encrypts the symmetric key using the sender's public key. Groove also digitally signs the message with Professor Que's private key so Frank can verify that the message came intact from the Professor.

5. The entire package of data is transmitted to Frank's Groove client. Upon receipt, Groove uses Frank's private key to decrypt the symmetric key contained within the package. After the symmetric key has been obtained, it can then be used to decrypt the message body in a second step. Groove then uses Professor Que's public key to verify the Professor's signature on the message.

Using this symmetric key, Groove can decrypt and display the message contents to Frank, as shown in Figure 2.20.

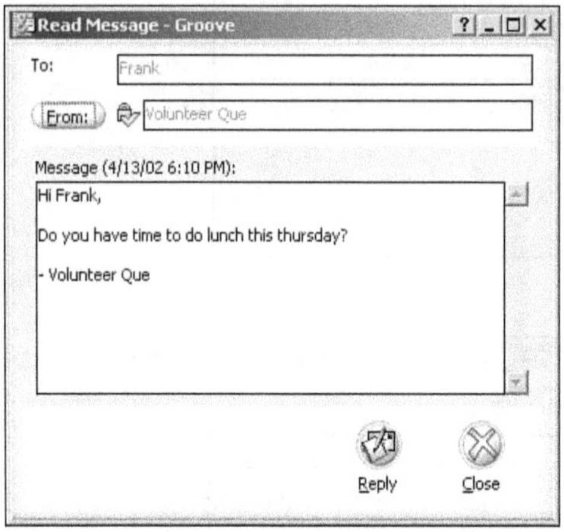

Figure 2.20
Frank receives the instant message from Professor Que without even being aware of the several security checks completed before the message's arrival.

The authentication process that Frank performed originally allows him to guarantee that all correspondence from Volunteer Que is truly from Volunteer Que and not someone impersonating him. Because Volunteer Que has already been authenticated, Groove will check the digital fingerprint on this message to ensure it's an exact match to the one originally authenticated. If it is an exact match, Groove will place a green check mark and padlock next to the From field on the message, as shown in Figure 2.20. Frank needs to do this manual fingerprint comparison only once in Groove for this digital fingerprint verification process to happen automatically with all communications.

NOTE

Although our example had Frank authenticate Volunteer Que prior to receiving the message, it is also possible to perform the authentication after you've received a message or invitation. Click the From button in the invitation and click the More button. Choose authentication from the drop-down menu and you can check the digital fingerprint.

To demonstrate the some of the security built into Groove, we'll try to "spoof" Volunteer Que by installing Groove Workspace on another machine and creating the Volunteer Que identity. Using the local directory, we find Frank and send him an instant message from our spoofed identity. Frank receives the message, as shown in Figure 2.21. As we can see in the figure, there is a red name conflict mark to the left of the spoofed Volunteer Que name in the message. This should indicate that messages have come from two identities with the same name, but different digital fingerprints.

NOTE

> If there truly is a situation where you may have more than one identity using the same name, at this point you would click the From: button and authenticate the individual. However, you should be sure to assign each identity a different name in the Authenticate As field.

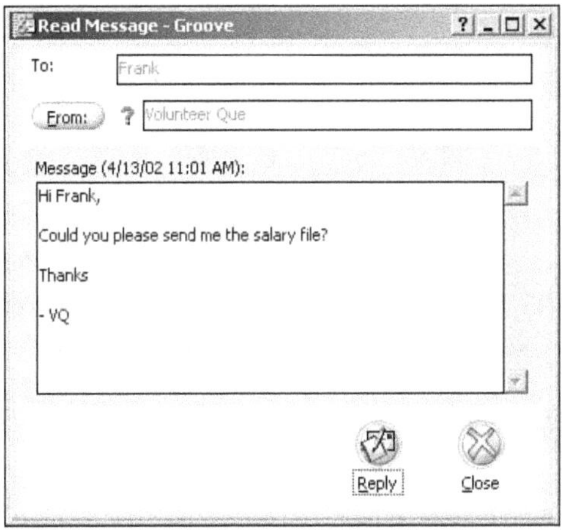

Figure 2.21
Using the digital fingerprint, Groove will alert you to a potentially spoofed account by placing a red name conflict mark next to the identity of the sender.

NOTE

> If Groove shuts down unexpectedly, such as in the case of a power failure, trying to run Groove may generate the error `Cannot open database c:\program files\Groove Networks\groove\data\\__XSSTemp__.xss (0)`. Find and rename the `__XSSTemp__.xss` file to something else, such as `XSSTEMP.BAK`, and this should resolve the issue. This is a temporary file used by Groove that is not deleted due to unexpected shutdown.

RUNNING GROOVE ON MULTIPLE COMPUTERS

If you'd like to use the same Groove Workspace account on different devices, such as at home and at work, there are some special steps you'll need to take. In fact, any time you want to preserve account information you'll need to follow these steps or create a completely new account. Groove accounts are an integral part of the security structure of Groove and need to be transferred properly if you want to use them on more than one device. It's not a difficult task, just one that requires you understand a little bit about how Groove accounts operate. We are assuming you already have some familiarity with Groove at this point, but for a refresher you can consult Chapter 3, "Starting to Groove," which outlines many of the application basics.

SAVING YOUR ACCOUNT INFORMATION

If you are moving Groove to a new machine while replacing an old one, I cannot stress how important it is to save your account information *prior* to uninstalling Groove on the first machine. Otherwise you may become what some call a "Groove orphan," and you'll need to reacquaint yourself with all your old contacts. The following steps outline how to save your account information:

1. First open the My Account area by clicking the GoTo drop-down list box and choosing My Account in the menu located in the upper-left corner of the Transceiver, as shown in Figure 2.22.

Figure 2.22
The GoTo button provides a quick way to reach the My Account area.

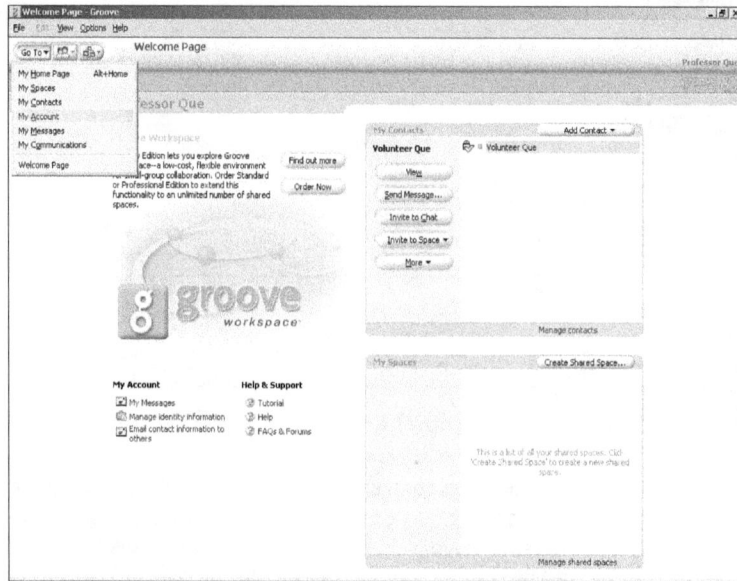

2. Once inside your account, you should click the Account tab at the bottom of the window, as shown in Figure 2.23.

3. Click the Multiple Computers button. This starts the wizard that will help you complete the rest of the process.

4. You should see the Multiple Computers wizard, as shown in Figure 2.24. First, choose whether you want to save your account information via the Internet or manually through a file. If you use the Via the Internet option you are transmitting your account information to groove.net so that you can simply download it on your new destination computer. Choosing the Manually, Through a File option does exactly what it says. Your account information is saved to a .grv file that you must be able to access from the destination computer to proceed. After you choose the appropriate radio button, click Next to continue.

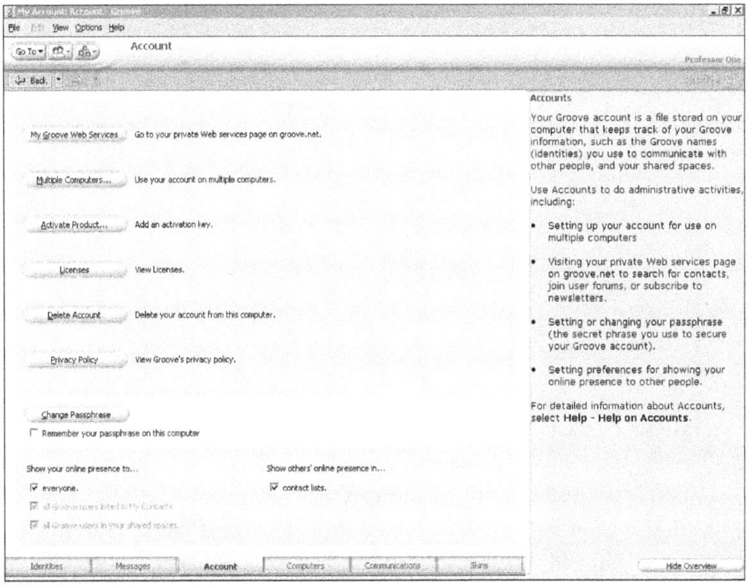

Figure 2.23
Clicking the Account tab lets you configure the current Groove account.

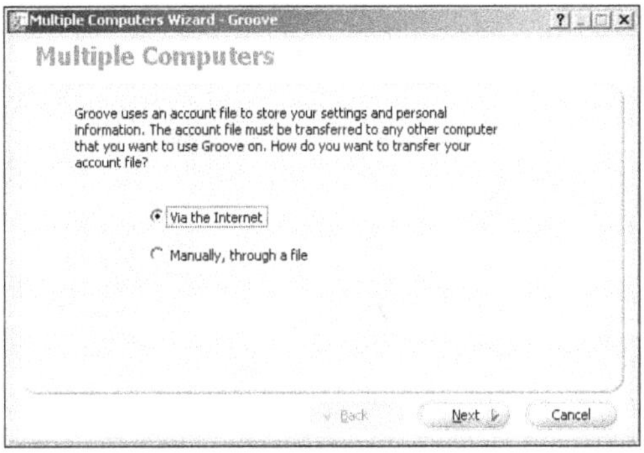

Figure 2.24
The Multiple Computers wizard requires you to choose a location where the current account information will be stored.

5. If you have chosen the Via the Internet option in the previous step, you should now see the screen in Figure 2.25. The Name field will be populated with the current account name. In the Passphrase field, enter your account passphrase. Enter your email address in the Email field provided. After you click the Next button, Groove will notify you that it is in the process of uploading your account information to groove.net. After this information has been saved, you will be taken to the finish screen and you can proceed to the next step.

NOTE

Remember the email address you've used here because it will be used later to retrieve the account.

Figure 2.25
Choosing to save your
account information to
the Internet will
prompt you for a
passphrase and email
address.

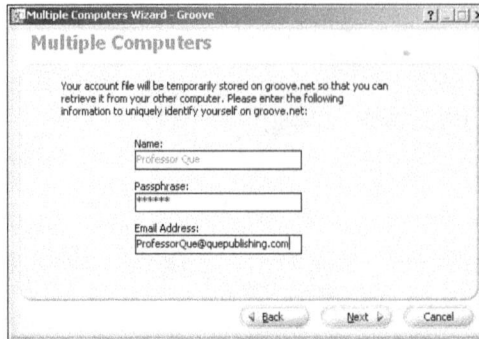

If you chose the Manually, Through a File option in step 4, you should now see the
Save Account As dialog box shown in Figure 2.26. Specify a location to save the file
that is accessible from the destination computer. Click the Save button once finished.
In this example, you'll use the floppy drive on this computer. The .grv file is relatively
small and can easily be transported by floppy disk.

Figure 2.26
Choose the location
where your Groove
account file should
be saved for later
retrieval.

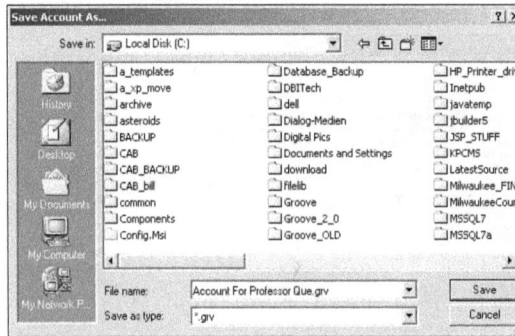

6. After the file has been saved in step 5, you can click the Finish button shown in Figure
   2.27. Your account information is now stored and ready to be moved to a different
   installation of Groove, or what we can refer to as a new *instance* of the Groove client.

Figure 2.27
Click Finish to end
the Multiple
Computers Wizard.

CAUTION

> Be sure to import the account soon after saving it. After an account is saved to a file, the file will eventually expire and you will be unable to import it.

IMPORTING YOUR ACCOUNT INTO GROOVE

After installing and launching Groove on the new destination computer, you'll see the familiar Create Account screen. This is where many people get confused, thinking that they can simply type in their old account information and access the account from the previous installation. Account information is not stored on a central server and is only maintained on devices on which it is installed, unless the user specifically saved the account information. This is why it was necessary to explicitly save your account information before doing the new install. The .grv file you saved to a file or to groove.net is your only link to the previous account data.

Click the Groove icon in the system tray on the new destination computer and choose the Import Account option from the drop-down menu. You'll then be prompted to choose where your account information resides. Reminiscent of the process used to save the account information, you need to choose whether you will be importing account information from a file or from the Internet on groove.net, as shown in Figure 2.28.

Figure 2.28
Specify where your account information was saved when using the Multiple Computers Wizard.

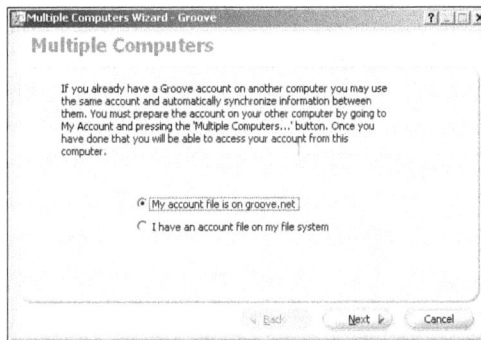

If you chose to save your account information in a file, you should choose I Have an Account File on My File System and click the Next button. Similar to the dialog used to save the file, you must locate the .grv account file. In Figure 2.29, you have located the .grv file on the floppy drive. Click the Open button and you should receive confirmation if the file was imported properly.

If you chose to save your information on groove.net, you will be prompted for the username, passphrase, and email address for the account, as shown in Figure 2.30. These are the keys used to retrieve your specific account data from groove.net. Information must be entered exactly, including spaces and capitalization. After you click the Next button, Groove will display a message indicating that it is retrieving your account information.

Groove should display a notification box with the message `Account <Identity Name> Imported!` indicating that it now recognizes the account, as shown in Figure 2.31.

Figure 2.29
Locate the `.grv` account file and click the Open button.

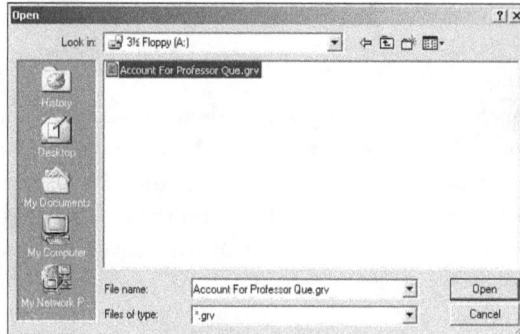

Figure 2.30
Enter the account information specified in the Multiple Computers Wizard.

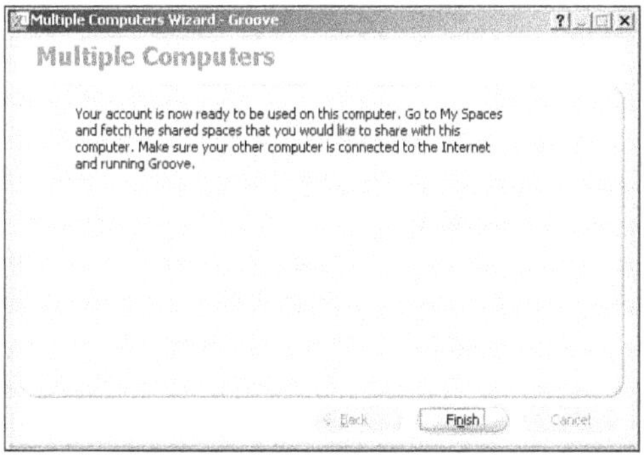

Figure 2.31
A Groove notification should display after the account has been successfully imported.

You may encounter errors at this point connecting to groove.net. Although it is entirely possible that the service is having problems, usually the problem is with the Groove client. See "Problems Accessing groove.net to Retrieve a Saved Account" in the Troubleshooting section at the end of this chapter.

At this point, you will have transferred your account information, including your contacts. Next, you'll move all the shared space data to this new instance.

CAUTION

> Be careful changing your passphrase on separate installations residing on different devices. This passphrase is valid for that device only. Without synchronizing your passphrases, it would be easy to have different passphrases for different machines accessing the same account.

After importing the previous account information, you should go to the My Spaces area by clicking GoTo, My Spaces. This will take you to a screen displaying all the spaces that existed on the instance of Groove the account was exported from, as shown in Figure 2.32. Because you haven't explicitly fetched all the Shared Space data, the status will be listed as Not on This Computer for each space. This indicates that Groove is aware of the space; however, all the data within it has not been retrieved. Highlighting a space and clicking on Fetch Space will initiate the process of retrieving all the space data. This will be indicated by the notification Fetching "*Space Name*", as shown in Figure 2.33.

TIP

> If the source computer (where the original account exists) is not online, the fetch will be queued using Groove relay services. The status will continue to say "Fetching" until the source computer is brought online again. While the space is being fetched, you can continue to use other Groove functions but should not enter the space being retrieved until the fetching process has completed.

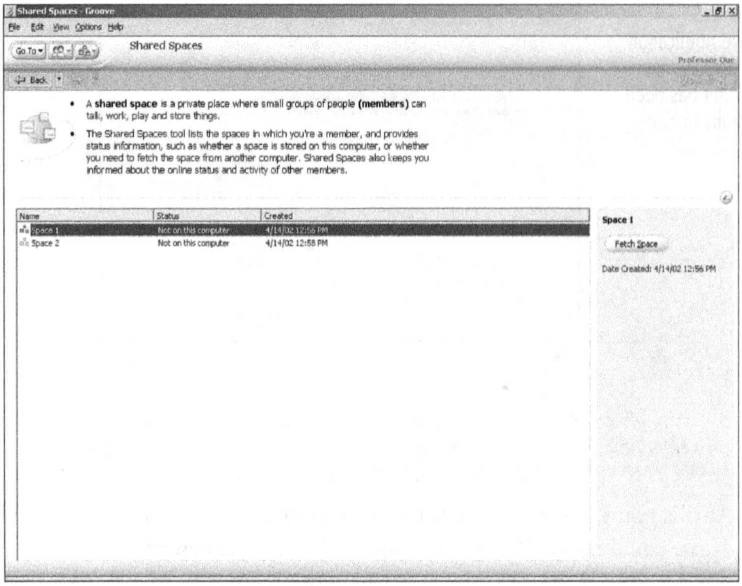

Figure 2.32
After importing your account, the My Spaces area will be displayed indicating the status of all shared spaces attached to your account.

Figure 2.33
As space data is being retrieved, you will receive status information next to the space name in the My Spaces area.

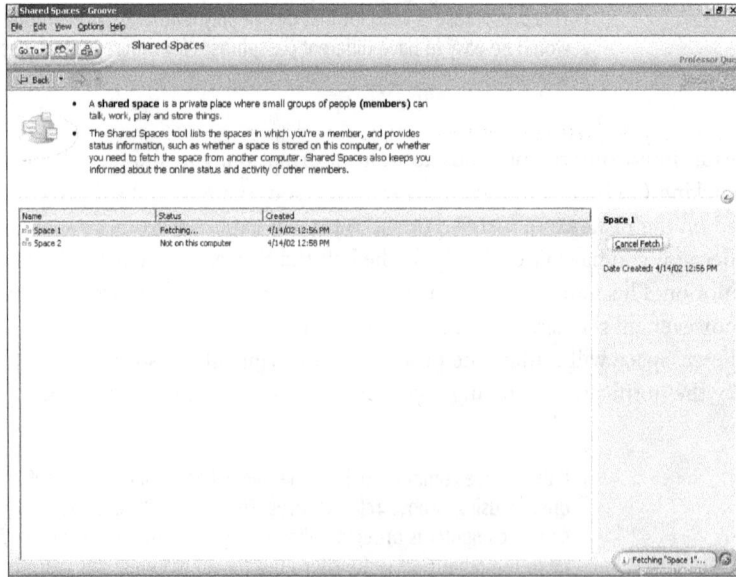

After the space data has been successfully retrieved, the status will change to Ready, as shown in Figure 2.34. This indicates the space data has been retrieved and you can now enter the space. You should do this for all shared spaces in which you will be participating.

Figure 2.34
After all space data has been retrieved, it will change to a status of Ready and is ready for use.

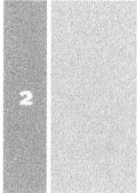

NETWORK CONNECTIVITY

Groove adapts to your particular network configuration. As such, there are several different scenarios that may apply to you at a given time. Depending on your situation, Groove may need a few things in place to allow it to operate most efficiently.

NOTE

> The Groove Management Server provides the same services as the relay services provided by groove.net. The following examples assume that the relay services provided by groove.net are being used. However, in situations where limited bandwidth is available, the Groove Management Server might be a good choice for enterprise customers. You can find full information about this product at `http://www.groove.net/products/enterprise/relay/`.

DIAL-UP

A typical dial-up user connects using a 56Kbps modem on a standard phone line. Most dial-up users are assigned an IP address automatically from a DHCP server when the connection is established. This IP address allows you to connect with other Groove users given that they have access to the Internet and are not in some way restricted by something in their environment, such as a firewall that has not been configured to support Groove. As shown in Figure 2.35, a typical dial-up user has access to the groove.net directory. Access to the local network directory would only be enabled if the user has a small home network with all machines on the same subnet.

Figure 2.35
A high-level depiction of a Groove user with a dial-up modem connection and no local area network installed.

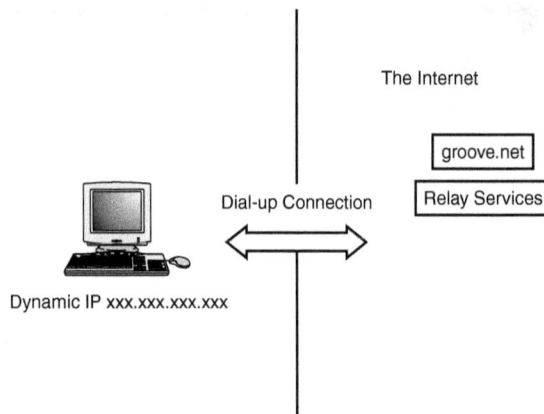

TIP

> When Groove is minimized (which places it into the system tray) it goes into "conserve" mode and generally will not use as much system resources or bandwidth. For 56Kbps modem dial-up users and other situations where resources might be scarce, it might be a good idea to minimize Groove when not in use to conserve some bandwidth. Of course, you can completely close the Groove application, but you will lose notification of new messages and other Groove events.

LOCAL AREA NETWORK WITH NO INTERNET ACCESS

In the scenario shown in Figure 2.36, Groove can be used to communicate with all other participants as long as they are in the same subnet. In most small offices, this is likely the case. However, in larger offices and those with WANs you may have users segmented into different subnets. Currently, Groove uses the relay service to enable communication between subnets, but in this case it would not be possible because Internet access is required to reach the relay server. However, participants can search and use the local network directory services to find other users in their own subnet on the network.

Figure 2.36
A high level depiction of a Groove user in a local area network with no Internet access.

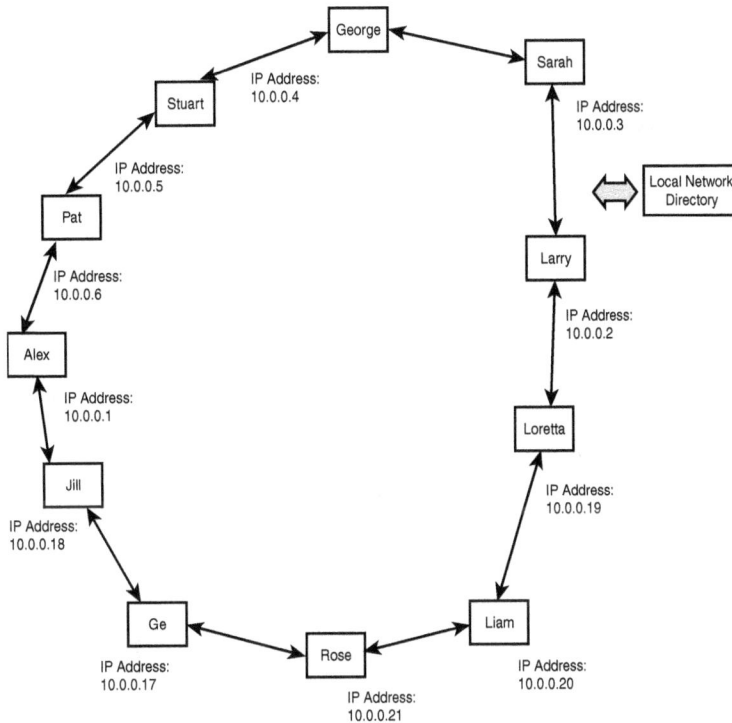

LOCAL AREA NETWORK WITH INTERNET ACCESS

This very common scenario, shown in Figure 2.37, is found in many offices that have Internet access enabled. In this case, communication with all internal colleagues and external participants should be possible, given the firewall is configured correctly. If the firewall is set to restrict access by IP address, it should be configured to allow access to the IP block 63.209.254.*. Groove is constantly adding new relay servers, so this should accommodate any new relay and component servers brought online. In addition, if TCP access on ports 80 and 443 has not been enabled already, have the administrator turn this on. Lastly, for optimal performance, the firewall should be configured to allow TCP access on port 2492. This allows Groove to use its efficient SSTP protocol, which can speed up synchronization. We talk more about this protocol and why it's better suited for peer-to-peer communications in Chapter 13, "Publishing a New Tool." In this situation, users can not only search for contacts from the local network directory, but can also access the groove.net directory because they have Internet access.

⚠ *Whether it is installed to a home or office computer, some people have reported problems running Groove if advertisement blocking software is installed. If you are encountering problems and have this type of software installed, see "Running Groove with Advertisement Blocking Software" in the Troubleshooting section at the end of this chapter.*

Figure 2.37
A common scenario
depicting a Groove
user in a local area
network with Internet
access.

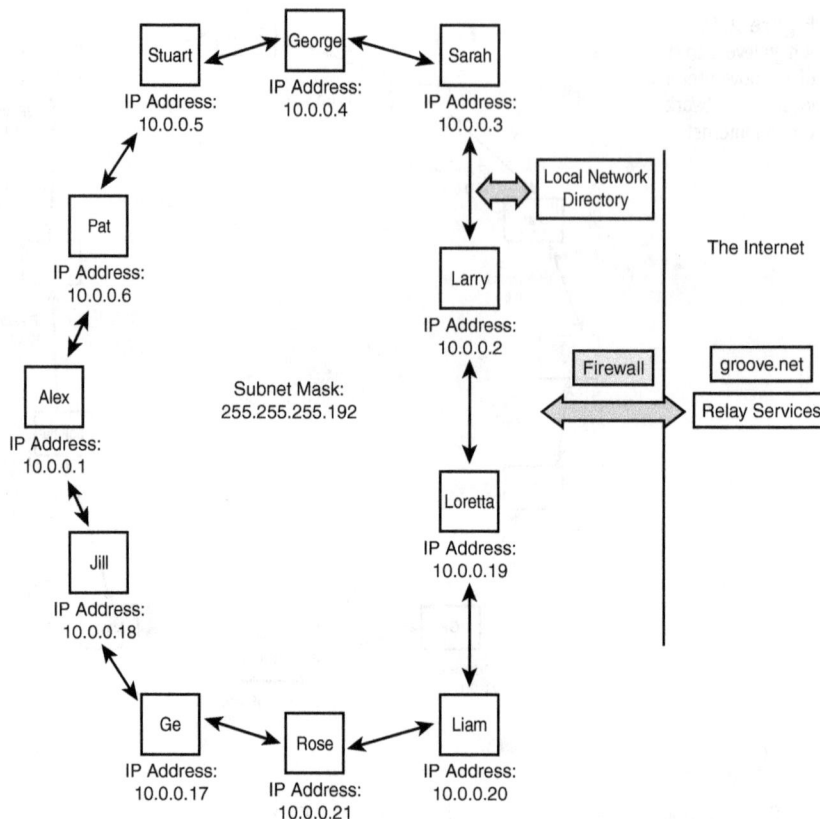

HOW TO UNINSTALL GROOVE

If you want to uninstall Groove from your computer, there are a few steps you need to follow instead of simply deleting the folders and the icons from your menu. If you do not uninstall the Groove application and all its data correctly, it can cause you some serious frustration later. The following steps demonstrate how to uninstall the Groove application and its related data storage:

1. Launch Groove and remove any identities that may be listed in the groove.net or LAN directory. You can find these in the My Account area under the Identities tab, as shown in Figure 2.38. You'll want to iterate through every identity listed in the drop-down text box at the top of the screen. After choosing an identity, simply select No Listing under both the groove.net and LAN directory options at the bottom portion of the screen. You'll receive a notification in the lower-right portion of your screen confirming they have been removed from the directory.

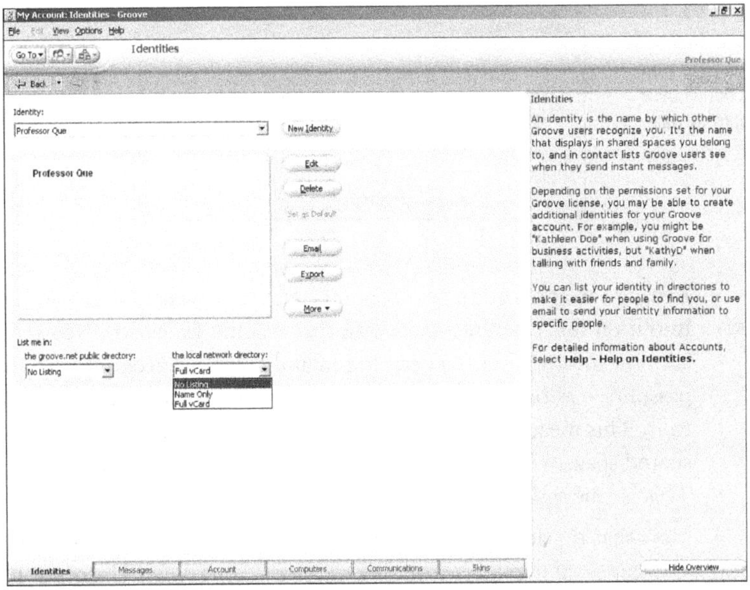

Figure 2.38
Configure all account identities so they are not listed in the local or groove.net directory.

CAUTION

Deleting your account is irreversible unless you explicitly save your account information to a file or to groove.net. Refer to the "Running Groove on Multiple Computers" section earlier in this chapter if you want to do this.

2. After you have disabled the listing of your identities in the local and network directories, you must now delete each identity individually. Similar to removing them from the directory, you must select each identity from the drop-down list at the top of the Identities window. Once selected, click on the Delete button and click Yes in the confirmation alert window that appears. You must do this for all the identities, except for the last one in the list, which you cannot remove because every Groove account must have at least one identity assigned to it. You will remove them both in the next step.

NOTE

Identities stored on groove.net are periodically removed after a certain period of inactivity. This also means inactive Groove users will no longer appear in the groove.net directory if they do not use an identity for extended period of time.

3. After removing all but one of the identities, you must now remove the account. You'll first need to select the Account tab within the My Account area you are currently in. On this screen you see a Delete Account button that you'll need to click. At this point, you should have saved all your shared space information in some manner, because this is an irreversible action. When you are sure, click the Yes button in the confirmation dialog shown in Figure 2.39. You'll receive one more box stating that deletion will occur when you shut down Groove.

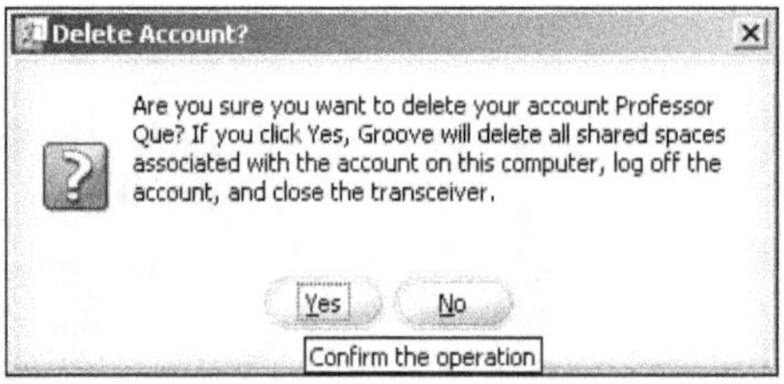

Figure 2.39
Clicking Yes here will not only delete your account but all other accompanying data.

Exiting the application at this point deletes the account and no longer allows you to log into it on this machine again with this account unless you've explicitly saved your account information. You can log in and create an account with the same username and passphrase as before; however, this new account has a new digital fingerprint attached to it. This means anyone who previously listed you as a contact or invited you to a shared space will need to add the new account or re-invite you to any shared spaced. This is true *unless* you've saved your account information in a file or on groove.net.

4. Now that the account references have all been cleaned up, it is time to remove the application and its data from your system. Shut down Groove if it is still running by right-clicking on the taskbar and choosing Shutdown Groove. Similar to other applications with uninstall support, you then need to choose Add/Remove Programs from your Control Panel. If you're running Windows 2000, you'll see a screen similar to Figure 2.40. Users of other Windows versions will see a screen similar to this. Choose the Groove application and click on the Change/Remove button.

Figure 2.40
Remove the Groove application using the Add/Remove Programs feature in Windows 2000.

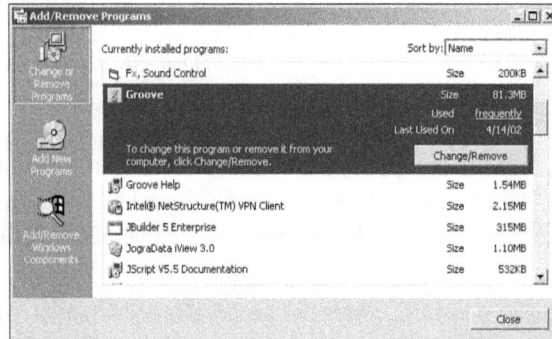

NOTE

Although not officially supported, stopping at this point often allows you to "refresh" your Groove installation without losing your account information and retaining all shared space content. If you do a little snooping, you'll see that although the Groove application may be gone, most of the data it uses isn't. One word of caution, however; any updates to tools (such as the addition of new functionality) will not be added to tools in existing spaces. Tools are *versioned*, meaning that to get the latest version you will need to add a new instance of the tool to a shared space to realize any features in the newest version.

5. To completely uninstall Groove, there are a few other loose ends you need to take care of. It is doubtful that the actual Groove program folder has been deleted. So using Windows Explorer or whatever you're comfortable with, you need to navigate to the installation folder and manually delete the Groove folder. In default installations, this is under the \Program Files\Groove Networks\ folder. This should remove all Groove data stored locally.

6. Run the Registry editor by choosing Start, Run and specifying "regedit" as the application to open. Clicking OK at this point will open the Registry editor. Navigate to the Registry under HKEY_LOCAL_MACHINE\SOFTWARE\Groove Networks, Inc. Highlight the entry and choose Delete under the Edit menu. You'll be prompted to confirm the deletion. Clicking Yes removes the Registry entry from your computer.

CAUTION

> Manipulating the Registry can have disastrous results. Remember that important information is stored in the Registry that is not only used by other applications, but by the operating system itself. If you are uncomfortable with this step, it can be skipped because it usually does not have any real adverse affects on future installations. It should be common practice for you to make a backup of your Registry prior to making any changes in case there are any problems.

NOTE

> If you receive an error message during the uninstall process about `groovutil.dll` being in use, it probably means that Groove is still running. Make sure you've shut it down properly by right-clicking the Groove icon in the taskbar and choosing Shutdown Groove. If you have already completed this step, but still receive the error, restart your computer and try the process again.

BACKING UP YOUR GROOVE DATA

Given the decentralized nature of a Groove installation, it does not currently have a backup utility included. However, there is a method you can use in the interim to give yourself a reasonable means of restoring all shared space and account information in the event of a problem. It just makes sense to back up regularly, especially before upgrading software or hardware components. This is not officially supported by Groove, but it seems to be a good interim solution until a more formal utility is introduced.

Save the Groove application \Data directory. This is found under the default installation path. For most users, this will be C:\Program Files\Groove Networks\Groove\Data. You can use the backup utility provided with Windows or any other suitable application for copying all the files and retaining the directory structure.

TIP

> Saving to CDR/W may present some problems due to the long filenames that Groove uses. Consult your CD manual to find out about accommodating extremely long file names, or you may try packing everything into a zip file with a shorter name or using some other compression method. Because shared space data can consume a lot of space, compressing it before backing up may make it easier to move around.

In case of a problem, often you can uninstall Groove and replace the \Data folder with a prior backup. Reinstalling Groove will replace all the application components, but should keep all data in shared spaces and account information intact.

TIP

> If you get errors or other peculiar occurrences in any of the restored shared spaces, this could indicate a corrupted space. The most common method of fixing this problem is to delete the space and have someone in the space re-invite you.

ADDITIONAL NOTES ON BACKING UP YOUR DATA

As you learned in Chapter 1, "What Is Groove?," Groove is designed to operate in dynamic network environments. Even though it's pretty resilient even with system and network configuration changes, it is entirely possible for strange errors to occur. As with most Windows applications, it is possible for an installation to become corrupted. In addition to the steps outlined previously, many individuals have made a habit of regularly saving shared space data. Although Groove does not have a built-in backup mechanism to save your data, it is as simple as copying some files to ensure you have a clean backup. Some recommendations for backing up include the following:

- For Windows 98/Me/2000/XP users:

  Under Start, Programs, Accessories, System Tools you can run the Backup utility. This will create a backup file (.bkf) that can be stored on permanent or removable media. This utility allows backup jobs to be scheduled to run at regular intervals. Pick a time to back up Groove when it is not running because files in use will be skipped during the procedure. For additional information on using this utility consult your Windows documentation.

- Windows NT (Workstation and Server):

  Many Windows NT users will purchase third-party backup utilities, but many of these may be too complicated for the home user and overly sophisticated for our needs here. Windows NT users may want to refer to the section on using ZIP compression.

- All operating systems:

  Using a compression utility such as ZIP provides a quick and easy way to back up your Groove directory and use the least amount of space. The PKZIP product is offered in Windows and DOS-based (command line) versions that can be used in conjunction with your Windows scheduler to make backups on regular intervals. For more information on PKZIP visit www.pkware.com.

A little bit of prevention can go a long way, especially when it comes to the valuable fruits of effective collaboration.

LISTING YOUR NAME IN THE DIRECTORY

Without knowing a username, users can discover other Groove users by searching the Groove directories. Groove gives users control over whether a particular identity is included in each type of directory. Groove has two types of directories: the *local network directory* and the *groove.net directory*. As the name suggests, the local network directory contains the names of all individuals around you. In a network setting, this would consist of only those individuals on your particular subnet. The groove.net directory is maintained remotely at groove.net, and you have the option to add or remove yourself when you are completing the Create Account form or at any other time you want. Only those with Internet access will be able to publish to and search this directory.

Groove's built-in directory feature is a very powerful function. Although users are connected in a decentralized manner, the directory provides a centralized point of contact for all users within a local network (local network directory) or even across different geographic regions (groove.net directory). Chapter 3 discusses the My Contacts area and how you can use the directory to build your contact list. In Chapter 10, "The Foundation for Development: The Groove Development Kit (GDK)," you'll look at the technical aspects of the underlying architecture that makes this all possible.

→ To learn about building your contact list using the directories and My Contacts, **see** "Using My Contacts," **p.97**

→ For more information on the variety of interconnected services that enable features such as the directory, **see** "The Groove Framework Architecture," **p.310**

> TIP
>
> Be sure to enter some contact information about yourself because usernames do not have to be unique. This will help everyone find you easier, but remember you must choose to list your entire vCard for this to work. It can make search results confusing when there are several instances of the same name. For example, in a company using Groove there may be two Groove users by the name "John Smith." Each "John Smith" should add additional information to his vCard, such as email address, so that other users can easily distinguish them. Without a unique identifier attached to each, a message would have to be sent to each to confirm that the selected "John Smith" is the intended recipient. For complete details on how to enter your personal and business contact information and more information on directory listings, consult Chapter 3.

→ For more information on updating personal and business information on your vCard, **see** "Editing Your Current Identity," **p.88**

> TIP
>
> Be very careful not to save any sensitive information you would not want others to see if you decide to list your entire vCard. Familiarize yourself with all the directory options and the use of identities in Chapter 3. Otherwise you may be publishing information, such as an unlisted phone number, that you may not want to share with others.

FINDING ADDITIONAL HELP

If you need additional support there are several places to get help. For installation support questions, Groove runs a moderated forum that allows users to post questions. Simply go to www.groove.net, choose Support from the home page, and there you will see an option to enter the forums. Groove Networks staff members or even other users generally answer questions in a timely manner.

Another good source of information is to enter a Learning Groove session. This is a regularly scheduled shared space that offers an interactive training session for those new to Groove. In addition, during regularly scheduled sessions you can pose questions to other members or the Groove employee running the session. Under the support option on the www.groove.net home page, click on the Training link and you'll see the option to download the Learning Space invitation.

In addition to these sources, Usenet offers several different newsgroups that are often used by other Groove users and peer-to-peer enthusiasts. If your news service provider offers these groups they may be a good place to go for help or general questions:

- `alt.gnutella`
- `alt.internet.p2p`
- `alt.music.mp3.napster`
- `comp.groupware`

In the Groove community, there are a few enterprising users who have set up their own less formal "water coolers" for Groove discussion. Not only can you get technical help with Groove, but you also can network with all types of Groovers:

- groovelog (`http://groovelog.agora.co.uk`)

  Sponsored by a business partner of Groove, this is a running log that has regular posts by several members of the Groove community. This also is a good place for links to the latest articles on Groove.

- Rendezvoo (`http://www.rendezvoo.net`)

  As a "launch pad" for members to invite others to active shared spaces, Rendezvoo is the beginning of a virtual community for Groove users from around the world to meet and share ideas. Discussions are categorized so you can easily find what you're interested in. This is presented by Agora, which also runs the groovelog forum.

EXERCISE: CONFIGURING GROOVE TO WORK BEHIND A PERSONAL FIREWALL

With the increasing popularity of broadband connections, many with static or rarely changing IP addresses, it's important to shield your computer from unwanted access. In addition to turning on security settings supported by some operating systems, firewalls offer protection against unauthorized intruders. Although Groove has been designed to work in a variety of different network scenarios, there are certain firewall configuration options that can ensure you are getting peak performance. In the following example, you'll look at configuring Norton Personal Firewall 2001.

Norton Personal Firewall is a popular choice for home computer protection because it uses something called the Rules Assistant to step you through configuration changes. If the Enable Automatic Firewall Rule Creation option has been turned on, it should immediately prompt you when a new application requests access to a network resource. Groove uses several different protocols that may require configuring your firewall settings. In this example I'll walk you through configuring the firewall to enable TCP communications on port 2492. The rest of the protocols and the appropriate firewall settings are summarized in the sections following the walk-through.

OUTBOUND TCP CONNECTION ON PORT 2492

When starting Groove, you'll receive the first of your automatic warnings from Norton Personal Firewall, as shown in Figure 2.41. It has detected outbound TCP communications on Port 2492. Although opening port 80 is the minimum Groove needs to operate, this forces Groove to use the HTTP protocol. Although optimized for Web browsing, HTTP is not optimized for the dynamic communication Groove needs to perform. The preferred protocol for Groove communication is called SSTP, or the *Simple Symmetrical Transmission Protocol*. SSTP is a bi-directional protocol that is highly optimized for peer-to-peer communications over low-bandwidth, high-latency networks.

Figure 2.41
Firewall applications, such as Norton Personal Firewall, will often notify you when Groove tries to communicate.

In the standard configuration, Norton Personal Firewall will prompt you when a new application tries to access the Internet. When the warning for Groove.exe is displayed, you can configure the firewall to permit Groove to communicate without repeatedly displaying a warning message by following these steps:

1. From the warning screen, click on Configure a Rule for the Future (Recommended) to begin the Rule Assistant.

2. Select the Always Permit This Network Communication option, as shown in Figure 2.42, and click Next.

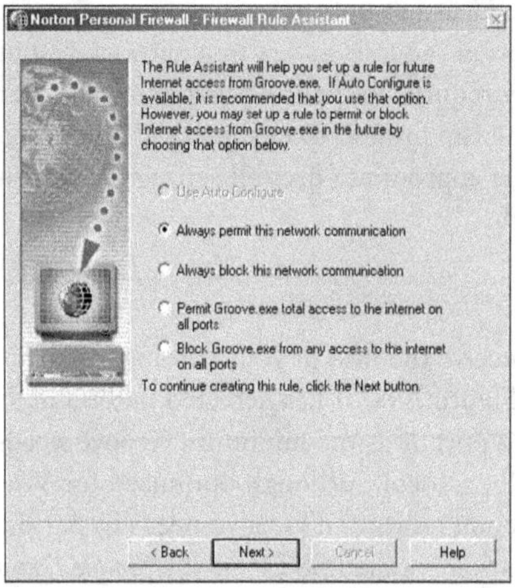

Figure 2.42
Choose Always Permit This Network Connection so that you will not be notified by subsequent Groove connection attempts on this port.

3. Select the Only This Service: Port 2492 option and click the Next button, as shown in Figure 2.43.

Figure 2.43
Choose only the port 2492 service and click the Next button to continue.

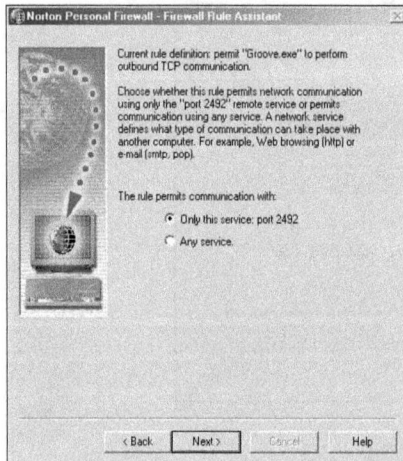

4. Select Any Address, which will allow Groove to communicate to any remote address, as shown in Figure 2.44.

Figure 2.44
You should allow this service to talk to any address and click the Next button to continue.

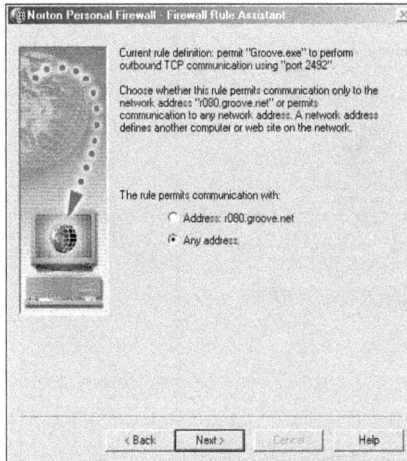

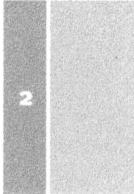

NOTE

In this example, you are allowing Groove to communicate to any remote address. If this setting is too permissive for your security requirements, you can create a more restrictive rule to permit access to only specific remote addresses. Check your documentation for instructions to permit communication to a range of IP addresses.

5. You can choose to leave the Category set to General, as shown in Figure 2.45, or change it to a more appropriate one. This is only used to group firewall settings and does not affect how it functions.

Figure 2.45
Choose a category to place the new firewall rule into.

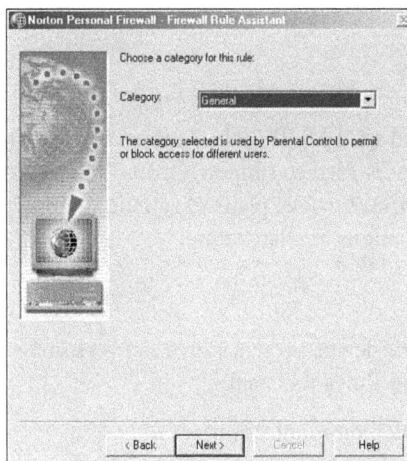

6. Finally, you will see the summary screen shown in Figure 2.46. Double-check that the correct options have been chosen.

Figure 2.46
This screen will summarize the firewall rule that you just added.

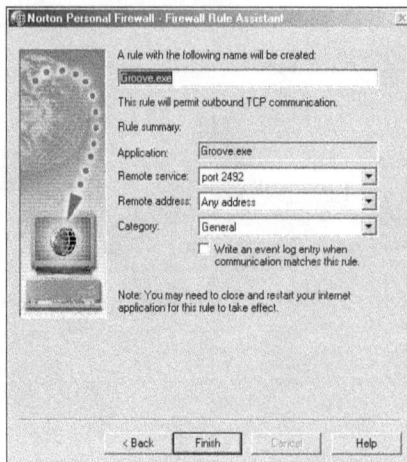

OUTBOUND TCP ON HTTP PORT 80

Groove uses port 80 to communicate to its relay servers. Relay servers are used when Groove cannot communicate to other users with the SSTP protocol. Creating a rule with the following options will allow the relay server communication in Norton Personal Firewall:

- Always Permit This Network Communication
- Only This Service: http, Port 80
- Permit Communication to Any Address
- General Category

UDP CONNECTIONS

At frequent intervals, Groove will send UDP packets on port 1211. This is part of the *Device Presence Protocol* (DPP) that is used to support Groove's device awareness and discovery on local and wide area networks. Groove plans to submit and publish the DPP protocol to the Internet standards organizations at a later time.

OUTBOUND UDP ON PORT 1211

This protocol is used to announce device presence on a network and should be configured using the following options in the Rules Assistant:

- Always Permit This Network Communication
- Only This Service: Port 1211

- Permit Communication to Any Address (see previous note)
- General Category

INBOUND UDP ON PORT 1211

This protocol is used to discover peer devices on a local area network and should be configured using the following options in the Rules Assistant:

- Always Permit This Network Communication
- Only This Service: Port 1211
- Permit Communication to Any Address
- General Category

TROUBLESHOOTING

USER PERMISSION PROBLEMS DURING INSTALLATION

Although not an issue with Windows 98 machines, in Windows NT/2000/XP you'll want to ensure that you are logged in with Administrator rights to perform the installation. If you are logged in with insufficient rights, you may get errors such as

```
Error: Setup Failed to Launch installation engine: Class Not Registered

Error extracting support files: Access denied
```

Subsequently, users of the Groove application must have read/write access to the Groove Data folder and subfolders in order to run Groove. Contact your system administrator if you're unsure about your current security settings.

INSTALLATION STOPS BECAUSE FILE IS IN USE

When installing Groove, you may receive error messages referring to issues with certain DLLs, such as GrooveHotKeys.dll or GrooveHooks.dll. This is due to libraries persisting in memory prior to the install. Usually these will not cause a problem as the installer unloads them properly. However, it may be a good idea to restart your computer and ensure Groove has not been started so that you won't have any problems with these lingering references in memory.

RUNNING GROOVE WITH ADVERTISEMENT BLOCKING SOFTWARE ENABLED

Some people have reported problems using Groove while running software designed to eliminate banner advertisements, cookies, JavaScript, and so on. If everything else about your installation seems fine, try turning off this software if you have it enabled. These often redirect your HTTP requests to a proxy through which Groove may have trouble communicating. If this solves the problem, consult the documentation to see if the blocking software can be configured to allow Groove full and unrestricted access. Also, many newer browsers such as Internet Explorer 6 have privacy options available that may be able to fulfill your needs without interfering with Groove.

PROBLEMS ACCESSING GROOVE.NET TO RETRIEVE A SAVED ACCOUNT

If your account information was saved on groove.net and after entering your username and passphrase information you receive a message such as Groove could not access groove.net, you need to check your Internet Explorer settings. Under the Tools menu, choose Internet Options. Click on the Connections tab and then the LAN Settings button near the bottom of the window. On this screen, ensure that the Automatically Detect Settings and Use Automatic Configuration Script options are not checked. Unchecking these will often resolve problems connecting to the groove.net server.

USING GROOVE TO COLLABORATE

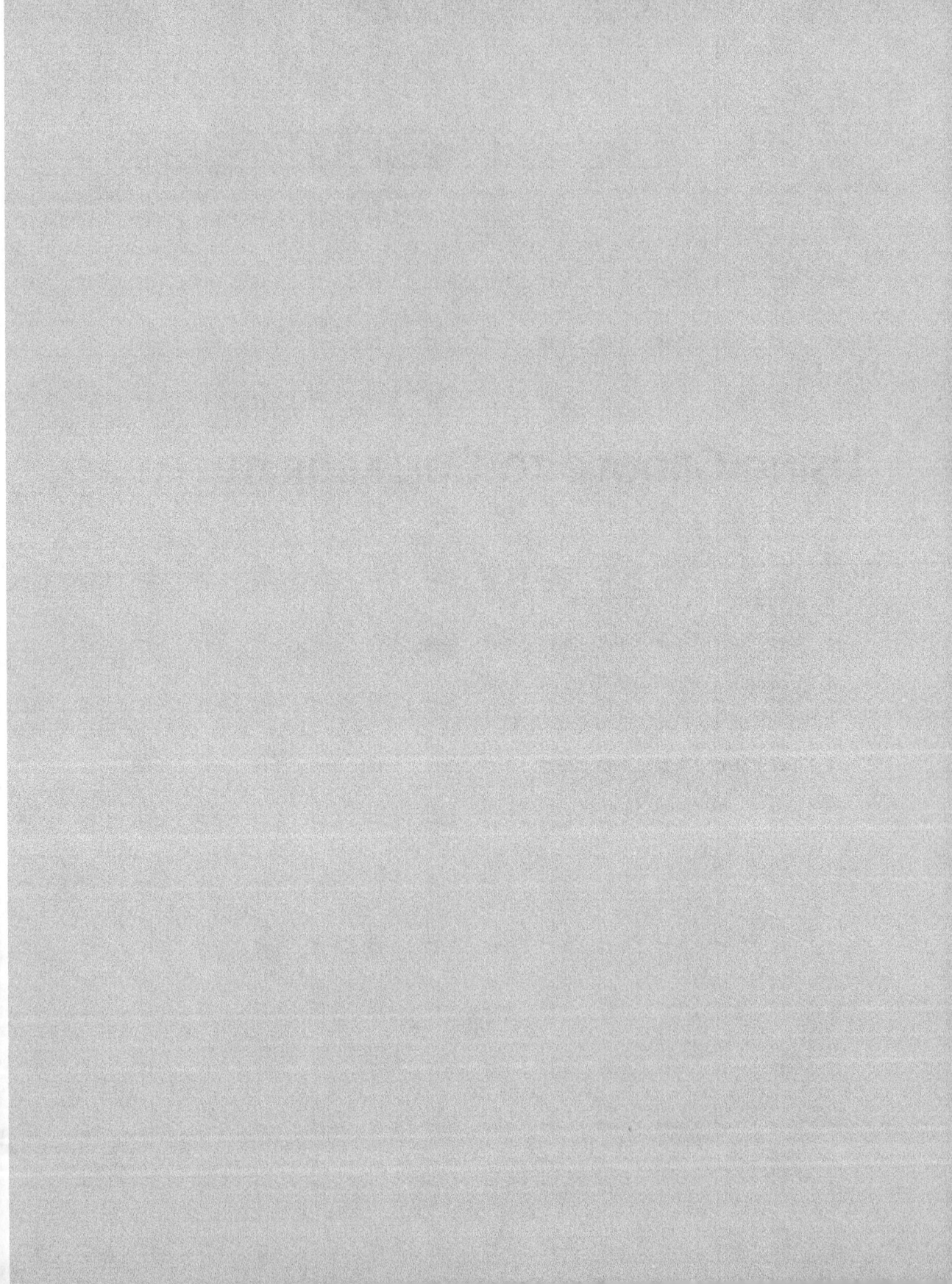

CHAPTER **3** ▶

STARTING TO GROOVE

In this chapter

OVERVIEW

Groove Workspace is designed to let users hit the ground running. An introduction to the Groove Workspace application and some navigation basics are all you need to begin collaborating with your colleagues. In this chapter, you look at some of the basic Groove configuration options and prepare yourself to begin collaborating with Groove.

You'll begin by examining the Transceiver, the interface that comprises the Groove client. You'll look at some of the important configuration settings from the start-up options to configuring Groove to work in offline mode. Once within the Transceiver, you'll look at how to navigate from Groove's Welcome Page to other areas in the application. After you're comfortable with the Groove interface you'll see how you can list yourself in the local and groove.net directories. Then, using your knowledge of user accounts you'll be able to send your first instant message (IM) to another user. Finally, you begin to explore Groove's customization capabilities as you see how to change the look and feel of the transceiver itself.

THE TRANSCEIVER

The Groove Workspace application is commonly referred to as the Transceiver. Although I'll primarily be discussing the user interface functionality it provides in this chapter, the Transceiver actually performs a variety of different functions. As the primary local system controller, it is responsible for managing communications, security, and account maintenance. A graphical overview of the Groove framework is shown in Figure 3.1. As you can see, the Transceiver encompasses all the other Groove system-level services. Within the Transceiver, you can also see that security is an integral piece that works in coordination with any access to local data stores, part of Groove's always present security features. The individual services and the role they play will become apparent in our detailed discussion of shared spaces in Chapter 4, "Understanding Shared Spaces," and also in our discussion of the Groove Framework in Chapter 10, "The Groove SDK."

Figure 3.1
The Transceiver is the common container for all Groove activities.

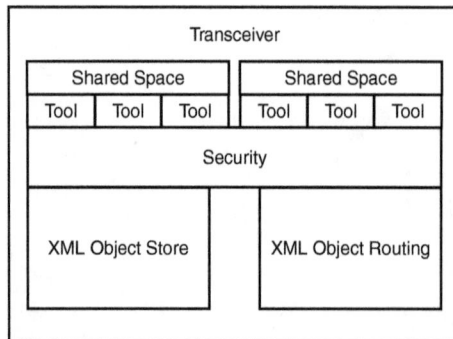

GROOVE ON YOUR DESKTOP

If you successfully installed Groove Workspace as outlined in Chapter 2, "Installing and Configuring Groove," you may have chosen to insert a shortcut to the application in your Startup folder. Unless you remove it, Groove services will start every time you boot your computer. You also had the opportunity to add the Groove icon shortcut to your desktop. If you right-click the Groove icon from the desktop or Start menu and choose Properties the target should look like Figure 3.2. The target is used to specify the application that will run when an icon is selected and any optional command line parameters that are passed to the application.

Figure 3.2
This is what the properties of the Groove icon looks like by default.

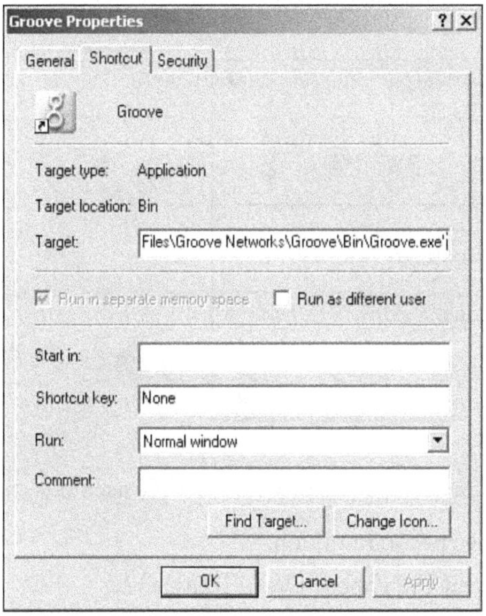

Adding a /trayonly command line parameter tells Groove to initialize its services, but to run in the background without displaying the user interface or logging into an account. For example, on a typical Groove installation the Target line would look like this to indicate that Groove should start in the system tray only:

```
"C:\Program Files\Groove Networks\Groove\Bin\Groove.exe " /trayonly
```

To change the Target line, simply select the current contents of the field and replace it with the previous example. Without this parameter, Groove opens the Transceiver itself. If you have multiple accounts on the same computer, you will be prompted to choose an account for this session. Note that even without the Transceiver open, you will still receive notifications alerting you of events such as shared space invitations and instant messages.

You will know Groove services are running when you see the Groove icon in your system tray.

STARTING THE TRANSCEIVER

To open the Groove transceiver on a machine with a single account, follow these steps:

1. Double-click the Groove program icon.
2. Click the system tray icon and choose Open Transceiver.

Opening the Groove Transceiver requires you to log in, as shown in Figure 3.3. You will not be prompted to sign in if the Remember My Passphrase on This Computer option was checked when the account was created. However, it is not recommended you turn off Groove's password verification. If it is disabled, anyone accessing your machine will have full access to your account and any data that resides within that account.

Figure 3.3
When initially opening the Transceiver, you will be prompted to sign into your account using your passphrase.

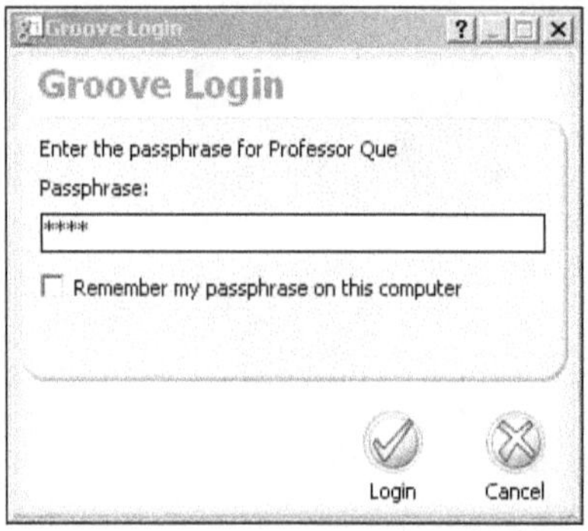

To open the Groove Transceiver on a device with multiple accounts, follow these steps:

1. Double-click the Groove program option.
2. Click the system tray icon and choose Open Transceiver.

After opening the transceiver, you may need to choose the account you want to use if you have multiple accounts on this device. If you have double-clicked the Groove program icon, you should select it from the Name drop-down list box shown in Figure 3.4. For devices with a single account, it will prompt you to sign into that account and no drop-down list will be displayed.

If you click the Groove icon in the system tray, you must click the proper account name to use and choose Open Transceiver, as shown in Figure 3.5.

NOTE

> After single-clicking the Groove icon, you may see a listing like "*Account Name* (logged off)". This indicates that account is not currently logged in and you'll need to log in to open the Transceiver under that account. In addition to this text, you will also notice the Groove icon in the system tray will become a lighter color to indicate all accounts are currently logged off.

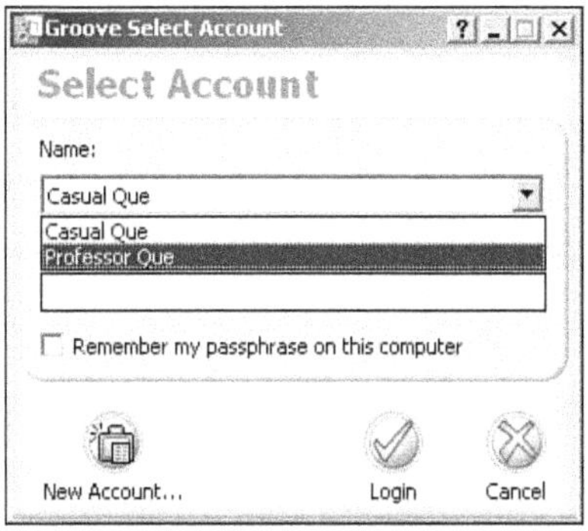

Figure 3.4
If there are multiple accounts on a device, you'll need to choose the account you want to log in to.

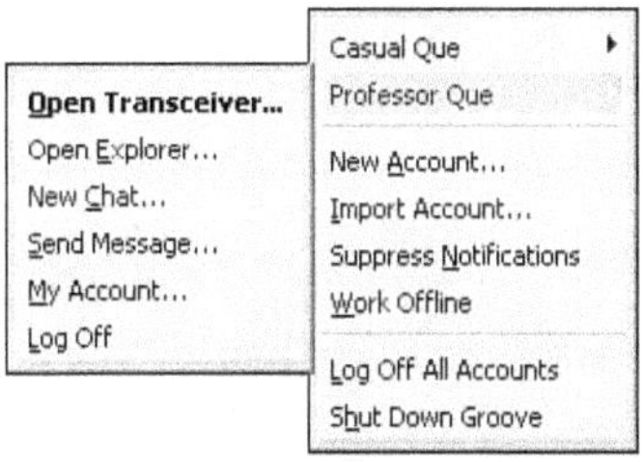

Figure 3.5
Clicking the Groove icon in the system tray provides an alternate way to open the Groove transceiver with a specific account.

After you open the Transceiver with the proper account password, Groove will open to the Welcome Page automatically. This page is a launch pad to most of the common Groove Workspace functions. You can have multiple Transceiver windows open at any time; the usefulness of this will become more apparent in our discussion of shared spaces and tools in Chapters 4 through 8.

WORKING IN OFFLINE MODE

By default, Groove is working in *online* mode. At any point while using the application, you may opt to work in *offline* mode. When Groove operates in online mode it will automatically attempt to synchronize changes with other users. Offline mode stores all changes locally and will not transmit them to other users. This is useful when you are working on a document you don't want to share until you've finished with it, when you need to conserve bandwidth, or know that you may not have network access for a period of time. Clicking on the Groove icon in the system tray and choosing Work Offline will place you in offline mode. The system tray will reflect this by displaying a red X. While you are offline, all changes to shared spaces and other activities such as invitations will be stored in the outbound queue that will be transmitted after Groove is brought back online.

CAUTION

You should switch back to online mode regularly as making changes to shared spaces while in offline mode can make your local data queue quite large and increase the time it takes to synchronize again.

THE TRANSCEIVER NAVIGATION BAR

As shown in Figure 3.6, the upper portion of the Groove window is used for common functions. Similar to a Web browser, no matter where you travel within the Groove application, you will always have quick and easy access to frequently used options. These are not unique to the Home page and will persist everywhere in the Groove application. This area of the screen consists of not only the top menu that is standard in many Windows applications, but also groups of buttons that provide recognizable graphics to aid in navigation.

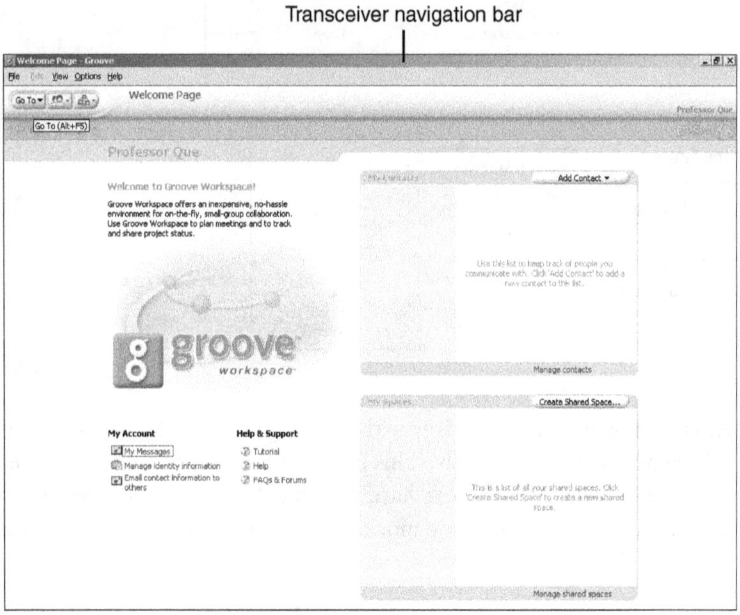

Figure 3.6
We've highlighted the portion of the transceiver where the standard navigation controls are found in the typical Groove interface.

Transceiver navigation bar

DROP-DOWN MENUS

Most of the drop-down menu items shown in Figure 3.7 can perform actions already available on-screen. Similar to most Windows applications, the menu provides an alternative means to perform many of the functions that are served by buttons and other links on the screen. The menu options are *contextual*, meaning that the available options will change depending on what area of the Groove application you are in. For example, while in a shared space you will find Rename Shared Space under the File menu. This same option would not be found while you are in the My Contacts area because it does not apply there.

BUTTON CLUSTER

This tightly grouped set of buttons is shown in Figure 3.8. These buttons allow you to go to a particular place within Groove or work with My Contacts or My Spaces; thus, they are called Go To buttons. Each uses a graphic for quick identification, but you may also hold the cursor over them for a short pop-up description of each one.

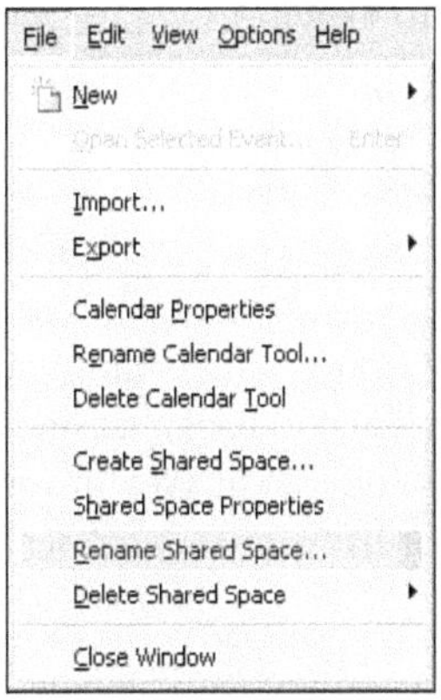

Figure 3.7
The Groove Transceiver provides the drop-down menus standard with most Windows-based applications.

Figure 3.8
The button cluster provides a quick way to access many common functions.

The following are additional descriptions of the options contained within each button:

- Go To. The Go To button is designed to allow quick access to many of the common areas within the Groove application. This button is always available, regardless of the current skin applied. Clicking this button allows you to link to the following:

  Home Page. Takes you back to the main Transceiver interface or the "Home" screen.

  My Spaces. Allows you to work with all shared spaces visible to your account.

  My Contacts. Where you can maintain your own list of Groove contacts and others you collaborate with.

  My Account. Maintenance area for all account information including identities, passphrases, skins, and can perform other account-related activities.

  My Messages. All instant message and shared space invitation history is maintained here.

  My Communications. An area for viewing and managing communications such as message delivery or shared space synchronization.

- My Contacts. The same as My Contacts that you can reach from the Go To button menu explained previously.

- My Spaces. Same as the link from the Go To menu.

  Create shared space. This allows quick creation of a shared space without navigating to My Spaces screen.

NAVIGATION BUTTONS

Another intuitive navigation control offered in Groove is the familiar forward and backward buttons. Shown in Figure 3.9, clicking the arrows allows backward and forward movement between recently visited screens. Similar to those offered in Web browsers, there are also drop-down arrows that allow jumping forward or backward several screens into the list.

Figure 3.9
Similar to a Web browser, the backward and forward buttons allow you to quickly navigate to screens that you've recently viewed.

WHO AND WHERE YOU ARE

Running multiple accounts can make it difficult to remember which account is currently logged in. As shown in Figure 3.10, your current account name is almost always displayed on the upper-right portion of the screen.

This area of the screen shows you where you are currently

Professor Que is the current account

Figure 3.10
You can usually tell the current account that is logged in by looking in the upper-right portion of the screen.

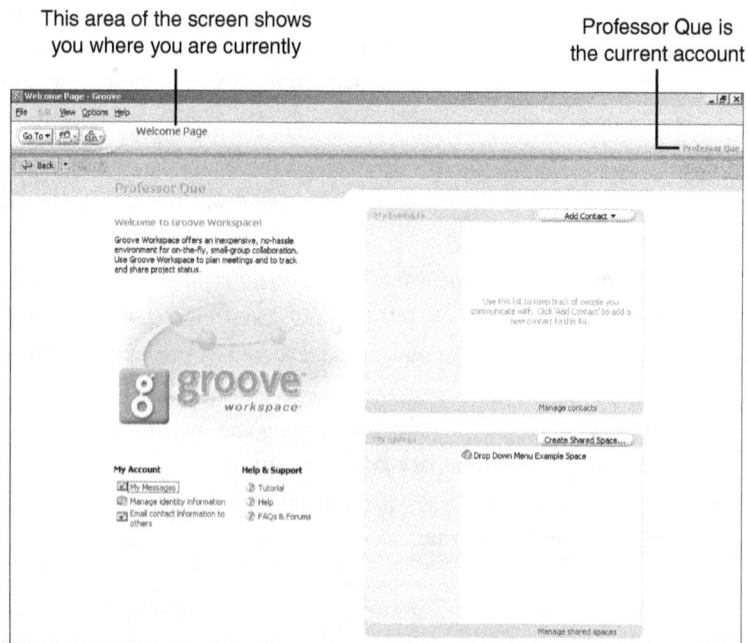

At the top of the screen, you can instantly see where you are in the application, as shown in Figure 3.10. In this example you are currently on the Welcome Page.

DATA EXCHANGE MONITORS

Two data exchange counters are displayed in the upper-right corner of the Transceiver when data is sent or received. The left counter shows the number of bytes remaining for transmission when data is being sent as shown in Figure 3.11. The right counter (not shown in Figure 3.11) shows the number of bytes left when data is being received. These counters will help you to determine how long it will take for data to transfer.

Figure 3.11
This Groove data counter shows that there is still 16KB to be transmitted, as indicated by the arrow pointing to the right.

THE OVERVIEW PANE

In order to assist you along the way, Groove has an overview pane that displays brief help information for some areas, as shown in Figure 3.12. This can be toggled off at any point by choosing View, Hide Overview from the drop-down menu. It can be re-enabled by choosing View, Show Overview.

Figure 3.12
The overview pane provides a brief overview designed to help you understand what each area of the Groove client is used for.

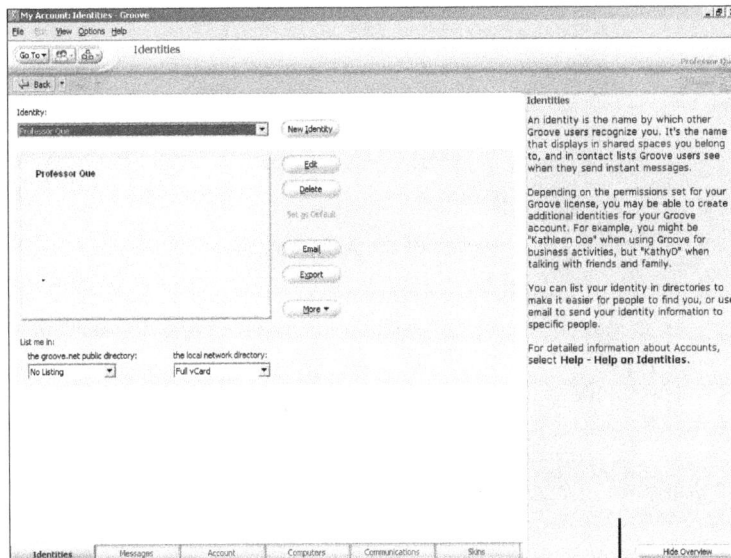

Overview pane

NOTE

In some areas, like My Spaces, the help overview may be shown at the top portion of the screen. This overview can be turned off by choosing View, Hide Overview and re-enabled in the same manner.

NOTIFICATIONS WITHIN GROOVE

You've probably noticed that some of your actions within the Transceiver result in a pop-up notification being posted to the lower-right portion of your screen, as shown in Figure 3.13. These text messages are displayed as hyperlinks and can perform different actions depending on their type.

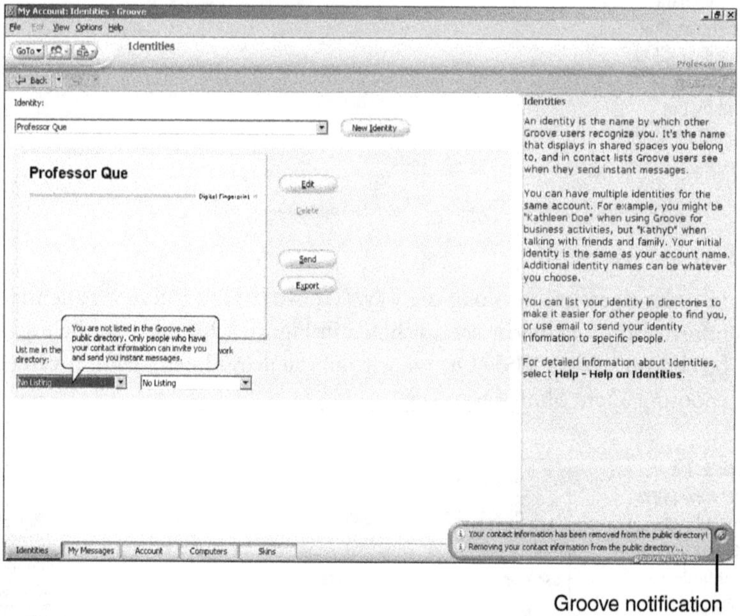

Figure 3.13
Notifications are displayed as small pop-up messages above the system tray in the lower-right corner of the screen.

Groove notification

All notifications fall into one of the following three categories:

- Information—These notifications, one of which is shown in Figure 3.14, are often used as additional information to indicate such events as account updates, directory listing changes, and so on. Often temporary in nature, many permanently disappear after a few seconds.

Figure 3.14
Groove Workspace will notify you of events, such as new instant messages, by displaying a notification above the system tray.

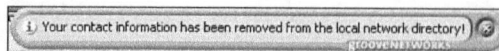

■ Instant message—This notification usually indicates an instant message is waiting for your retrieval (see Figure 3.15). You'll be looking at opening and working with instant messages later in the "Instant Messaging" section later in this chapter.

Figure 3.15
This notification shows that this Groove user has an instant message waiting to be retrieved.

■ Shared Space Notification—As shared space invitations are processed, you will receive a series of notifications informing you of the status (see Figure 3.16). You'll learn about the messages associated with these notifications in Chapter 4.

Figure 3.16
Notifications will alert you during the different stages of shared space invitation processing.

→ For a complete listing of the notification messages associated with shared spaces, **see** "Shared Space Delivery Notifications," **p. 128**

Most notifications are visible for only a few seconds and then disappear. You can redisplay most notifications by holding your mouse pointer over the Groove tray icon. Some notifications, such as the addition of an identity to a directory, will only display for a predetermined amount of time and can't be recalled.

Although some notifications are removed automatically, you can always close a notification by clicking the red X to the right of the message.

SUPPRESSING NOTIFICATIONS

Groove notifications can be disabled at any time by single-clicking the Groove icon in the system tray and clicking Suppress Notifications, as shown in Figure 3.17. Clicking this option places a minus sign to the left of the Suppress Notifications option when the Groove system tray icon is clicked. To turn notifications back on, simply click the Groove system tray icon and select Suppress Notifications. After this is selected, the check mark will be removed. Groove queues any notifications sent when suppression is turned on. So once re-enabled, all missed notifications will be displayed from the queue.

Figure 3.17
Clicking Suppress Notifications will turn off notifications for this Groove client.

Casual Que	(logged off) ▶
Professor Que	▶
New Account...	
Import Account...	
Suppress Notifications	
Work Offline	
Log Off All Accounts	
Shut Down Groove	

NOTE

Even with suppress notifications turned on you will still be notified when receiving an instant message by a flashing mail icon over the Groove logo in the system tray. However, this is all you will see. No detailed information such as sender or subject will be displayed until notifications are turned back on.

AN OVERVIEW OF THE HOME PAGE

The Welcome Page, as shown in Figure 3.18, is intended to be your "launch pad" when Groove Workspace is started. It has been designed so you can easily access the most commonly used Groove features. This includes not only seeing your current contacts, but also a listing of shared spaces that can be entered and quick links to your account information. We'll look at the elements that make it up in the following sections.

Figure 3.18
The Groove Welcome Page is shown in the Transceiver when the Groove Workspace application is first started.

MY ACCOUNT

These links allow direct access to most of the account-level functions found within the My Account area of Groove:

- My Messages—This link takes you to the My Messages area within My Account where instant messages can be retrieved and maintained.

- Manage Identity Information—This link takes you to the area in which you can manage your identities and directory listing options.

- Email Contact Information to Others—This link takes you to the area where you can send a contact's vCard file as an attachment in an email message.

HELP AND SUPPORT

These links provide different types of Groove support:

- Tutorial—This links to an excellent Flash presentation that visually demonstrates many of the common Groove tasks.

> **NOTE**
>
> You may be prompted to install Flash if you don't have it already.

- Help—This link will open an HTML version of the Groove documentation with an index and searching capability.

- FAQ's and Forums—This link will take you to Groove's online support area from where you can participate in support forums, view Frequently Asked Questions, and access other support information.

> **TIP**
>
> Many of the FAQs contained online can also be found in the offline HTML documentation provided with the installation.

MY CONTACTS

This is a stripped down version of the full My Contacts area. Its inclusion on the home page allows you to quickly see everyone's online presence and send messages. In the "Using My Contacts" section later in this chapter you will discover in more detail how to build and use the My Contacts area.

MY SPACES

This window displays all the shared spaces you have participated in. This provides an easy way to create a shared space. By right-clicking on a shared space in the list you can perform many of the shared space options described in detail in Chapter 4.

FINDING OTHER GROOVE USERS

Unlike traditional centralized collaboration tools such as a chat room, communicating with other Groove users is a more personal undertaking. Participants must be individually invited to events in a Groove shared space, and these members can reach others in one of two ways:

- Actively—In this case a Groove user sends his contact information to another user, thus actively initiating the communication. This can be via an instant message, email, or some other transmission of the account file data.

- Passively—Groove users can be listed in either a local network directory or the public groove.net directory. In this way, the Groove user is passive whereas other users discover them by searching the directory.

Either way, an individual Groove user has total control over whether or not they will allow others to discover them. They also have control over what information is visible to other users. You'll first look at how you update your account information and later discuss how you can share it with other users.

MAINTAINING YOUR ACCOUNT AND IDENTITY INFORMATION

In Groove's collaborative environment, accounts, and identities are used for each Groove user. The following sections highlight the distinctions and relationships between the two along with the basic steps you'll take to maintain them.

THE DIFFERENCE BETWEEN ACCOUNTS AND IDENTITIES

During installation in Chapter 2, one of the last steps in the process was to create an account by specifying your username and passphrase. When you create an account, you are also creating an identity with exactly the same name. It's easiest to think of identities as "display names" because they are what other users will recognize you by. Several identities can be attached to one account. For instance, you may have two different identities to distinguish your work from your personal communications. Although each identity is attached to the same account, people that you communicate with do not know that there is any link between the two identities unless you tell them. Each identity has its own separate vCard, which we discuss in more detail in the following section "About your vCard." This separation of identities closely mimics the different ways you may act in social versus business situations.

Your account is stored on disk and can consist of the following information:

- Your identity or identities and the cryptographic private keys that define them.
- Other cryptographic information, such as your master key, which is used for securing your shared spaces.

- A listing of all the other devices that run Groove (if they are all connected to the Internet).
- References to all the shared spaces of which you are currently a member.
- Information about all the individuals you communicate with (including contacts).

A good illustration involving the fictional Professor Que is shown in Figure 3.19. As you can see, Professors Que's account and the identities attached to that account are represented on the left. The Professor uses this account and the Professor Que identity when participating in the Classroom Space shown on the upper right. However, when the Professor communicates with his skydiving club members in the Skydiving Space he uses another persona, Skydiver Que. It's a similar situation in the Social Space, where the Professor masquerades as Partier Que. As you can see, the same account can have more than one identity attached depending on the context of the shared space in which you are participating.

Figure 3.19
The relationship between an account and its related identities.

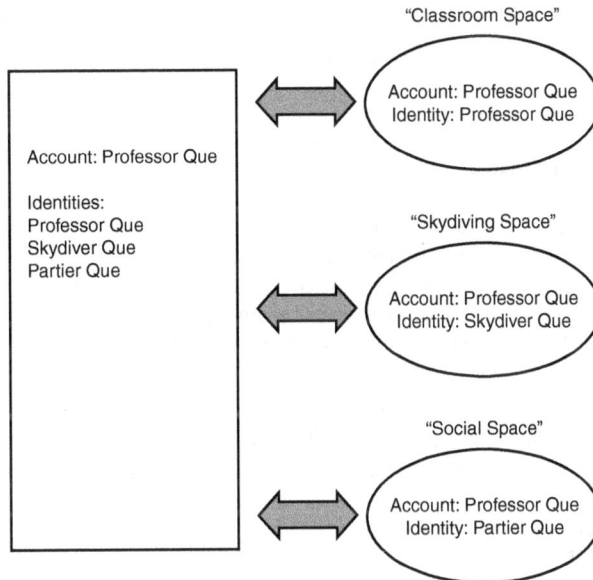

Account: Professor Que

Identities:
Professor Que
Skydiver Que
Partier Que

"Classroom Space"

Account: Professor Que
Identity: Professor Que

"Skydiving Space"

Account: Professor Que
Identity: Skydiver Que

"Social Space"

Account: Professor Que
Identity: Partier Que

THE MY ACCOUNT AREA WITHIN GROOVE

The My Account area allows you full control over many aspects of your account. The My Account area can be reached by clicking Go To, My Account from the Welcome Page. As shown in Figure 3.21, you can perform many account related tasks here including:

- Managing identity information
- Viewing and manipulating instant messages you've received
- Running the Multiple Computers Wizard
- Deleting accounts on a particular device

- Changing how your presence is relayed to other participants
- Viewing other computers currently running the same account
- Activate your copy of Groove Workspace
- Monitor and control Groove Workspace communications
- Changing the look and feel of Groove with skins

USING THE IDENTITIES TAB

You've seen how identities are used in communication with other Groove users. Now you'll learn about identity maintenance in more detail.

ABOUT YOUR vCARD

As I've stated, each identity has its own vCard. A *vCard* is an electronic business card, based on the published vCard 2.1 specifications. This vCard contains the data about an identity, including such things as physical addresses, phone numbers, or email addresses. Included in Groove's version of the vCard, denoted by its .vcg extension, is the inclusion of your unique digital fingerprint.

About Groove's Implementation of the vCard 2.1 Standard

Personal Data Interchange, or PDI, occurs when two individuals communicate. This interchange involves the exchanging of personal information to identify each other, including business and personal information. This exchange of contact information is at the heart of the Groove application. This results in the formation of a network of individuals communicating with one another in trusting relationships. Groove opted to use the vCard 2.1 specifications to facilitate the exchange of identity information because it is a standard that will allow some data to be shared with other applications. Version 3.0 is on the verge of adoption, and this may even be the accepted standard by the time you read this.

A vCard is a collection of properties. The property name is separated from its value with a colon. Property values or names with multiple components are delimited using the semicolon. Looking at the vCard for the Professor Que identity we've used so far as an example, you can examine the format used:

```
BEGIN:VCARD
VERSION:2.1
FN:Professor Que
N:Que;Professor
ADR;POSTAL;HOME:;;123 Main Street;Cincinnati;OH;45238;USA
TEL;HOME;VOICE:513-555-1212
TEL;HOME;FAX:513-555-1212
TEL;PAGER:513-555-1212
EMAIL;INTERNET:groovester@yahoo.com
URL:www.quepublishing.com
ADR;POSTAL;WORK:;;123 Main Street;Cincinnati;OH;45238;USA
TEL;WORK;VOICE:513-555-1212
TEL;WORK;FAX:513-555-1212
EMAIL;PREF;INTERNET:groovester@quepublishing.com
TITLE:Chief Groovester
ORG:Que Publishing
X-GROOVE:PAA/ARgBmAFoAADoAQwBTAGUAYwB1AHIAaQB0AHkAPgA8AC8AZwA6AEMAbwBuA ......
END:VCARD
```

The X-Groove property is unique to Groove. Within a vCard this is treated as an extension to the specification. This extension is used by Groove to store application-specific information. In Groove's case, this stores XML information in base64 format that holds a variety of information such as the public keys used for encryption. In addition, this also contains device and relay URLs that are important for Groove communication. The Internet Mail Consortium has taken on the responsibility of development and adoption of the standard. You can view the latest developments on its Web site at http://www.imc.org.

Similar to the physical world, you can exchange your vCard with those with whom you want to communicate. After an individual receives your vCard, they can add you to their personal list of contacts and also view any information you've wanted to save on the card. Let's first look at editing your vCard contents and then you'll look at how you can share your contact information with others.

Editing Your Current Identity

Just like an entry in an address book, Groove allows you to add personal and business information to your vCard. After entering the My Account area, the Identities tab will be selected by default, as shown in Figure 3.20. Normally you would choose the identity you want to edit in the drop-down list near the top of the screen, but if this is a new account you should only have one identity currently available.

Figure 3.20
The Identities tab in the My Account area is selected by default.

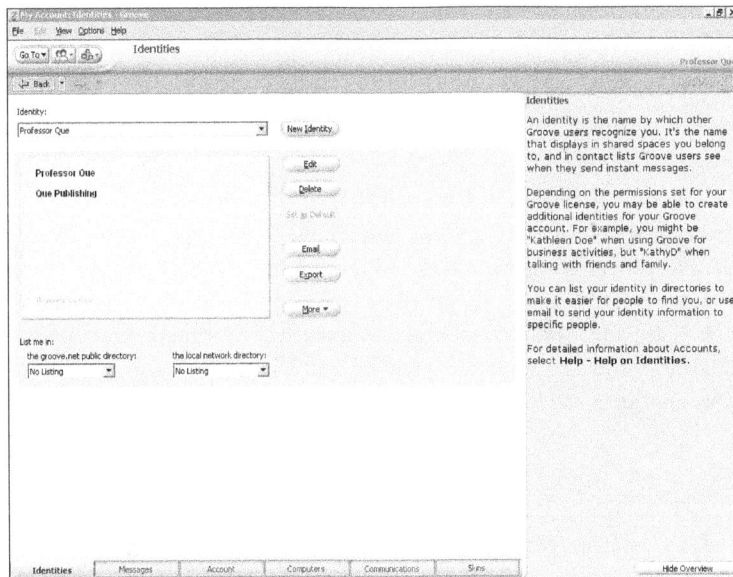

Click on the Edit button and you'll receive the pop-up window shown in Figure 3.21. This is where all your demographic information for your vCard can be entered. It is divided into two sections, for personal and business information respectively, that you select via the tabs at the bottom of the window. You can enter as much or as little information as you would like. In the figure, I've typed in some sample information for demonstration. After you've completed editing the fields, click on the OK button and everything will be saved to your account.

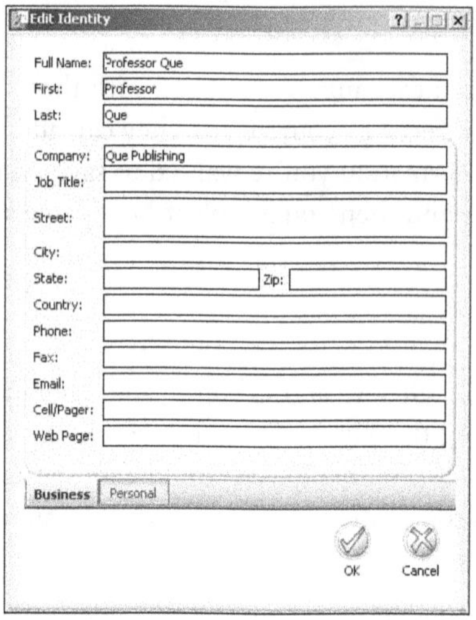

Figure 3.21
Clicking the Edit button opens this pop-up window where vCard personal and business information can be entered.

3

Once back at the main Identities screen, you'll now see the information displayed on the left side of the screen in what looks like a virtual business card. This will be very important as we discuss directory-listing options after demonstrating how to create a new identity.

CREATING A NEW IDENTITY

Creating a new identity in Groove is simple. Click on the New Identity button to display the New Identity screen shown in Figure 3.22, which except for its name is the same screen you saw in the previous figure when editing your identity. The first field is the full name that is the effective name of this new identity. From there, you can complete all additional fields you'd like to appear on your vCard. Clicking OK will save this identity, which should now appear in the Identity drop-down list near the top of the window.

SETTING YOUR DEFAULT IDENTITY

When you launch Groove, your identity that was generated during account creation will be used by default. However, you can change the default identity that is used. Choose an identity from the drop-down list box and click the Set as Default button shown in Figure 3.23 to make it your new default identity. You'll know which one is currently the default because this button will be grayed out when the identity is viewed.

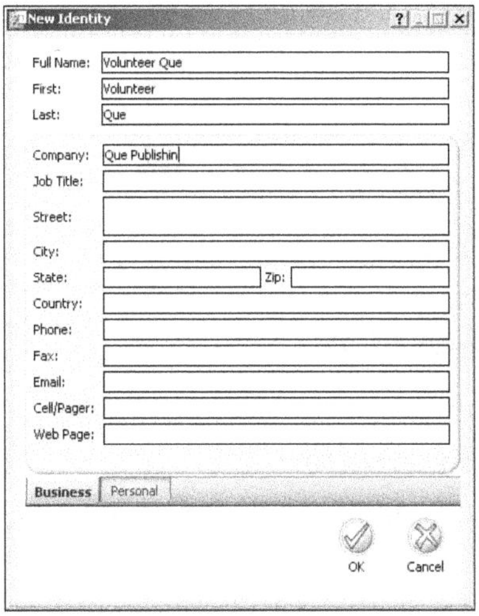

Figure 3.22
Clicking the New Identity button shown will allow you to create a new identity that will be attached to your account.

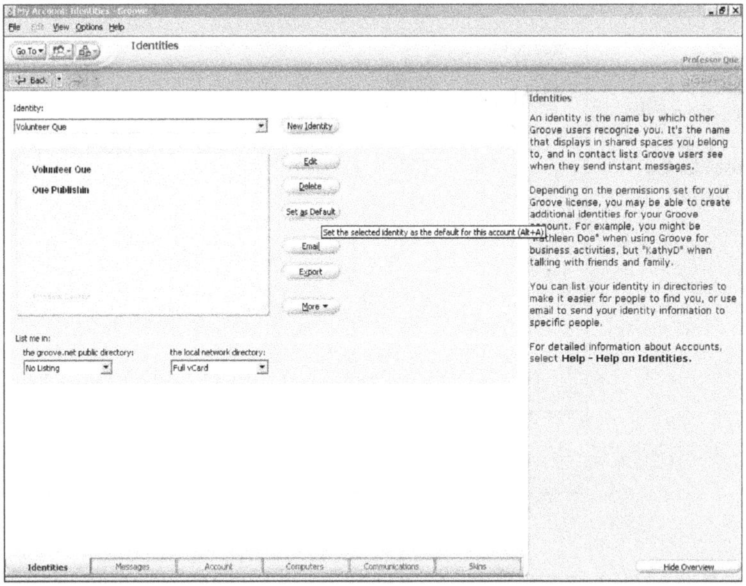

Figure 3.23
Clicking the Set as Default button shown will make the currently selected identity the default for all Groove interactions.

LISTING YOUR IDENTITY IN THE DIRECTORY

Listing yourself in a Groove directory allows others to find you easily. In the My Account screen, choose the identity you'd like to modify from the drop-down list at the top of the screen. At the bottom of the screen, as shown in Figure 3.24, are drop-down list boxes for the groove.net public and local network directory listings.

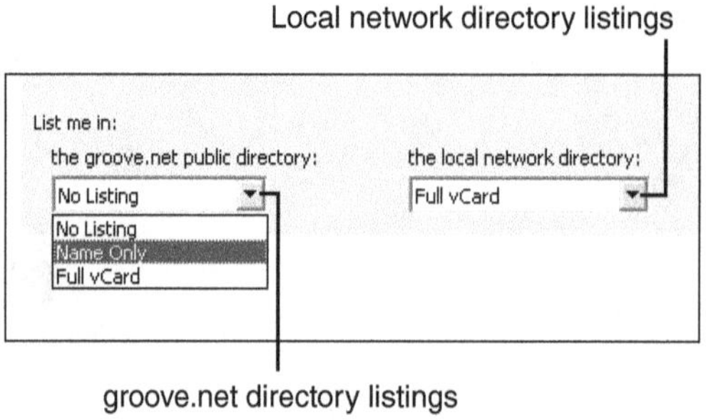

Local network directory listings

Figure 3.24
These drop-down list boxes indicate what type of information should be displayed in each directory for this particular identity.

List me in:

the groove.net public directory:

No Listing
No Listing
Name Only
Full vCard

the local network directory:

Full vCard

groove.net directory listings

The following options are available for each directory:

- No Listing—You are not listed in the directory at all. This is what you would choose to "unlist" your identity.

- Name Only—Only your identity name and digital fingerprint will be shown to other users. Users adding you to their contacts will only see what's shown in Figure 3.25.

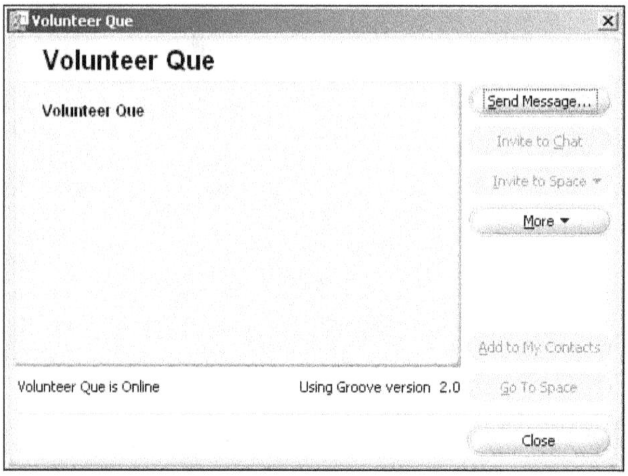

Figure 3.25
The vCard that is displayed when the Name Only option was chosen for the type of directory listing.

Volunteer Que

Volunteer Que

Volunteer Que

Send Message...

Invite to Chat

Invite to Space ▼

More ▼

Add to My Contacts

Volunteer Que is Online   Using Groove version 2.0   Go To Space

Close

- Full vCard—All vCard information will be shown to other users. This includes any personal and business address information you've entered, as shown in Figure 3.26.

LISTING NOTIFICATION

Listing yourself in the groove.net directory, whether just by name or the entire vCard, should trigger the two notifications shown in Figure 3.27. These are only notifications that the listing has been added to the directory and will disappear shortly after they appear.

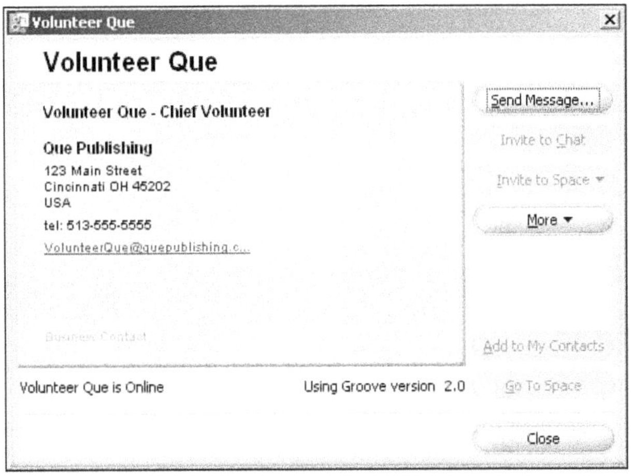

Figure 3.26
The vCard that is displayed when the Full vCard option was chosen for the type of directory listing.

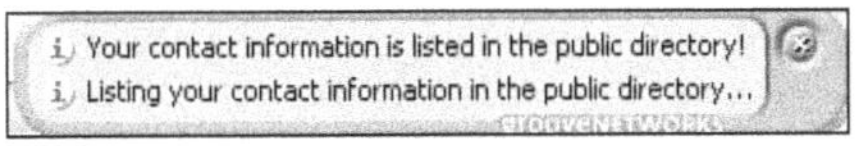

Figure 3.27
Users listing an identity in the groove.net directory should see these two notifications.

TIP

If you get the notification "Contact listing failed," verify that you are not working offline and that your Internet connection is active.

Listing yourself in the local network directory will only provide one notification, as shown in Figure 3.28. The message will disappear shortly after the notification appears.

Figure 3.28
Users listing themselves in the local network directory should receive this single notification.

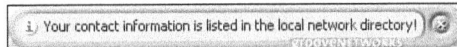

REMOVING YOURSELF FROM A DIRECTORY

Choosing the No Listing option above removes your identity from the appropriate directory. To verify that you have been removed, you should receive notification as shown in Figure 3.29. This will not remove the identity from your account, just the listing in the directory.

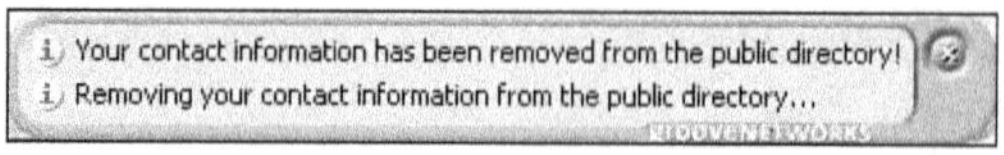

Figure 3.29
After this notification has been displayed, you will know that your listing has been successfully removed from a directory.

> i) Your contact information has been removed from the public directory!
> i) Removing your contact information from the public directory...

SENDING YOUR IDENTITY INFORMATION TO OTHERS

There are cases where you will want to send your contact information directly to other users. In the My Account area under the Identities tab, clicking the Email button creates the email shown in Figure 3.30. Essentially, it is creating an email with your vCard (.vcg) file attached with instructions to the recipient. You'll need to fill in the To portion of the email with the intended recipient's email address(es).

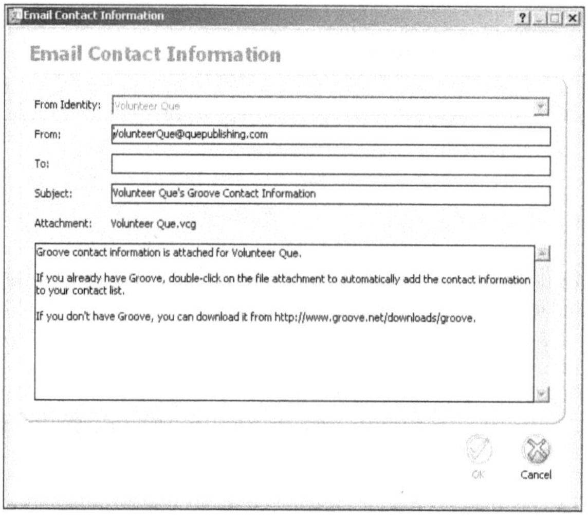

Figure 3.30
Clicking the Email button will prompt you with the following form that allows you to specify the details of the email message with your vCard attached.

If sending your contact information via an instant message or through email will not work in your situation, you still have the option of exporting your vCard. Because your vCard information is stored in a file, simply clicking the Export button and specifying a location will allow you to save the vCard file to disk. Once saved, you have the option of using another email application, instant messaging software, or some other means to transmit the file.

OTHER ACCOUNT OPTIONS

In addition to maintaining your identities, there are a few other options available on the Account tab within the My Account area, including those described in the following sections.

ACCESSING MY GROOVE WEB SERVICES

Clicking the My Groove Web Services button will open up your default Web browser and take you to the My Groove Services Web site. From here users can

- Change their passphrase.
- Find contacts.
- Join online forums.
- Subscribe to informative Groove newsletters on different topics.

USING YOUR GROOVE ACCOUNT ON MULTIPLE COMPUTERS

By clicking the Multiple Computers button you'll start the Multiple Computers Wizard. Using this wizard allows a single Groove account to be used on multiple computers, such as at home and at work.

→ For a complete discussion of the entire process for using a single Groove account on multiple computers, including using the Multiple Computers Wizard, **see** "Running Groove on Multiple Computers," **p.47**

ACTIVATING GROOVE WORKSPACE

Clicking the Activate Product button allows you to activate your copy of Groove Workspace so that you can enjoy all the features of the licensed version.

→ To learn how to activate your copy of Groove, **see** "Activating Your Copy of Groove Workspace," **p.41**

VIEWING YOUR LICENSE(S)

For licensed users of Groove, you can click the Licenses button to open the License Viewer window. This screen will show all the current licenses for your copy of Groove as shown in Figure 3.31.

Figure 3.31
Clicking the Licenses button will display all current licenses in the License Viewer window.

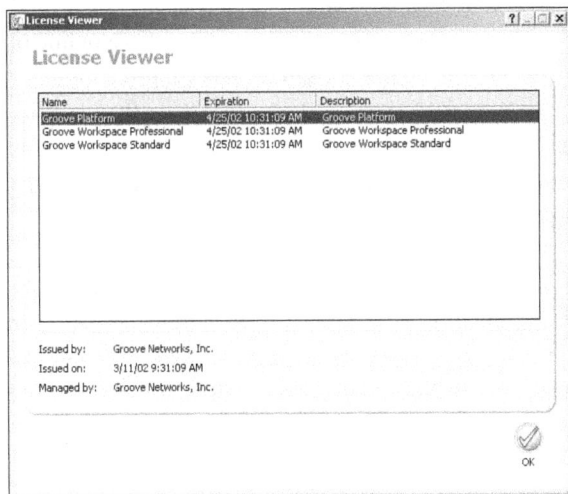

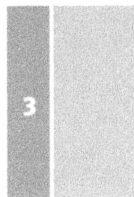

DELETING YOUR ACCOUNT

Clicking the Delete Account button removes the current Groove account and all its identities from this computer. The changes will not take effect until you shut down and restart Groove.

READING GROOVE'S PRIVACY POLICY

Privacy is very important to Groove Networks. Clicking the Privacy Policy button will take you to an area on the Groove Web site that explains the core principle to which Groove adheres. This is a good read that goes into great detail about steps Groove takes to ensure your privacy.

CHANGING YOUR PASSPHRASE

Clicking the Change Passphrase button enables you to change your passphrase for this device. Though not required, it is recommended that you do this at regular intervals to keep your account secure. Chapter 2 describes the process in detail.

SAVING YOUR PASSPHRASE ON THIS DEVICE

Although not recommended, you have the option of saving your passphrase on a device by checking the Remember Your Passphrase on This Computer check box from the Account tab in the My Account area. This enables you to open the Groove transceiver without entering a passphrase for the account.

ONLINE PRESENCE OPTIONS

Depending on your personal preference, you may want to control when your online presence is displayed to others. At the bottom of the Account screen shown in Figure 3.32 you can choose from the following options:

- Everyone—Every Groove user can tell whenever you are online or offline.
- All Groove Users Listed in My Contacts—Only users whom you've added to My Contacts can see when you're online. Everyone else will always see an offline icon next to your name.
- All Groove Users in Your Shared Spaces—Any Groove user who is a member of any of your shared spaces will see your status.

In addition, you also have the option of controlling when other users' online presence is displayed. By unchecking the box under Show Other's Online Presence In label, contacts will always show as offline in any contact list. This is checked by default, meaning that each user's online presence will display in any contact list of which they are a part.

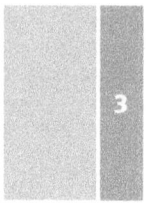

Figure 3.32
At the bottom of the Account screen, you have several options for displaying your online presence.

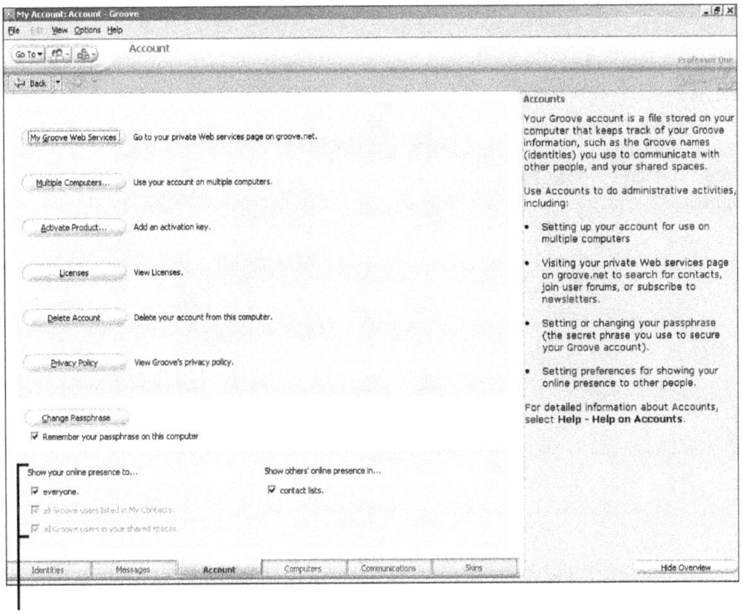

Online presence options

USING MY CONTACTS

Similar to the contact lists you build in applications, Groove allows you to build your own personal list of other Groove users. In this way, you'll be able to easily find colleagues to whom you send instant messages and invite into your shared spaces. In addition, you'll be able to find other information about these users such as their addresses, phone numbers, and other important data.

You can add new contacts by clicking on the Add Contact button on the home page or from within the My Contacts area. After this button is clicked, you have several different options including the following:

- Add a Groove Contact
- Paste
- Import
- Add Email Contact

These options are described in detail in the following sections.

ADDING A NEW GROOVE CONTACT

Clicking the Add Contact button from the Welcome Page and choosing Add a Groove Contact from the drop-down menu brings you to the Add Contacts screen shown in Figure 3.33.

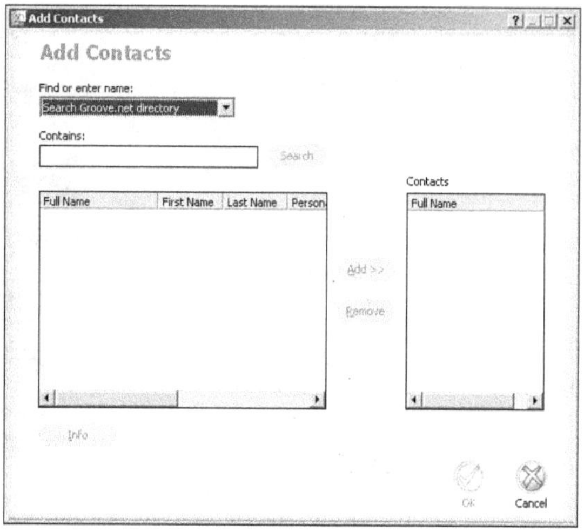

Figure 3.33
Choosing Add a
Groove Contact brings
you to the Add
Contacts screen that
allows you to find con-
tacts from several dif-
ferent sources.

You can obtain contacts from several different sources including the following:

- Known Groove Contacts—This is a listing of your current entries in My Contacts and members of your shared spaces.

- groove.net—This is Groove's own public directory of users.

- Local Network Directory—This is the directory of members on the local subnet (if you are part of a local area network).

Choosing groove.net directory in the Look In field allows you to find contacts in this public directory. Filling in the Contains field and clicking the Search button will query the directory for any matches. Results will be displayed in the list box at the bottom of the screen.

NOTE

> If your search returns more than 50 results, it may not return all of them. Try refining your keyword(s) and search again. For example, try using the first and last name of the user instead of simply the last name. For example, "Smith" may return too many results, but "John Smith" will help narrow the results considerably.

Choosing either the Local Network Directory or Known Groove Contacts from the Look In field displays all the contacts found in the results list box. They are sorted by first name and typing anything in the Starts with: box will automatically position you within the list by the beginning characters in the Full Name.

By highlighting any result row and clicking the Info button you can view the information for that individual. Clicking on the Add button will add the contact to your My Contacts list for this account. This includes automatically adding it to any other machines running this account. Any erroneous additions can be deleted by highlighting the entry and clicking the Remove button.

PASTING A NEW GROOVE CONTACT

When participating in a shared space, right-clicking on any user in the member panel gives you the option to copy the contact. Clicking on the Add Contact button from the home page or My Contact area allows you to choose the Paste option. We'll also be discussing this in Chapter 4 in our discussion of the member panel within a shared space.

→ For a discussion of all the different activities possible within the member's panel, **see** "Member's Panel Functions," **p.136**

> **TIP**
>
> Simply right-clicking on a user in the member pane and choosing Add to Contacts does exactly the same thing with one less step.

IMPORTING A GROOVE CONTACT

If a Groove user has exported his vCard to a .vcf or .vcg file, you can import his information. Simply click on Add Contact from the Welcome Page, choose Import from the drop-down menu, and specify the file location. Clicking Open will then add the identity contained in the file. See the section "Sending Your Identity Information to Other Users" earlier in this chapter for an explanation of how to export a vCard to a file.

> **TIP**
>
> You can export contacts from other email applications, such as Outlook, and import the information into Groove. Just export the contact to a .vcf file and Groove can read it.

ADDING A NON-GROOVE CONTACT

If you are using Groove as your primary communication tool, you may want to keep all contact information in one place. By choosing Add Contact from the Welcome Page and choosing Add Email Contact from the drop-down menu, you can manually enter an individual's information. You won't be able to use Groove features like Instant Messaging with this type of contact, but can still send an email using Groove's built-in emailing capability.

CREATING ALIASES FOR CONTACTS

If you prefer, you can assign an alias to any contact to make it more recognizable. Simply right-clicking a member in your My Contacts list and choosing Alias from the menu will prompt you for the alias name. Enter some text and click the OK button. Your contact list will reflect the new name with the original identity in brackets [ ].

> **NOTE**
>
> Clicking the More button in My Contacts provides access to several different functions including creating aliases, exporting contacts, emailing contact information, and viewing a contact's digital fingerprint.

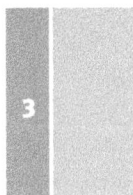

HANDLING CONTACT CONFLICTS

Groove removes all non-alphanumeric characters and spaces in order to find out if there is a potential conflict between two identity (contact) entries. If Groove detects a conflict, it will place a red question mark indicator next to the name, as shown in Figure 3.34. In this example, we have two contacts named "Richard" and each has a red question mark before his usernames. To resolve this conflict you should assign one of the conflicting names an alias as discussed in the "Creating Aliases for Contacts" section earlier in this chapter.

The question mark
indicates an identity conflict

Figure 3.34
A red question mark indicates an identity conflict that must be dealt with by creating an alias for one of the contacts.

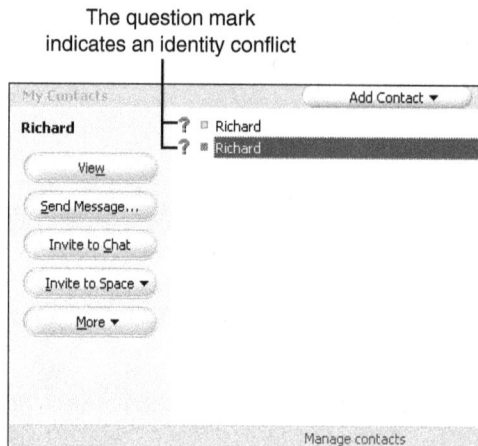

DETERMINING WHEN A CONTACT'S INFORMATION HAS CHANGED

It's possible that a contact has changed her vCard information since you last viewed it. Groove notifies you that a change has been made by placing an unread icon in front of the contact's name, as shown in Figure 3.35. In this example, we can see that our contact, The Dean, has changed his vCard information since it was last viewed. The navigation buttons provide an easy way to cycle through any unread contacts you may have in your list. After a vCard is viewed for more than five seconds, the unread icon will disappear.

Figure 3.35
If a contact changes her contact information, Groove will notify you by placing an unread icon next to her name.

These unread markers can be set manually, allowing you to mark a contact as unread. The unread marker looks like a small document with a new indicator behind it as shown in the figure to the left of the contact name. This is useful if you want to "mark" the vCard for viewing later. This can be accessed by clicking the Unread Options button shown in Figure 3.36.

KEYBOARD SHORTCUTS

Table 3.1 lists some of the commonly used keyboard shortcuts within the My Contacts area.

TABLE 3.1   MY CONTACTS KEYBOARD SHORTCUTS

Keyboard Shortcut	Action
Alt+G	Add a new contact to the list.
Alt+S	Send an instant message to the selected contact(s).
Alt+C	Start a chat with the selected contact(s).
Alt+I	Invite contact(s) to an existing shared space with the Invite Space drop-down menu.
Alt+M	Select the More drop-down menu.
Alt+A	Select all contacts in the list.
Alt+F	Open File from the main menu.
Alt+E	Open Edit from the main menu.
Alt+V	Open View from the main menu.
Alt+T	Open Contact from the main menu.
Alt+O	Open Options from the main menu.
Alt+H	Open Help from the main menu.
Insert	Toggle the unread status of the currently selected contact.
Delete	Delete the currently selected contact(s).

STATUS INFORMATION

While online, Groove provides status information to allow you to know a user's current online or offline status. This is available both in the My Contact area and when working in a shared space. Shared spaces offer additional information about space participants that will be covered in Chapter 4. An icon instantly relays a status of one of the following:

- Offline—User is currently offline.
- Online—User is currently online.
- Online but Idle—User is online but has been idle for some time. Holding the mouse pointer over the icon will display the amount of time he has been inactive.

- No Status Available—Groove has not "read" the user's status. This could be due to other network activity, such as shared space synchronization, taking priority.

- Email Only (Non-Groove User)—This is not a Groove user and can only be reached via email.

TIP

> If you find all your contacts have a status of Offline at all times, even when you know they are online, double-check your online presence settings. A full description of these settings can be found earlier in this chapter in the section "Online Presence Options."

INSTANT MESSAGING WITHIN GROOVE

Similar to other services such as AOL Instant Messenger and ICQ, Groove allows you to send instant messages to other Groove participants. Obviously, you must first know the identity of the recipient before you can send the message. Finding these recipients was described in the "Using My Contacts" section earlier in this chapter. For everyone except for those contacts added only by email address, you can send an instant message to them at any time.

Unlike standard instant messaging software, you can send instant messages to other Groove users even if they are offline. If the user sending the message has Internet access, Groove automatically uses the Groove Relay Server to queue the message for later delivery. In a local area network setting without Internet access, these messages are also queued up in the sender's local data store for later transmission. This provides a more robust messaging system that doesn't require all participants to be online at the same time.

CREATING AN INSTANT MESSAGE

After you've added someone as a Groove contact, you can begin sending him or her instant messages. There are several ways to create a message:

- Click the Send Message button in the My Contacts area of the home page.
- Right-click Groove user(s) in a shared space or My Contacts and choosing the Send Message option.
- Press the Shift key twice in rapid succession.
- Choose Options, Send Message.
- Reply to an instant message that you've already received.

NOTE

> You can use the Ctrl and Shift keys to select multiple recipients for a message.

Creating an instant message prompts you with the pop-up window shown in Figure 3.36. Although the To box has been filled in automatically, you do have the option of selecting a different identity if there is more than one attached to this account. The Send Message button will remain grayed-out until you specify something in the body of the message.

Figure 3.36
The Instant Message screen will prompt you for all the details of an instant message, including the sender (identity), recipient, body of the message, and any attachments.

ADDING TEXT TO THE MESSAGE

In the Message text box within the Instant Message window, you can enter the text for your message. At this point you can use only standard text because at this time HTML tags and other special characters are not supported. You can use standard cut and paste functions in the Message area using the standard right-click menu or the following key combinations:

- Cut—Ctrl+X
- Copy—Ctrl+C
- Paste—Ctrl+V

ADDING AN AUDIO FILE TO THE MESSAGE

If you don't have time to type, Groove allows you to attach an audio file to an instant message. This is a great feature for quick communication and for verifying users. Before using this feature, you should run the Audio Tuner Wizard that is outlined in Chapter 4.

→ To understand how to use the Audio Wizard, **see** "Using the Audio Tuner Wizard," **p.149**

Clicking the red circle shown in Figure 3.37 will start the recording. You'll know recording has started when the red circle changes to a gray square. Clicking this gray square icon will stop the recording and return it to its original state.

After a message is recorded and you've clicked the gray icon, the triangle icon shown in Figure 3.37 should now be enabled. Clicking the triangle icon will then replay the message in its entirety.

Clicking the red icon at any time will allow you to re-record the audio message. If you decide you no longer want to include an audio message, clicking the Delete Voice Memo button shown in Figure 3.37 will remove any audio that has been recorded.

CAUTION

> Re-recording a message will overwrite the previous audio message because there is no way to start the recording at a particular point in the message.

USING THE WINDOWS SOUND RECORDER

Although we discuss Groove's own audio tuner in Chapter 4, using Windows Sound Recorder is another quick way to ensure your microphone is functioning properly. You can try this by following these steps:

1. Click on the Windows Start menu and choose Run.

2. In the Open text box type **sndrec32.exe** and click OK.

   You should now see the Windows sound recorder interface shown in Figure 3.37. All the buttons are labeled for reference in the following steps.

Figure 3.37
The Windows sound recorder is a utility provided with Microsoft Windows that is useful for troubleshooting audio problems.

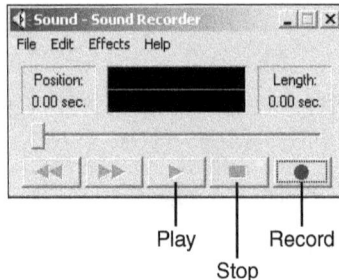

3. Click the Record button and talk into your microphone for a couple of seconds. The green bar will fluctuate as you talk.

4. Click the Stop button, which should now have changed from light gray to black.

5. Click the Play button (assuming your speaker volume is turned up).

This should give you a good idea of how you sound to other Groove users.

ATTACHING A FILE TO AN INSTANT MESSAGE

Similar to an email, you can also attach a file to an instant message. Clicking on the File button prompts you for the location of the file to attach. After you've attached a file, an attachment area, as shown in Figure 3.38, will appear showing what files have been attached. Files are preceded by a folder icon.

Figure 3.38
When an instant message has multiple attachments, the attachments will open in the bottom of the message.

Many users have found this to be a very powerful feature because you can attach files that are prohibited in some email systems due to their size.

ADDING A URL

Just like attaching a file, you may attach Web URLs to a message. Clicking on the URL button will prompt you for the address. Attached URLs are similar to attached files except they are preceded by a URL link icon.

REMOVING ATTACHED FILES AND URLS

At any time, you may click a URL or file in the Attachments area to select it and click the Remove button to purge them from the message.

INSTANT MESSAGE NOTIFICATIONS

When sending an instant message you will receive several notifications as its status changes. These are outlined in Table 3.2.

TABLE 3.2   INSTANT MESSAGE NOTIFICATIONS

Notification	Meaning
Message for sendee: Waiting to send	Groove is not yet sending the message because the sender is offline.
Message for sendee: Sending...	Groove is sending the message either to the sendee's computer or to the relay service (if the sendee's computer is offline).
Message for sendee: Sent, waiting for delivery...	The message left the sender's computer and will be delivered if the sendee is online. If the sendee is offline, the invitation is routed to the relay service.
Message for sendee: Delivered...	The message has reached the sendee's computer.
Message for sendee: Opened	The sendee has opened the message.

RECEIVING INSTANT MESSAGES

When you receive an instant message from another Groove user, you should see a flashing "letter" on top of your Groove icon in the system tray, as shown in Figure 3.39.

Figure 3.39
Groove notifies
you that there is
an instant message
waiting by flashing a
mail icon over the
Groove icon in the
system tray.

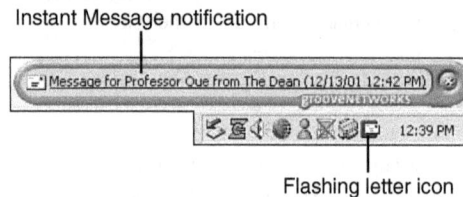

Instant Message notification

Message for Professor Que from The Dean (12/13/01 12:42 PM)

groveNETWORKS

12:39 PM

Flashing letter icon

In addition, unless notifications are suppressed, you will also receive a notification as shown in the figure. This will detail who the message is from (the sender), who the message is to (the sendee) and the date/time it was received. This notification is a link to the message. Clicking this will display the Instant Message window, as shown in Figure 3.40.

NOTE

Because you can receive notifications regardless of whether you are logged in, you may be prompted to log into your account to retrieve the message.

TIP

You can delete an instant message without opening it by right-clicking the notification and choosing Delete from the menu.

Figure 3.40
Clicking the link within the notification for an instant message will open the instant message and its contents in a pop-up window.

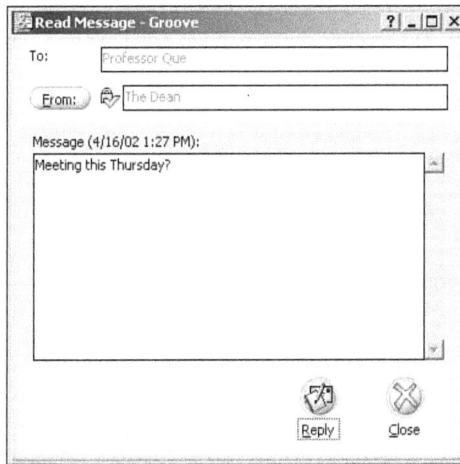

VIEWING THE SENDER'S VCARD

Clicking the From button within the Instant Message window will display the vCard of the user who sent the message. This is a good way to positively ID another user if you haven't previously authenticated them.

→ To understand how user authentication is used to provide a high level of security for Groove instant messages, **see** "Groove's Unspoofable Identities," **p.44**

REPLYING TO THE MESSAGE

Clicking the Reply button in an Instant Message window will reply to the sender. This will include the original text of the message by default, but you can delete this original text if you desire.

TIP

> A reply will only include the original message text. Any files or URLs attached will be removed. You'll need to save them from the original message should you want to include them in the reply.

MANAGING YOUR MESSAGES

Instant messages you've received are stored in the My Messages area. Also included are some messages pertaining to shared space invitations you've either sent or received. There are several ways to access this area:

- Click Go To and choose My Messages.
- Follow the My Messages link from the home page.
- Choose the My Messages tab in the My Account area.

The My Messages area is shown in Figure 3.41. A list of messages is displayed at the top of the screen showing each instant message that has been received and sent from this account. The following columns are displayed:

Figure 3.41
The My Messages area is used to manage all messages relating to a particular account.

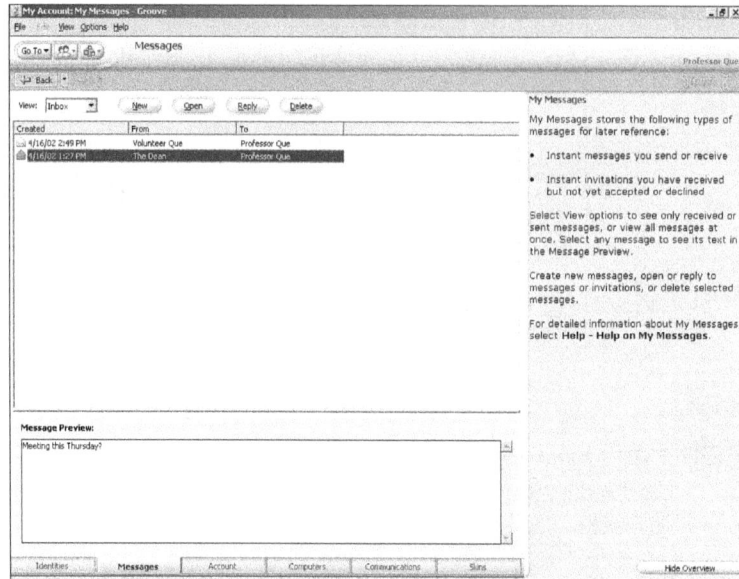

- Created—The time the message was created or received.
- From—The message sender (sender).
- To—The message's intended recipient (sendee).

NOTE

> The time on each message is from the recipient's machine. When you are corresponding with users across different time zones this is an important fact to remember.

Directly preceding each message is an icon representing its status:

- Unopened message
- Unopened voice message
- Previously opened voice message with attached file
- Previously opened message with attached file
- Previously opened voice message
- Invitation to a shared space that has been received but not accepted *or* a response to a shared space invitation you've sent
- Message you've sent

The Preview area at the bottom of the screen allows you to preview the text message without explicitly opening the entire message.

You can choose which messages are displayed in the My Messages screen by choosing one of the options from the View drop-down list box:

- Inbox—Instant messages and invitations not yet accepted or declined that have been received by this account
- Sent—Instant messages and invitations not yet accepted or declined that have been sent from this account to other users
- All—All instant messages and invitations

Clicking the New button will allow you to create a new instant message. Clicking the Open button will open the currently selected message. Messages you've sent cannot be opened in this manner; you may only view the message via the preview window at the bottom. Clicking the Reply button will reply to the currently selected message.

You should clean up instant messages that are no longer needed. Clicking on a single message or multiple messages (using Ctrl and Shift) and clicking the Delete button will permanently remove them.

By default, messages are sorted by the date and time they were received. By clicking one of the column headings, as shown in Figure 3.41, you may re-sort the messages.

USING LITE CHAT WITHIN GROOVE

There are times when you may want to chat in real time with a certain user or groups of users. Instant messaging is a great tool, but there are times when you need to discuss items in an interactive setting. Groove provides a feature called Lite Chat, which in reality is a stripped down version of a shared space. You can't add tools to this space that only provides text and audio messaging capability. Because Lite Chat ultimately is a shared space, using the feature is outlined in Chapter 4, the chapter that explains shared spaces in more detail.

→ For a complete discussion of using Groove's Lite Chat feature, **see** "Using Lite Chat Within Groove," **p.109**

USING SKINS IN GROOVE

Everyone has his or her own preferences when it comes to the look and feel of an application. Luckily, Groove gives you some choices when you decide how your particular instance of the application will look. They are called skins, and in this section we'll show you how to change the default Groove skin and even go through a simple example of creating your own.

GETTING TO THE SKINS AREA

Skin maintenance is part of the My Account area under the Skins tab. You can usually get there one of two ways:

- Click on the Change the Look of Groove link from the home page.
- Click on Go To, choose My Account, and then select the Skins tab at the bottom of the screen.

PREVIEWING AND CHOOSING A SKIN

By default, the Skins area should look like Figure 3.42. In this example, the Default Groove skin is still selected. Notice that there is a preview section at the bottom that will give you a feel for what the skin looks like. Clicking on the different selections will not change the skin at this point; it simply toggles the preview graphic at the bottom. After you see a skin that you might like, click on the Apply button and you'll change the skin within your Groove instance.

Figure 3.42
Groove's Skins area allows you to preview and choose new skins that can be used to tailor the client's look and feel.

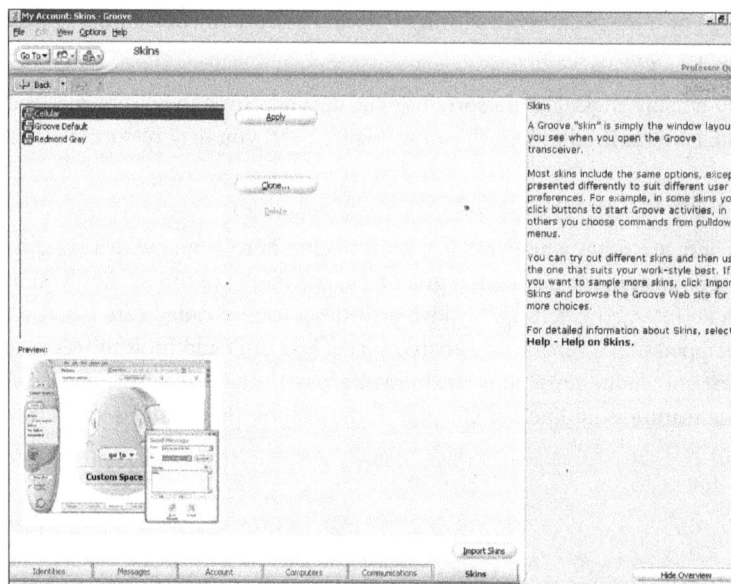

FINDING ADDITIONAL SKINS

Clicking on the Import Skins button takes you to the area on the Groove Networks site where you can download additional skins. You'll see a screen similar to Figure 3.43 with several skins from which to choose. Clicking the Install Now link next to a skin will begin the process of injecting the skin. If Groove has not been started already, clicking this link should automatically launch Groove. If there are several accounts on this device, you'll need to choose the account for which the skin will apply and enter the passphrase if required.

Figure 3.43
Clicking the Import Skins button will take you to the Groove Networks site that offers several different skins that may be downloaded and injected.

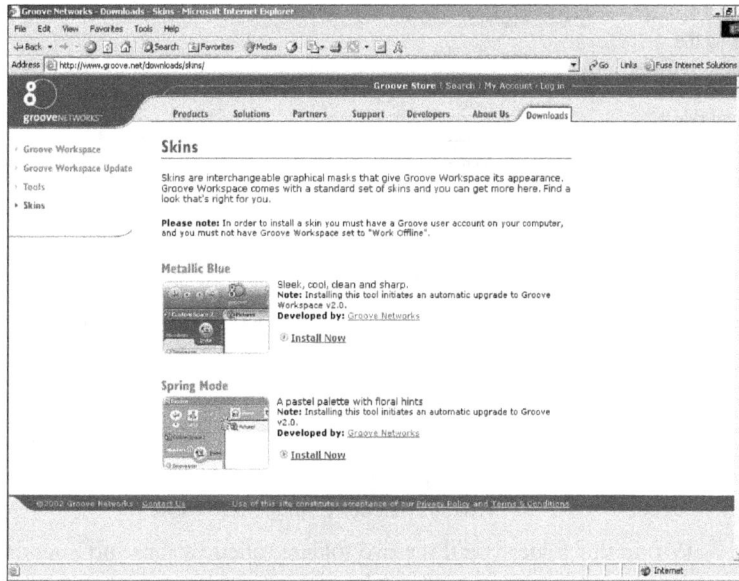

NOTE

At the time of this writing there were several Internet sites offering additional Groove skins for download. Backward-compatibility can become an issue if the skin developer used non-traditional means to create the skin. You may want to back up your system as outlined in Chapter 2 before injecting any skins from sources other than groove.net.

After clicking on the installation link, you'll receive a pop-up window with a status bar detailing the download progress. Once finished, it will notify you that the installation has completed successfully. This new skin should now be available within the account to which it was added. It can be applied by following the steps listed previously.

→ The injection process in Groove is very important. For more information, **see** "What Is Tool Injection?" **p.142**

CHANGING ONE OF YOUR CURRENT SKINS

If you've ever used themes in Windows, you'll understand that it can be nice to have the flexibility to tweak your current settings slightly to make the look and feel more appealing. In a similar fashion, Groove allows you to also modify the sounds and images that make up a Transceiver skin. An example of changing a skin is described in the following steps:

1. You will want to clone a skin that is most similar in design to the new one you want to create. From the Skins screen, highlight the source skin and click the Clone button. You'll be prompted to give it a new name and description, as shown in Figure 3.44. Click the Clone button after filling in these fields and a duplicate skin with a new name will be created.

Figure 3.44
After clicking the
Clone button you'll be
prompted to give the
new, cloned skin a
name and description.

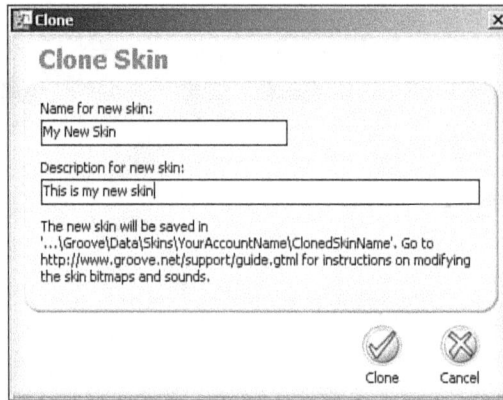

2. Using Windows Explorer, navigate to the new folder that was created in step 1 at *app folder*\Groove\Data\Skins*Account Name**Skin Name*\.

   Within this folder you'll see two folders called Images and Sounds. These hold the images and sounds used throughout Groove.

3. At this point, you may modify the images and sounds to suit your preferences. All .jpg files are the actual images you see within the Transceiver, whereas any .bmp images are used for masking and shading. Pay attention to the following characteristics when editing the images; otherwise, you may see unpredictable results:

   - Width
   - Height
   - Horizontal Resolution
   - Vertical Resolution
   - Bit Depth
   - Color Representation

4. Restart the Transceiver and you can see your changes.

EXAMPLE: CHANGING THE MEMBER PANE BACKGROUND

In this example you'll change the member pane background that is shown on the left side while participating in a shared space:

1. Clone the Groove Default skin and name it My Tile Skin, as shown in Figure 3.45.

Figure 3.45
After clicking the Clone button, we've decided to name the newly cloned skin My Tile Skin.

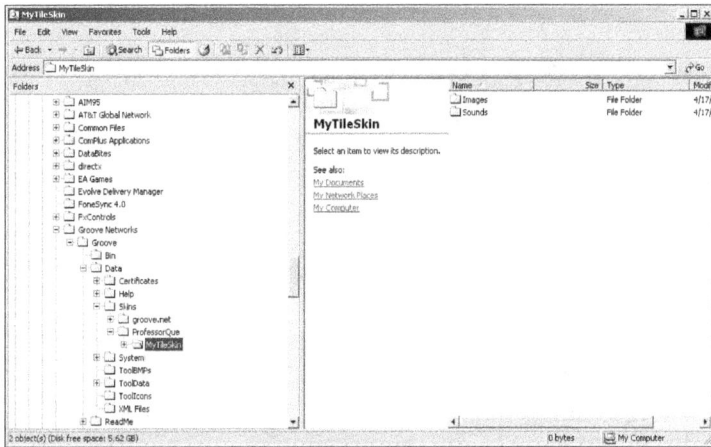

2. Use Windows Explorer to navigate to the new Tile Skin folder created under *app folder*\Data\Skins*Account Name*\My Tile Skin\, as shown in Figure 3.46.

Figure 3.46
You have navigated to the folder that contains all the graphics related to My Tile Skin.

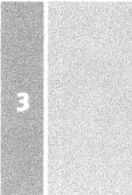

3. Open MemberPaneBackground.jpg located in the Images folder using Adobe Photoshop, as shown in Figure 3.47.

4. Check the width in pixels, height in pixels, horizontal resolution, and vertical resolution by choosing Image, Image Size. In this case it has not been changed so it is correct at 150 pixels wide, 515 pixels high, and with 72 pixels/inch resolution.

5. Verify RGB Color with 24-bit depth by choosing Image, Mode and ensuring that RGB Color and 8 bits/channel are checked (8 bits × 3 channels = 24 bit).

6. Apply the mosaic tiles filter as shown in Figure 3.48.

Figure 3.47
Using Adobe
Photoshop, you are
opening the
`MemberPaneBackgro`
`und.jpg` graphics file.

Figure 3.48
Applying the mosaic
tiles filter to the
graphics for the mem-
ber pane background.

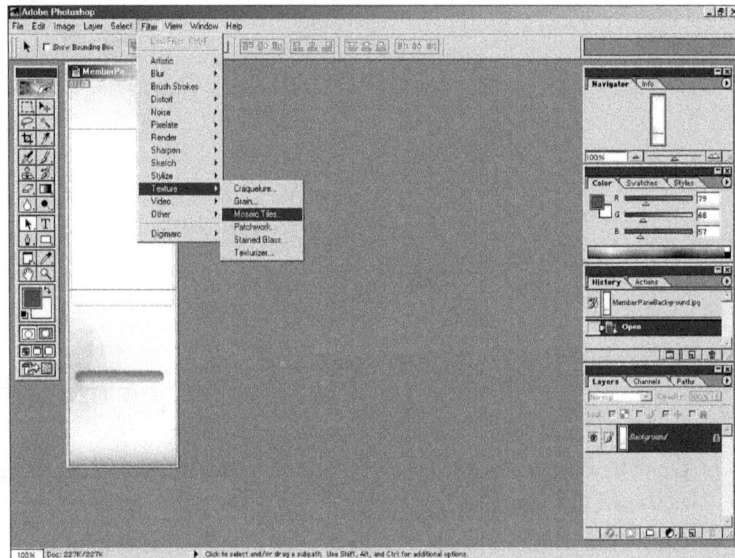

7. Save the image.

8. Restart the Transceiver and enter a shared space. Your space should now look like Figure 3.49.

Figure 3.49
This is how the newly created skin should look.

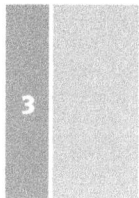

3

CHAPTER 4

UNDERSTANDING SHARED SPACES

In this chapter

WHAT IS A SHARED SPACE?

So far, you've seen how the basic features of Groove Workspace let you collaborate with other users. However, the Instant Messaging features only scratch the surface of Groove's collaborative capabilities. Groove's capability to facilitate ad hoc discussions is enabled primarily by something called a *shared space*. A good definition of a shared space is provided by Groove's own documentation:

> "A shared space is a private place where people can engage in purposeful activities and share information. A shared space is always available to any Groove member who has been invited to participate in that space, though all invited members don't need to participate at the same time."

Shared spaces have inherent security because all members must be explicitly invited to the space. Purposeful activities include everything from text/audio chat, sharing documents and other files, and the use of other shared applications. This chapter begins a discussion of the different tools available for use within a space. This will be a good precursor to the detailed discussion of the default tools in Chapters 5 through 8.

Figure 4.1 provides a high level overview of how shared spaces are created.

Figure 4.1
These are the steps involved in the creation of a shared space.

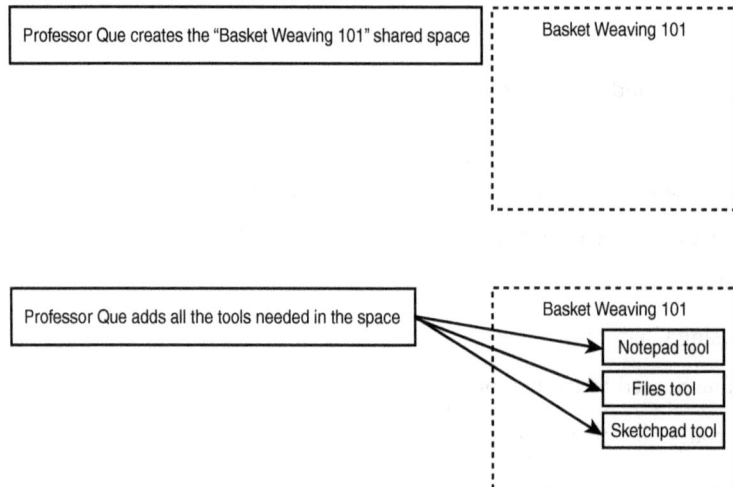

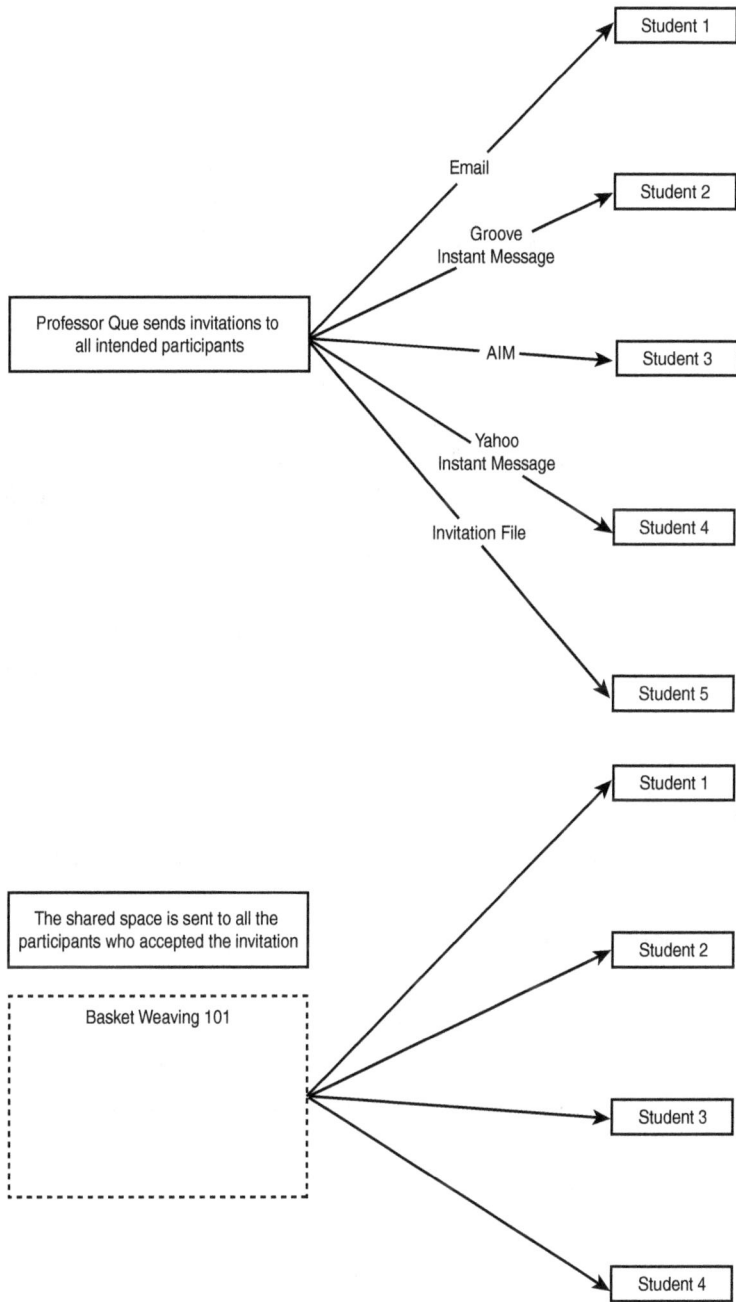

After receiving the shared space, all participants can begin using the shared space

Basket Weaving 101

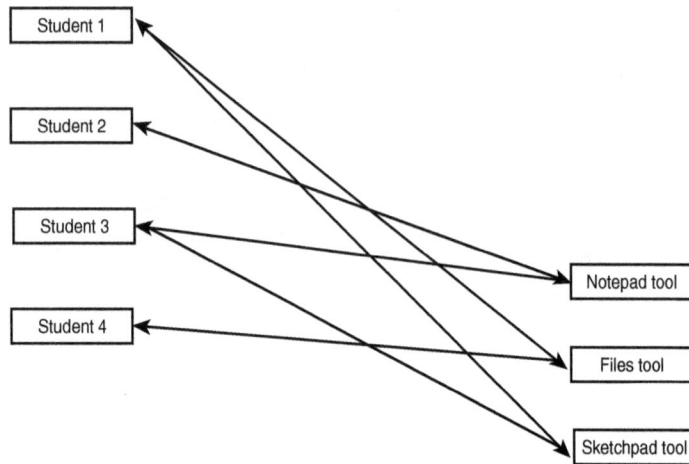

| Student 1 |

| Student 2 |

| Student 3 |

| Notepad tool |

| Student 4 |

| Files tool |

| Sketchpad tool |

CREATING A NEW SHARED SPACE

Creating a new shared space involves naming your new space, choosing the tools that make it up, and inviting other participants to the space. There is a wizard provided to help you that can be started in several different ways, including the following:

- Click the Create Shared Space button on the home page in the My Spaces area.
- Choose File, Create Shared Space.

CHOOSING THE RIGHT TOOLS

When the Shared Space Wizard is started, you're asked to choose the tools the space will use, as shown in Figure 4.2.

The following are the standard individual tools:

- Calendar—Useful for tracking appointments, events, birthdays, anniversaries, and so on.
- Chess Game—Play a game of chess against other participants.
- Contact Manager—Useful tool for sharing contact information with other space members. Contact Manager works just like an address and telephone book that can be viewed by anyone within the space.

- Discussion—Used for creating a review cycle for a document or set of documents.
- Document Review—Allows for hierarchical discussion of topics very similar to a message board or online forum.
- Files—Tool for sharing files, documents, and pictures.
- Forms—Tool for designing forms and views to share data.
- Meetings—Tool for managing agendas, meetings, actions, minutes, and so on.
- Notepad—A basic collaborative text creation tool.
- Outliner—Enables participants to share ideas in a structured outline format.
- Pictures—Enables participants to share and view images in common formats.
- Project Manager—A tracking tool to manage project tasks and phases.
- Sketchpad—Like a virtual whiteboard, members can do freehand sketches, mark up these sketches, add text, and use some preformatted tools to graphically illustrate ideas.
- Tic-tac-toe—The popular game in which competitors have to place Xs and Os strategically on the board.
- Web Browser—Enables participants to browse the Web together and collect a group of shared favorite links.
- Welcome Page—Enables you to create description of the purpose of the space and the tools used.

Figure 4.2
You must choose the tools that will make up your shared space.

In addition to individual tools, some tools have been grouped together to form a toolset. Toolsets have been created for many different types of tasks, saving you the trouble of adding each individual tool to a shared space. Multiple toolsets can be added to a shared space and individual tools added and removed as desired. Many of the tools are given aliases depending on the manner in which they are used within a space. For instance, the Outliner tool has been given the alias "Brainstorming" when used within the Project toolset to more accurately describe its function. The alias is given with the real tool name used in parentheses "( )". Some of the toolsets and the tools that make them up include the following:

- Documents—Assemble a group of documents for reviewing, discussion, and revision.

  Tools included: Welcome Page, Discussion, Files, Document Review, Browser (Web Browser).

- Meetings Organizer—Organize and conduct an effective meeting.

  Tools included: Welcome Page, Meetings, Calendar, Browser (Web Browser), Sketchpad

- Project—Collaborate on a project for work, school, or home.

  Tools included: Welcome Page, Project Manager, Meetings, Files, Browser (Web Browser), Discussion, Calendar.

> **NOTE** You can add and remove tools once the space is created so it's not an issue if you forget to choose one or add tools that won't necessarily be used at this point.

Click the Next button after you've finished choosing the tools for the space.

NAMING YOUR SHARED SPACE

After choosing the tools that make up your space, you'll need to assign a name to your shared space as shown in Figure 4.3. In the text box at the top of the screen, you can enter the name for your shared space. You'll want to assign a meaningful name for the space so recipients can better understand the purpose of the space they've been invited to. In this example, it is named the "Classroom Space."

Figure 4.3
You must assign a name to your shared space that will be meaningful to the other members.

SETTING OPTIONS FOR THE SPACE

As was discussed in Chapter 3, "Starting to Groove," you can attach multiple identities to a single Groove account. Depending on the types of shared spaces you'll be participating in, you may opt to create separate identities for different uses such as home, school, or work. Clicking the Options button underneath the shared space name text box displays the screen shown in Figure 4.4. Any one of the identities attached to your current account can be selected from the drop-down list box. This is the identity recipients will see when they are invited to the space.

Figure 4.4
Choose the identity that you will use within the shared space from the Shared Space Options dialog.

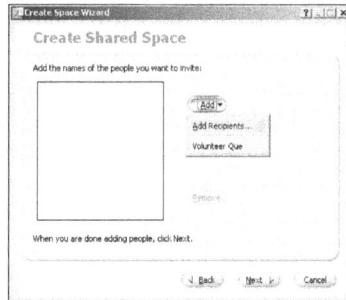

INITIALLY INVITING OTHERS TO YOUR NEW SPACE

At this point, you also have the option of choosing to invite others into the shared space upon its initial creation or to invite no one at this time by choosing the appropriate radio button. Selecting the Invite People to Your Shared Space option and clicking Next takes you to a screen where you build the recipients list, as shown in Figure 4.5.

Figure 4.5
Use this screen to invite people initially to the new shared space.

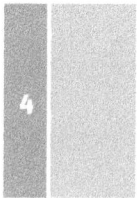

SELECTING THE RECIPIENTS

Clicking Add and choosing Add Recipients from the drop-down menu displays the pop-up window shown in Figure 4.6.

In a similar fashion to how you searched for contacts to add to the My Contacts list in Chapter 3, you have the same options for finding recipients here including the following:

- Look in My Contacts—Contacts that you have added to your contact list in the past.
- Look in Known Groove Contacts—Individuals who are members in shared spaces you participate in and users who have been added to My Contacts.
- Look in Local Network Directory—Individuals listed in the directory maintained on the local network.
- Search groove.net Directory—Individuals listed in the groove.net public directory.

- Enter Email Address—Choosing this option enables you to send an invitation using Groove's built-in email capability.
- Look in My Messenger Contacts—Choosing this option enables you to send an invitation to contacts who are contained within your MSN Messenger installation.

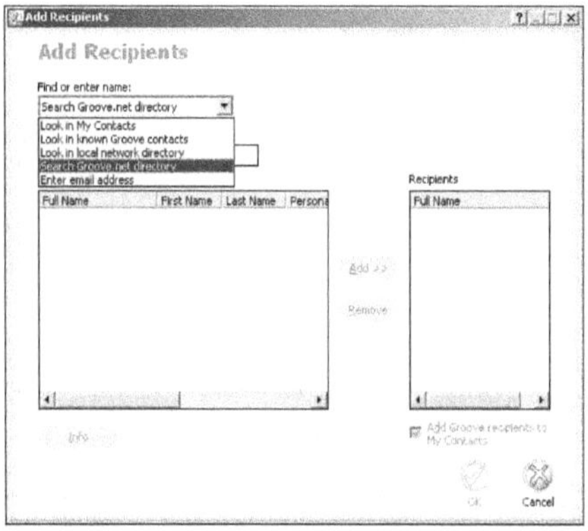

Figure 4.6
You can choose recipients from several different sources.

After you've chosen all the intended recipients, click the OK button to return to the prior screen. After clicking the Next button to continue, you'll need to assign roles to everyone who is invited and whether the invitation requires confirmation before sending the shared space content. An overview of roles is provided in the following section, "Roles Assignment."

ROLES ASSIGNMENT

Roles are used in Groove to assign permissions to participants of a shared space. There are three different roles from which to choose:

- Manager—A manager is the highest permission level that can be granted. This is automatically assigned to the creator of a space, but can be granted to anyone invited. Someone with a manager role can do the following by default:
  - Invite new participants
  - Uninvite participants
  - Add tools
  - Delete tools
  - Shut down the shared space
  - Keep archive of shared space after uninvited

- Participant—This is the default role assigned to any new members in a shared space. Individuals assigned to this role can do the following by default:
  - Invite new participants
  - Add tools
  - Keep archive of shared space after uninvited

> The primary difference between the participant and manager roles is the capability to delete tools and uninvite guests. What this can mean is that any tool added erroneously by a participant may only be deleted by someone in a manager role.

- Guest—With the lowest level of permissions, the guest role is used for read-only access to a shared space. Guests can only view discussions and are limited in their interaction with other members. Guests can do little more than use the audio and text chat features within a space. This is useful for shared spaces that have been "closed" because this enables participants to view all the shared space historical data, but without the capability to modify any of the contents. Like managers and participants, guests are usually given the capability to retain an archive of a shared space after they are uninvited.

INITIAL ASSIGNMENT OF ROLES

Initially, all members invited to a space are given the role of Participant, as shown in Figure 4.7. Clicking the Change Role button enables you to assign a new role to invitees. The example shown in Figure 4.8 shows how you change the role of The Dean to a Guest. After clicking the OK button, the change is reflected in the invitee list. Clicking the Next button takes you to the final step in the process. All assigned roles are granted to the invitees when they enter the space.

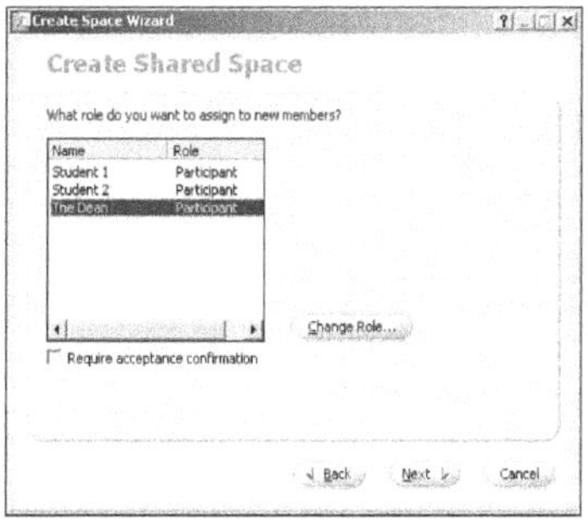

Figure 4.7
By default, all users invited to a shared space are given the role of Participant.

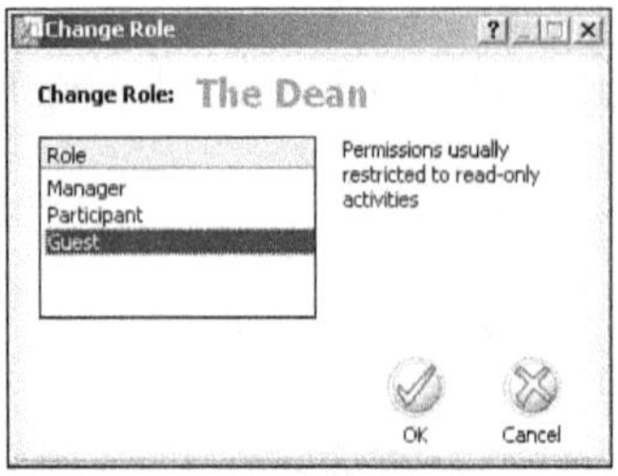

Figure 4.8
In this example, the
role of The Dean has
been changed to
Guest.

MODIFYING ROLES IN AN EXISTING SPACE

After a user enters a shared space, the manager can modify his role at any time. After right-clicking a user in the member pane to the left of the screen, as shown in Figure 4.9, you can choose Role to change their given role. In addition, you can also choose Options, Roles from the drop-down menu while you are in the shared space. This enables you to see all members in the space and change multiple role assignments, as shown in Figure 4.10. By default, only managers can assign new roles or change existing roles for participants.

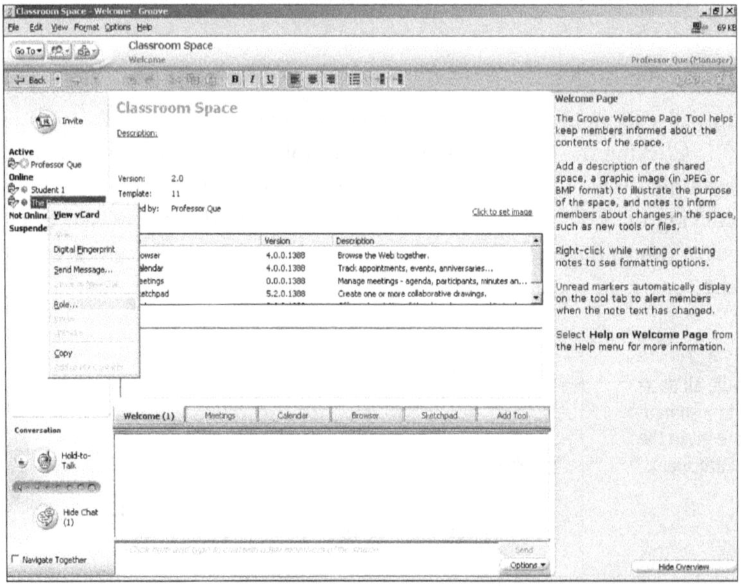

Figure 4.9
Within a shared
space, you can right-
click a user in the
member pane to
change an existing
participant's role.

NOTE

Previously, the use of roles and permissions was only available to licensed users of Groove Workspace. Beginning with Version 2.0, Preview Edition users are also given this ability.

Figure 4.10
By choosing Roles in the Options menu you can easily change multiple role assignments instead of clicking on each individual user.

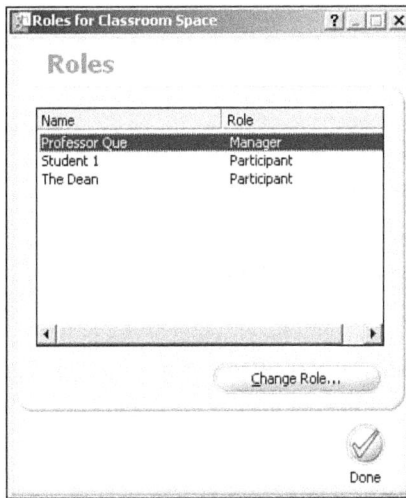

CHANGING SHARED SPACE ROLE PERMISSIONS

You can change the default permissions assigned to each role in a shared space. Choosing Options, Shared Space Permissions takes the manager of a shared space to the screen shown in Figure 4.11, where the permissions for each role can be modified. After any modifications are made, all users assume the new rights (if any) assigned to each role.

Figure 4.11
The manager of a shared space can change the permissions attached to each role within the shared space.

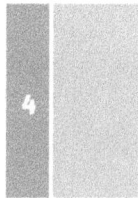

Managers can modify the following permissions assigned to each role:

■ Adding a new tool

■ Deleting a tool in the space

■ Inviting a user to the space

■ Uninviting a current member from the space

■ Shutting down the shared space

■ Keeping an archive after they have been uninvited

In addition, more granular permissions can be assigned at the individual tool level. For more information on this, see the "Modifying Tool Permissions" section later in this chapter.

SHARED SPACE DELIVERY NOTIFICATIONS

After shared space invitations are sent, there are several different notifications that are displayed on the inviter's machine. These depend on the inviter's and invitee's current status and are listed in Table 4.1.

TABLE 4.1   NOTIFICATIONS ASSOCIATED WITH SHARED SPACE INVITATIONS

Notification	Meaning	Applies to These Types of Invitations
Inviting *invitee*: Waiting to send	Groove is not yet sending the invitation because the sender is offline.	Groove Instant Message
Inviting *invitee*: Sending...	Groove is sending the invitation either to the invitee's computer or to the relay service. If the invitee's computer is offline, it will go to the relay service for later transmission.	Groove Instant Message
Inviting *invitee*: Sent, waiting for delivery...	The invitation left the sender's computer and will get delivered if the invitee is online. If the invitee is offline, the invitation is routed to the relay service.	Groove Instant Message

Notification	Meaning	Applies to These Types of Invitations
Inviting *invitee*: Delivered, waiting for invitee to open	The invitation has reached the invitee's computer.	Groove Instant Message
Inviting *invitee*: Opened, waiting for reply...	The invitee has opened the invitation, and now must decide whether to accept or decline it.	Groove Instant Message
Inviting *invitee*: Accepted, waiting to send space	The invitee has accepted the invitation but Groove is not yet sending the shared space because the inviter is offline.	Groove Instant Message Email File-based Other Instant Messengers
Inviting *invitee*: Accepted: Sending shared space, XX% complete	The invitee has accepted the invitation and the shared space is now being sent.	Groove Instant Message Email File-based Other Instant Messengers
Inviting *invitee*: waiting for delivery	The shared space has left the inviter's computer, though the invitee is still receiving it.	Groove Instant Message Email File-based Other Instant Messengers
Inviting *invitee*: Shared space delivered!	The shared space is successfully delivered to the invitee.	Groove Instant Message Email File-based Other Instant Messengers

NOTE

If the invitee goes offline before receiving the entire shared space, the shared space gets sent to the relay service. The next time the invitee goes online, the shared space is routed from the relay service to his or her computer.

NOTE

You can stop the display of these status messages by right-clicking the notification and choosing Stop Tracking. If you are inviting a large number of users to a space, the pop-up can become pretty large.

SENDING AND RECEIVING SHARED SPACE INVITATIONS

Groove allows shared space invitations to be sent using many different methods. In the text, those sending an invitation are referred to as inviters and recipients as invitees. The following sections outline the different ways invitations can be transmitted.

SENDING SHARED SPACE INVITATIONS VIA GROOVE INSTANT MESSAGES

Sending an invitation by Instant Message provides the most feedback to the inviter. An invitee receives notification, as shown in Figure 4.12. The notification states "Invitation for *Invitee* from *Inviter Date/Time*". The Invitee can click on the link to open the Invitation dialog shown in Figure 4.13.

Figure 4.12
The recipient of an invitation using a Groove instant message will receive a notification after the invitation has arrived.

Figure 4.13
Clicking on the notification for a shared space invitation opens this screen, which enables the invitee to accept or decline the invitation.

At this point, the invitee can choose to accept or decline the invitation. Clicking the Response button toggles the response field at the bottom so a personal text or audio message can accompany an acceptance or denial of the invitation. Clicking the vCard button can help further identify the sender by displaying his vCard and digital fingerprint. For more information on the shared space, including the size, date created, and number of members, click the Info button.

TIP

> If you accidentally close the invitation window prior to accepting or declining, you can retrieve it from the My Messages inbox area. After viewing an invitation, the notification message disappears so you can no longer select it.

SENDING INVITATIONS BY EMAIL AND BY FILE

Groove invitations can be saved to a `.grv` file. When you choose the email delivery method for an invitation, Groove creates an email for you and attaches the file to your email message automatically. A recipient running Microsoft Outlook would receive an email like Figure 4.14. Double-clicking the attached invitation, or right-clicking and choosing Open, brings up the Respond to Invitation dialog box. Instructions are provided within the email body for recipients that do not currently have Groove installed.

Figure 4.14
An invitation sent via email would look like this to a Microsoft Outlook user.

NOTE

> Invitees have the option of requiring confirmation for invitations. If confirmation has been enabled, a member accepting an invitation is not able to enter the space until the inviter confirms the invitee acceptance.

SENDING SHARED SPACE INVITATIONS VIA MSN MESSENGER

MSN Messenger users can send shared space invitations using that service. Assuming MSN Messenger is already started, choose Actions, Start Groove from within MSN Messenger, as shown in Figure 4.15. This should open the window shown in Figure 4.16. From here, you can select an online contact by clicking the My Contacts tab at the top of the window. This

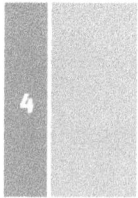

should be used to invite contacts who are currently online with the MSN Messenger service. For offline contacts, you'll need to click the Other tab and specify the email address and messenger service to use, as shown in Figure 4.17. After you've specified the contact, click the OK button to continue. The MSN Messenger service delivers the invitation to the user and notifies you in a new chat window, as shown in Figure 4.18. You can click Cancel at any time to revoke the invitation.

Figure 4.15
Choose Actions, Start Groove to send an invitation using MSN Messenger.

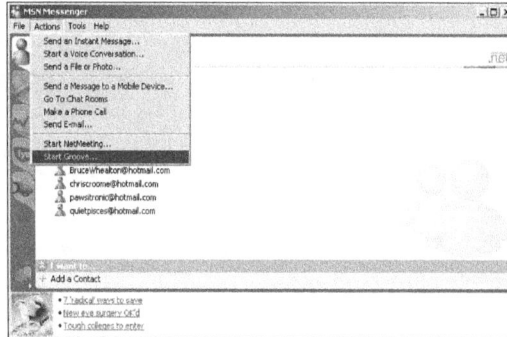

Figure 4.16
You can choose to send an invitation to any online MSN Messenger contacts.

Figure 4.17
By selecting the Other tab, you can send an invitation to offline users by their email address.

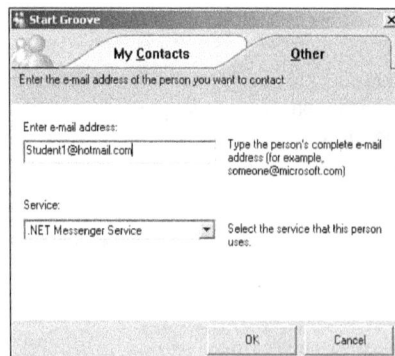

Figure 4.18
When you specify the recipients of the invitation, a new chat window opens in MSN Messenger that enables you to display or cancel the invitation.

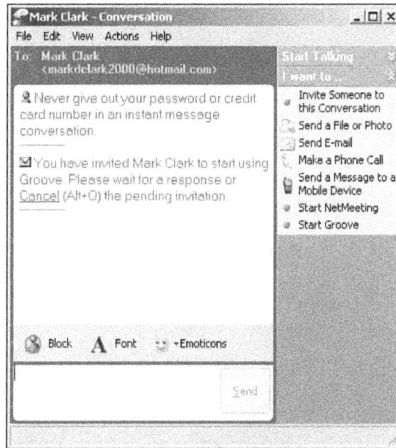

TIP

If the user does not have Groove Workspace installed, he is given a link to follow where he can download the software.

CONFIRMING ACCEPTANCE OF THE INVITATION

If the user accepts the invitation, you need to confirm the invitation, as shown in Figure 4.19. In this window, you see the recipient's name in the top part of the window. You can click the View vCard button to help authenticate the individual. After you have confirmed the identity, you can choose the recipient's destination shared space in the drop-down list along with the role he will assume. If you want to create a new shared space at this time, you can select the Create New Shared Space check box. Also, you can select the Navigate to Space check box to instruct Groove to navigate to the space when the OK button is clicked.

Figure 4.19
After an invitation sent via MSN Messenger is accepted, the inviter must confirm the invitation.

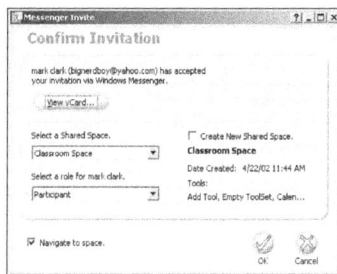

SHARED SPACE RECEIPT NOTIFICATIONS

When you receive and accept a shared space invitation from a Groove instant message, you will receive several notifications as your reply is processed. You'll find a listing of these messages and a description of each in Table 4.2.

TABLE 4.2   NOTIFICATIONS DISPLAYED WHILE A SHARED SPACE INVITATION IS PROCESSED

Notification	Meaning
Waiting for *Shared Space*: Waiting to send acceptance	Groove is preparing to send a response to the invitee.
Waiting for *Shared Space*: Sending Acceptance...	Groove is sending the invitation acceptance to the sender.
Waiting for *Shared Space*: Acceptance sent...	The invitation acceptance has left your computer.
	If the sender goes offline before receiving your acceptance, it gets routed to the relay service until the next time the sender goes back online.
Downloading *Shared Space*: 50% complete	Groove is downloading the shared space from the sender's computer. The percentage changes to show the progress of the transmission.
	If the sender goes offline before the entire shared space is sent, the shared space does not get sent. Groove will try again to send the shared space the next time the sender goes online.
	If you go offline before receiving the entire shared space (and if the sender stays online), the shared space gets routed to the relay service, and will be forwarded to your computer then next time you go online.
Installing *Shared Space*	Groove is installing the downloaded shared space.
"Shared Space" ready (click to open)!	The shared space is installed and ready. You can go to it by clicking the notification or by double-clicking it in My Spaces.

If you were sent an invitation through email and the sender checked the Confirmation Acceptance Required box, this indicates that your acceptance must be confirmed by the inviter before it is processed further. After receiving notification that your acceptance was sent you will receive the following message:

"Acceptance sent, awaiting confirmation from *Inviter*"

After it is confirmed, processing will continue and you may download the space.

4

ENTERING AN EXISTING SHARED SPACE

Your account maintains a list of all the shared spaces in which you've participated. There are several different ways to enter a shared space including the following:

- Click the Shared Space icon in the Go To button group and choose the space name from the drop-down list.

- Select the shared space under My Spaces on the home page and click Goto Space or double-click a shared space in the list.

- Choose View—Goto from the menu and click the space name.

- Highlight a shared space in the My Spaces area and click Goto Space or double-click a space in the list. The My Spaces area is discussed in detail in the "Managing My Spaces" section later in this chapter.

THE SHARED SPACE INTERFACE

Now that you've learned how to create and invite participants to your shared space, let's look at the interface that creates this "complete environment for group interaction." Shared spaces have the following sections, as shown in Figure 4.20:

- Member's Panel—This shows all the current participants in the shared space. They are grouped into different categories depending on whether they are online or offline.

- Tool Area—Tools are applications used within a shared space. All interaction with a tool is performed in the middle of the shared space interface.

- Chat Pane—Shared space participants can use the audio and text chatting features while they are performing other shared space activities.

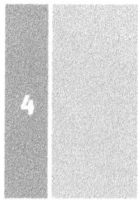

THE MEMBER'S PANEL

At any time while participating in a shared space, the member's panel on the left side of the screen will show you the status of all participants. As shown in Figure 4.21, Groove classifies users into four categories:

- Active—A user is online and is actively participating in the space.

- Online—A user is online, but is not active in the space at this time.

- Not online—A user is either not logged in to Groove or has chosen to work in offline mode.

- Suspended—The user has been inactive in the space for an extended period of time and will have to be re-invited to participate.

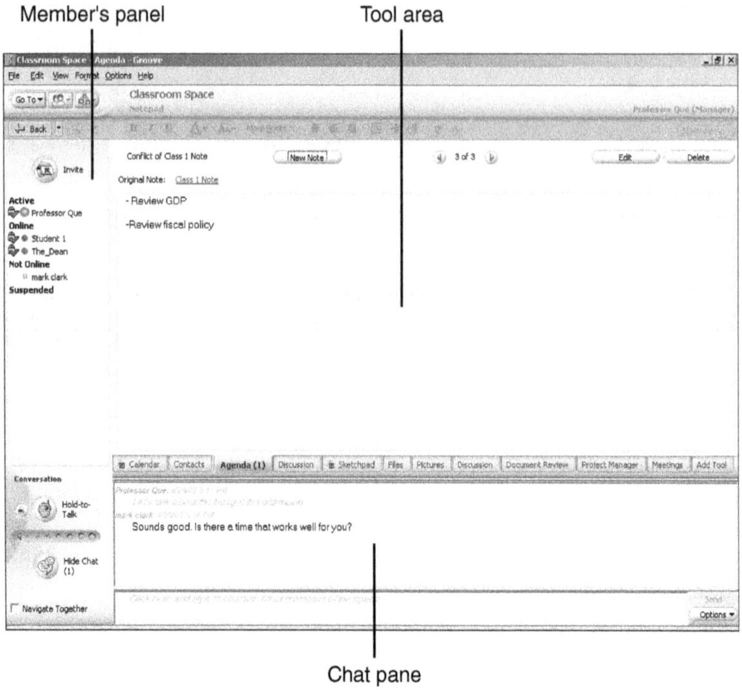

Member's panel   Tool area

Figure 4.20
These are the differ-
ent areas within a
shared space.

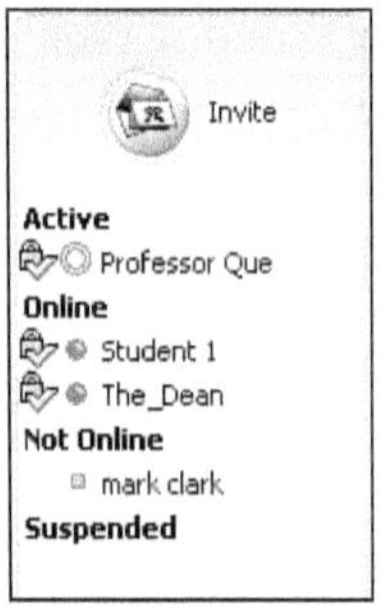

Chat pane

Figure 4.21
Shared space mem-
bers can fall into one
of four categories
depending on their
current status.

Holding the mouse pointer over a user in the member panel can reveal different information about a user, including what tools they are currently using, their role, and their
online/offline status. In the "Viewing Presence Information" section later in this chapter
you take a look at what the current tool usage indicator means.

→ For a summary of the icons used to represent a user's current online or offline status, **see** "Status
Information," **p.101**

MEMBER'S PANEL FUNCTIONS

By right-clicking a member's name in the member panel, as shown in Figure 4.22, you can
perform the following functions:

Figure 4.22
Right-clicking a user in the member panel enables you to perform several different functions.

- View vCard—Choosing this option from the menu displays the member's vCard. This is very useful for not only viewing contact information but for verifying a user's digital fingerprint. You can also double-click the user to display this screen.

- Alias—This enables you to assign an alias to the user. This is helpful when there is another identity with the same or a similar name.

- Authenticate—For users who have yet to be authenticated, this enables you to confirm the identity of the user within the shared space.

→ For more information on the authentication process, **see** "Groove's Unspoofable Identities," **p.44**

- Send Message—This option enables you to compose and send a Groove instant message to that user. All instant messages can be sent to online or offline users.

- Invite to New Chat—This creates a new chat space and sends an invitation to the member. This is a lightweight shared space with only chat and audio capabilities that is opened in a new window (or can later be converted into a shared space).

- Role—This option enables you to change the role of any member. You must be assigned to the manager role to perform this function.

- Invite—This option sends a message to the user inviting him to join you within the shared space. This is a subtle way to let others know that their presence is requested within the shared space.

- Uninvite—This option uninvites someone from this shared space and makes a copy of the space on their device. An uninvited participant can enter the copy of the shared space but cannot enter the "live" space as long as he remains uninvited. You must have adequate permission to perform this function.

- Copy—This copies the member's name to the Clipboard so it can later be pasted in such areas as the Contact Manager tool.

THE TOOLS AREA

Tools are applications designed to facilitate quick and effective collaboration. Being developed around the Groove framework, they are built to take advantage of all the Groove services from synchronization to security. Although Groove provides many tools out of the box, there can also be custom tools developed using the Groove Development Kit (GDK). This is why Groove is so powerful; developers are freed from worrying about these complex technical issues and can concentrate on creating a robust tool with rich functionality.

THE TOOL TABS

The current tool is displayed prominently in the middle of a shared space. Along the bottom of this space are the Tool Tabs that let you choose the tool you'd like to use. Each tab contains the name of the tool and the number of members currently accessing it. Looking at Figure 4.23, you can see the Calendar tab indicates that there are two people currently viewing the document, as evidenced by the "(2)" next to the tab name. Tabs are spaced and sized automatically. Periods are appended to the name if the tab is too small to display the entire string.

Figure 4.23
The Tool tab not only displays the name of the space but also indicates the number of active users in parentheses.

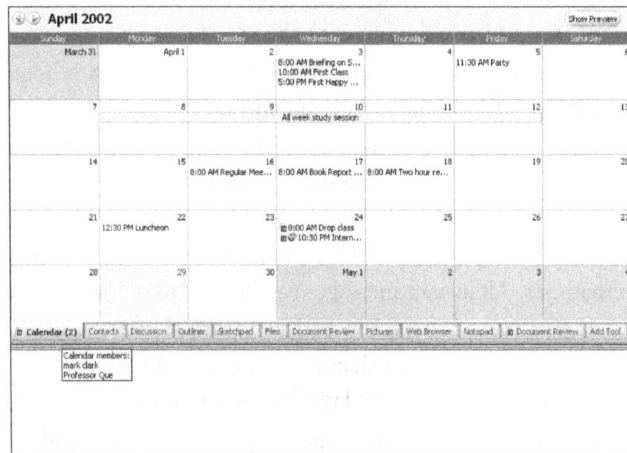

Clicking a tab activates the tool and places it into the central tool area. You can think of this tool area as an application running right in the middle of your shared space, except that this application is instantly synchronized with all members of the space. As you type in Notepad, all other currently active space members with that tool open will see the changes and can simultaneously edit the text. If changes are made within a tool by another member, the tab displays an unread icon to alert you that changes have been made.

TIP

> If for some reason you want to turn off the unread markers that display on the tool tabs, right-click the tab and uncheck the Mark Space Unread on Changes option. The unread markers take up space on the tab and with constant changes happening within a shared space some users might find them distracting.

NOTIFICATION WHEN A TOOL CONTENT CHANGES

Unread markers, if enabled, are useful because they can quickly alert you to changes to tool content while you are within the shared space. If you'd like to be notified of tool content changes even when you are not within the shared space, it is possible to turn on Tool Changes notification. After right-clicking a Tool tab, you may select the Send Notification On Changes option. Every time the tool content changes you receive a notification via Groove instant message as shown in Figure 4.24. This notification shows that the Classroom Space has unread content. Clicking the notification takes the user directly into the space and selects the tool that has changed.

Figure 4.24
By enabling the Send Notification On Changes option, the user is notified via instant message that the tool content has changed since it was last viewed.

Classroom Space - Sketchpad has unread content.

RENAMING A TAB

By default, tabs are populated with the name of the tool such as Files, Sketchpad, and so on. However, this is often not an accurate description of how it is being used within the space. You can rename a tool by choosing File, Rename *Tool Name* tool or by right-clicking a Tool tab and choosing the Rename option. You are then prompted for the new tool name displayed on the tab. In Figure 4.25, the Notepad tool is renamed with the new tool display name "Agenda." After clicking OK, you can now see in Figure 4.26 that the tab reflects the new tool display name. This doesn't change the actual tool (Notepad tool) but only the text that displays on the tab. Note that this changes the name for everyone in the space, not just within your copy of the space.

DELETING A TOOL

If your role has proper permissions assigned, you can delete tools that are no longer needed in a shared space. You can remove a tool from a space by choosing File, Delete *Tool Name* tool or by right-clicking a Tool tab and choosing Delete. You are prompted for confirmation before the tool is actually deleted and must be assigned the permission to do so.

Figure 4.25
Right-clicking a Tool tab and choosing Rename prompts you to assign a new name to the tool.

Figure 4.26
The Notepad tool has been renamed to Agenda because of its intended purpose within the shared space.

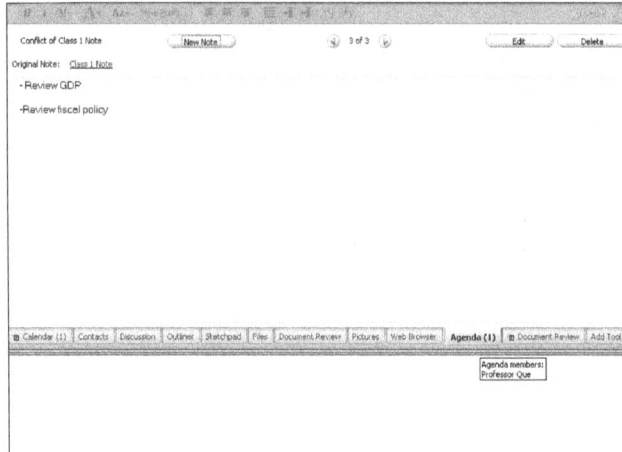

CAUTION

Deleting a tool removes all data it may have contained from everybody's shared space. So be very careful taking this step!

REARRANGING TAB ORDER

Tabs can be arranged by simply dragging the tab to a new location. A vertical placeholder is displayed indicating the new insertion point.

TIP

If you accidentally drag a Tool tab into a text area (such as Notepad) it will probably insert some text like "groove Telespace:...". This can be easily undone by pressing Ctrl+Z (undo) and trying to drag the tab again.

N O T E

Because tools can get rather crowded if they are all part of the same row, it would be nice to have multiple rows in which to place the tools. Although not very elegant, it is possible to create additional rows using the custom toolset feature. When adding a new toolset (not an individual tool) you will note that it places all the tools it contains in its own new row. This new row can have tools added and deleted from it as your needs dictate. In addition to the standard toolsets, there is a blank toolset called Custom that initially contains no tools and is intended to help in situations where the number of tools has made the display overly crowded.

ADDING A NEW TOOL

If your role has been assigned the appropriate permissions, you may add a new tool to the space. Clicking the Add Tool tab opens the tool selection screen shown in Figure 4.27. You may remember this screen because it is similar to a step during the initial creation of a shared space. After the appropriate tool(s) or toolset is selected, clicking Add Selected Tool adds it to the shared space.

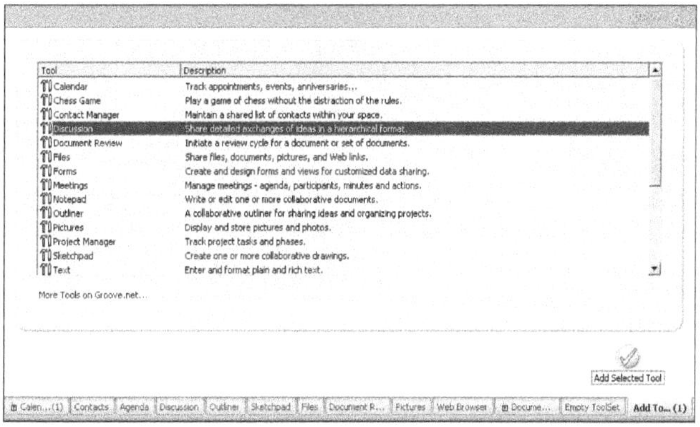

Figure 4.27
The tool selection screen enables you to add new tools and toolsets to a shared space.

TIP

Remember that Groove is designed for fast interaction. Don't add every tool to the space, only the ones you need. Extra tools can not only distract users, but also can add synchronization overhead to the space. Lean and mean spaces make for effective communication.

FINDING ADDITIONAL TOOLS

While Groove provides an impressive array of standard tools with both the licensed and preview editions of their software, they also offer some additional tools on their site. Clicking the More Tools on groove.net link in the Add Tool screen shown in Figure 4.27 opens a browser and takes you to the Partner Tools area on the Groove Web site. Clicking on the More info link for each tool will provide more information on obtaining and injecting the tool. Many of these tools offer a free demonstration period so you can see if the tool suits your needs. To better understand how the tool injection process works, see the sidebar called "What Is Tool Injection?" for more information. In addition, Chapter 10, "The Foundation for Development: The Groove Development Kit (GDK)," outlines how you can begin developing your own tools and publishing them for others to use.

What Is Tool Injection?

Although the term "injection" might give many people the shivers, within Groove it is a very important concept. Groove has been designed to be extensible, meaning that its component-based structure allows new features to be added without requiring the entire application to be replaced. When talking about shared spaces and tools, the term *injection* describes the addition of new tools to Groove with a new set of features. However, injection is used to describe many other Groove processes including the following:

- Adding a new contact into Groove by "injecting" a vCard (.vcg) file
- Downloading and "injecting" a new skin into your installation
- Accepting a shared space invitation and "injecting" the space
- Saving your account to a file or on groove.net and "injecting" it into another device to use it on multiple computers

Behind the scenes, Groove's injection process is designed to fit within a strict security framework and thus injection subscribes to the following rules:

- Injecting a component only adds it to one account. It will not "cross over" and be added to other accounts even if they are on the same device.
- If a tool injected by another member is added to a shared space, other participants will receive the tool in that space *only*. However, it is not added to their accounts unless they explicitly inject the tool themselves.
- Tools must be signed for injection (unless Component Authentication has been turned off).

COPYING A TOOL AS A LINK

Right-clicking and choosing Copy Tool as a Link or choosing the Edit, Copy Tool as Link from the top menu enables you to insert a tool reference in other places. This is useful because it provides a quick hyperlink for other space members. Once copied, simply right-click and choose Paste or choose Edit, Paste from the menu to place the link at the current insertion point. Notice in Figure 4.28 that I have copied the Sketchpad tool as a link inside the Agenda. Users can simply click on the link and it will take them to the tool just as if they had clicked on the Tool tab itself. These links can be used in text chat, the Discussion tool, the Notepad tool, and just about anywhere else within the shared space that supports a text message.

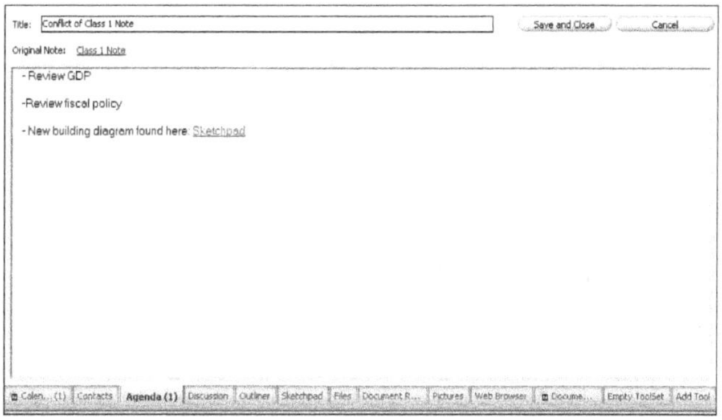

Figure 4.28
A link to the Sketchpad tool has been placed within the Agenda Note page for easy reference by other users.

OPENING A TOOL IN A NEW WINDOW

There might be times when you need to have several tools open at once. Right-click on a Tool tab and choose Open Tool in New Window to open the selected tool in a new window. This can also be accessed from the menu by choosing View, Open in New Window, *Tool Name*, but this only enables you to open the currently selected tool or the chat tool. All data will still be synchronized, but now you can switch between the windows using Alt+Tab or the Windows taskbar.

CAUTION

> You should only open tools in multiple windows using the steps listed previously. Opening separate transceivers at the same time under the File, New Window option can cause some strange synchronization issues if you enter a shared space in more than one window.

VIEWING PRESENCE INFORMATION

In addition to seeing the number of users within a tool reflected on the Tool tab, you can also find out exactly which users are accessing a tool. Hold your mouse pointer over a Tool tab to display a status pop-up showing the names of the users who are viewing the tool. As you can see in Figure 4.29, this message shows that Professor Que and The Dean are currently viewing the Calendar tool.

Figure 4.29
Holding your mouse pointer over a Tool tab displays the names of all users currently active within the tool.

You can also tell what tools a particular user is viewing. By holding the mouse over a user's name in the member panel, as shown in Figure 4.30, you can not only see the tools being used, but also the Role assigned to the user (if applicable).

Figure 4.30
Holding your mouse pointer over a user-name in the member's pane displays what tools they are using and their currently assigned role.

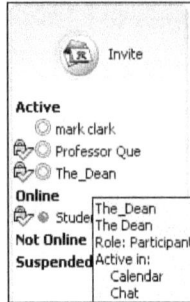

GETTING HELP WITH A TOOL

If the Hide Overview option has not been selected, you should see a brief overview of the tool features on the right of the screen. To display the Overview again after it has been hidden, choose View, Show Overview from the main menu. For more detailed help, you can choose Help, Help on *Tool Name* from the main menu.

NOTE

> The default tools provided with Groove include their own help text. However, it is possible that custom tools may not always have help because it is created at the developer's discretion.

MODIFYING TOOL PERMISSIONS

In the earlier discussion of shared space creation, you saw how initial assignment of roles could be used to control permissions of shared space participants. Each tool within a space has its own set of permissions attached to it. Although default permissions are set for each tool, it might be necessary to further modify the tool permissions. Right-clicking a Tool tab and choosing Permissions or choosing Options, *Tool* Permissions from the menu displays the screen shown in Figure 4.31.

At the top of the screen is a drop-down list box that contains all the current roles: Manager, Participant, and Guest. Below this is a list of activities and check boxes indicating the permissions granted to that role. After you have set the permissions, click the Apply button to update the tool permissions for everyone within the space. Table 4.3 lists the standard tools and default permissions assigned to each role.

Figure 4.31
Modify the permissions for an individual tool from this dialog.

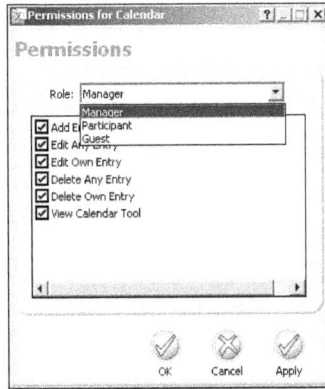

TABLE 4.3   STANDARD GROOVE TOOLS AND THE DEFAULT PERMISSIONS ASSIGNED TO EACH ROLE

Tool	Manager	Participant	Guest
Calendar	Add Entry	Add Entry	View Calendar Tool
	Edit Any Entry Edit Own Entry Delete Any Entry Delete Own Entry View Calendar Tool	Edit Own Entry Delete Own Entry View Calendar Tool	
Chess Game	N/A	N/A	N/A
Contact Manager	Add Contact Edit Own Contact Edit Any Contact Delete Own Contact Delete Any Contact View Contacts Tool	Add Contact Edit Own Contact Delete Own Contact View Contacts Tool	View Contacts Tool
Discussion	Create Documents Edit Own Document Edit Any Document Delete Own Document Delete Any Document View Discussion Tool	Create Documents Edit Own Document Delete Own Document View Discussion Tool	View Discussion Tool
Document Review	N/A	N/A	N/A

continues

Table 4.3   Continued

Tool	Manager	Participant	Guest
Files	Add Files/Folders Modify Permissions Modify Files Delete Files View Files Tool	Add Files/Folders Modify Files View Files Tool	View Files Tool
Forms	Designer Access View Forms Tool	View Forms Tool	View Forms Tool
Meetings	N/A	N/A	N/A
Notepad	Edit Text View Notepad Tool	Edit Text View Notepad Tool	View Notepad Tool
Outliner	Edit Outline View Outliner Tool	Edit Outline View Outliner Tool	View Outliner Tool
Pictures Rename Pictures Picture	Add Pictures Rename Pictures Delete Pictures View Pictures Tool	Add Pictures Rename Pictures View Pictures Tool	View Pictures
Project Manager	Add New Tasks Edit Any Task Edit Created Tasks Edit Project Information Edit Created Tasks Edit Assigned Task Status Edit Assigned Task Schedule Delete Any Task Delete Created Tasks View Project Manager Tool	Add New Tasks Edit Assigned Task Status Delete Created Tasks View Project Manager Tool	View Project Tool Manager
Sketchpad	Create, Edit, and Delete Sketches View Sketchpad Tool	Create, Edit, and Delete Sketches View Sketchpad Tool	View Sketchpad Tool
Text	Edit Text View Text Tool	Edit Text View Text Tool	View Text Tool
Tic-tac-toe game	N/A	N/A	N/A
Web browser	N/A	N/A	N/A
Welcome Page	N/A	N/A	N/A

THE CONVERSATION PANE WITHIN A SHARED SPACE

All shared spaces have text and audio chat capability. Located below the tool area in Figure 4.32, users can use text chat as they navigate and utilize different tools within the space. Chat is actually a tool itself, but it's unique because it does not appear on the Tool tabs and is automatically injected at space creation. All members in the space can see text chat, but audio chat is only available to those with a properly configured sound card.

Figure 4.32
The Chat pane enables you to engage in text conversations with other shared space members.

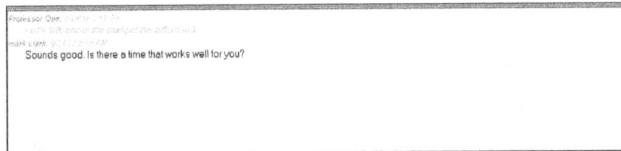

USING TEXT CHAT

Text messages can be sent to all the members in a shared space by entering your message in the text box at the bottom of the chat pane. After the message is finished, you can press Enter or click the Send button. Your message appears in the chat window, preceded by your name and the time it was sent. Online users within the space will see the message almost immediately. Offline users will receive all chat messages once they are back online.

FORMATTING TEXT CHAT

Text formatting options enable you to personalize your chat messages. Highlighting the text to change, clicking the Options button, and choosing Font, as shown in Figure 4.33.

Figure 4.33
You can change the style of text within the chat pane to suit your needs.

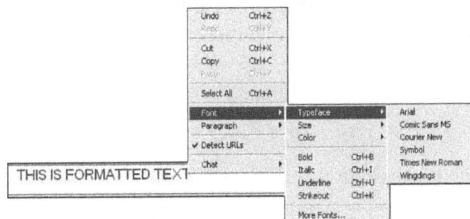

This gives you the following options:

- Typeface—This can be used to change the font typeface.
- Size—The point size of your text can be changed anywhere from 8 to 72.
- Color—A whole array of color choices is provided to make text stand out.

In addition, you are given standard choices for bold, italic, underline, and strikethrough text. Font changes only apply to the current entry; once the text is sent it reverts to the default font.

NOTE

> If you don't find what you want in the standard font choices, you can choose More Fonts from the drop-down menu for the complete collection of fonts available.

OTHER TEXT OPTIONS

By clicking the Options button and choosing Paragraph, you can access several other text options:

- Align Left—Align text to the left of the chat pane.
- Center—Center the text within the chat pane.
- Align Right—Align text to the right of the chat pane.
- Bullets—Place a bullet to the left of the text. You must choose this for every line that needs a bullet because it does not repeat.
- Increase Indent—Indent the text to the right.
- Decrease Indent—Makes the indentation smaller by one indentation. This does nothing if there is no indentation present.
- Detect URLs—By checking this option, any URL appearing in a chat transcript becomes a hyperlink.
- Chat—This opens another menu with a few different options including the following:
  - Undo—Undo the last thing that was typed.
  - Redo—Remove the last undo.
  - Delete Transcript—Delete all the chat currently in the Chat Pane.

CAUTION

> The Delete Transcript function deletes all the text chat, not just the currently highlighted portion, in all shared spaces. Use with caution!

DETERMINING WHO IS CURRENTLY USING TEXT CHAT

As a user begins to type a chat message, other users in the space will receive a chat alert pop-up indicating that the user is currently typing a message. As you can see in Figure 4.34, Student 3 has begun typing a chat message and the other space members have been alerted.

Figure 4.34
Groove is alerting other shared space members that Student 3 is currently typing a message within the chat pane.

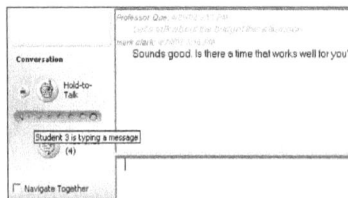

HIDING THE CHAT PANE

Because the chat pane takes away some of the available screen area, you may want to hide it when not in use. Clicking the Hide Chat icon hides the chat area. The number of users with the Chat pane open is also displayed here in parentheses. The Chat pane only collapses out of view, but any chat transcript within it is not lost. Clicking the Show Chat button restores the Chat pane to its previous location.

USING AUDIO CHAT

Like your own online conference call, Groove provides the capability to use audio chat while members participate in a shared space. If your system meets the System Requirements outlined in Chapter 2 you can use the Audio Tuner provided with Groove to properly configure your microphone and speakers.

USING THE AUDIO TUNING WIZARD

If you want to participate in audio discussion within a shared space, you should first choose Options, Audio Tuning Wizard to properly configure your audio options. If you do not run the wizard, you are prompted to do so when first trying to use the audio features. The initial wizard screen shown in Figure 4.35 outlines three steps you should take prior to beginning:

1. Close all programs that play or record sound. This includes any MP3 players like Winamp or other jukebox-type applications that may be running in the background.

2. Verify that your microphone and speakers are properly connected, turned on, and well positioned. This includes making sure the microphone is not too far away so you may speak in a comfortable tone. Also, you may want to use headphones because speakers can cause feedback when using the microphone.

3. If your speakers have a volume knob, ensure it is turned to a reasonable setting. The volume can also be lowered to help eliminate feedback.

After you've completed these initial steps, click Next to continue.

Figure 4.35
You must complete several steps before you can use the Audio Tuning Wizard.

ADJUSTING THE SPEAKER VOLUME   After clicking Next, you are taken to the Adjust Speaker Volume screen shown in Figure 4.36. Click the Play button and you can begin adjusting the volume slider to the left and right until the sound is playing at a reasonable volume. If you don't hear any sounds or the slider isn't responding, click the Volume Controls button to open the Windows Volume Control panel and double check your settings. Click Next when you're satisfied with the audio volume.

Figure 4.36
The first step when running the Audio Tuning Wizard is to adjust your speaker volume. Clicking the Play button enables you to hear your new audio volume.

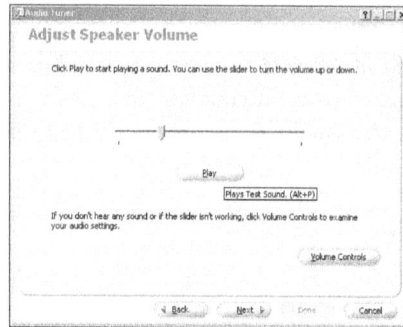

ADJUSTING YOUR MICROPHONE VOLUME   The next screen enables you to test your microphone input volume as shown in Figure 4.37. If your microphone is plugged in, speak the following phrase into the microphone:

> "I am using the Audio Tuner to tune my microphone volume. Then I will be able to talk to others with Groove."

As you speak, the blue bar should fluctuate. If the blue bar moves very little, try moving the slider to the right. Likewise, if the blue bar fills the status bar the entire time, try moving the slider to the left. Once you are satisfied that the bar is responding as you speak, click the Next button.

Figure 4.37
You must adjust your microphone volume within the Audio Tuning Wizard to ensure others can hear you.

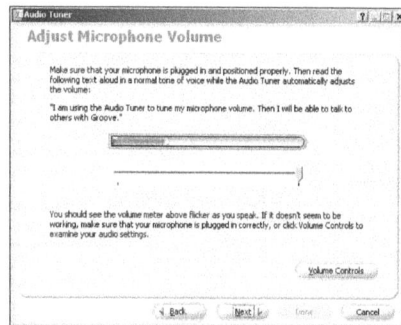

MAKING A TEST RECORDING   In this step, you make a test recording so you may play it back. Click the red circle shown in Figure 4.38. Speak a short message into the microphone and click the gray square when you are finished. Once stopped, you can click the gray triangle to play the memo. The quality of the audio you hear should closely resemble how other Groove users will hear you. You can click the gray X at any time to delete the audio message and start over. When the quality of the audio is satisfactory, click Next to proceed.

Figure 4.38
Record a test message and play it back to test your audio settings.

MAKING FINAL ADJUSTMENTS   On the screen shown in Figure 4.39, click the Begin button to allow Groove to make its final adjustments. Do not speak into the microphone at this time. You will know it has finished when the Begin button text changes to Repeat. You can click this to rerun the process. Clicking the Next button takes you to the final step.

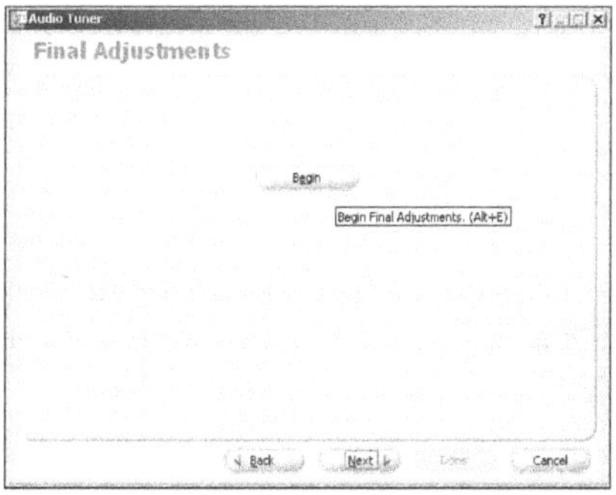

Figure 4.39
Click the Begin button and Groove will make all its final adjustments.

If you've reached the screen in Figure 4.40, your audio tuning should be completed. If you make any changes to your system's audio configuration, you can rerun the Audio Tuning Wizard for readjustments. Click the Done button to exit the wizard and return to the shared space.

Figure 4.40
Now that the Audio Tuning Wizard is complete you should be able to begin using Groove's audio chat feature.

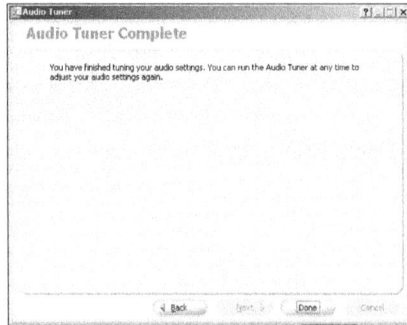

USING THE AUDIO CHAT IN A SHARED SPACE

While in a shared space, you can click the Hold-to-Talk button and it will change to the Talk button, as shown in Figure 4.41. It will now transmit anything you say into your microphone to the other online and active Groove members within the space. You must hold down the button while you speak, unless you click the Lock button. This "locks" the Hold to Talk function until you are finished speaking. Click it again to release it.

Figure 4.41
Clicking the Hold-to-Talk button transmits anything you say into the microphone to other space members who have the appropriate audio configuration.

DETERMINING WHO IS CURRENTLY USING AUDIO CHAT   Unless conferencing is turned on, while others are using the audio chat within a space, you will find the Hold-to-Talk button disabled. You know who is using it at any given time because a status message will display indicating "Now Talking: *User Name*," as shown in Figure 4.42.

Figure 4.42
While someone is transmitting Groove displays his username over the Hold-to-Talk button.

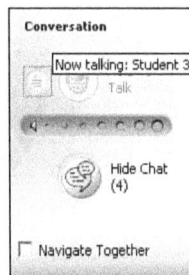

TURNING ON CONFERENCE MODE   By default, only one member can speak at a time within a shared space. This "one-to-all" configuration means that while one person is speaking, all other space members can only listen until he/she releases the Hold-to-Talk button. By choosing the Options, Conference Mode from the menu, all users can speak at the same time.

TIP

> You should probably use this sparingly. Just like a physical meeting without a moderator, things can get pretty chaotic when everyone tries to talk at once.

NAVIGATING TOGETHER   Another useful Groove feature is the capability to turn on the Navigate Together feature by selecting the check box shown in Figure 4.43. All members with this feature turned on "follow" one another as they navigate through the space. This means as one user clicks a new Tool tab, all others with the feature turned on move to that tool as well. This is useful for demonstrations and for training such as introducing others to space features.

Figure 4.43
The Navigate Together feature is useful because it allows others to "follow along" as you navigate through the tools within a space.

TIP

> You can hold the Shift key while clicking to navigate on your own while Navigate Together is checked.

INVITING USERS TO AN EXISTING SHARED SPACE

After a shared space has been created, you can invite new members or re-invite suspended members by clicking the Invite button as shown in Figure 4.44. This displays the Send Invitation dialog, as shown in Figure 4.45. You can choose to invite members in My Contacts by choosing them from the drop-down list provided. Clicking the Recipients button provides additional invitee options including:

- Look In My Contacts—Contacts that you have added to your contact list in the past.
- Look In Known Groove Contacts—Individuals who are members in shared spaces you participate in and users who have been added to My Contacts.
- Look In Local Network Directory—Individuals listed in the directory maintained on the local network.

- Search groove.net Directory—Individuals listed in the groove.net public directory.

- Enter Email Address—Choosing this option enables you to send an invitation using Groove's built-in email capability.

Figure 4.44
Click the Invite button while in a shared space to invite new members or to reinvite existing members.

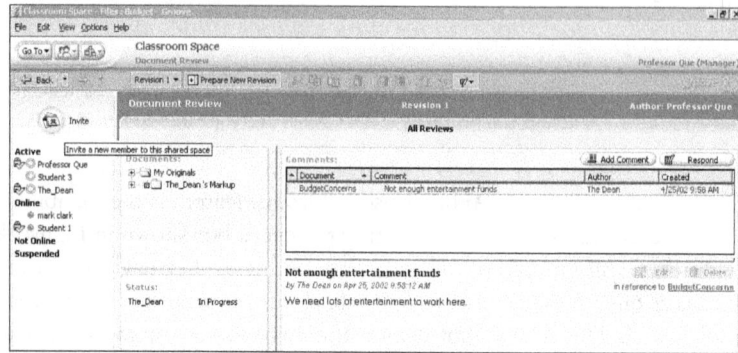

Figure 4.45
Use the Send Invitation dialog to invite members to the current space.

After you've chosen all the intended recipients, click the OK button to return to the Send Invitation screen. From here you may also include a text messages and/or attachments. After you are satisfied with the invitation, clicking the Invite message sends the invitation to the invitee(s).

ASKING USERS TO RETURN TO A SPACE

There may be times when there are users who are online, but are not actively involved in a shared space. If you need to collaborate with these individuals, you have the option of asking them to return to the space. Inviting someone who is already a member of a shared space will ask them to re-enter the space. If they decide to return, they can click the link or right-click the notification and choose Go There. To reject the offer, they can right-click the notification and choose Decline. The inviter will receive a notification that the offer has been declined.

NOTE

> Declining an invitation to return to a space will not delete or uninvite the user from the space. This simply indicates that the user does not wish to return to the space at this time.

UNINVITING A SPACE MEMBER

You have the option of uninviting a member from a shared space. By right-clicking a user in the member's panel, you can choose uninvite from the menu. After confirmation, the member will be removed from this shared space. The uninvited member will be notified and will be left with a duplicate copy of the space without any other members. If you want to invite the member to the space again, instruct her to remove the space before you send another invitation.

NOTE

> After uninviting this member, she immediately ceases to receive any updates in the space. However, she still has access to any previous activity in the space in the duplicate copy.

MANAGING MY SPACES

The My Spaces area within Groove enables you to manage all the spaces in which you participate. You can access it several different ways:

- Click the GoTo button and choose My Spaces.
- Click the My Spaces button within the Go To button group and choose My Spaces.
- Press Alt+F8.

Figure 4.46 shows the My Spaces area that contains a list of all spaces you've created or been invited to in the past. Each row represents a space and contains the following information in each column:

- Name—The current name of the shared space.
- Status—The current status of the shared space. This is in addition to an icon that is displayed preceding the space name. These icons, the status they represent, and the meaning of each is listed in Table 4.4.
- Created—The date and time the shared space was originally created.

Figure 4.46
The My Spaces area shows all the shared spaces that you have either created or participated in.

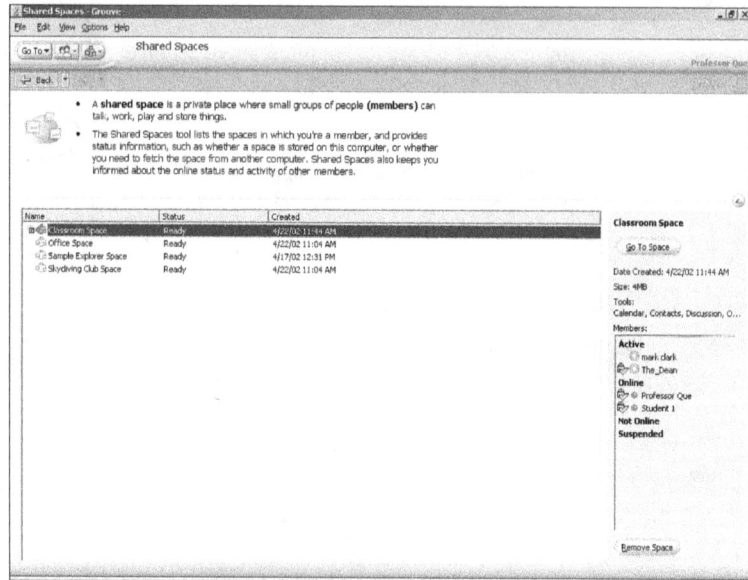

TABLE 4.4   SHARED SPACE STATUS ICONS AND DESCRIPTIONS

Icon	Status	Meaning
	Ready	The shared space is stored locally on your computer and is ready for you to open. You can open the space.
	Ready	The same as "Ready" in the previous entry, except that another member of the shared space has changed or added information that you have not yet opened for reading or viewing.
	Not on this computer	The shared space is not yet stored locally on this computer. This is common when an account has been moved to a new computer but the shared space data has not been fetched.
	Fetching...	The space is being fetched from another Groove device. When completed the status changes to "Ready."

Icon	Status	Meaning
	Synchronization alert	There are two possible meanings: One or more other members of the shared space have been inactive for an extended period of time. As a result, the log file that tracks changes in the shared space is growing too large and you should take measures to reduce it. This can happen if members decide to work in offline mode for an extended period of time. You were inactive in this shared space for an extended period of time and your membership has been suspended. To restore your resynchronization, you must request that another member re-invite you to the shared space.

ADDITIONAL SHARED SPACE INFORMATION

Highlighting a shared space in the list populates the right side of the window with additional information that is illustrated in Figure 4.46. You'll find the following information:

- Space Name—The name of the highlighted shared space.
- Date Created—The date and time the shared space was created.
- Tools—A list of the tools within the shared space. If the tool names cannot fit in the space provided, it is truncated and an ellipsis added to the end "…". In this case, you may hold your mouse over it to display the entire name.
- Members—The current members in the space. This is very similar to what you see in the member pane within a shared space. Member names are displayed and categorized appropriately along with presence icons to the left of the name indicating the member's online/offline status.

OTHER MY SPACES FUNCTIONS

By right-clicking a shared space in the My Spaces list you can choose from several options (see Figure 4.47).

Figure 4.47
Right-click a shared space in the My Spaces area to perform various actions on the highlighted space.

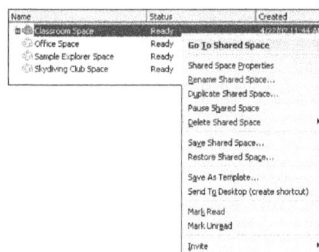

- Go To Shared Space—Immediately open the shared space.

- Shared Space Properties—Display the details of the shared space including the date the user created it.

- Rename—Rename a space. Because this changes the name for all current members, you may want to notify them prior to changing it to avoid confusion.

- Duplicate—Create a copy of this shared space with a new name (will not copy the names of any invited members).

- Pause—Pause all updates for the shared space. This includes the sending and receiving of updates for changed data within the space.

- Delete Shared Space—Choosing Delete opens another menu with the following options:

  - From This Computer—This option deletes the shared space and all associated data from this computer. To re-enter the space, someone in the shared space will need to send you another invitation.

  - From All My Computers—This applies to Multiple Computer Configurations. This deletes the space from all computers sharing the account.

- Save Shared Space—This saves a copy of the shared space along with all the data. You are required to enter a passphrase that will be needed to decrypt the space later.

- Restore Shared Space—This is used to restore a previously saved shared space. You are required to enter the passphrase use to encrypt the space when it was saved.

- Save As Template—By choosing to save the space as a template, you are prompted for the location to save the template (.grv) file. This option only preserves the following:

  - The toolset from the original space. The toolset is then included in every new shared space created from that template.

  - If applicable, the roles and permissions assigned to tools.

  - The name of the original space.

  - Tool aliases.

> NOTE
> No shared space activity data or the member list is saved in the template file.

- Send Shortcut to Desktop—This sends a shortcut to your Windows desktop so that the space can be opened directly by double-clicking the icon. If the account from which the shortcut was created is not logged in, you are prompted to log in at this point (unless the passphrase is stored on this device).

- Mark Read—If the current space is marked as "unread" this option marks it as "read."

- Mark Unread—Marks the current space as "unread."

■ Invite—This is used to invite members to the space. See the "Inviting Users to an Existing Shared Space" section earlier in this chapter.

ABOUT SHARED SPACE SYNCHRONIZATION

Groove stores the information needed to synchronize a space with other members within a log file. It's possible, if many users continue to work in Offline mode or are inactive for a long period of time, that this log file can become extremely large. Not only can this log file take up a significant amount of disk space but also the eventual transmission of the changes could take a long time to complete. Groove has a mechanism built in to provide a synchronization alert and enable you to purge the log if it becomes too large.

USING CHAT

Chat is provided as a lightweight version of a shared space that enables text and audio conversation between two individuals or a small group of users.

STARTING THE CHAT

You can start chat in several different ways:

■ Right-click the user while in a shared space and choose Invite to a New Chat.

■ Choose Options, New Chat from the top menu.

■ Select a contact in the My Contacts area and click the Invite to Chat button.

You can highlight several users at a time by holding the Ctrl key while selecting them. This enables you to send the invitation to several users at the same time.

CHAT NOTIFICATION

Like a shared space notifications, as soon as you invite someone to chat you will receive notifications as the invitation is sent and processed. Refer to the "Shared Space Notifications" section earlier in this chapter for the status notifications that are displayed.

THE CHAT INTERFACE

The Chat interface itself looks exactly like a shared space, except that chat is the only tool available. Shown in Figure 4.48, the space consists of only the chat pane as outlined in the "Using the Chat Pane" section earlier in this chapter. You'll want to consult this section for information regarding what text and audio options are available. Like a shared space, you can also invite new members to the chat space using an instant message in Groove or a third-party application, by email, or by saving the space to a file.

Figure 4.48
The Chat interface is a shared space with only a chat pane so that you may hold private chat conversations with other user(s).

AUDIO OPTIONS

You don't have menus within a chat space, so you are given an audio options button, as shown in Figure 4.48. From this button you can run the Audio Tuning Wizard that I outlined in the "Using the Audio Tuning Wizard" section earlier in this chapter. In addition, you can also choose the Conference option discussed in the "Conference Feature" section also found earlier in this chapter.

CHAT MEMBER'S PANEL

Similar to a shared space, you can view all the chat participants in the list on the left side of the chat window. When a user closes the space, you will note that his status will have changed from Active to Online but not Active.

SAVING YOUR CHAT AS A SHARED SPACE

Because the Chat feature is a lightweight shared space, it's only natural that you can save it as a shared space. By clicking the Save as Space button shown in Figure 4.41 you can give the space a name that is stored in My Shared Spaces. Using this, you can take the current discussion and move it into a space where many other options are available. For example, if you find your discussion could use Sketchpad to illustrate ideas, saving it as a shared space can provide this capability by adding that tool without losing the current chat transcript or members already invited to chat.

NOTE

> Saving your Chat to a shared space is the only way to preserve the contents. Otherwise, once all members close the chat window all data within it is lost.

THE SHARED SPACE EXPLORER

For some users, it might be desirable to have a Groove Workspace interface similar to Windows Explorer. Groove Workspace 2.0 provides a new feature called the Shared Space

Explorer. You can open the Shared Space Explorer, shown in Figure 4.49, by clicking the Groove icon in the system tray and choosing Open Explorer.

Figure 4.49
The Shared Space Explorer offers an alternative way to view and manage spaces.

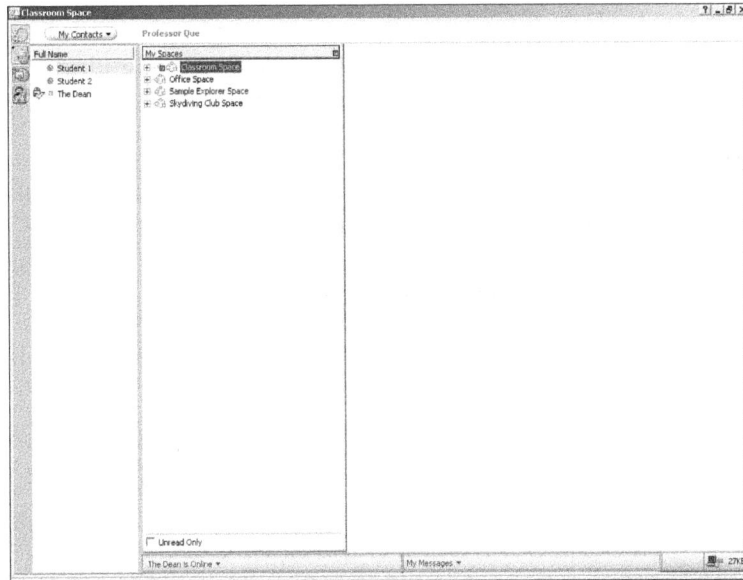

THE SHARED SPACE EXPLORER INTERFACE

When you open the Shared Space Explorer, you should see the interface shown in Figure 4.49. You can change what the Explorer shows by clicking one of the four buttons on the left:

- Groove system menu—Clicking this button displays a drop-down menu with a variety of different options. From here, you can perform many of the shared space tasks, such as creating a new space, examining roles and permissions, and renaming or deleting a shared space.

- Communications panel—This button is used to hide or show the communications panel. Showing the communications panel shows the Members Awareness pane, which enables you to see the online/offline status of each shared space member. Also displayed are the audio chat options so that you can talk with other members.

- Status bar—This button is used to hide or show the status bar that is displayed at the bottom of the Shared Space Explorer interface.

- My Contacts—This button hides or shows My Contacts.

Determining Which Spaces Have Changed

The shared space explorer is useful if you'd like to quickly see what spaces have changed since you've last entered them. When Professor Que opens the Shared Space Explorer, as shown in Figure 4.49, he can quickly see that something has changed in the Classroom Space because there is an unread marker to the left of the space name in the list. To find out which tool data has changed, Professor Que can then click the + sign to the left of the shared space name as shown in Figure 4.50. This expands the list and shows all the tools currently contained within the space. An unread marker is shown next to the tool(s) that have had data changed within them. In this figure, you can quickly tell that the Calendar tool has been updated in the Classroom shared space.

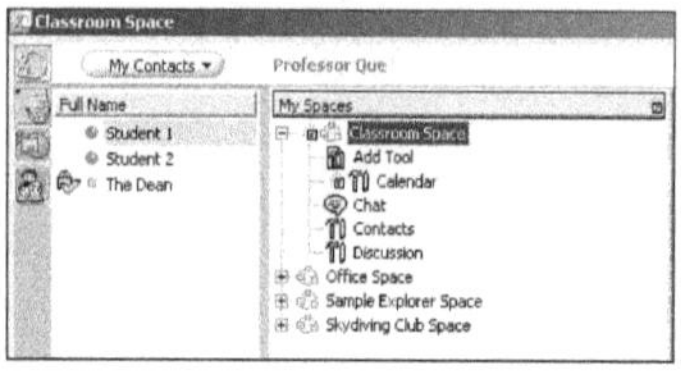

Figure 4.50
Click the + symbol to the left of a shared space to expand the list and show all the tools within the space.

Opening a Tool Within a Shared Space

In the example shown in Figure 4.50, you would probably like to open the Calendar tool in the Classroom Space because you know the contents have changed. To open the tool within the Shared Space Explorer, simply select the Calendar tool in the list and the high-lighted tool is displayed in the right pane, as shown in Figure 4.51. For more information on the different tools available within Groove Workspace, see "Choosing the Right Tools" earlier in this chapter or for more detailed information see Chapters 5 through 8.

Figure 4.51
After selecting the Calendar tool, you can see the contents in the right side of the Shared Space Explorer window.

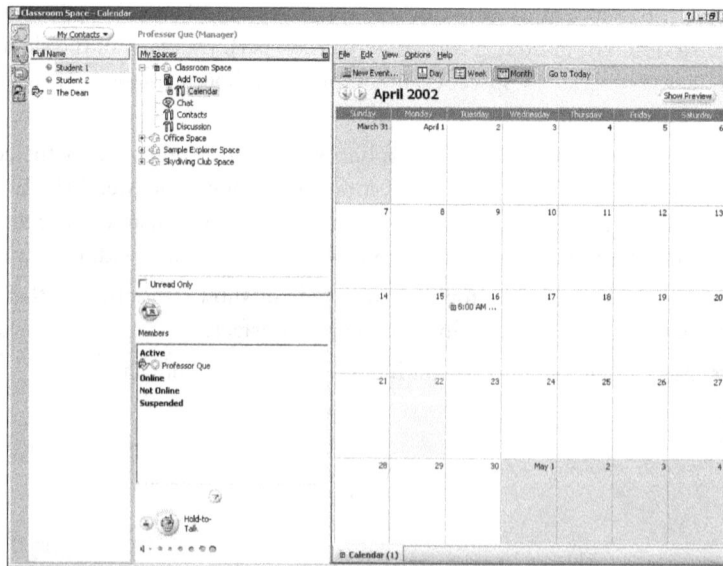

TIP

It's possible that you might not see all the shared space members when you select a tool within a shared space. The members area displays directly below the list of spaces and tools. You might need to drag the divider from the bottom by positioning the cursor over the split until you see the directional arrows, clicking the mouse button, and dragging the divider upward.

ADDING A NEW TOOL TO THE SHARED SPACE

Using the Shared Space Explorer, it is also possible to add a new tool to a shared space, assuming your account has permission to do so. Within the tool list for a shared space, you can select the Add Tool entry in the list and the traditional Add Tool window is displayed in the right pane on the screen as shown in Figure 4.52. For more information on tools, see "The Tools Area" earlier in this chapter.

Figure 4.52
Select Add Tool in the list to display the list of available tools and toolsets.

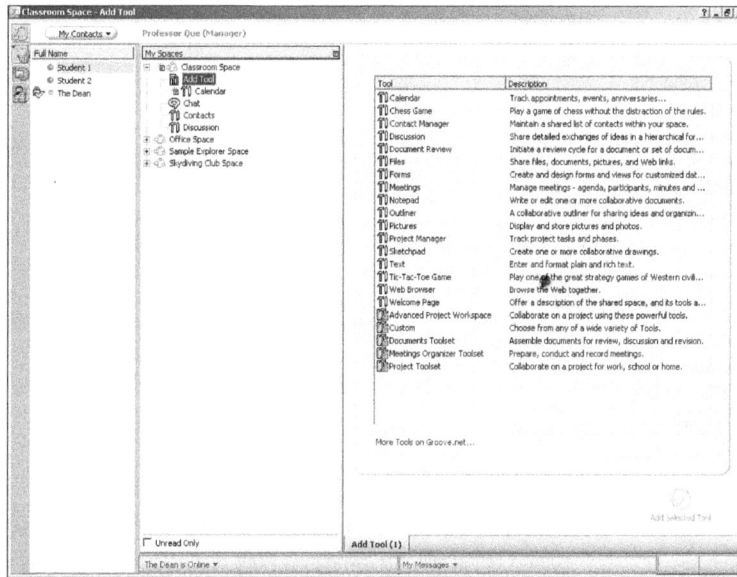

VIEWING AND MANAGING CONTACTS

Within the Shared Space Explorer, you can show or hide the Contact list by clicking on the Show/Hide Contact button as shown in Figure 4.53. You can view the awareness information for each contact and right-click each entry for additional options. A new contact can be added by clicking the Add Contact button.

→ For more information about working with contacts within Groove Workspace, **see** "Using My Contacts," **p.97**

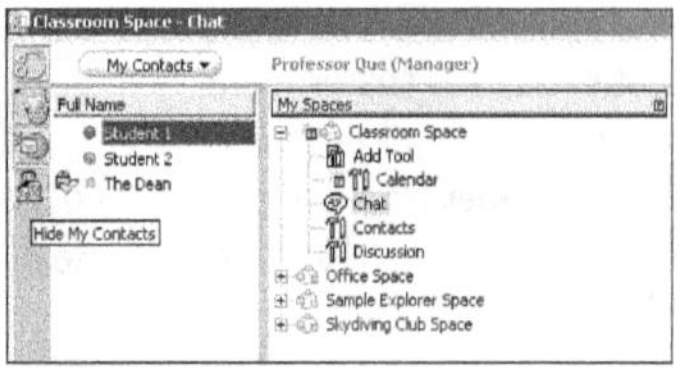

Figure 4.53
Clicking the
Show/Hide contact list
button displays your
contact list.

ABOUT THE STATUS BAR

At the bottom of the Shared Space Explorer is a status bar. It can be displayed or hidden by clicking the Show/Hide status bar button as shown in Figure 4.54. The status bar contains two drop-down menus that contain the status of each contact and a listing of all messages contained within the My Messages area. Click each section to display the drop-down list as has been done for the contacts in Figure 4.55.

Figure 4.54
Clicking the
Show/Hide Status Bar
button controls the
display of the status
bar at the bottom of
the Shared Space
Explorer window.

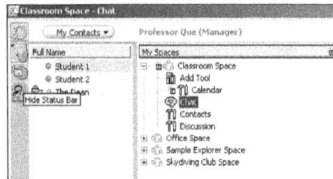

Figure 4.55
Clicking an item in
the status bar dis-
plays the same listing
as the contacts listing
shown in Figure 4.53.

TIP

> Using the status bar might not be intuitive for many users. You might prefer to use the contact listing with the awareness icons that is displayed directly below the shared space listing.

ACCESSING THE REST OF THE SHARED SPACE EXPLORER FEATURES

Because the Shared Space Explorer provides exactly the same functionality as a shared space, it would be redundant to discuss all of these features here. To access most of the common tasks, you can click the System Menu button, as shown in Figure 4.56.

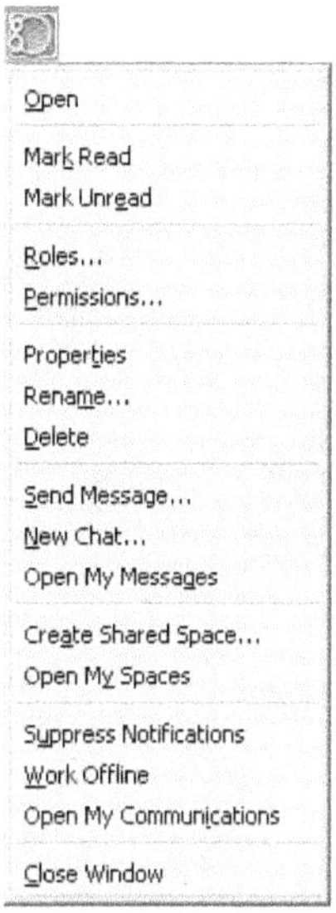

Figure 4.56
You can access all
Shared Space func-
tions by clicking the
System Menu button.

Open

Mark Read
Mark Unread

Roles...
Permissions...

Properties
Rename...
Delete

Send Message...
New Chat...
Open My Messages

Create Shared Space...
Open My Spaces

Suppress Notifications
Work Offline
Open My Communications

Close Window

TROUBLESHOOTING

A SHARED SPACE SEEMS TO BE LOSING DATA THAT I'VE ENTERED. IT IS A SHARED SPACE THAT I
HAVE NOT ENTERED IN A LONG TIME.

Go to the My Spaces area from the Welcome Page by clicking the Go To button and
choosing My Spaces. Check the status of the page to ensure there is not a synchronization
alert. The alert icon is shown in Table 4.4 along with the other icons you might see here. If
the problem continues, delete the shared space from all computers and have someone re-
invite you to the space.

WHEN I ATTEMPT TO ACCESS A TOOL, I ONLY SEE A MESSAGE THAT SAYS You do not have
permission to view this tool.

Have the Manager of the shared space check the assigned permissions. Regardless of any
other rights granted, each role must have the View *Tool Name* permission to access the tool.

WHEN USING THE AUDIO CHAT FEATURE, MY AUDIO QUALITY IS VERY POOR.

Access the Audio Tool Wizard when within a shared space by choosing Options, Audio
Tool Wizard. Run the wizard again as outlined in the section "Using the Audio Tuning
Wizard" earlier in this chapter.

WHEN I AM ONLINE, OTHERS SAY THAT THEY STILL SEE MY USERNAME AS OFFLINE.

Check your online presence options in the My Account area. These are discussed in
Chapter 2 in the section "Online Presence Options."

USING THE CALENDAR AND CONTACT MANAGER TOOLS

TOOLS TO GET THE JOB DONE

As you've seen in Chapter 4, "Understanding Shared Spaces," shared spaces are places where people can gather online to get things done. The creator of the shared space, the space manager, invites others into the space for group activities. This manager is responsible for ensuring that all the proper tools are available for participants to collaborate effectively. Groove is shipped with a wide variety of tools that provide an extensive array of functionality that will fulfill most common business needs. This chapter covers the Contact Manager and Outliner tool features and how to use them. These are only two of the tools available; the next few chapters will discuss the rest of the tools that can be used within Groove Workspace.

→ For details on the Outliner and Sketchpad tools, see Chapter 6, "Using the Outliner and Sketchpad Tools."

→ For details on the Files and Discussion tools, see Chapter 7, "Using the Files and Discussion Tools."

→ For details on the Pictures, Web Browser, and Notepad tools, see Chapter 8, "Other Shared Space Tools."

Although an impressive selection of tools is available, it is very possible that your particular needs warrant something not found in any of the tools shipped with Groove Workspace. Remember that you are buying the Groove Workspace platform, and not just an inflexible application. Using the robust Groove services, you can build new tools around the framework provided. In Chapter 10, "The Groove SDK," we'll look at using the Groove development toolkit to create your own tools. With some imagination and a little education on the framework, you can further refine Groove to best suit your business or personal needs.

USING THE CALENDAR TOOL

Scheduling is an essential function within any organization. Good timing will be very important to your group collaboration within Groove. The Calendar tool is provided so that participants can document upcoming events. An event can be a meeting, an important milestone, a pending task, and anything else that is date-driven. Although every member of the shared space has at least read-only access, adding and deleting events depends on your role and the assignment of permissions within the space. The first time the Calendar tool is opened it defaults to a view of the entire month, as shown in Figure 5.1.

THE DIFFERENT CALENDAR VIEWS

Views enable you to change how the calendar looks. This is useful for getting a look at the month at a glance or examining the details of a particular day. You can choose from the following views:

- Day—The Day view enables you to view a detailed list of the day's events. As shown in Figure 5.2, this view shows all the hours in a particular day. You can apply this view by clicking the Day button, choosing View, Day from the main menu, or right-clicking on the calendar and choosing Day View from the drop-down menu. As shown in the example, events are scheduled at 8:00 a.m., 10:00 a.m., and 5:00 p.m.

Figure 5.1
By default the Calendar tool provides a view of the entire month at a glance.

NOTE

As shown in Figure 5.2, if events appear off the visible part of the screen, a More button will appear enabling you to scroll up or down to see the entries.

Figure 5.2
The Day view enables you to see descriptions and the times of events scheduled during the current day.

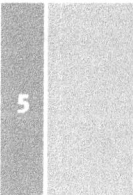

5

- Week—If you would like to see all the events for the upcoming week at a glance, you can switch to the Week view shown in Figure 5.3. You can apply this view by clicking the Week button, choosing View, Week from the main menu, or right-clicking on the calendar and choosing Week View from the drop-down menu. All the days of the week will be spread across two columns.

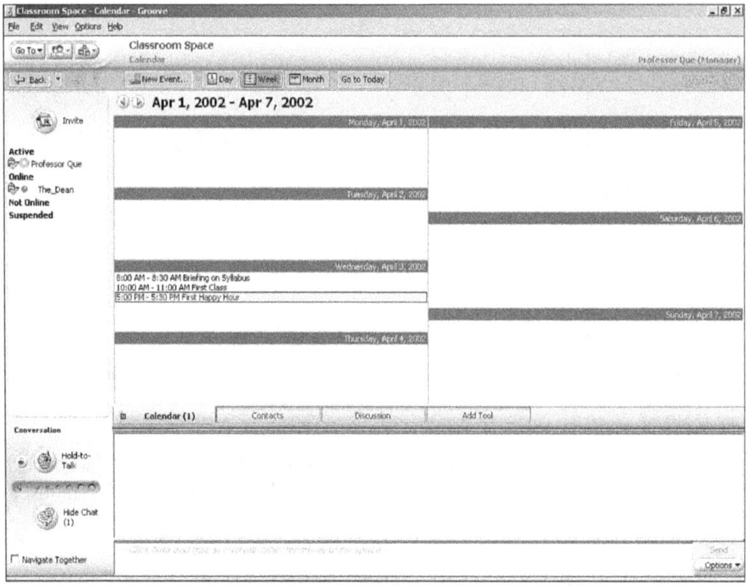

Figure 5.3
If you need to see the events for an entire week, you can switch the Calendar tool to Week view to see events scheduled in the current week.

- Month—If you need to see the events for the entire month, you can also switch to the Month view. The days of the month are shown with a white background (refer to Figure 5.1). Days from the previous or subsequent month are indicated by a gray background. You can apply this view by clicking the Month button, choosing View, Month from the main menu, or right-clicking on the calendar and choosing Month View from the drop-down menu. Because space is limited, event descriptions will be brief but you can easily switch back to Week or Day view for more detail.

- Business Week—Similar to the Week view, there is a Business Week view that simply condenses the space available for the weekend days. You can apply this view by choosing View, Business Week from the main menu or right-clicking on the calendar and choosing Business Week View from the drop-down menu.

- Business Month—Similar to the Month view, there is a Business Month view that simply condenses the space available for weekend days. You can apply this view by choosing View, Business Month from the main menu or right-clicking on the calendar and choosing Business Month View from the drop-down menu.

USING THE PREVIEW FUNCTION IN THE MONTHLY VIEWS

While viewing the calendar in Month view or Business Month view, clicking the Show Preview button will break down the day's details on the right side of the screen as shown in Figure 5.4. Clicking the Hide button takes you back to the original display. In the daily view to the right, you can view and edit entries like the Day view. The Preview area size can be adjusted by positioning your mouse over the divider and resizing as needed.

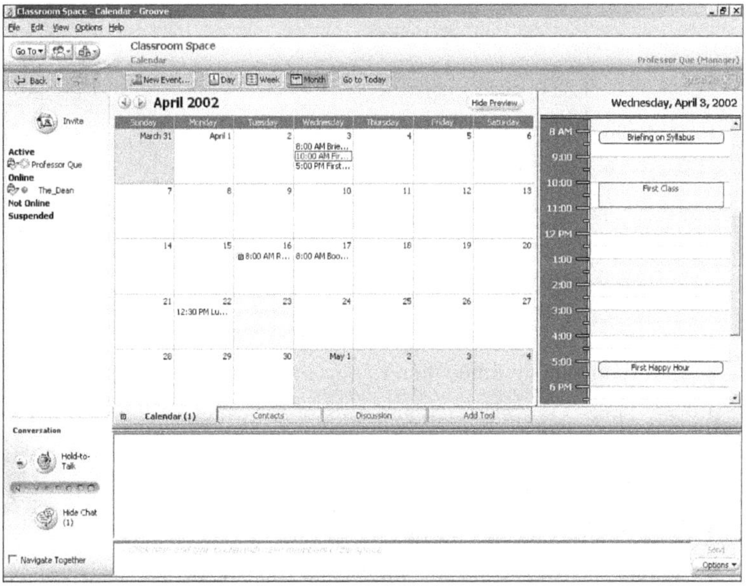

Figure 5.4
Clicking the Show Preview button enables you to see the details of a day when you click it within the Month or Business Month view.

CREATING A SINGLE CALENDAR EVENT ENTRY

By clicking the New Event button or double-clicking somewhere on the calendar you can insert a new event into the Calendar tool. You will be prompted for the entry details, as shown in Figure 5.5.

Entry details include the following information:

- Description—A description for the entry. This will be shared with other members of the space, so it should describe the entry accurately, but succinctly, because it will display in most calendar views.
- Start Date—The date on which the event will occur.
- End Date—The expected end date of the event.

NOTE
You can click the Show Calendar button next to the text box to choose the dates from a small calendar interface. This has been highlighted in Figure 5.5.

Show Calendar buttons

Figure 5.5
Clicking the New
Event button will
prompt you for the
details of the event
you want to add to
the calendar.

- Start Time—The time when the event starts.
- End Time—The expected end time of the event.
- All Day Event—Checking this box makes the start and end time boxes disappear and the event will span the entire day(s) for the date(s) specified.
- Details—More details about the event.
- Author—This is read-only and shows your identity. This is visible to others viewing the event.

SELECTING DATES IN THE CALENDAR AND CREATING AN EVENT

By clicking and dragging your mouse across days in the calendar you can quickly create an entry that spans several days. As shown in Figure 5.6, we've highlighted several days in this month. After the range is highlighted, right-clicking the selection and choosing New Entry or choosing File, New, Event from the main menu, displays the New Calendar Event dialog box with the dates already filled in.

NOTE

This assumes an all day event. To specify a specific time, uncheck the All Day Event check box.

Highlighted date range

Figure 5.6
You can easily create events that span several days by clicking a day in the calendar and dragging your mouse to highlight several days at a time.

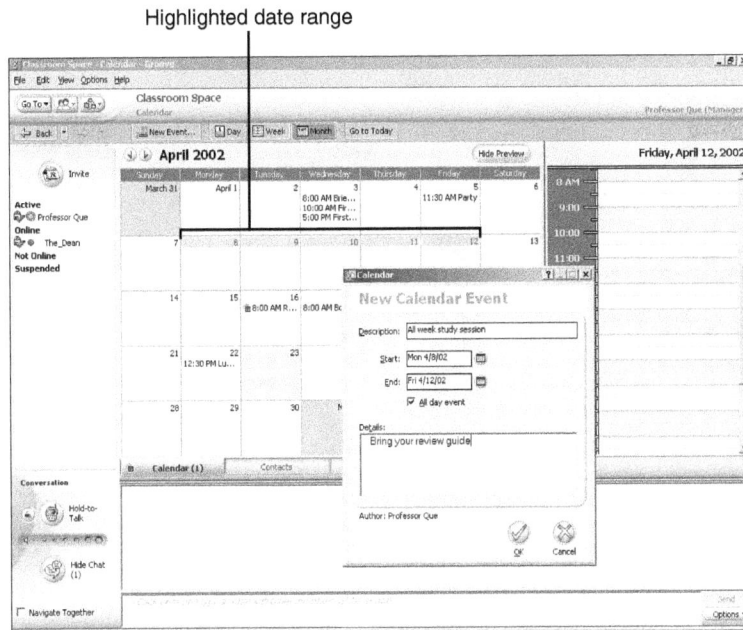

SELECTING A TIME FRAME AND CREATING AN ENTRY

Similar to creating an event that spans several days, you can also do the same with times in the Day view. As shown in Figure 5.7, we've highlighted from 8:00 a.m. to 10:00 a.m. After the time range is highlighted, right-clicking the selection and choosing New Entry or choosing File, New, Event from the main drop-down menu creates a new event for the day and time range selected.

VIEWING OR EDITING A CALENDAR EVENT

Provided your current role has edit capability, you can easily edit any entry in any of the views. You can open the Edit dialog box using one of the following methods:

- Double-click an event in the Calendar.
- Right-click an event and choose Open Detail.
- Highlight an event in the calendar and choose File, Open Selected Event.
- Highlight an event in the calendar and press Enter.

TIP

> Holding the mouse pointer over an entry displays the subject, date, and details in a small pop-up window.

Highlighted time range

Figure 5.7
When creating an event on the Day view, you can click and drag the selection area to create an event that spans a period of time. In this example, we've highlighted from 8 a.m. to 10 a.m. for this new event.

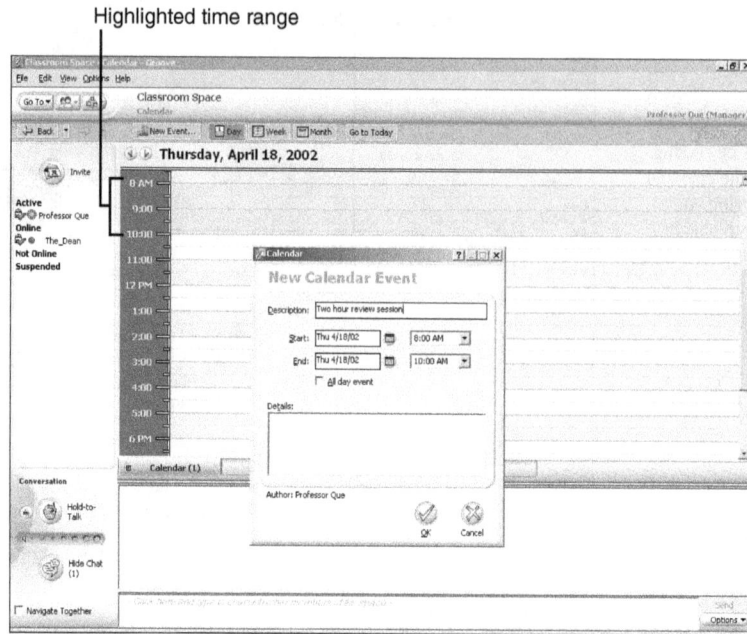

This Edit dialog is exactly the same as you used to create a new entry. After you've edited the entry, click the OK button to save the changes or click Cancel. If the changes are saved, all other members in the space will receive the update when they are online.

NOTE

> In the Day view, you can easily change the start and end times for an event. Position your mouse over the edge of a highlighted entry and an arrow appears enabling you to extend or decrease the starting/ending times as appropriate.

MOVING CALENDAR ENTRIES

In addition to viewing and editing a calendar entry, you can also drag and drop entries in any of the five views. Simply click an entry and drag it into a new position. The dates and times will be adjusted accordingly.

DETERMINING WHEN AN ENTRY HAS BEEN CREATED OR MODIFIED

When a member edits or creates a new calendar entry, Groove will display an unread icon to alert others in the space of the change. As shown in Figure 5.8, you see the unread icon for an entry that has changed since you last opened it. You can also manually set Read and Unread statuses from the right-click drop-down menu and by choosing the options under Edit in the main menu.

Figure 5.8
The unread icon next to the Drop Class entry tells you that you have not read this entry since it was last updated.

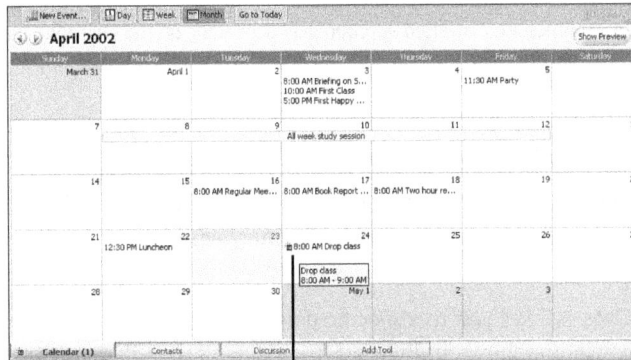

Unread icon

Additional options for unread markers are provided under the Edit menu including the following:

- Mark Selected Read—Removes the unread icon from the currently selected entry.
- Mark Selected Unread—Marks the currently selected entry as unread.
- Mark All Read—Removes an unread icon from the entry.
- Mark All Unread—Marks every entry unread.

HANDLING DIFFERENT TIME ZONES

It's entirely possible that some of the other shared space members will be in different time zones. Groove alerts shared space members that a calendar entry has been made from a different time zone by displaying a global icon as shown in Figure 5.9. Professor Que's colleague in India has created this entry and because the Professor is in the Eastern Time zone, the global icon is displayed.

Figure 5.9
The global icon next to this entry alerts you that someone in a different time zone created it.

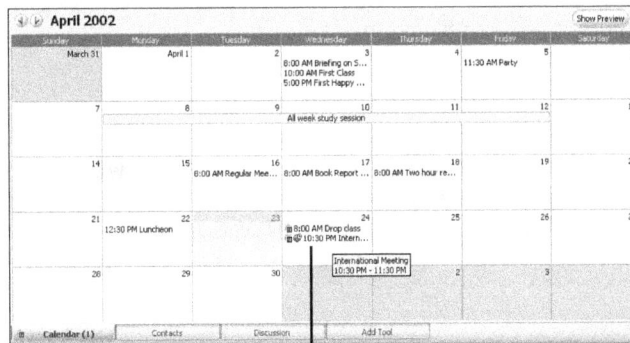

Global icon

5

NOTE

Times are converted appropriately depending on the time zone on the Groove device viewing the entry.

Navigating the Calendar

There are several different ways to navigate through the days on the calendar. Right-clicking any space on the calendar unoccupied by an entry or choosing the View menu gives you the following options:

- Go to Date—Takes you to a specific date in the view you specify. You will be prompted with the window shown in Figure 5.10. Clicking the OK button instantly takes you to that date and changes the current view if need be.

Figure 5.10
You can jump immediately to any date on the calendar by clicking the Go To Date button.

- Today—Always returns you to the current day in the active view no matter where you are in the calendar.
- Next—Depending on the view selected, this takes you forward one unit in that length of time. For instance, clicking Next while in Week view takes you to the next week in the Calendar.
- Previous—Depending on the view selected, this takes you back one unit in that length of time. For instance, clicking Previous while in Week view takes you to the previous week in the Calendar.

NOTE

Using the right and left arrow keys on the keyboard will take you forward and back a day, respectively. Also, Previous and Next buttons are provided near the top of the screen that will take you back or forward a unit depending on the current view selected.

Deleting an Entry

By highlighting an entry, choosing Edit, Delete, pressing the Delete key, or right-clicking and choosing Delete, you can remove an entry from the calendar. This delete will be reflected on everyone's calendar, so use it cautiously.

CUTTING AND PASTING CALENDAR ENTRIES

You can move an entry by right-clicking a calendar entry and choosing Cut and then Paste or choosing Edit, Copy from the main menu. Although the description and details will remain the same, the pasted entry will inherit the date and time of where it is inserted.

COPYING A CALENDAR ENTRY AS A LINK

Sometimes it is useful to provide links to specific calendar entries. Links can be posted elsewhere in a space by right-clicking and choosing Copy as Link or choosing Edit, Copy from the main menu. This will function as a hyperlink that will open the calendar tool and take the member to the entry when it is clicked. For example, in Figure 5.11 we've used a link to easily direct others in chat to a meeting we are having.

Figure 5.11
To direct others to events, you can create a link that will take others directly to the event. In this example, we're using a link within the chat pane that will take members directly to the Revised Test Period entry.

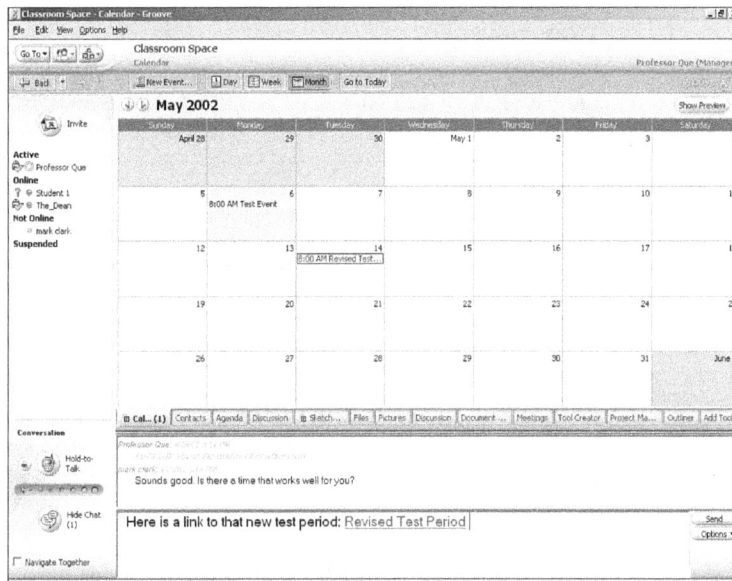

EXPORTING EVENTS TO AN XML FILE

Exporting Calendar tool entries to a file is usually used when moving events from one version of Groove to another. To export to an XML file, choose File, Export from the main menu and select one of the following options:

- Exporting a Single Event—You may export an event into an XML file for later import into another Groove calendar. Highlight the event you want to export and choose File, Export, Selected Event from the main menu. You will then be prompted for the name and location in which to store the XML file.

- Exporting All Events—Instead of exporting just a single event, you can export all events by choosing File, Export, All Events from the main menu. You will then be prompted for the name and location in which to store the XML file.

IMPORTING EVENTS

After you've exported the event(s) as shown previously, simply choose File, Import from the main menu from a Calendar tool. Specify the location of the XML files created during the export and click Open. Groove will import all calendar entries and place them within the shared space.

NOTE

There are no options for dealing with duplicate entries. If there are identical events scheduled, they will show up twice in the calendar. You will have to manually delete the duplicate entries.

KEYBOARD SHORTCUTS

Table 5.1 lists some of the commonly used keyboard shortcuts within the Calendar tool.

TABLE 5.1 CALENDAR TOOL KEYBOARD SHORTCUTS

Keyboard Shortcut	Action
Ctrl+N	Creates a new event. This can be used for a single event or for a range depending on what is highlighted.
Enter	Opens the details for the currently selected event.
Ctrl+L	Copies the selected event as link.
Ctrl+F4	Marks the selected event as read.
Ctrl+Shift+F4	Marks all unread events as read.
Ctrl+G	Enables you to go directly to a specified date.
Page Down/Page Up	Scrolls forward or backward one unit (depending on the Calendar view).
Ctrl+T	Jumps to today's date.
Ctrl+D	Displays the Day view.
Ctrl+W	Displays the Week view.
Ctrl+M	Displays the Month view.
Alt+F	Opens File from the main menu.
Alt+E	Opens Edit from the main menu.
Alt+V	Opens View from the main menu.
Alt+O	Opens Options from the main menu.
Alt+H	Opens Help from the main menu.
F1	Opens Calendar Tool help.

PERMISSIONS IN THE CALENDAR TOOL

Your role and the permissions assigned to it affect what capabilities you have within the Calendar tool. The default permissions are found in Table 4.3 (see p. 145). Table 5.2 gives a more detailed explanation of the permissions.

TABLE 5.2   PERMISSIONS IN THE CALENDAR TOOL

Permission	Allows
Add Entry	Addition of a new entry into the calendar.
Edit Any Entry	Editing of any entry, even those created by other members.
Edit Own Entry	Editing of entries created by the current user only.
Delete Any Entry	Deleting of entries, including those created by other members.
Delete Own Entry	Deleting of entries created by the current user only.
View Calendar Tool	The capability to view the contents of the tool.

THE CONTACT MANAGER TOOL

In just about any group project, it's common practice for a Project Manager or other group leader to create a contact list giving the contact information for all team members. Teams in a Groove shared space also have this same capability in the Contact Manager tool. As demonstrated in Chapter 3, "Starting to Groove," each Groove user can use the My Contacts area to easily contact anyone with whom they usually collaborate. The Contact Manager tool is very similar, except that it is used within the context of a space. The Contact Manager tool only exists for the duration of the shared space (versus being tied to an account like My Contacts). As you can see in Figure 5.12, the interface should look familiar because it's very similar to My Contacts. In fact, it's so similar that we'll keep the discussion of it brief.

→ For a more complete reference to My Contacts, **see** "Managing My Contacts," **p.97**

On the left side of the screen is a listing of all contacts currently contained within the tool. Each contact represented by a Groove vCard will have a status indicator icon showing his online or offline status. The vCard for the selected member in the list occupies the largest part of the screen. Non-Groove contacts can be added manually and are fully editable.

VIEWING CONTACT INFORMATION

Selecting a contact in the contact list to the left side of the screen will display his vCard. The level of detail you see depends on the directory listing preferences of the contact added (unless it has been imported from a file). You can view a Groove user's digital fingerprint by double-clicking the Digital Fingerprint label on the vCard or by clicking the More button and choosing Digital Fingerprint.

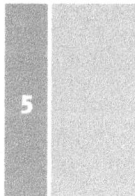

Figure 5.12
The Contact Manager tool is very similar to the My Contacts area except that the contacts are shared with other members of a shared space.

If a member is active in a space that you are also a member of, it will display the message "*User* is active in: *Shared Space Name*," as shown in Figure 5.12. Clicking GoTo Space will take you immediately to that space.

NAVIGATING THROUGH THE CONTACTS

You may navigate through the contacts one at a time by doing the following:

■ Clicking the Next and Previous buttons shown in Figure 5.13.

Previous button ⌐   ⌐ Next button

Figure 5.13
You can quickly navigate through the Contact Manager tool contacts by using the Next and Previous arrow buttons.

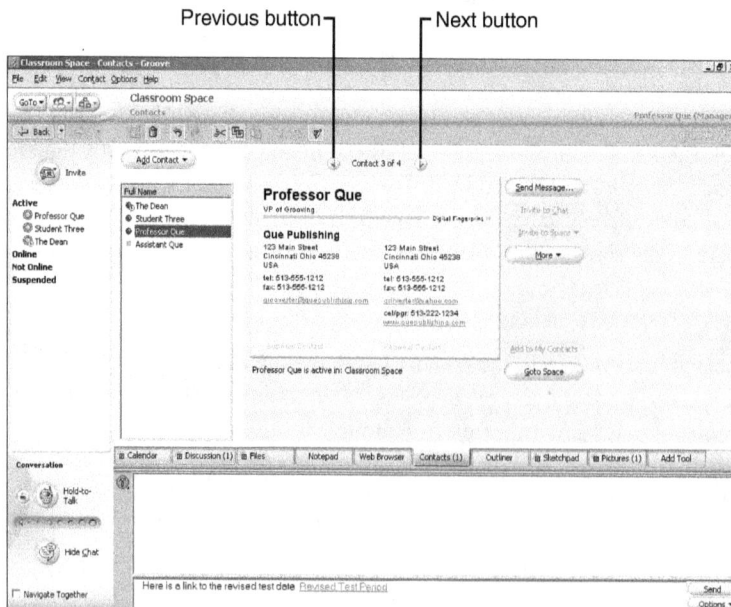

- Pressing the up and down arrow keys on the keyboard.
- Pressing F3 and Shift+F3 on the keyboard.
- Choosing View, Next Entry or View, Previous Entry from the main menu.

Your current position and the total number of contacts will be displayed between the navigation buttons as shown. Pressing the Page Up button will take you to the very top of the list, whereas the Page Down button jumps to the last contact in the list.

> **TIP**
>
> When you first enter the tool, the up and down arrow keys will not work until you actually select a contact in the list.

ADDING A NEW GROOVE CONTACT

Just like My Contacts, you can add contacts who are currently Groove members whether they are online or offline. By clicking File, New, Groove Contact from the main menu or clicking the Add Contact button and choosing Groove Contact, you will be given the option of choosing who you want to add. Like My Contacts, you can choose contacts from the directories or known contacts. After a contact is selected, click the Add button for each member you want to add. After you've chosen the contacts, click the OK button and they will be added to the shared Contact Manager tool and visible to other active members within the space.

ADDING A NEW EMAIL CONTACT

You also have the option of adding contacts by email address only. By choosing File, New, Email Contact from the main menu or clicking the Add Contact button and choosing Add Contact, you will be taken to the New Contact screen shown in Figure 5.14. At the minimum, you need to enter at least a Full Name and Email Address for the contact. You can toggle between personal and business information by clicking the tabs at the bottom of the window.

> **NOTE**
>
> Although Groove calls this tool "Shared Contacts" in some of the documentation, it is referring to the Contact Manager tool we are using.

IMPORTING A GROOVE CONTACT

You can import a vCard saved in the .vcg or .vcf format. Simply click on Add Contact, choose Import, or choose File, Import and specify the file location. Clicking Open will then add the identity contained in the file.

Figure 5.14
Contacts added to the Contact Manager tool do not have to be Groove users. In this example, the Non-GrooveGuy contact only has an email address to identify him.

DETERMINING WHEN A CONTACT HAS BEEN EDITED

If a new contact has been added or an existing contact has been modified, the unread icon will be displayed next to his name in the contact list. You have a few more options by clicking the Unread Options button shown in Figure 5.15.

Unread Options button

Figure 5.15
As indicated by the unread icon to the left of his username, the Assistant Dean contact record has not been viewed since it was last updated.

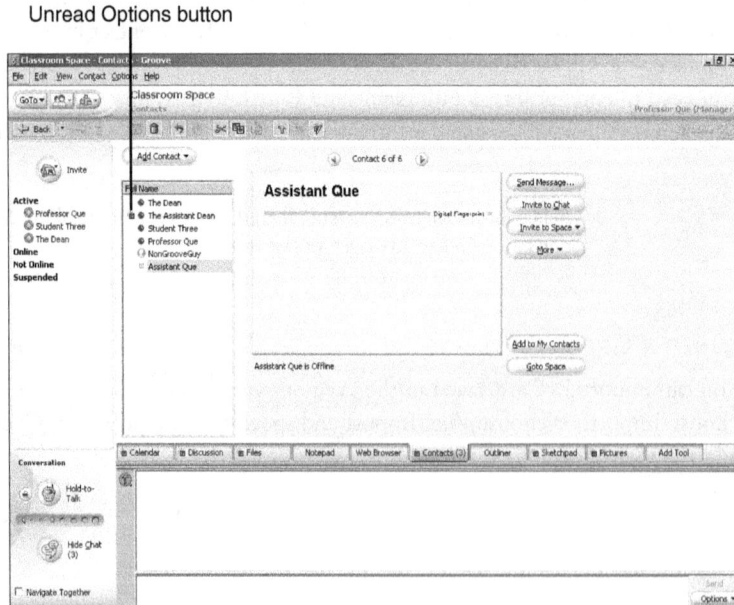

These options are

- Mark All Read—Removes an unread icon from all contacts in the list.
- Mark All Unread—Marks every contact within the list as unread.
- Mark Selected Read—Removes the unread icon from the currently selected contact.
- Mark Selected Unread—Marks the currently selected icon as unread.

ADDING A CONTACT TO MY CONTACTS

Remember that any contacts added within this tool are only available within the shared space. However, a contact can be added to your personal My Contacts list by selecting a contact within the tool and clicking the Add to My Contacts button as shown in Figure 5.16. You may also add a contact by right-clicking a name in the list and choosing Add to My Con-tacts from the drop-down menu. You will receive a notification message once the contact has been added.

Figure 5.16
Contacts within the Contact Manager tool can be moved into your own personal My Contacts area by clicking the Add to My Contacts button.

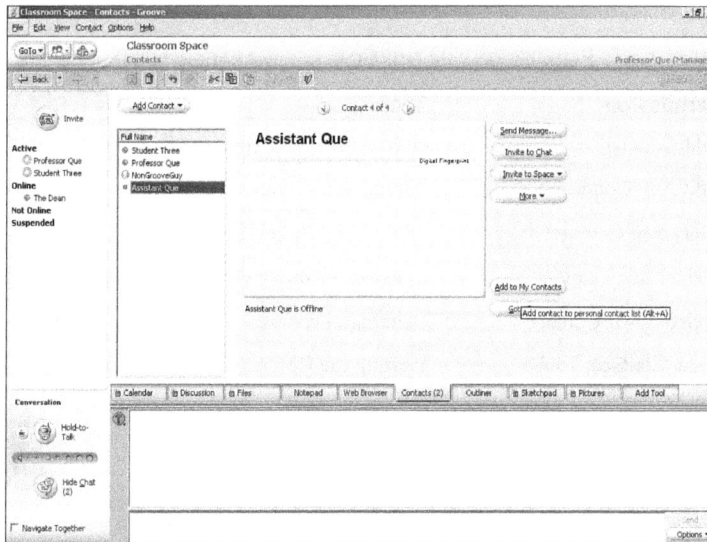

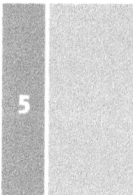

KEYBOARD SHORTCUTS

Table 5.3 lists some of the commonly used keyboard shortcuts within the Contact Manager tool.

TABLE 5.3   CONTACT MANAGER TOOL KEYBOARD SHORTCUTS

Keyboard Shortcut	Action
Alt+G	Go to the shared space the selected contact currently has open (if you have been previously invited to the shared space).
Alt+S	Send an instant message to one or more selected contacts.

TABLE 5.3	CONTINUED
Keyboard Shortcut	**Action**
Alt+C	Start a chat with one or more selected contacts.
Alt+I	Open the Invite to Space menu to invite a contact to an existing shared space.
Alt+M	Select the More menu.
Alt+A	Add selected contacts to My Contacts.

PERMISSIONS IN THE CONTACT MANAGER TOOL

Your role and permissions assigned to it affect how you can use the Contact Manager tool. The default permissions are found in Table 4.3 (see p. 145). Table 5.4 gives a more detailed explanation of the permissions.

TABLE 5.4	PERMISSIONS IN THE CONTACT MANAGER TOOL
Permission	**Allows**
Add Contact	Addition of a new contact into the Contact Manager.
Edit Any Contact	Editing of any contact, even those created by other members.
Edit Own Contact	Editing of only contacts created by the current user.
Delete Any Contact	Deleting of contacts, including those created by other members.
Delete Own Contact	Deleting of contacts created by the current user only.
View Contacts Tool	Viewing the Contacts Manager tool.

TROUBLESHOOTING

WHEN TRYING TO ADD NEW CONTACTS TO THE CONTACT MANAGER TOOL FROM THE GROOVE.NET DIRECTORY, I CAN'T SEEM TO FIND ANYONE.

First, you should ensure that the users you are trying to find are in the groove.net directory. If you are on a corporate network, try searching the local network directory first in case they are listed. If everything else fails, try making your search less restrictive by entering less in the search field.

AFTER EXPORTING A CONTACT FROM MICROSOFT OUTLOOK IN VCARD FORMAT, I KEEP GETTING ERRORS WHEN I TRY TO IMPORT IT INTO THE CONTACT MANAGER TOOL.

When trying to import a vCard into the Contact Manager tool, you must make sure the Full Name and at least one email address has been entered. Make these changes to the contact in Microsoft Outlook, export to a vCard, and try the import process again.

PARTICIPANTS IN A SHARED SPACE ARE HAVING PROBLEMS WITH THE DATES AND TIMES OF EVENTS WHEN WE USE THE CALENDAR TOOL. THEY DON'T SEEM TO MATCH UP, CAUSING US GRIEF WHEN APPOINTMENTS ARE MISSED.

A common problem when participants in different geographic regions use the Calendar tool is that some users might not have the correct time zone set on their machine. It is common for users to reset the time but not set the actual time zone correctly. Refer to your Windows documentation for information on setting the Regional Settings.

CHAPTER 6

Using the Outliner and Sketchpad Tools

In this chapter

MORE TOOLS TO GET THE JOB DONE

Starting with Chapter 5, we began looking at some of the tools that can be used in a shared space. This chapter continues that discussion by looking at the Outliner and Sketchpad tools.

→ For details on the Calendar and Contact Manager tools, see Chapter 5, "Using the Calendar and Contact Manager Tools."

→ For details on the Files and Discussion tools, see Chapter 7, "Using the Files and Discussion Tools."

→ For details on the Pictures, Web Browser, and Notepad tools, see Chapter 8, "Other Shared Space Tools."

OUTLINER TOOL

The Outliner is a great tool for brainstorming because it enables you to begin giving ideas a basic structure. Thoughts can be entered in a rather free-form fashion and then indented depending on their relation to other thoughts. The example in Figure 6.1 shows how students could use the tool to brainstorm a project in their class.

Indent and Outdent buttons

Indented space   Move Row buttons

Figure 6.1
The Outliner tool can be used to collaborate quickly on items by representing them in a hierarchical list, such as the outline for this project presentation.

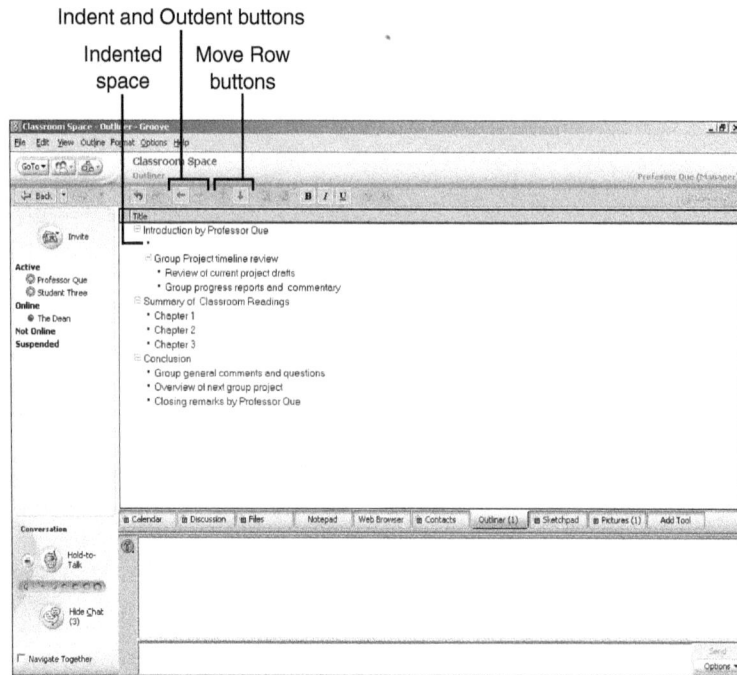

ADDING A NEW ROW TO THE OUTLINE

To create a new row, place the insertion point somewhere in the outline and press Enter or choose Outline, Insert Row from the main menu. This row will be added after the initial insertion row and will have the same level of indentation. As you can see in Figure 6.1, we've placed a new record immediately after our introduction.

ARRANGING THE OUTLINE

An outline is arranged in hierarchical order by indenting and outdenting the rows within it. You can also easily move rows around by selecting them, dragging them, and using cut and paste.

SELECTING RECORDS

By selecting records, you can easily manipulate them. They will be highlighted with a green background. You can select rows using several methods including the following:

- Click to the left of the record or hold Ctrl while clicking to select several records at a time.
- Place the cursor in a record and press the F2 key (called changing the edit mode).
- Choose Edit, Select All Rows from the main menu.
- Right-click a row and choose Select All to highlight the current row.

DEMOTING AN ENTRY

The act of indenting an entry further to the right is called demotion. You can demote single or multiple rows by positioning your cursor on a row or highlighting the row(s) to indent. Then by pressing the Tab key, choosing Outline, Indent Row, or clicking the Indent button shown in Figure 6.1, the row(s) will be indented a predetermined number of spaces to the right.

PROMOTING AN ENTRY

The act of removing an indent, or moving a row to the left, is called promotion or outdenting the row. You can promote single or multiple rows by positioning your cursor on a row or highlighting the row(s) to outdent. Then by pressing the Shift+Tab keys, choosing Outline, Outdent Row, or clicking the Outdent button shown in Figure 6.1, the row(s) will be moved back to the left.

MOVING ROWS

You can move rows up and down in the outline by clicking the Move Row Up/Down buttons illustrated in Figure 6.1 or by choosing Outline, Move Row Up/Down from the main menu. Familiar cutting and pasting is also supported. After selecting single or multiple rows, you can cut and paste them using the Cut, Copy, and Paste functions from the Edit menu.

FORMATTING ENTRIES

Like the Notepad and Sketchpad Text tools, you can change the format of the text in your outline. By highlighting text, you can click the Bold Text, Italic Text, or Underline Text button to change the text formatting. In addition, by right-clicking selected text you can choose the following options from the Font selection in the drop-down menu (similar formatting options are also available by choosing Options from the main menu):

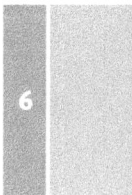

- Typeface—This can be used to change the font typeface.
- Size—The point size of your text can be changed anywhere from 8 to 72.
- Color—A whole array of color choices is provided to make text stand out.
- Bold—Bold the current selection (same as the Bold Text button).
- Italic—Italicize the current selection (same as the Italic Text button).
- Underline—Underline the current selection (same as the Underline Text button).
- Strikeout—Strikethrough the current selection.

By choosing Paragraph from the drop-down menu, you are also given these options:

- Align Left—Align text to the left.
- Center—Center the text within the margins.
- Align Right—Align text to the right.
- Bullets—Place a bullet to the left of the text. You must choose this for every line that needs a bullet because it does not repeat. You can highlight an area and select Bullet, which will bullet a number of lines in a repeat fashion.
- Increase Indent—Indent the text to the right by inserting a tab. This will not affect the beginning of this record in the outline.
- Decrease Indent—Remove an indentation. This does nothing if there is no indentation present. This will not affect the beginning of this record in the outline.

COLLAPSING AND VIEWING ENTRIES

The Outliner tool gives you the capability to collapse and expand entries and their subordinates. This enables you to concentrate on only the records you need to while collapsing the others you're not currently using. Clicking the + and − buttons next to a row will expand and collapse rows appropriately. As shown in Figure 6.2, you can see where we have collapsed the Introduction section and have expanded the Conclusion section of the outline. Rows with no indented rows beneath them will have a simple bullet icon to the left of them like the Overview section.

SORTING THE ROWS

At any time, you can sort all rows alphabetically in descending or ascending order by clicking the Title column heading. An arrow within the Title bar itself indicates the current sort order.

KNOWING WHEN RECORDS HAVE BEEN CHANGED

Similar to the way unread markers function within other tools, new additions to an outline or modified records will display an unread icon to the left of the entry. As shown in Figure 6.3, the section on Report Findings was just added by another member so all entries display the icon.

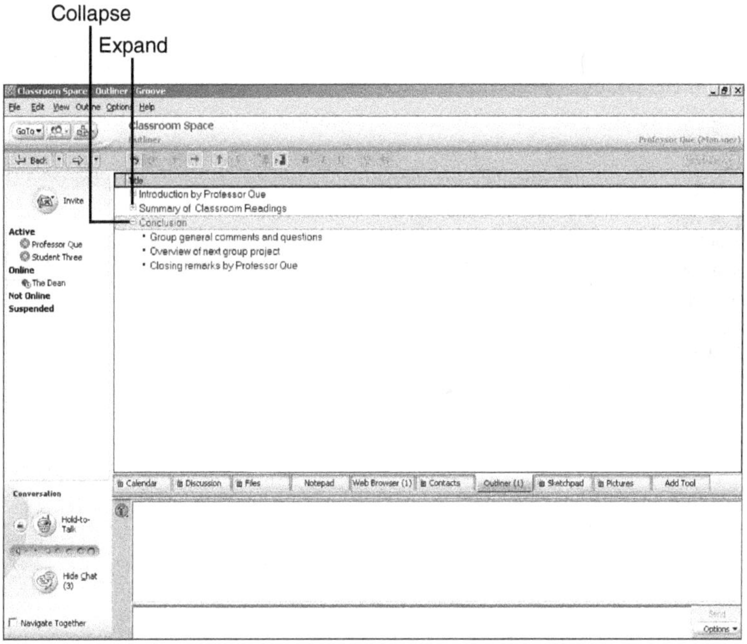

Collapse

Expand

Figure 6.2
Clicking the – button next to a row will enable you to collapse all the entries below it. In this example, we have collapsed all the entries except the Conclusion group that we are currently working on.

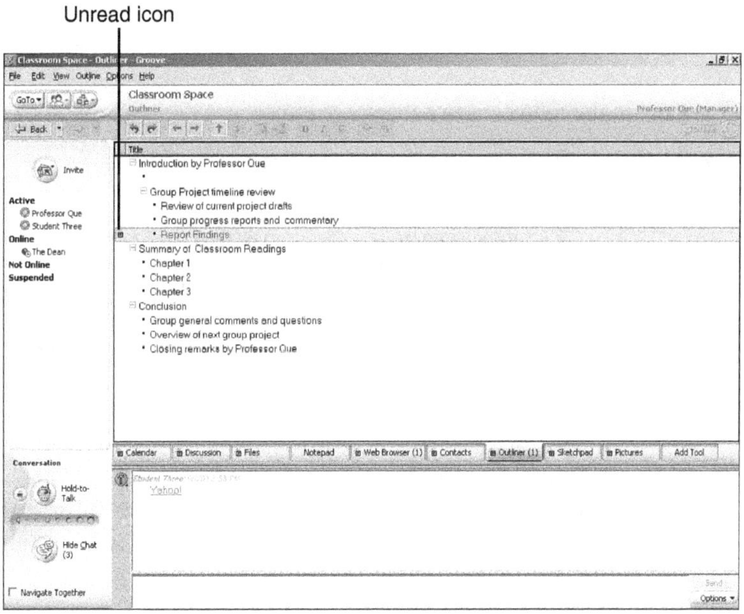

Unread icon

Figure 6.3
As others modify entries within the Outliner tool, Groove will alert you to updates by displaying the unread icon next to the line.

SHOWING AND HIDING DETAILS ABOUT ENTRIES

Although the unread icons will show that a record has been modified, it is helpful to know when the changes were made and by whom. By choosing View, Show/Hide Details you can toggle the entry detail columns (see Figure 6.4).

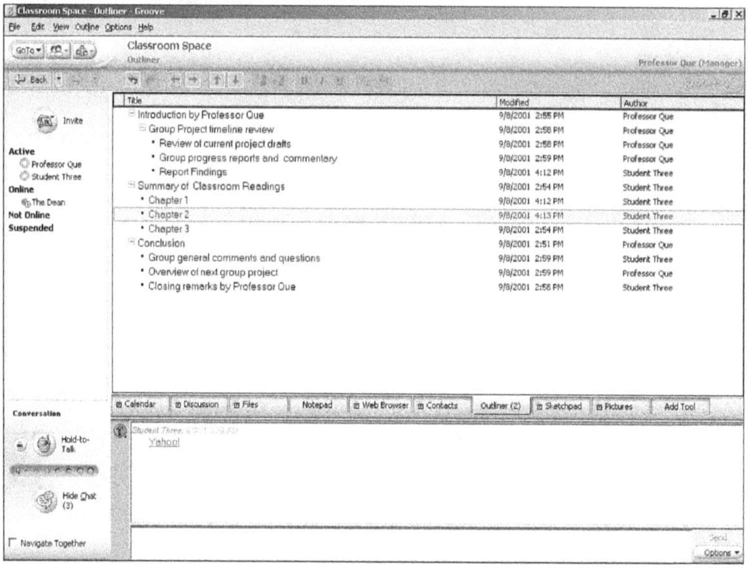

Figure 6.4
Clicking on View, Show/Hide Details will enable you to see the last update date/time for each line and the user who made the modification.

You can see the following two detail columns:

- Modified—The date and time the record was modified.

> NOTE
>
> Even if someone made a change in another time zone, the time reflected here is relative to the machine viewing the entry.

- Author—The user who last modified the record.

CREATING LINKS TO ENTRIES

You can create links to a record in the Outliner tool. Although not a link to the record itself, it will enable you to paste a hyperlink so that other members can be directed to the outliner item. Select a record and choose Edit, Copy Row as Link. The link can then be pasted into any other Groove tools that support rich text such as the text area, chat, or the discussion tool.

IMPORTING A TEXT FILE

You can import standard ASCII text files into the Outliner by choosing File, Import Text File from the main menu. After specifying the name and location of the text file, clicking the Open button places it into the Outliner at the current insertion point.

> **NOTE**
>
> Groove will create new lines where it finds carriage returns and will indent where it finds tabs.

EXPORTING AS XML

You can export the current outliner contents into a binary XML file for later import into another Outliner tool. After choosing File, Export as Binary XML File from the main menu, you'll be prompted for the name and location of the file. Clicking Save will save the file in the specified location.

IMPORTING AN XML FILE

If the contents of another Outliner tool have been exported as binary XML, they can be imported into another Outliner tool by choosing File, Import XML File from the main menu. After choosing the name and location of a previously exported XML file, click Open and the contents will be placed at the current insertion point.

KEYBOARD SHORTCUTS

Table 6.1 lists some of the commonly used keyboard shortcuts within the Outliner tool.

TABLE 6.1   OUTLINER TOOL KEYBOARD SHORTCUTS

Keyboard Shortcut	Action
Ctrl+Z	Undo last change
Ctrl+Y	Redo last change
Ctrl+L	Copy outline as link
Ctrl+F4	Mark selected read
Ctrl+Shift+F4	Mark all read
(+)	Expand row
(–)	Collapse row
Ctrl+1 through Ctrl+9	Expand the outline 1 through 9 levels
F3	Move to the next entry
Shift+F3	Move to the previous entry
F4	Move to next unread entry
Shift+F4	Move to previous unread entry

6

TABLE 6.1 CONTINUED

Keyboard Shortcut	Action
Alt+Home	Go to Home page
Enter or Insert	Create a new record/row
F2	Toggle Edit/Read mode for a selected record
Tab	Indent row
Shift+Tab	Outdent row
Ctrl+<	Move row up
Ctrl+>	Move row down
(+)	Expand a collapsed section
(–)	Collapse a section
Shift+ (+)	Expand All
Shift+ (–)	Collapse All
Home/End	Select the first topic/last record in the list
↓	Select the next/previous record in the list
↑	Select the previous record in the list
PgDn	Display the next screen of topics in the list
PgUp	Display the previous screen of topics in the list
Alt+F	Opens File from the main menu
Alt+E	Opens Edit from the main menu
Alt+V	Opens View from the main menu
Alt+L	Opens Outline from the main menu
Alt+R	Opens Format from the main menu
Alt+O	Opens Options from the main menu
Alt+H	Opens Help from the main menu
F1	Open up help for the Outliner tool

PERMISSIONS IN THE OUTLINER TOOL

Your role and its permissions assigned affect how you can use the Outliner tool. The default permissions for the Outliner tool are found in Table 4.3 (see p. 145). The Outliner tool only has two permissions available: Edit Outline and View Outliner tool. The Edit Outline permission enables or prevents a member from editing the outline contents. The View Outliner Tool permission is used to enable someone to view the Outliner tool within a shared space.

SKETCHPAD TOOL

Just like a whiteboard in a conference room, the Sketchpad tool enables all members in a space to share ideas on a virtual canvas. Not only are changes instantly relayed to other active members within the shared space, but members can also save the contents of the Sketchpad to their local file system for later reference.

CREATING A NEW SKETCH

By clicking the New Sketch button you will create a new blank sketch, as shown in Figure 6.5. The Sketchpad tool can hold several sketches at a time. The Previous and Next buttons can be used to cycle through all the sketches, while a counter is displayed showing which sketch is currently displayed.

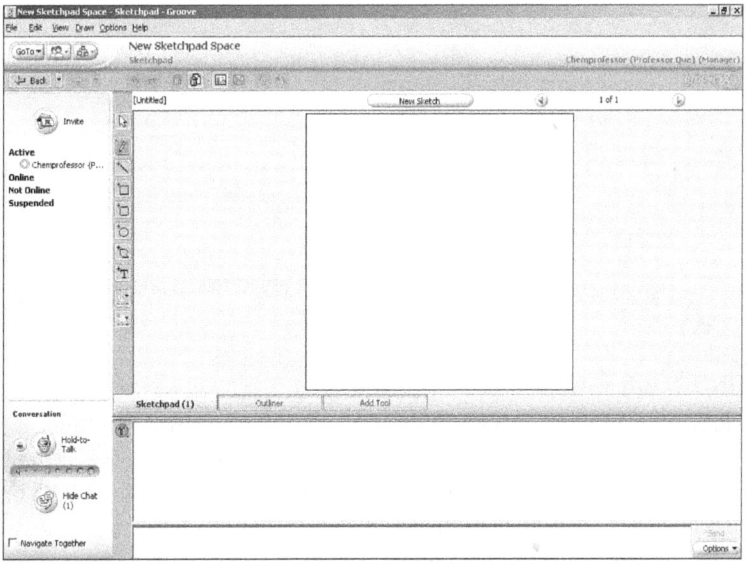

Figure 6.5
Clicking the New Sketch button will create a new blank sketch for you to work with.

NOTE

If you need to view more than one sketch at a time, right-click the Sketchpad tool tab and choose Open Tool in New Window. You can open several of these at a time and use Alt+Tab to cycle through them.

6

LOADING A BACKGROUND IMAGE

Although you can start out with a completely "clean" canvas, the Sketchpad tool enables you to load a picture to begin with. By clicking the Background Image button or File, Background Image, you can select a JPEG or Bitmap image from the file system. After it has been loaded, other shared space members can draw literally on top of the picture. As shown in Figure 6.6, Professor Que is using the Sketchpad to annotate an image.

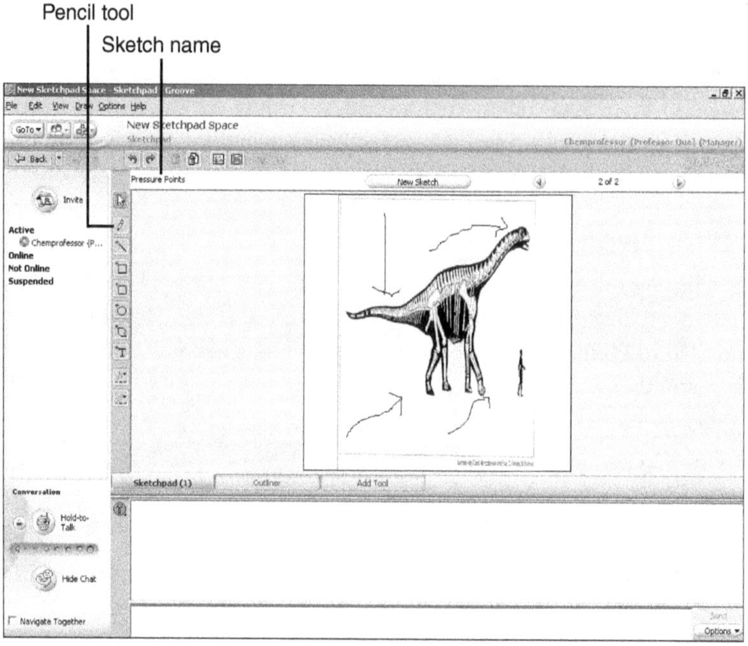

Pencil tool

Sketch name

Figure 6.6
By clicking the
Background Image
button we were able
to specify a new back-
ground image of a
dinosaur that we
could use.

NOTE

When images are imported, the aspect ratio is preserved to prevent distortion.

NAMING YOUR SKETCH

Because you can have multiple sketches in the Sketchpad at a time, you should assign a
name to your sketch. The name of a sketch is found to the left of the New Sketch button as
shown in Figure 6.6. Originally, all sketches are named "[Untitled]" but can be changed by
clicking this name and entering a new one. Pressing Enter after the name is entered will
save the new name of the sketch.

USING THE DRAWING TOOLS IN SKETCHPAD

Everything created within the Sketchpad tool is an individual element. This means the element can be selected and manipulated on the Sketchpad's virtual canvas. The different tools
available are outlined in Table 6.2. You can select each drawing tool by clicking the button
with the appropriate icon, choosing the drawing tool from the Draw option in the main
menu, or simply pressing the shortcut key as outlined in the table.

TABLE 6.2   SKETCHPAD TOOL BUTTONS

Tool Icon	Name	Description
	Selection	Selects drawn objects.
	Pencil	Used for freehand drawing.
	Line	Used for creating straight lines.
	Rectangle	Makes a rectangle with angled corners.
	Rounded Rectangle	Makes a rectangle with rounded corners.
	Ellipse	Used for making an ellipse.
	Polygon	Used for making a polygon.
	Text	Used to add text.
	Line Color	Changes the color of lines.
	Fill Color	Will change the fill color of the currently selected object, or the color of subsequently created objects such as polygons or rectangles.

FREEHAND DRAWING

By selecting the Pencil tool shown in Table 6.2, you can draw freely on the canvas. Select the Pencil tool by clicking it and then hold the left mouse button to draw. See the "Changing the Line Color" section later in this chapter for information on changing the pencil line color.

DRAWING LINES

By selecting the Line tool shown in Table 6.2, you can draw lines on the canvas. Select the Line tool by clicking it and then hold the left mouse button to draw a line.

DRAWING SHAPES

In addition to freehand drawing, Groove enables you to create several predefined shapes. By default the background of the shape is transparent, but will use the current fill color if one has been selected. The shape tools available and the buttons to activate them are shown in Table 6.2.

DRAWING A RECTANGLE

By clicking the Rectangle tool icon shown in Table 6.2, you can draw a rectangle. Clicking on the Sketchpad canvas and holding the left mouse button activates the tool. From here, you drag the shape until it is the desired size and release the button.

DRAWING A ROUNDED RECTANGLE

By clicking the Rounded Rectangle tool icon shown in Table 6.2, you can draw a rectangle with rounded corners. Clicking on the Sketchpad canvas and holding the left mouse button activates the tool. From here, you drag the shape until it is the desired size and release the button.

DRAWING AN ELLIPSE

By clicking the Ellipse tool icon shown in Table 6.2, you can draw an ellipse. Clicking on the Sketchpad canvas and holding the left mouse button activates the tool. From here, you drag the shape until it is the desired size and release the button.

DRAWING A POLYGON

By clicking the Polygon tool icon shown in Table 6.2, you can create a polygon with as many sides as you would like. To begin, you need to click on the Sketchpad canvas and hold the left mouse button dragging it to create the first side. From here, you can continue to click on the canvas to create the rest of the sides. The final side should be connected to the starting point to enclose the shape. Figure 6.7 shows examples of a completed rectangle, rounded rectangle, ellipse and six-sided polygon.

Figure 6.7
Within the Sketchpad tool you can create a variety of predefined shapes including a rectangle, rounded rectangle, ellipse, and polygons.

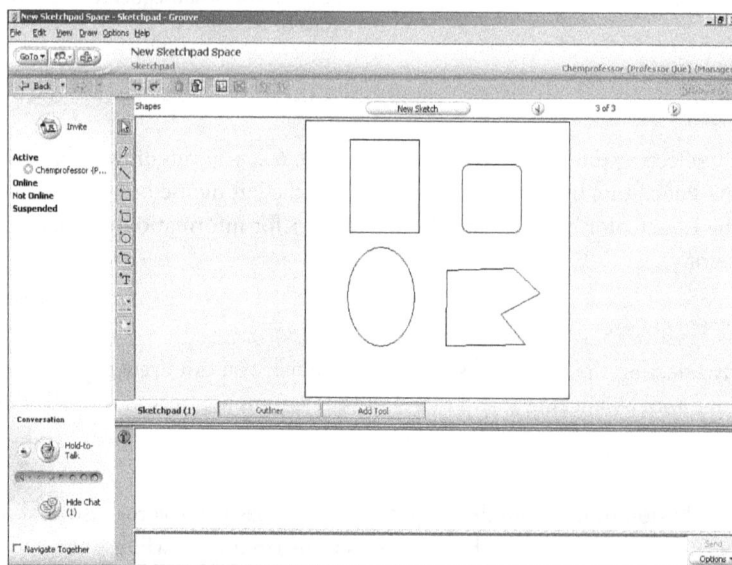

NOTE

It's important to close the polygon because if it is not closed, choosing another tool will delete the shape. If a fill color is chosen, you'll know the polygon is closed when it is automatically filled in.

ADDING TEXT

By clicking the Text tool icon shown in Table 6.2 or using the shortcut key, you can add text to a sketch. Clicking on the Sketchpad canvas and holding the left mouse button activates the tool. From here, you drag the box until it is where you would like it placed in the Sketchpad canvas and release the button. A text editing window will appear for your text entry as shown in Figure 6.8. After completing the text editing window and clicking OK, Figure 6.9 shows what the completed text box looks like on the Sketchpad canvas.

Figure 6.8
The Text tool within the Sketchpad tool enables you to create and format text that will be used within the sketch.

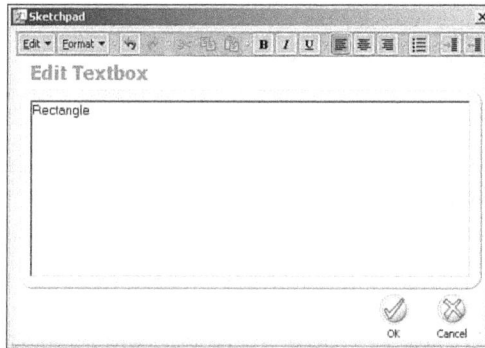

Figure 6.9
Clicking the OK button has added the text "Rounded Rectangle" to the sketch.

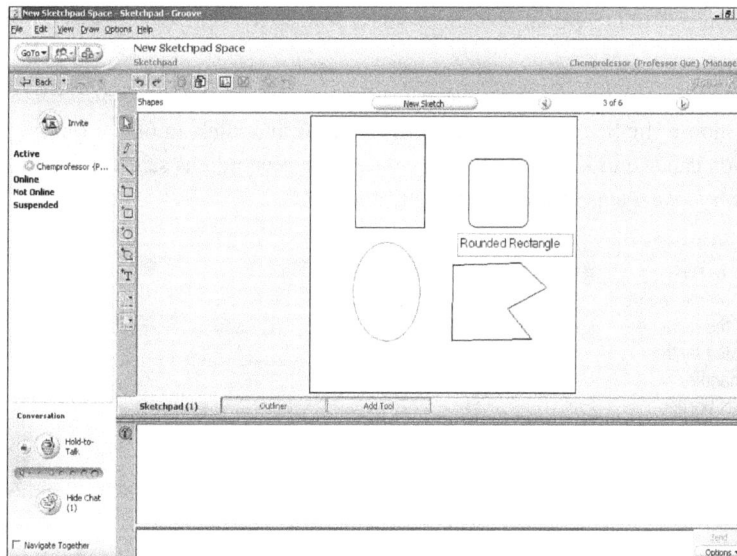

When the text box appears on the Sketchpad, it will display text with a border around it. If you decide that you do not want the border around the text, right-click the text box and choose Line Color, None. You may also change border color by choosing Line Color, *Color*.

EDITING TEXT

By clicking the Selection tool and double-clicking the text box on the Sketchpad canvas or choosing Edit, Edit Textbox from the main menu, it is possible to edit the text that appears on the sketch in a text box. When the text editing window appears, make your changes and click OK.

RESIZING A TEXT BOX

After a text box is selected, position your Pointer over one of the outline handles. You should see a two-way arrow indicating the direction you may resize the text box. Holding the left mouse button, you may drag and resize the object in either direction. The corners can be used to resize the object equally in two directions.

FORMATTING TEXT

Like the Notepad and Outliner tools, you can change the format of the text on your Sketchpad canvas. Formatting options are available in the Text Editing window. By clicking OK after selecting your format options, formatted text will be transferred to your sketch.

SELECTING DRAWN OBJECTS

The Selection tool shown in Table 6.2 enables you to select any drawn object in the Sketchpad. This is useful for moving, resizing, and changing the color of items you've drawn. You can manipulate individual objects or select several to apply changes to more than one at a time.

SELECTING OBJECTS INDIVIDUALLY

Choose the Selection tool from the toolbox and click an object on the Sketchpad canvas. As you can see in Figure 6.10, you can tell the rectangle is selected because white squares or *outline handles* appear around the perimeter.

Figure 6.10
In this example, we've selected the rectangle as indicated by the outline handles around its border.

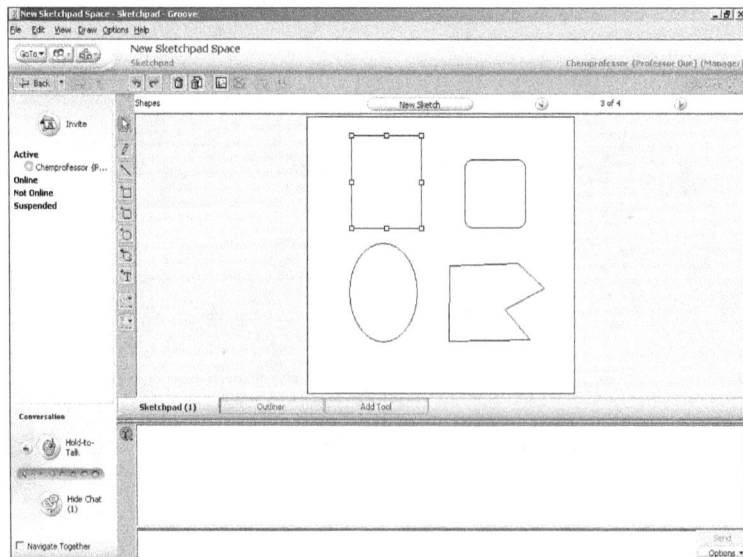

SELECTING MULTIPLE OBJECTS

Holding down the Shift key enables you to select several objects at once. You may also select several objects at a time by choosing the Selection tool and dragging the selection box around the objects by holding the left mouse button down. As shown in Figure 6.11, we are using the selection box to "lasso" the ellipse and rectangle. To select every object in the Sketchpad, choose Edit, Select All or right-click on the canvas and choose Select All.

Figure 6.11
By clicking on the sketch and dragging the selection "lasso" you can select several objects at a time.

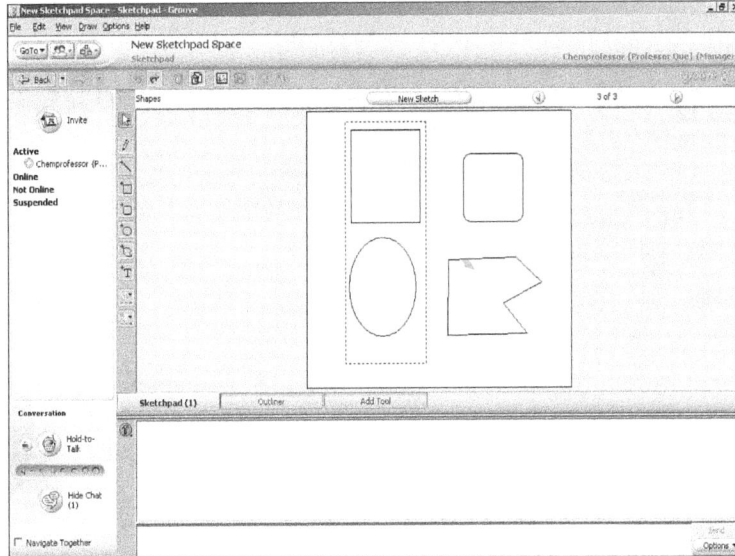

UNSELECTING OBJECTS

By clicking a selected object, you can unselect it. Also, by clicking on any white space within the Sketchpad, you will unselect any currently selected objects.

RESIZING OBJECTS

After an object is selected, position your pointer over one of the outline handles. You should see a two-way arrow indicating the direction you may resize the object. Holding the left mouse button, you may drag and resize the object in either direction. The corners can be used to resize the object equally in two directions.

MOVING OBJECTS

After an object is selected, you are free to move it around the Sketchpad's canvas. Position your pointer on top of the object until you see the four-way splitter icon. By holding the left mouse button, you can then drag the object and place it by releasing the button.

Other users will not see the new position of the object until it is actually released.

CHANGING THE LINE COLOR

You can change the line color used when drawing shapes, lines, or pencil strokes with the Line Color button as shown in Figure 6.12. First, select the line using the Selection tool. Then click the Line Color button and choose the color from the drop-down menu. Subsequent lines will also be drawn using this color.

Figure 6.12
Clicking the Line Color button will enable you to change the line color for a selected object and the line color used for all subsequently drawn objects.

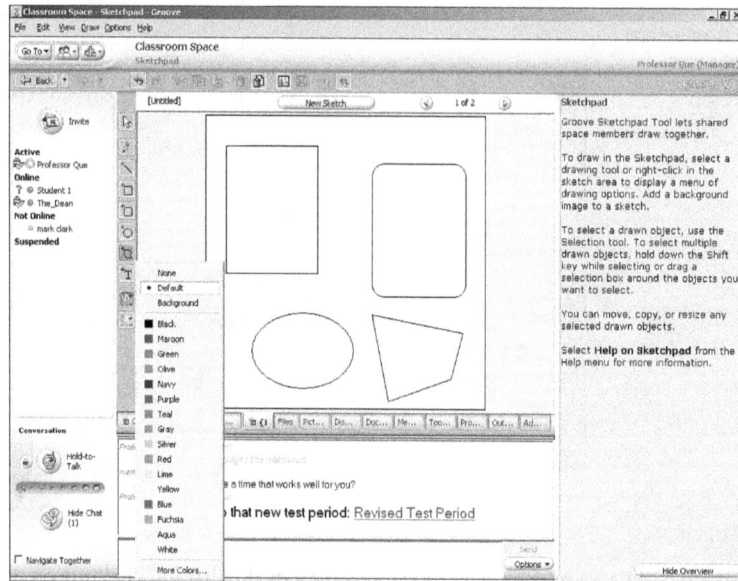

CHANGING THE FILL COLOR OF A DRAWN OBJECT

By default, closed shapes will be drawn with a transparent fill. This means that any background image will show through and only the lines that make up the shape will be visible. To change the fill color, click the shape with the Selection tool to select it. White squares will appear to indicate it has been selected. Click the Fill Color button shown in Figure 6.13. Choose a color from the drop-down list or More Colors to define a custom color. After you click OK, the shape will be filled with the selected color. All subsequent shapes drawn will be filled with this color by default.

Figure 6.13
By choosing the Fill
Color button we were
able to change the fill
color of the rectangle.

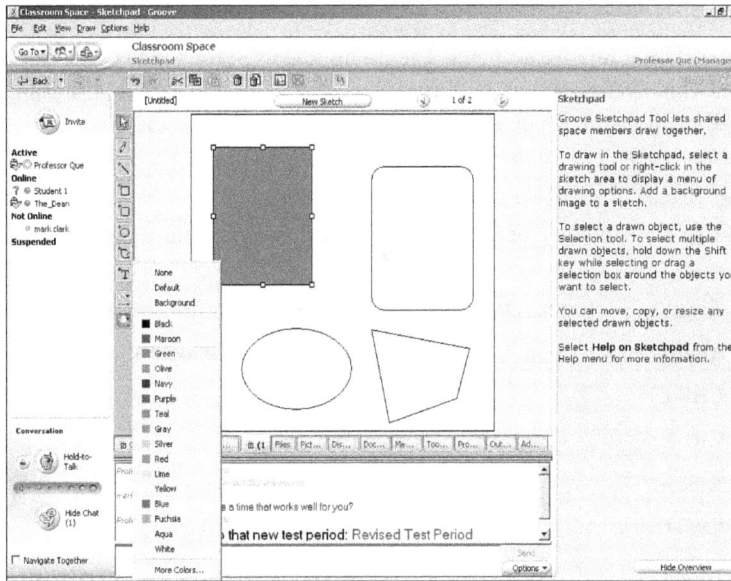

DELETING A DRAWN OBJECT

After selecting an object, you can delete it from the drawing by clicking the Delete button
shown in Figure 6.14 or choosing Edit, Delete from the main menu. This action can be
undone by clicking the Undo button.

Figure 6.14
The Delete button
can be used to delete
the currently selected
object. In this exam-
ple, clicking the
Delete button would
remove the rounded
rectangle.

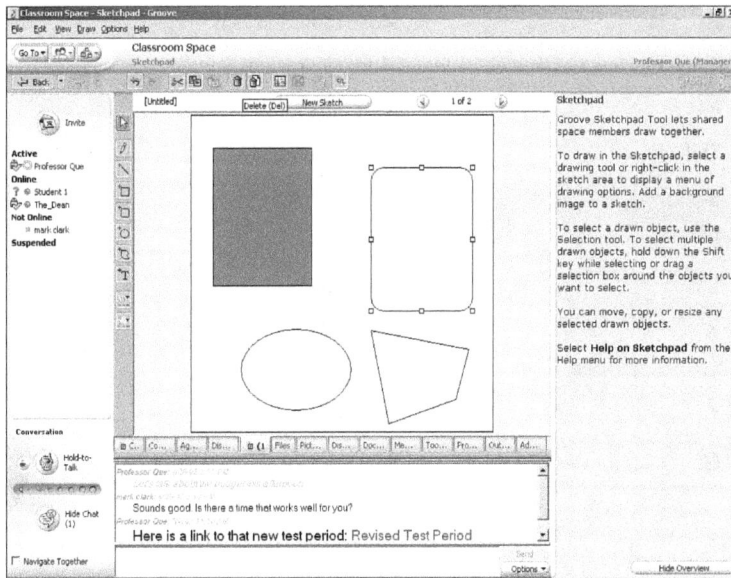

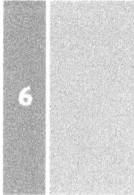

Deleting a Sketch

You should remove sketches that are no longer needed. Select the sketch to remove and click the Delete Sketch button as shown in Figure 6.14 or choose Edit, Delete Sketch from the main menu. If you delete a sketch accidentally, you can click Undo to bring it back.

Keyboard Shortcuts

Table 6.3 lists some of the commonly used keyboard shortcuts within the Sketchpad tool.

TABLE 6.3   Sketchpad Tool Keyboard Shortcuts

Keyboard Shortcut	Action
Ctrl+Z	Undo last change
Ctrl+Y	Redo last change
Delete	Delete the current selection
Ctrl+Delete	Delete the current sketch
Ctrl+S	Create shared space
Ctrl+F4	Mark sketch read
Ctrl+Shift+F4	Mark all read
Alt+F2	Show/hide Chat pane
Alt+F1	Show/hide Overview
Alt+Home	Go to Home page
F3	Move to next sketch
Shift+F3	Move to previous sketch
F4	Next unread
Shift+F4	Previous unread
S	Selection tool
P	Pencil tool
L	Line tool
R	Rectangle tool
O	Rounded rectangle tool
E	Ellipse tool
G	Polygon tool

PERMISSIONS IN THE SKETCHPAD TOOL

Your role and its permissions assigned affect how you can use the sketchpad tool. The default permissions for the Sketchpad tool are found in Table 4.3 (see p. 145). The Sketchpad tool contains only two permissions: Create, edit, and delete sketches or View Sketchpad Tool. Essentially, the first permission determines whether a shared space member can use the Sketchpad tool or have read only access to sketches already created. The View Sketchpad Tool permission is used to enable a user to view the tool within a shared space.

TROUBLESHOOTING

I AM TRYING TO COPY A ROW AS A LINK FROM THE OUTLINER TOOL TO INSERT IN ANOTHER GROOVE WORKSPACE TOOL. HOWEVER, WHEN I TRY TO CHOOSE THE OPTION FROM THE EDIT MENU, THE COPY ROW AS LINK OPTION IS GRAYED OUT.

To copy a row as a link, you need to select the entire row. Simply having the cursor on the line will not work. Select the entire row by clicking to the left of the bullet or place the cursor on the row and press the F2 key. You'll know it has been selected when the entire row has a green background.

I AM UNABLE TO DRAG AND DROP A ROW TO A NEW POSITION IN THE OUTLINER TOOL.

The Outliner tool does not support dragging and dropping rows. To move lines, simply select the line with F2 and use the Cut/Copy/Paste features from the Edit menu.

CHAPTER 7

USING THE FILES AND DISCUSSION TOOLS

In this chapter

MORE TOOLS TO GET THE JOB DONE

Starting with Chapter 5 you began looking at some of the tools that can be used in a shared space. This chapter continues that discussion by looking at the Files and Discussion tools.

→ For details on the Calendar and Contact Manager tools, see Chapter 5, "Using the Calendar and Contact Manager Tools."

→ For details on the Outliner and Sketchpad tools, see Chapter 6, "Using the Outliner and Sketchpad Tools."

→ For details on the Pictures, Web Browser, and Notepad tools, see Chapter 8, "Other Shared Space Tools."

THE FILES TOOL

There may be times while collaborating on projects with multiple project members that you want to share files with the others. Using the Files tool within a Groove shared space, you can easily "post" files that can be viewed and downloaded by other members. These can be documents, images, spreadsheets, or any other type of file. As shown in Figure 7.1, the Files tool enables you to organize files within folders and subfolders similar to a standard file system.

Figure 7.1
The Files tool enables you to create folders that can be used to organize collections of files.

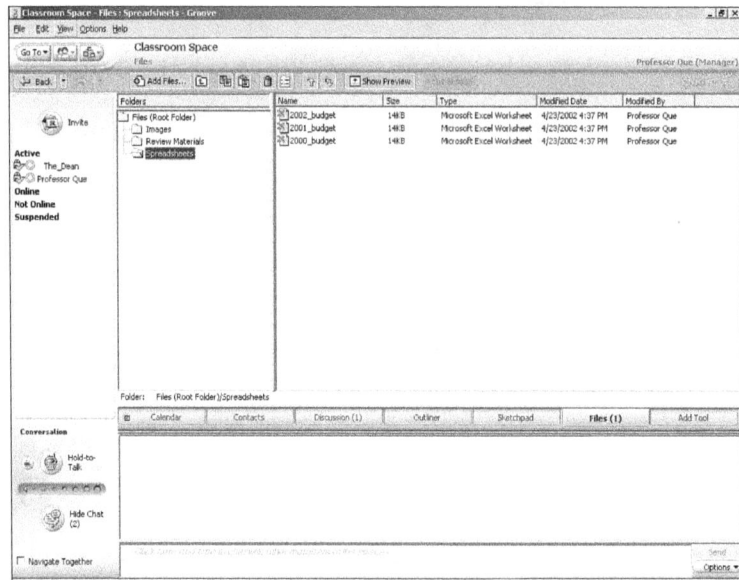

THE FILES TOOL INTERFACE

The left side of the Files tool is a list of all the folders. They can be nested many levels deep. Folders that have subfolders beneath them will be indicated by a + button to the left of the folder name. Clicking this button expands the list to show all the subfolders beneath it. Once expanded, clicking the – button will collapse the expanded folder.

HIDING THE FOLDERS LISTING

You can hide or show the folders list by choosing View, Folders from the main menu. When this option is checked, the folders will be visible on the left. When it is unchecked, the files window will expand to the full size of the tool.

NOTE

Even with the folders list hidden, you are still able to navigate throughout the folders by double-clicking folders and using the Up One Folder button.

CREATING FOLDERS

Folders should be used to categorize files so that others within the space can find them easily. Folders will always be created below the current level selected, so ensure you have selected proper level prior to insertion. You can create a new folder from the folders list by choosing File, New, Folder from the main menu. The new folder will be highlighted and you can enter an appropriate name for it. You can also create new folders from the file listing on the right. Right-click in the white space of the listing and choose New, Folder from the drop-down menu.

NOTE

At any time if you create something accidentally, you can click the Undo button as shown in Figure 7.2 or choose Edit, Undo from the main menu to undo your last action.

Figure 7.2
The Undo button is useful because it can quickly undo any mistakes, such as the accidental deletion of a file.

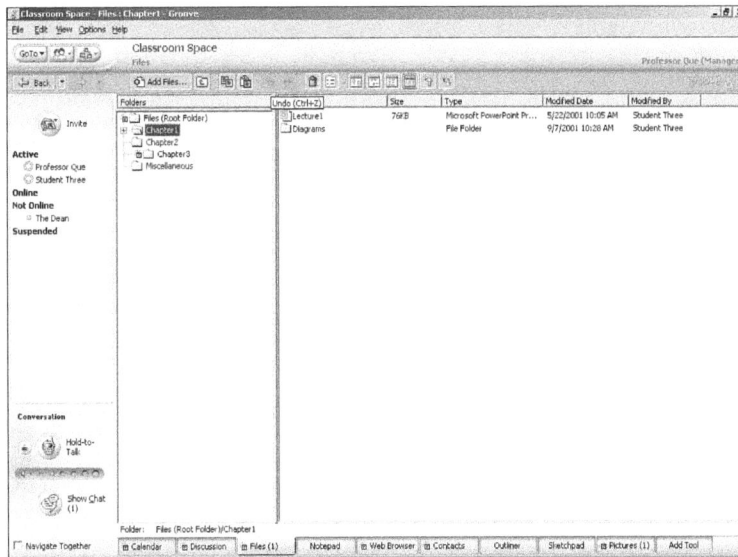

ADDING FILES TO THE LIST

You can add files at any time by performing the following:

1. Click the folder where you want to insert the files. As you can see in Figure 7.3, we've highlighted the Department folder.

Figure 7.3
In this example we've highlighted the Department folder so we can add new files to this folder.

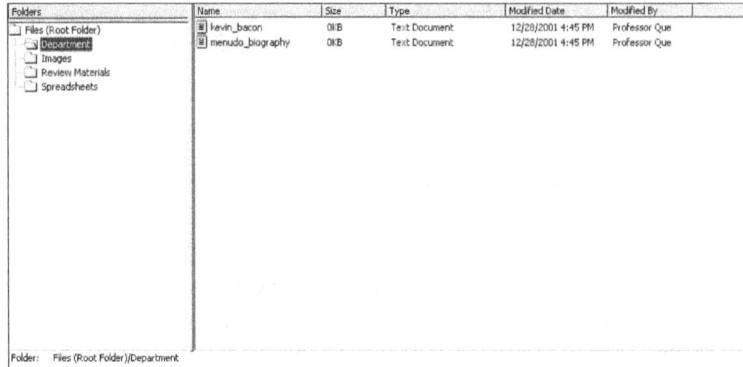

2. Once highlighted, you can insert files by clicking the Add Files button or by choosing File, Add Files from the main menu. At this point you will be prompted to choose the appropriate files to add as shown in Figure 7.4. You can select several files at a time by using the Ctrl and Shift keys. Click the Open button to add the files.

Figure 7.4
Clicking the Add Files button will prompt you to choose the files to be added from the file system.

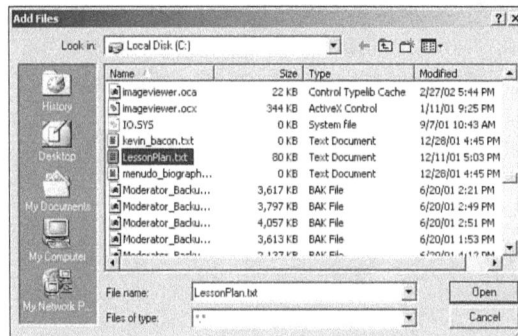

You can also move files into the tool by dragging them from another application, such as Windows Explorer, or by cutting and pasting them from another location.

TIP

> Keep in mind that files will need to be synchronized with other space members, so extremely large files could result in long synchronization times.

3. Verify the correct files have been added in the file listing window. As you can see in Figure 7.5, both LessonPlan.txt and Class1.doc have been added. When synchronized, other members of the shared space will be able to view and retrieve them.

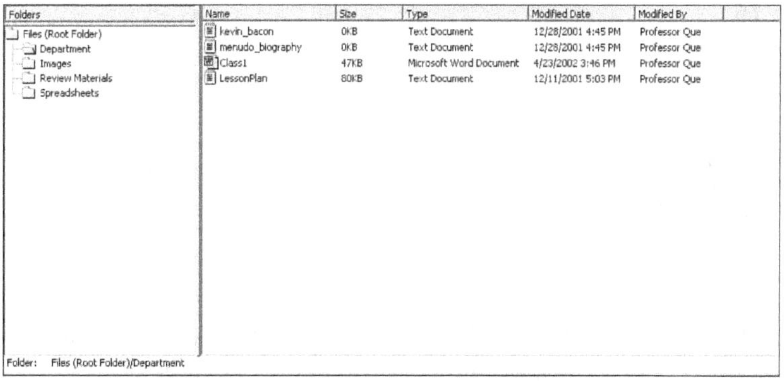

Figure 7.5
In this example,
`LessionPlan.txt`
and `Class1.doc`
have been added to
the Files tool.

Folders	Name	Size	Type	Modified Date	Modified By
Files (Root Folder)	kevin_bacon	0KB	Text Document	12/28/2001 4:45 PM	Professor Que
Department	menudo_biography	0KB	Text Document	12/28/2001 4:45 PM	Professor Que
Images	Class1	47KB	Microsoft Word Document	4/23/2002 3:46 PM	Professor Que
Review Materials	LessonPlan	80KB	Text Document	12/11/2001 5:03 PM	Professor Que
Spreadsheets					

Folder: Files (Root Folder)/Department

NOTE

Time and date stamps indicate when the file was actually added to the tool, not the Windows date/time stamp that is attached to the file in the file system.

CREATING NEW FILES IN THE LIST

You can create files directly from the files list. For example, you could create files for a document, a spreadsheet, a presentation, and so on. The file types that can be created depend on the file associations defined in your Windows installation. By selecting the folder in which you want to place the file and choosing File, New or right-clicking the whitespace within a folder and choosing New, you will be given a list of file types that can be created. Consult your Windows documentation for more information.

OPENING FILES

The Files tool uses your Windows settings, including any file associations that have been previously defined. Generally, you can open a file by double-clicking it or right-clicking it and choosing Open from the drop-down menu. If the association has been set up properly, the files will open in the appropriate application. If not, you will be prompted to choose the application needed to open the file. In addition, depending on your Windows configuration, you may have other options available when you right-click the file. Consult your Windows documentation for more information on this topic.

SAVING EDITED FILES

When editing files, it is important to note that your edits are not automatically updated in Groove when you save them in the application. Groove gives you the option of transferring your changes to other Groove members when you save an edit file. After editing a file and saving the changes within the application, Groove will prompt you whether to transfer the changes to other members as shown in Figure 7.6.

7

Figure 7.6
When saving changes in an external application, Groove will ask you if you'd like to share the changes with other members within the space.

You have two options:

- Clicking Yes will save the edits and transfer them to other shared space members when they subsequently open the file within the Files tool.

- Clicking No will not save the changes into Groove and other members will not see the new edits.

CAUTION

> Clicking No will not save your changes after you close the application in which the file was edited. You must be careful when choosing this option because the edits cannot be retrieved again after the application is closed unless you've chosen to save the file somewhere else in the file system by choosing Save As. This process seems a little awkward for some, but was added to prevent excessive traffic generated by large files being repeatedly saved. In earlier versions, each time a document was saved, perhaps using an auto-save feature, the entire file would be queued and sent to other users.

ABOUT FILE CONFLICTS

Groove enables multiple members to edit a file at the same time. Although it's very flexible, it can also present some problems when changes are saved. The following scenario illustrates how Groove handles this situation:

8:10 a.m.: Professor Que opens the Class1.doc file.

8:10 a.m.: The Dean also opens the Class1.doc file.

8:15 a.m.: The Dean closes and saves his changes to the file.

9:00 a.m.: Professor Que attempts to save his changes and receives the message shown in Figure 7.7.

When Professor Que tried to save the file, Groove alerted him to the fact that someone else had made changes to the file while he had it open. To resolve this situation, Groove automatically creates a new copy of Class1.doc and appends the text "(Professor Que's Copy)." Although this ensures no data is lost, it does mean that Professor Que and The Dean must manually merge the two documents.

Figure 7.7
If multiple members are changing a file at the same time, Groove will notify the last member trying to save her changes so she can attempt to reconcile changes.

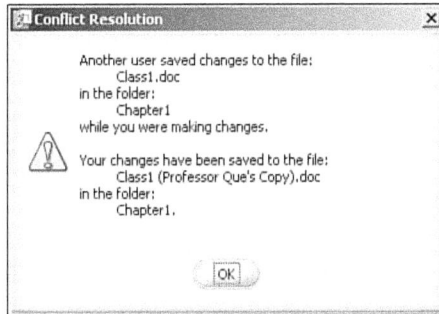

Proper communication among shared spaced participants can help prevent problems with document versioning control using the Files tool. In Version 2.0, Groove Workspace enables more control over simultaneous editing in Microsoft Word and Microsoft PowerPoint documents using the co-editing feature which is described in the "Using Co-editing with the Files Tool" section. However, if you need to implement a more sophisticated document review process, you may want to look into using the Document Review tool which is discussed in the section "Using the Document Review Tool" in Chapter 8. This tool should also be used to edit documents that are not created in Microsoft Word or Microsoft PowerPoint.

ADDITIONAL FILE FUNCTIONS

There are a few additional functions available by right-clicking a file or selecting it and choosing Edit from the main menu:

- Copy as Link—Copies a link to the file onto the Clipboard. This link can then be pasted giving other members a quick link to the file. Clicking the link opens the file in its associated application.

- Delete—Removes the file from the shared space. (if user has proper permissions).

CAUTION

> Delete will remove the file from all shared spaces.

- Rename—Renames the file. This will be reflected in all shared spaces.

PRINTING A FILE

You can open and print a file directly from within its associated application. By right-clicking the file(s) and choosing Print from the drop-down menu, Groove will prompt you for the printer to receive the output.

TELLING WHEN FILES HAVE CHANGED

Groove will notify you when a file has changed since the last time you accessed it. An unread icon will display to the left of any new or recently modified files. Arrow buttons are provided to step through all files having an unread status. By clicking the Unread Options button, you can also force an Unread or Read status for any and all the files.

KEYBOARD SHORTCUTS

Table 7.1 lists all the keyboard shortcuts that can be used within the Files tool.

TABLE 7.1 FILES TOOL KEYBOARD SHORTCUTS

Keyboard Shortcut	Action
Ctrl+M	Add a file to the currently selected folder
Ctrl+Z	Undo last change
Ctrl+Y	Redo last change
Ctrl+L	Copy selected file or folder as a link
Ctrl+F4	Mark the selected read
Ctrl+Shift+F4	Mark everything read
F4	Move to next unread
Shift+F4	Move to previous unread
Alt+F	Open File from the main menu
Alt+E	Open Edit from the main menu
Alt+V	Open View from the main menu
Alt+O	Open Options from the main menu
Alt+H	Open Help from the main menu
F1	Open help for the Files tool

PERMISSIONS IN THE FILES TOOL

Licensed Groove users can also use folders to control access to files. Your role and its permissions assigned affect the capabilities provided to you within the Files tool. The default permissions are found in Table 4.3 (see p. 145). Table 7.2 gives a more detailed explanation of the permissions.

7

TABLE 7.2 PERMISSIONS FOR FOLDERS IN FILE TOOL

Permission	Description	Manager	Participant	Guest
Add Files/Folders	Add new file(s) and folder(s).	Yes	Yes	No
Modify Permissions	Change permissions for a folder and the file(s)s within it.	Yes	No	No
Modify Files	Edit files content within the tool (does not stop a user from editing local copy).	Yes	Yes	No
Delete Files	Remove file(s).	Yes	No	No
Delete Folder	Remove folder(s).	Yes	No	No
View Files tool	View the Files tool in a shared space.	Yes	Yes	Yes

By right-clicking on a folder and choosing Permissions, or by choosing Options, File Permissions from the main menu, you can choose a role and edit the current permissions assigned to it. Assigned permissions will be checked, while unchecking a particular permission will remove that capability from the role.

CAUTION

Remember that even users with the Guest role can always view and save files locally. At this time, files added to the tool cannot be completely protected from someone invited into the space. In other words, documents you do not want certain shared space members to access should not be added to the files tool. However, it is possible to secure files outside of Groove to enable access to only certain members. A common approach is to use the security mechanisms built into Microsoft Office. Consult your Microsoft Office documentation for more information on this feature.

NOTE

Permissions are not inherited. Even if a folder gives no permissions to any roles, this does not apply to any subfolders beneath it. You must set permissions individually for every folder.

USING CO-EDITING WITHIN THE FILES TOOL

There are many times when several users need to edit a document at the same time. However, without proper controls this can cause major headaches for all participants. In Groove Workspace 2.0, co-editing capability is provided for Microsoft Word and Microsoft PowerPoint documents. The following sections describe the co-editing process for a document that has been added to the Files tool within a shared space.

INITIATING A CO-EDITING SESSION

For our example, we have a scenario where users The Dean and The Professor need to interactively edit a Microsoft Word document entitled BudgetConcerns.doc. The document has been added to the Files tool, as shown in Figure 7.8. Professor Que initiates the co-editing session by right-clicking the BudgetConcerns.doc file and choosing Start Co-Edit from the drop-down menu. This will prompt Professor Que to select the names of the users who will be co-editing and click OK, as shown in Figure 7.9. In this example, he has selected The Dean as the only user doing the co-editing.

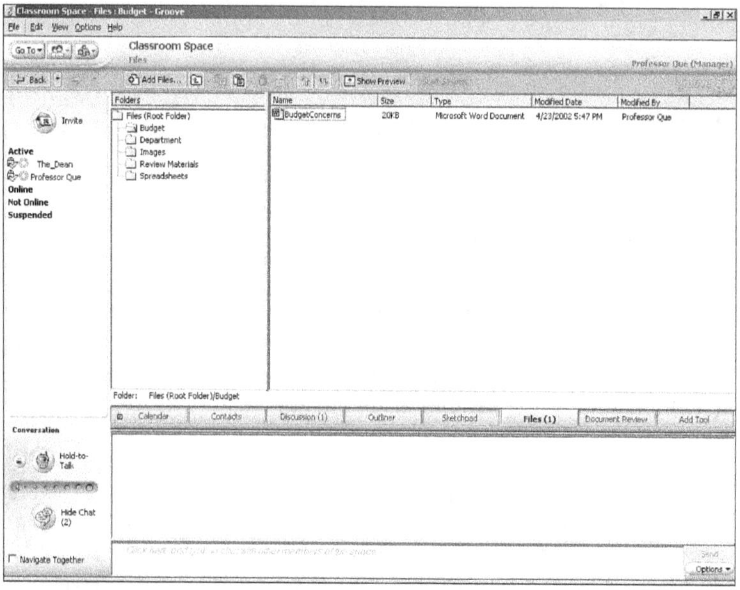

Figure 7.8
Add the document to be co-edited to the Files tool.

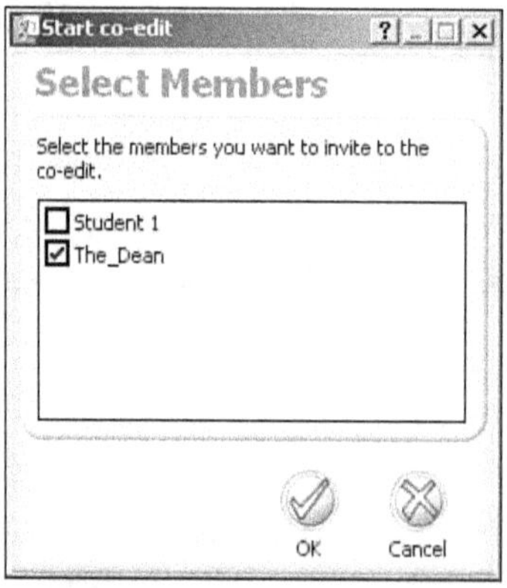

Figure 7.9
Select the members you want to invite to co-edit the document from this dialog.

ACCEPTING THE INVITATION

When a co-edit session is started all participants will receive a notification alerting them. As shown in Figure 7.10, the user The Dean has been notified that a co-editing session has been started by Professor Que. Similar to accepting a shared space invitation, The Dean can click the notification to start the co-editing session on his machine. Along with the floating Groove toolbar, this also opens a Groove Chat tool that will contain all participants as they enter the co-editing session.

Figure 7.10
A notification arrives that a co-editing session has begun.

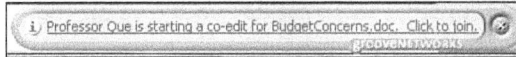

USING THE FLOATING GROOVE TOOLBAR IN A CO-EDITING SESSION

When a Groove user enters a co-editing session, the document for editing will be opened for him in Microsoft Word or Microsoft PowerPoint. While within the document, each participant will see a floating Groove toolbar, as shown in Figure 7.11. This will be used by participants to control the review and editing process.

Figure 7.11
Each member within a co-editing space will see this floating toolbar.

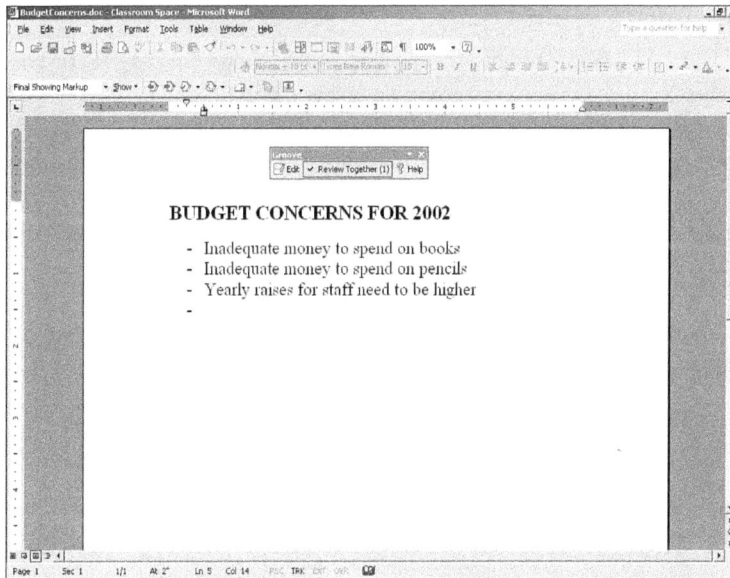

REVIEWING DOCUMENTS TOGETHER

The co-editing feature enables you to review interactively with the other participants. By clicking the Review Together button, all scrolling within the document will occur within each participant's session. It is necessary for all participants to select this in order to review the document interactively with other participants. At any time, the number of users with this selected is shown in parentheses after the Review Together label. This option is selected by default.

CONTROLLING DOCUMENT EDITING

By default, all participants in a co-editing session have read-only access to the document. Clicking the Edit button within the floating Groove toolbar enables that user to edit the document, while keeping all other participants at read-only access. The user currently editing the document is shown within the document caption. When the user has finished editing the document, he can click the Done button to return to read-only access. If another participant clicks the Edit button while the document is being edited, he will be notified with a pop-up window that the document is currently being edited by another user. Only once the original editor clicks the Done button will he be allowed to edit the document.

ACCESSING HELP WITH CO-EDITING

At any time, you can click the Help button on the Groove floating toolbar to access help with the co-editing function.

DISCUSSION TOOL

Group discussions tend to evolve over time. Discussions usually become fragmented, with several different subtopics going on at any given time. The Discussion tool works very much like an online forum, enabling members of a shared space to begin new discussion threads so that others may respond. The discussion text can include links to other places in Groove and can contain attached files. The discussion tool promotes free form discussion of topics and a level of organization enabling posts to be naturally grouped by relevance.

DISCUSSION TOOL INTERFACE

Looking at the Discussion tool interface in Figure 7.12, you can see how it resembles an online forum. The following elements have been illustrated in this figure:

- Unread—This column displays the unread icon for messages that have not been viewed.
- Created—The time and date a topic or response was created.
- Attachment—A paperclip is displayed in this column if the message has a file attached.
- Subject—The subject of a topic or response. These are indented to indicate their relationship to other messages.
- Preview Pane—A preview of the currently selected discussion item.

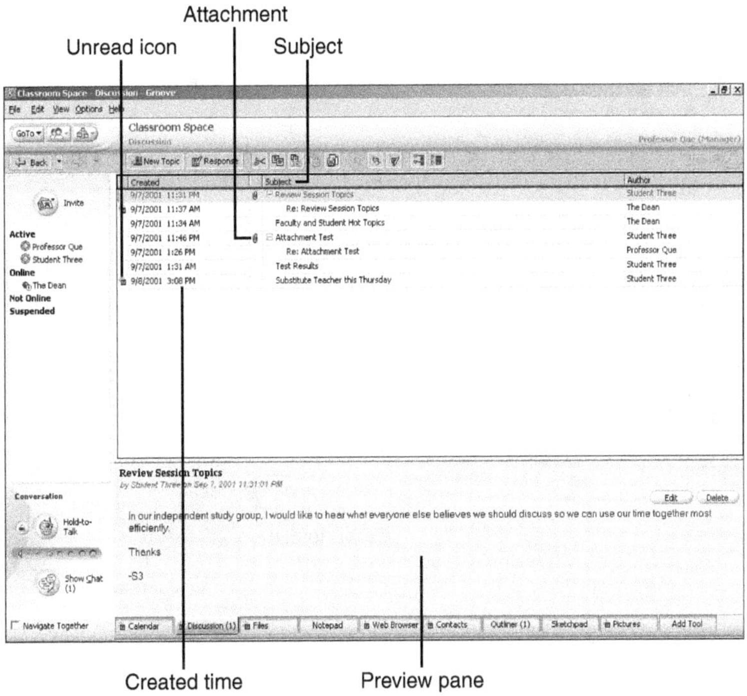

Attachment

Unread icon   Subject

Figure 7.12
The Discussion tool
provides threaded
discussion capability
for shared space
members.

Created time   Preview pane

READING A MESSAGE

Double-clicking any message will display the message in the entire tool window. Once
opened, you have different options depending on permissions assigned to your account.
The following options are shown in Figure 7.13.

- Save—Save the current message if any edits have been made and return the user to the
  initial Discussion tool screen.

- Cancel—Cancel any current edits and return the user to the initial Discussion tool screen.

- Attach—Attach a file to the message. The Save button must be clicked after this action
  or the file will not be attached.

- Response—Create a response to the message.

  The new subject will be preceded by Re: unless the title is edited, and will be indented
  to show its relationship to the original message.

- Import/Export—Import messages saved in binary XML format. You are also given the
  option to export messages in binary XML, tabular text, structured text, or rich text format.

- Navigate Previous—Jump directly to the previous message in the list, if there are any;
  otherwise it's grayed out.

7

- Navigate Next—Jump directly to the next message in the list, if there are any; otherwise it's grayed out.

- Navigate Previous Unread—Jump directly to the previous unread message in the list, if there are any.

- Navigate Next Unread—Jump directly to the next unread message in the list, if there are any.

Figure 7.13
By double-clicking a message within the Discussion tool, you'll be shown the message along with several different options depending on your permission level.

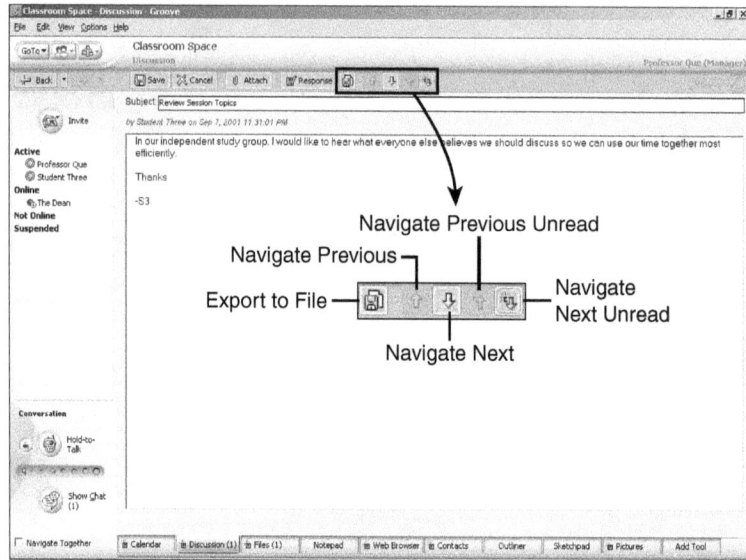

PREVIEWING A MESSAGE

By choosing View, Show Preview from the main menu, you can preview the contents of any messages in a pane at the bottom of the tool window. Clicking View, Hide Preview will disable this feature. This feature enables you to quickly see the contents of a message as you select them within the tool.

CREATING A NEW TOPIC

By creating a new topic, you are "kicking off" the discussion of a subject. Other members can reply to this topic so that it becomes a running thread of (hopefully) relevant communication on the subject matter. Clicking the New Topic button shown in Figure 7.14 or choosing File, New Topic from the main menu will prompt you for the subject and the body of the topic as shown in Figure 7.15. The subject should be a concise description of what the thread is about. The body will contain all other information pertaining to the topic.

Figure 7.14
Clicking the New Topic button will enable you to begin a new discussion thread.

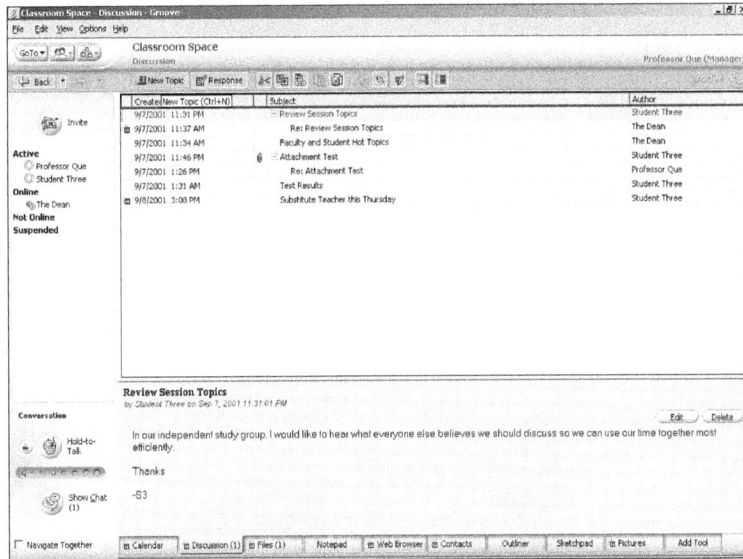

Figure 7.15
After clicking the New Topic button you'll be prompted for the subject and body of the message.

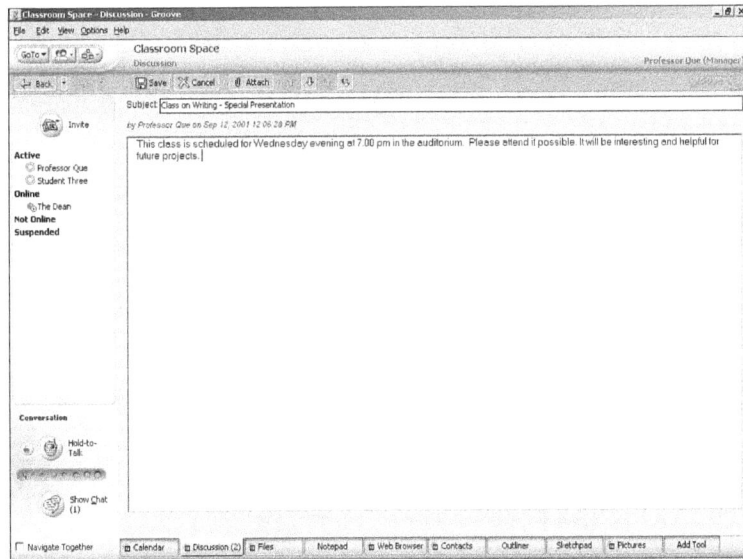

RESPONDING TO TOPICS

Topics are posted to encourage discussion. Replies to topics run in the same thread and are called responses within the Discussion tool. Choose a topic and click the Response button to reply to a message. The response will open as shown in Figure 7.16, prompting you for the subject and body of the message. The response will appear indented below the topic to show that it is part of the threaded discussion. Users may click the + and – buttons to expand or collapse the display of all topic responses.

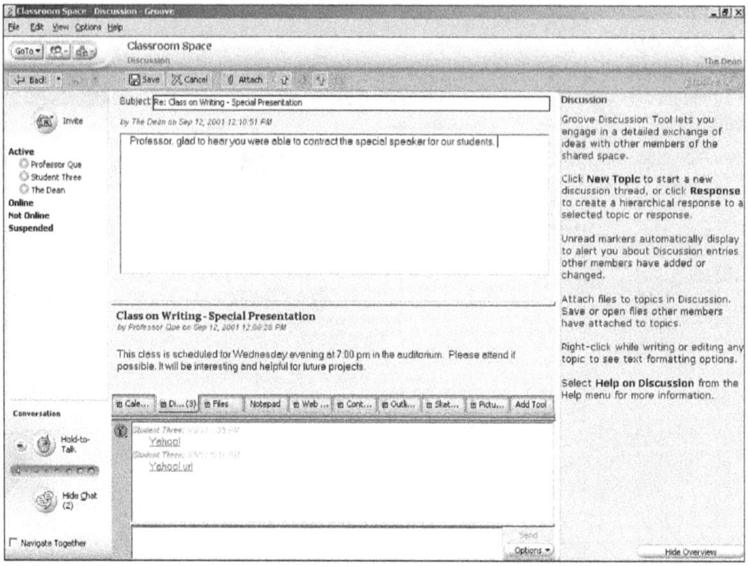

Figure 7.16
Clicking the Response button enables you to add an additional response to a thread.

NOTE

Topics and responses can use all the rich-text formatting features. You can right-click any selected text and choose the Font and Paragraph options from the drop-down menu for the different formatting options.

MANAGING ATTACHMENTS

When creating a new topic or editing an existing one, you can add and remove the message file attachments. Within a message, clicking the Attach button will prompt you for the name and location of the file to attach. After you've found the file, click the Open button to attach the file. The Attachments window will open with the following buttons:

- Save Selected—Save the currently selected file to disk.
- Save All—Save all the message attachments to disk.
- Remove Selected—Remove the currently selected attachment from the message.
- Remove All—Remove all attachments from the message.

In addition, by right-clicking on an attachment you can perform the following functions:

- Open—Open the file in the associated application.
- Print—Open the file in the associated application and send it to the printer.
- Copy—Copy the file for pasting into the Groove Files tool within a shared space or any other Windows application that accepts files from the Clipboard.
- Copy as Link—Copy a link to the message, not the file, so that it can be later pasted to enable others in the shared space one click access the message containing the file. A member clicking the link is taken directly to the message.

- Delete—Remove the attachment from the message.
- Rename—Rename the attachment.
- Properties—Display the file details of the attachment such as size and type.

NOTE

> The Delete and Rename functions only affect the attachment and not the file saved on disk. For example, if an attachment is deleted the file will not be removed from its initial location in the file system.

TIP

> You can rename and delete files attached to messages but the links to them will still work. The links point to the message and not the attached file. The only way the links will be invalidated is by deleting the message itself.

- Properties—Display information about the file including the filename, type, location, size, and the last modified date.

SORTING DISCUSSION TOPICS

Clicking a column heading enables you to sort the discussion topics in ascending or descending order in the following ways:

- Chronological order—Click the Created column heading to sort the messages by the date and time they were created.
- Subject—Click the Subject column heading to sort all messages by their subject.
- Author—Click the Author heading to sort messages by the member that created it.

REMOVING ITEMS

If you have proper permission, you may remove topics and responses. Highlight the items you want to delete and click the Delete button or choose Edit, Delete from the main menu.

CAUTION

> This also deletes any responses underneath the message you delete, so use with caution if there are other messages in the thread you want to preserve.

EXPORTING DISCUSSION TOOL CONTENTS

For both topics and their responses, you have the option of exporting the documents and responses by choosing File, Export To from the main menu or click the Import/Export button and choose Export To from the drop-down menu. You can choose from several different formats, including the following:

- Binary XML—Exports the message in binary XML and is most useful when it will be imported into another instance of Groove.

7

- Tabular Text—Exports only the subject, date created, and the body of the message separated by tabs.

- Structured Text—If exported in structured text format, all message properties will be displayed on a new line along with the property name.

- Rich Text—Exports the message in Rich Text Format (rtf) that is recognized by most word processors.

KEYBOARD SHORTCUTS

Table 7.3 lists all the keyboard shortcuts that can be used within the Discussion tool.

TABLE 7.3   DISCUSSION TOOL KEYBOARD SHORTCUTS

Keyboard Shortcut	Action
Ctrl+T	Create a new main topic
Ctrl+R	Create a new response to the selected topic
Ctrl+O	Open the selected topic
Ctrl+E	Open the selected topic for editing
Esc	Cancel an edit
Ctrl+L	Copy the selected topic as a link
Ctrl+F4	Mark the selected topic read
Ctrl+Shift+F4	Mark all topics read
Plus (+)	Expand a collapsed section
Minus (–)	Collapse a section
Shift+Plus (+)	Expand All
Shift+Minus (–)	Collapse All
F3	Move to next topic
Shift+F3	Move to previous topic
F4	Move to next unread
Shift+F4	Move to previous unread
Home/End	Select the first topic/last topic in the list
↓/↑	Select the next/previous topic in the list
Page Down/Page Up	Display the next/previous "screenful" of topics in the list

ABOUT PERMISSIONS IN THE DISCUSSION TOOL

Your role and its permissions assigned affect how you can manage discussion topics. The default permissions for the Discussion tool are found in Table 4.3 (see p. 145). Table 7.4 gives a more detailed explanation of the permissions available.

TABLE 7.4   PERMISSIONS IN THE DISCUSSION TOOL

Permission	Description	Manager	Participant	Guest
Create Documents	Create a new topic or response.	Yes	Yes	No
Edit Any Document	Edit any document, including those created by other members.	Yes	No	No
Edit Own Document	Edit documents that were created by the current user.	Yes	Yes	No
Delete Any Document	Delete any document, including those created by other members.	Yes	No	No
Delete Own Document	Delete only documents created by the current user.	Yes	Yes	No
View Discussion Tool	Enable user to view the Discussion tool in a shared space.	Yes	Yes	Yes

7

CHAPTER 8

OTHER SHARED SPACE TOOLS

In this chapter

MORE TOOLS TO GET THE JOB DONE

Starting with Chapter 5, you began looking at some of the tools that can be used in a shared space. This chapter continues that discussion by looking at the Pictures, Web Browser, Notepad, Document Review, Project Manager, and Meeting tools.

→ For details on the Calendar and Contact Manager tools, **see** Chapter 5, "Using the Calendar and Contact Manager Tools."

→ For details on the Outliner and Sketchpad tools, **see** Chapter 6, "Using the Outliner and Sketchpad Tools."

→ For details on the Files and Discussion tools, **see** Chapter 7, "Using the Files and Discussion Tools."

PICTURES TOOL

Like a virtual photo album, the Pictures tool enables you to share BMP or JPG images with others within a space. Like the Sketchpad tool, several images can be stored within the tool and "flipped through" by other shared space members. However, unlike the Sketchpad tool, the Pictures tool does not provide sketching capability and is provided for display only.

PICTURES TOOL INTERFACE

The Pictures tool is shown in Figure 8.1. Most of the interface is used to display the picture, whereas Next and Previous buttons are provided to flip through the current set of images. Each picture is assigned a name or short description in the text box provided.

Figure 8.1
Using the Pictures tool you can easily share images with other shared space members.

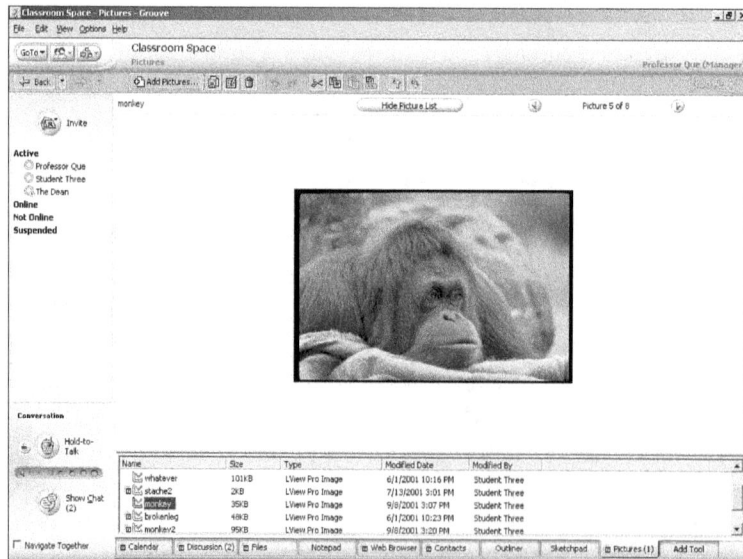

ADDING A NEW PICTURE

The Pictures tool originally takes its image from another location such as a file and makes a copy of the image in Groove's local data storage. You can add a new image to the tool in several ways, including the following:

- Click the Add Pictures button and provide the name and location of the BMP or JPG image to add. Using the Ctrl and Shift keys allows you to add several at a time.
- Drag an image directly into the tool from another application such as Windows Explorer.
- Choose File, Add Pictures from the main menu.
- Cut/Copy an image from another location and choose Edit, Paste from the main menu or click the Paste button.

Pictures added are appended as the last picture in the set. To rearrange the order, see the "Using the Picture List" section later in the chapter.

DELETING A PICTURE

You can delete the current picture by choosing Edit, Delete from the main menu or by clicking the Delete button. If you accidentally delete a picture, choosing Edit, Undo from the main menu or clicking the Undo button can restore it.

NAMING YOUR PICTURES

You can assign names or short descriptions to your pictures to make them more recognizable by other shared space members. By default, all pictures are given the same name as their source file minus the extension. To rename a file, click the Rename button, enter a name in the pop-up window, and click the OK button. You can also edit the name by clicking directly on the current name or choosing Edit, Rename picture from the main menu or right-clicking on the current name and choosing Rename.

EXPORTING PICTURES

By clicking the Export button or choosing File, Export from the main menu, you can save a picture to disk. After specifying the name and location, you can click the Save button to save the image to disk.

TIP

> Groove resizes images so they fit in the tool. This means that a file exported may not be the same size as the original. If you need to preserve images in their original format, use the Files tool to share image files.

LINKING TO YOUR PICTURE

The Pictures tool allows you to embed links directly to pictures from other Groove tools such as the Chat and Discussion tools. Select the picture you want to create a link to and

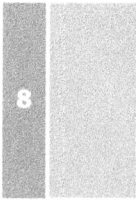

8

click the Copy as Link button, or choose Edit, Copy Picture as Link, or right-click and choose Copy as Link. This will place the link on the Clipboard so that it can be pasted later. As you can see in Figure 8.2, Professor Que has referenced one picture in a discussion topic he has created.

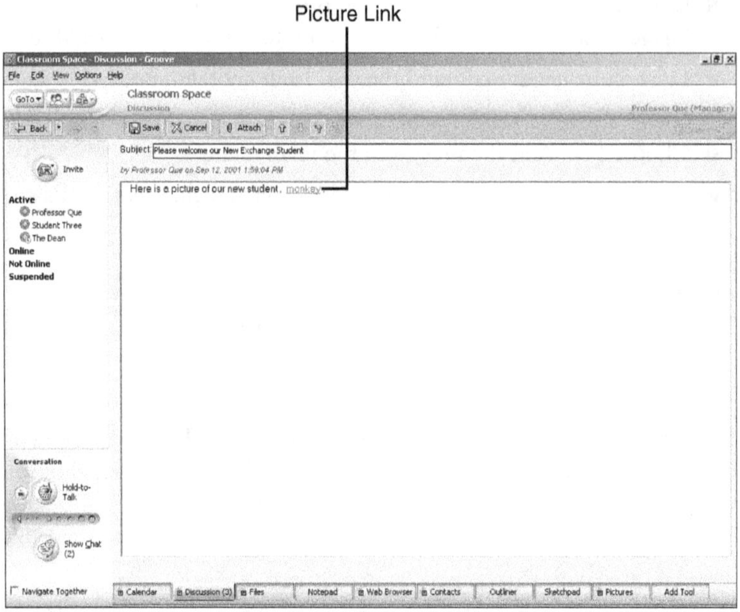

Picture Link

Figure 8.2
Using the Copy as Link function, you can insert links to Pictures tool images within other areas such as this Discussion tool message.

USING THE PICTURE LIST

By clicking the Show Picture List button or selecting View, Show Pictures List from the main menu, the Pictures tool will display a list of all the images currently stored within the tool. As shown in Figure 8.3, the Pictures list provides the following details about each image:

- Name—The name of the picture.
- Size—The size of the image.
- Type—The type of image (BMP, JPG).
- Modified Date—Usually this will contain the modified date from the file when it was added.
- Modified By—The person who added the image.

NOTE

If an image has been renamed, the Name shown in the picture list may not be the same as the original name of the file stored on disk.

Figure 8.3
Clicking the Show Picture List button will show all the images contained with the Pictures tool along with the name, size, type, modified by, and modified date fields.

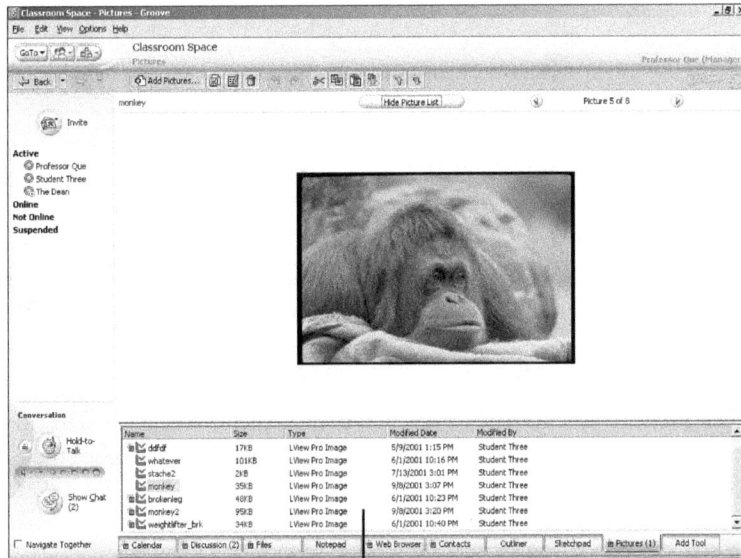

Pictures list

Click the Hide Picture List button or select View, Hide Pictures List from the main menu at any time to hide the list and restore the currently selected image to its previous size.

FUNCTIONS AVAILABLE IN LIST VIEW

While in list view, right-clicking an image gives you several options including the following:

- Open—Opens the image file in the associated viewer for that file type. For help with file associations, consult your Windows documentation.

- Print—Open the image file in the associated viewer for that file type and sends it directly to the printer.

- Copy—Copy the image onto the Clipboard.

- Copy as Link—Copy a link to the image onto the Clipboard. This can later be pasted within other places in Groove so other members can hyperlink to the picture.

- Delete—Delete the selected image.

- Rename—Rename the selected image.

- Mark Read—Removes the unread icon from the image.

- Mark Unread—Forces the current picture to unread status.

- Properties—Displays all the properties of the image including File Name, Type, Unread Status, Location, Size, Modified Date, and Modified By.

8

If you do not have proper permissions, you may not have permission to use the Cut feature. Because cutting actually deletes the picture you must have delete permission for the picture you want to move.

SHARING PICTURE TOOL IMAGES WITH OTHER APPLICATIONS

In addition to exporting pictures to a file as outlined previously, you may also drag and drop images stored within the tool. From the File List, you can drag the images to other Windows applications by clicking an image name and dragging it to the destination.

REARRANGING THE ORDER OF PICTURES IN THE SET

The Pictures tool does not allow you to drag pictures to a new location in the list. Instead, to move pictures you must delete them and re-add the files from their original source (usually a file).

KEYBOARD SHORTCUTS

Table 8.1 lists all the keyboard shortcuts that can be used within the Pictures tool.

TABLE 8.1   THE PICTURES TOOL KEYBOARD SHORTCUTS

Action	Keyboard Shortcut
Open the selected file and add picture	Ctrl+O
Undo last action	Ctrl+Z
Redo last action	Ctrl+Y
Copy the selected picture as a link	Ctrl+L
Mark selected read	Ctrl+F4
Mark all read	Ctrl+Shift+F4
Show/hide Chat pane	Alt+F2
Show/hide Overview	Alt+F1
Go to Home page	Alt+Home
Next picture	F3
Previous picture	Shift+F3
Next unread	F4
Previous unread	Shift+F4
Navigate together	Alt+F9

PERMISSIONS IN THE PICTURES TOOL

Your role and its permissions assigned affect how you can manage the Pictures tool. The default permissions for the Pictures tool are found in Table 4.3 (see p. 145). Table 8.2 gives a more detailed explanation of the permissions.

TABLE 8.2   PERMISSIONS IN THE PICTURES TOOL

Permission	Description	Manager	Participant	Guest
Add Pictures	Add new pictures into the tool.	Yes	Yes	No
Rename Pictures	Rename a picture.	Yes	Yes	No
Delete Pictures	Remove a picture.	Yes	No	No
View Pictures Tool	Enable the user to view the Pictures tool within a shared space.	Yes	Yes	Yes

WEB BROWSER TOOL

Members of a shared space can use the Web Browser tool to surf the Web and share favorite links with the other shared space members. In addition, by using the Browse Together feature, you can navigate the Web while others follow along. This enables the Web Browser tool to be used for collaboration and instructional purposes within a shared space.

THE WEB BROWSER INTERFACE

The Web Browser interface shown in Figure 8.4 is a simple, stripped down browser with only basic features available. Along with the familiar URL address box, you are presented with the following buttons along the top of the browser:

- Back—Takes you back to the previous site in the page history. Not to be confused with the Groove Back button that will take you to the previous area visited in the application.
- Forward—Takes you forward one page in the history so it only applies when the Back button has been used previously. Not to be confused with the Groove Forward button that will take you to the previous area visited in the application.
- Stop—Stops loading the current Web page.
- Refresh—Refreshes the current Web page.
- Copy as Link—Copies a link to the current Web page to allow a hyperlink to the page to be pasted elsewhere within Groove.
- Favorites List—Opens the Favorites List window.
- Add Favorite—Adds the current Web page to the Favorites List.
- Up One Folder—Used for navigation within folders in the Favorites List.

- Previous Unread—Moves to the previous unread entry in the Favorites List.
- Next Unread—Moves to the next unread entry in the Favorites List.
- Browser Together—Allows all members in a shared space to use a shared browser.

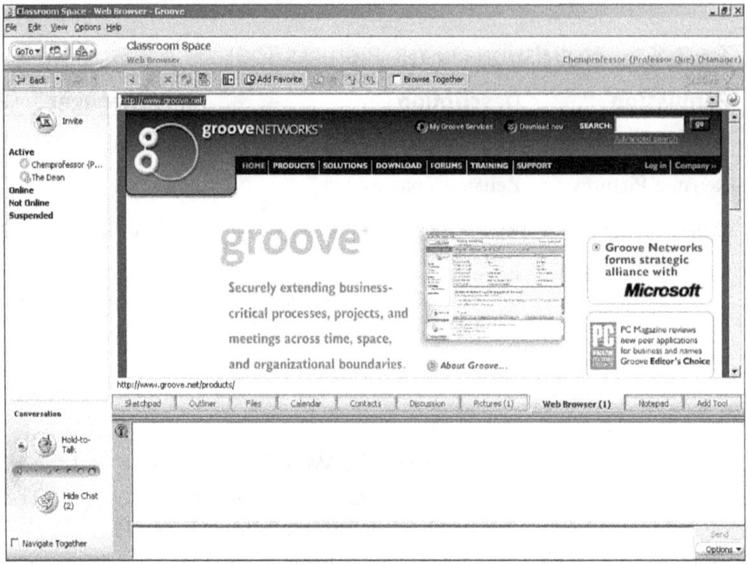

Figure 8.4
The Web Browser tool allows users to browse the World Wide Web from within a shared space.

VISITING A NEW WEB PAGE

Typing a Web page URL in the URL address box and pressing the Enter key or clicking Go will take you to that page.

> **NOTE**
>
> Although Groove actually uses your browser components, some features may not be available. For instance, those who regularly use RealName "keywords" may find they are not supported within the Web Browser tool interface.

THE FAVORITES LIST

You can save shortcuts to pages by adding them to your favorites list. Favorites can be categorized by using folders and are accessible by all members in the shared space.

OPENING THE FAVORITES LIST

Clicking the Favorites List button opens the Favorite Lists split screen shown in Figure 8.5. The left side of the screen will show all favorites by their description and can be categorized into folders.

Favorites list

Figure 8.5
By clicking the
Favorites List button
you can see all
favorites that have
been added and cate-
gorized into folders.

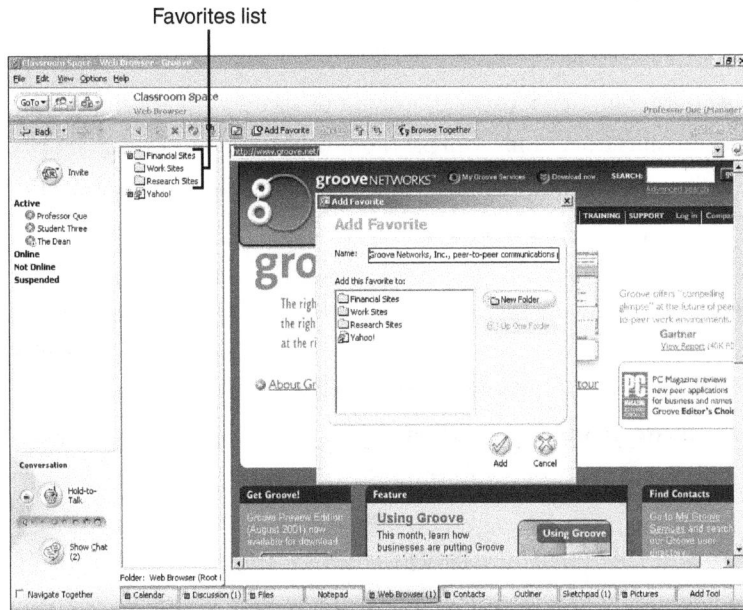

ADDING A NEW FAVORITE

Clicking the Add Favorite button displays the Add Favorite dialog, which prompts you
for the name of the new favorite and where it should be stored within the list (refer to
Figure 8.5). Folders can be several layers deep and you can navigate by double-clicking them
or clicking the Up One Folder button as shown. In this example Professor Que has already
characterized sites into Financial Sites, Work Sites, and Research Sites. You choose to keep
the default page name or enter something more descriptive. After you've selected the folder
in which to place the favorite, click the Add button to complete the process.

CREATING A NEW FAVORITES FOLDER

Instead of one very long flat list of favorites, you can group them together by creating folders. Because folders can be several layers deep, you must navigate through the folders list
and specify where you want the new folder to be created. It will be created as a subfolder
under the selected folder. Choosing File, New Folder from the main menu will create the
new folder.

You also have the option of creating a new folder when adding a favorite. You can click the
New Folder button on the Add Favorites dialog to create a folder.

8

WEB BROWSER LIMITATIONS

The Web Browser has a few limitations including the following:

- Entries in Web form fields will not be seen by other members.
- Submits from forms with password field(s) will not work.
- It is not possible to browse secure sites (any site with the HTTPS protocol).

KEYBOARD SHORTCUTS

Table 8.3 lists all the keyboard shortcuts that can be used within the Web Browser tool.

TABLE 8.3 WEB BROWSER KEYBOARD SHORTCUTS

Keyboard Shortcut	Action
Ctrl+O	Open a URL
Ctrl+S	Create a shared space
Ctrl+D	Add a Favorite URL name
Ctrl+L	Copy current site as link
Ctrl+F4	Mark selected read
Ctrl+Shift+F4	Mark all read
Alt+F2	Show/hide Chat pane
Alt+F1	Show/hide Overview
Ctrl+I	Show/hide Favorites pane
Alt+Home	Go to Home page
Esc	Stop
F5	Refresh

PERMISSIONS IN THE WEB BROWSER TOOL

The Web Browser does not have any permissions that can be assigned.

NOTEPAD TOOL

The Notepad tool is a text editor that allows all shared space members to edit documents in rich text format. Because it supports rich text, a variety of different formatting options are provided. All notes are saved as new pages that can be cycled through by users.

THE NOTEPAD TOOL INTERFACE

When you first enter a Notepad tool that contains note pages, there are several buttons that perform the following functions (see Figure 8.6):

- New—Creates a new note page.
- Previous—Displays the previous note page in the list.
- Next—Displays the next note page in the list.
- Edit—Allows you to edit the current note page displayed.
- Delete—Deletes the current note page displayed.

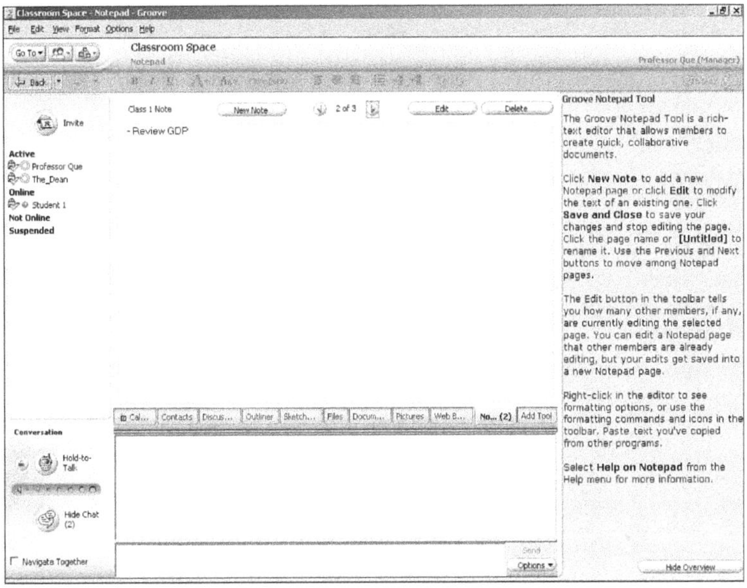

Figure 8.6
The Notepad tool enables users to enter Note Pages in rich text format that are stored as pages that can by cycled through.

ADDING A NEW NOTE

To add a new note to the Notepad tool, you must first click the New Note button as shown in Figure 8.6. This will open the note editing screen, as shown in Figure 8.7. You must then enter a title for the new note page and the text that make up the body. On the top of the screen are several buttons used for editing, including

- Bold—Bold the current selection.
- Italic—Italicize the current selection.
- Underline—Underline the current selection.
- Font Color—Change the color of the text within the note body.
- Font Size—Change the size of the font within the note body.

8

- More Fonts—Displays a variety of font types from which to choose.
- Align Left—Align text to the left.
- Center—Center the text within the margins.
- Align Right—Align text to the right.
- Bullets—Place a bullet to the left of the text. You must choose this for every line that needs a bullet because it does not repeat.
- Increase Indent—Indent the text to the right by inserting a tab.
- Decrease Indent—Remove an indentation. This does nothing if the text is not already indented.

When you have entered the details for the note page, you should click the Save and Close button to save the note page. To exit the note without saving the changes, click the Cancel button.

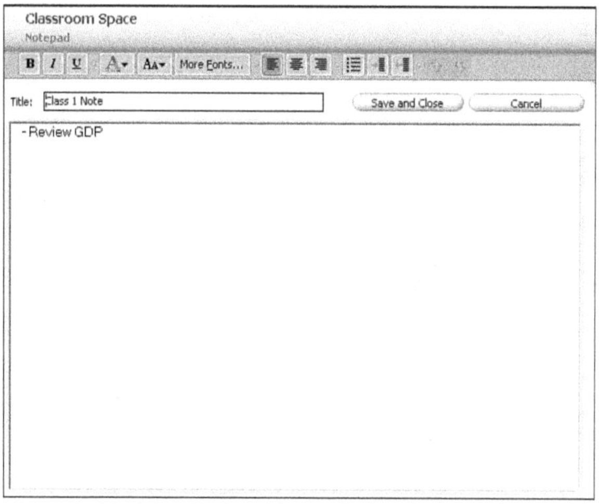

Figure 8.7
After clicking the New Note button, the user is shown the Note Page editing screen that provides the assorted formatting options.

SIMULTANEOUS EDITING BY USERS

The Notepad tool enables multiple users to edit a document at the same time. To notify one user that another user is editing a document, Groove will display a number in parentheses next to the Edit button. For example, because Professor Que has already begun editing the "Class 1 Note" note page, user The Dean will see the user count next to the Edit label, as shown in Figure 8.8. This will alert him of the potential for conflict should he begin editing the document simultaneously.

If The Dean does decide to edit the document by clicking the Edit button, he can do so. However, each user will be unaware of changes as they occur because changes are not dynamically updated on each machine when multiple users are in edit mode. The first user to save the note page "Class 1 Note" will be saved in the same place as the original note page. However, any subsequent edits and saves to the same note page will be saved into a new conflict note page. For example, in Figure 8.9 you can see that a new note page was created with a name prefixed by "Conflict of." This indicates that simultaneous edits occurred that conflicted with one another and that someone may need to reconcile the net result of the changes.

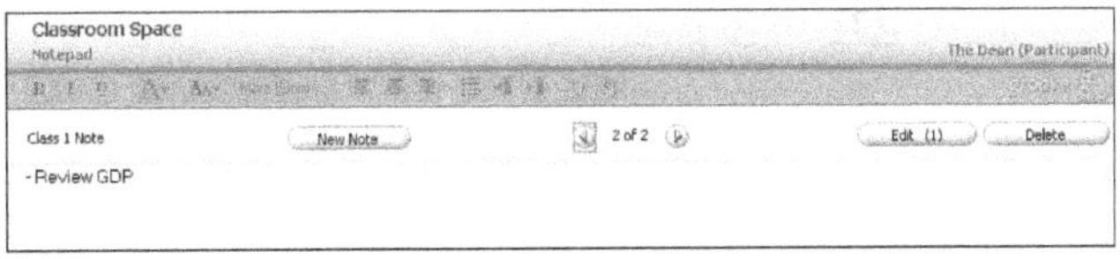

Figure 8.8
If other users are editing a particular note page, the user counted will be included in parentheses.

Figure 8.9
A conflict note page is created when simultaneous editing of a note page occurs.

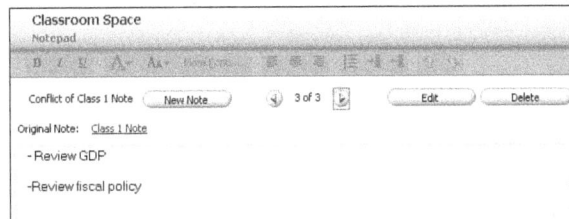

KEYBOARD SHORTCUTS

Within the Notepad tool, you have shortcuts for cutting, pasting, undo, bold, italic, underline, and so on as outlined in Table 8.4.

TABLE 8.4   NOTEPAD KEYBOARD SHORTCUTS

Keyboard Shortcut	Action
Ctrl+N	Create a new note page.
Esc	Cancel the current edit.
Ctrl+L	Copy the current note page as a link.
Ctrl+E	Edit the current note page.
Ctrl+F4	Mark the current note page as read.
Ctrl+Shift+F4	Mark the current note page as unread.
F3	Move to the next note page.
Shift+F3	Move to the previous note page.
F4	Move to the next unread note page.
Shift+F4	Move to the previous unread note page.

8

PERMISSIONS IN THE NOTEPAD TOOL

Your role and its permissions assigned affect how you can manage the Notepad tool. The default permissions for the Notepad tool are found in Table 4.3 (see p. 145). Table 8.5 gives a more detailed explanation of these permissions.

TABLE 8.5   PERMISSIONS FOR NOTEPAD TOOL

Permission	Description	Manager	Participant	Guest
Create Notes	Create new note pages.	Yes	Yes	No
Edit Any Note	Edit any note page created by any user.	Yes	Yes	No
Delete Any Note	Delete any note page by any user.	Yes	Yes	No
View Notepad Tool	View the Notepad tool within a shared space.	Yes	Yes	Yes

USING THE DOCUMENT REVIEW TOOL

There will be times when a document needs to be reviewed by several different Groove Workspace users. To facilitate the process in an orderly fashion, Groove provides the Document Review tool. This tool is designed to enable several reviewers to examine documents, provide feedback, and examine and incorporate suggested changes.

STARTING THE DOCUMENT REVIEW PROCESS

First, a Groove Workspace user must initiate the document review process. After adding the Document Review tool to a shared space, he should be greeted with the tool interface shown in Figure 8.10. At this time, the person leading the review session should add all the documents to be reviewed during this stage of the process. Click the Add Files button to choose the appropriate documents. They will be added to the Documents listing, as shown in Figure 8.11.

Figure 8.10
The Document Review tool when it is first added to space.

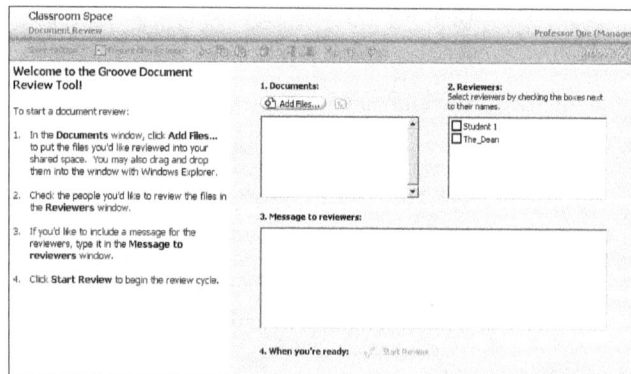

Figure 8.11
As documents to be reviewed are added, they will appear in the Documents listing.

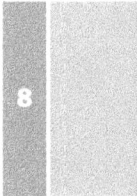

NOTE

> The user who adds the Document Review tool to the shared space becomes the author. This determines who adds documents and initiates the review process. This means that the document author does not necessarily have to be the manager within the shared space.

TIP

> Instead of clicking the Add Files button, you can also drag the files from Windows Explorer into the Documents window.

After all documents have been added, select the check box next to each user name as shown in Figure 8.11. You also have the option of entering text in the Message to Reviewers section. This is a good place to inform the reviewers of any special instructions because the message will be displayed to them when they enter the reviewing session. When the Start Review button is clicked, notifications are sent to all reviewers and the review cycle for the selected documents begins.

ENTERING A REVIEW SESSION

When the document review process is begun, each of the reviewers selected will receive a notification, as shown in Figure 8.12. Clicking the notification will take the reviewer to the Document Review tool in the appropriate shared space.

THE REVIEW PROCESS

After clicking the notification, the reviewer is taken to the Document Review tool interface, as shown in Figure 8.12. The following steps demonstrate how the review process works from the reviewer's perspective:

1. To keep others in the review process informed of your progress, you should always set the status field. Because The Dean is beginning to review the documents, he should select In Progress from the Status drop-down list, as shown in Figure 8.13. Initially, the status is set to Not Started to indicate he has not begun the review process.

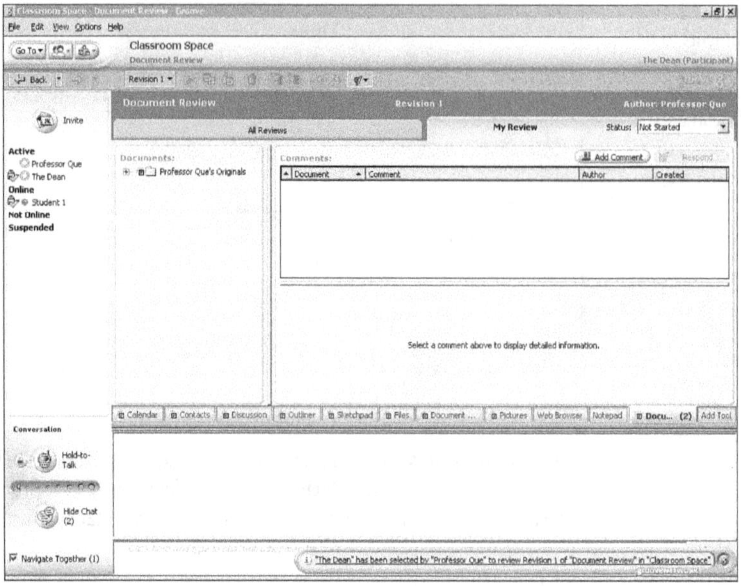

8

Figure 8.12
When a reviewer is invited to review a document, clicking the invitation will take them to a Document Review tool that looks like this.

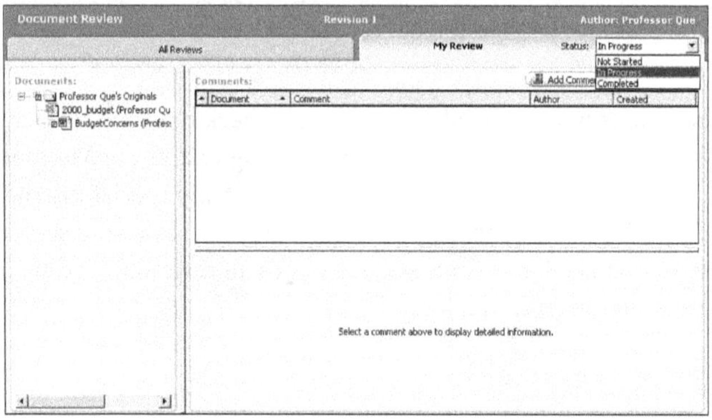

Figure 8.13
When starting the review process, the reviewer should change the status to In Progress.

2. On the left side of the screen is a list containing all the documents to be reviewed. The Dean must first select the document to be reviewed, as shown in Figure 8.14. He has selected the BudgetConcerns.doc document. Right-click the file to choose Edit Markup from the drop-down menu as shown in the figure.

3. The example document is a Microsoft Word document. Microsoft Word launches automatically when the Edit Markup option is chosen, as shown in Figure 8.15. You can see that the window caption contains "My Markup for Rev1," which helps identify the current revision. The Dean should now review the document and make any edits needed.

Figure 8.14
The Dean has selected the `BudgetConcerns .doc` document to review.

Figure 8.15
After selecting the Edit Markup option, the document will open within the native application, which in this case is Microsoft Word.

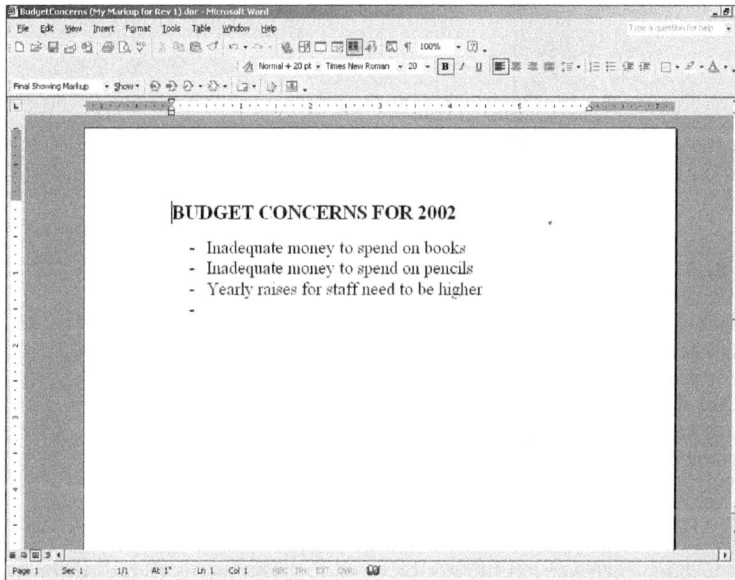

4. In applications such as Microsoft Word, you can turn on track changes so others can tell what has been edited. In this example, you can enable this in Microsoft Word by choosing Tools, Track Changes from the main menu, as shown in Figure 8.16.

5. When The Dean has completed the edits, he should save the document within Microsoft Word. If changes have been made, he will be prompted to save the changes back into Groove, as shown in Figure 8.17. Clicking Yes will save the edits that The Dean has made. To cancel the changes, click the No button and the edits will not be saved back into Groove.

At this point, the reviewer has finished all the edits for the current revision and saved the changes back into Groove. Groove will create a new folder in the reviewer's version of the tool called My Markup that will contain the newly edited version of the document. Looking at Figure 8.18, you can see the newly created folder in the Documents area of the Document Review tool in The Dean's copy of the shared space.

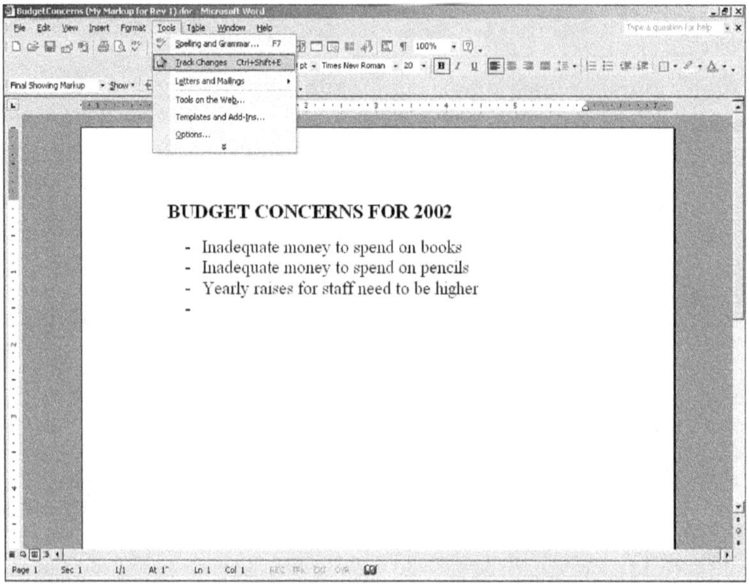

Figure 8.16
Selecting Track Changes enables you to use the tracking features within Microsoft Word.

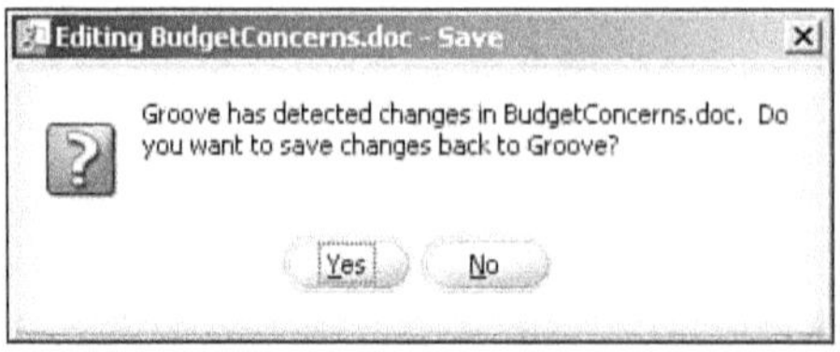

Figure 8.17
When changes have been made to a document, Groove will prompt you to decide whether they should be saved back into the Document Review tool copy.

6. Each reviewer has the option of adding comments to the review to explain what changes have been made. By clicking the Add Comment button, the user will be presented with the screen shown in Figure 8.19. After entering a title for the comment and the body of the note, the reviewer can indicate what document this comment refers to by clicking the arrow as demonstrated. Click the Save button to save the comment or click Cancel to abort the comment addition. All comments will be visible to the author who initiated the review process.

7. In order for reviewers to signify they have finished the review process for all documents assigned to them, they should change the status to Completed as shown in Figure 8.20. In the next section, you see how the author can inspect the reviewer's changes.

LOOKING OVER THE REVIEWER'S WORK

After all reviewers have completed the review process, they should have changed their status to Completed. The author who initiated the review will then know that all edits for this round have been completed. In this example, the author Professor Que can tell that The Dean has completed reviewing the documents by the Completed status shown in Figure 8.21. The following steps illustrate how Professor Que might proceed to examine the edits made by The Dean:

Figure 8.18
A new folder called My Markup is created to hold copies of the documents after the reviewer had edited them.

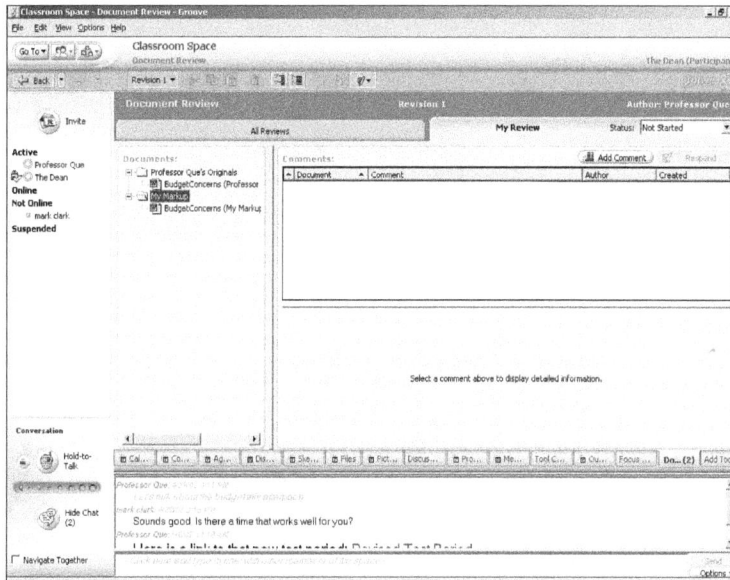

Figure 8.19
Comments can be attached to documents being reviewed to provide more information about the edits being performed.

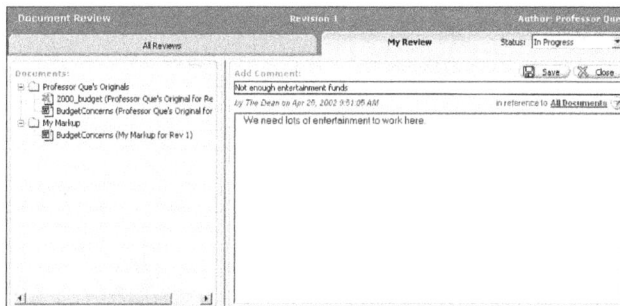

1. All documents edited by reviewers will be place in their own folder entitled User's Markup, as shown in Figure 8.21. Right-click and choose Open or double-click the BudgetConcerns.doc document to open the document in its native application so Professor Que can review the edits.

NOTE

Unread markers will appear to the left of documents that have edits you have not viewed yet.

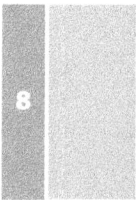

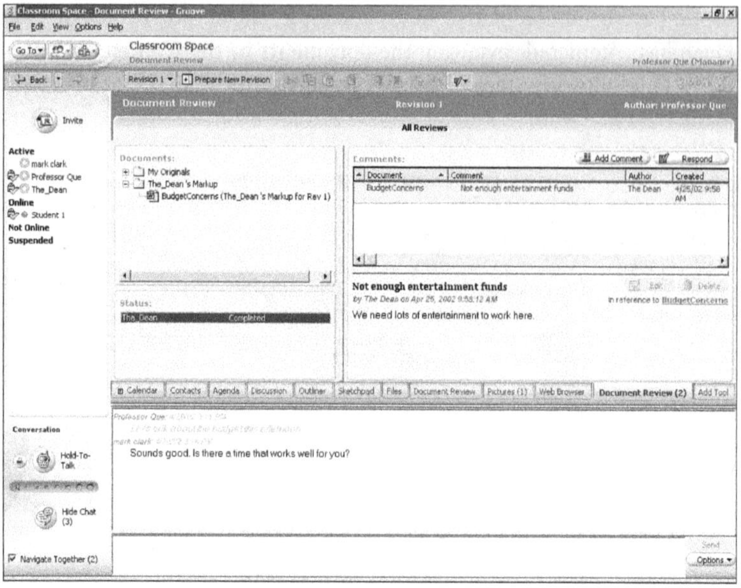

Figure 8.20
When a reviewer has finished all the edits, the status should be changed to Completed.

Figure 8.21
Professor Que knows The Dean has completed his edits because of the Completed status shown in the Status area.

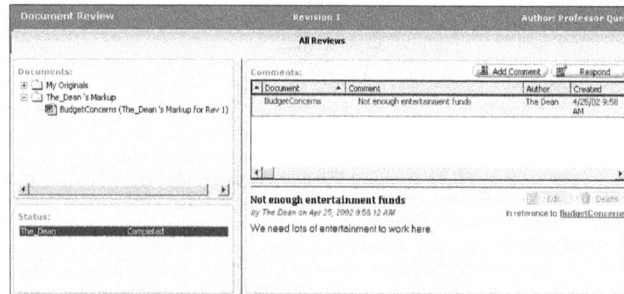

2. Each reviewer should enter comments describing what edits have been made. This will provide the author initiating the review with more information so he/she can easily find the edits. Looking in the comments section shown in Figure 8.21, Professor Que can double-click on the comment attached to BudgetConcerns.doc and should see the detail shown in Figure 8.22. When viewing comments, you can respond to them by clicking the Respond button or simply click Close to return to the comments listing.

3. With BudgetConcerns.doc open in Microsoft Word, the author Professor Que can view the edits made by The Dean. If not already enabled, Professor Que should turn on markup by choosing View, Markup, as shown in Figure 8.23. With this option enabled, all edits by reviewers will be highlighted.

Figure 8.22
Double-clicking a comment will show the details, including the document to which the comment is attached.

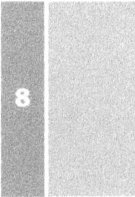

NOTE

The author only has read-only access to the documents edited by the reviewers. The author should compare and make modifications to the original documents (in the Originals folder) if they need to be saved back into the Document Review tool.

Figure 8.23
By enabling View Markup, Professor Que can easily see what edits have been made to the document.

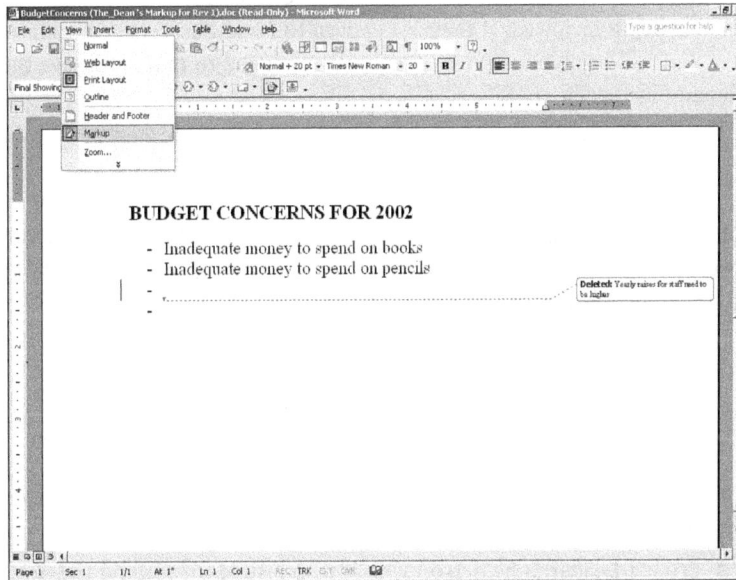

KEYBOARD SHORTCUTS

Within the Document Review tool, there are several shortcuts as shown in Table 8.6.

TABLE 8.6   DOCUMENT REVIEW TOOL KEYBOARD SHORTCUTS

Keyboard Shortcut	Action
Enter	Open a document.
Ctrl+C	Copy a document.
Del	Delete the selected document.
Ctrl+F4	Mark the selected document as read.
Ctrl+Shift+F4	Mark all items as read.

PERMISSIONS IN THE DOCUMENT REVIEW TOOL

Although there are no permissions to set in the Document Review tool, you should understand that there are implied permissions depending on how the review session was started. The user who adds the Document Review tool to a shared space becomes the "author" or the person initiating the review. This user is responsible for adding documents and assigning the reviewers. All other users within the space are only allowed read-only access to any documents being reviewed. If they are chosen to review a document they will be sent an invitation and will be able to review documents assigned to them and save them back into the Document Review tool.

THE PROJECT MANAGER TOOL

The Project Manager tool is designed to help Project Leaders break down and manage the tasks that make up a project. We'll look at using some of the Project Manager tool features in the following sections.

DEFINING THE PROJECT

After adding the Project Manager tool to a shared space, the Project Manager will be prompted for the following information (see Figure 8.24):

- Project Name: A short descriptive name outlining what the Project is supposed to accomplish.
- Project Leader: The person who is responsible for leading the project.
- Start Date: The intended starting date for the project.
- Objective: Longer text detailing the objective of the project.

When you click the OK button, the wizard closes and the Project Manager tool opens with this basic information.

THE PROJECT MANAGER TOOL INTERFACE

After completing the wizard, the Project Manager tool interface should open to a screen that looks like Figure 8.25. At the top of the screen is a list of all the current tasks. These can be indented to indicate whether certain tasks fall under another task as subtasks. Highlighting a task displays its details in the lower half of the screen. In this example, you can see the values entered in the wizard comprise the first task in the list. Because the Meeting Task is indented, you can recognize that it is a subtask under the primary task "Budget for 2002."

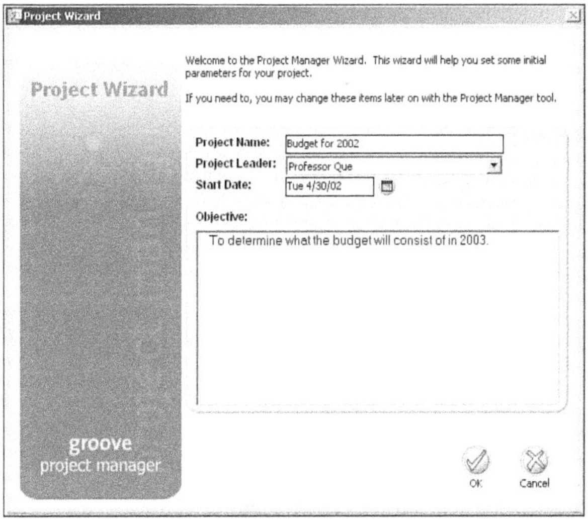

Figure 8.24
When the Project Manager tool is first opened, the Project Leader is prompted for some of the project information.

New task

Task list

Figure 8.25
The primary Project Manager tool interface is broken down into two sections.

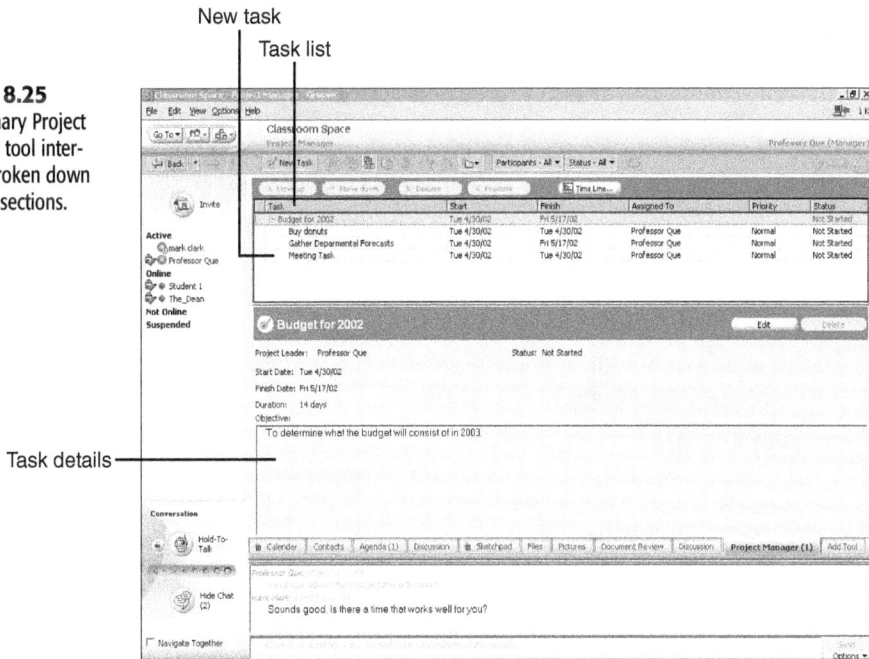

Task details

8

CREATING NEW TASKS

Now that you have the primary project task, "Budget for 2002," you must define all the subtasks required to meet the object. You define a new subtask under the Budget for 2002 task in the following steps:

1. Highlight the Budget for 2002 task and click the New Task button. This should open the window shown in Figure 8.26.

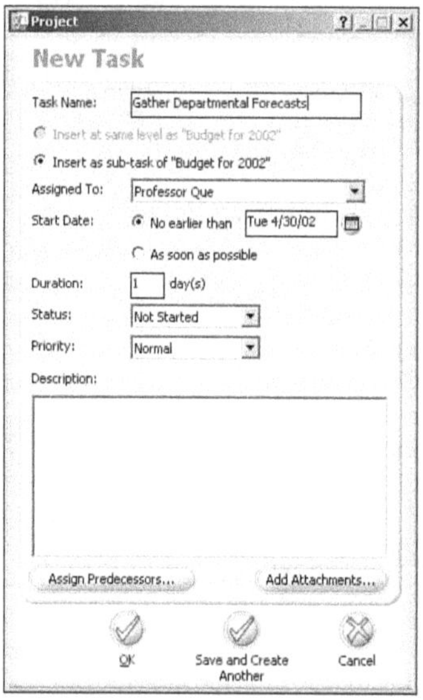

Figure 8.26
Enter the task details in this window.

2. In the Task Name text box, enter a meaningful name for the task to be completed. It is important to name the task carefully so that it is not too long, yet fully describes what the task entails. In this example, we'll call this the "Gather Departmental Forecasts" task.

3. Because tasks are contained within a hierarchy, it is important to specify that this will be a subtask under the Budget for 2002 task. You can specify this by choosing the radio button next to Insert as a sub-task to Budget for 2002. If you choose the Insert at same level as Budget for 2002 option, this creates a new primary task that would not be a subordinate of the Budget for 2002 task.

4. In this step, you must choose who will be assigned the task. Choose a username from the drop-down list. You can only choose names of users who have accepted the invitation to the shared space in which this instance of the Project Manager tool resides.

5. It's important to specify a realistic start and end date for the task. You have the option of either specifying a date by entering it in the No Earlier Than space or selecting As Soon as Possible. The duration for the task must be provided in days in the Duration text box.

6. To determine the status of a particular task, you have the option of setting the status. By default, each task has a status of Not Started. When a task is underway, you will want to set the status to In Progress. When the task is finished, you should indicate this by setting the status to Completed.

7. It's important to prioritize tasks so that other members can understand their relative importance. You can assign one of the following priorities: Critical, Important, Normal, or Low.

8. In the description text area provided, you can enter a lengthy description about the task. If you already have documents that outline the task details, you might want to use the attachments feature described shortly.

9. Often, it's possible that tasks must happen in a certain order. In cases like this, you should click the Assign Predecessors button. This displays the window shown in Figure 8.27. From this screen, you should select all tasks that must be completed prior to beginning the current task. You can choose more than one predecessor task. After clicking the OK button, you'll see that the number of predecessors for a task will be displayed in parentheses next to the Assign Predecessors' label.

CAUTION

> Remember that predecessor settings are used when determining start dates for dependent tasks. Be careful when using these that you don't cause dates to automatically be reset that you didn't want to change.

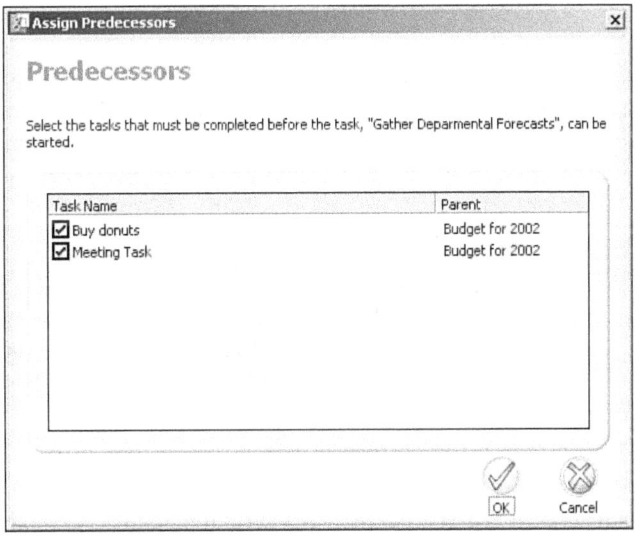

Figure 8.27
Clicking the Assign Predecessors button will enable you to select all the tasks that must happen prior to the current task.

10. By clicking the Add Attachments button, you can add documents to the task. When a document has been added, it shows up in the Attachments window as shown in Figure 8.28. In this example, you've attached a form that will be needed to collect the forecast information.

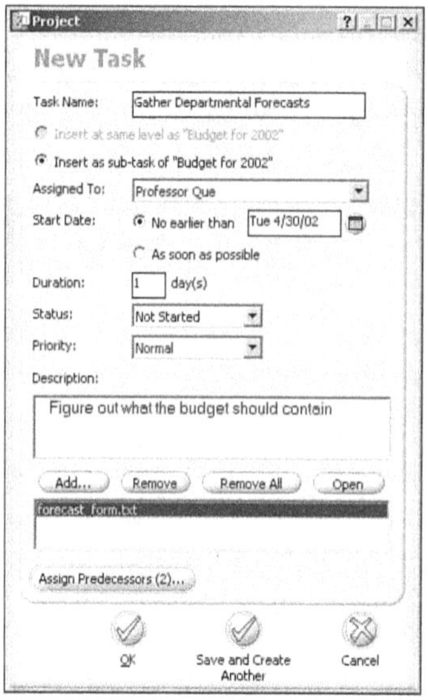

Figure 8.28
After clicking the Add Attachments button, you can attach text documents to a task.

When all the task information has been entered, you can click the OK button to save the task. If you plan on entering several tasks at a time, clicking the Save and Create Another button will save the task and prompt you for the next task's details. To cancel entry of the new task, click the Cancel button.

EDITING TASKS

After a task has been created, it is often necessary to edit the task. By highlighting a task in the Task list and clicking the Edit button, you can edit the task details. This is often used to edit the task status. After you're finished making changes, click the Save button and the task edits will be saved. If you want to abort the changes, click the Cancel button.

NOTE

If the status of a subtask is changed, it is possible that the primary task status will change. The primary task status reflects a cumulative status for the project. For example, assume the primary task Budget for 2002 has a status of Not Started. Changing a subtask status to In Progress will also change the primary Budget for 2002 task to In Progress. Create a project with some subtasks and try changing the statuses of each to see this in action.

MANIPULATING TASKS IN THE LISTING

Depending on where a task resides, there are several functions available for manipulating the tasks. By highlighting a task in the list and using the buttons shown in Figure 8.29, you can perform the following functions:

- Move Up—Move the task up the list. This will not affect the start date of the task, only the visual position in the list.

- Move Down—Move the task down the list. This will not affect the start date of the task, only the visual position in the list.
- Demote—Demote the current task. This will make the task a subtask of the task directly above it in the listing.
- Promote—Promote the current task. This will move a subtask to the level of the task directly above it in the listing.

Figure 8.29
These buttons are used to manipulate tasks within the task listing.

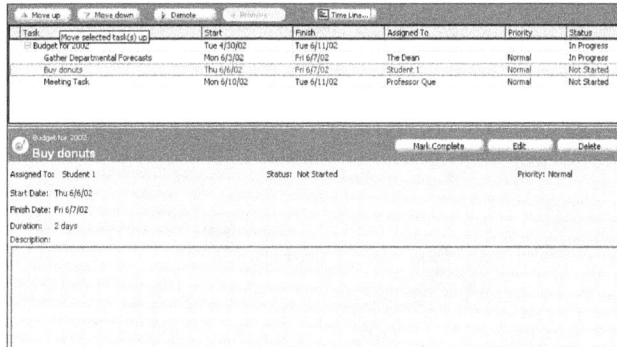

FILTERING WHAT'S DISPLAYED IN THE TASK LISTING

You can easily filter what is shown in the Task Listing. As shown in Figure 8.30, you have an option of filtering by a participant name or by task status. Click the filter button you want to use and select the filter value from the drop-down list. The task listing will immediately change to display only the tasks that match the filter(s) value.

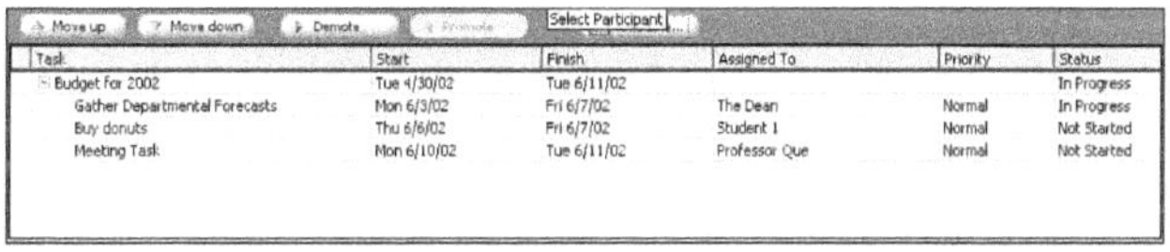

Figure 8.30
The Participant and Status filters can be used to quickly display tasks that match certain criteria.

VIEWING THE TIMELINE

Sometimes it is helpful to graphically see a timeline of all the tasks within a project. This can make it easier to see where there is potential overlap or other issues that may need to be resolved. Clicking the Time Line button will display a graph similar to Figure 8.31.

In the timeline window, you also have the option of changing the display using the following functions:

- View By—Choosing Days or Weeks from this drop-down list will change the time interval displayed in the Time Line. Although it is set to Days by default, for longer projects you may want to change the setting to Weeks.

Figure 8.31
The Time Line is useful because it can graphically show how the tasks relate to one another.

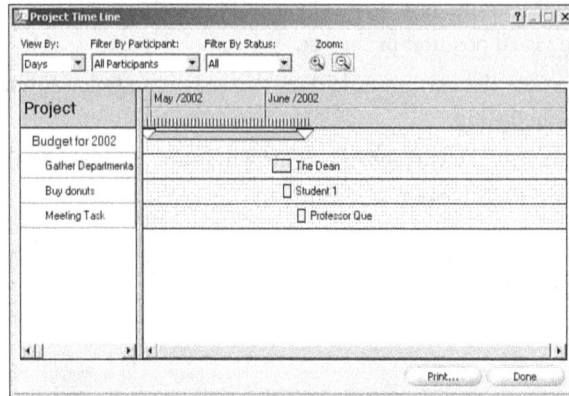

- Filter By Participant—If you want to see only the tasks assigned to one individual, you can choose a username from this drop-down list.

- Filter By Status—This enables you to see only tasks that have a certain status. For instance, you can choose Completed from this drop-down list to see only tasks that have been marked as Completed.

- Zoom—By clicking the + and – buttons, you can change the amount of time that is displayed within the timeline window.

- Print—If you want to print the Time Line, you can click the Print button and choose the printer you want to send it to.

NOTE

> The printing options provided for the Time Line are rather limited. You might want to click the Properties button in the Print pop-up window. Most printers will enable you to set options such as Scale to fit that may make the printed Time Line much more readable. Refer to your printer documentation for more information about configuration settings.

Click the Done button when you are finished viewing the Time Line. Unfortunately, no view settings within the Time Line will be saved and subsequent views of the Time Line will require reconfiguration of any changed settings.

USING THE MEETINGS TOOL

Just about anywhere that you work has its share of meetings to attend. Some are productive and some are not so productive. A productive meeting requires that some objectives be set that are to be accomplished at the meeting. Using the Meetings tool, you can easily define a meeting, the participants, and the planned agenda, keep minutes, and define any of the action items that resulted from the meeting. The following sections describe how to use these features within the Meetings tool.

CREATING A NEW MEETING

After adding the Meetings tool to a shared space, you should see the interface shown in Figure 8.32. Because there are no meetings defined yet, create a new one by clicking the Add Meeting button. This should open the Meeting Wizard window, as shown in Figure 8.33. You can enter the following meeting details in the first screen of the wizard:

- Title—The title of the meeting. Usually, this will include the purpose of the meeting.
- Date—The date the meeting will be held.
- Start Time—The time the meeting will start.
- End Time—The anticipated time the meeting will end.
- Location—Where the meeting will be held.
- Overview—Text describing what the meeting will be about.

Figure 8.32
The Meetings tool will look like this when it is first opened and no meetings have been entered.

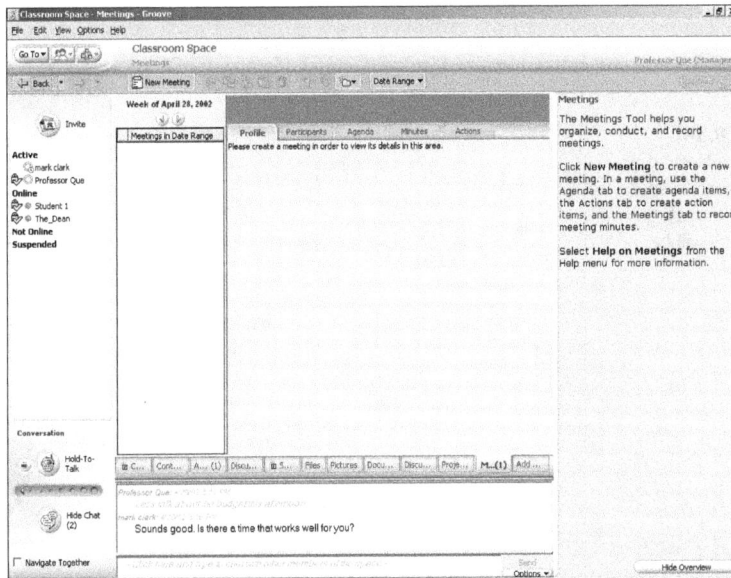

After you have entered the details, you can click the Next button to be taken to the screen that enables you to describe the participants, as shown in Figure 8.34. You should select the chairperson for the meeting and the person who will be taking minutes by choosing them from the drop-down lists provided. You can indicate who the other participants will be by selecting the check box next to their name. A free-form text box is provided at the bottom of the screen for including non-Groove participants. Click the Finish button after you've selected the participants and the meeting will be saved.

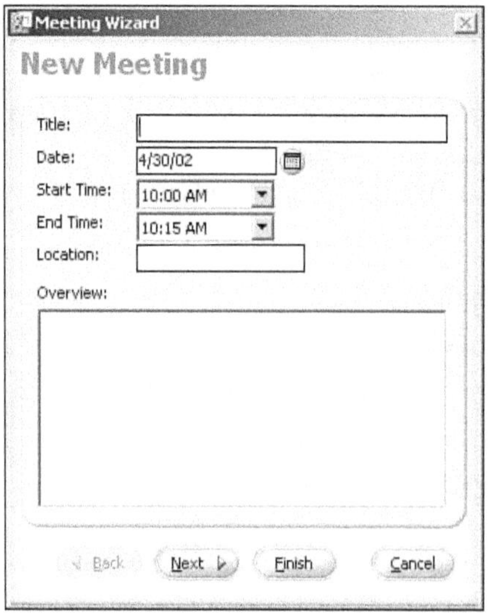

Figure 8.33
After you click the Add Meeting button the Meeting Wizard is launched.

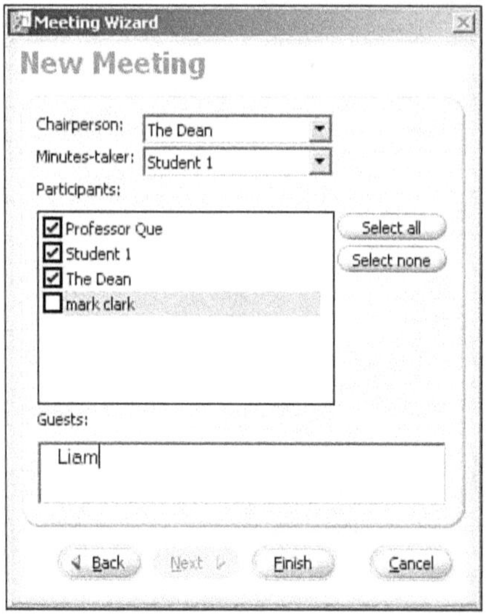

Figure 8.34
Within the Meeting Wizard, you can specify who the meeting participants will be.

NOTE

> The Chairperson and Minutes-taker selections will be checked automatically in the participants listing.

VIEWING A MEETING'S DETAILS

After entering a meeting, you can examine a meeting's details. In the Meetings tool interface, shown in Figure 8.35, all current meetings are shown in a list on the left side of the screen.

Figure 8.35
The Meetings tool shows all current meetings in a list on the left side of the screen with tabs containing all the details on the right side.

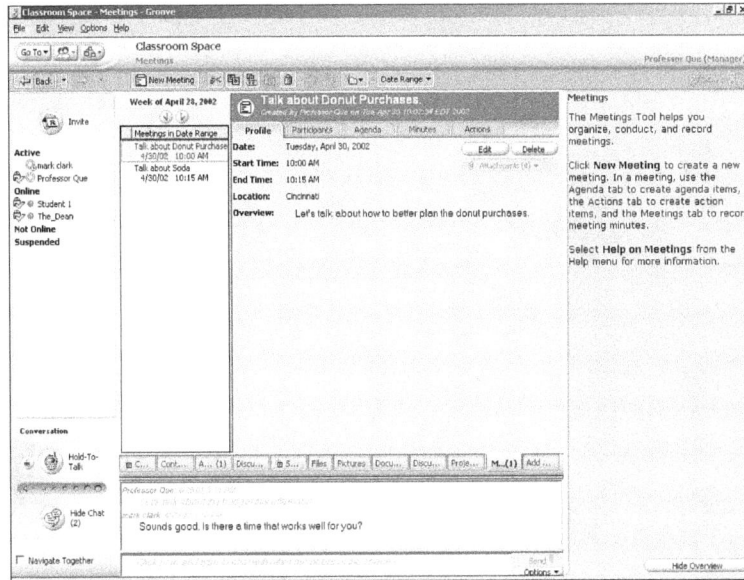

When a meeting is highlighted, you can click one of the following tabs to view the different details attached to the meeting:

- Profile—When the Meeting Wizard is run, this tab is populated with information such as the title of the meeting, the start date, the start and end times, and the objective of the meeting.

- Participants—The users who will be attending the meeting. This is populated when the Meeting Wizard is run and also contains the Chairperson, Notes-taker, and any guests who will be participating.

- Agenda—The detailed agenda for the meeting. The agenda consists of a list of topics, the time it will take, and the person doing the presentation.

- Minutes—The minutes are taken after the meeting has ended. Only the person designated as the Minutes-taker will be able to edit the text contained on this tab.

- Actions—After the meeting, there is usually a list of "action items" that must be performed by different members. Using this tab, actions can be assigned an owner, given a due date, tracked using a status code, and assigned a priority.

You should complete the Profile and Participants tabs after running the Meetings Wizard. You look at how to set the rest of the meeting details in the following sections.

ENTERING AN AGENDA

An agenda describes what will take place at the meeting. To enter a new agenda, highlight the meeting you want to edit and click the Agenda tab, as shown in Figure 8.36. In the

8

figure, you can see we have not entered any agenda items yet. Click the New Agenda Topic to enter a new item as shown in Figure 8.37.

Figure 8.36
Click the Agenda tab to view and enter new agenda items.

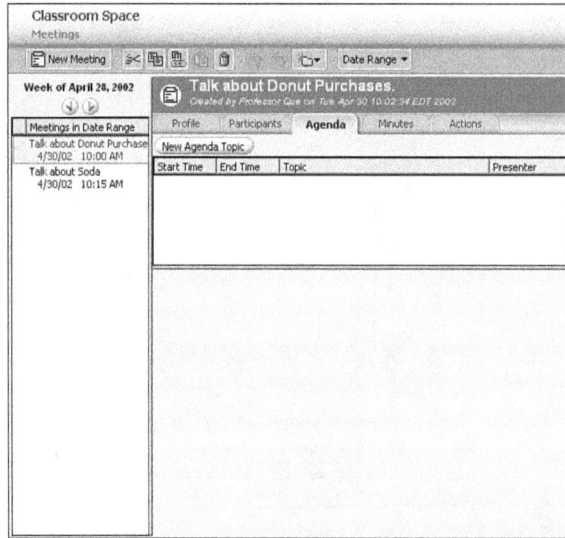

Figure 8.37
Click the New Agenda Topic button to enter details about the new agenda item.

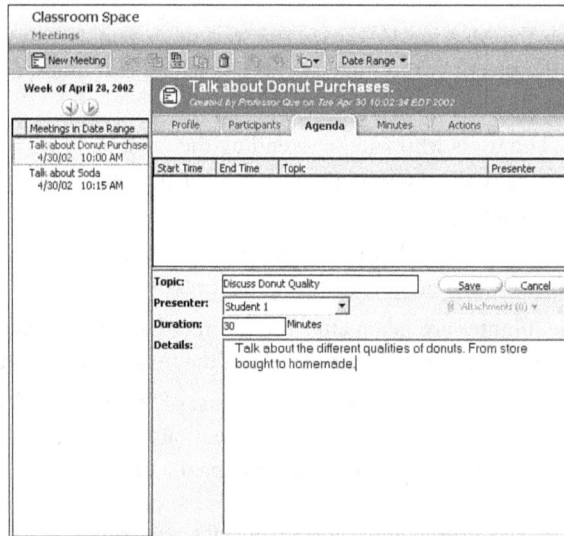

You can enter the following information about each new agenda item:

- Topic—The topic of this agenda item.
- Presenter—The participant who will be responsible for presenting this item. Initially, this will be *unassigned* so you should choose a participant from the drop-down list.

- Duration—How long the presentation will take in minutes.
- Details—The details of this agenda item.
- Attachments—Any necessary attachments can be included by clicking this button. It is common for a presenter to attach an outline of his presentation so participants can follow along.

Click the Save button and the agenda item will be added to the list. Clicking the Cancel button will abort the addition of the item. Once saved, the Move Up/Move Down buttons can be used to arrange items in the agenda topic listing.

Editing the Meeting Minutes

During a meeting, it is common practice to note what has been discussed in a minutes document. Clicking the Minutes tab will allow an appointed Minutes-taker to enter this information. As shown in Figure 8.38, clicking the Edit button allows the Minutes-taker to enter notes in the space provided.

Figure 8.38
The Dean has clicked the Edit button and has begun entering notes for the meeting.

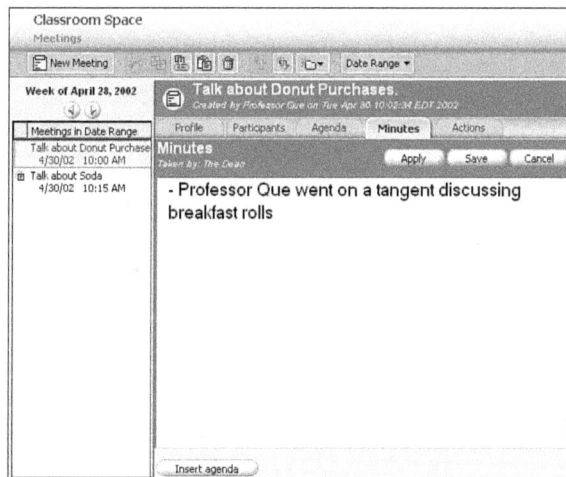

Entering Action Items

Many meetings have action items that must be assigned an owner and address. To access the action items for a meeting, highlight the meeting you want to edit and click the Actions tab as shown in Figure 8.39. You can see that no action items have been entered yet. Click New Action Item to enter a new item as shown in Figure 8.40.

You can enter the following information about each new action item:

- Action item—A short title to explain what the action item is.
- Due—The date by which this action item should be completed.
- Owner—The participant assigned to be the owner of this action item.

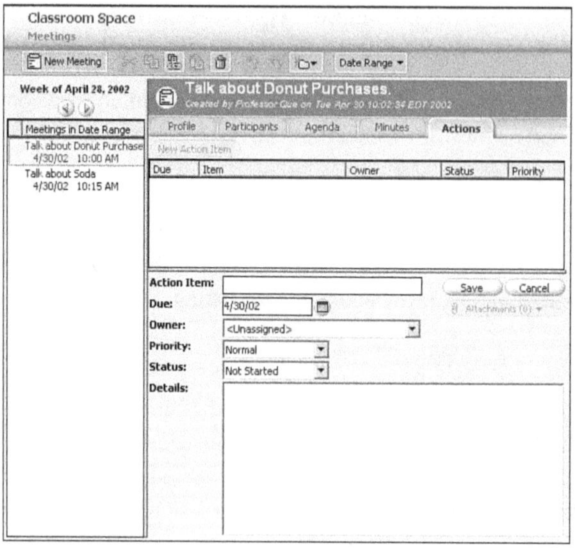

Figure 8.39
Click the Actions tab to view and enter new action items.

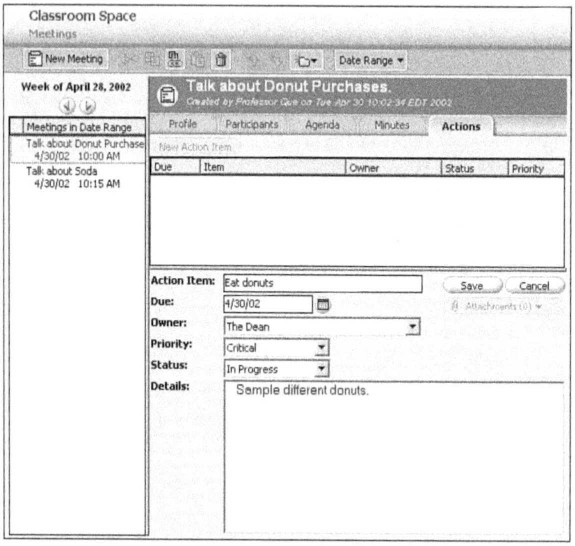

Figure 8.40
Click the New Action Item button to create and assign an owner to a new action item.

- Priority—The priority assigned to this action item. You can choose to assign it a priority of Critical, Important, Normal, or Low from the drop-down list.

- Status—The current status of this action item.

- Details—Details outlining what the action item is about.

Click the Save button and the action item will be added to the list. Clicking the Cancel button will abort the addition of the item.

Filtering the Meetings That Are Displayed

As the number of meetings increases, you may want to filter what is displayed so you don't have to sift through older meetings. As shown in Figure 8.41, you can click the Date Range button and choose to display only meetings from the current day, the last week, the last month, or from the entire last year.

Figure 8.41
By clicking the Date Range button you can control what timeframe of meetings will be displayed within the Meetings tool.

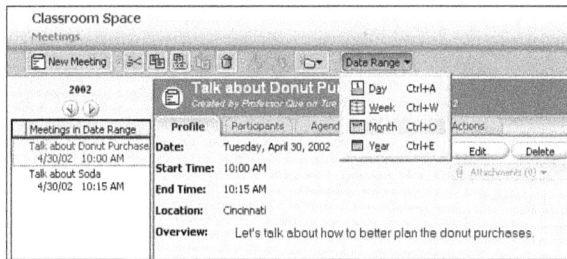

Keyboard Shortcuts

Table 8.7 lists all the keyboard shortcuts that can be used within the Meetings tool.

TABLE 8.7   Meetings Tool Keyboard Shortcuts

Keyboard Shortcut	Action
Ctrl+M	Create a new meeting
Ctrl+A	Display Day date range
Ctrl+W	Display Week date range
Ctrl+O	Display Month date range
Ctrl+E	Display Year date range
Ctrl+L	Copy selected item as a link
Ctrl+F4	Mark the selected meeting read
Ctrl+Shift+F4	Mark all meetings read
F4	Proceed to next unread meeting item
Shift+F4	Proceed to previous unread meeting item
Ctrl+T	Add the current date and time in the text
Del	Delete the currently selected item
F1	Launch Meetings tool help

CHAPTER

9

GROOVE ENTERPRISE NETWORK SERVICES

In this chapter

STARTING TO MANAGE YOUR GROOVE DOMAIN

Although Groove operates in true peer-to-peer fashion without the need for a central server, Groove's developers realized that enterprise applications of their software would require a centralized administration component. Not only do system administrators need a way to manage users, but they also need a way to oversee system usage because internal networks have limited resources available for use. This functionality is currently provided by a Web-based service called Groove Host Services.

Currently offered on the Groove.net site, this interface allows administrators to

- Manage Groove domains
- Set component download and installation policies
- Remove members from your domain
- Run various reports on how Groove is being used within your company
- Report on the Groove Relay Servers

NOTE

> Although currently hosted externally by Groove, the same services on the hosted site are offered for deployment on an organization's own servers or for hosting by other third parties. Contact Groove Networks for more information on the availability of this product.

Like network domains, a Groove domain is a group of users and devices that use Groove. You may have a single domain or several, depending on the particular needs of your company and the purchase agreement with Groove. Members of a domain have access to licenses granted to a domain and operate within the bounds of any policies that have been defined by the administrator.

ACCESSING GROOVE'S HOSTED SERVICES

Groove's Hosted Services is part of the secure My Groove Services section of the Groove Web site. To access this, first click on the My Account link at the top of the www.groove.net page as shown in Figure 9.1.

LOGGING IN

Because this is a secure area of the site you need to log into your account as shown in Figure 9.2. After purchasing licenses from Groove, you should have received a sign-on and password from Groove services for your account.

NOTE

> If you are having trouble logging in, contact your Groove sales representative to verify your account name and password.

My Account

Figure 9.1
Click on My Account to access the Log In page.

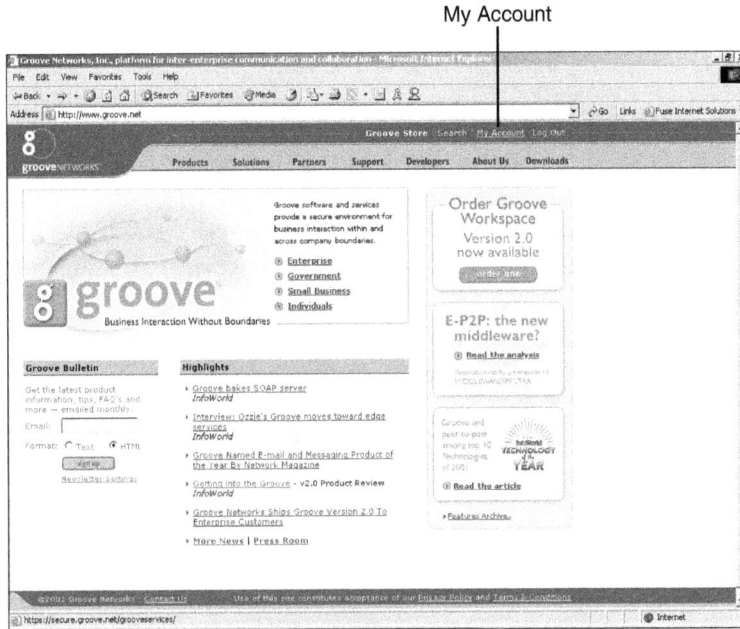

Figure 9.2
You must log into Groove's Hosted Services to access the services provided.

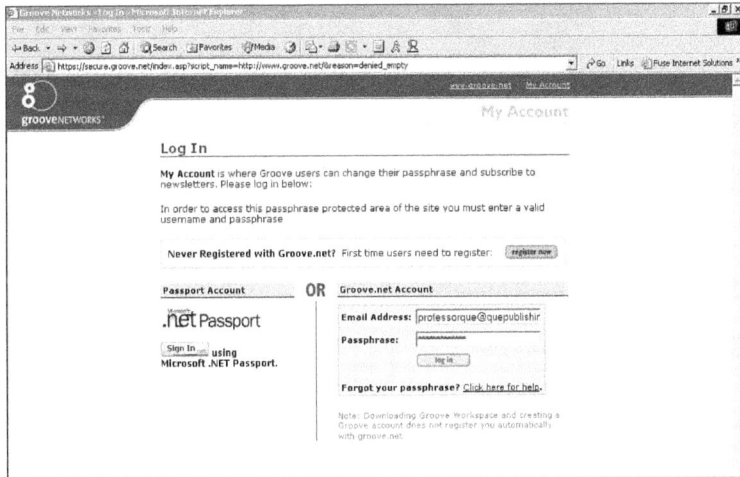

NOTE

At the time of writing, you could also sign in using your Microsoft .NET account. Contact Groove Networks for more information on whether this can be implemented for your account.

9

CHOOSING A DOMAIN

After successfully logging in, you will be taken back to the Groove Networks home page. You must click on the My Account link at the top of the screen to take you to the My Account area. Click on the Go to Hosted Services link to enter the Hosted Services area as shown in Figure 9.3. The current domains managed by your account should be listed on the left in the Domain Administration menu as shown in Figure 9.4. At this time, domains are created by Groove during initial account creation. In this example, the administrator controls the Bill Pitzer domain. Clicking one of the domain hyperlinks will take you to the management tasks menu for that domain as shown in Figure 9.5.

Figure 9.3
Click the Go to Hosted Services link to enter the Hosted Services area.

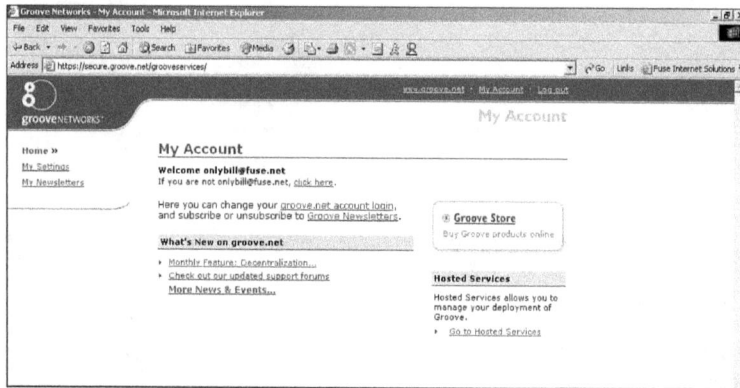

Figure 9.4
All domains you currently manage will be listed on the left side of the screen in the Domain Administration menu.

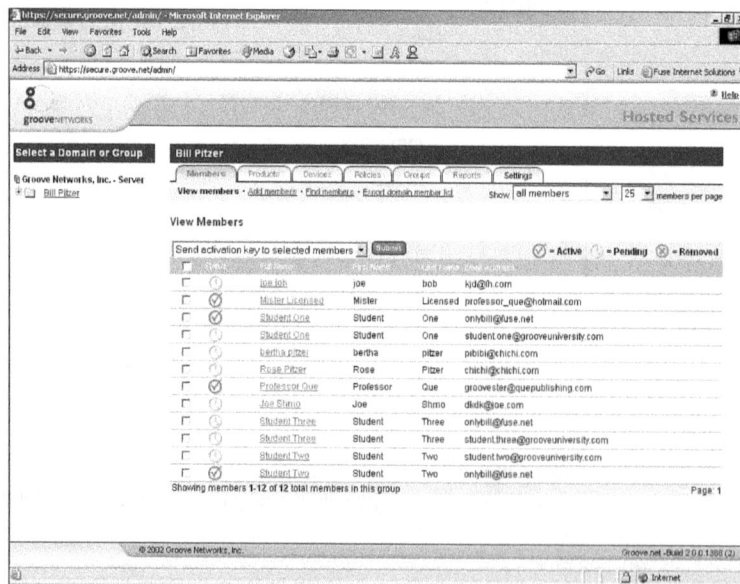

DOMAIN MANAGEMENT TASKS

After a domain has been selected on the left side of the screen, you can access different domain management functions via the tabs at the top of the page. The different areas include

- Members: View and maintain members within the domain.
- Products: Manage the products available within the domain.
- Devices: Manage individual devices within the domain.
- Groups: Create groups that enable you to segment users for easier administration.
- Reports: Run a variety of reports on domain activity.

VIEWING MEMBERS IN THE DOMAIN

By default, clicking the Members tab takes you to the View Members screen, as shown in Figure 9.5. You can filter what members are shown by choosing a value from the drop-down list shown in Figure 9.6.

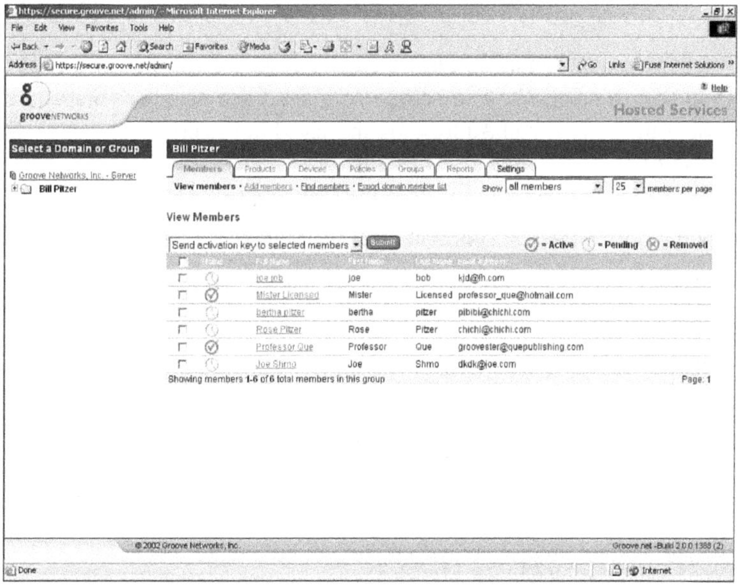

Figure 9.5
The View Members screen enables you to see all the members of the currently selected domain.

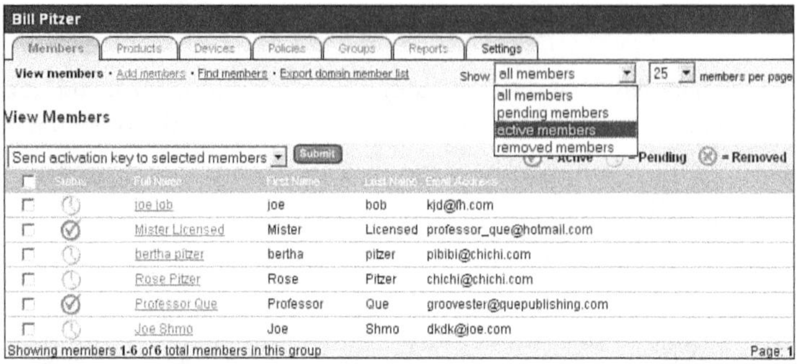

Figure 9.6
Use the Show drop-down list to view only particular sets of members.

9

You can display members with these specific statuses:

- All Members: Displays all members, even those who have been removed.
- Pending: Displays members for whom an identity has been issued to the user but not injected.
- Active: Displays users who have successfully injected the license file.
- Removed: Displays members who have been removed from the domain.

In addition, you can choose how many members display on each page by choosing a value from the Members Per Page drop-down list. Each member's Status, Full Name, First Name, Last Name, and Email Address are displayed in the list. For a list of the status icons see Table 9.1.

TABLE 9.1   STATUS ICONS FOR DOMAIN MEMBERS

	Identity has been created, but not injected.
	User is an active member.
	User has been removed.

ADDING MEMBERS TO THE DOMAIN

By clicking the Add Members link, you can add new members to the domain. As shown in Figure 9.7, you have the option to add a single member or a group of members at once.

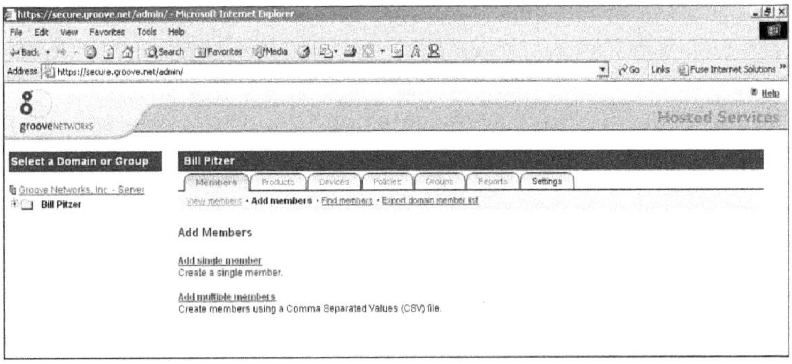

Figure 9.7
You can choose whether to add a single member or a batch of members to your domain at this screen.

ADDING A SINGLE MEMBER

If you only need to add a single member to the domain, proceed with the following steps:

1. Click the Add Single Member link shown in Figure 9.7.
2. Complete the Groove identity information form shown in Figure 9.8 with the following required information:
   - Full Name: The name of the user. This is an important field because this will become the original identity that will be attached to the account.
   - Email Address: A valid email address for the user.

Click the Add Members button when you are finished. This will take you back to the View Members screen where the new name, Student One, has been added with a status of Pending.

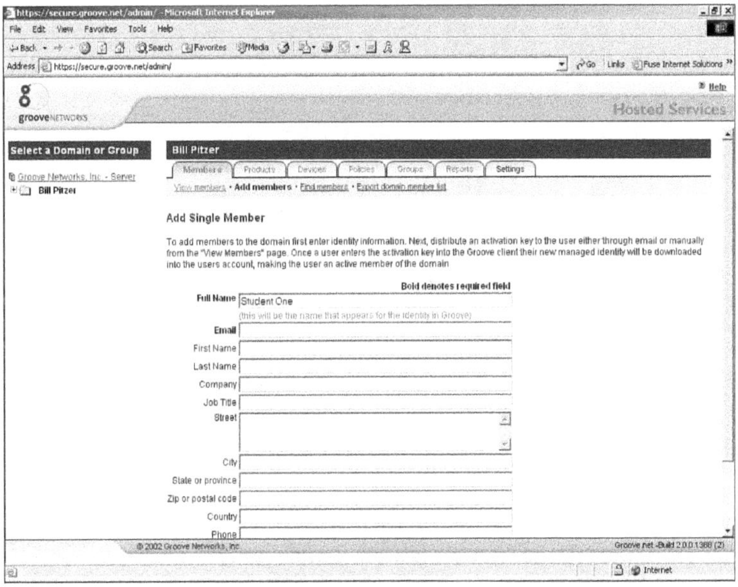

Figure 9.8
When adding new members you can add additional details about the individual on this screen.

Now that the new member has been added to the domain, you need to send the activation key to the email address specified. To do this, check the box next to the new member in the list, as shown in Figure 9.9. Choose Send Activation Key to Selected Members in the drop-down list box and click the Submit button. This should open the email screen shown in Figure 9.10.

> **NOTE**
>
> Although we are only sending an activation key to a single member in this example, remember that it is possible to check several members and send the activation keys all at once.

- Email From: A return email address for the Groove administrator.
- Email Subject: The subject for the email. This should be completed automatically.
- Email Body: The body of the email. This should already be complete with instructions for injecting the new Groove account.

Figure 9.9
Select the check box next to the newly added member and click the Submit button to open the email activation key form.

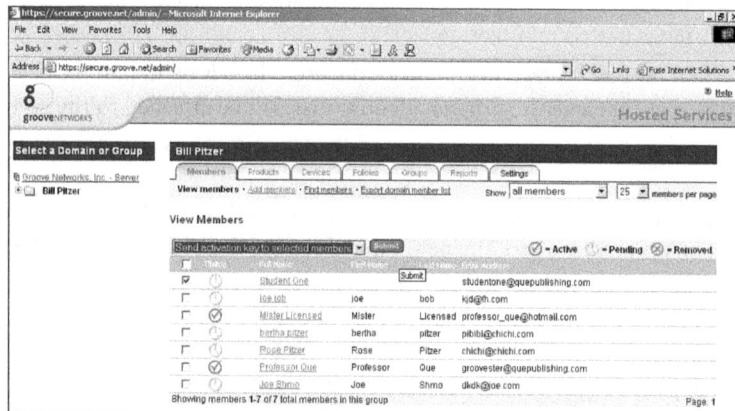

> **NOTE**
>
> If a user's email is invalid when sending the activation key to the new member, an email stating that the email delivery was unsuccessful will be forwarded to the address specified in the Email From field.

ADDING MULTIPLE MEMBERS

If you know you will be adding several new members at once, Groove Network Services provides a batch import feature to expedite the process.

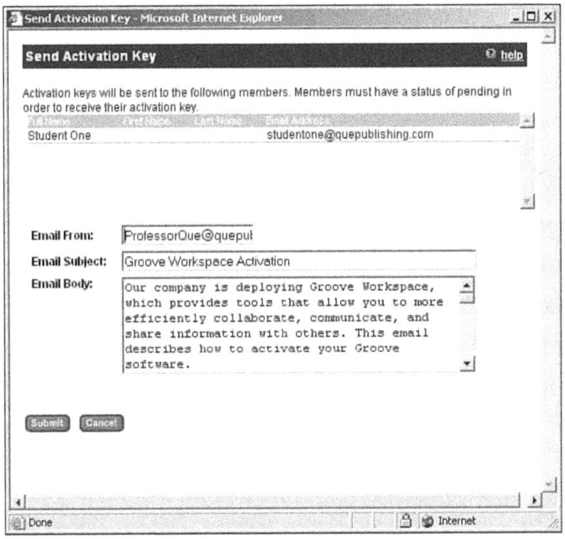

Figure 9.10
Fill in the fields and click the Submit button to send an activation key to the new member of the domain.

Create a comma-separated file with seven columns. You can use Notepad, which comes with Microsoft Windows, or any editor of your choice. The columns in order should be:

- Full Name
- First Name
- Last Name
- Email Address
- Job Title
- Company Name
- Street
- City
- State
- Postal Code
- Country
- Phone Number
- Fax Number
- Cell Number

For example, if you want to add the following three students to the domain:

User #1

> Full Name: Student One
>
> First Name: Student
>
> Last Name: One
>
> Email Address: student.one@grooveuniversity.com
>
> Title: Full Time Student
>
> Company Name: ABC Corporation
>
> Street: 123 Main Street
>
> City: Cincinnati
>
> State: OH
>
> Postal Code: 45238
>
> Country: USA
>
> Phone Number: 513-555-5551
>
> Fax Number: 513-555-5551
>
> Cell Number: 513-555-5551

User #2

> Full Name: Student Two
>
> First Name: Student
>
> Last Name: Two
>
> Email Address: student.two@grooveuniversity.com
>
> Title: Full Time Student
>
> Company Name: ABC Corporation
>
> Street: 123 Main Street
>
> City: Cincinnati
>
> State: OH
>
> Postal Code: 45238
>
> Country: USA
>
> Phone Number: 513-555-5552
>
> Fax Number: 513-555-5552
>
> Cell Number: 513-555-5552

User #3

        Full Name: Student Three

        First Name: Student

        Last Name: Three

        Email Address: `student.three@grooveuniversity.com`

        Title: Full Time Student

        Company Name: ABC Corporation

        Street: 123 Main Street

        City: Cincinnati

        State: OH

        Postal Code: 45238

        Country: USA

        Phone Number: 513-555-5553

        Fax Number: 513-555-5553

        Cell Number: 513-555-5553

The comma-separated file for these three users would look like this:

```
BatchUsers.csv
Student One,Student,One,student.one@grooveuniversity.com,Full Time Student,
XYZ Corporation,123 Main Street, Cincinnati, OH, 45238, USA, 513-555-5551,
513-555-5551,513-555-5551
Student Two,Student,Two,student.two@grooveuniversity.com,Full Time Student,
XYZ Corporation,123 Main Street, Cincinnati, OH, 45238, USA, 513-555-5552,
513-555-5552,513-555-5552
Student Three,Student,Three,student.three@grooveuniversity.com,
Full Time Student,XYZ Corporation,123 Main Street, Cincinnati, OH, 45238,
 USA, 513-555-5553,513-555-5553,513-555-5553
```

NOTE

> Make sure you save the file as a plain text, or `.txt`, file. Different formats such as rich text format (`.rtf`) will not work properly because of the formatting within them.

Click the Add Multiple Members link shown in Figure 9.7. You should now be looking at the screen shown in Figure 9.11. Click the Browse button to locate the CSV file you created.

If some members will be receiving an email with the license file attached, complete the following fields:

- Email From: A return email address for the Groove administrator.
- Email Subject: The subject for the email. This should be completed automatically.
- Email Body: The body of the email. This should already be complete with instructions for injecting the new Groove account.

Figure 9.11
By specifying a batch upload file you can easily add multiple members at a time.

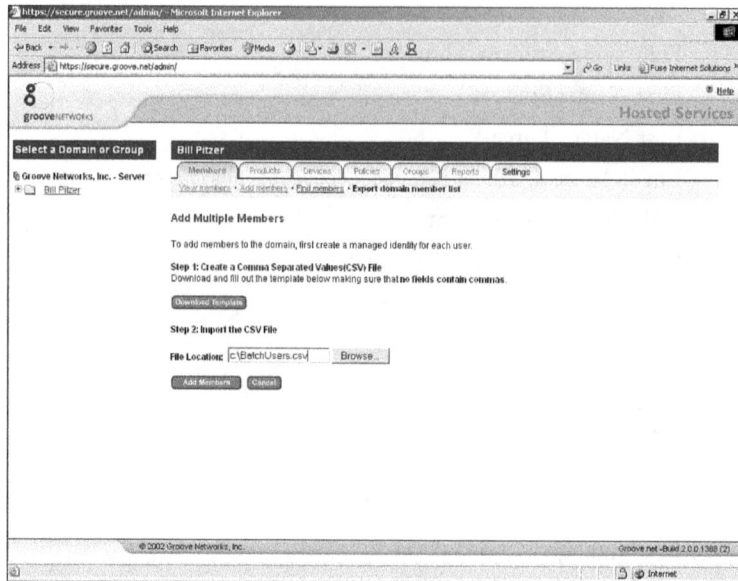

Click the Preview button to double-check the CSV format and to visually preview the members that will be added. If the .CSV file is formatted correctly, you will see the members added with a status of Pending, as shown in Figure 9.12.

Figure 9.12
After uploading the batch file, you can see that the new members have been added and have a status of Pending.

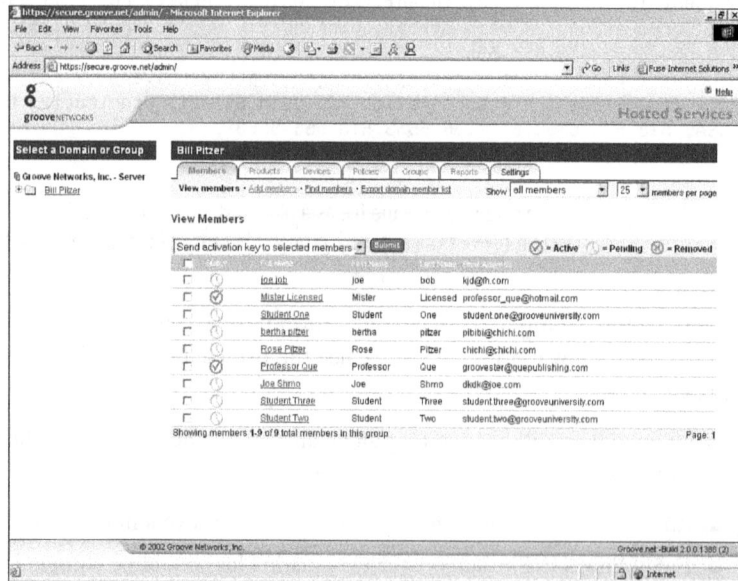

CAUTION

> If you get an error page, there is a problem with the CSV file format. The most common mistakes are as follows:

- Incorrect number of fields
- Putting titles in the first record (these should not be included)
- Spaces before field values
- Other invalid characters in the file (like commas or escape characters)

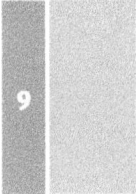

FINDING MEMBERS IN THE DOMAIN

When the number of users within a domain grows, finding an individual member becomes more difficult. Clicking the Find Members link will take you to the search screen shown in Figure 9.13. Enter any part of a name or email address and click the Search button to return the results of the search.

Figure 9.13
Search for members within a domain by entering a name or email address in the text box and clicking the Search button.

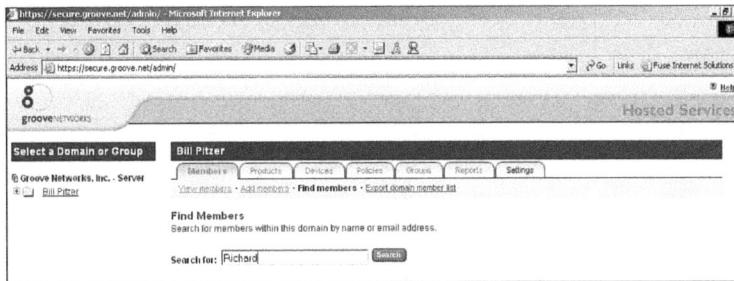

EXPORTING A LIST OF DOMAIN MEMBERS

You can export a comma-separated (.CSV) file of all domain members. Click the Export domain member list link and you will be prompted for where to save the file. Clicking the Save button will save it to disk. As you can see in the example shown in Figure 9.14, this list is useful because it not only contains member information but the activation key used for each member. As an administrator, this activation key can be used to manually install and activate user installations of Groove Workspace.

Figure 9.14
When the domain member list is exported, it will create a file like this example.

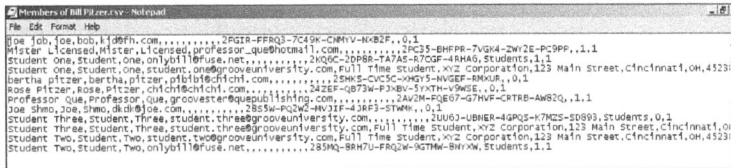

DELETING A MEMBER

To delete a member, first check the box to the left of the Full Name in the list. Then choose Remove Selected Members from the drop-down list at the top of the screen as shown in Figure 9.15. Click the Submit button and a confirmation window will appear as shown in Figure 9.16. Click the Submit button to perform the deletion or Cancel to keep the member.

Figure 9.15
Choose Remove Selected Members from the drop-down list at the top of the screen to remove a member of the domain.

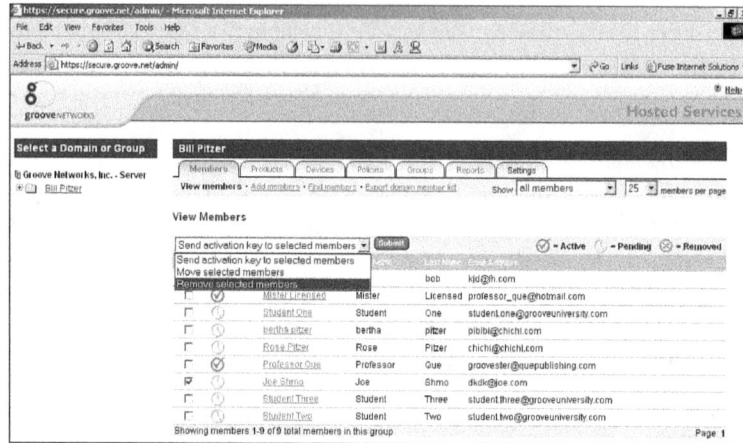

Figure 9.16
You must confirm the deletion of a member of domain by clicking the Submit button on this confirmation window.

MANAGING PRODUCT PACKAGES

Different product packages are offered with Groove depending on your license agreement. By clicking the Products tab at the top of the screen, you can see all the product packages available to the members in your domain, as shown in Figure 9.17. Each package name will be displayed along with the date it was issued. A green check mark icon indicates a package that is active while a red X icon indicates that it has been revoked by the administrator of the domain.

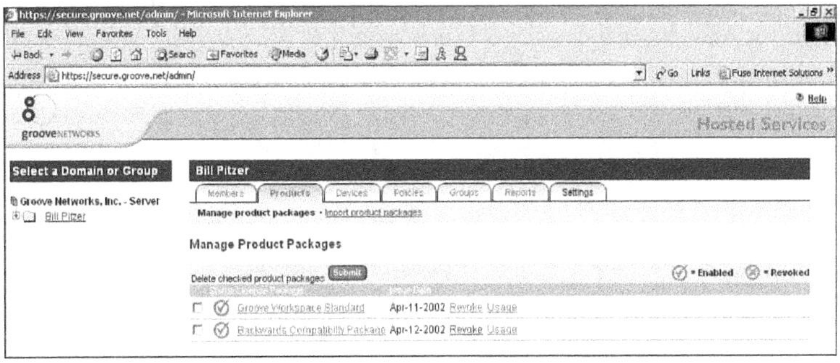

Figure 9.17
Clicking the Products tab will show all the product packages available for members within your domain.

REVOKING A PRODUCT PACKAGE FOR ALL DOMAIN MEMBERS

If for some reason a product package must be revoked due to changes in licensing or other reasons, you can revoke the product package through this interface. To revoke a package, you only need to click the Revoke link next to the product package. In Figure 9.18, you can see that the Groove Workspace Standard package has been revoked as indicated by the X icon in the status column. You can enable a revoked package by clicking the Enable link that now appears to the right of the package name.

Figure 9.18
In this example the Groove Workspace Standard package has been revoked as indicated by the status icon.

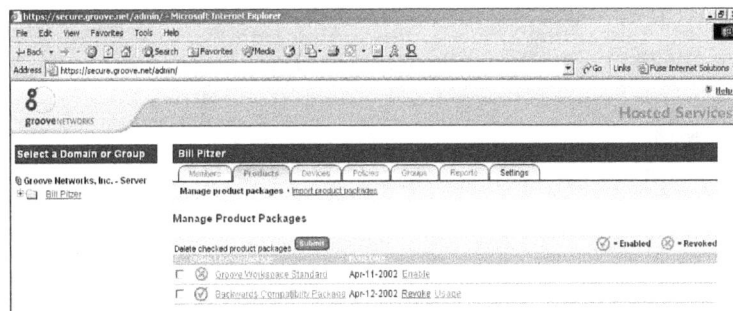

REVOKING A PRODUCT PACKAGE FOR SPECIFIC DOMAIN MEMBERS

In addition to revoking a product package for all members of a domain, it is also possible to revoke the package from specific members. Click the Usage link next to a package on the main product package page. This will open the page shown in Figure 9.19, which lists all domain members using that product package. Check the members from whom you want to revoke the package, choose Revoke Package from Selected Users, as shown in Figure 9.20, and click the Submit button. You will be asked to confirm the revocation and this user will now show a status of revoked, as indicated by the red X icon shown in Figure 9.21. Reinstating a package involves exactly the same process except that you should choose Reinstate Package to Selected Users from the drop-down list before clicking the Submit button.

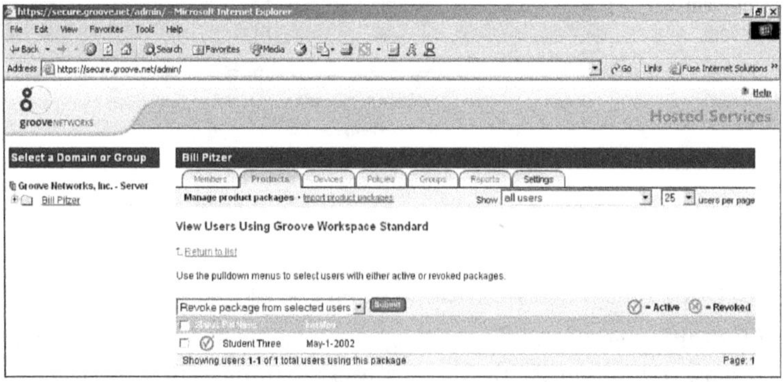

Figure 9.19
After clicking the Usage button, this screen is displayed showing all members using the product package.

Figure 9.20
Choose Revoke Package from Selected Users in the drop-down list at the top of the screen and click the Submit button to revoke the product package from the checked member(s).

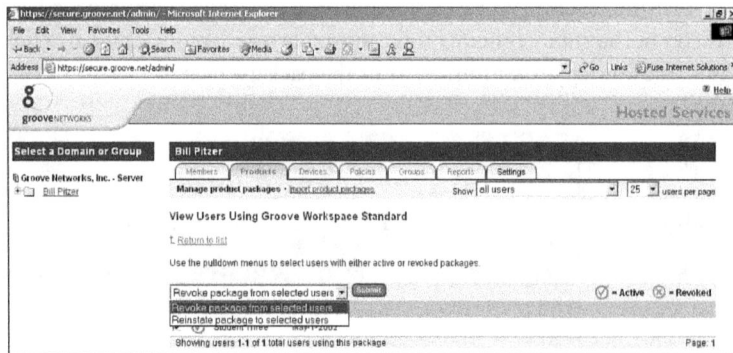

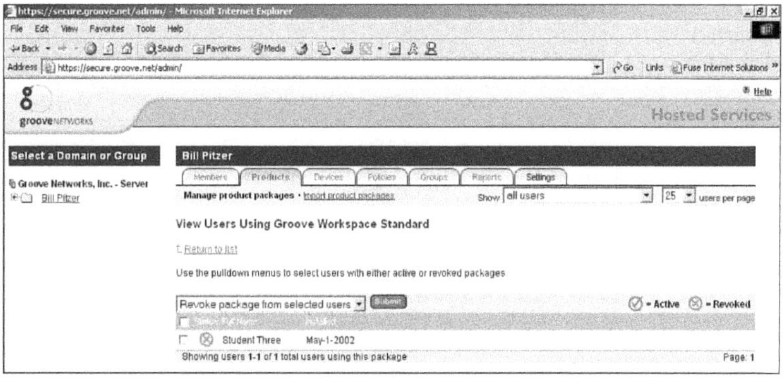

Figure 9.21
After revoking a product package from a specific member a red X icon will be displayed in the status column.

TIP

Like other screens, there is filtering available should the list of users become extremely large. You can filter on status by choosing a value from the drop-down list next to the Show Label on the Product Package usage screen. In addition, you can control how many users display per page by choosing a value in the Users Per Page drop-down list provided.

TIP

Users will be alerted with a notification when a product package is removed from their accounts. You should alert members to the changes before you make them; otherwise, you might find yourself answering a lot of support calls over the notification message displayed.

AN ALTERNATIVE METHOD TO ADD PRODUCT PACKAGES TO A SPECIFIC ACCOUNT

There is an alternative means to add a product package to a member's account using the Activate Product feature provided within the Groove Workspace transceiver. From the Manage Product Packages screen shown in Figure 9.22, click the Product Package link. In this example, we'll click the Groove Workspace Standard package, which will display the pop-up window shown in Figure 9.23. In the figure, along with details about the product package usage, you will be provided with an Activation Key and Activation Server address. After sending this information to a domain member, have him choose Help, Activate Product from the main menu within the Groove transceiver. This will open the Activate Product screen shown in Figure 9.24. Have the member enter the Activation Key and server address in the spaces provided. When he clicks the Next button, the product package will be added to his account.

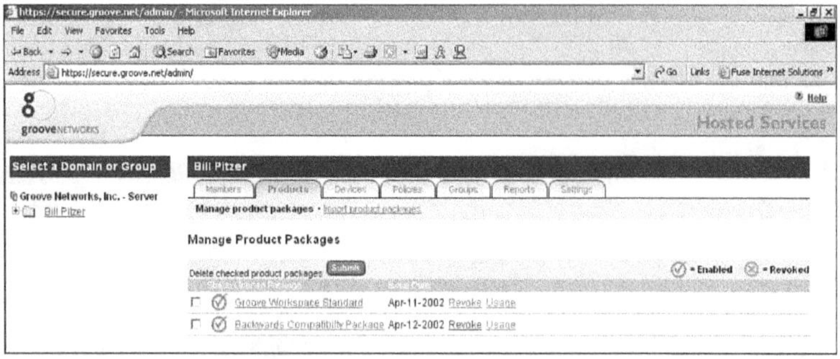

Figure 9.22
Clicking a product package link will take you to the package details screen.

Figure 9.23
This product package details screen provides an activation key and activation server address that will be used to manually add a package to a member's account.

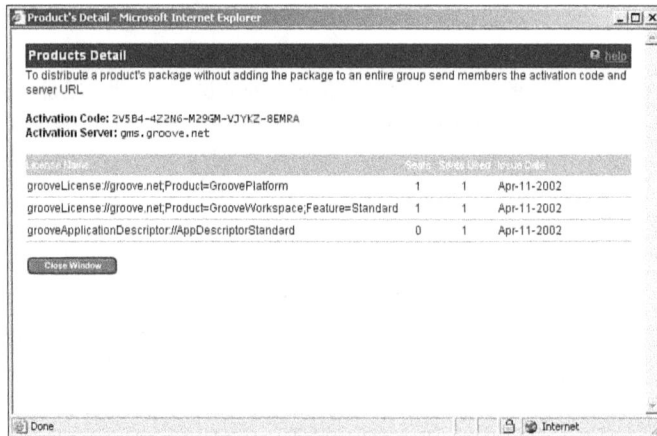

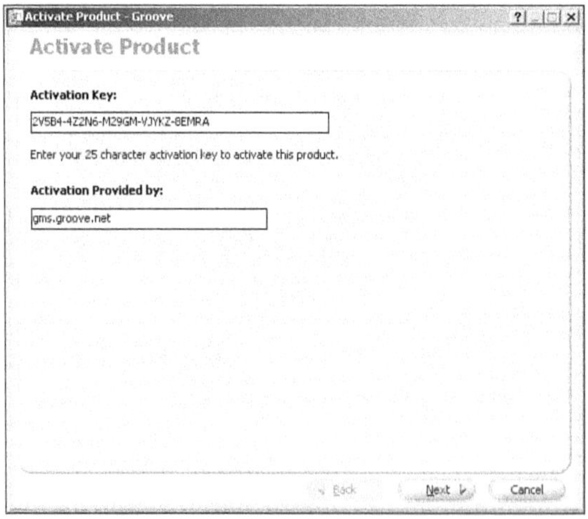

Figure 9.24
From the Activate Product screen, a domain member can specify an activation key used to install a specific product package into their account.

IMPORTING ADDITIONAL PRODUCT PACKAGES

It is possible you may need to add additional packages offered within your domain. By clicking the Import Product Packages link shown in Figure 9.25 you will be taken to the import screen shown in Figure 9.26. Click the Browse button to locate the product package file provided to you. After you've located the file, click the Open button to return to the import screen. Click the Submit button and the product package will be imported and available to all members of the domain.

Figure 9.25
Click the Import product packages link to find and import new product packages for members of your domain.

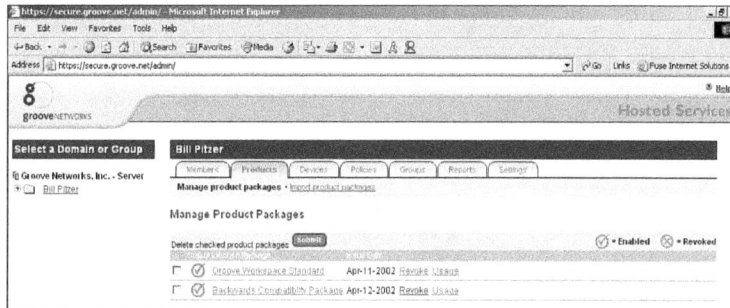

Figure 9.26
Clicking the Import Product Packages link takes you to this screen where you specify the file to be imported.

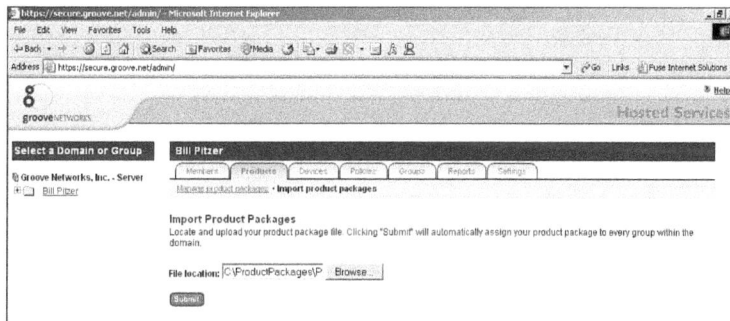

DELETING PRODUCT PACKAGES

Generally, you will manage members in your domain by revoking and reinstating product packages. Rarely, you may need to completely remove a product package from your domain. From the main product package maintenance screen shown in Figure 9.24, click the Submit button to delete the package. In the pop-up confirmation window, click the Submit button to perform the deletion or Cancel to abort the task.

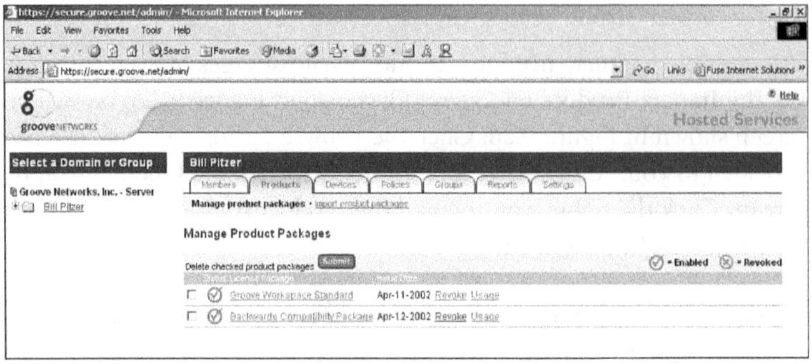

Figure 9.27
Click the Submit button from this screen to completely remove a product package from a domain.

MANAGING DEVICES WITHIN A DOMAIN

Up to this point, we've discussed how to manage individual users. However, there is also a means for managing individual devices that have Groove Workspace installed. By managing devices, you can set policies that apply to every Groove account and identity on a specific device. This is in contrast to policies that apply to specific identities within a particular managed domain. In this section, we'll discuss how to add new devices to a domain. Setting policies will be defined in the following section.

VIEWING DEVICES WITHIN A DOMAIN

Clicking the Devices tab at the top of the Hosted Services screen will display all devices within the domain or group, as shown in Figure 9.28. The device name and date installed are displayed for each device. You can change the number of devices displayed per page by choosing a value in the devices per page setting in the upper-left corner of the screen.

ADDING A DEVICE TO THE DOMAIN

To manage a specific device, click the Add Device link shown in Figure 9.28. This will take you to the Add Device screen shown in Figure 9.29. The actual addition of a managed device involves changing Registry key settings on the target machine. You should right-click the Download the Registry Key (.reg) link as shown in the figure and save it to disk. This file should be executed on the device that you intend to manage. After the Registry changes are made, the device should now show up in the managed devices listing indicating it is now part of the managed domain.

Figure 9.28
Clicking the Devices tab will show all managed devices within the domain.

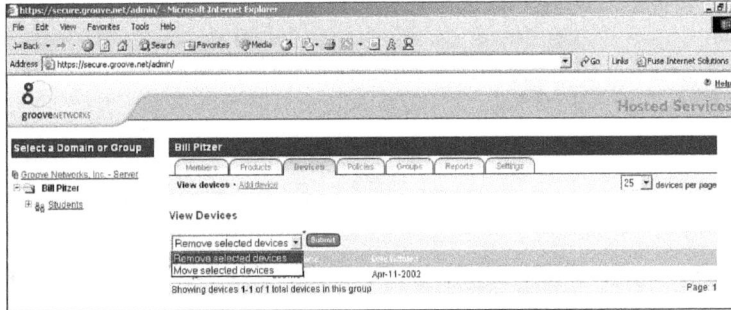

Figure 9.29
From the Add Device screen, you can download the Registry file needed to add a new managed device.

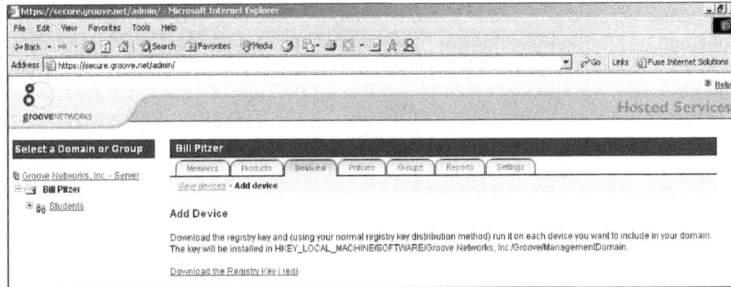

NOTE

After the Registry key has been inserted, it will not be reflected on the device listing until Groove has been started on that device.

REMOVING DEVICES FROM THE DOMAIN

To remove a device from the domain, check the device (or devices if you want to remove more than one) to be removed. After the device is checked, select Remove Selected Devices from the drop-down list box on the View Devices screen, as shown in Figure 9.30. Click Submit on the confirmation pop-up and it will be removed from the list of managed devices.

MOVING DEVICES

Devices can be moved between domains and groups. To move device(s) check the devices that will be moved. When the devices are checked, select Move Selected Devices and click the Submit button as shown in Figure 9.31.

Figure 9.30
Selecting Remove
Selected Devices
enables you to
remove devices from
a domain.

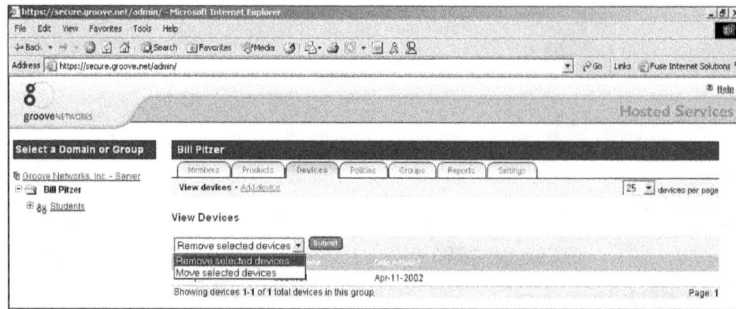

Figure 9.31
Selecting Move
Selected Devices
enables you to move
devices to another
domain or group.

MANAGING DOMAIN POLICIES

Within a managed domain, you can set policies at an identity and a device level. You can access the policy management administration screen by clicking the Policies tab at the top of the screen, as shown in Figure 9.32.

Figure 9.32
Clicking the Policies
tab will take you to
the policy manage-
ment area.

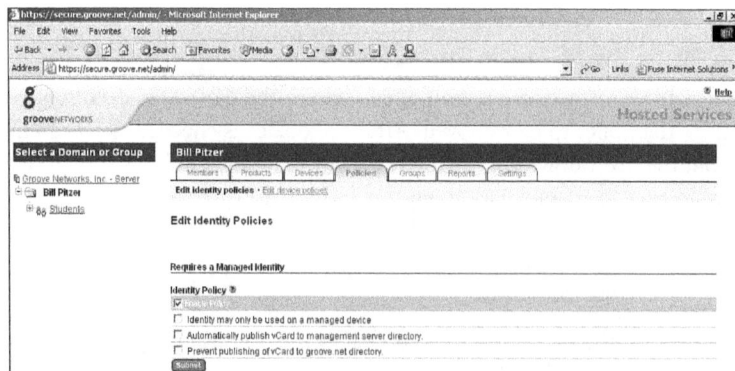

At an identity level, you can set the following policies:

- Specify whether an identity can only be used on a managed device
- Determine whether each identity's vCard is automatically published to a management server directory
- Prevent or allow the publishing of vCards to the public groove.net directory

Devices have several policies that can be set, including the following:

- Define passphrase restrictions such as mandatory length and expiration time period
- Enforce various account policies such as the creation of multiple accounts
- Define installation policies for component upgrades

Setting Identity Policies

After clicking the Policies tab, you are automatically taken to the area where you can modify identity policies as shown in Figure 9.33. Policies set here will apply to all managed identities within the current domain.

Figure 9.33
You have the option of enabling or disabling identity policies for the domain.

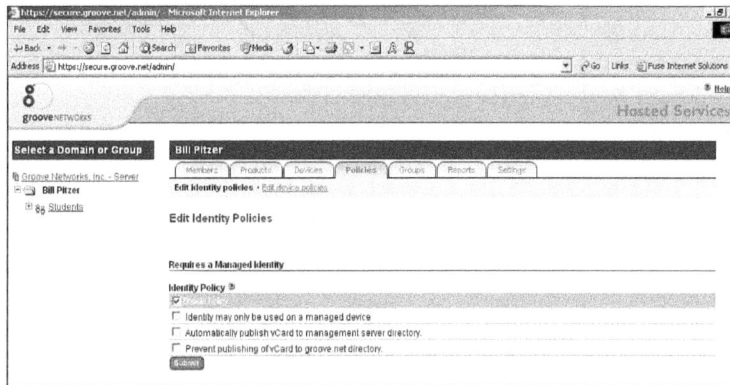

Enabling Identity Policies

The identity policies must be enabled by selecting the check box shown in Figure 9.33. If this box is not checked, the policies will not be enforced for this domain. The policies are as follows:

- Identity may only be used on a managed device: In order for an identity to be used, it must have been added to the listing of managed devices. This will prevent the identity from being created on any other devices not listed, thus eliminating the possibility of "spoofing" by other domain members.

- Automatically publish vCard to management server directory: Publishes users' vCards to management server directory automatically.

- Prevent publishing of vCard to groove.net directory: This prevents users from publishing their vCard information to the groove.net public directory.

SETTING DEVICE POLICIES

For all managed devices that were added using the instructions in the "Adding a Device to the Domain" section earlier in this chapter, it is possible to define a variety of policy rules. Clicking on the Edit Device Policies link will take you to the Edit Device Policies screen shown in Figure 9.34. The policies set here will apply to all devices that have been added to the domain regardless of the identities contained on the device. Device and identity policies can be used in conjunction with one another.

Figure 9.34
After clicking the Edit Device Policies link you will be taken to this screen.

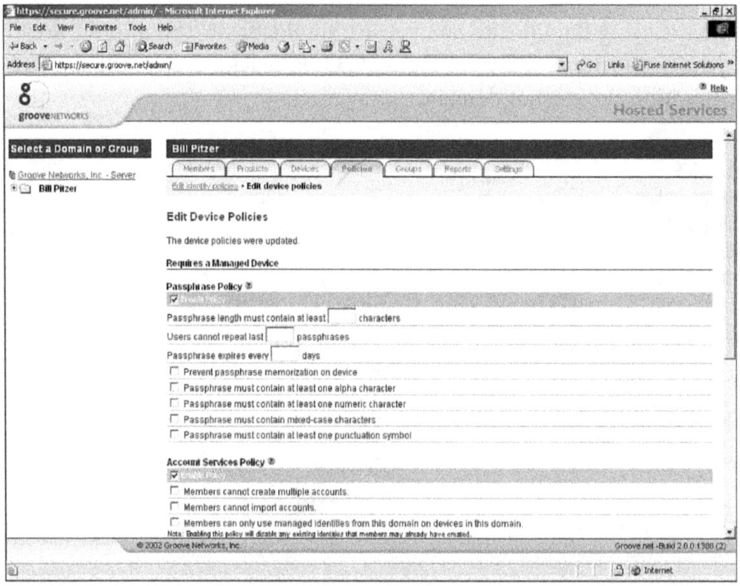

The device policies are grouped into four sections: Passphrase policy, Account Services policy, Data Recovery policy, and Install policy. Each group has an Enable Policy check box that must be selected to enable the policies set in that group. These check boxes are shown in Figure 9.35.

Figure 9.35
Each group of policy items must be enabled by selecting the appropriate check box.

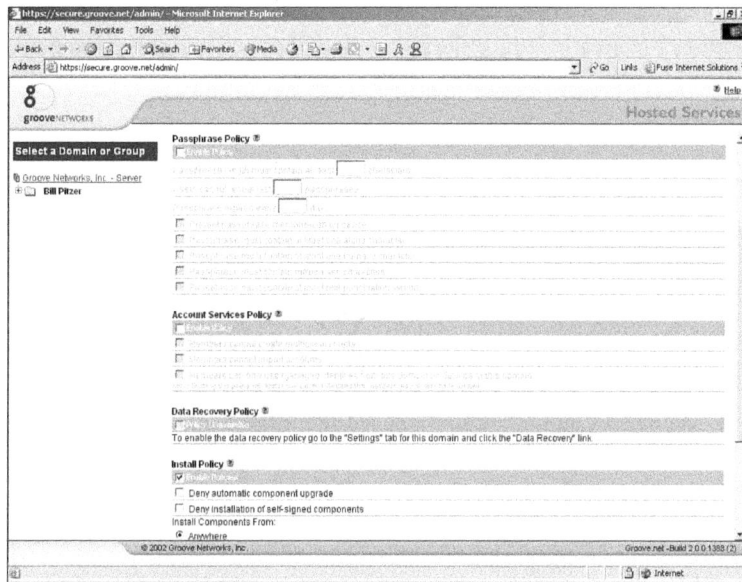

The Passphrase Policy Options

There are a number of restrictions that can be enforced when domain members specify the account passphrase on a managed device, including the following:

- Passphrase Length Must Contain at Least X Characters: This restricts users from using passphrases that are too short. A typical value for this field is at least six characters.

- Users Cannot Repeat Last X Passphrases: This stops users from using previous X number of passphrases when their old one has expired.

- Passphrase Expires Every X Days: It is recommended you set an expiration period to prevent access if a previous password has been compromised.

- Prevent Passphrase Memorization on Device: By selecting this option you prevent a user from selecting this feature on a device. When passphrase memorization is enabled, anyone with access to a device could start Groove and enter any of the account's shared spaces.

- Passphrase Must Contain at Least One Alpha Character: This requires a passphrase to have at least one non-numeric character.

- Passphrase Must Contain at Least One Numeric Character: When this is selected, passphrases must have one numeric character.

- Passphrase Must Contain Mixed-case Characters: A mixed case passphrase makes the passphrase harder for intruders to guess.

- Passphrase Must Contain at Least One Punctuation Symbol: Selecting this option forces the user to add at least one non-alphanumeric character to the passphrase.

Although some of these options may be considered a nuisance by many users, these policy settings can greatly reduce the risk of unauthorized persons gaining access using a compromised passphrase.

THE ACCOUNT SERVICES POLICY OPTIONS

These settings place restrictions at an account level for each managed device. They include the following:

- Members Cannot Create Multiple Accounts: Selecting this prevents users from creating multiple accounts on the same device.
- Members Cannot Import Accounts: Selecting this prevents users from importing accounts on this device.
- Members Can Only Use Managed Identities from This Domain on Devices Within This Domain: This restricts users from using any identities that are not currently managed within the domain.

CAUTION

> This option will disable any unmanaged identities users have created. This could prevent them from entering any shared spaces these identities were a part of. Before selecting this option, ensure that users with unmanaged identities understand the impact this will have on them.

THE DATA RECOVERY POLICY OPTIONS

The options for this policy are managed and set from the Settings tab that is discussed in the "Settings Area" section later in this chapter.

THE INSTALL POLICY OPTIONS

Groove's component-based design allows it to easily update itself with enhancements without requiring the whole application to be replaced. However, in some corporate environments it might be desirable to restrict how these components are updated. Groove Hosted Services enables you to define download, installation, and custom component policies. You can define the following policy options:

- Deny Automatic Component Upgrade: Selecting this check box will not allow any automatic component upgrades to occur. Some Groove tools have been designed to automatically search for updated components. This setting stops this search from occurring.
- Deny Installation of Self-signed Components: This prohibits installation of any components that have been signed by the component developer.
- Install Components From: This specifies where components can be installed from. You can choose one of the following options:

- Anywhere: Components can be downloaded and installed from any location. This is not recommended because it does increase the risk of rogue components.
- The HTTP Server: This specifies the only URL that components may be downloaded and installed from.
- The UNC File Server: In a corporate network, this specifies the Universal Network Connection from which components can be downloaded and installed from.
- Nowhere: Selecting this option prevents the download of any new or updated components.

TIP

> I don't recommend that you select Nowhere, because the automatic update feature is extremely valuable in that it ensures all users have the most updated components.

- **Allow Users to Install**: This specifies what components users may install with the following options:
  - Every Component: Every component can be installed.
  - No Components: This stops the user from installing any components, including components installed via automatic updating.
  - Prompt User: Each time a new or updated component is to be installed, prompt the user whether the installation should proceed.

TIP

> The Prompt user setting is very useful when a user has limited bandwidth because it allows the user more control over new component installation.

DEFINING A CUSTOM INSTALLATION POLICY

The default installation policies are not likely to provide enough granular control in most corporate installations. Because of this, administrators also have the option of defining custom installation policies that will override the default policy chosen. By clicking the Create a Custom Install Policy link from the Edit Device Policies screen, the administrator can define a custom policy from the screen shown in Figure 9.36.

DEFINING A CUSTOM INSTALL POLICY BASED ON THE DIGITAL THUMBPRINT

The following example demonstrates how to define a custom installation policy based on the digital fingerprint from the software provider. This does not take into account the version number of the component. If you need this type of control, see the Adding Version Control to your Custom Install Policy version. Follow these steps from the Custom Install Policy screen shown in Figure 9.36:

1. Give your new policy a name and enter it in the Display Name text box provided. This name should contain a description of what the policy allows.

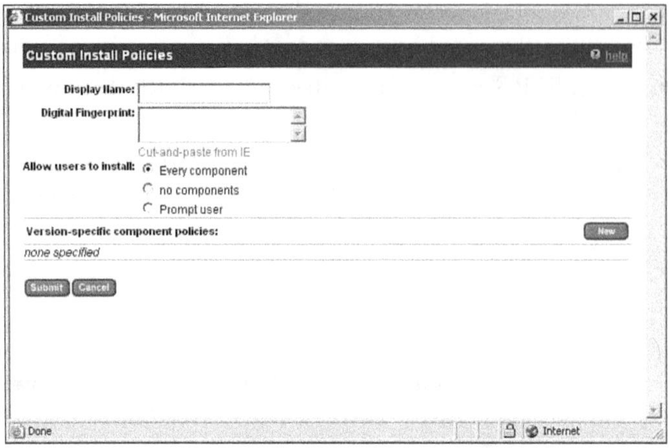

Figure 9.36
Groove enables you to define installation for specific third-party components by entering the component's Digital Fingerprint.

NOTE

The name should be descriptive because in the future this will override any default installation policies that have been defined.

2. Enter the company's digital fingerprint in the box provided. This is also called the thumbprint that can be obtained from the company's digital certificate. See "Examining a Company's Digital Certificate" for more information about where this can be found.

3. Select the radio box corresponding to the installation policy you want to use. These are the same as the choices for the default installation policy except that this applies only to the software provider with the digital thumbprint specified. You have the following choices of what you allow users to install, including:

   - Every Component: All components from this software provider are installed without prompting the user.

   - No Components: Users will be unable to download any components from the software provider with the digital thumbprint specified.

   - Prompt User: Users will be prompted to install components from this software provider. They also have the option to choose the "trust always" option for this provider to allow automatic installation without prompts in the future.

4. Click the Submit button to create the policy. All managed devices will now be forced to adhere to this policy when installing components with the digital thumbprint specified.

ADDING VERSION CONTROL TO A CUSTOM INSTALL POLICY

If you want to control what versions of components that members can or cannot download, you can follow these steps:

1. You first need to enter the digital fingerprint for the software provider, as in step 2 in the preceding section; however, do not click the Submit button at this time.

2. Add a new version-specific component policy by clicking the New button shown in Figure 9.36. This should add a new row shown in Figure 9.37.

Figure 9.37
After clicking the New button, a new row is added where version-specific criteria can be entered.

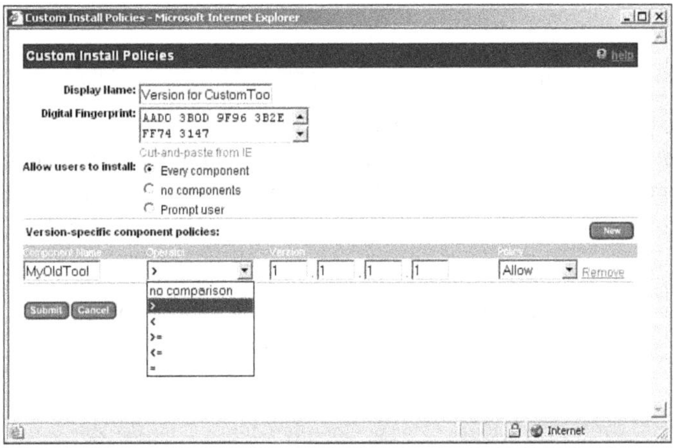

3. Now you must complete the row shown in Figure 9.37 with the following information:

   • Name: Give this component policy a name

   • Operator: A logical operator that will be used when comparing version numbers for installation. As shown in the figure, you can choose from all the basic operators including >, <, >=, <=, or =.

   • Version: This is the version number of the component given in the standard major, minor, custom, build format. For example, 1.1.1.1.

   • Policy: Similar to the options provided for non–version-specific policies. You can choose from the following:

     Allow: Allow installation of any components with this digital fingerprint *and* match the version criterion.

     Prohibit: Do not allow installation of any components that have this digital fingerprint *and* match this version criterion.

     Prompt: Prompt the user for installation of any components that have this digital fingerprint *and* match this version criterion.

CAUTION

> You must specify all criteria you want to be checked. By default, Groove Workspace allows installation of components that fall outside any version criteria specified. For example, if you define a policy that prohibits installation of any components from Business X that are = (equal) to version 1.1.1.1 this means that version 2.1.1.1 can be installed. This also allows installation of version 3.1.1.2, 4.1.1.2, and so on.

EDITING AND DELETING CUSTOM POLICIES

9

After a custom installation policy has been defined using the steps outlined previously, it should now appear by name in the Custom Installation Policies area on the device management page. Clicking the remove link next to a policy will remove that policy from the domain.

CAUTION

> You will not be prompted when deleting and it cannot be undone. Use care when choosing this link.

EXAMINING A COMPANY'S DIGITAL CERTIFICATE

Groove allows all components to be digitally signed to prevent the downloading of rogue components. Certificates contain a variety of information so that you can inspect and verify that the components are coming from a trusted software provider. For a simple example, you can find a Web site that uses Secure Sockets Layer (SSL) and examine its certificate from within Internet Explorer. In this example, you'll look at the certificate Groove Networks uses on its secure pages.

After logging into My Groove Services, I have been taken to a secure area as indicated by the padlock in the lower-right corner (see Figure 9.38). This padlock means that I have accepted the digital certificate and trust that I am exchanging information with Groove Networks. Right-clicking the page, choosing Properties, and clicking the Certificates button on the Properties dialog shown in Figure 9.39 will display the current certificate. The certificate has three different tabs, each containing a variety of information that we'll outline in the following sections.

GENERAL TAB

This tab gives some of the basic certificate information, including:

- This Certificate Is Intended To: Outlines what the certificate is intended to secure. In our example, it is used to ensure the identity of the groove.net server for individuals accessing the site.
- Issued To: The company that the certificate was issued to by the Certificate Authority (CA).
- Issued By: The type of organization that granted the certificate.
- Valid From: The date range that the certificate is valid. Certificates must usually be renewed annually.

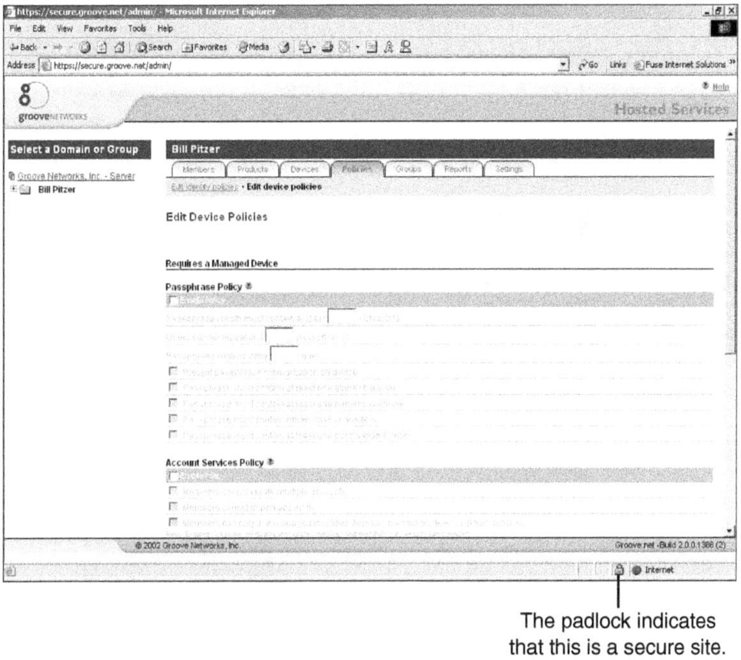

Figure 9.38
We can tell we are in a secure site by the padlock shown in the browser.

The padlock indicates that this is a secure site.

Figure 9.39
Clicking the Certificate button will display all the certificate details organized under three different tabs.

Details Tab

Within the Details tab, you can find the details attached to a particular certificate. Most of these fall under the X.509 standard for digital certificates. As shown in Figure 9.40, the Show drop-down list at the top can be used to filter the details displayed by standard X.509 Version 1 fields, extensions only, critical extensions only, or properties only:

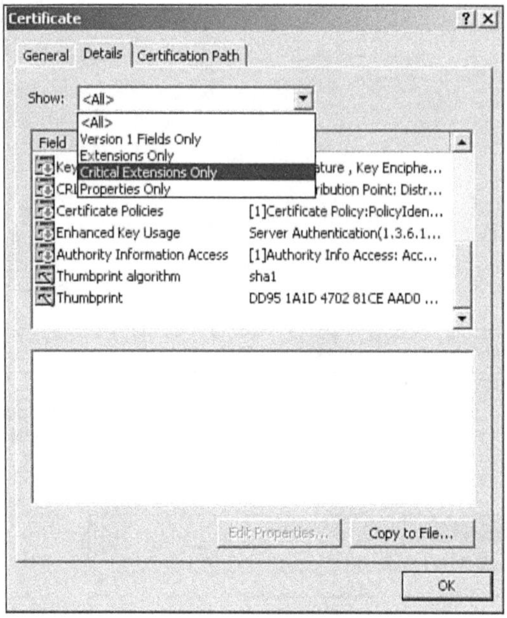

Figure 9.40
The drop-down list box on the top of the certificate screen enables you to filter what certificate details are displayed.

The following list explains these options in detail:

Version 1 Fields Only: This will display all the standard X.509 Version 1 fields attached to the certification, including

- Version: The X.509 version number of the certificate.
- Serial Number: This number, assigned by the certification authority, will be unique for all certificates assigned by that particular authority.
- Signature Algorithm: The hash algorithm used to digitally sign the certificate. In this case, the sha1RSA algorithm is used.
- Issuer: Some details of the certification authority that issued the certificate. In this case, it is RSA that resides in the United States.
- Valid From: The beginning date the certificate is considered valid.
- Valid To: The last date the certificate is considered valid.
- Subject: A distinguished name identifier telling to whom the certificate was issued.

- Public Key: The type of public key used with the certificate and its length. In this case it is 1024 bits.

Extensions Only: This will display all non-critical extensions, including

- Basic Constraints: This defines whether the subject of the certificate can act as a Certificate Authority.
- Key Usage: Purposes for which the key can be used.
- CRL Distribution Points: Where Certification Revocation Lists (CRL) can be found.
- Certificate Policies: The policies for this certificate.
- Enhanced Key Usage: Purposes for which this key can be used. This was added after it was determined the key usage field by itself was not sufficient to convey all intended uses.
- Authority Information Access: This specifies the location where the certificate can be obtained for this Certificate Authority.

Critical Extensions Only: This will contain all critical extensions for the certificate. A certificate with critical extensions that are not recognized will usually be rejected. However, unrecognized non-critical extensions are usually ignored. There are no critical extensions in our example.

- Properties Only: Other attributes attached to the certificate.
- Thumbprint Algorithm: The hash algorithm that generates a digest of data (or thumbprint) for digital signatures
- Thumbprint: The digest (or thumbprint) of the certificate data.

NOTE

> For adding custom installation policies, this is the fingerprint field that needs to be pasted in the text box.

CERTIFICATION PATH TAB

The Certification Path Tab shown in Figure 9.41 enables you to see all intermediate certificates in the path to the final entity certificate. In this example, there is only one anchor certificate that originated at the Certificate Authority (CA). The screen contains the following elements:

- Certification Path: A hierarchy representing the anchor certificate and all intermediate certificates.
- Certificate Status: The current status of the certificate. If there are no problems with the certificate you should see "This certificate is OK."

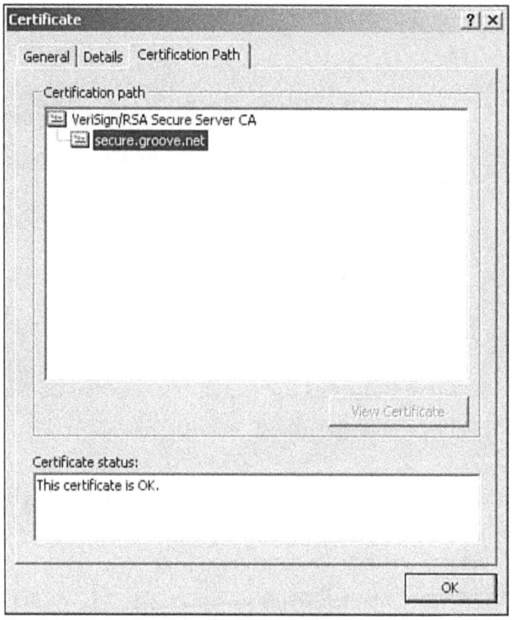

Figure 9.41
The certification path enables you to tell where a certificate originated from.

USING GROUPS

Within a domain, in order to simplify management of members you might want to segment them into groups. *Groups* are arbitrarily named containers that members can be placed into. For instance, you might want to create groups to identify the members of various departments in an organization. Clicking the Groups tab will take you to the View Groups screen shown in Figure 9.42.

Figure 9.42
The View Groups screen will show all the groups that have been created such as the Students group in this example.

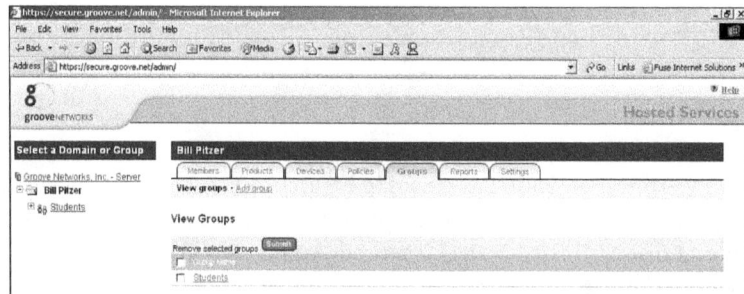

ADDING A NEW GROUP

You can add your own group(s) by first choosing where you want the group to be place by clicking a domain or existing group on the left side of the screen. Groups can be nested, so placing them under a domain is not a requirement. After you've decided where to place the group, click the Add Group link at the top of the screen, which will look like Figure 9.43. In this example, we are adding a group under the existing Students group. After you click the Submit button, the group will be added and the listing on the left will show the new group, as shown in Figure 9.44.

Figure 9.43
From the Add Group screen you must enter the name of the new group and click the Submit button.

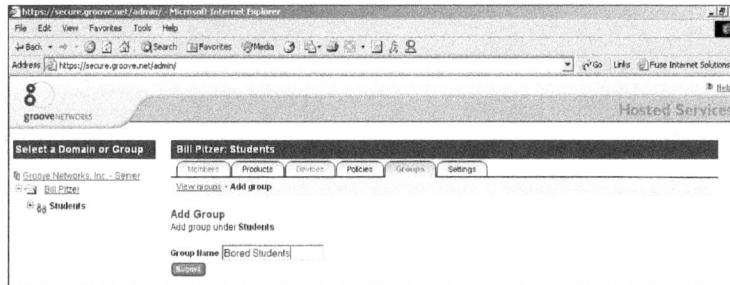

Figure 9.44
You can now see the new Bored Students group is nested under the existing Students group.

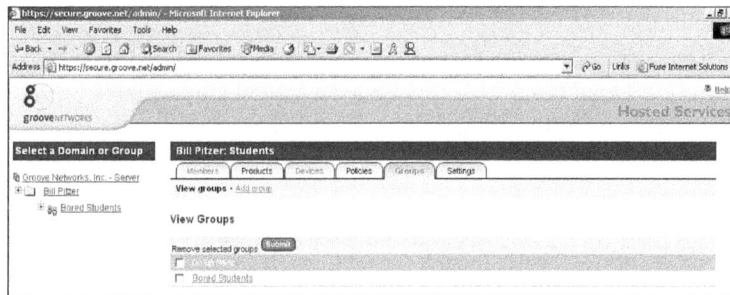

MOVING USERS INTO THE NEW GROUP

With the Bored Students group created, we can move an identity into the group. Click the Members tab to see a list of members within the domain. Select the check box next to Student One and choose Move Selected Members from the drop-down list at the top of the screen. Click the Submit button and you will receive a confirmation pop-up window, as shown in Figure 9.45. Click the Submit button the user will be moved from his or her original location to the new group.

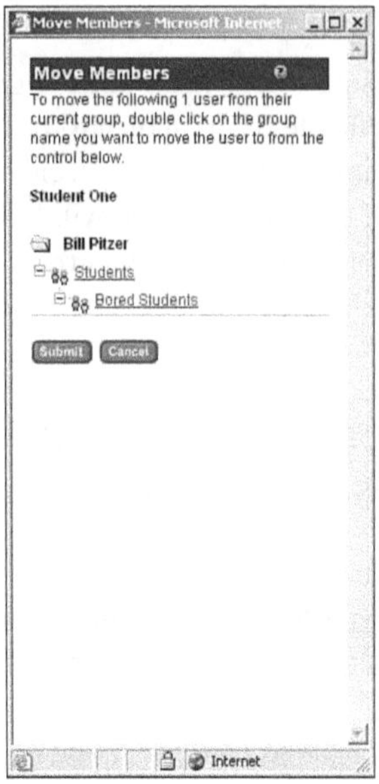

Figure 9.45
Click Submit in this confirmation window and Student One will be moved to the Bored Students group.

USAGE REPORTS

For each domain within a company, it can be very useful to track usage. The usage reports provided within Groove Network Services allow administrators to run reports on a domain's shared spaces, users, and tools. Several different usage reports are provided, including the following:

- Shared Space: The Shared Space report enables you to track usage for each shared space within the domain.
- Users: The Users report enables you to track participation of users within the domain.
- Tools: The Tools report enables you to display the usage statistics for tools used by domain members within shared spaces.

RUNNING THE REPORTS

Administrators can access the reports by clicking the Reports tab as shown in Figure 9.46 and following these steps:

1. Click on a domain from the Domain Administration on the Domain Administration menu on the left of the screen.
2. Choose the Report to run from the Report drop-down list. You can choose from the Shared Spaces, Users, or Tools usage reports.
3. Choose a report period as shown in Figure 9.47. You can choose from a preset length of time from the drop-down menu or specify the starting and ending dates.

Figure 9.46
Clicking the Reports tab will take you to this screen from where the usage reports can be launched.

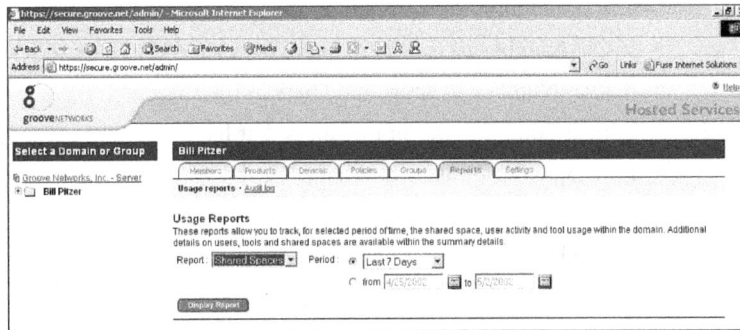

Figure 9.47
You can choose the timeframe you want to report on for the Shared Space, Tool, and Users reports.

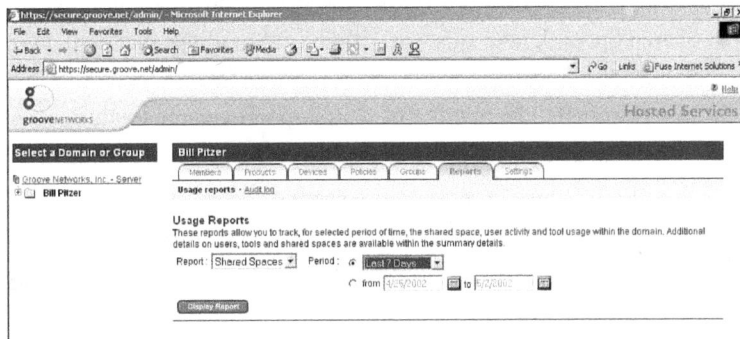

NOTE

You can also click the Date Pickers next to each date text box to choose the dates from a calendar.

4. Click the Display Report button to generate the report.

The following data is contained in the shared space usage report:

- Space Name: The name assigned to the shared space.
- Created: Contains information about the shared space creation:
- By: The Groove user who created the space and its creation date.
- Time Spent (minutes): Time spent in the space by domain members:
  - Total: Total cumulative time spent in the space by domain members.
  - Average: The average time spent in the space by a domain member.

- Members: A summary of members in the space:
  - Visits: Number of members that have visited the space at least once.
  - Active: Number of active members in the space.
  - Joined: Total number of members that have joined the space since it was created.
  - Left: Number of users that have left the space.
  - Current: Number of current users in the space.
  - Age: The number of days the space has existed.

The following data is contained in the user report:

- User Name: The name of the domain member.
- Devices: The number of devices that the member's account has been installed on.
- Shared Space: Under this you will find subheadings that contain information related to the member's shared space activity:
  - Created: The number of shared spaces created by this user.
  - Joined: The number of shared spaces this user has joined.
  - Left: When a user deletes a space or deletes the identity used in the space.
  - Active: The number of shared spaces that this user actively participates in.
  - Total Time: The total time the user has spent actively participating in shared spaces.
  - Average Time: The average time this user has spent in each shared space.
  - Total Visits: The total number of visits to shared spaces this user has made.
- Date
  - Created: Date the domain member's account was injected.
  - Last Contacted: Date the account last contacted the groove.net server(s).

The following data is contained in the Tools report:

- Tool Name: The name of a tool.
- Time Spent (minutes): The time a tool was used.
- Total: The cumulative time all members used this tool.
- Average: The average time each member used the tool.

NOTE

You can also click the Date Pickers next to each date text box to choose the dates from a calendar.

DISPLAYING THE AUDIT LOG

By clicking the Audit Log link on the top of the Reports area, you will be taken to the Audit Log Reporting screen shown in Figure 9.48. Clicking the Display Audit Log button will display all activity in a report similar to the one shown in Figure 9.49. When the report is displayed, you can filter the results shown by clicking the Filter button and choosing the appropriate criteria.

TIP

Picking too large of a date range can make the report take a long time to finish. If there has been a lot of activity within the domain, be sure to choose the date range carefully to eliminate unwanted results.

Figure 9.48
You can run an audit log that will detail all changes made from the Hosted Management Services interface.

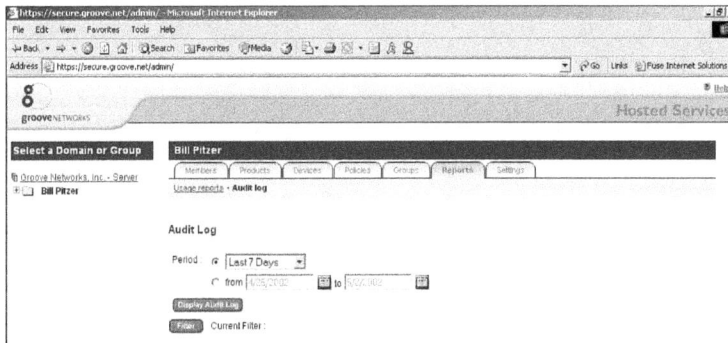

Figure 9.49
The audit log will display activity by username in this report.

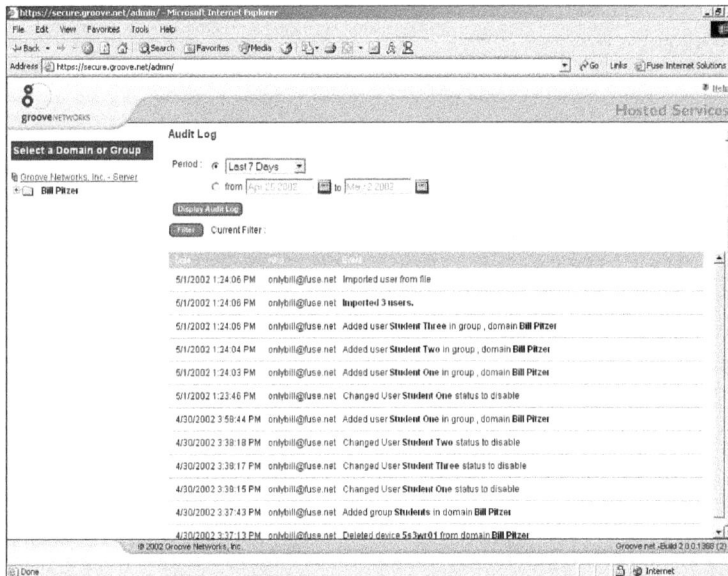

PART III

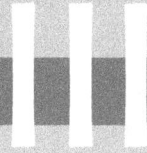

CREATING YOUR OWN CUSTOM TOOLS

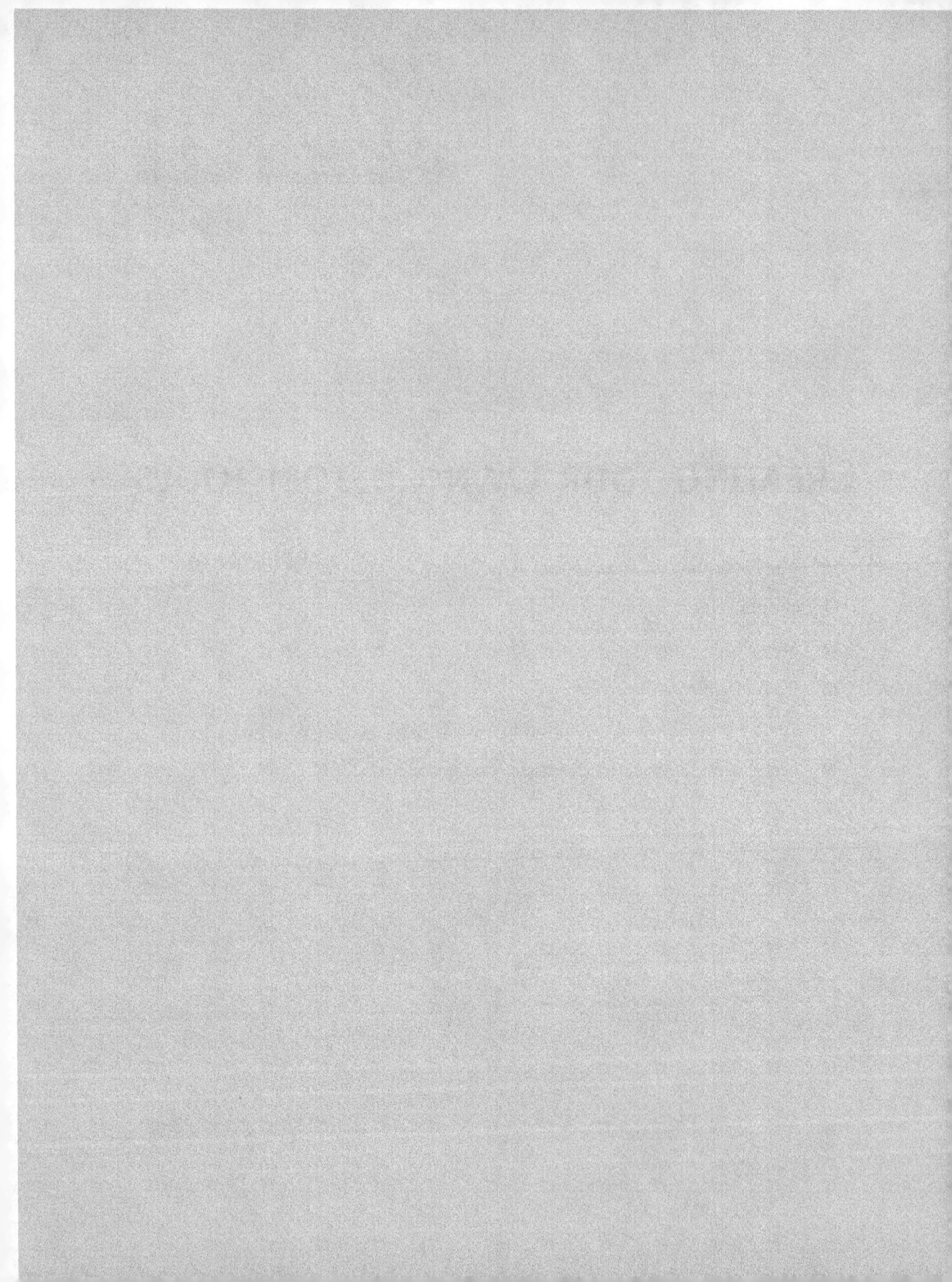

CHAPTER **10**

THE FOUNDATION FOR DEVELOPMENT: THE GROOVE DEVELOPMENT KIT (GDK)

In this chapter

GETTING STARTED WITH THE GROOVE DEVELOPMENT KIT

Writing a new tool template from scratch can be a very daunting task. Luckily, Groove provides the Groove Development Kit (GDK) to get you off to a great start. The tools provided with the GDK are the same tools that the Groove Network's own developers have created to facilitate their development of Groove's standard collection of tools. Like any work in progress, you may find some of these tools and their documentation a little rough around the edges but the benefits of using them far outweigh any of these minor inconveniences.

The overall goal for this chapter is to ensure that you become completely acquainted with the Groove Development Kit and what it has to offer. After showing you where to find the GDK and how to install it, this chapter will give you a thorough understanding of the components of the Groove Development Kit and the underlying architecture of the Groove Workspace client by describing

- The services and subsystems that compose the Groove Framework Architecture
- The concept of the Model-View-Controller structure and Groove's implementation of it
- How you can explore the different Groove components by using the Groove Object Model

After you've been given some background information on the Groove client and structure, you'll start using some of the tools provided. This part of the chapter will demonstrate just how quickly you can begin developing tools with the GDK utilities by showing you

- How to create a simple tool using the Tool Creator tool
- How you can use the Tool Publisher tool to publish your own tool templates
- How to explore the Groove databases using the Database Navigator tool

Finally, you will learn some additional tricks of the trade that you can use during development, such as

- Debugging a tool by attaching to the process with Microsoft Visual InterDev
- Finding the source of application errors by using the tracing functionality provided with the Customer Service Manager application

THE GROOVE FRAMEWORK FOR BUILDING TOOLS

Groove is more than just an application; it's an entire framework for building peer-to-peer collaborative applications. Groove provides its own development kit, aptly named the Groove Development Kit (GDK). The kit provides everything you need to quickly develop and test your new Groove tools. Within this kit, you'll find

- A step-by-step tutorial describing how to create your first tool with sample code
- API references for different languages
- Sample programs and code snippets
- Type libraries (.tlb) containing headers for Groove's own COM components such as the Groove user interface component
- Various utilities to help in tool development such as the Tool Creator and the Tool Publisher
- Registry files to enable or disable various Groove features that might be required during different stages of development
- A copy of the Groove Object Model

The minimum hardware requirements for the GDK are as follows:

- A Pentium II or equivalent 600Mhz or higher (900Mhz or higher is recommended)
- 256MB System RAM (380MB RAM recommended)
- 300MB of disk space available for Groove (1GB recommended).
- A video card capable of 800×600 resolution or higher with at least 15-bit color.
- A sound card and microphone to enable voice-messaging and audio features. A full-duplex sound card required for some voice chat features.

→ For more information about Groove's sound card requirements, **see** "Preparing for the Groove Workspace Installation," **p.30**

The GDK supports the same operating systems the Groove application supports:

- Microsoft Windows 95 (requires OSR2 or greater and DirectX 3.0)
- Microsoft Windows 98
- Microsoft Windows NT (Service Pack 3 or greater must be applied)
- Microsoft Windows 2000
- Microsoft Windows XP

Internet Explorer 5.01 or greater is required. Because Groove uses many of the libraries included with Internet Explorer, using a later version ensures that Groove will be able to leverage any of the latest enhancements to the Internet Explorer libraries it shares.

A 56Kbps connection is the minimum for dial-up usage. A LAN connection with an Internet or broadband (DSL, cable, T1) connection is suggested.

NOTE

> You can develop tools without an Internet connection. However, publishing a tool requires either an intranet or Internet connection.

BASIC SKILLS REQUIRED TO DEVELOP TOOLS WITH THE GDK

Although not absolutely required, the Groove Development Kit utilities and documentation have been developed with the assumption that you at least have the following experience:

- You know what the Windows Registry is and how to apply changes to it.
- You have experience with a scripting language such as JavaScript or Perl.
- You have had some exposure to the Extensible Markup Language (XML) and are familiar with how to construct well-formed XML documents.
- You know how to use an Advanced Programming Interface (API) reference manual.
- A basic understanding of how to incorporate Component Object Model (COM) object calls within scripts.

NOTE | You really only need to know how to use COM from a scripting language. How to instantiate a component, make method calls and property changes, and destroy the object when you are finished with it is all you need to know.

This and the following chapters will properly introduce new concepts as they are encountered.

INSTALLING THE GROOVE DEVELOPMENT KIT

The Groove Development Kit is provided separately from the Groove Workspace client. You can download and install it by following these steps:

1. Make sure you have installed the latest version of Groove. Refer to Chapter 2, "Installing and Configuring Groove," for more details on installation.

CAUTION | If your client installation of Groove and the GDK are not the same version, this can cause you some considerable headaches later. For example, some of the Groove components might change in the Groove client. Without the latest copy of the GDK you might find only dated specifications for some components, or none at all.

2. Point your Web browser to http://www.groove.net/devzone/. This is the Groove DevZone where you'll not only find the GDK, but other development resources such as technical notes, recent news, technical presentations, and the popular development forums.

3. Click the link Downloads, as shown in Figure 10.1. From the next page shown in Figure 10.2, click the Download Groove Development Kit link. After filling out a short survey and submitting it the download will begin. Save the file to disk when prompted.

Figure 10.1
You can link to the download page for the GDK from the home page of Groove's DevZone.

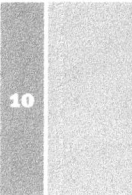

Figure 10.2
Click the Download Groove Development Kit link of the right side of this screen to begin downloading the Groove Development Kit.

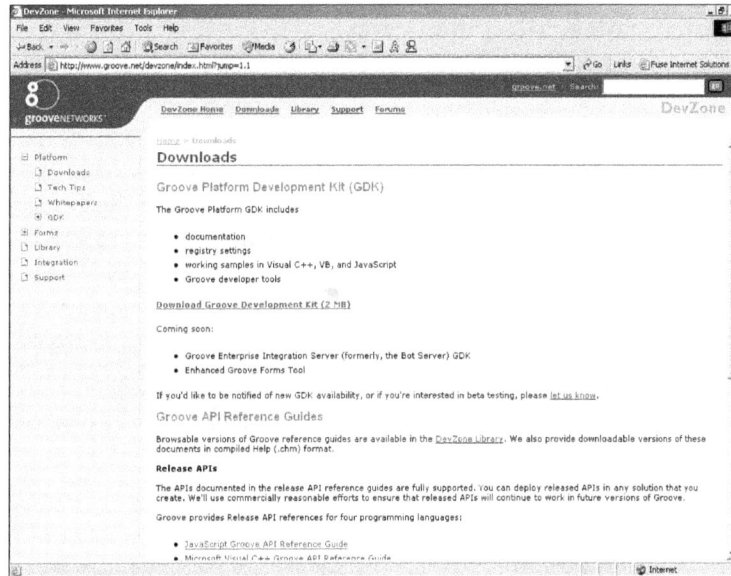

4. Run the executable you've just downloaded.

5. Follow the steps within the installation wizard.

Once installed, you should have a GDK folder installed within your Groove folder on the Start menu. By default, the GDK should have been installed under your *Groove Application* \groove\Data\localhost\GDK folder. This folder contains a number of subfolders created by the GDK including the following:

- Documentation: GDK and general information useful for developers. Not all documentation is installed with the GDK; refer to the DevZone site for additional documents for download.

- RegistryFiles: A variety of Registry files that are outlined in the "Registry Files" section later in this chapter.

- Samples: Different sample applications and code snippets. Usually they are provided in several different languages. Many of the samples are written in JavaScript, Visual Basic, and C++.

- TypeLibs: Type library files (.tlb) that contain information about the types, modules, and interfaces exposed by an object.

- Utilities: Different development utilities, which we'll be discussing in the "Development Utilities" section later in this chapter.

THE GROOVE FRAMEWORK ARCHITECTURE

Before writing your first line of code, you should understand the Groove architecture. Groove is a complex collection of different components designed to work together seamlessly to enable collaboration in a peer-to-peer network. Normally, Groove hides the details of how it works from the user by defining simple interfaces to components that actually perform a variety of complex processes. For example, Groove allows you to send shared space changes to other members of a shared space without having to worry about their online or offline status, the protocol they are using, their IP address, and so on. Although developers need not be concerned about Groove's lowest level of functioning, a basic understanding of it is necessary to develop tools that work efficiently within the Groove framework.

Although we'll provide a brief overview of the architecture here, a more detailed examination can be found in the Groove Application and Architecture Overview document supplied with the GDK.

ACCOUNT AND USER IDENTIFICATION SUBSYSTEM

In Chapter 2, we introduced you to account creation. Later, in Chapter 3, "Overview of Shared Spaces," we explored creating different identities attached to a single account. This was all enabled by the Account and User Identification Subsystem within the Groove Framework. In addition to these responsibilities, it also performs a variety of other tasks from device awareness to the storage of keys. As a special type of shared space, the Account Database stores all account-related data. Requests from other subsystems are handled by the Groove Account Manager, which resides in the Account Database itself.

USER INTERFACE (UI) SERVICES

The User Interface Services, as the name implies, is responsible for managing all windows and other interfaces within the Groove application. This includes managing the display and application of Groove's own and custom developed skins. Also as part of these services is the *idle manager*, which handles any requests for idle processing time that is available.

CUSTOMER SERVICES SUBSYSTEM

Provided as a proactive error handler, this subsystem is used to handle errors, provide resolutions if possible, and enable other diagnostics to be performed. Developers will become familiar with some of the CSM subsystem as they use it to debug injection problems and other issues during tool development.

SHARED SPACE TOOL FRAMEWORK

There are lots of processes working behind the scenes to implement the collaborative working environment of a shared space. As changes occur in a space, Dynamic Services utilizes a component called the Dynamics Manager to perform these different types of tasks:

- Data maintenance and space cleanup
- Executing commands in outbound/inbound deltas

> **NOTE**
>
> You may be familiar with the term *delta*, which usually refers to the difference between two numbers and is signified by a triangle. Deltas in Groove are the same concept. Whenever there are changes to a shared space, these changes are packaged in "deltas" to be transferred to other shared space members. Other actions, such as account changes and invitations, also use the principle of deltas to neatly package (and process) different types of data changes.

- Notifying views that underlying data has changed
- Disseminating deltas to other shared space members
- Coordinating the processing order of received and transmitted deltas

DATA STORAGE AND PERSISTENCE SUBSYSTEM

All shared space and account data is stored in a local XML documents database that is managed by the Data Storage and Persistence Subsystem. This subsystem is made up of several different components, including the following:

- Storage Manager—All data in shared spaces is stored in XML documents. It is the Storage Manager's job to ensure the integrity and consistency of these documents. It also ensures that all these documents are secured using encryption before anything is written to disk. The Storage Manager provides an interface that allows tool creators to manipulate these documents using the XML Object Model.

- Groove Collection Services—These services provide a persistent data model for tool data storage using XML. This provides tools with the interface needed to view and manipulate data. Because multiple collections can be created, it allows tools to easily provide users with alternate views of the data.

- Storage Service and Log Service—Similar to database logging, Groove provides these services to allow rollbacks should a problem occur between operations. This is automatically performed by Groove without tools explicitly calling it.

> NOTE
>
> The term *rollback* generally refers to database changes. For example, if the database supports it, you can perform a rollback at any time. Any data that has been inserted or updated since the last commit will be "rolled back" or revert to the value it was immediately after the last commit was performed. The term "commit" refers to the action that actually makes changes to the underlying data.

- Transactions—Very similar to what the Storage Service and Log Service provides, this enables tool developers to utilize transactional capabilities. Just like databases use transactions to control data changes, Groove uses transactions to control its own data modifications. An important acronym to describe the properties of Groove transactional support is ACID, which stands for:

- Atomicity—All operations must occur or they are all rolled back. A good phrase to describe atomicity is "all or nothing."

- Consistency—Data is left in a consistent state after a transaction.

- Isolation—Operations cannot interfere with one another. Within the Groove documentation you may see this referred to as "independent," which means the same thing.

- Durability—Regardless of other operations' success/failure the transaction must be committed once started.

COMPONENT SERVICES SUBSYSTEM

This subsystem is responsible for managing the download of all components. This is the subsystem that will be responsible for reading the files created for publishing our tool in Chapter 13, "Publishing a New Tool." This subsystem comprises many different components, including:

- Component Manager—The Component Manager determines all the components that are required at any point in time. For example, it can tell if a tool needs additional components and will then attempt to acquire them locally or initiate the process to download them from the Internet.

- Download Manager—When requested by the Component Manager, the Download Manager will retrieve the component from the Internet from the location specified in the OSD.

■ Install Manager/System Install Manager—After the Download Manager retrieves component(s) it is the responsibility of the Install Manager to coordinate the actual installation. System-level components have their own separate Install Manager.

WEB SERVICES

This term is used to describe a whole array of services that are hosted by Groove Networks. Depending on your organization's needs, you may decide to deploy these services within their own organization using Groove's Management Server and Relay Server products. Some of the services offered include the following:

■ Relay services:

■ Object queues

■ Fan out

■ Firewall transparency

■ Presence services

■ Management services for enterprises:

■ License management

■ Account management

■ Device management

■ Usage reporting

■ Groove.net services:

■ The My Groove Services area

■ The Groove.net directory services

Groove Networks is constantly expanding the services they offer. Future services could include

■ E-commerce applications and billing services for partners.

■ Resource backup and other archival services.

■ Hosting of additional licensed tools for download.

SECURITY SUBSYSTEM

This subsystem performs security services for the entire Groove application. Not only does it provide encryption for data stored on disk and transferred over the wire, but also it provides authentication services for all user interactions.

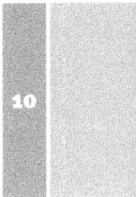

COMMUNICATIONS SUBSYSTEM

Acting as a sort of traffic cop, the communication subsystem gets data where it needs to go. This not only involves the transmission of deltas for a shared space, but also anything else that must be transmitted over the network for normal Groove operation. A good example of such a transmission is the data sent for presence information. This presence information is a feature in Groove that allows you to see whether a particular member is online or offline at any point in time. It is this subsystem that allows Groove to work efficiently in a variety of different network environments.

GROOVE'S MODEL-VIEW-CONTROLLER (MVC) STRUCTURE

The Groove application uses a slightly modified version of the Model-View-Controller structure. The Model-View-Controller structure is a simple yet powerful technique that allows you to *decouple* the parts that make up an application to allow greater flexibility and encourage reuse. Decoupling separates the parts of an application according to what function they perform. Before this structure was widely used, all functions were provided by one large program. Although this worked fine for applications written and maintained by one individual, these huge collections of code made it more difficult to maintain and understand by subsequent developers. Most software applications today use this structure which is divided into three parts:

- Model—All processing occurs on this end of the structure. This includes all computation and data storage routines. For example, this is where routines for crunching numbers and pulling data from a database would reside. Within Groove, components called *engines* are responsible for this type of processing. In Figure 10.3 we can see two-way interaction that occurs between the Model and View.

Figure 10.3
The Model-View-Controller structure is followed by many applications developed today.

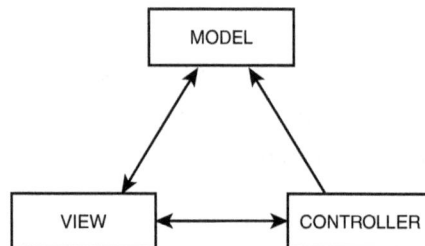

- View—As the name implies, this is the graphical interface that the user sees and interacts with. The View is dynamic because as the underlying Model changes it may have to reflect the modifications. This interaction is illustrated in Figure 10.3.

- Controller—The easiest way to imagine the Controller is to think of it as the linkage between the Model and View. It acts as a virtual traffic cop by interpreting input from different devices (keyboard, mouse, and so on) and directing the interpreted input to the Model or View so that the appropriate changes can be made to each. In Figure 10.3 you can see that the controller talks to both the Model and View in the structure.

Groove uses a version of the MVC structure, but the application has some unique challenges because it allows *simultaneous access* to the same application. For example, users in a shared space can simultaneously make changes to a Notepad document. Groove must somehow replicate these changes to other users within the shared space in almost real time. For this, Groove has extended the Model-View-Controller structure and created its own version, the Mediated Model-View-Controller structure.

THE GROOVE MEDIATED MODEL-VIEW-CONTROLLER STRUCTURE

Because Groove allows shared access to data and applications within a shared space, there were a few necessary changes that had to be made to the traditional Model-View-Controller structure. They needed a new service which all model and data changes could be funneled through. This is the job of Groove's Dynamics Services component. This component is responsible for replicating changes to a shared space. In addition to this service, several other elements had to be added to enable shared space interaction including the following:

- A Command Processor—Processes changes between the Controller and Model in the structure. These changes can come from the local Controller or the Controller on a peer computer. Within Groove, all of these commands are in the form of XML objects.
- Virtual Message Queue—Because not all users in a Shared Space are required to be connected at all times this queue is used to store messages for later forwarding to these disconnected users. Offline users should receive all changes once they come back online.
- XML Object Routing—Groove is designed to work in a variety of different network configurations. The XML Object Routing service is responsible for finding the most efficient path for communication. This can involve a variety of different transmission speeds (T1, 56k, ADSL, and so on), protocols, firewalls, and proxy servers.
- XML Object Store—This is Groove's underlying data repository. It can store data that originally existed in a variety of different formats.

THE GROOVE OBJECT MODEL

The Groove Development Kit contains a valuable diagram of the Groove Object Model. The object model graphically illustrates relationships between the different Groove components at runtime. This is a great companion to the API reference, or manual describing the

Groove objects' interfaces. Looking at the diagram allows you to quickly view object relationships and graphically illustrate them to others.

OPENING THE MODEL

The model itself is an extremely large GIF image. You can open it by pointing your Web browser to *GDK Installation Folder*\Utilities\GOM\HTML\GrooveGOMChart.htm. The portion of the object model showing the relationship of the GrooveForm to other objects is shown in Figure 10.4.

Figure 10.4
This portion of the Groove object model shows how it can be a valuable resource for determining the different objects used at runtime.

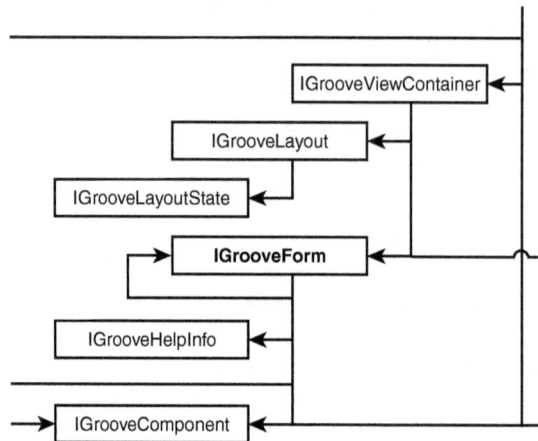

CHANGING THE CURRENT PAGE

Because the model is very large, it's contained on several different pages. Choose a page number from the drop-down list in the bottom center of the screen to jump to a new page.

RESIZING THE DISPLAY

Because it is such a large image, you can zoom in and out of the image using the drop-down list box on the lower right portion of the screen. You can choose either to fit it into the current window or choose a percentage of the original image size.

OTHER TOOLS USED IN DEVELOPMENT

Even though the GDK provides most of what you need to begin developing tools, there are a few other things you should have before starting development.

A TEXT EDITOR

Even though the GDK provides graphical tools like the Tool Creator and the Tool Publisher, there will be times you need to edit the text files Groove uses for tool injection. Although Microsoft Notepad works fine, there are other very inexpensive or free tools out there you can use. Some of the more useful features you may want to look for when choosing a text editor include the following:

- The ability to open multiple files simultaneously because tools consist of several different files and being able to see all of them at once is a real timesaver
- The ability to compare files, which can save time when you are trying to find code changes
- The capability to FTP files (useful when publishing components to a server on the Internet)
- Syntax highlighting that can make it easier to find syntax problems with XML and script

Some other popular text editors include

- UltraEdit (www.idmcomp.com)
- TextPad (www.textpad.com)
- NoteTab (www.notetab.com)

AN XML EDITOR

An XML editor is an application used to aid in the creation and editing of documents written in the Extensible Markup Language. Because XML documents rely on being structured correctly, an XML editor can ensure that you are adhering to the principle of well-formedness. Although XML editors can vary, many offer the following benefits:

- Closing tags automatically
- Ensuring that you have created a well-formed XML document. A well-formed document exhibits the following characteristics:
  - Every start tag has a corresponding end tag.
  - Elements do not overlap.
  - The document has one, and only one, root element that is unique.
  - All attribute values are surrounded by quotes (double or single). This is unlike HTML, which often allows things like `<TD align=center>`. This format would not be permitted in a well-formed XML document since attributes must be contained within quotes like `<TD align="center">`.
  - There are no isolated starting markup characters such as & and <.

- An XML document should begin with a processing instruction that declares it is an XML document. For example, most Groove XML documents will start with this line: `<g:Document Name="MyTool.xml" xmlns:g="urn:groove.net">`. This line also indicates any element using the g prefix will be contained within the groove.net namespace.

■ Expanding and collapsing branches within your XML document for ease of viewing

It is very common to spend a considerable amount of time debugging a problem only to find that there is a missing tag! There are many good XML editors on the market. Two of my favorites are

■ XML Notepad by Microsoft (`www.microsoft.com`)—Although not the most full-featured editor you'll find, anyone with some experience with XML will appreciate XML Notepad's simple interface and small size.

■ XML Spy by Altova (`www.xmlspy.com`)—A full-featured editor, it's a favorite of many because it offers a complete suite of tools for working with XML, DTD, Schema, and XSL documents.

> **NOTE** Internet Explorer 5.x and later can also be used to display an XML document and verify that the document is well formed.

AN INTEGRATED DEVELOPMENT ENVIRONMENT FOR SCRIPTING

Again, although you can develop your tools completely with a text editor, an Integrated Development Environment (IDE) such as Microsoft's Visual InterDev can provide additional functionality such as:

■ Script debugging

■ Syntax checking

■ The capability to visually compose and view HTML results immediately

■ Integrated source control and other change management features when working on a team

CREATING TOOL TEMPLATES WITH THE TOOL CREATOR

The Tool Creator provides a graphical interface for creating new tool templates and editing existing ones. It's a great way to learn the syntax of tool templates because you can view the source as you make modifications. Although the template files created may need a little tweaking, becoming familiar with this tool can greatly speed up the development process.

→ To understand the steps required to build a sample tool template and get a more detailed explanation of the elements that make it up, **see** "Building a Focus Group Tool," **p.365**

INJECTING THE TOOL CREATOR

The Tool Creator is a tool itself, so you must inject it into Groove before you can use it. Within the GDK Installation\Utilities\GrooveToolCreator folder you will find the ToolCreatorTool.grv file. Double-click this file to inject it into Groove.

USING THE TOOL CREATOR WIZARD

Once the Tool Creator tool is added to the shared space, you will be greeted with the Create Tool wizard shown in Figure 10.5. Follow the steps described in the following sections to use this wizard.

STEP 1: CREATING THE TOOL

In the Create Tool screen shown in Figure 10.5, you will need to specify a name for your tool. We're using the default MyTool value in our example, but you should give your tool a more unique, descriptive name. In addition to naming your tool, you also have the option of checking the box that indicates whether this tool should be created with a view container. If you plan on having a user interface for your tool you'll want to check this box.

Figure 10.5
In the first screen of the Create Tool wizard, you need to give your tool a name and specify whether you will be using a view container.

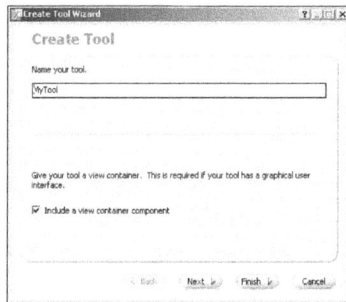

STEP 2: CHOOSING THE TYPE OF VIEW CONTAINER

If you decided in Step 1 that you would like to use a view container, you must now choose the type of layout you would like to use. As shown in Figure 10.6, you can choose from the following three standard layouts:

- HTML Layout: This layout uses standard HTML tags to position form elements.
- MultiCell Layout: This layout consists of a number of cells and columns. Unlike a table in the HTML Layout, you can have an uneven number of cells and columns.
- XY Layout: The XY allows for exact position of form elements by specifying the exact X and Y coordinates of each component.

Figure 10.6
In the Create Tool Wizard you can choose from three common layouts: the HTML layout, the MultiCell layout, and the XY layout.

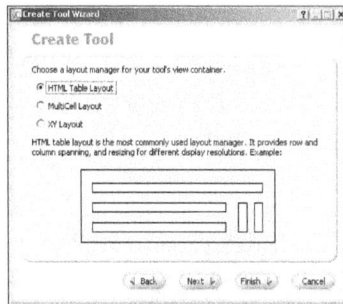

After you've made your selection, click Next to continue.

→ For more information about the different layouts available for use within your tool, **see** "Creating a Tool," **p.346**

NOTE

If you read the Groove documentation you may have seen the Splitter layout. This layout allows you to split the screen into two windows, either horizontally or vertically. As you can see, the Splitter Layout is not provided as an option. To incorporate this into your tool, you'll need to add the Splitter component by following the directions provided in the "Adding a Component" section later in this chapter.

STEP 3: INCLUDING A FORM DELEGATE

On the next screen shown in Figure 10.7, you must specify whether you want to include a form delegate. A *form delegate* ties together all the form's components and specifies all the events and behaviors for the form. Most forms that accept input from the user and need to respond to user events will need a delegate.

Figure 10.7
In this step of the Create Tool Wizard, you can specify whether you will be using the scripting host or a compiled binary.

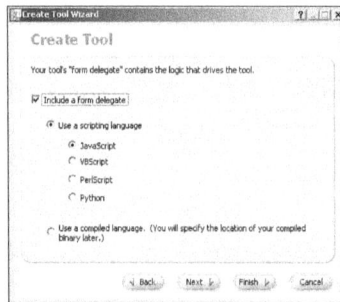

If you decide to use a delegate you then have the option of choosing whether to use a scripting language or a compiled binary (versus an interpreted module containing script). Groove currently supports scripting in JavaScript, VBScript, PerlScript, and Python. Using a compiled binary, such as C++, is for advanced users only. For our example we'll stick with JavaScript as our scripting language because it is one of the most common script languages in use today.

After you've made your selection, click Next to continue.

STEP 4: CHOOSING ONE OF THE STANDARD GROOVE ENGINES

You now have the option of including a standard Groove engine within your tool. You have two choices, which are shown in Figure 10.8.

Figure 10.8
The Create Tool Wizard allows you to include one of the standard Groove engines.

- **PropertyListEngine:** This is included by default with every Groove tool so it does not have to be defined in your tool template. This engine can be used to store and retrieve properties within the shared space.
- **RecordSetEngine:** This engine is used to manipulate persistent data within Groove.

After you've made your selection, click the Finish button to end the wizard.

STEP 5: MAKE ADDITIONAL MODIFICATIONS TO THE TOOL

You have reached the end of the Tool Creator Wizard and your tool template should now contain some of the most basic components. You should have been taken to the Tool Creator interface as shown in Figure 10.9. Using this interface, you can now make additional changes to the tool as outlined in the next section.

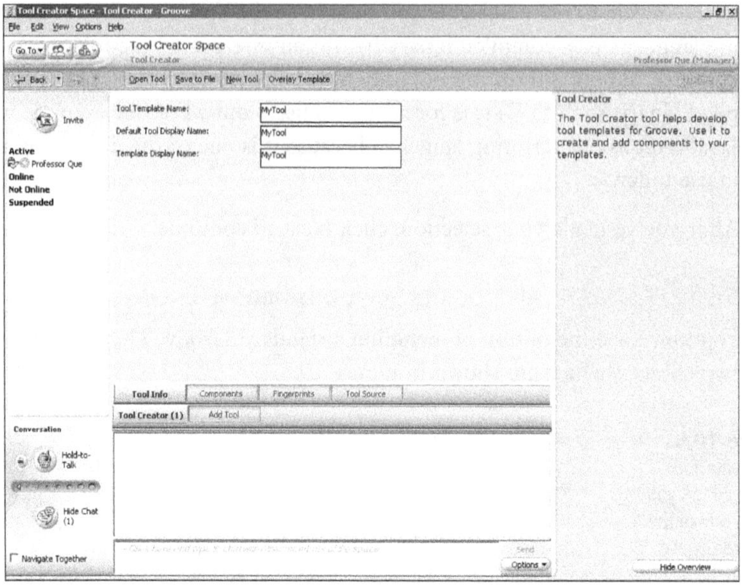

Figure 10.9
After you've finished with the Create Tool Wizard, you'll be taken to the actual Tool Creator tool interface.

MAKING ADDITIONAL MODIFICATIONS TO YOUR TOOL TEMPLATES

After you have created the basic foundation for your tool template by following the wizard prompts, you can now make additional modifications using the Tool Creator interface. The next few sections outline the different tabs and the tool properties that can be modified within each area.

THE INFO TAB

After you complete the wizard, the Tool Creator tool should now be open to the Tool Info tab shown in Figure 10.9, which contains the following fields:

- Tool Template Name—This will be assigned to the Name property attached to the ToolTemplate tag and is used to name the tool template file when it is saved to disk.

- Default Tool Display Name—This will be assigned to the DefaultToolDisplayName property attached to the ToolTemplate tag. This is the name used on the Tool Tab when the tool is added to a shared space.

- Template Display Name—This will be assigned to the TemplateDisplayName property attached to the ToolTemplate tag. While you must fill in this field, it is not used internally but accessed through the API.

THE COMPONENTS TAB

Clicking the Components tab takes you to the screen shown in Figure 10.10. You can choose from most of the components provided by Groove. This includes such things as the user interface components, engines, and layout. In fact, you'll see that the wizard has automatically added a few components for you. This screen contains a row of tabs, which you will use to set properties for each component you add. The following sections describe the different options available for adding, removing, and modifying tool template components.

Figure 10.10
Clicking the Components tab will take you to this screen where you can add, modify, and remove components.

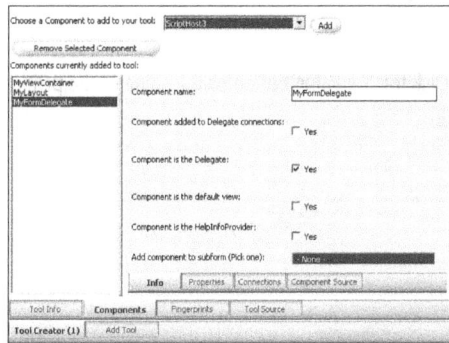

NOTE

It is also possible to specify components at runtime. However, this is outside the scope of our discussion here. Refer to the Groove Development Kit documentation and the examples it provides for more information on adding components dynamically at runtime.

ADDING A COMPONENT

Choose a component from the drop-down list at the top of the screen. After you've selected the appropriate tool, click the Add button and the component will be added to the list on the left of the screen.

You can download the complete details of the API from Groove's DevZone at www.groove.net/devzone by clicking on the Library link at the top of the page. After clicking this link, open the Platform branch of the hierarchical menu on the left as shown in Figure 10.10. From here you can click the API Reference link and download the documentation.

REMOVING A COMPONENT

Highlighting a component in the list on the left side of the screen and clicking Remove Selected Component will remove the component from the tool.

NOTE

> This also deletes any property values for this component.

SETTING COMPONENT PROPERTIES

By selecting a component in the list on the left, you can edit the properties attached to it. Different groups of configuration options are accessed through the tabs at the bottom of the screen. In the example we've created in Figure 10.11, we're modifying the Label property of the StaticText component in a sample tool.

CAUTION

> Don't forget to click the Set Value button or the value of the property will be lost when you leave the screen.

Figure 10.11
From the Components screen, you can modify the Label property of a StaticText component that has been added to our tool.

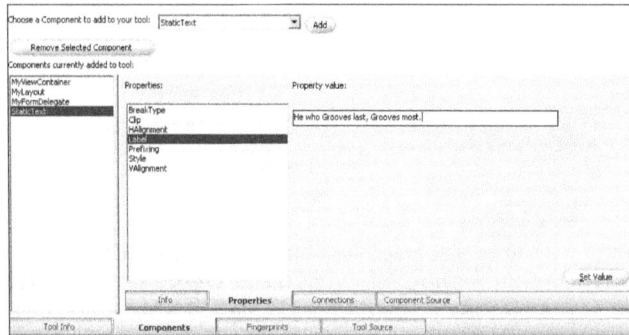

INFO TAB   Within the Info, or information tab, you can set the following properties for each component:

- Component Name—This is the name by which this component will be referenced elsewhere in the tool template. It takes the original component name by default.
- Component Added to Delegate Connections—If this check box is selected, the component will be added to the delegate connections.
- Component Is the Delegate—This check box indicates that this component is the delegate for the component group.
- Component Is the Default View—If this check box is selected, this will become the default view for the tool.
- Component Is the HelpInfoProvider—If this check box is selected it indicates that this component will be the one providing help text. Most Groove tools will use the RTFHelpProvider component here to provide a tool with Help Overview text.

- Add Component to Subform (Pick One)—For tools that have subforms defined, this will add the component to one particular subform. If there are no subforms defined, the only selection will be "None."

PROPERTIES TAB

This tab will display all the properties available for a component. The property value will be adjusted according to the data type of the value expected. For example, in Figure 10.12 the Sort value for a Combobox component expects a true or false Boolean value so only True and False radio buttons are shown. Click the Set Value to change the property value.

Figure 10.12
Different properties take different types of values. In this example, we see that the Sort property only takes a Boolean value of true or false.

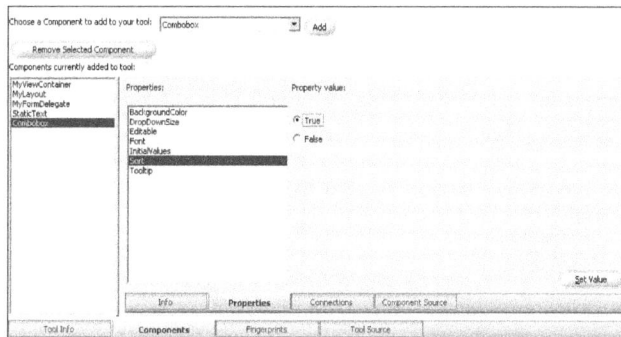

CAUTION

The property value box will only do simple validation checks to ensure property settings you use are valid. Refer to Groove's Component Catalog or API reference to ensure that the value you are using for a property is correct. For example, it will allow you to set "Cincinnati" for the BackgroundColor property of the Combobox component even though it is not a valid property value. Incorrect property values can cause errors or other strange problems within your tool.

CAUTION

If you do not click the Set Value button, the property change will not take effect and clicking anything else will cause you to lose the value you've entered.

CONNECTIONS TAB   This enables you to specify dependencies between tool components. For example, in Figure 10.13 you have specified that your view container will be connected to the MyLayout component. Click the Apply Connection to Component button to make the connection(s) specified. Not all components expect connections so some components will not offer any options on this screen. Consult the API and Programming reference to determine if a component you are using supports and/or expects a connection to be established.

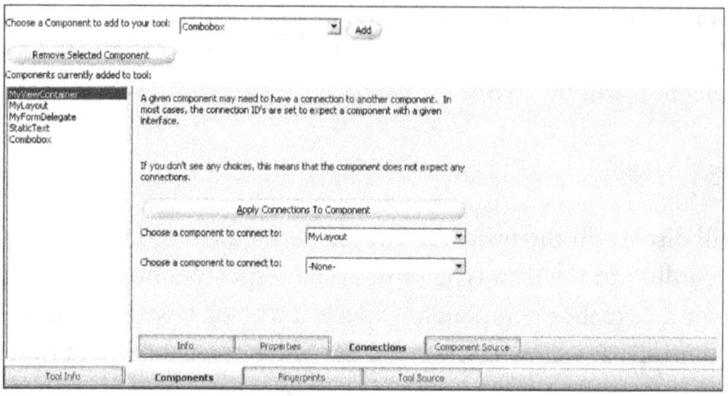

Figure 10.13
In this example we've defined a connection between the view container component and a layout component.

COMPONENT SOURCE TAB Clicking this tab will display the current source for the component. In a template, this is everything between the `<g:Component></g:Component>` tags. An example is shown in Figure 10.14.

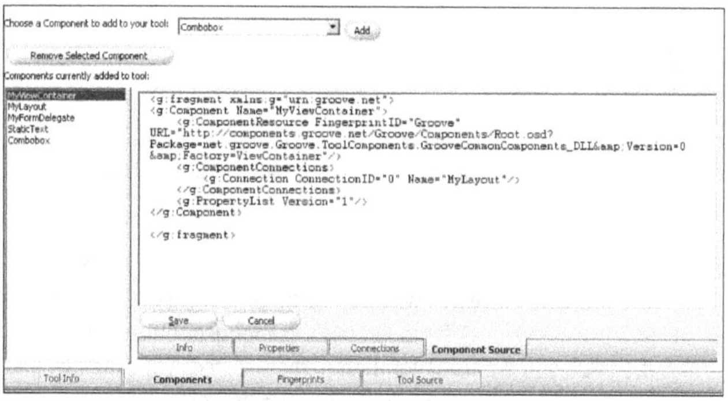

Figure 10.14
Clicking the Component Source tab will enable you to see the XML document created by the component type and property settings.

NOTE

> You will probably see `<g:fragment></g:fragment>` tags around the source code. This is because the component source is only a fragment from within a complete tool template. If you are cutting and pasting source into a template from this screen be sure to remove these tags.

FINGERPRINTS TAB

Groove enables you to digitally sign your components using a digital fingerprint. Signing a component provides a means for others to ensure that a component has come from you and not from some other, untrusted source. A single certificate can be used to sign many components so you don't need a new certificate for each component. The Groove Tool Publisher, which we'll be discussing shortly, enables you to generate a short-term certificate for use during development. Figure 10.15 shows a list of all the fingerprints defined for a single tool.

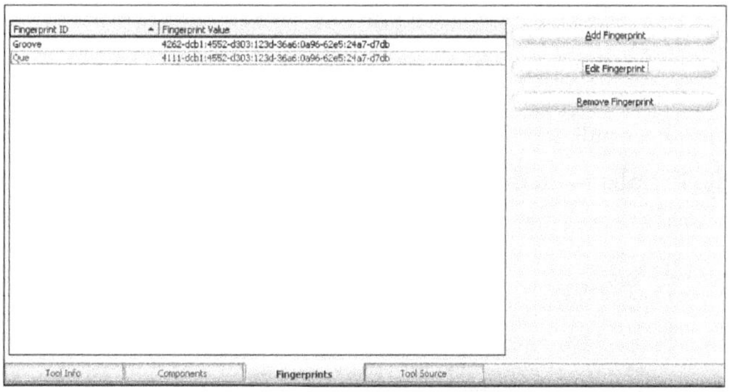

Figure 10.15
Clicking the
Fingerprints tab will
enable you to main-
tain fingerprints used
within the tool.

ADDING A FINGERPRINT

Click the Add Fingerprint button to add a new fingerprint to the tool's `FingerprintTable` element. You will be prompted for the following two fields:

- Fingerprint ID—The ID that uniquely identifies the fingerprint within this tool. You can choose whatever name you like but remember that you must use the same name later when referencing it within a tool template.
- Fingerprint Value—The hash value of the public key pairs for a digital fingerprint.

TOOL SOURCE

Clicking this tab will show the Tool Template source (`.tpl`) that the Tool Creator has generated for you. At any time in the Tool Creator tool you can click this tab to see how your changes have been reflected in the tool template source.

> **NOTE**
>
> You cannot edit the source directly in this window. To edit the source, you'll need to save the file to disk and open it in another editor. We'll talk about the Save to File option in the following section, "Additional Tool Creator Options."

ADDITIONAL TOOL CREATOR OPTIONS

The buttons highlighted in Figure 10.16 allow you to perform the following functions:

- Open Tool—Clicking this opens an existing Tool Template (`.tpl`) file into the Tool Creator tool.

> **CAUTION**
>
> Some templates developed outside of the Tool Creator tool (such as ones written manually in a text editor) may have properties that will be not reflected properly within the Tool Creator tool. Unless you originally created the tool template using the Tool Creator tool, be careful to check that no template elements got lost in the translation.

- Save to File—Clicking this allows you to save the current Tool Template source to disk.

- New Tool—Clears the current tool template being worked on and creates a new tool template file for modification. You will be prompted to save any changes in the current template. This will start the Create Tool wizard that we discussed earlier.

- Overlay Template—If this button is chosen, the Tool Creator will replace any templates in the `template.xss` file with the same name as the template currently in memory.

Figure 10.16
This row of buttons enables you to open a tool template in the Tool Creator, save the current tool template to disk, start a brand new tool template, and overlay the tool template in the Groove database.

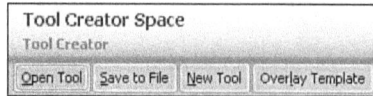

PUBLISHING TOOLS YOU'VE CREATED WITH THE TOOL PUBLISHER

To share your new tool with others, it needs to be published. Included with the GDK is the Tool Publisher tool, which can greatly simplify the process. It's a great timesaver for most basic tool publishing requirements. See Chapter 13 for more details on publishing tools.

INJECTING THE TOOL PUBLISHER

The Tool Publisher is a tool itself, so you must inject it into Groove to use it. Within the `GDK Installation\Utilites\GrooveToolPublisher` folder you will find the `ToolPublisherTool.grv` file. Double-click this file and it will be injected into your Groove account.

CREATING A NEW PROJECT

To begin using the tool, you must create a new project. A project includes all the information needed to successfully publish a tool. Click the New button and you will be prompted for the project name. This name will be used to reference your project within the Tool Publisher, so choose something descriptive. After specifying the name, click the OK button and the project will be added. From here, you must specify the following project information as shown in Figure 10.17:

- Current Project—The name of the current project being edited in the Tool Publisher tool. Choosing a project from the drop-down menu makes it the "active" project that is being edited.

- Root Package Name—The Root Package Name that will be specified in the OSD (Open Software Description) file and used to qualify any references to the package.

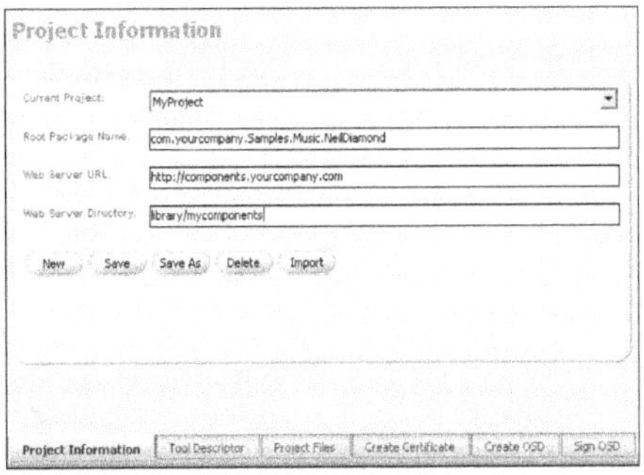

Figure 10.17
The Project Information tab is where you can maintain all the details for this current Tool Publisher project.

NOTE

Although not explicitly required. Groove recommends using reverse domain notation to create a name that identifies the path to your tool's descriptor file. This means taking the standard domain notation and reversing it. For example, the path to `http://www.mycompany.com/tools` would become `com.mycompany.tools` using reverse domain notation.

- Web Server URL—The URL where the tool files will be located. For example, `http://www.yourcompany.com`.

NOTE

Do not include any slashes at the end of the name. A slash at the end is assumed, so adding an additional slash will cause the URL to contain double-slashes, which indicates a folder with no name. For example, `http://www.yourcompany.com/` would be interpreted as `http://www.yourcompany.com//`. Note the empty folder name at the end which causes the problem. Because you usually cannot have an "unnamed" folder, references to files will be invalid.

- Web Server Directory—The directory path where the tool template files can be found. Appending this to the Web Server URL will provide the link to the files. Using the previous example, if components were found at `http://www.yourcompany.com/library/mycomponents` you would specify `/library/mycomponents`.

NOTE

Do not include any slashes at the end of the directory. For example: `/library/mycomponents/` would be incorrect.

OTHER FUNCTIONS OF THE TOOL PUBLISHER TOOL

Included at the bottom of the screen is a row of buttons that perform the following functions:

- New—As discussed earlier, this creates a new project.
- Save—Saves all the settings for the current project.
- Save As—Clicking this button allows you to create a copy of the currently active project with a new name. This is useful if you wish to use a "boilerplate" project example to start with.
- Delete—Clicking this will delete the currently active project and any information contained within it.
- Import—Clicking this button will prompt you for a file in the file system. You can then choose an already existing .grv, .osd, or .xml file to import into the project.

SPECIFYING THE TOOL DESCRIPTORS

Clicking the Tool Descriptor tab will display the screen shown in Figure 10.18. All the templates that make up the tool will be displayed. Selecting a tool template from the drop-down list on the left enables you to specify the following properties for each one including

- Name—The name used to reference this template file.
- Long Name—The longer, more descriptive name for the tool.
- Description—A description of the tool template.
- Author—The author of the template.

Figure 10.18
From the Tool Descriptor tab you can edit some basic information for the tool templates within your project.

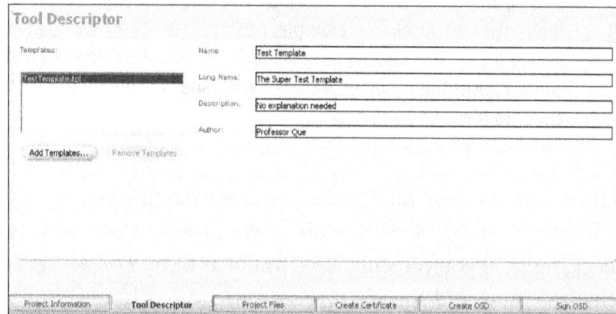

ADDING A NEW TEMPLATE WITHIN THE TOOL PUBLISHER TOOL

You can add a new template by clicking the Add Templates button and specifying the location of the .tpl file you want to add.

REMOVING A TEMPLATE

By selecting a template and clicking the Remove Templates file, you will remove the template from this project. This only removes the tool template from this project. The actual tool template file on disk will not be deleted.

PROJECT FILES LISTING

Clicking the Project Files tab displays all the files included in a project, as shown in Figure 10.19. Many of the fields will be filled in automatically depending on other settings you've made and not all fields may be required depending on the type of installation.

To change the settings for a file, select the file in the list in the list box on the left of the screen. Once selected, there are four different tabs for setting project file options. Short descriptions are provided in the following sections. For more information consult Chapter 10 or the documentation provided with the GDK.

Figure 10.19
By clicking the Project Files tab, you can see all the files associated with a project, including the tool templates and tool descriptors.

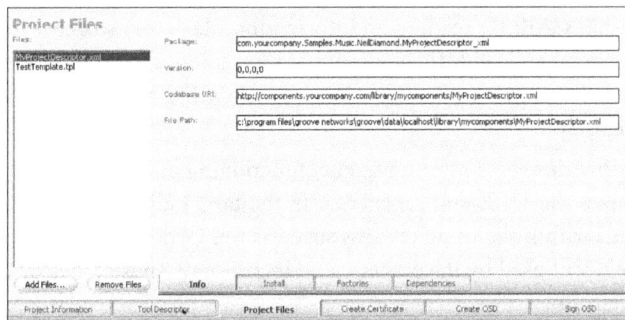

INFO TAB

On this tab you can specify the following information:

- Package—The name of the software package within the OSD.
- Version—The version number in "major, minor, custom, build" format. For example, "1,1,0,0" would indicate a major version of 1, a minor version of 1, and customer and build numbers of zero. These numbers are important so that Groove knows when a newer version of a component is available.
- Codebase URI—Specifies the location of the file for installation using the Uniform Resource Identifier (URI) standard. A URI is a string of characters in a standard format used to describe the location of a physical or logical resource. For our purposes here, it will typically contain a standard URL to the resource.
- File Path—Where the file actually resides in the file system (read-only).

INSTALL TAB

Under the Install tab, you must specify the type of installation and any other information required for that type. The fields include

- Type—The installation type, which can be chosen from the drop-down menu. The different types of installations include

  - Import to XSS: This option is used to import the tool template (.tpl) into a Groove database (.xss).

  - Copy: Copy is often used to copy the tool descriptor file into Groove's XML data directory. However, this can also be used to copy other files needed for your tool, including graphics files and dynamic link libraries (DLLs).

  - Unpack CAB: Cabinet or CAB files are compressed archives that contain files in a particular directory structure. This is often more convenient than deploying individual files. If you are familiar with the Microsoft Windows installation and update process, you may have noticed that it uses cabinet files extensively.

  - Install CAB: By reading an information file (.inf) stored within a cabinet file, Groove can install the contents of the cabinet file automatically. This not only includes copying necessary files but also other tasks such as modifying the Registry.

  - InProc Server: For components functioning as in-process servers, this install type copies the DLL and registers it in the target client system. An in-process server runs within the same process space as the Groove Workspace application. This field will used by developers who incorporate these types of COM components in their tool.

  - External: For installations with an executable file such as INSTALL.EXE or SETUP.EXE, this type will execute the program to begin the installation.

- Target Directory—The target installation directory (if applicable).
- Database URI—The URI to a database resource (if applicable).
- Document Name—The name of the project file.
- Schema URI—The URI to a schema file.

FACTORIES TAB

The Open Software Description provides for the definition of different factory elements. You can define several different types of them within the Tool Publishing tool and you can set the following properties if applicable:

- Type—Describes the type of factory being used. This can either be a Program ID, an XML document, or a temporary XML document.
- Name—The name used to reference this project element.
- Database URI—Location of a database using the Universal Resource Identifier format.

10

NOTE

> For a more detailed explanation of the URI syntax, see the Internet Engineering Task Force memo on the subject at `http://www.ietf.org/rfc/rfc2396.txt`.

- Document Name—The name assigned to this document.
- Filename—The actual filename used for the document.

DEPENDENCIES TAB

On this screen you can create dependencies among your files. For example, in Figure 10.20 we have created a dependency between our tool template and its XML descriptor. Dependencies are part of the Open Software Description and illustrate when files are dependent on one another.

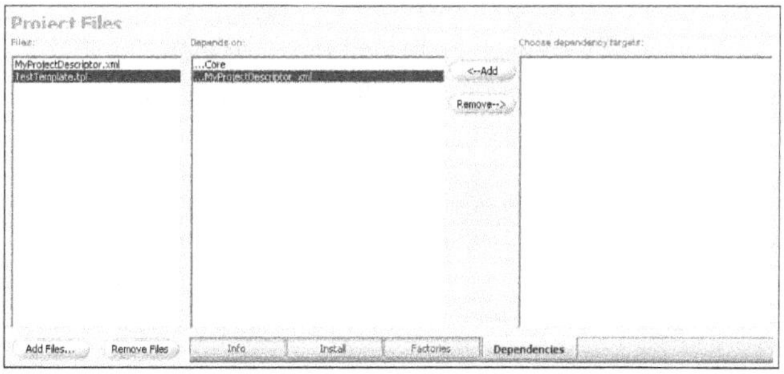

Figure 10.20
Within the Dependencies tab, you can define dependencies within the project such as this example where you associate a tool template with a tool descriptor file.

To create a dependency, select the project file in the list on the left side of the screen. Select the file it depends on from the list on the right side of the screen and click the Add button. It should now appear in the Depends On list in the center of the screen.

To remove a dependency that is no longer needed, highlight the selection in the Depends On list and click the Remove button.

NOTE

> Removing a project file automatically destroys any dependencies of which it is part.

THE DATABASE NAVIGATOR TOOL

Earlier in this chapter, we discussed how Groove stores its data locally in XML databases. These data stores serve a variety of purposes, from storing persistent space data to account data to data used in space synchronization. It's often helpful to examine and directly modify this data during the development process. Using the Database Navigator tool, Groove developers can

- View the contents of an XSS database to ensure a tool was injected correctly.
- Delete database documents.
- View and copy the source code from an already existing template.
- Import tool templates (.tpl), libraries (.gsl), and XML document (.xml) files.
- Export database documents to a file.

CAUTION

> The Database Navigator, if used improperly, can corrupt your Groove installation. If you are careless, you could find yourself needing to reinstall your Groove client. For example, using the Delete Document button carelessly can remove entire tools from the installation and usually requires reinstallation to restore the tools.

THE DATABASE NAVIGATOR INTERFACE

The Database Navigator tool itself is divided into two panes as shown in Figure 10.21. The top pane is used to navigate the XML databases whereas the bottom is used to display the contents of any database document.

Figure 10.21
Within the Database Navigator tool, you can see all available databases in the top pane and view individual XML documents in the bottom pane.

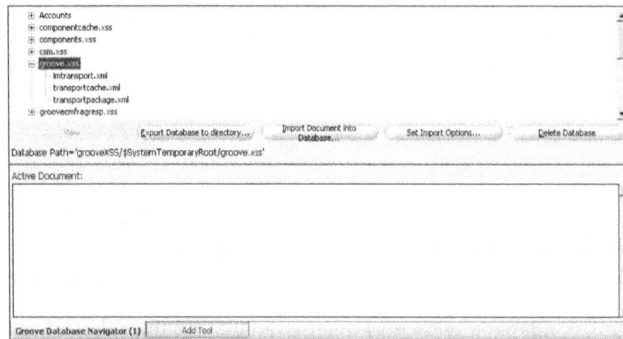

INJECTING THE GROOVE DATABASE NAVIGATOR

The Database Navigator is a tool, so you must inject it into Groove and add it to a shared space. Within the *GDK Installation*\Utilites\GrooveDBNav folder you will find the GrooveDBNav.grv file. Double-click this file to inject it into Groove. Once injected, you should now see the Groove Database Navigator in the list of available tools.

NAVIGATING AND VIEWING A DATABASE DOCUMENT

Using the top pane of the tool, you can navigate through the various branches that represent the different XML databases. Branches can be expanded and compressed by double-clicking the branch itself or clicking the + and [ms] buttons next to the branch. In Figure 10.22, we have expanded the templates.xss branch to find the chesstemplate.tpl object.

By selecting this template and clicking the View Document button, we can view the template source in the bottom pane as shown.

Figure 10.22
In this example we display the chess game tool template by highlighting the document and clicking the View Document button.

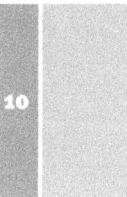

SAVING A DOCUMENT TO A FILE

Although we can view a document directly in the tool, you can also save it to disk. After selecting a document in the database, click the Export Document to File button and you will be prompted for the location in which to save the file.

SAVING AN ENTIRE DATABASE TO A DIRECTORY

Instead of saving individual documents, it is possible to export all the documents within a particular database to a directory. Simply select the .xss file you'd like to export and click the Export Database to Directory button. You'll be prompted to enter a database name at this point. Click the Save button and the export process will begin.

NOTE
> There is no status bar showing the current progress. However, this could take several minutes to complete depending on the number of documents in the database.

IMPORTING A DOCUMENT INTO A DATABASE

This feature is very useful during tool development. As shown in Chapter 8, importing a document into the database allows you to "manifest" the document. When the document is placed in the manifest, Groove has become aware of it. For example, when a tool template is added to the manifest the tool defined can be added to a shared space. Select the database

(.xss) file where the document will be placed and click the Import Document into Database button. In the pop-up window displayed, you have several different options for the import process as shown in Figure 10.23. Refer to the GDK documentation for an explanation of the different import options provided. After they have been set, you will not be prompted again for them during this Groove session. If you need to modify them again, clicking the Set Import Options button will allow you to change them at any point.

Figure 10.23
When importing a document into the database, you can tailor the import from the Import Options screen.

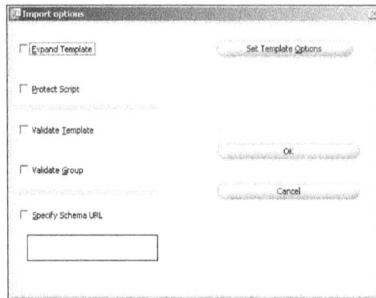

Deleting a Document from the Database

By selecting a document in the database and clicking the Delete Document button, you will permanently remove the document from the database.

CAUTION

> This does not delete any files that the document may have dependencies on. You may end up orphaning files that were referenced in the original document. For example, a tool template may use an instance of another tool in its tool template. If this is not used anywhere else, deleting the "parent" tool will effectively create another tool that is not referenced anywhere (the "orphaned" tool).

Deleting a Database

By selecting a database and clicking the Delete Database button, the database will be removed from this installation of Groove.

CAUTION

> Use extreme caution with this function; many of the databases are required and deleting one could render your installation inoperable. Unless you've created the database yourself, consider it to be an important part of the installation. Creating and using your own database is an advanced topic that is beyond the scope of this book. Refer to the documentation provided within the GDK for more information on this topic.

REGISTRY FILES INCLUDED IN THE GDK

Sometimes there are settings not readily accessible that can be very useful for developing, testing, and debugging tools. These are not meant for deployment into production clients, but can be very valuable for the developer trying to build a component. These are enabled via the following Registry edits that are provided in the `GDK Install Folder`\RegistryFiles folder:

- `DisableWebAccess.reg`—This forces Groove to download all components from the `\localhost` folder instead of trying to download them from the Web. This is useful for developers because they will not have to publish their components to a Web server to inject them.

- `EnableWebAccess.reg`—This reverts Groove to the normal configuration in which it will check the Web for component updates.

- `DisableComponentAuthentication.reg`—This stops Groove from checking authentication information before injecting components. This is useful so developers will not have to sign their components until they are published for others.

CAUTION

> You should not have this enabled when injecting components from other sources because the authenticity has not been verified.

- `EnableComponentAuthentication.reg`—This will again require Groove to check authentication before injecting any components.

- `DisableMyTemplates.reg`—This enables the default setting in which Groove will not check the `Data\My Templates` folder for tool templates.

- `EnableMyTemplates.reg`—This is very useful for rapid prototyping. When enabled, this instructs Groove to check the `Data\My Templates` folder for any tool templates. If any are found, it will allow the developer to add the tool without going through all the other steps need for formal tool injection. In Chapter 8, we'll discuss how to use this as we use rapid prototyping to developer our sample tool.

- `DisableCellBorders.reg`—Makes cell borders invisible.

- `EnableCellBorders.reg`—Although usually invisible, this Registry entry turns on the borders and that can be very helpful when trying to "tweak" the layout for a tool.

- `DisableScriptDebugging.reg`—Disables the script debugging feature.

- `EnableScriptDebugging.reg`—Because Groove tools can use the scripting host, these scripts can be debugged using such tools as Microsoft's Visual InterDev.

EXAMPLE: USING SCRIPT DEBUGGING WITH VISUAL INTERDEV

Groove uses the Microsoft Windows Script Components (Active Scripting) as the scripting engine for tools and has implemented Active Debugging, so a tool like Microsoft's Visual InterDev can allow you to easily track down runtime errors. In this example, we'll show how to add a breakpoint to some simple JavaScript code, tell exactly on which line a script error has occurred, and use the immediate window to view some variable values. These following steps demonstrate how to attach to the Groove client process using Microsoft Visual InterDev:

1. Shut down Groove if it is running.

2. Double-click the EnableScriptDebugging.reg file to enable script debugging. You will receive confirmation if it is successfully entered into the Registry.

3. Add the SampleDebug.tpl tool code to the *Groove Installation Folder*/Data/My Templates folder.

4. Start Groove and add the SampleDebug tool to a shared space.

5. Open Microsoft Visual InterDev and enter the debug processes option by choosing Debug, Processes from the main menu or clicking the Processes icon as shown in Figure 10.24.

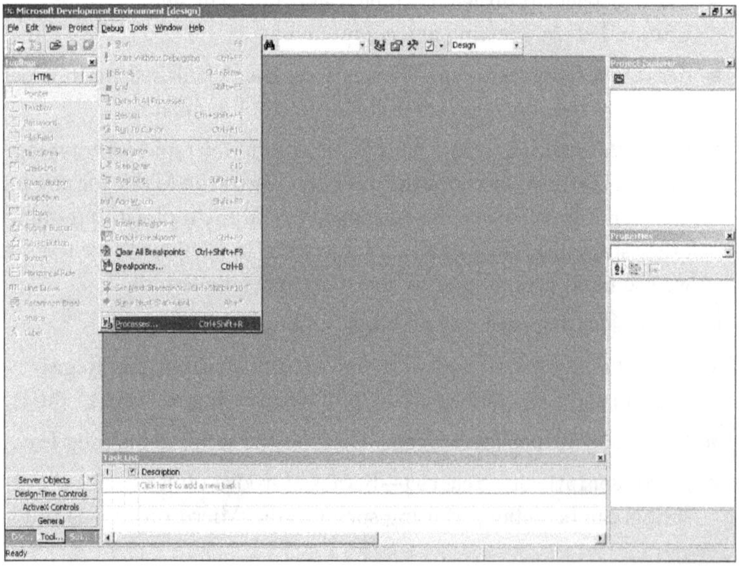

Figure 10.24
Clicking the Processes button will allow us to see all processes that we may attach to.

6. As shown in Figure 10.25, highlight Groove.exe from the list of processes and click the Attach button. It will appear in the bottom list of attached processes. Click the Close button and return to the Groove transceiver.

Figure 10.25
From the list of processes, highlight Groove.exe and click the Attach button to debug.

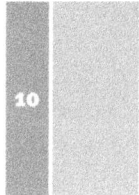

The Visual InterDev debugger is now attached to the Groove process.

ADDING A BREAKPOINT TO THE SCRIPT

Now that Visual InterDev is attached to the Groove.exe process, you can add a break to the script. Breaks are useful for stopping a script during execution so that you can check variable contents or examine the flow of program execution. Follow these steps to add a breakpoint to your code for debugging by using Microsoft Visual InterDev:

1. Open the SampleDebug tool that was added to the shared space in step 4 of the previous numbered list if it is not open already.

2. Open the Visual InterDev window. If the previous steps were followed correctly, it should be attached to the Groove.exe process.

3. Open the Running Documents windows by choosing View, Debug Windows, Running Documents in Visual InterDev. A window should open as shown in Figure 10.26 that shows all the attached processes that are hosting active scripting on this machine. In this example, you will find the Groove process with documents representing the shared space, tool, and the script component underneath it.

TIP

> By default, the window showing the running documents is rather small. You can resize the window by placing your mouse pointer at the top of the running documents window and dragging it toward the top of the screen.

4. Double-click the script component document which is named AppGlue in our example. This opens the script in the primary Visual InterDev window as shown in Figure 10.26.

Figure 10.26
You need to choose
Debug Windows,
Running Documents to
view what is currently
executing.

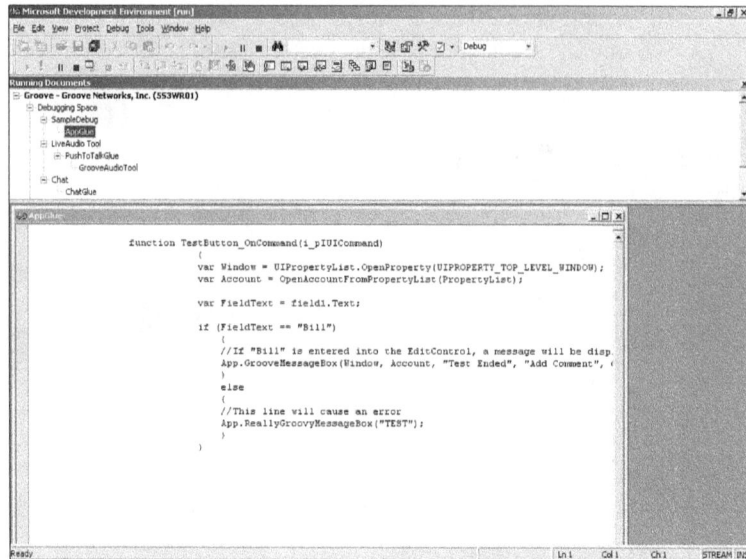

5. Now set a breakpoint in your code to suspend execution temporarily. Place the cursor on the line and choose Debug, Insert Breakpoint from the main menu. In our example, we have placed a break on the If statement line that checks the contents of the edit control as indicated by the circle to the left of the script as shown in Figure 10.27.

Figure 10.27
In this figure we've
clicked to the left of
the code where we
want the breakpoint
to be inserted as indi-
cated by a red circle.

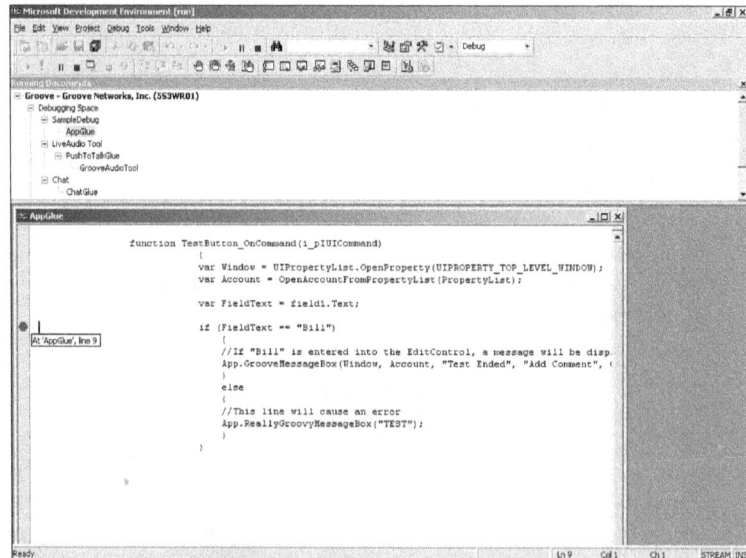

6. In the SampleDebug tool in your shared space type **Liam** into the edit control provided and click the Test button.

7. Clicking the Test button executes the script. The script will break at the point that was set in step 5 and open the Visual InterDev window. Examine the contents of the `FieldText` variable by opening the Immediate Window by choosing View, Debug Windows, Immediate as shown in Figure 10.28.

Figure 10.28
In this step we open the Immediate Window by choosing View, Debug Windows, Immediate from the main menu.

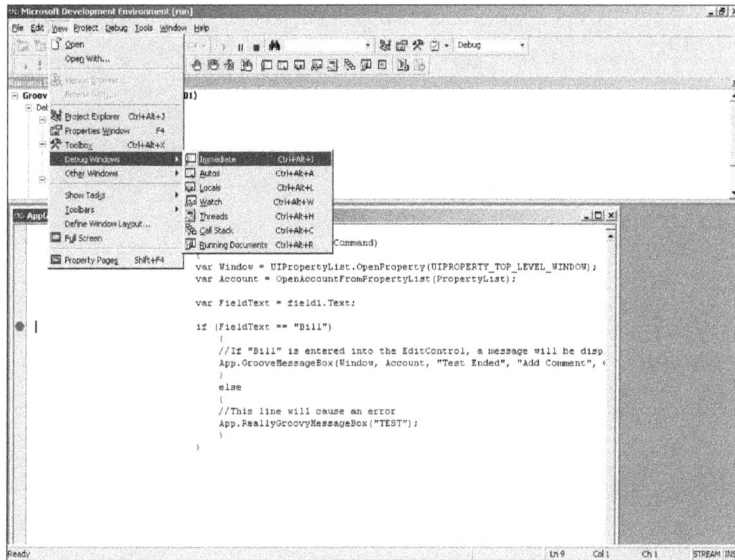

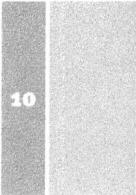

8. In the Immediate Window, type ? `FieldText` as shown in Figure 10.29. This will print the current contents of the `FieldText` variable.

Figure 10.29
With the code at the breakpoint we can now view the contents of the `FieldText` variable from the Immediate Window.

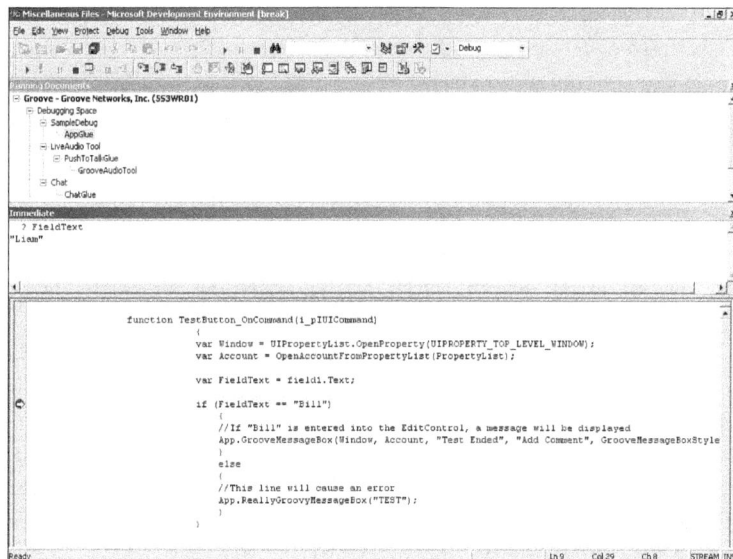

TIP

> You can also modify the contents of a variable in the Immediate Window by using the equals (assignment) operator. For example, you can set `FieldText` to "Bill" by typing `FieldText = "Bill"` in the Immediate Window.

9. Continue the script execution by clicking the Continue button as shown in Figure 10.30.

Figure 10.30
Clicking the Continue button will allow the process to continue execution.

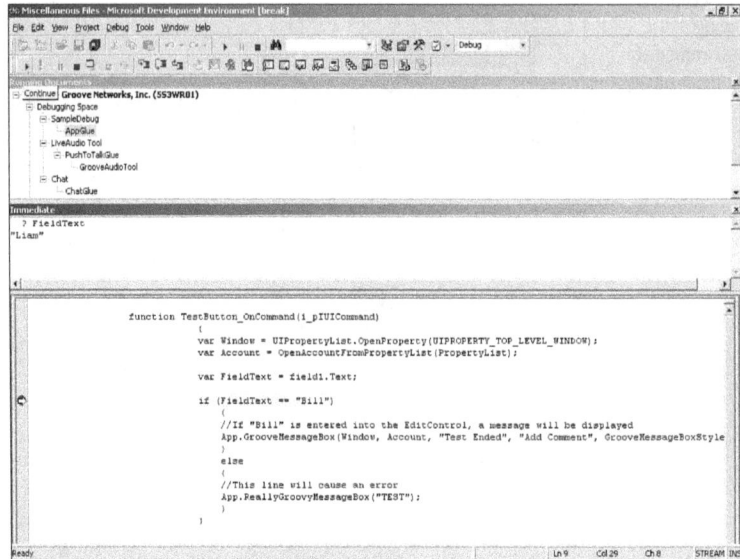

As you can see in this simple example, using a tool like Visual InterDev is a great way to interactively debug scripts. Being able to stop execution and view and change variables can help you root out those elusive script bugs. Refer to your Microsoft Visual InterDev documentation for the additional debugging features that are available.

GROOVE CUSTOMER SERVICE MANAGER VIEWER

Many problems can occur when injecting a tool. Even when a tool had been taken through several successful test runs during rapid prototyping, it can still encounter numerous problems during the injection process. Some are simple such as mistyped URLs in the OSD, although others can be more elusive such as Fingerprint format problems. Groove includes the GrooveCSMViewer to provide information that can usually help pinpoint where the problem lies. This is actually not part of the GDK, but is important to know about now that you've begun to look at the tool creation process. This tool has actually been very valuable not only for tool developers, but for Groove support as a means to remotely troubleshoot problems with the client and tools. These next few steps demonstrate how to open the viewer and enable the tracing feature:

1. Shut down Groove if it is currently running.

2. Navigate to your Groove installation folder. This is the same folder that contains the main Groove executable (`groove.exe`). Run the program entitled `GrooveCSMViewer.exe` by double-clicking it.

3. This should open the Select Account screen as shown in Figure 10.31. Highlight the row which contains "(Device Account}" in Default Identity column. Click the OK button to select this account.

Figure 10.31
From this screen you must select the account with which you wish to use the Customer Service Manager.

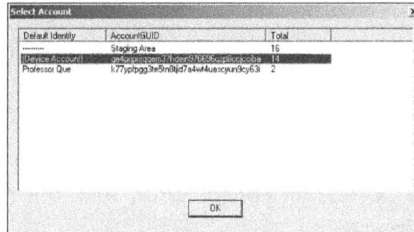

4. You should now see the screen shown in Figure 10.32. By clicking the Settings button near the bottom of the window, you can select for the trace as shown in Figure 10.33. Highlight the `ComponentMgr` module and click the Edit button. Check the Enable Tracing button and choose a Severity Level of "Trace" from the drop-down list box. Do the same for the `DownloadMgr` module.

Figure 10.32
After selecting an account, you'll be greeted with all the tabs that the Customer Service Manager has to offer.

Figure 10.33
We have selected the `DownloadMgr` as the component for which we'd like to enable tracing.

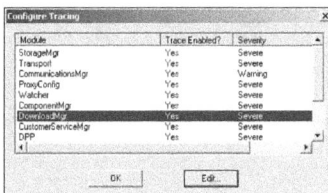

TIP

For injection problems, it is usually a good idea to start tracing on the ComponentMgr and DownloadMgr modules.

5. After all the settings have been configured properly, click the OK button to close the viewer.

6. Try to reinject the tool with the error.

7. After the error has been re-created, shut down Groove and reopen the viewer as explained in step 2.

8. This should open the Select Account screen as we saw in Figure 10.31. Highlight the row which contains "(Device Account}" in Default Identity column. Click the OK button to select this account.

9. Click the Trace tab and you can examine the trace log. Looking at the example in Figure 10.34 you can see the "URL Not Found" error. So in this example, you should double-check all URLs for accuracy.

Figure 10.34
The Trace tab in the Customer Service Manager shows us the error logged by the Download Manager.

CHAPTER 11

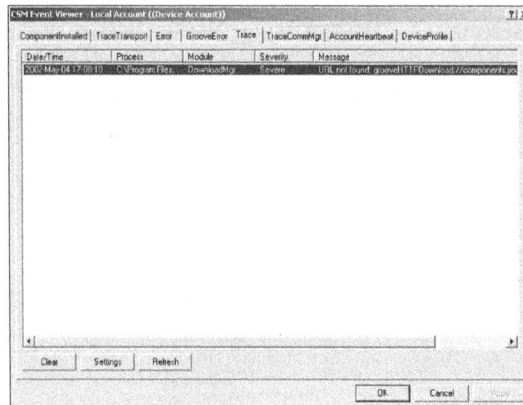

CREATING NEW TOOLS IN GROOVE

In this chapter

TAILORING GROOVE WITH YOUR OWN CUSTOM TOOL

As you saw in Chapters 5 through 8, tools are the building blocks used to create a collaborative forum within a Groove shared space. As shared space managers and participants add tools to a space they are able to tailor the environment to match their particular needs as they arise. Although Groove provides a great variety of tools for many common tasks, organizations and individuals often have needs that may not be satisfied by Groove's default set of tools. This is where the similarities between Groove and many other collaborative tools end. Tool developers have the capability to create tools quickly that can take advantage of Groove's already rich set of components and a collaborative platform that works hand in hand with Groove's strong set of security features.

In this chapter, you see how to develop a tool for Groove Workspace that requires the real-time collaboration of a small group of users. You develop a virtual focus group tool that enables all participants to view a product's photograph. While viewing the image, each participant will take a survey that provides feedback on the product they are viewing. As in the real world, the participants will also be able to chat with one another while they are in session using Groove Workspace's provided audio and chat capabilities. In this chapter you build the tool template, which takes advantage of several of Groove's runtime features, including

- The capability to easily place user interface components within the tool interface.
- Using glue code to react to events, such as a user clicking a button.
- Storing data in Groove's local database that will be disseminated to all other users within the space automatically.
- Using a subform pop-up window to collect information from the user.

Although we'll start by introducing some of the important concepts you should know, this chapter is primarily intended to present a tool development exercise. With a step-by-step approach broken down into sections, we'll complete a tool that takes advantage of many Groove features. Chapter 12 extends the lesson even further by showing you some of the additional functionality that can be added to your tools.

SKILLS REQUIRED FOR THIS CHAPTER

In this chapter, you learn what components make up a tool template and the syntax used. Using the Tool Creator, you can easily create a tool template with most the elements required without having to code them by hand. Using the Tool Creator tool only requires you to have a basic knowledge of how a tool works within a shared space. You learn more about the Tool Creator tool itself in Chapter 10, "The Groove SDK," which discussed the Groove Development kit. However, after you have created a base template, you will need to modify it slightly. Although I will detail the exact changes in this chapter's example, the following skills are helpful:

- Understanding of basic HTML syntax for using the HTML Layout component
- Some experience with JavaScript and familiarity with the language syntax
- A basic understanding of proper XML syntax
- Experience working with database records

THE FILES THAT MAKE UP A TOOL

In the simplest terms, a tool is the instantiation of something called a tool template file. Although the tool template is the emphasis of this chapter, several files are necessary to make a completely functional tool that can be deployed to other Groove users. These include the following:

- Tool template—A tool template is the file that most developers will become intimately familiar with. It contains information needed by Groove at run-time to instantiate components and define the layout of the user interface, and can contain logic that comprises the tool's behavior. The file itself is a well-formed XML document.

- XML Schema—For tools using Groove's own local data storage, the XML schema is used to define the underlying data structure. Using the schema, Groove's own data storage and dissemination services can handle synchronization and persistence of the data. For our Focus Group tool in this chapter you create a simple schema that defines the fields used when storing user feedback.

- Tool Descriptor—The tool descriptor's name gives a good indication of what it contains. Used to describe the tool, it contains information such as the tool name, the version, and what type of tool it is. In addition, it also directs Groove where to find the tool's template and OSD files. You'll be exploring this file in depth when you examine publishing in Chapter 13, "Publishing a New Tool."

- OSD File—OSD stands for Open Software Description. This XML standard, originally pioneered by Microsoft, is used to instruct Groove where to obtain all needed software components for the tool and their intended destination. Also, it provides additional configuration information directly related to the installation of any and all software packages. You'll learn more about Groove's implementation of this standard in Chapter 13.

- GRV File—When injecting a tool, skin, or other Groove component, the GRV file is the file that "kicks off" the injection process. For tools, this tells the Component Services where to find the OSD file, which subsequently is used to inject the tool into the user's account. The GRV files are also used for injecting shared spaces, adding licenses, and for other components that must undergo the injection process. This is usually one of the last files created when preparing for distribution and will be covered in Chapter 12.

11

A BASIC OUTLINE OF A GROOVE TOOL TEMPLATE

Although there are other files that make up a tool, the tool template is where you find the real guts of a tool. It is made up of an assortment of component definitions. A Groove component can be a user interface component, such as a button, a layout component that determines where the various user interface components will be placed, or a scripting host component, which contains the code that makes the tool an interactive collaborative tool that exhibits its own behaviors. Just like other software components, a tool does not need a user interface. However, for our purposes here, you will be creating a tool with a graphical interface that will interact with the user.

For simplicity's sake, you'll examine how a tool template is structured to perform just some basic tasks. The diagram shown in Figure 11.1 illustrates a simple design of a tool with one button and the underlying structure.

Figure 11.1
A very basic tool template structure contains these elements.

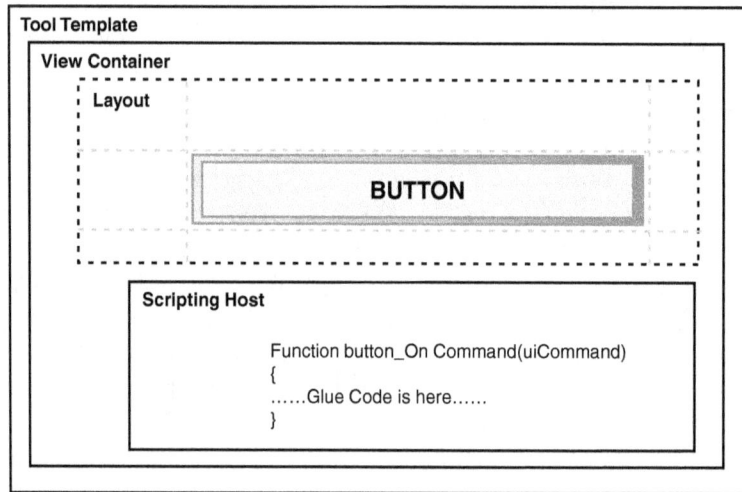

A very integral part of most tool templates is the View Container. What you could consider a blueprint for the tool interface, this is used to present a form with form elements to the user. Roughly analogous to a form on a Web page, this holds all the screen elements such as a textbox, label, button, etc.

These graphical elements are the Components that are the building blocks of every Groove tool. These are objects that are instantiated by Groove when the tool is accessed. In this simple example you can see that your sample tool has three components: the layout, the button, and the scripting host. The button shown is one of the standard user interface components that Groove provides. It's a simple button that can be formatted a variety of different ways and can be used to run code when the user clicks it. Two very important components that you'll be hearing a lot about are

- Layout: This determines where everything should be placed. You'll be examining the different types of layouts shortly. In this example, just think of it as the blueprint for your screen design. The layout itself is one of the components within your tool template.

- Scripting Host: Actions and behaviors in Groove are performed by *glue code*. Glue code is aptly named because it is the "glue" that holds pieces of a Groove tool together. In our example, we show the glue code that responds to the button's click event. Many of the standard Groove tools use JavaScript as the scripting language.

While we are discussing the basic tool template here, there are some other features you can use that can make your tool template powerful and extremely complex. Although these fall outside the scope of the examples you'll see in this book, some of these include the following:

- Enterprise Integration: Using features called connectors and bots with the Groove Enterprise Integration Server, you can seamlessly integrate Groove Workspace with other applications and data stores within the Enterprise.

- Extending Groove Tools with External Applications: Using COM, you can develop applications that interface with Groove tools using popular development platforms, such as Microsoft Visual Basic or C++.

THE TOOL TEMPLATE STRUCTURE ELEMENTS

Every tool template is a well-formed XML document that follows the same basic structure. Figure 11.2 provides a high-level overview of the elements that compose a tool template file.

Figure 11.2
This is a figure showing the different XML elements that make up a tool template.

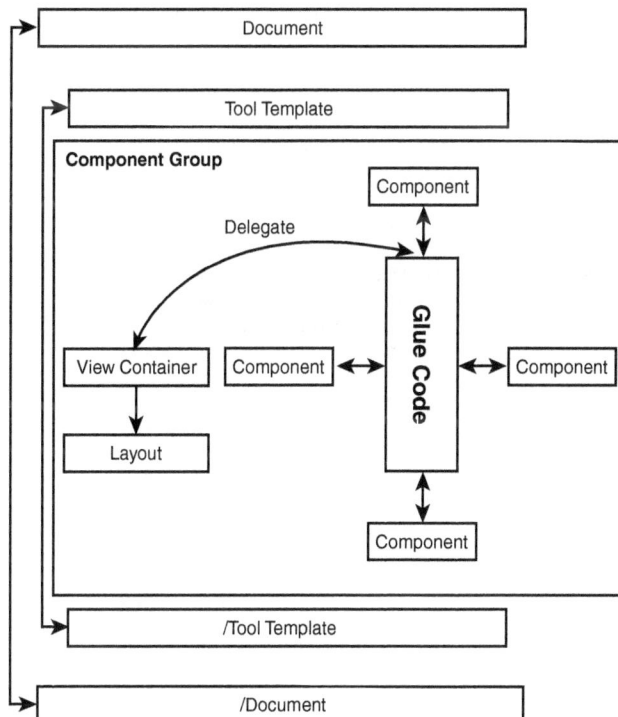

THE XML Document TAGS

Each Groove Template File (and any XML file Groove uses) will be surrounded by a document tag or element. They always look like this:

```
<g:Document Name="ToolTemplate.tpl" xmlns:g="urn:groove.net">
Contents of document
</g:Document>
```

Those familiar with XML will recognize the xmlns attribute, which specifies the namespace that is used to qualify element and attribute names. This is required for all the Groove XML documents that you'll be creating for your tool. An XML document is primarily a collection of elements and attributes. It would be very easy for there to be a problem of duplicate elements and attributes being used in XML document. To help avoid this problem, namespaces are used along with an element to define the element to which you are referring. For example, it is very likely another Document element is used in another XML schema that has been created. To distinguish Groove tool template document from one in another schema, specify the groove.net namespace with xmlns:g="urn:groove.net", as you can see in the preceding XML.

THE ToolTemplate TAGS

The ToolTemplate element tells Groove that it is reading a tool template file and should treat it accordingly. Within these tags, Groove will expect to find the view container, layout, and all the components that will make up the tool. To demonstrate how rapid prototyping works, you'll look at a simple tool template that has already been created for you in the file TestTemplate.tpl. Examine the code for this tool template in Listing 11.1. This tool template contains only one StaticText component that will display "You are using rapid prototyping" when the tool is opened.

LISTING 11.1 THE TestTemplate.tpl TOOL TEMPLATE DEMONSTRATE RAPID PROTOTYPING

```
<g:Document Name="TestTemplate.tpl" xmlns:g="urn:groove.net">
   <g:ToolTemplate DefaultToolDisplayName="Test Template"
➡Name="TestTemplate.Tool" TemplateDisplayName="Test Template">
       <g:ViewInfo Lifetime="Limited"/>
       <g:ComponentGroup DefaultView="TestViewContainer">
           <g:Component Name="TestViewContainer">
               <g:ComponentResource
➡URL="http://components.groove.net/Groove/Components/Root.osd?Package=net.groove.
➡Groove.ToolComponents.GrooveCommonComponents_DLL&amp;Version=0&amp;
➡Factory=ViewContainer"/>
               <g:PropertyList Version="1">
                   <g:Property Name="Background">
                       <g:BackgroundStyle Style="SectionBackground"/>
                   </g:Property>
                </g:PropertyList>
               <g:ComponentConnections>
                   <g:Connection ConnectionID="0" Name="HTMLLayout"/>
               </g:ComponentConnections>
           </g:Component>
```

```
        <g:Component Name="HTMLLayout">
            <g:ComponentResource
➥URL="http://components.groove.net/Groove/Components/Root.osd?Package=net.groove.
➥Groove.ToolComponents.GrooveCommonComponents_DLL&amp;Version=0&amp;
➥Factory=HTMLTableLayout"/>
            <g:PropertyList Version="1">
                <g:Property Name="Layout">
                    <g:PropertyValue>
                      <TABLE CELLPADDING="2">
                          <TR>
                              <TD>Label1</TD>
                          </TR>
                      </TABLE>
                    </g:PropertyValue>
                </g:Property>
            </g:PropertyList>
        </g:Component>
        <g:Component Name="Label1">
            <g:ComponentResource
[ic:ccc}URL="http://components.groove.net/Groove/Components/Root.osd?Package=net.g
roove.
➥Groove.ToolComponents.GrooveCommonComponents_DLL&amp;Version=0&amp;
➥Factory=Static"/>
                <g:PropertyList Version="1">
                    <g:Property Name="Style" Value="Normal"/>
                        <g:Property Name="Label" Value=
➥"You are using rapid prototyping!"/>
                    </g:PropertyList>
            </g:Component>
        </g:ComponentGroup>
    </g:ToolTemplate>
</g:Document>
```

Looking at this code, you can see the following attributes are defined within the
ToolTemplate element:

- **DefaultToolDisplayName**: The value that will appear on the Tool tab when the tool is used within a shared space. Because Tool tabs are limited in size you should make the attribute value descriptive yet brief. For example, "Focus Group with tons of amazing features" would probably be better named as "Focus Group."

- **Name**: The unique name of the tool within the shared space. Tool templates are usually identifiable by a .Tool extension in the name.

- **TemplateDisplayName**: The name of the tool shown in the Add Tool listing.

THE ComponentGroup ELEMENT

This element is used to group a number of components together within the tool. This element will contain the name of the default view component that we'll be discussing shortly in the "Common Components" section. In addition, each component group can specify a component as a delegate, a concept that was first introduced when we created a tool template using the Tool Creator tool in Chapter 10. Each tool can have several different component groups, each with their own specific delegate.

→ For the introduction to form delegates, **see** "Using the Tool Creator Wizard," **p. 319** (Chapter 10)

Each tool with a user interface must have at least one view container defined. In Listing 11.1, you can see that this is contained within the `ComponentGroup` element and defined with the `DefaultView` attribute. In this example, it is expecting a view container entitled `TestViewContainer`.

TOOL COMPONENTS

Groove provides an entire library of reusable COM components with the base client installation. We used several in the previous simple tool template structure section. COM stands for *Component Object Model*. I describe this type of software architecture a little later in this chapter. All of Groove's components are documented in the API Reference provided with the Groove Development Kit. It's easy to classify every component into one of five general categories:

- Views: These are user interface components that interact with the user. This includes the text boxes, buttons, and other components users will see on the screen.

- Engines: These are responsible for data storage and dissemination. For example, you will be using the `RecordSetEngine`, which is responsible for not only storing data locally for the tool but creating deltas that are sent to other shared space members. You were first introduced to these in Chapter 9 when we discussed using the Tool Creator tool.

- Delegates: These specify an outgoing interface for the tool. Each form and subform can have one of these. In fact, most tools will require one of these to enable your different tool behaviors in response to user interaction and other events.

- Code Components: These are other components that contain script that allows a form to exhibit different behaviors. You will be using the scripting host component in your example, which enables you to create your own customer JavaScript functions and other routines.

- Helper Components: These are other components that do not fit neatly into one of the other categories, such as the layout component, which is used for positioning interface components. As you'll see, Groove has several different components that are designed to work in conjunction with these "helper" components.

If you need functionality not provided by Groove's own reusable component library, you can also develop your own custom COM components. This is often the case when you need to access other external applications and data storage. You can develop your COM components in several different languages, including Visual Basic, C++, and Delphi. Describing the custom development of COM components is beyond the scope of this book, but I will briefly discuss COM in the next section and what is most important for you to know about it.

WHAT IS THE COMPONENT OBJECT MODEL?

This chapter refers to COM frequently. The Component Object Model, or COM, is a software architecture that is an integral part of the Groove client and is used extensively by third-party developers creating exciting new Groove products. So what is COM and what makes it so special?

In the early days of computing, each software developer created new tools as they were needed. A big reason for this was the fact that either

- The program with the correct functionality didn't exist
- The program existed but was in a format that was unusable with the original software

As stated in the second point above, trying to use existing software was often made difficult by integration issues. Software can be developed on many different platforms and in many different languages that are often not compatible. Add to this the fact that historically most software was developed to meet immediate needs without concern for future integration with different or newer versions of software. These are the issues the Component Object Model hopes to address.

The Component Object Model, or COM, is a standard software component architecture model. This model was introduced in a group of technologies that Microsoft has collectively called ActiveX. While surfing the Internet, you've probably been prompted to download several of these as add-in components to Internet Explorer. All components that adhere to this model are guaranteed to be interoperable with other COM components. For example:

> *Liam the developer has created a robust system for tracking expenses in Microsoft Visual Basic. His company has decided to expand into an overseas market that uses different currency. Unfortunately, Liam has very limited time to implement the changes. Knowing that his friend Konrad has written this code for some of his own applications in another language called Delphi, Liam gives him a call. Luckily, Konrad has packaged his currency conversion routine in a COM component. With the COM component, Liam is able to leverage the routines written by Konrad for currency conversion.*

What you see in this example is the power of using the Component Object Model. Even though the currency conversion routines were written in a different language, Liam was still able to use them because they were packaged as COM components.

The actual technical details for creating your own COM component are outside the scope of this book. The only thing you need to know is that if something is written using COM, it can likely be used within your own tool templates. If you want to learn more about the Component Object Model, visit Microsoft's COM site at `http://www.microsoft.com/com/about.asp`. For those who desire more of a hands-on introduction, Microsoft Visual Basic is a popular choice to create your first COM component. A complete ActiveX (COM) component development tutorial in Microsoft Visual Basic can be found at `http://msdn.microsoft.com/library/default.asp?url=/workshop/components/activex/tutorial.asp`.

DEFINING THE COMPONENTS WITHIN YOUR TOOL TEMPLATE

Luckily, most component definitions can be created by using the Tool Creator tool that Groove provides. However, it's important to understand what each component definition consists of because you may find yourself having to modify some component definitions that the Tool Creator provides. In our Focus Group tool example we'll show how to tweak the Tool Creator–generated code.

Each component is defined within the tool template file by specifying the factory, library, and the FingerprintID (if signed) within Component tags. Looking at the following example you can see how a component tag is structured:

```
<g:Component Name="StaticTextComponent">
  <g:ComponentResource FingerprintID="Groove"
➥URL="http://components.groove.net/Groove/Components/Root.osd?Package=net.groove.
➥Groove.ToolComponents.GrooveCommonComponents_DLL&amp;Version=0&amp;
➥Factory=Static"/>
    <g:PropertyList Version="1">
      <g:Property Value="Groove is great" Name="Label"/>
      <g:Property Value="LabelText" Name="FontStyle"/>
      <g:Property Value="Left" Name="HAlignment"/>
    </g:PropertyList>
</g:Component>
```

Figure 11.3 illustrates the some basic elements that make up a component.

Figure 11.3
The typical structure of a component definition in a tool template.

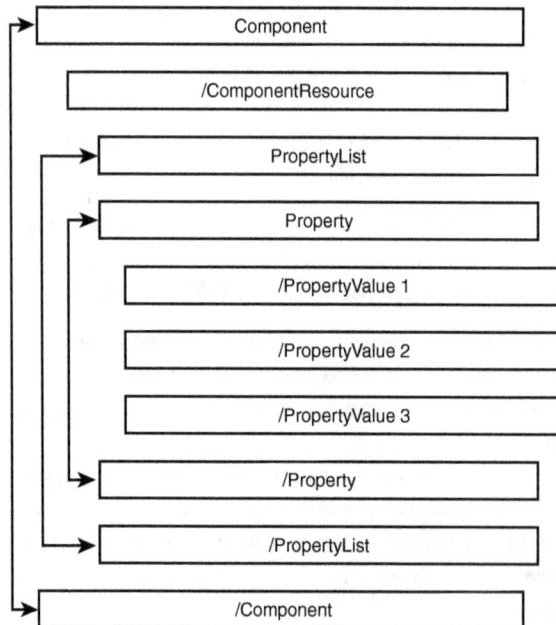

- **Component:** These tags are the container for the entire component. All the other elements are contained within the Component opening and closing tags. This element contains the Name attribute that is used to name the component. In our example, we have named the component StaticTextComponent.

- **ComponentResource:** This is the element that actually points to the component resources. The URL attribute contains a link to the component resource. Also, for signed components you will also find a FingerprintID attribute used to define the Fingerprint used by this component.

- **PropertyList:** Each component has properties that can be defined. Because some components can have different sets of properties, they are contained within the PropertyList elements. The Version attribute is used to define the version number of the properties that you will be using.

- **Property:** Within the PropertyList, you define each individual property with a Property element. The Name attribute is used to define the property value you want to set. The Value property contains the actual value that the property should be set to. If an available property is not set here, the property will use a default value determined by the component developer.

In this example we are instructing Groove to use the GrooveStatic component, which is a user interface component we are using to display the text "Groove is great." If Groove has an earlier version of the component, it will attempt to download it from the address specified in the URL attribute. You can see that we are modifying several of the properties of the component. We have defined the text to be displayed in the Label property, the style of font in the Style property, and the alignment it will use in the HAlignment property. Table 11.1 lists some of the more common interface components, in what library they are found, and a description of their function.

TABLE 11.1   COMPONENTS FOUND WITHIN THE GrooveCommonComponents LIBRARY

Component Name	Description	Factory
GrooveButton	A standard button.	Button
GrooveComboBox	A drop-down combo box.	ComboBox
GrooveEdit	A editable text box.	Edit
GrooveImage	Displays images in JPG, JPEG, or GIF format.	Image
GrooveListBox	Similar to a ComboBox except it is not editable.	ListBox
GrooveListView	Displays a list of text entries.	ListView
GrooveMenu	A standard menu with drop-down options.	Menu

TABLE 11.1 CONTINUED

Component Name	Description	Factory
GrooveProgressBar	Displays a horizontal bar that can be used to show process status.	ProgressBar
GrooveSlider	Provides a horizontal line that has an indicator that can be moved left or right by the user.	Slider
GrooveStatic	A static text box or label.	Static
GrooveTabControl	Provides visual tabs that can be used within a form.	TabControl
GrooveRecordSetEngine	Preferred method for storing a tool's data.	RecordSetEngine

THE VIEW CONTAINER COMPONENT

Every tool must define at least one view container. View containers are used to create the look and feel of a tool. Most tools will have a particular view container designated as the default view, which is displayed when the tool is first used. Like the GrooveStatic component in Table 11.1, the view container component is also contained in the library of the GrooveCommonComponents package in the ViewContainer factory. For some view containers to properly function, they must also be "connected" to a layout using the ComponentConnections element. The following sections briefly explain the different layout options available to a tool developer.

> NOTE
>
> View containers can also be nested within one another. This technique is helpful because it can make complex layouts much simpler to read and maintain.

THE DIFFERENT LAYOUTS SUPPORTED WITHIN A GROOVE TOOL

The layout component, one of Groove's several "helper" components, is used to position the user interface components within a view container. You can choose from several different types of layouts. Generally, you can use any of the layouts provided in your own tool template. However, depending on the complexity of the layout, you might find one of them easier to work with. It will take some trial and error to find which layout is best suited for your application. Even though each layout provides a great deal of flexibility, you are not limited to one layout per tool. The different types offered can be nested and arranged in a combination that suits your needs. The different choices are described in the following sections. Refer to the GDK documentation provided for more details on each of the layouts.

HTML LAYOUT   This layout, as the name implies, enables you to place user interface (UI) components on your form using common HTML table tags. This is a common choice because the structure is easy to understand with even basic HTML experience.

A WYSIWYG HTML editor such as Microsoft FrontPage can be used to prototype screen layouts prior to placing them into the template. Unlike HTML, the HTML Layout is case-sensitive (owing to the fact we are truly using XML within the tool template) so all tags must be in UPPERCASE letters.

Incorrect:

```
<td>MyComponent></td>
```

Correct:

```
<TD>MyComponent></TD>
```

Like HTML, you should ensure all the rows in your table (defined with the `<TR>` tag) have the same number of columns (defined with a `<TD>` tag) throughout the table.

Incorrect:

```
<TABLE>
    <TR>
        <TD>Row1 Column1</TD>
        <TD>Row1 Column2</TD>
    </TR>
    <TR>
        <TD>Row2 Column1</TD>
    </TR>
</TABLE>
```

Correct:

```
<TABLE>
    <TR>
        <TD>Row1 Column1</TD>
        <TD>Row1 Column2</TD>
    </TR>
    <TR>
        <TD>Row2 Column1</TD>
        <TD>Row2 Column2</TD>
    </TR>
</TABLE>
```

You'll note that the first example is not correct because it has a different number of columns in each row.

You should also be aware that the HTML Layout does not enable you to enter text into the layout to be displayed. The HTML Layout will assume anything other than the table tag elements is a component and will attempt to place the component at the position specified.

Incorrect:

```
<TABLE>
    <TR>
        <TD>Groove is great</TD>
        <TD>MyButtonComponent</TD>
    </TR>
</TABLE>
```

Correct:

```
<TABLE>
    <TR>
        <TD>StaticTextComponent</TD>
        <TD>MyButtonComponent</TD>
    </TR>
</TABLE>
```

The first example is incorrect because it tries to place text within the layout. Because there is no Groove is great component, this will generate an error. The second example references a component that will contain the text to display. The GrooveStatic component example in the "Component Definition" section would work well here.

> **TIP**
>
> A common source of errors is referencing the same component more than once in a layout. At this time you can only reference a component with the same name once per layout. The workaround is to create the exact same component but give it a new, unique name.

Because the HTML Layout and tool templates use XML, you can also define empty tags with a single element. For example, the following HTML

```
<TD></TD>
```

can be represented in the HTML Layout like this:

```
<TD/>
```

You'll see this often in tool template elements. Another good example can be found in the "Component Definition" section where we use this nomenclature to define our single ComponentResource element, set some attributes, and close it at the same time like this:

```
<g:ComponentResource FingerprintID="Groove"
➥URL="http://components.groove.net/Groove/Components/Root.osd?Package=net.groove.
➥Groove.ToolComponents.GrooveCommonComponents_DLL&amp;Version=0&amp;
➥Factory=Static"/>
```

Just like standard HTML table elements, you can also use formatting options, such as the following:

- HSPACE: Adds whitespace above and below the table.
- VSPACE: Adds whitespace before and after the component table.
- CELLPADDING: Places whitespace between the border of each cell and component contained within it.

In this example, you create a table with one row and one column with the HSPACE and VSPACE properties set on the TABLE element:

```
<TABLE HSPACE="5" VSPACE="3">
    <TR>
        <TD>
        Name
        </TD>
```

```
    </TR>
</TABLE>
```

However, you cannot include other HTML formatting properties, such as BGCOLOR and BOR-DERCOLOR, which are used to change the color of a table.

> **TIP**
>
> When resizing cells using the HEIGHT and WIDTH properties, you must understand that the largest value within the row or column is ultimately used. For example:
>
> ```
> <TR>
>     <TD HEIGHT="100">Button1</TD>
>     <TD HEIGHT="150">Button2</TD>
>     <TD HEIGHT="100">Button3</TD>
> </TR>
> ```
>
> This example will create a column with a HEIGHT of 150 and not of 100. If you need different HEIGHTs for each cell you would probably choose another type of layout such as the MultiCell layout, which is described in the next section.

For more advanced formatting using the HTML Layout, you do have the capability to use nested tables to produce the desired formatting. However, you must still adhere to the requirement that each row must have the same number of columns or an error will occur.

> **TIP**
>
> Like standard HTML, you can nest tables to create more complex layouts.

MULTICELL LAYOUT   The MultiCell layout enables you to specify a series of *cells* in a row or a column. Like a spreadsheet, each cell can contain an item. In this case, the cells will contain user interface components. It does not require that each row contain the same number of cells. The MultiCell layout is used in many of Groove's own system tools because of its flexibility.

There is one very basic requirement when using the MultiCell layout. Each column or row must have at least one cell defined. There cannot be columns or rows with zero cells in them. This example would be incorrect because the second row does not have a cell defined:

```
<g:Property Name="Layout">
    <g:PropertyValue>
        <MULTIROW>
            <ROW>
                <CELL WIDTH="10"/>
                <CELL HEIGHT="30">
                MyComponent
                </CELL>
            </ROW>
            <ROW>
            </ROW>
        </MULTIROW>
    </g:PropertyValue>
</g:Property>
```

Unlike HTML, the MultiCell layout does support uneven numbers of cells or columns within each row. In addition, each CELL supports the following attributes to change how the cell is displayed, including the following:

- WIDTH: The horizontal size of the cell.
- HEIGHT: The vertical size of the cell.
- LEFTPAD: How much space, or padding, to place to the left of the cell.
- TOPPAD: How much space, or padding, to place in the top of the cell.

Although it's flexible, you must be aware that there are a few things the MultiCell layout does not support, including the following:

- Any static text (text must come from a component, such as the Static component)
- Prototyping of layouts within a WYSIWYG editor
- Column and row spanning

XY LAYOUT This is used for precise placement of components. Coordinates for each component are specified in Left (horizontal or X) and Top (vertical or Y) format. A PropertyList is defined with each component name, position, and size.

NOTE

A powerful feature of the XY Layout is that new components can be added at runtime. The cell-based layouts, such as the HTML Layout, require cells to be positioned at design time.

SINGLECELL LAYOUT The SingleCell layout is used for tools that only contain one component. It serves as both a view container and layout.

SPLITTER LAYOUT This layout divides a tool vertically or horizontally into two separate windows. Like the SingleCell Layout, this component acts as both a view container and a layout.

OTHER IMPORTANT TOOL CONCEPTS

In addition to the basic tool template structure, there are a few other concepts you should be familiar with before beginning tool development. Delegates and connections are two very important concepts that will be required for even the most basic of tools.

DELEGATES

Delegates are used to specify the behaviors and/or events that a component exhibits. Two common examples include the Form Delegate and the Data Model Delegate.

FORM DELEGATE

There are certain behaviors you'll want to implement within your forms, such as the script that runs when a button is clicked. This is accomplished through the `Delegate` attribute in the `ComponentGroup` element. This attribute will provide the name of the scripting host component that provides the glue code for actions within the form. For instance, the following code illustrates how the `FormGlue` Delegate is defined and the sinking of the event when the button is clicked:

```
<g:ComponentGroup Delegate="FormGlue" DefaultView="ViewContainer"
➥HelpInfoProvider="">
    ....
        <g:Component Name="AddButton">
            <g:ComponentResource FingerprintID="Groove"
➥URL="http://components.groove.net/Groove/Components/Root.osd?Package=net.groove.
➥Groove.ToolComponents.GrooveCommonComponents_DLL&amp;Version=0&amp;
➥Factory=Button"/>
            .....
        <g:Component Name="SurveyGlue">
            <g:ComponentResource FingerprintID="Groove"
➥URL="http://components.groove.net/Groove/Components/Root.osd?Package=net.groove.
➥Groove.ToolComponents.GrooveCommonComponents_DLL&amp;Version=0&amp;
➥Factory=ScriptHost3"/>
                <g:ComponentConnections>
                    <g:Connection ConnectionID="0" Name="AddButton"/>
                    ....
                        <SCRIPT>
                        <![CDATA[
                            function Button_OnCommand(i_UICommand)
                            {
                            //Button was clicked
                            ..Actions in response to button being clicked go
here...
                            }
                        ]]>
                        </SCRIPT>
        </g:Component>
</g:ComponentGroup>
```

The `Delegate` attribute has been set to `FormGlue`, which is the name of a scripting host component. In this example, the scripting host component is contained in the same group of component, or `ComponentGroup`, for the view container itself. Because it has been defined as the delegate, all events are passed to the appropriate handlers within the delegate component. Figure 11.4 illustrates this concept by showing how a view container implements a form delegate. After establishing the component connection as shown, you can write glue code in response to events. This example responds to the click event on Button1.

11

Figure 11.4
A form delegate is used to tie glue code to a button component.

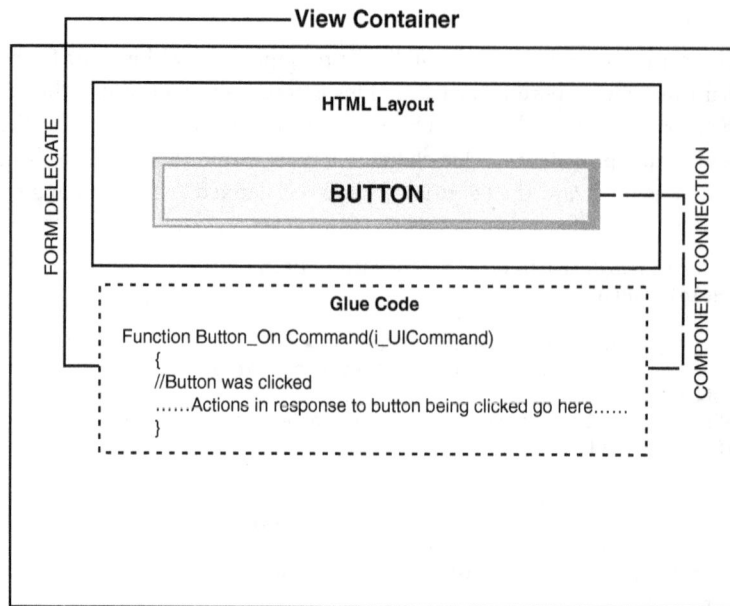

View Container

FORM DELEGATE

HTML Layout

BUTTON

COMPONENT CONNECTION

Glue Code
Function Button_On Command(i_UICommand)
{
//Button was clicked
......Actions in response to button being clicked go here......
}

DATA MODEL DELEGATE

Most forms are data-driven with users viewing, editing, or adding data in a recordset. Often, you might need to implement certain behaviors depending on events fired from the recordset engine itself. This is accomplished through the use of a Data Model Delegate, which is also specified at the ComponentGroup level. Also, the data model delegate is the means by which your model (using the Model-View-Controller structure paradigm discussed in the previous chapter) is exposed externally for other applications to use.

→ For more about the Model-View-Controller structure, **see** "Groove's Model-View-Controller (MVC) Structure," **p. 314**

THE STANDARD TOOL DEVELOPMENT CYCLE

Because tool development is an iterative process, Groove allows developers to construct tools using rapid prototyping. It's not uncommon that during the development process you'll find yourself tweaking screen layouts and debugging numerous lines of code. As you've seen in the first part of this chapter, tools need quite a few files to make them complete and available to other Groove users. Fortunately, most tool templates you develop will be able to take advantage of this efficient design and development method. However, there are a few limitations when using the rapid prototyping process, including the following:

- External components can only use rapid prototyping if you started with a fully injectable version of the tool.

- You must add any XML schemas to the database manually using the Database Navigator tool. You see how to do this shortly.

TURNING ON RAPID PROTOTYPING

In the discussion of the GDK in Chapter 10, you saw several Registry files included that can aid in development. By shutting down Groove and double-clicking the EnableMyTemplates.reg file found in the *GDK Install Folder*\RegistryFiles folder, you can enable rapid prototyping. This feature will remain turned on for this installation until it is explicitly disabled.

→ For more information about EnableMyTemplates.reg file and the other Registry files provided with the Groove Development Kit, **see** "Registry Files Included in the GDK," **p.337**

CREATING A FOLDER FOR PROTOTYPE TEMPLATES

The EnableMyTemplates.reg file is named appropriately because this is the folder where prototype templates should be placed. If it was not created during GDK installation, you should create a new folder called My Templates under the *Groove Install Directory*\Groove\Data directory. For most installations, this is probably C:\Progam Files\Groove Networks\Groove\Data\My Templates.

NOTE

This folder should have the same permissions as the *Groove Installation*\Data directory.

HOW RAPID PROTOTYPING WORKS

After rapid prototyping has been enabled with the EnableMyTemplates.reg Registry file, you should place prototype tool templates in the My Templates folder. The Groove installation is "aware" of any well-formed templates placed in the directory. When the Add Tool tab is chosen, any templates in this folder should appear in the list of available tools. Click the Add Selected Tool button and the tool will be added to the space if there are no errors in the template that prevent it from running. This section demonstrates rapid prototyping using a simple tool we've provided.

TIP

When the rapid prototyping function is turned on, Groove will use any tool template found in the My Templates folder. When making backups of tool templates, you should place them in another folder to avoid confusion. Copying templates into the same folder can cause several tools to appear with the same name in the Add Tool list. This could make it difficult to determine which tool is currently being edited.

Prior to beginning the Focus Group tool tutorial, let's step through a simple example to show how rapid prototyping works:

1. Shut down Groove if it is running.

2. Double-click on EnableMyTemplates.reg in the *GDK Installation Folder*\RegistryFiles\ folder. Click OK when asked for confirmation for the Registry edit.

3. Create a file called TestTemplate.tpl in the *Groove Installation Folder*\Data\My Templates folder. Enter the code in Listing 11.1 and save the file in the same location.

> **NOTE**
>
> Be sure the file has a .tpl extension when saved. Some text editors may change the extension automatically.

4. Start Groove and enter a new or existing shared space. Click the Add Tool tab and highlight the Test Template tool. Click the Add Selected Tool button.

When the tool is added you should see the screen in Figure 11.5.

Figure 11.5
This is what your simple rapid prototyping will look like when it's added to a shared space.

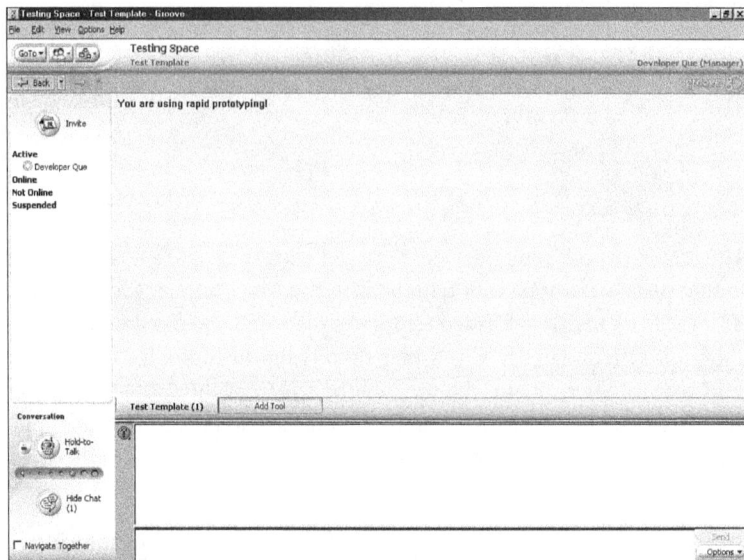

Any changes to the tool template will now instantly be reflected in the tool. For example, modify the TestTemplate.tpl file by replacing

```
Value="You are using rapid prototyping!"
```

with

```
Value="We are all using rapid prototyping!"
```

Save the file again in the same directory. Delete the tool from the shared space and add it again. When the tool is added again, the new text should display in the tool window. Congratulations! You've just used rapid prototyping to edit a tool template.

CREATING THE FOCUS GROUP TOOL

In this example, we'll be demonstrating how to rapidly prototype a tool for a focus group. In this scenario, Professor Que has decided to create a focus group for marketing analysis. Using the Focus Tool group that we will create, Professor Que hopes to gather data on the group's thoughts and feelings about a particular product idea.

HOW IT WILL WORK

Professor Que will create a space and add the newly created Focus Group tool to the space. After a student is invited to the space, he will receive a copy of the space including the Focus Group tool. Members selecting the tool will see the screen shown in Figure 11.6. In the center is an image they will be examining. Through the use of the arrow buttons, members can rotate the image to see the product from different angles.

Figure 11.6
This is how the Focus Group tool will appear once completed.

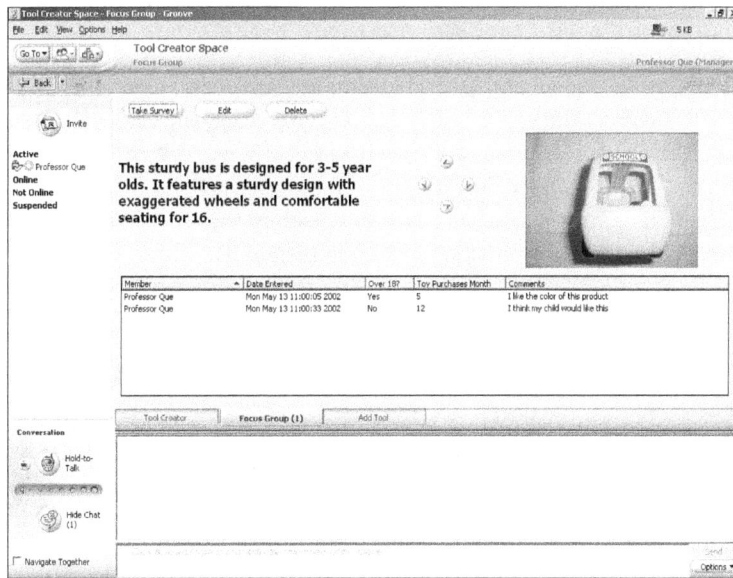

After a member has inspected the product, clicking the Vote button enables him to provide feedback about the featured product through the pop-up window shown in Figure 11.7. Not only will he answer a series of questions, but have the capability to provide some freeform comments at the end. Users will have the capability to go in and modify their vote at any time, whereas other members have read-only capability.

Figure 11.7
Clicking the Take Survey will display this pop-up window that will enable users to take a survey about the product image they are viewing.

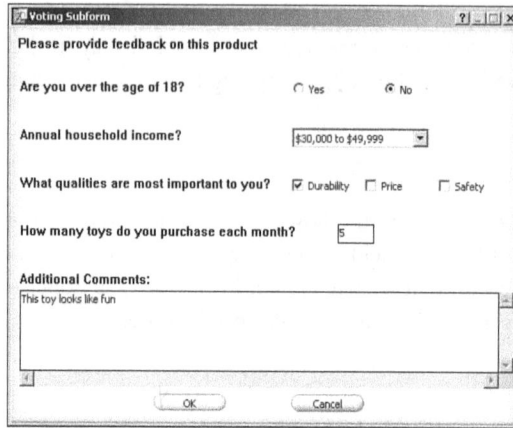

PLANNING THE INITIAL LAYOUT AND ADDING SOME COMPONENTS

One of the first steps in any software development is designing the screen layout. With the Focus Group tool it is no different. First of all you will be visually designing your tool before coding it. After you've decided the screen layout, it will be time to create the layout and add the user interface components.

Defining the interface should be one of the first steps a developer takes. For our example, we'll construct the screen using the user interface components that Groove provides. Using the Sketchpad tool, Professor Que has sat down with his colleagues and collectively worked on the initial interface. The results of their brainstorming are shown in Figure 11.8. This initial planning can save time later by deciding what user interface components will be required and the best method for laying them out.

Figure 11.8
It's helpful to lay out your tool interface like in this example before you begin creating the tool template.

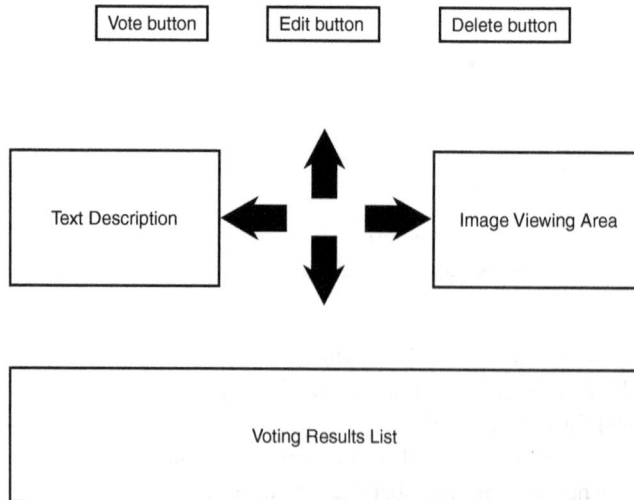

CREATING THE FOUNDATION FOR YOUR TOOL

Now that you've decided how the tool will look, the components you will need, and their layout, it's time to start creating the tool. One of the easiest ways to create a tool template is to use the Tool Creator tool that introduced in the discussion of the Groove Development Kit in Chapter 10. The following steps assume that you've already followed the steps in Chapter 10 to successfully install the Tool Creator.

→ For more information on the installation of the Tool Creator tool, **see** "Injecting the Tool Creator," **p. 328**

STEP 1—RUNNING THE TOOL CREATOR WIZARD

The Tool Creator Wizard enables you to create the base for your tool. When the Tool Creator tool is first added to a space or the New Tool button is clicked, the wizard will be started. As shown in Figure 11.9, you first need to specify a name for the tool. You must also check the check box because you will need a view container. When the wizard looks like Figure 11.9, click Next to continue.

Figure 11.9
After starting the Tool Creator tool, you'll first need to provide a name for your tool and whether a view container component will be used.

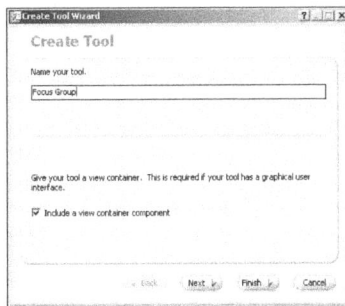

STEP 2—SPECIFYING THE LAYOUT

After clicking the Next button, you should be prompted for the type of layout to use. For your main form, choose the XY Layout, as shown in Figure 11.10. Click the Next button to continue.

STEP 3—SPECIFYING THE FORM DELEGATE AND SCRIPTING LANGUAGE

You will be asked whether you would like to use a form delegate or a compiled binary. For this example, you will be using a form delegate with JavaScript as the scripting language. After making the proper selections, the screen should look like Figure 11.11. Click the Next button to continue.

Figure 11.10
Within the Tool Creator, you can choose from one of three layouts for your tool.

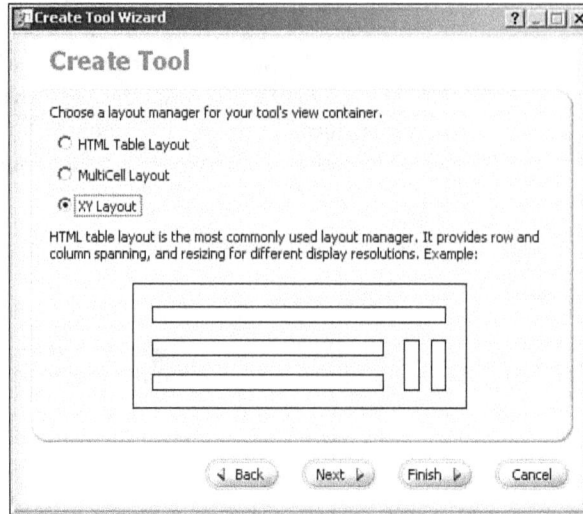

Figure 11.11
During this step you can choose whether you want to use the scripting component or a compiled language.

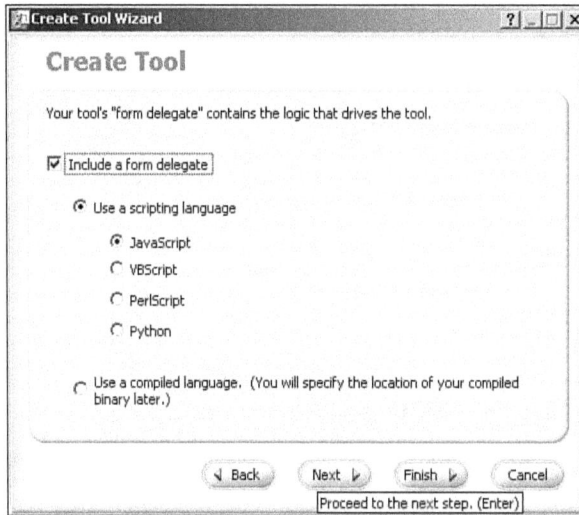

STEP 4—CHOOSING AN ENGINE

You will be prompted for the type of Groove engine you'd like to use. Because you plan on saving information gathered in your tool, choose the RecordSetEngine, as shown in Figure 11.12. The other choice available, the PropertyListEngine, is included by default with all Tool Templates, so selecting that option would not add any engines to the template. After you click the Finish button you've laid the groundwork for your new Focus Group tool.

Figure 11.12
For the final step in the series of Tool Creator prompts, you must choose the type of engine to be included.

ADDING ALL THE COMPONENTS

Now that you've finished the wizard, you've created a simple "shell" for your tool. At this point it really doesn't do anything because you still have to add many more user interface components to make it complete. After finishing the wizard, you should have been returned to the Tool Creator tool main screen with the fields completed, as shown in Figure 11.13. In the following steps, you'll begin adding the various user interface components you'll need within the tool.

Figure 11.13
After completing all the Tool Creator tool prompts, you'll be taken to the initial screen in Tool Creator interface.

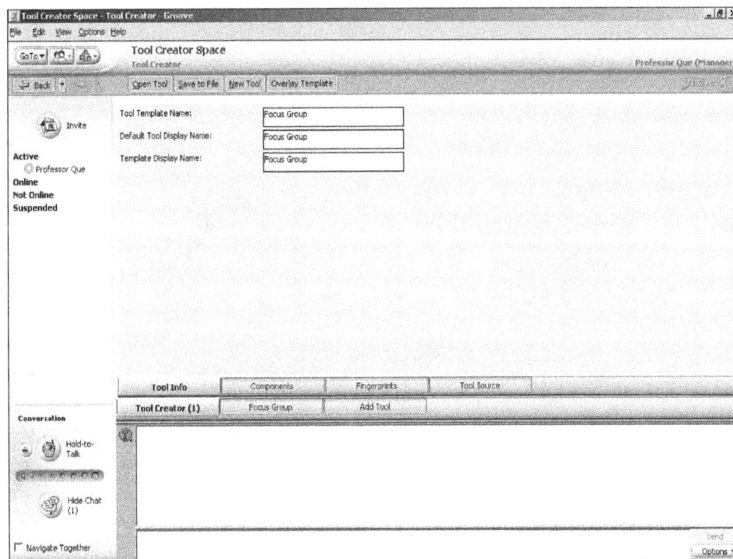

STEP 1—CHOOSING THE COMPONENTS TAB

By clicking the Components tab, you should be taken to the components listing, as shown in Figure 11.14.

Figure 11.14
After following the prompts, you can see that a set of components has already been added to your tool after clicking the Components tab.

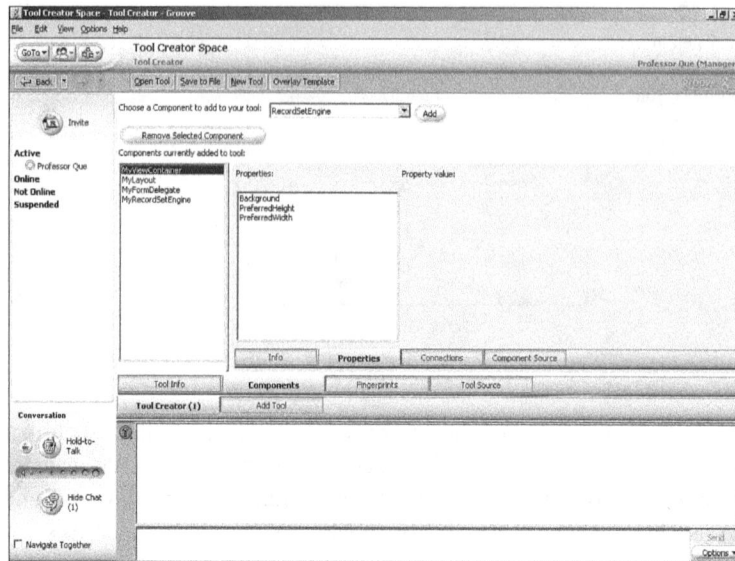

As you can see, the following components have been added by the wizard already:

- **MyViewContainer:** This was added to the tool because all visual tools must have at least one view container component defined.
- **MyLayout:** The Layout works in conjunction with the View Container to determine the actual placement of user interface components on the screen.
- **MyFormDelegate:** The MyFormDelegate component will be used to hold JavaScript code used to respond to user events within your tool.
- **MyRecordSetEngine:** This component provides a convenient way to access data in Groove's local shared data repository.

STEP 2—ADDING THE TOP ROW OF BUTTONS

Recall your Focus Group tool design from Figure 11.8: You want three buttons along the top of the tool to enable users to take the survey, edit the survey, or delete the survey. By selecting the Button component in the drop-down list at the top of the Components screen and clicking the Add button, you can add the three buttons required for your Focus Group tool's main form. Click the Add button on this Component screen three times and three new Button components will be added.

STEP 3—SETTING THE GENERAL PROPERTIES OF THE TOP ROW BUTTONS

In the last step, you added three button components and they should now appear in the list on the left side of the screen. You can change the details of each button by highlighting it in the list of the left and setting the appropriate values on the right. Because each button was named "Button" by default, you need to change the name of each one by selecting it and typing a new name in the Component Name text box on the right, as shown in Figure 11.15. You need to do this for all three buttons; they should be named voteButton, editButton, and deleteButton, respectively.

Figure 11.15
Using the Tool Creator interface, you can rename one of the button components to the voteButton.

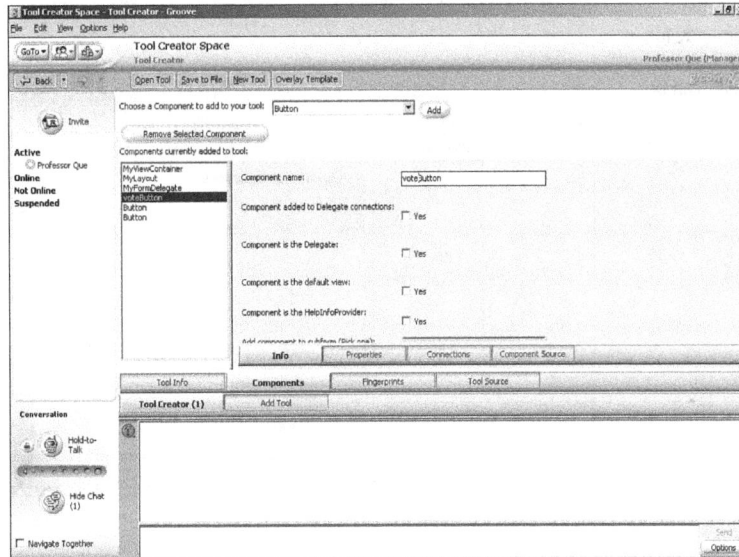

STEP 4—SETTING THE OTHER TOP ROW BUTTON PROPERTIES

After renaming each button in the previous step, you should click the Properties tab, as shown in Figure 11.16, to show the available properties for each component. By highlighting one of the three buttons on the left side of the screen, you can click a property to modify. In the figure you can see that we've edited the Label property. After a property has been changed, you can click the Set Value button to save the change.

Change the properties of the VoteButton component as follows:

- Autosize: False
- Cancel: False
- Checkbox: False
- Default: False
- Enabled: True
- Label: Take Survey
- LinkButton: False
- Radiobutton: False
- SingleLine: True

- `Style`: StandardButton
- `Tooltip`: Click this to take the survey

Figure 11.16
This figure demonstrates how the `Label` property for one of the button components can be changed.

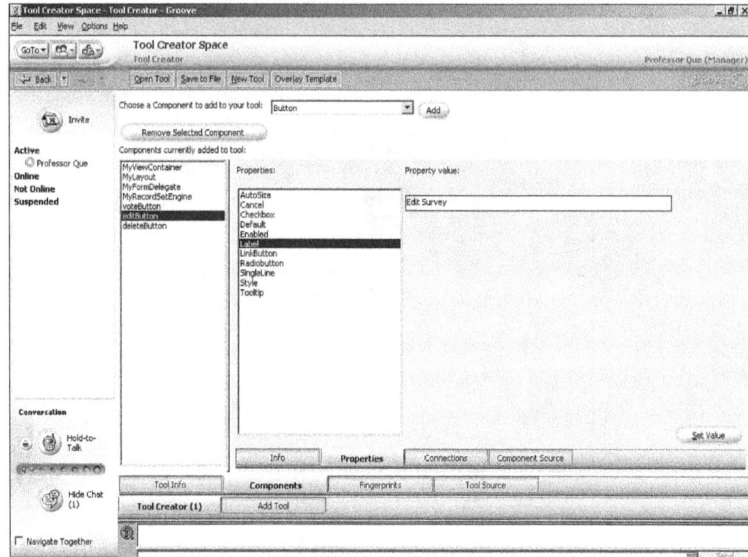

Change the properties of the `EditButton` component as follows:

- `Autosize`: False
- `Cancel`: False
- `Checkbox`: False
- `Default`: False
- `Enabled`: True
- `Label`: Edit Survey
- `LinkButton`: False
- `Radiobutton`: False
- `SingleLine`: True
- `Style`: StandardButton
- `Tooltip`: Click this to edit the selected survey

Change the properties of the `DeleteButton` component as follows:

- `Autosize`: False
- `Cancel`: False
- `Checkbox`: False

- `Default`: False
- `Enabled`: True
- `Label`: Delete Survey
- `LinkButton`: False
- `Radiobutton`: False
- `SingleLine`: True
- `Style`: StandardButton
- `Tooltip`: Click this to delete the selected survey

A button component has many different properties that you can use to change its appearance. For buttons, the `Style` property indicates what type of button will be displayed. In this case, you are displaying a standard "push button" indicated by the `StandardButton` style. Refer to the API reference for the `IGrooveButton` interface under the `GrooveCommonComponents` for a list of the properties available.

STEP 5—ADDING THE IMAGE CONTROL COMPONENT

To display the picture of the product featured in your Focus Group tool, you need to add an image control component to the component list. Like you did in step 2 for the form buttons, you can select the `ImageControl` component from the drop-down list at the top of the screen and click the Add button. Then, change the Component Name in the Info tab to `productImage` to make it more recognizable. The image control accepts only one property, `AcceptedFileTypes`, which you should set to the value `.bmp,.jpg,.jpeg`.

STEP 6—ADDING THE IMAGE ROTATION BUTTONS

To enable users to "rotate" the image presented in the image control, you need to add components that will display the rotation images on a button. If you recall from the design in Figure 11.8, the screen contained four arrow buttons pointing to the left, right, upwards, and downwards. The `Button` component you used earlier for the `Vote`, `Edit`, and `Delete` buttons will work fine for what you need to do. However, you will use the `SmallIconButton` component for the rotate buttons so you can display an arrow image on the top of each one. Other than that, they function exactly the same as the `StandardButton` style used in step 2. So first you must add four new Button Components to the tool and name them `leftButton`, `rightButton`, `upButton`, and `downButton`.

STEP 7—MODIFYING THE IMAGE ROTATION BUTTONS' PROPERTIES

Similar to step 4, you need to modify each of image rotation button properties. Change the properties of the `leftButton` component as follows:

- `Autosize`: False
- `Cancel`: False
- `Checkbox`: False

- **Default**: False
- **Enabled**: True
- **Label**: <none>
- **LinkButton**: False
- **Radiobutton**: False
- **SingleLine**: False
- **Style**: SmallIconButton
- **Tooltip**: Rotate product image to the left

Change the properties of the `rightButton` component as follows:

- **Autosize**: False
- **Cancel**: False
- **Checkbox**: False
- **Default**: False
- **Enabled**: True
- **Label**: <none>
- **LinkButton**: False
- **Radiobutton**: False
- **SingleLine**: True
- **Style**: SmallIconButton
- **Tooltip**: Rotate product image to the right

Change the properties of the `upButton` component as follows:

- **Autosize**: False
- **Cancel**: False
- **Checkbox**: False
- **Default**: False
- **Enabled**: True
- **Label**: <none>
- **LinkButton**: False
- **Radiobutton**: False
- **SingleLine**: True
- **Style**: SmallIconButton
- **Tooltip**: Rotate product image upward

Change the properties of the `downButton` component as follows:

- `Autosize`: False
- `Cancel`: False
- `Checkbox`: False
- `Default`: False
- `Enabled`: True
- `Label`: <none>
- `LinkButton`: False
- `Radiobutton`: False
- `SingleLine`: True
- `Style`: SmallIconButton
- `Tooltip`: Rotate product image downward

These buttons use the same component as the Vote, Delete, and Edit buttons mentioned before. However, you are indicating that these will be the small icon buttons by setting `Style` to `SmallIconButton`. Refer to the API reference for the `IGrooveButton` interface under the `GrooveCommonComponents` for a list of the properties available.

STEP 8—ADDING THE ROTATE BUTTON IMAGE URLS

Not every component property is listed in the Tool Creator. There might be some that need to be added manually. This is true for the image properties used on the rotate buttons. When you encounter a situation like this you need to modify the component source directly. By clicking on one of the rotate buttons, such as the `upButton`, and then clicking the Component Source tab, you can see the source code, as shown in Figure 11.17. From this screen you can modify the source directly and click the Save button to apply it to the component. For each image button you need to insert the code that defines what image to use.

For example, this code will be inserted for the left button:

```
<g:Property Value="grooveFile:///ToolBMPs\Arrows16X16Images.jpg" Name="ImageURL"/>
<g:Property Value="grooveFile:///ToolBMPs\Arrows16X16ImagesMask.bmp"
Name="ImageMaskURL"/>
<g:Property Value="0" Name="ImageIndex"/>
```

This example shows how to use an image with mutiple icons contained within it. The offset for finding the specific image will be the (ImageIndex * size of the image). For more information on the use of images on buttons, refer to the Component Catalog provided with the GDK.

Because in this example you are using an image file containing multiple icons, you can use the same block of code for the other rotation buttons as well. Only the `ImageIndex` property will need to change. For the `rightButton`, you will use an index of 1. For the `upButton` you will use an index of 2. For the `downButton`, you will use an index of 3.

11

Figure 11.17
Clicking the Component Source tab enables you to see the source generated for each component added to the tool template.

This code is used to specify the arrow image to use on each button. You can see an example of what the finished code looks like in the Tool Creator for the upButton in Figure 11.18.

Figure 11.18
Here is what the Component Source should look like for the upButton after you've made your changes to support the icon image.

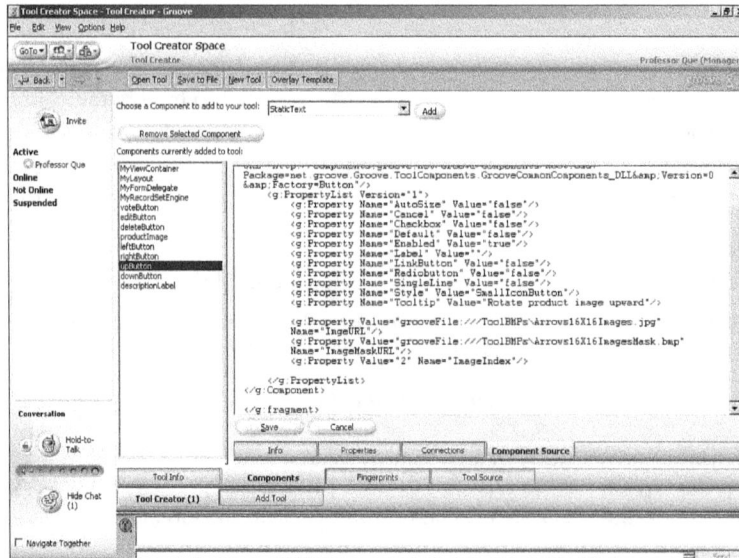

STEP 9—ADD THE PRODUCT DESCRIPTION LABEL

For your Focus Group tool you need an area that will describe the product being shown. Because you cannot put text directly on a Groove form, you must use a `StaticText` component to display the text. Like you did in step 2 for the form buttons, you can select the `StaticText` component from the drop-down list at the top of the screen and click the Add button. Then, you can change the Component Name in the Info tab to `descriptionLabel`, as shown in Figure 11.19, so that you can reference it later.

Figure 11.19
You must make the `StaticText` component name `DescriptionLabel` so you can reference it later within the tool template.

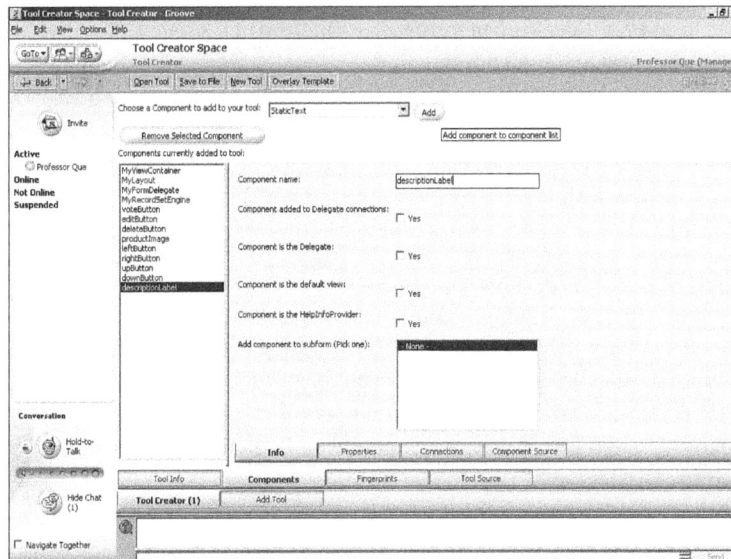

STEP 10—MODIFYING THE STATIC TEXT COMPONENT PROPERTIES

By clicking the Properties tab, you can now modify the properties of your `StaticText` component you added in step 8 as follows:

- `BreakType`: WordBreak
- `Clip`: EndEllipsis
- `HAlignment`: Left
- `Label`: This sturdy bus is designed for 3–5 year olds. It features a sturdy design with exaggerated wheels and comfortable seating for 16.
- `Prefixing`: NoPrefix
- `Style`: Normal
- `VAlignment`: Top

ADDING THE COMPONENTS TO THE XY LAYOUT

Now that you've defined a majority of the user interface components, you are ready to add them to the layout. The layout is used to position the components within the interface. In this next example, you will use the XY Layout to accurately position your components using X and Y coordinates. In addition, you will follow this with examples of how the same layout could be achieved using the HTML Layout and MultiCell layout components.

DETERMINING THE POSITION FOR EACH COMPONENT

Using the XY Layout, you must determine the horizontal (X) and vertical (Y) position for each component. The coordinates 0,0 are in the upper-left portion of the tool window. As you move down the screen one pixel either horizontally or vertically, the X or Y coordinate is incremented. It can be hard to guess at the coordinates for each component you need to place on the screen. However, there are a few tools available that you can use when designing a Groove tool layout (and just about any other Windows-based application) that requires coordinates to position elements on a user interface.

There are some tricks to help you quickly determine what X and Y coordinates will be used when positing your components within a tool form. A simple utility called Screen Calipers by Nico Westerdale is an excellent tool to help determine where elements should be placed and what size they should be. It can be downloaded from http://www.iconico.com/caliper/. Refer to the documentation provided for complete installation instructions. The following steps will show how you place and size the up arrow rotation button on your screen.

STEP 1—START THE CALIPERS APPLICATION   After you've downloaded the application, running it should give you a pop-up set of calipers that will always remain in front of other windows. Figure 11.20 shows the calipers in front of your instance of Groove. If you'd like to change the appearance of the Calipers utility, right-click the tool and you will be given a variety of display options. For example, right-click the Calipers tool and select Stay on Top to enable or disable the display of the tool on top of all other windows.

STEP 2—DETERMINE THE HORIZONTAL COORDINATES   Figure 11.21 shows what should be considered the left border of the tool window. Probably the easiest place to see the separation is between the chat pane on the bottom of the screen and the conversation pane on the left side of the screen. Starting from this border, you need to calculate how many pixels to the right of it the component should be placed. You can drag the ends of the onscreen caliper to find the distance by simply positioning the mouse pointer over any piece on the right side of the Caliper and holding down the left mouse button. In Figure 11.21, 450 shows in the Calipers tool display. For future reference, this will be the value used for the Left property, indicating where the left side of the component will be placed.

Figure 11.20
The Calipers tool will always remain in front of other windows by default.

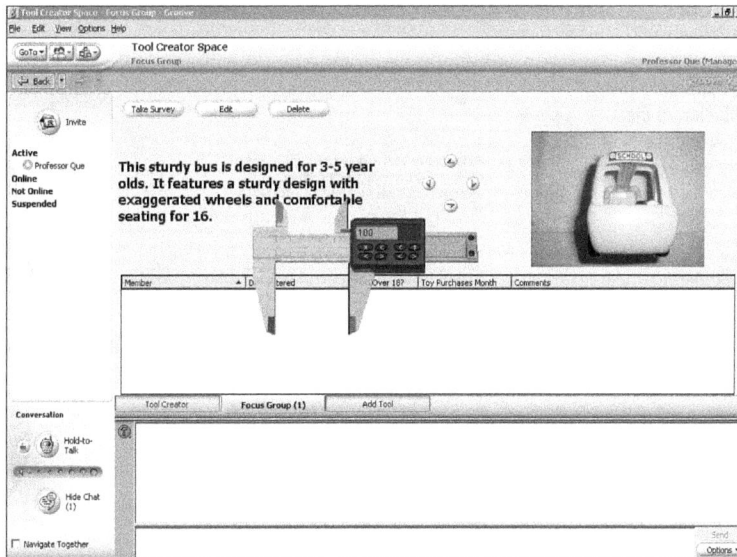

Figure 11.21
Using the Calipers utility, you can determine the amount of space between the left border and the component you want to place.

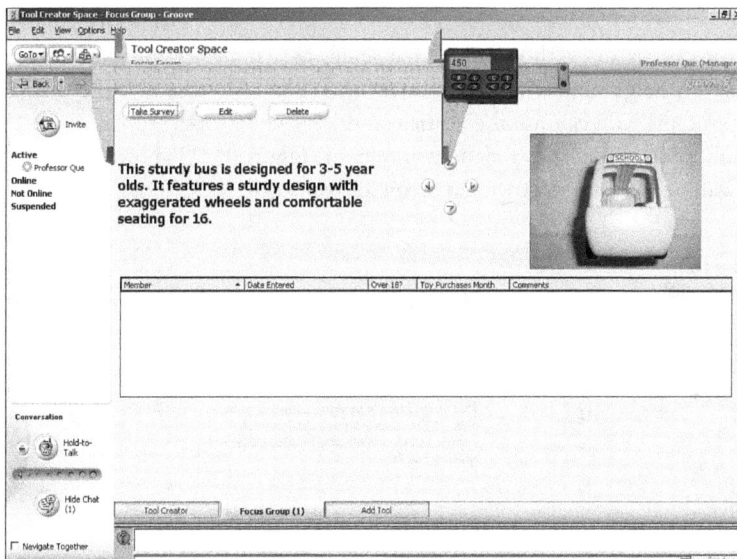

STEP 3—DETERMINE THE VERTICAL COORDINATES   In a similar manner to step 2, you also need to determine the vertical (Y) coordinate. To do this, you need to know where the top border of the tool window ends. This is shown in Figure 11.22. Clicking the two-ended vertical arrow on the Calipers tool causes the onscreen calipers to flip 90 degrees, which enables you to make vertical measurements. Looking at the onscreen display, you can see that the Top property value you will need to use is 80 pixels.

Figure 11.22
Using the Calipers utility, you can determine the space required between the top of the tool window and the component you want to place.

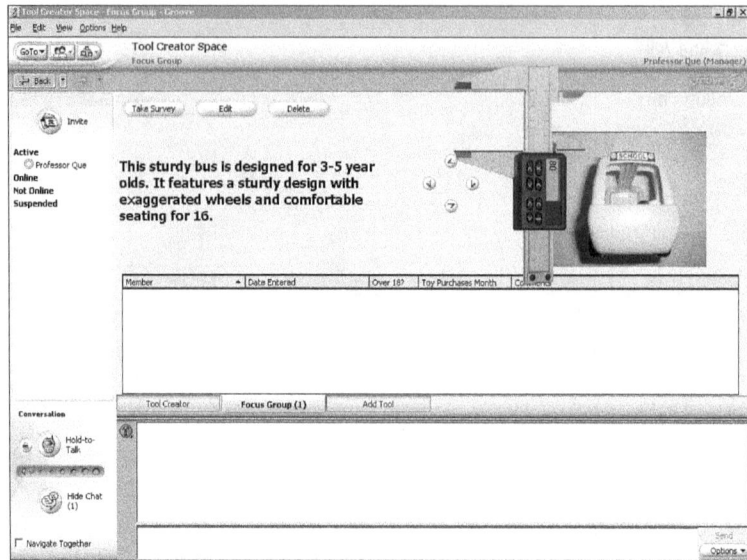

11

STEP 4—DETERMINE THE SIZE OF THE COMPONENT Using the same Calipers tool, you can also get an idea of how large a particular user interface item should be. Most components have a height and width component. Just like you measured the vertical and horizontal positions, you can use the vertical and horizontal onscreen caliper to determine the height and width properties for the component. Figure 11.23 shows that you'll want to use a width of 18 pixels for the up arrow in your tool.

Figure 11.23
The Calipers utility can also determine the height and width of your component.

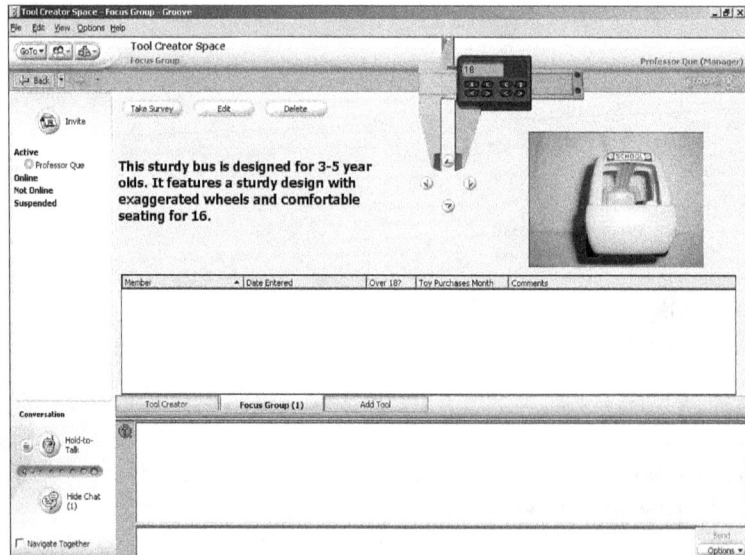

PLACING YOUR COMPONENTS WITHIN THE XY LAYOUT

Now that you've defined the necessary components and determined the positioning and size for each, you are ready to place them within the layout. In the following steps you'll see how to add the `upArrow` component to the layout using the Tool Creator tool. This example assumes you have followed the steps in the "Adding All Components" section earlier in this chapter.

STEP 1—OPEN THE COMPONENTS TAB AND SELECT THE LAYOUT While in the Tool Creator, click the Components tab at the bottom of the screen and select the `MyLayout` component, as shown in Figure 11.24. After the component has been selected, click the Info tab at the bottom of the window. Check the box entitled Component Is the Default View to indicate this is the view you want to display when the tool is opened.

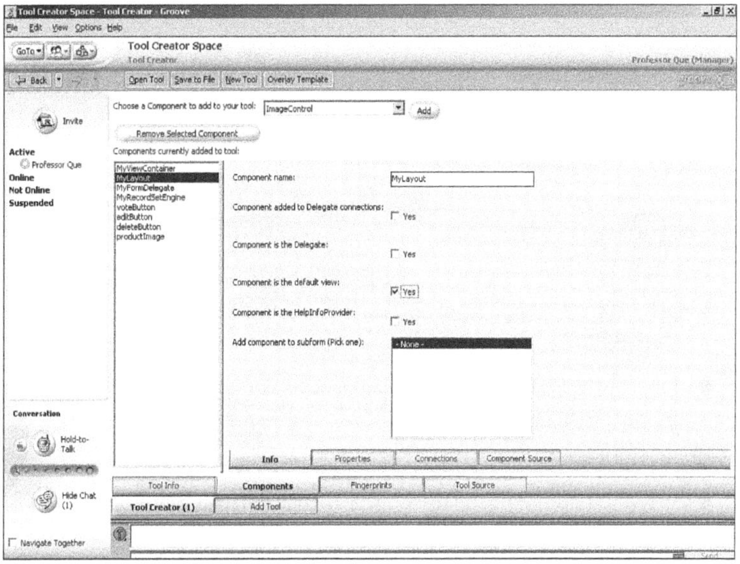

Figure 11.24
Because you want the `MyLayout` component to be the default view when the tool is opened, you must select the Component Is the Default View check box.

STEP 2—SELECT THE LAYOUT PROPERTY Now that you've designated this layout as the default view, you need to set the `Layout` property using the component names you've established along with the sizing and coordinate values. Click the Properties tab at the bottom of the screen and select `Layout` from the Properties list, as shown in Figure 11.25.

STEP 3—ADD THE `upButton` TO THE LAYOUT With the `Layout` property highlighted, you can add the `upButton` component by adding the following code in the Property Value text area on the right side of the screen:

```
<g:Control Name="upButton" Left="450" Top="80" Width="18" Height="18"/>
```

Figure 11.25
From the Properties tab you can select the Layout property where you will be inserting the appropriate layout code.

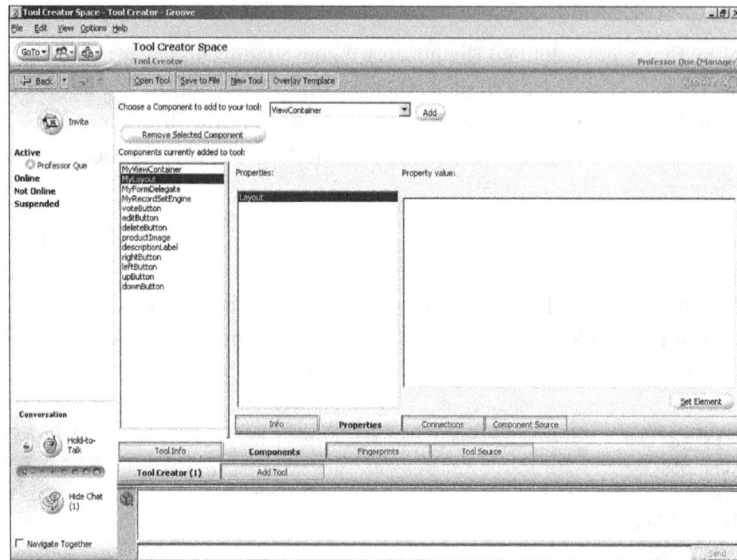

Define the following properties for each component:

- Name: The name assigned to the component in the component definition.
- Left: The distance in pixels from the left side of the tool window where the component should be placed.
- Top: The distance in pixels from the top of the tool window where the component should be placed.
- Width: The width of the component in pixels.
- Height: The height of the component in pixels

The complete layout for the rest of the buttons is as follows:

```
<g:Control Name="voteButton" Left="5" Top="5" Width="90" Height="30"/>
<g:Control Name="editButton" Left="105" Top="5" Width="90" Height="30"/>
<g:Control Name="deleteButton" Left="205" Top="5" Width="90" Height="30"/>
<g:Control Name="descriptionLabel" Left="2" Top="85" Width="370" Height="200"/>\
<g:Control Name="upButton" Left="450" Top="80" Width="18" Height="18"/>
<g:Control Name="leftButton" Left="420" Top="110" Width="18" Height="18"/>
<g:Control Name="rightButton" Left="480" Top="110" Width="18" Height="18"/>
<g:Control Name="downButton" Left="450" Top="140" Width="18" Height="18"/>
<g:Control Name="productImage" Left="570" Top="20" Width="240" Height="240"/>
```

ADDING YOUR COMPONENTS TO AN HTML LAYOUT

The previous set of steps showed how you could position the components using an XY Layout. You will now see how you can use the HTML Layout in your Focus Group tool. This is a popular choice because it's created in much the same way as HTML tables. In fact, you'll see how you can use a WYSIWYG editor such as Microsoft FrontPage to quickly draft a rough layout of how the descriptionLabel, rotate buttons, and product image control can be placed. This example uses Microsoft FrontPage to design the table, but the steps outlined here should transfer easily to many other popular HTML editors.

If you've already added the XY Layout, you'll want to remove it. Click the Components tab in the Tool Creator tool, highlight MyLayout, and click the Remove Selected Component button, as shown in Figure 11.26. These steps assume that you've already defined and named all the components in the tool per our previous explanation.

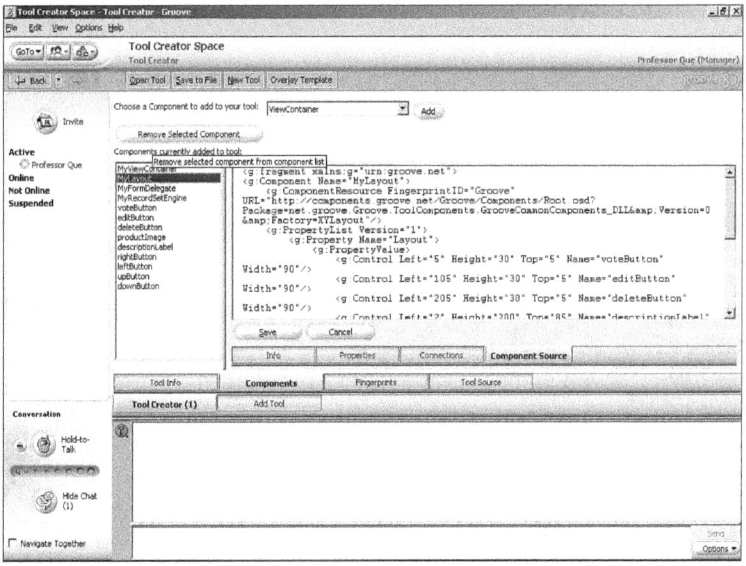

Figure 11.26
By clicking the Remove Component button you can remove the XY Layout from your tool template.

STEP 1—START THE EDITOR AND CREATE A TABLE

Choose Start, Programs, Microsoft FrontPage to open the application to a blank page. Choose Table, Insert, Table from the main menu to open the Insert Table window. Choose the number of rows, columns, and any cell padding properties you would like to set for your table. The table settings for this example are shown Figure 11.27. You can see that there are going to be four columns to hold the interface components.

For this example, use the following values in the Insert Table window:

- Rows: 1
- Columns: 4
- Alignment: Default
- Border size: 0
- Cell padding: 0
- Cell spacing: 0

- Specify width: Checked
- Width: 100 (in percent)

These default settings should create the table shown in Figure 11.28.

Figure 11.27
After choosing to insert a table, Microsoft FrontPage will prompt you for the default settings.

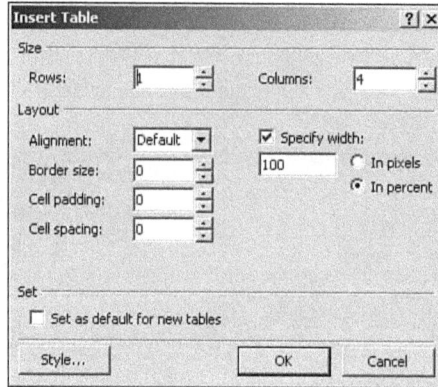

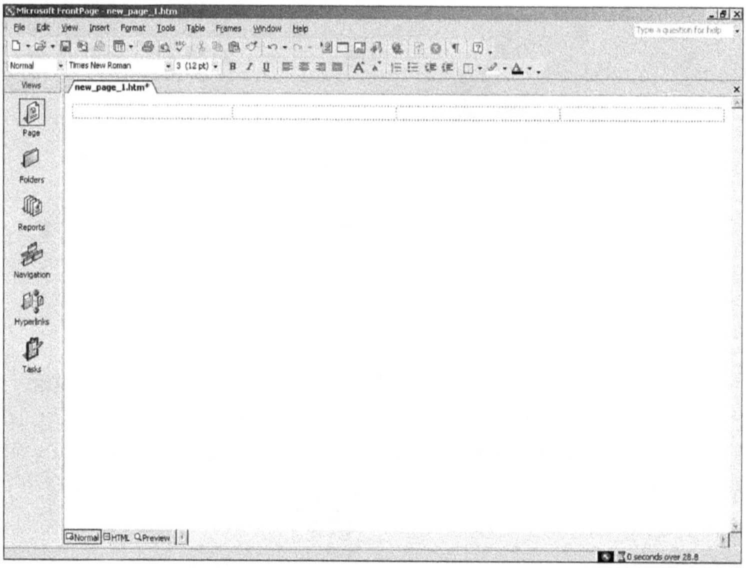

Figure 11.28
After inserting the table, your HTML page should look like this.

STEP 2—INSERT YOUR PLACEHOLDER IMAGE

Because Groove components themselves are not something that can be natively dropped into an HTML page, you need to insert something that you can easily resize to visualize how the component will appear in relation to other objects on the screen. Images work very well because you can easily resize them so you will use one in this example. Just about any

.jpg, .gif, or .bmp image will work fine. For this example, place the blinking cursor (insertion point) in the first cell in the table row that you've created. Then insert an image by choosing Insert, Picture, From File from the main menu and you will be prompted for the image to insert. I've used the setup.bmp image found in my *Windows installation*/system32 directory, as shown in Figure 11.29.

Figure 11.29
In this example, you've used the setup.bmp image in the Microsoft Windows installation as a placeholder image.

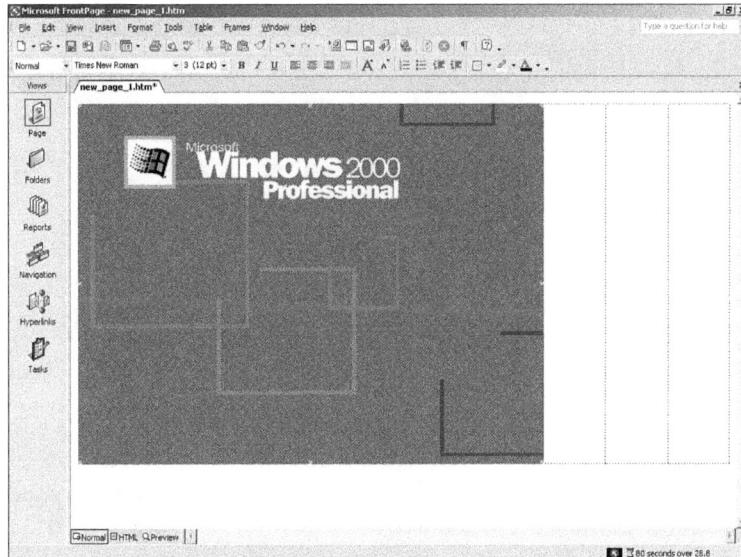

STEP 3—SET THE PLACEHOLDER IMAGE SETTINGS

Now that you've inserted the placeholder image, you need to resize it to accurately represent the buttons. First of all, double-click the image that you inserted in step 2. As shown in Figure 11.30, ensure the following image properties are set:

- Wrapping Style: None should be selected
- Alignment: Default
- Border thickness: 0
- Horizontal spacing: 0
- Vertical spacing: 0
- Specify size: Checked (by default this is not checked)
- Keep aspect ratio: Not checked (by default this is checked)

Click OK once these settings are correct.

Figure 11.30
After double-clicking the image, you can set the different image properties.

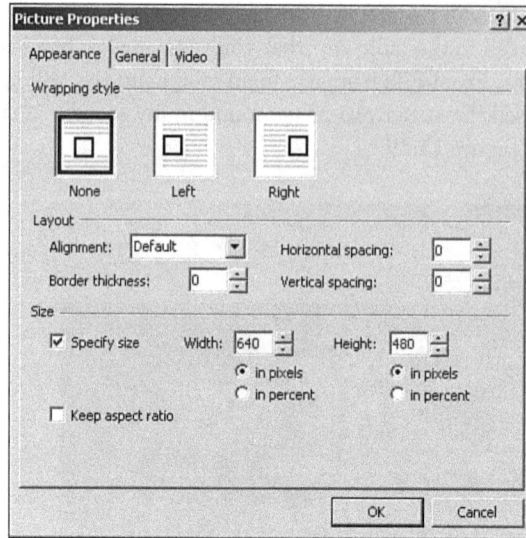

STEP 4—RESIZE AND PLACE YOUR PLACEHOLDER IMAGES

With the correct settings, you can now begin to size and place your image placeholder. The first image will represent the Take Survey button. The image has handles so you can drag the edges until the image is the right size. For the Edit Survey and Delete Survey buttons you also follow the directions from step 2, placing images in the two adjacent table cells. The three images representing your button components are now shown in Figure 11.31.

Figure 11.31
After resizing the component place-holders, you can place them into the correct columns.

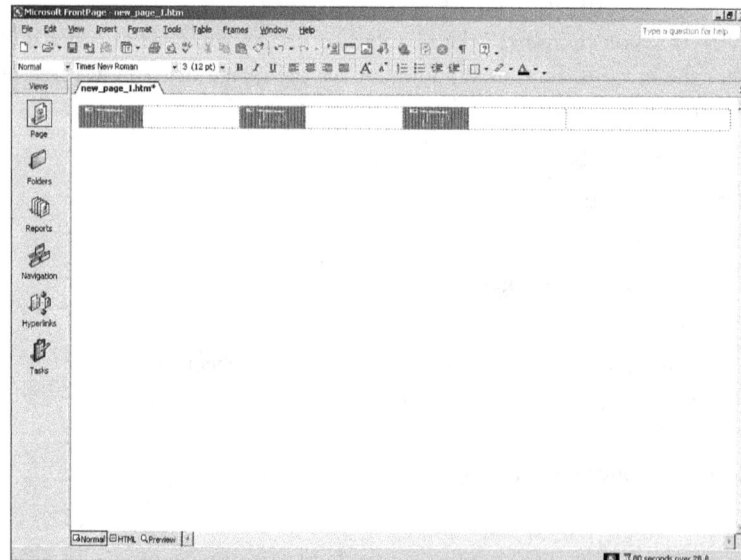

STEP 5—RESIZE THE TABLE COLUMNS

With your three images in place, you now need to size the table columns appropriately. By dragging the dashed lines that represent the table cell's borders, you can position the three buttons and create the empty space required in the cell farthest to the right. The results of the column sizing are shown in Figure 11.32. The layout of this part of your screen is finished; now you must transfer your work to the tool template.

Figure 11.32
To properly space the components, we've resized the column widths by dragging them to the appropriate width.

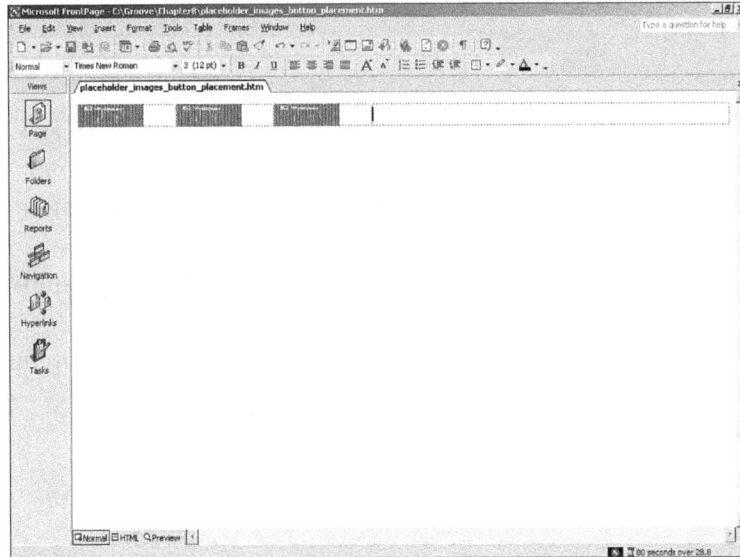

STEP 6—VIEW THE HTML SOURCE FOR YOUR TABLE AND REMOVE UNSUPPORTED PROPERTIES

By clicking the HTML tab at the bottom of the screen, you can see the HTML code created by Microsoft Frontpage. There are a few things added by the editor that you'll want to remove at this point because they are not supported by the Groove HTML Layout:

- Non-breaking spaces: Remove any and all occurrences of   from the HTML.
- Style attributes: Oftentimes, FrontPage will insert style attributes for tables. Remove any Style="xxxxxx" attributes from the HTML.
- Border color: Remove any Bordercolor="xxxx" attributes.
- All uppercase: All tags used within the HTML should be in uppercase.

The cleaned up HTML code is shown in Listing 11.2.

LISTING 11.2 THE HTML CODE GENERATED BY MICROSOFT FRONTPAGE CLEANED UP FOR USE WITHIN THE TEMPLATE

```
<HTML>

<HEAD>
<META NAME="GENERATOR" CONTENT="MICROSOFT FRONTPAGE 5.0">
<META NAME="PROGID" CONTENT="FRONTPAGE.EDITOR.DOCUMENT">
<META HTTP-EQUIV="CONTENT-TYPE" CONTENT="TEXT/HTML; CHARSET=WINDOWS-1252">
<TITLE>NEW PAGE 1</TITLE>
</HEAD>

<BODY>

<TABLE BORDER="0" CELLPADDING="0" CELLSPACING="0" WIDTH="100%">
  <TR>
    <TD WIDTH="15%">
    <IMG BORDER="0" SRC="../../WINNT2/SYSTEM32/SETUP.BMP" WIDTH="90"
    ➥HEIGHT="30"></TD>
    <TD WIDTH="15%">
    <IMG BORDER="0" SRC="../../WINNT2/SYSTEM32/SETUP.BMP" WIDTH="90"
    ➥HEIGHT="30"></TD>
    <TD WIDTH="15%">
    <IMG BORDER="0" SRC="../../WINNT2/SYSTEM32/SETUP.BMP" WIDTH="90"
    ➥HEIGHT="30"></TD>
    <TD WIDTH="55%"></TD>
  </TR>
</TABLE>

</BODY>

</HTML>
```

STEP 7—ADD THE HTML CODE TO A HTML LAYOUT COMPONENT

Assuming you've already added an HTML Layout component within Tool Creator, you can now copy the layout into your tool template. Select your HTMLTableLayout component within the Tool Creator tool and click the Properties tab. Highlight the Layout property and cut and paste the HTML code found between the <TABLE> tags into the Property value text area.

STEP 8—REPLACE IMAGES WITH THE GROOVE COMPONENTS

All the image tags used were designed to temporarily hold the place for your real components. At this point you can begin replacing the <IMG> tags with the real component names. Look for any <IMG> tags in the layout and replace them with the name used during component definition. For example, this code:

```
<TD WIDTH="15%">
    <IMG BORDER="0" SRC="../../WINNT2/SYSTEM32/SETUP.BMP" WIDTH="90"
➥HEIGHT="30"></TD>
```

Would now become:

```
<TD WIDTH="15%">voteButton</TD>
```

The code with all necessary replacements is shown in Listing 11.3.

LISTING 11.3   THE HTMLLAYOUT CODE WITH THE COMPONENT NAMES ADDED

```
<TABLE BORDER="0" CELLPADDING="0" CELLSPACING="0" WIDTH="100%">
  <TR>
    <TD WIDTH="15%">voteButton</TD>
    <TD WIDTH="15%">editButton</TD>
    <TD WIDTH="15%">deleteButton</TD>
    <TD WIDTH="55%"><TD/>
  </TR>
</table>
```

MULTICELL LAYOUT

The MultiCell layout component enables you to place components in multiple rows or columns. Unfortunately, it is not possible to easily draft your page layout using Microsoft FrontPage because it is not standard HTML. However, the MultiCell layout is a popular choice because, unlike the HTML Layout, you do not need to have the same number of columns and rows throughout the layout. Using the tags <MULTIROW> and <MULTICELL>, components are placed with <CELL> tags that comprise the columns or rows depending on the type of layout.

As an example, we have taken the Focus Group screen and segmented it in a fashion similar to what was done with the HTML layout. As shown in Figure 11.33, we are treating the entire screen as a MULTIROW layout containing three rows with a different number of cells in each row. For the rotation buttons, you will be nesting a MULTICOL layout after dividing the buttons themselves into the three different columns. The code for the MultiCell layout is shown in Listing 11.4.

Figure 11.33
Due to the complexity of the button placement, you have created a nested MultiCell layout with the following structure.

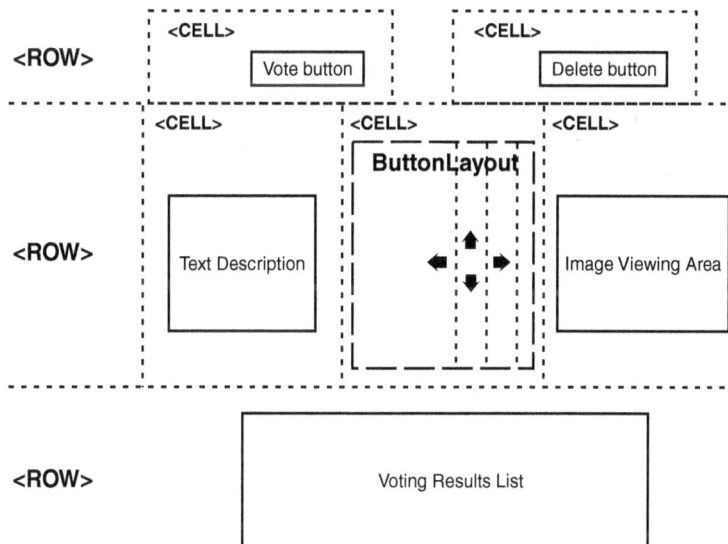

LISTING 11.4 PLACE YOUR FOCUS GROUP TOOL COMPONENTS BY USING THE MULTICELL LAYOUT COMPONENT

```
                        <g:Component Name="buttonLayout1">
                            <g:ComponentResource
➡URL="http://components.groove.net/Groove/Components/Root.osd?Package=net.groove.
➡Groove.ToolComponents.GrooveCommonComponents_DLL&amp;Version=0&amp;
➡Factory=MultiCellLayout" FingerprintID="Groove"/>
                            <g:PropertyList Version="1">
                                <g:Property Name="Layout">
                                    <g:PropertyValue>
                                        <MULTICOL>
                                            <COL>
                                                <CELL HEIGHT="100%" WIDTH="33%">
                                                leftButton
                                                </CELL>
                                            </COL>
                                            <COL>
                                                <CELL HEIGHT="50%">
                                                upButton
                                                </CELL>
                                                <CELL HEIGHT="50%">
                                                 downButton
                                                </CELL>
                                            </COL>
                                            <COL>
                                                <CELL HEIGHT="100%" WIDTH="33%">
                                                rightButton
                                                </CELL>
                                            </COL>
                                        </MULTICOL>
                                    </g:PropertyValue>
                                </g:Property>
                            </g:PropertyList>
                        </g:Component>
```

SAVING YOUR TOOL AND VIEWING THE LAYOUT

With the components defined and placed on the layout, you can now save your template. Click the Save to File button located near the top of the Tool Creator tool interface. When prompted, give the tool a name of focusgroup.tpl and specify the location of your \My Templates directory. After you've saved the file, open a new or existing shared space and add the Focus Group tool to the space from the tools list.

> **NOTE**
>
> You may have noticed the productImage component did not show up in the tool at this time. Certain components will not show up until they have been completely configured. The ImageControl component used here requires an image file be specified for display before the control becomes visible.

STEP 1—ADDING THE REST OF THE COMPONENTS

In the previous step, you created your layout that determines where the user interface components will be placed. However, you have not defined the components themselves. These will be placed within the `ComponentGroup` tags within the tool template where they are used. Listing 11.5 shows the component definition code that will be inserted at this point. Refer to the Groove API reference included with the GDK for more information about the properties that can be set for each component.

LISTING 11.5 ADDING ALL THE COMPONENT DEFINITIONS

```
            <g:Component Name="descriptionLabel">
                    <g:ComponentResource FingerprintID=""
➡URL="http://components.groove.net/Groove/Components/Root.osd?Package=net.groove.
➡Groove.ToolComponents.GrooveCommonComponents_DLL&amp;Version=0&amp;
➡Factory=Static"/>
                    <g:PropertyList Version="1">
                        <g:Property Name="Style" Value="Normal"/>
                        <g:Property Name="HAlignment" Value="Left"/>
                        <g:Property Name="VAlignment" Value="Top"/>
                        <g:Property Name="BreakType" Value="WordBreak"/>
                        <g:Property Name="Label" Value="This sturdy bus is designed
for
➡3-5 year olds. It features a sturdy design with exaggerated wheels and
comfortable
➡seating for 16."/>
                        <g:Property Name="Font">
                            <g:FontDesc Typeface="Tahoma" Height="18"
➡StyleBold="true"/>
                        </g:Property>
                    </g:PropertyList>
            </g:Component>
            <g:Component Name="rightButton">
                    <g:ComponentResource FingerprintID=""
➡URL="http://components.groove.net/Groove/Components/Root.osd?Package=net.groove.
➡Groove.ToolComponents.GrooveCommonComponents_DLL&amp;Version=0&amp;
➡Factory=Button"/>
                    <g:PropertyList Version="1">
                        <g:Property Value="grooveFile:///ToolBMPs\
➡Arrows16X16Images.jpg" Name="ImageURL"/>
                        <g:Property Value="grooveFile:///ToolBMPs\
➡Arrows16X16ImagesMask.bmp" Name="ImageMaskURL"/>
                        <g:Property Value="1" Name="ImageIndex"/>
                        <g:Property Value="16" Name="ImageHeight"/>
                        <g:Property Value="16" Name="ImageWidth"/>
                        <g:Property Value="SmallIconButton" Name="Style"/>
                        <g:Property Value="Rotate Right" Name="Tooltip"/>
                    </g:PropertyList>
            </g:Component>
            <g:Component Name="leftButton">
                    <g:ComponentResource FingerprintID=""
➡URL="http://components.groove.net/Groove/Components/Root.osd?Package=net.groove.
➡Groove.ToolComponents.GrooveCommonComponents_DLL&amp;Version=0&amp;
➡Factory=Button"/>
                    <g:PropertyList Version="1">
```

continues

LISTING 11.5 CONTINUED

```
                                  <g:Property Value="grooveFile:///ToolBMPs\
➥Arrows16X16Images.jpg" Name="ImageURL"/>
                                  <g:Property Value="grooveFile:///ToolBMPs\
➥Arrows16X16ImagesMask.bmp" Name="ImageMaskURL"/>
                                  <g:Property Value="0" Name="ImageIndex"/>
                                  <g:Property Value="16" Name="ImageHeight"/>
                                  <g:Property Value="16" Name="ImageWidth"/>
                                  <g:Property Value="SmallIconButton" Name="Style"/>
                                  <g:Property Value="Rotate Left" Name="Tooltip"/>
                          </g:PropertyList>
                  </g:Component>
                  <g:Component Name="upButton">
                          <g:ComponentResource FingerprintID=""
➥URL="http://components.groove.net/Groove/Components/Root.osd?Package=net.groove.
➥Groove.ToolComponents.GrooveCommonComponents_DLL&amp;Version=0&amp;
➥Factory=Button"/>
                          <g:PropertyList Version="1">
                                  <g:Property Value="grooveFile:///ToolBMPs\
➥Arrows16X16Images.jpg" Name="ImageURL"/>
                                  <g:Property Value="grooveFile:///ToolBMPs\
➥Arrows16X16ImagesMask.bmp" Name="ImageMaskURL"/>
                                  <g:Property Value="2" Name="ImageIndex"/>
                                  <g:Property Value="16" Name="ImageHeight"/>
                                  <g:Property Value="16" Name="ImageWidth"/>
                                  <g:Property Value="SmallIconButton" Name="Style"/>
                                  <g:Property Value="Rotate Upward" Name="Tooltip"/>
                          </g:PropertyList>
                  </g:Component>
                  <g:Component Name="downButton">
                          <g:ComponentResource FingerprintID=""
URL="http://components.groove.net/Groove/Components/Root.osd?Package=net.groove.
➥Groove.ToolComponents.GrooveCommonComponents_DLL&amp;Version=0&amp;
➥Factory=Button"/>
                          <g:PropertyList Version="1">
                                  <g:Property Value="grooveFile:///ToolBMPs\
➥Arrows16X16Images.jpg" Name="ImageURL"/>
                                  <g:Property Value="grooveFile:///ToolBMPs\
➥Arrows16X16ImagesMask.bmp" Name="ImageMaskURL"/>
                                  <g:Property Value="3" Name="ImageIndex"/>
                                  <g:Property Value="16" Name="ImageHeight"/>
                                  <g:Property Value="16" Name="ImageWidth"/>
                                  <g:Property Value="SmallIconButton" Name="Style"/>
                                  <g:Property Value="Rotate Downward" Name="Tooltip"/>
                          </g:PropertyList>
                  </g:Component>
                  <g:Component Name="productImage">
                      <g:ComponentResource FingerprintID=""
➥URL="http://components.groove.net/Groove/Components/Root.osd?Package=net.groove.
➥Groove.ToolComponents.GrooveCommonComponents_DLL&amp;Version=0&amp;Factory=Image"
/>
                          <g:PropertyList Version="1">
                              <g:Property Name="AcceptedFileTypes" Value="
➥.bmp,.jpg,.jpeg"/>
                                  <g:Property Name="Background">
                                    <g:BackgroundStyle Style="SectionBackground"/>
```

```
                    </g:Property>
                    <g:Property Name="Scaling" Value="ScaleDownOnly"/>
                    <g:Property Name="Image" Value="grooveFile:///localhost/
➥FocusGroupTool/product1.jpg"/>
                </g:PropertyList>
            </g:Component>
            <g:Component Name="voteButton">
                <g:ComponentResource FingerprintID=""
➥URL="http://components.groove.net/Groove/Root.osd?Package=net.groove.Groove.
➥ToolComponents.GrooveCommonComponents_DLL&amp;Version=0&amp;Factory=Button"/>
                <g:PropertyList Version="1">
                    <g:Property Name="Style" Value="StandardButton"/>
                    <g:Property Name="Label" Value="Vote"/>
                    <g:Property Name="Tooltip"
➥Value="Ctrl+V to vote on this item"/>
                    <g:Property Name="Mnemonic" Value="CTRL+V"/>
                    <g:Property Name="Enabled" Value="true"/>
                </g:PropertyList>
            </g:Component>
            <g:Component Name="editButton">
                <g:ComponentResource FingerprintID=""
➥URL="http://components.groove.net/Groove/Root.osd?Package=net.groove.
➥Groove.ToolComponents.GrooveCommonComponents_DLL&amp;Version=0&amp;
➥Factory=Button"/>
                <g:PropertyList Version="1">
                    <g:Property Name="Style" Value="StandardButton"/>
                    <g:Property Name="Label" Value="Edit"/>
                    <g:Property Name="Tooltip"
➥Value="Ctrl+E to edit this item"/>
                    <g:Property Name="Mnemonic" Value="CTRL+E"/>
                    <g:Property Name="Enabled" Value="true"/>
                </g:PropertyList>
            </g:Component>
            <g:Component Name="deleteButton">
                <g:ComponentResource FingerprintID=""
➥URL="http://components.groove.net/Groove/Root.osd?Package=net.groove.
➥Groove.ToolComponents.GrooveCommonComponents_DLL&amp;Version=0&amp;
➥Factory=Button"/>
                <g:PropertyList Version="1">
                    <g:Property Name="Style" Value="StandardButton"/>
                    <g:Property Name="Label" Value="Delete"/>
                    <g:Property Name="Tooltip"
➥Value="Ctrl+D to delete this item"/>
                    <g:Property Name="Mnemonic" Value="CTRL+D"/>
                    <g:Property Name="Enabled" Value="true"/>
                </g:PropertyList>
            </g:Component>
```

STEP 2: TESTING YOUR TOOL

At this point, you're ready to see how the page looks. Using the XY Layout, you can see what the final code should look like in the file FocusGroup_With_Components.tpl. You can download this file from the Que Publishing Web site. First, navigate to http://www.quepublishing.com. Type the book's ISBN (0789726777) in the search text field provided and click the Search link to go to the book's home page. Click the Source Code link and download the FocusGroup_With_Components.tpl file (as well as the rest of the code examples in this book) by clicking the link. In this code snippet, you've defined your view container, layout, and the other user interface components that comprise the page. All appropriate closing tags have been added so you should now be ready to test this basic tool by adding it to a shared space.

Start Groove and enter an existing shared space or create a new one. After clicking the Add Tool button within the space, you should see Focus Group Tool in the list of available tools. Add the tool to the space and you should see something that looks like Figure 11.34.

Figure 11.34
Your tool now has all the user interface components on the screen but they are not enabled yet.

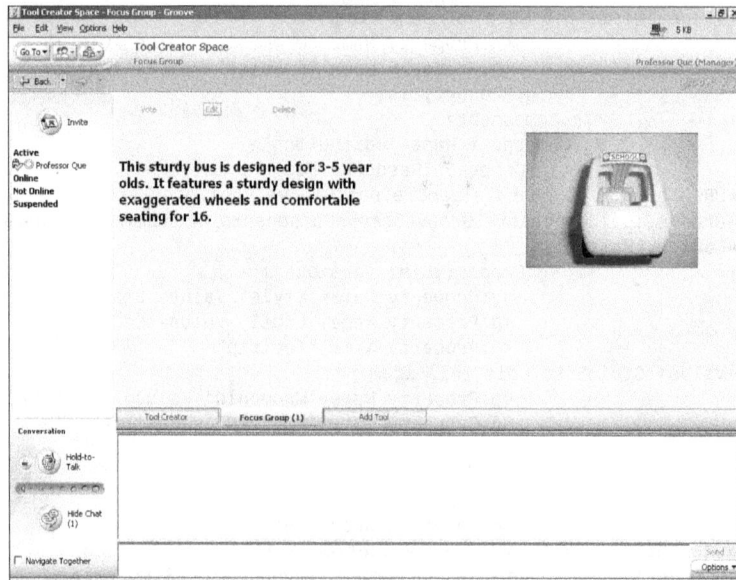

At this point, you have a form with several components but clicking the buttons has no effect. You still need to *sink* events on the form so you can respond to different actions, such as the clicking of a button. The act of sinking an event enables you to respond to the event in script, such as a function that is executed when a button is clicked.

READYING YOUR TOOL TO ACCEPT GLUE CODE

Up to this point, you've defined your primary form and placed several different user interface components onto it. These buttons will perform different tasks, from rotating the product image to enabling a member to vote on the current product. Within a tool template, you must sink the events within a form so that you can code a response to the event. The following series of steps will add the scripting host component and prepare it for the addition of some glue code to script specific tool behaviors.

STEP 1—ADDING THE SCRIPTING HOST COMPONENT

To run script in response to user events, such as the clicking of a button on a form, you need to define a Scripting Host component. Click the Components tab in the Tool Creator tool, select ScriptHost3 from the drop-down list at the top of the screen, and click the Add button. On the Info tab, rename this component to AppGlue.

STEP 2—ADDING THE CONNECTION FOR THE SCRIPTING HOST COMPONENT

To establish that functions will be called in response to user interface actions (such as clicking a button) a connection must be established from the form to a script host component. This requires that component connections be defined from the view container to the scripting host component you defined in the previous step. By selecting the MyViewContainer component and clicking the Connections tab, you should see the screen shown in Figure 11.35. In the second drop-down list, labeled Choose a Component to Connect To, specify the AppGlue component, as shown in Figure 11.36. Click the Apply Connections to Component button to apply the changes.

Figure 11.35
Click the Connections tab to add a connection to your scripting host component.

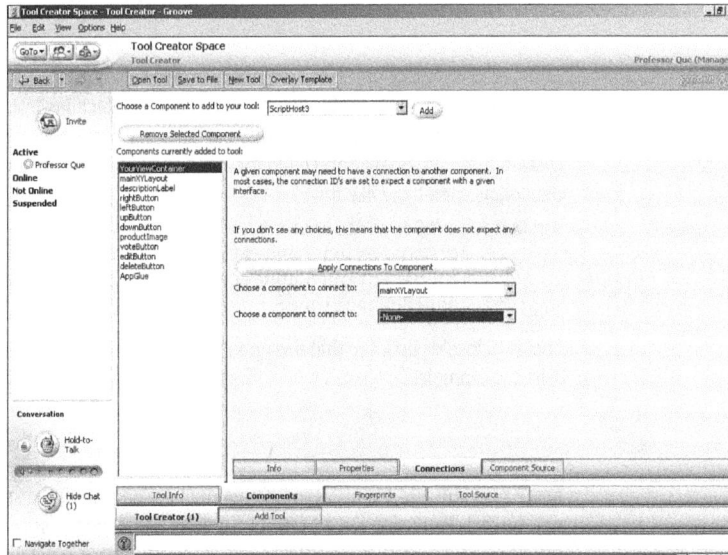

Figure 11.36
Specify a connection to the `AppGlue` component.

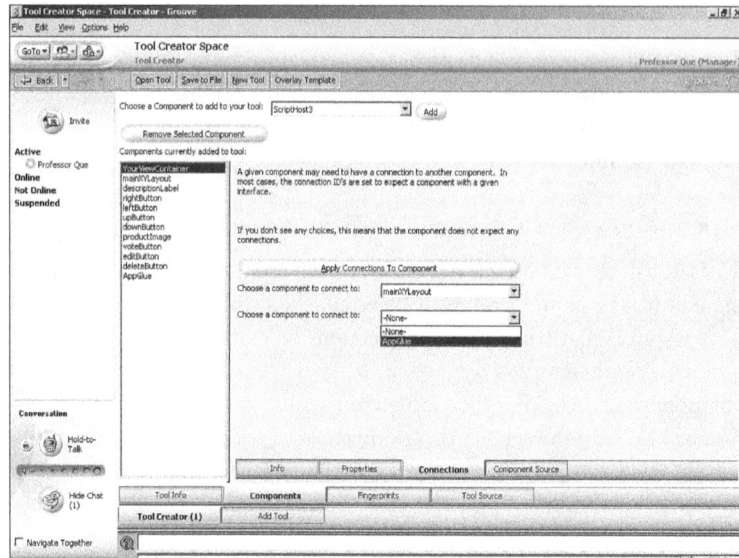

The Tool Creator tool enables you to specify two connections from any component. Each connection will receive its own unique connection ID. You can visually inspect this by clicking the Component Source tab for `MyViewContainer`. You will see the connections defined as something like this:

```
<g:ComponentConnections>
        <g:Connection ConnectionID="0" Name="mainXYLayout"/>
        <g:Connection ConnectionID="1" Name="AppGlue"/>
</g:ComponentConnections>
```

Looking closely you'll see that the `AppGlue` has been given a unique `ConnectionID` of 1 in this example.

Make sure you add the `AppGlue` component connection in the second drop-down list, not the first. Removing the XY Layout from the first connection will disconnect your layout from the view container. Essentially, your tool won't have a default display so it won't work properly.

Always use the latest numbered version of a component. In this case you used `ScriptHost3`, even though it's likely you had a `ScriptHost2` component. As a rule of thumb, you should always check release notes with Groove and the Groove Development Kit to learn any issues that might arise if you use a different component version.

STEP 3—DEFINING THE AppGlue COMPONENT CONNECTIONS

For your scripts to run within this scripting engine, you need to make the AppGlue component "aware" of them. This is done by defining component connections within the AppGlue component. The Tool Creator tool does not enable you to add these using the graphical interface. However, they are pretty easy to add manually. Select the AppGlue component in the Tool Creator and click the Component Source tab. Look for this line:

```
<g:ComponentConnections/>
```

This is an empty ComponentConnections element. Replace this line with the following:

```
<g:ComponentConnections>
    <g:Connection ConnectionID="0" Name="productImage"/>
    <g:Connection ConnectionID="1" Name="rightButton"/>
    <g:Connection ConnectionID="2" Name="leftButton"/>
    <g:Connection ConnectionID="3" Name="upButton"/>
    <g:Connection ConnectionID="4" Name="downButton"/>
    <g:Connection ConnectionID="5" Name="voteButton"/>
</g:ComponentConnections>
```

Each component you want to access via your script must have a connection defined. Each is given a unique ConnectionID because these are used internally by Groove to reference each connection. You'll be adding some more connections later as add functionality to the tool, but for now this gives you access to all the buttons and the main product image that is being displayed.

> **NOTE**
>
> With this step, you will begin to dive into writing some simple JavaScript. If you don't have much of a background in writing JavaScript, don't despair. If you don't understand all of the syntax, you can simply follow along and type the script in at this point. The script itself is simple enough that you should be able to start picking up some of the details.
>
> There are many books and Web sites available that can have you writing JavaScript functions in no time. One great example of such a book is *Javascript 1.5 By Example*, also published by Que. It's a great way to learn JavaScript in an intuitive manner by using examples to demonstrate the various concepts you'll need to know.

STEP 4—CREATING A PLACE TO PUT OUR SCRIPT

A tool template is an XML document. However, the JavaScript you are about to code does not fit into a well-formed document. Luckily, this has been accounted for with the XML standard. The <!CDATA[tag is an XML standard that tells the parser "ignore me." In this case, this is where you will be adding your script, which is not meant to be in well-formed XML format. This is the first thing you need to add to the AppGlue component. Again, you must add this directly to the component source code. Click the AppGlue component and select the Properties tab and you will see the Source code area where you will place all of your script. Enter the following into the text area, as shown in Figure 11.37:

```
//glue code goes here
```

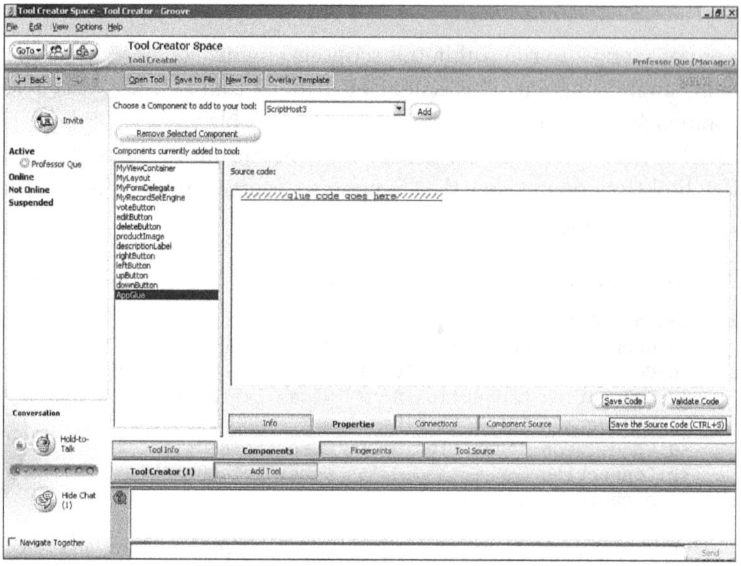

Figure 11.37
Add a comment to
your source code to
indicate where all the
glue code will be
placed.

Click the Save Code button to save the source code into your tool template. The line you just entered doesn't do anything because it is commented out. Any line that begins with // is a comment in JavaScript. Using this same source code area, you can begin adding specific behaviors to your tool by creating some script functions in JavaScript.

For a listing of the code, you can download the `FocusGroup_Before_Glue.tpl` code from the Que Publishing Web site.

ADDING GLUE CODE FOR THE IMAGE ROTATION BUTTONS

In the previous section you prepared the tool for your glue code. In the next section you begin adding script so that the image rotation buttons will change the current picture contained in the image control. If you look at your tool in its current state, as shown in Figure 11.38, the buttons are no longer grayed out but are unresponsive when they are clicked. This indicates that a connection has been established to the component, but there is no function defined to respond to the event. The next set of steps will show how you can define these functions that respond when a user clicks a button in the Focus Group tool.

STEP 1—INITIALIZE ANY GLOBAL VARIABLES

If used sparingly, global variables are a good way to pass values between functions because they persist until the tool is unloaded. The scope of these variables is within the `AppGlue` component itself. The only way such a value could be shared with another component would be to expose a method that returns the value that will be demonstrated later. In our example, you will use this to store the path to your `productImage` graphics file and a few index variables used to keep track of the current image file being viewed. Insert the following code after the `<SCRIPT>` tag in the Component Source for your `AppGlue` component:

```
//Globals for product image
var g_productID = 1;
var g_imageLocation = "grooveFile:///localhost/FocusGroupTool/product";
var g_imageFace = "";
```

Figure 11.38
The buttons have been defined, but at this point there is no glue code to respond to user actions.

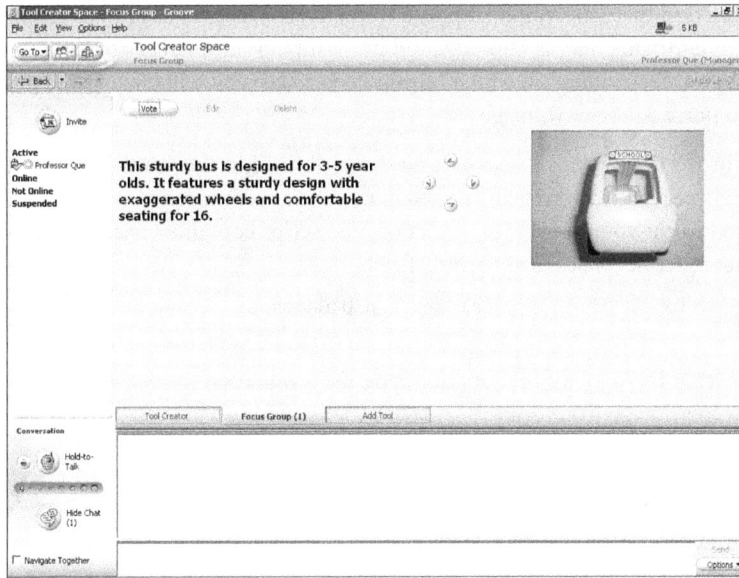

NOTE

> The `grooveFile:///` specifies that this will be a directory under the *Groove Installation*/Data directory.

STEP 2—DEFINING INITIALIZATION CODE

You can define some code that will run automatically when the tool is selected by placing it within the `Initialize` function. In this example, you'll use it to set the original image source for your product image. Add the following code after the global variables you defined in step 3:

```
function Initialize()
    {
    // Load the original image
    productImage.ImageURL = g_imageLocation + g_productID + ".jpg";
    }
```

The name of the image control in our example is `productImage`. This was defined when you added the component to the tool. The `ImageURL` is a property attached to the image control that enables you to specify where the current image file is located. You'll notice that we are using the `g_imageLocation` global variable that was just defined in the previous step.

STEP 3—ENABLING THE ROTATION BUTTONS

So far, you've only assigned one graphic to the image control in your Initialize function. This image will be displayed when the tool is first added to the space and until you explicitly change it within your code. To enable members to rotate the image, you need to define a function that will run in response to the click event on each button component. A rather crude rotate effect is implemented by swapping out pictures of the product taken at different angles. Depending on which button is checked, you will change the productImage.ImageURL to point to the new image.

For the leftButton, because it has been defined in the ComponentConnections section, you can create script that will run when the click event is triggered. By adding the following code after your Initialize function, the script contained within will run when the leftButton's OnCommand event is fired:

```
function leftButton_OnCommand(i_pIUICommand)
{
```

Within the body of the function, you find code used to set the index that is used to pull the proper image from disk:

```
if (g_productID != 1)
{
        g_productID—;
        }
    else
        {
        g_productID = 4;
        }
```

Finally, the image location, the current index number, and the extension are concatenated and assigned to the imageURL property of the image component:

```
productImage.ImageURL = g_imageLocation + g_productID + ".jpg";
}
```

When clicked, the image will change to the newly assigned image file stored locally on disk. The rest of the image rotation functions work in a similar fashion. If you'd like to see the entire code listing for the Focus Group tool template, you can download FocusGroup_Final.tpl from the Que Publishing Web site.

STEP 4—TESTING YOUR TOOL

Delete the tool from any existing shared spaces and save the file to the /My Templates folder. Add the Focus Group tool to a shared space and you can view the results. Figure 11.39 shows how the image has changed after the left arrow button has been clicked.

Figure 11.39
After you add script in response to the click event, clicking the left rotate button will change the image displayed as shown.

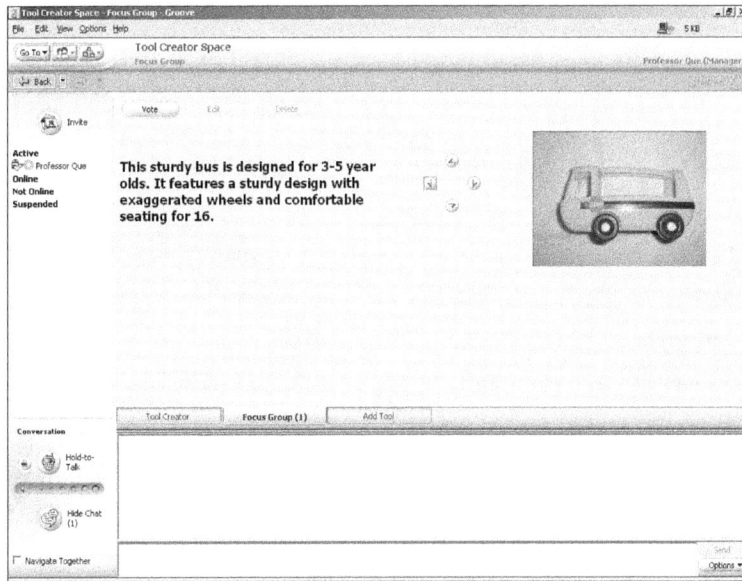

DEVELOPING YOUR SCHEMA

So far you've added some basic functionality to your tool. You can respond to click events and replace the image control contents at runtime. However, your tool also needs a way to store data that can be modified and viewed by all members. In this case, you need to store data relating to votes about the image. A good way to collect data is through another form that's subordinate to your main form; this is called a subform. We'll discuss the form (actually a subform in a pop-up window) for collecting this data later but first we need to define the schema for the data.

Those familiar with relational databases know that you must create tables in which to store your data. At the most basic level, you must name your table and fields. Each field must be assigned a data type, such as a string, number, and so on. Storing data within the Groove data store is very similar, except that you are storing them in Groove's own XML document store. Using a subset of the XML schema language, you must define what data elements you will need to store. Schemas store a variety of information including any indexes and bindings that need defined. As data is written (encrypted) to disk, the data is compared to the field date types defined in this file so that data is stored using the appropriate data type.

Let's examine the data that you need to store for the Focus Group tool and turn it into a valid Groove XML schema.

OVERVIEW OF DATA NEEDED

There are several types of information you'll want to collect when a member decides to take the brief survey offered. These are outlined and described in Table 11.2.

TABLE 11.2 FIELDS COLLECTED FROM THE USERS TAKING THE SURVEY

Field Name	Data Type	Description
member_name	String	The name of the member who posted the vote.
date_entered	Date	The date the vote was input.
age_group	String	The age group selected.
income_range	String	The income range selected.
useful_rating	Number	The rating on how useful the product is.
buy_flag	Number	Whether the user would buy the product displayed (0=no, 1=yes).
comments	String	Comments about the product.

CREATING YOUR FOCUS GROUP TOOL SCHEMA

With all the fields and their data types mapped out, you can begin to create your own Groove XML schema document. Unfortunately, this is not something that can be created using any of the tools provided with the GDK. However, there are many examples that can be found in the samples provided with the GDK in the `<Groove Installation>/Data/local-host/samples` subfolders. This is a great place to look for examples that are more advanced than our discussion here. You can use a text editor or XML editor for the following examples. An XML editor is recommended because it can help you verify that your creation is well-formed XML.

STEP 1—CREATE A NEW TEXT FILE TO HOLD THE SCHEMA   Using an XML editor or a simple text editor, create a new file called `focusgroupschema.xml`. A handy place to save this might be in a folder that you create called `GDK Install Folder\MySchemas`.

STEP 2—IDENTIFY THE FILE AS CONTAINING A SCHEMA DOCUMENT   First of all, you need to tell the parser that this is an XML schema document with the following container tag:

```
<g:Schema URL="focusgroupschema.xml" xmlns:g="urn:groove.net" Version="1,0,0,0">
```

Within this tag, you find a reference to the URL where the schema is stored (usually locally), the namespace, and the current version of the Groove schema language.

STEP 3—INCLUDE GROOVE'S OWN STANDARD RECORD SCHEMA   Groove provides its own standard recordset schema. This is used to provide the hierarchical nature of records that you'll see in the discussion tool, but also includes other important system-generated fields. The `IncludeSchemas` tag works in a similar fashion to the `#INCLUDE` statement provided by many programming languages. The following lines include the standard recordset schema:

```
<g:IncludeSchemas>
    <g:AdditionalSchema
URI="grooveDocument:///GrooveXSS/$PersistRoot/Schemas.xss/GrooveStandardRecordsSch
ema2.xml"/>
    </g:IncludeSchemas>
```

STEP 4—NAME THE RECORD   Your record should have a name; in this case we will call it the focusgrouprecord. It is defined with the following elements:

```
<g:ElementDecl Name="urn:groove.net:Record" ElementTemplate="true">
    <g:ElementRef Element="urn:groove.net:focusgrouprecord" IsChildElement="0" />
```

STEP 5—DEFINE THE FIELDS WITHIN THE RECORD   Within this element declaration, you will find the attribute definitions or *fields* that make up your records. The data you mapped out previously will be translated into the schema format with the following lines of code:

```
<g:AttrGroup>
 <g:AttrDef Name="member_name" Type="String"/>
 <g:AttrDef Name="date_entered" Type="Date"/>
 <g:AttrDef Name="over_18" Type="String"/>
 <g:AttrDef Name="durability_flag" Type="Bool"/>
 <g:AttrDef Name="price_flag" Type="Bool"/>
 <g:AttrDef Name="safety_flag" Type="Bool"/>
 <g:AttrDef Name="income_range" Type="String"/>
 <g:AttrDef Name="toys_per_month" Type="Single"/>
 <g:AttrDef Name="comments" Type="String"/>
</g:AttrGroup>
```

All the attribute definitions (`<AttrDef>` tags) are enclosed with the attribute group container (`AttrGroup`). Each definition must provide a name unique within the group and specify the data type within the `Type` attribute. Finally, you must close the element declaration that contained all elements pertaining to the record with the following closing tag:

```
</g:ElementDecl>
```

The completed schema definition is shown in Listing 11.6.

LISTING 11.6   THE ENTIRE RECORD SCHEMA USED WITHIN THE FOCUS GROUP TOOL

```
<g:Schema URL="focusgroupschema.xml" xmlns:g="urn:groove.net" Version="1,0,0,0">
    <g:IncludeSchemas>
        <g:AdditionalSchema
URI="grooveDocument:///GrooveXSS/$PersistRoot/Schemas.xss/GrooveStandardRecordsSch
ema2.xml"/>
    </g:IncludeSchemas>
    <g:ElementDecl Name="urn:groove.net:Record" ElementTemplate="true">
        <g:ElementRef Element="urn:groove.net:focusgrouprecord" IsChildElement="0"
/>
        <g:AttrGroup>
            <g:AttrDef Name="member_name" Type="String"/>
            <g:AttrDef Name="date_entered" Type="Date"/>
            <g:AttrDef Name="over_18" Type="String"/>
            <g:AttrDef Name="durability_flag" Type="Bool"/>
            <g:AttrDef Name="price_flag" Type="Bool"/>
            <g:AttrDef Name="safety_flag" Type="Bool"/>
            <g:AttrDef Name="income_range" Type="String"/>
```

continues

LISTING 11.6   CONTINUED

```
            <g:AttrDef Name="toys_per_month" Type="Single"/>
            <g:AttrDef Name="comments" Type="String"/>
        </g:AttrGroup>

    </g:ElementDecl>

</g:Schema>
```

IMPORTING THE SCHEMA INTO THE DATABASE

In order for you to use the schema, it has to be imported into Groove. Chapter 12 discusses how to automate this process during injection. However, during development you'll manually import the schema using the Groove Database Navigator tool provided with the GDK:

1. If you haven't done so already, inject the Groove Database Navigator as outlined in Chapter 10.

2. Add the Groove Database Navigator to a shared space.

3. In the list of databases on the top portion of the screen, highlight the schemas.xss database. This is where Groove stores most of its XML schemas and where you'll store the Focus Group tool schema for consistency.

4. Click the Import Document into Database button. If asked for the Import Options, click OK to continue. Choose the location of the focusgroupschema.xml file, which can be downloaded from http://www.quepublishing.com. Click the Open button and the schema will be imported.

> **NOTE**
>
> If the schema fails to load, there may be a problem in the XML. Double-check your syntax and ensure you have a well-formed XML document. This is where tools like XML Notepad and XML Spy can come in handy.

After the schema has been imported, you will see an entry in the schemas.xss database as shown in Figure 11.40. Now that the schema has been imported into the database, you can begin referencing it from your script using the Groove RecordSetEngine.

USING THE RECORDSET ENGINE

Each tool has its own XML database and so far you've defined the schema outlining some of the custom data fields you need to store. Groove provides the RecordsetEngine for accessing this data. Not only does this engine enable you to access data from your script, but it also works in conjunction with other components, such as the DataViewer control, to provide users with a current view of the data. Using the Model-View-Controller structure paradigm, you can think of the RecordsetEngine as the controller that updates the view when the underlying data model changes. For its data storage and dissemination capabilities, this should be the preferred method for storing data within a tool.

Figure 11.40
After importing the schema you can view it using the Database Navigator tool.

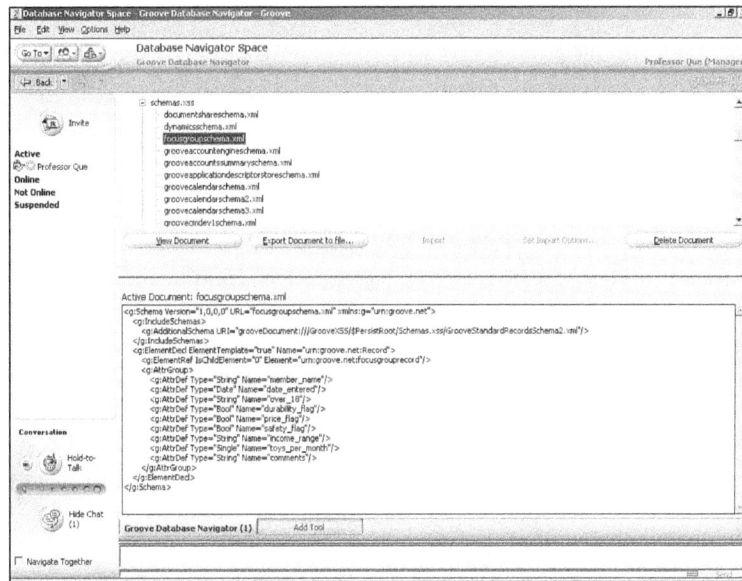

Data can be visualized in the `RecordSetEngine` as a series of records, each record having its own unique ID. Using records, developers have a familiar interface for retrieving and updating records. Also, the `RecordSetEngine` provides built-in indexing to allow more efficient manipulation of large recordsets.

DEFINING THE `RecordSetEngine` COMPONENT

Like other components, you can add the `RecordSetEngine` component to our tool template using the Tool Creator tool. Within the Tool Creator, click the Components tab at the bottom of the screen. Choose the `RecordSetEngine` from the component drop-down list and click the Add button to add this component to the tool template.

Replace:

```
<g:Property Name="ClassInfoList"/>
```

with:

```
<g:Property Name="ClassInfoList">
    <g:PropertyValue>
        <g:ClassInfo
URL="http://components.groove.net/Groove/Components/Root.osd?Package=net.groove.Gr
oove.ToolComponents.GrooveListComponents_DLL&amp;Version=0&amp;Factory=Record"
Name="urn:groove.net:focusgrouprecord"/>
    </g:PropertyValue>
</g:Property>
```

You are also creating a connection to the `ToolCollections` component. This is often used in conjunction with the `RecordSetEngine` because it provides useful functionality when dealing with records such as indexing, bulk retrieval, cursor support, and searching capabilities. Wrapping up the `RecordSetEngine`, you create the connection and close the Component tag:

```
<g:ComponentConnections>
    <g:Connection Name="ToolCollections" ConnectionID="0"/>
</g:ComponentConnections>
</g:Component>
```

ADDING THE `ToolCollectionsComponent`

As stated earlier, the `ToolCollectionsComponent` component offers additional useful functionality when used in conjunction with the `RecordSetEngine`. It can be added to the tool template by choosing the `ToolCollections` component from the component drop-down list and clicking the Add button. No additional properties must be set for this component.

ADDING A SAMPLE RECORD TO THE DATABASE

Later you'll be adding the voting subform and retrieving real data from it. However, you can quickly check to make sure the schema definition, the recordset engine component, and the collection component are working properly. Similar to the event sink used with the left rotate arrow, you can quickly place some code behind the Vote button to place a dummy record into the database.

Follow these steps to add a sample record to the database:

1. Within the `AppGlue` component, add a connection to the `voteButton` and `RecordSetEngine` so they can be accessed within your script. You can add these to the `AppGlue` component source within the Tool Creator. Click the `ApplGlue` component in the list on the left side of the screen and add the following connections:

```
<g:Connection ConnectionID="5" Name="voteButton"/>
<g:Connection ConnectionID="6" Name="RecordSetEngine"/>
```

The last `ConnectionID` used in the Focus Group tool for the `downButton` was 4, so we've numbered these two components sequentially with 5 and 6. Click the Save button to save these additional connections.

2. Now define a script function in response to the `surveyButton OnCommand` event. This will fire when the Take Survey button is clicked. You can define the code in the `AppGlue` component by adding the following code to the source code area:

```
function voteButton_OnCommand(i_pIUICommand
{
```

Click the Save Source button once you've added the code to save it within the tool template. All of the code in the following steps will be placed within these braces.

3. All changes to data using the `RecordSetEngine` should be put into a transaction. This is very important so that in case an error occurs, you can abort the transaction before it is actually committed. A transaction is opened as a method on the current telespace with the following code:

```
var appTelespace = PropertyList.OpenProperty(PROPERTY_TELESPACE);
var myTransaction = appTelespace.OpenTransaction(false);
```

This code should be placed within the function braces in step 2.

4. In JavaScript, you can place script within a `try...catch` block to handle any exceptions. In our case this block will be used to abort the transaction if an error occurs. The block of code and the transaction operations are shown in the following code:

```
try
    {
    //CODE TO UPDATE RECORD GOES HERE
    myTransaction.Commit();
    }
catch(e)
    {
    //IF AN ERROR OCCURS, ABORT THE TRANSACTION
    myTransaction.Abort();
    Error("error occured writing record:" + e);
    }
```

After aborting the transaction, you also write an error message to the log that is a useful tool for debugging. This code should be placed directly after the code in step 3.

NOTE

It is also possible to "throw" an error to an outside handler within your tool. For example, you could change your `catch` block to the following to throw an error:

```
catch(e)
    {
    throw e;
    }
```

5. Now that you've created a transaction, you can build the record to be inserted into the tool's data store. Using the `RecordFactory` found within the `RecordSetEngine`, you can call the `CreateRecord` method:

```
//Create a new record using the focusgroup schema we have defined
var fgRecord =
RecordSetEngine.RecordFactory.CreateRecord("urn:groove.net:focusgrouprecord");
```

The `CreateRecord` method accepts the record type as a parameter. This is the same record type that was defined in your schema in the `ElementRef` element. This code will be placed within the try block defined in step 4.

NOTE

You can explore the many different types of schemas that Groove has defined by exploring the `schemas.xss` database within the Groove Database Navigator tool.

6. Using the `SetField` method on the record object, you can pass the name of the field (as defined in the XML schema) and its new value:

```
//Set all the field values
fgRecord.SetField("member_name", "Dummy User");
fgRecord.SetField("date_entered", Date());
fgRecord.SetField("over_18", "Yes");
fgRecord.SetField("durability_flag", 1);
fgRecord.SetField("price_flag", 0);
```

```
fgRecord.SetField("safety_flag", 1);
fgRecord.SetField("income_range", "$20,000 to $29,999");
fgRecord.SetField("toys_per_month", 2);
fgRecord.SetField("comments", "Greatest tool ever");
```

This code should be appended to the code in step 5 (within the try block).

7. After the record object has been defined, the AddRecord method on the RecordSetEngine component will insert a new record. The only parameter it requires is the Record object that you've just defined. Add the following code after the code you've just entered in step 6.

```
// Add the record
RecordSetEngine.AddRecord(fgRecord);
```

8. Using a standard message box, you can verify the new number of records by displaying the NumRecords property of the RecordSetEngine:

```
GrooveScriptFunctions.DoMessageBox(RecordSetEngine.NumRecords);
```

After closing all the tags and functions properly, you can view the code by downloading FocusGroup_Before_Dataview.tpl. Clicking the Vote button will now add a bogus record to the database and display the current number of records. You can click the button repeatedly and you'll see the number continuously increment by one each time. For example, after clicking the Vote button several times you will receive a message box that increments by 1 each time. Although this shows that records are being added to the database, you won't see the data contained within until you've configured the DataViewer component in the next section. You can download at copy of the Focus Group tool code at this point in the file FocusGroup_dummy_record.tpl from http://www.quepublishing.com.

CREATING THE DataViewer COMPONENT

At this point you've successfully added a record to the local data store. Now you need to get the data into the columnar format shown at the bottom of the screen in Figure 11.41. For this functionality, Groove provides the DataViewer component that is designed to work in conjunction with the RecordSetEngine:

1. Like the other components you've added to the tool up to this point, the DataViewer component must be added to your tool template. Within the Components area of Tool Creator, select the DataViewer component and click the Add button to add the component to your tool template.

   We have chosen to name the component the DataViewerControl, although it can be given any unique name within the telespace.

2. There are several properties that need to be defined to ensure your DataViewer component works properly. Clicking the Properties tab will enable you to see all the properties available as shown in Figure 11.42.

Figure 11.41
In this figure you can see the columns that will make up your `DataViewer` control in the bottom of the tool form.

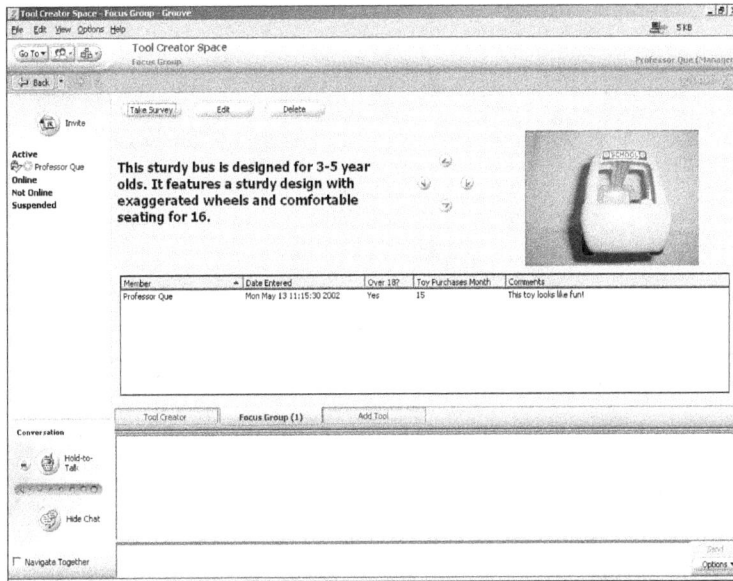

Figure 11.42
Clicking the Properties tab will enable you to see all the properties that can be set for this component.

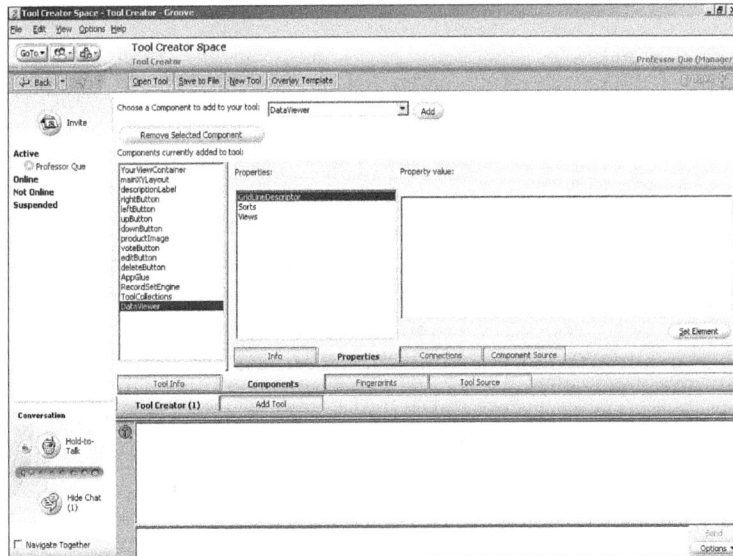

3. The `DataViewer` component can have several different views. This allows it to be "reused" in applications where members can choose between several different view layouts. You must set the Views property in the `DataViewer` component to the following:

```
<g:Property Name="Views">
<g:PropertyValue>
    <g:DataViewerView Name="Main" Default="True">
        <g:DataViewerColumn Name="member_name" Label="Member"
```

```
DataType="String" Width="20%" ShowTwisty="0" Indent="15" ReadOnly="1"/>
        <g:DataViewerColumn Name="date_entered" Label="Date Entered"
DataType="Date" Width="20%" ShowTwisty="0" Indent="15" ReadOnly="1"/>
        <g:DataViewerColumn Name="over_18" Label="Over 18?"
DataType="String" Width="8%" ShowTwisty="0" Indent="15" ReadOnly="1"/>
        <g:DataViewerColumn Name="toys_per_month" Label="Toy Purchases
Month" DataType="Single" Width="15%" ShowTwisty="0" Indent="15" ReadOnly="1"/>
        <g:DataViewerColumn Name="comments" Label="Comments"
DataType="String" Width="42%" ShowTwisty="0" Indent="15" ReadOnly="1"/>
      </g:DataViewerView>
    </g:PropertyValue>
</g:Property>
```

The following attributes have been defined for each column in this view:

- Name: A name to uniquely identify the column that corresponds to the field in the schema.

- Label: The heading that appears at the top of the column.

- DataType: The DataType that the column will hold (same as schema type).

- Width: The width of the column.

- ShowTwisty: Flag used to determine if cursor indicates that column widths can be changed.

- Indent: Size of space to be inserted before the value is displayed.

- ReadOnly: Whether the column is read-only or editable. For our example, we will not allow editing within the DataViewer itself.

After the Views property code has been added be sure to click the Set Value button to save the new value.

4. A very nice feature of the DataViewer control is that it enables users to sort rows of data by clicking the column header. The DataViewer control takes care of the sorting without the need to write additional script. To enable this feature, set the Sorts property of the DataViewer control to this value:

```
<g:DataViewerSort Name="ByAscmember_name" Column="member_name"
DataType="String" Order="Ascending"/>
<g:DataViewerSort Name="ByDescmember_name" Column="member_name"
DataType="String" Order="Descending"/>
<g:DataViewerSort Name="ByAscdate_entered" Column="date_entered"
DataType="DateTime" Order="Ascending"/>
<g:DataViewerSort Name="ByDescdate_entered" Column="date_entered"
DataType="DateTime" Order="Descending"/>
```

Each of the following attributes must be set:

- Name: A unique name given to each sorted field.

- Column: The name of the corresponding column (from the column definition in step 3).

- `DataType`: The data type of values within this column.

- `Order`: Whether the column can be sorted in ascending or descending order.

In this example, we have allowed ascending and descending order sorting for the `member_name` and `date_entered` columns. Be sure to click the Set Value button after you've changed the `Sorts` property.

NOTE

> To allow sorting in both ascending and descending order, you must create two `DataViewerSort` elements, each with a unique name. Using the same `Name` attribute more than once in a view is incorrect.

USING THE MODEL GLUE COMPONENT WITH THE `DataViewer`

Now that the `DataView` control has been defined, it needs to be attached to the `RecordSetEngine` that holds the underlying records. The Model Glue component is what enables the `DataViewer` component to display the contents of your saved survey data. This cannot be added through the Tool Creator tool directly, so you must first save your tool template to disk. Within the Tool Creator click the Save to File button and you will be prompted to save the template to disk. Name the file `focusgroup.tpl` and save the file in the *Groove Installation*/Data/My Templates folder at this time. Follow these steps to enable the `DataViewer` component to work with the underlying `RecordsetEngine` data:

1. First of all, the `ModelGlue` component must be defined using a standard component container:

```
<g:Component Name="ModelGlue">
    <g:ComponentResource
➥URL="http://components.groove.net/Groove/Components/Root.osd?Package=net.groo
ve.
➥Groove.ToolComponents.GrooveDataViewerTool_DLL&amp;Version=0&amp;
➥Factory=ModelGlue" FingerprintID="Groove"/>
    <g:PropertyList Version="1"/>
</g:Component>
```

This code can be added anywhere alongside the other components you've defined, but a good place to put it would be directly following the `RecordSetEngine` component.

2. In order to label each column and to provide sort functionality, you also need to add the `ColumnHeaders` component with the following code:

```
<g:Component Name="ColumnHeaders">
    <g:ComponentResource
➥URL="http://components.groove.net/Groove/Components/Root.osd?Package=net.groo
ve.
➥Groove.ToolComponents.GrooveCommonComponents_DLL&amp;Version=0&amp;
➥Factory=Header"/>
</g:Component>
```

Again, it can be added anywhere alongside the other components in the template. However, for consistency you may want to place it directly after the `ModelGlue` component you defined in step 1.

3. Within the `ModelGlue` component that you just created, you need to set up the appropriate connections to the `Collection` and `RecordSetEngine` components:

```
<g:ComponentConnections>
    <g:Connection Name="Collection" ConnectionID="0"/>
    <g:Connection Name="RecordSetEngine" ConnectionID="1"/>
</g:ComponentConnections>
```

4. The last connection that must be established is between the `DataView` and `ModelGlue` components. Remember that when the underlying data model changes, you want these to be reflected in the data view component (or the View in the MVC structure). This is accomplished by adding this connection within the `ModelGlue` component container:

```
<g:ComponentConnections>
    <g:Connection Name="ModelGlue" ConnectionID="0"/>
    <g:Connection Name="ColumnHeaders" ConnectionID="1"/>
</g:ComponentConnections>
```

5. At this point, you can edit the tool template using the Tool Creator tool. Save the current tool template file within your editor.

6. Open the Tool Creator tool and click the Open Tool button to be prompted for the tool template file you wish to open. Choose the `focusgroup.tpl` file you saved to disk in step 5. After clicking the Open button the Tool Creator tool should now contain the tool template information.

7. Lastly, you must tell Groove where to place the `DataViewer` control itself. The component has already been defined so you must now add it to the `MyLayout` component properties with its appropriate horizontal and vertical position. Click the `MyLayout` component and select the `Layout` property. Add the following line to this property:

```
<g:Control Name="DataViewerControl" Left="5" Top="240" Width="850"
Height="160"/>
```

Your code should look like the file `FocusGroup_dummy_record.tpl`, which is available from this book's Web page at www.quepublishing.com. To test out the new tool, add it to a shared space. Click the Vote button several times and the records should be displayed in the `DataViewer` control as they are added to the underlying recordset. In Figure 11.43, we've added a few records to illustrate this. For now, because we are adding "dummy" records, they all have the same data. This will change as we now discover how to create a voting subform that will be used by the members.

Figure 11.43
Clicking the Take Survey button several times will insert a few dummy records that are displayed in the `DataViewer` control.

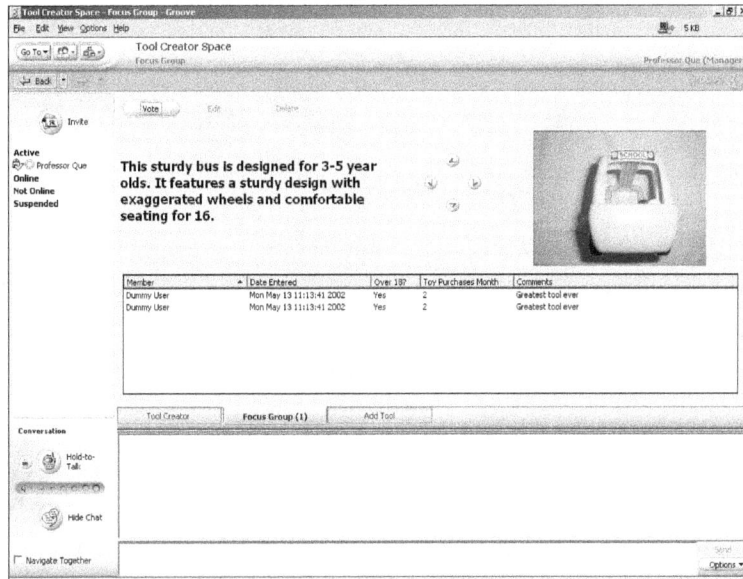

CREATING THE VOTING SUBFORM

When a user clicks the Vote button, you want to take her to a subform in order to collect feedback on the current product she is viewing. Groove provides a `Subform` component that you can use to create a pop-up window that will contain a variety of different controls used to collect the information:

1. A `Subform` is a component that can be added via the Tool Creator tool. In the Components area of the Tool Creator choose the Subform component from the drop-down list and click the Add button.

2. You need to specify a view container for the subform. In the components area, choose `ViewContainer` from the drop-down list box and click the Add button. After the component is added, click the Info tab and rename this view container to `SubformView`. Also, you need to specify that this component will be part of a subform by choosing Subform in the Add This Component to a Subform list box. Click the Properties tab and assign the following values to these properties:

   Background: <Leave this field blank>

   PreferredWidth: 400

   PreferredHeight: 400

   Be sure to click the Set Value button after the properties have been changed.

3. Like your primary form, you must define all the components for your subform. The following listing shows all the components to add, the names they should be assigned, and any property settings. The full source code for all the definitions can be found in

```
http://xxxx.txt.
Component: StaticText
Component Name: titleLabel
Properties:
        Label: Please provide feedback on this product

Component: StaticText
Component Name: ageLabel
Properties:
        Label: Are you over the age of 18?
Component: StaticText

Component Name: commentsLabel
Properties:
        Label: Additional Comments:

Component: StaticText
Component Name: incomeLabel
Properties:
        Label: Annual household income?

Component: Button
Component Name: ageRadio1
Properties:
        Radiobutton: True
        Label: Yes
        Style: Radiobutton
        Enabled: True
        Tooltip: <blank>

Component: Button
Component Name: ageRadio2
Properties:
        Radiobutton: False
        Label: No
        Style: Radiobutton
        Enabled: True
        Tooltip: <blank>
Component: Button
Component Name: qualityDurability
Properties:
        Checkbox: False
        Label: Durability
        Style: Checkbox
        Enabled: True

Component: Button
Component Name: qualityPrice
Properties:
        Checkbox: False
        Label: Price
        Style: Checkbox
        Enabled: True

Component: Button
Component Name: qualitySafety
```

```
Properties:
        Checkbox: False
        Label: Safety
        Style: Checkbox
        Enabled: True

Component: ComboBox
Component Name: incomeCombobox
Properties: <NONE>

Component: StaticText
Component Name: qualitiesLabel
Properties:
        Label: What qualities are most important to you?

Component: StaticText
Component Name: toysPerMonthLabel
Properties:
        Label: How many toys do you purchase each month?

Component: Edit
Component Name: toysPerMonthEdit
Properties:
        Enabled: True

Component: Edit
Component Name: commentsEdit
Properties:
        Style:      Multiline
                    VerticalScrollbar
                    HorizontalScrollbar
        ReadOnly: Enabled
        Enabled: True

Component: Button
Component Name: OKButton
Properties:
        Style: SmallTextButton
        Label: OK
        Tooltip: Click this once completed (Control-O)
        SingleLine: True
        Mnemonic: CTRL-O
 Component: Button

Component Name: cancelButton
Properties:
        Style: SmallTextButton
        Label: CANCEL
        Tooltip: Click to cancel (Control-C)
        SingleLine: True
        Mnemonic: CTRL-C
<g:ComponentConnections>
<g:Connection Name="VoteSubformLayout" ConnectionID="0"/>
    <g:Connection Name="VoteSubformDelegate" ConnectionID="1"/>
</g:ComponentConnections>
</g:Component>
```

The view container must have a layout defined and added to the component connections. In addition, the delegate component must be added to the component connections. This delegate will be responsible for processing events on the subform.

4. Your subform will have a variety of different components whose position will be determined by the layout. For this example, you will use the XY Layout and components defined in the file subform_layout_and_components.tpl, which is available from this book's Web page at www.quepublishing.com.

5. Previously, you inserted some code into the voteButton_OnCommand function to insert a dummy record into the database. Delete all the script within this function.

6. Very similar to the AppGlue component that housed the glue code for your default form, you need to define a similar scripting host component for your subform with the following code:

```
<g:Component Name="VoteSubformGlue">
                        <g:ComponentResource FingerprintID="Groove"
➥URL="http://components.groove.net/Groove/Components/Root.osd?
➥Package=net.
➥groove.Groove.ToolComponents.GrooveCommonComponents_DLL&amp;
➥Version=0&amp;
➥Factory=ScriptHost2"/>
                        <g:ComponentConnections>
                            <g:Connection ConnectionID="0"
➥Name="ageRadio1"/>
                            <g:Connection ConnectionID="1"
➥Name="ageRadio2"/>
                            <g:Connection ConnectionID="2"
➥Name="incomeCombobox"/>
                            <g:Connection ConnectionID="3"
➥Name="qualityDurability"/>
                            <g:Connection ConnectionID="4"
➥Name="qualityPrice"/>
                            <g:Connection ConnectionID="5"
➥Name="qualitySafety"/>
                            <g:Connection ConnectionID="6"
➥Name="toysPerMonthEdit"/>
                            <g:Connection ConnectionID="7"
➥Name="commentsEdit"/>
                            <g:Connection ConnectionID="8"
➥Name="OKButton"/>
                            <g:Connection ConnectionID="9"
➥Name="CancelButton"/>
                        </g:ComponentConnections>
                        <SCRIPT
➥SRC="http://components.groove.net/Groove/Components/Root.osd?Package=net.
➥groove.Groove.ToolComponents.GrooveGlobalHelperFunctions_GSL&amp;
➥Version=0&amp;Factory=Open" FingerprintID="Groove"/>
                        <SCRIPT>
                            <![CDATA[
        <<<<<<<<<<<<<<<<<Glue Code goes here>>>>>>>>>>>>>>>>>
            ]]>
                        </SCRIPT>
                </g:Component>
```

7. On your subform you have a Combobox used to collect the user's income level. You will populate this at runtime using the initialize function within your VoteSubformGlue component:

```
function Initialize()
        {
        // Load the income combo box
        incomeCombobox.AddItem("Less than $20,000");
        incomeCombobox.AddItem("$20,000 to $29,999");
        incomeCombobox.AddItem("$30,000 to $49,999");
        incomeCombobox.AddItem("$50,000 to $79,999");
        incomeCombobox.AddItem("$80,000 to $99,999");
        incomeCombobox.AddItem("Over $100,000");
        }
```

With this code in place, the Income combo box will be automatically loaded with values for the user to choose from.

8. Your form contains a variety of different check boxes and radio buttons. You must code the behavior for each using the following code:

```
function ageRadio1_OnCommand(i_UICommand)
            {
            if (ageRadio1.CheckState == 0)
                {
                ageRadio1.CheckState = 1;
                ageRadio2.CheckState = 0;
                }
            }

        function ageRadio2_OnCommand(i_UICommand)
        {
        if (ageRadio2.CheckState == 0)
            {
            ageRadio2.CheckState = 1;
            ageRadio1.CheckState = 0;
            }

        }

        function qualityDurability_OnCommand(i_UICommand)
        {
        if (qualityDurability.CheckState == 0)
            {
            qualityDurability.CheckState = 1;
            }
            else
            {
            qualityDurability.CheckState = 0;
            }
        }
        function qualityPrice_OnCommand(i_UICommand)
        {
        if (qualityPrice.CheckState == 0)
            {
            qualityPrice.CheckState = 1;
            }
```

11

```
                    else
                    {
                    qualityPrice.CheckState = 0;
                    }
              }
              function qualitySafety_OnCommand(i_UICommand)
              {
              if (qualitySafety.CheckState == 0)
                    {
                    qualitySafety.CheckState = 1;
                    }
                    else
                    {
                    qualitySafety.CheckState = 0;
                    }
              }
```

This code is pretty straightforward. Refer to the documentation provided with the GDK for other properties of radio buttons and check boxes.

ADDING THE CODE TO OPEN THE SUBFORM

Before you completely finish the subform, it would be nice to test it. To test the subform, you must add some code to the voteButton_onCommand function in response to the click event. If you remember, this is the same location that previously held the code that added a dummy record to the underlying database:

1. First of all, there are several global variables that you need to define. The global variables are defined outside any of the function definitions. A good place to put them is right before the initialize function:

```
//Globals for survey form
var g_appWindowManager;
var g_appComponentContainer;
var g_strSubformName;
```

2. In the AppGlue component, add the following script to define the function:

```
function surveyButton_OnCommand(i_pIUICommand)
{
```

Groove provides a window manager to handle things such as opening a new pop-up window. You can assign these objects to the global objects created in step 1:

```
// Initialize globals
g_appWindowManager = GrooveScriptFunctions.
➥CreateNewObject("Groove.WindowManager");
g_appComponentContainer =
PropertyList.OpenProperty(PROPERTY_COMPONENT_CONTAINER).ComponentContainer;
```

3. First of all, you need to create an instance of the WindowProperties object:

```
// Create the window
var WindowProperties = GrooveScriptFunctions.
➥CreateNewObject("Groove.WindowProperties");
```

Using this you'll be able to set some properties of the new window you create. In addition, you also want to grab a few other properties including the top-level window property and the window account:

```
var ParentWindow = UIPropertyList.
➥OpenProperty(UIPROPERTY_TOP_LEVEL_WINDOW);
var WindowAccount = UIPropertyList.
➥OpenProperty(UIPROPERTY_WINDOW_ACCOUNT);
```

4. Using the global component container you defined earlier, you may now get a reference to the subform and place it into the DialogSubForm variable:

```
var DialogSubForm = g_appComponentContainer.
➥OpenComponentByName("VoteSubform");
```

> **NOTE** You have not actually created a visible window yet; this is only a reference to the VoteSubForm component.

5. Before opening the window, you need to define some properties such as the style and size of window. These are all properties of the WindowProperties object:

```
WindowProperties.Style = "PopupWindow";
WindowProperties.ParentWindow = ParentWindow;
WindowProperties.Resizable = true;
WindowProperties.CaptionVisible = true;
WindowProperties.Caption = "Voting Subform";
WindowProperties.Visible = false;
WindowProperties.InitialWidth = 550;
WindowProperties.InitialHeight = 430;
```

Refer to the GDK documentation for a complete listing of properties and their valid settings. In your case, you are using the settings needed for your pop-up window.

6. Using a Window Manager method, you are able to create your voting subform window. It will assume all the window properties you defined earlier and take your reference to the VoteSubForm as a parameter:

```
// Create window
g_VoteWindow = g_appWindowManager.CreateGrooveWindowForForm
        (
            WindowAccount,
            "",
            WindowProperties,
            DialogSubForm
        );
```

7. You are now able to open the window itself. Using the DoModal method, you can open the window with the following line of code:

```
//Display the window in a modal state and retrieve the result
var surveyFormResult = g_VoteWindow.DoModal();
```

The surveyFormResult is used to store the return value from the window. With this, you can tell if the user exited the window by clicking OK or Cancel.

PROCESSING THE SUBFORM DATA

Up to this point, you've created the voting subform to open when the user clicks the Vote button. However, you now need to enable the OK and Cancel buttons and process the results accordingly. The following steps enable the subform buttons. You'll also add a script to process the user-entered data on the subform:

1. Sinking the events from the OK and Cancel buttons is simple. Add the following code to the `VoteSubformGlue` scripting host:

```
function OKButton_OnCommand(i_UICommand)
        {
        //  Close window if OK button is clicked
        var pITopLevelWindow =
UIPropertyList.OpenProperty(UIPROPERTY_TOP_LEVEL_WINDOW);
        pITopLevelWindow.Close(GrooveWindowResult_OK);
        }

function CancelButton_OnCommand(i_UICommand)
        {
        //  Close window if Cancel button is clicked
        var pITopLevelWindow =
UIPropertyList.OpenProperty(UIPROPERTY_TOP_LEVEL_WINDOW);
        pITopLevelWindow.Close(GrooveWindowResult_Cancel);
        }
```

   In each function you must first get a reference to the topmost window, which is the subform window, and store it in `pITopLevelWindow`. When you have a reference to this window, you can call the `Close` method. The `Close` method takes a single parameter that is the value passed back to the code where the window was opened. In each case, you can pass the appropriate Groove constant depending on which button was clicked.

2. Returning to the `AppGlue` component, you can add the logic to process the window results directly after the `DoModal()` method call:

```
//Check if the OK button was clicked on the survey subform
if (surveyFormResult == GrooveWindowResult_OK)
    {
    //OK Button logic goes here
    }
else
    {
    //Cancel Button logic goes here
    }
```

   This `if` statement will branch accordingly depending on the result value passed from the modal window that contains the subform.

3. You cannot directly retrieve values from the subform itself. However, by using a script dispatch you can reference any functions within the subform glue code. Adding the following simple functions to the `VoteSubformGlue` component will provide a simple way to retrieve each form value by returning the data entered into each user interface component:

```
function returnQualityDurability() { return qualityDurability.CheckState}
function returnQualityPrice() { return qualityPrice.CheckState}
```

```
function returnQualitySafety() { return qualitySafety.CheckState}
function returnToysPerMonth() { return toysPerMonthEdit.Text}
function returnComments() { return commentsEdit.Text}
function returnIncome() { return
incomeCombobox.GetItemText(incomeCombobox.GetSelectionIndex())}
function returnAge()
{
if (ageRadio1.CheckState == 1)
        {
        return "Yes";
        }
    else
        {
        return "No";
        }
}
```

Each function contains a simple return statement to return the field value. For the returnAge function we have added some additional code to translate the check box state into a Yes or No string for entry into the database.

4. If the user clicks the OK button, you will want to update the underlying data within the space. All shared data updates should be contained within a transaction. A transaction is created on the Telespace object using the following code:

```
var appTelespace = PropertyList.OpenProperty(PROPERTY_TELESPACE);
var myTransaction = appTelespace.OpenTransaction(false);
```

5. In JavaScript, you can use a try-catch block to control the database commit should a problem occur:

```
try
    {
    <<<<<<<<CODE TO DO THE DATABASE UPDATE AND COMMIT>>>>>>>>>>>>
    }
catch(e)
    {
    myTransaction.Abort();
    Error("error occurred writing record");
    }
```

If any problems occur you can abort the transaction within the catch block. This is where you can place any error reporting routines and other cleanup processes that must take place. In this example, you will simply abort the transaction.

6. Create a new record using the focusgrouprecord that is defined by the schema within the try block:

```
//Create a new record using the focusgroup schema we have defined
var fgRecord =
RecordSetEngine.RecordFactory.CreateRecord("urn:groove.net:focusgrouprecord");
```

7. In step 3, you defined functions to return the values entered by the user on the sub-form. To use these functions you must get a reference to the delegate's script dispatch:

```
var appDelegate = g_VoteWindow.OpenDelegateComponent();
var appScriptDispatch = appDelegate.GetScriptDispatch();
```

11

Remember that the `VoteWindowSubform` uses the `VoteSubformGlue` component as its delegate. Using this script dispatch, you can code the following in the `try` block to place the subform values (returned by functions) into variables:

```
//Place subform values into variables
var subformAge = appScriptDispatch.returnAge()
var subformQualityDurability = appScriptDispatch.returnQualityDurability();
var subformQualityPrice = appScriptDispatch.returnQualityPrice();
var subformQualitySafety = appScriptDispatch.returnQualitySafety();
var subformIncome = appScriptDispatch.returnIncome();
var subformToys = appScriptDispatch.returnToysPerMonth();
```

8. Using the variables defined in the last step, you can begin setting the field values for the new record that has been created:

```
//Set all the field values
fgRecord.SetField("over_18", subformAge);
fgRecord.SetField("durability_flag", subformQualityDurability);
fgRecord.SetField("price_flag", subformQualityPrice);
fgRecord.SetField("safety_flag", subformQualitySafety);
fgRecord.SetField("income_range", subformIncome);
fgRecord.SetField("toys_per_month", subformToys);
fgRecord.SetField("comments", subformComments);
```

For the `member_name` field, you can get the current identity of the user and modify the record with the following code:

```
//Get the current user's identity
var appCurrentIdentity = appTelespace.OpenCurrentIdentity();
var appCurrentIdentityContact = appCurrentIdentity.Contact;
var myUserName = OpenFullNameFromContact(appCurrentIdentityContact);
fgRecord.SetField("member_name", myUserName);
```

Finally, using the built in `Date()` function you can add the date to the record:

```
//Set the current date for when the record is added
fgRecord.SetField("date_entered", Date());
```

9. If all goes well, you have now modified all the fields within the record. You can now add the record and commit the transaction using the following code:

```
// Add the record
RecordSetEngine.AddRecord(fgRecord);
myTransaction.Commit();
```

If everything is working properly, the data should be modified in the underlying database. This change to the data (the Model) should instantly be reflected in the DataViewerControl (the View).

10. Up to this point you've only closed the subform window, but the subform itself still remains. (This is why you could call functions using the script dispatch even after it was closed). You must properly destroy the subform window object with the following code:

```
//Destroy the subform window
g_VoteWindow.Destroy();
```

CAUTION

> Be sure to explicitly destroy objects when you are finished with them. This is a step commonly missed by many beginning tool developers.

A full listing of the code for our tool template can be found in the file `FocusGroup_subform.tpl`, which is available from this book's Web page at `www.quepublishing.com`. As an example, code has been added to the subform and is automatically reflected in the `DataViewer` control as shown in Figure 11.18.

TROUBLESHOOTING

I'M DEVELOPING A TOOL USING RAPID PROTOTYPING. HOWEVER, WHEN I TRY TO ADD THE TOOL TO MY SHARED SPACE I RECEIVE AN ERROR.

Did you shut down Groove after applying the `EnableMyTemplates.reg` file? Did you create the My Templates folder in the proper place? Does the My Templates folder have appropriate rights?

If you've done all of these things and the problem persists, run CSMViewer.exe in the Groove program directory. Tracing can be enabled to help pinpoint the problem, as shown in Chapter 10.

I HAVE CREATED A TOOL TEMPLATE WITH AN INTERFACE THAT CONTAINS SEVERAL OF THE STANDARD BUTTONS. HOWEVER, WHEN I RUN THE TOOL THESE BUTTONS "GRAYED OUT" AND CANNOT BE CLICKED.

Double-check the component connections for the glue code to ensure the component(s) are listed and make sure the `Enabled` property for each button is set to True.

I AM USING RAPID PROTOTYPING TO DEVELOP MY TOOL. I HAVE ADDED THE TOOL TEMPLATE FILE TO THE MY TEMPLATES FOLDER BUT IT STILL DOES NOT APPEAR IN THE ADD TOOLS LIST.

Make sure you have run the `EnableMyTemplates.reg` file and have restarted Groove. You have added user interface components to an XY Layout, but not all components appear in the tool.

I HAVE CREATED A FORM USING THE XY LAYOUT COMPONENT WITH SEVERAL DIFFERENT USER INTERFACE COMPONENTS, INCLUDING BUTTONS, CHECK BOXES, AND STATIC TEXT FIELDS. SOME OF THE FIELDS DO NOT DISPLAY ONSCREEN, ALTHOUGH I CAN SET THE PROPERTIES SUCCESSFULLY FROM GLUE CODE.

Check component positioning in the XY Layout. Some components can become "hidden" behind other components if they are not placed properly.

CHAPTER **12**

ADVANCED DEVELOPMENT TOPICS

In this chapter

GROOVE SECURITY

Although Groove is built on an inherently secure platform, there are additional steps you can take to restrict access within individual tools. It's called the Access Control Framework and is designed to provide the means to create a roles-based access system for your custom Groove components.

ROLES WITHIN GROOVE

You were first introduced to Groove roles in Chapter 4, "Understanding Shared Spaces," when we discussed inviting users to a shared space. You had three roles to choose from:

- Manager: Usually the person who created the shared space. Has full authority to add and delete tools, uninvite members, and so on.

- Participant: A standard member of a shared space. Usually given all rights needed to actively participate and contribute within the shared space.

- Guest: Usually given only minimal rights, often with only read access for browsing shared space content.

For using the default Groove tools, this set of roles serves its purpose. However, as an organization develops custom tools three roles might not be enough to satisfy the different levels of access required for the application. This is where the Access Control Framework comes into play.

→ For information on inviting others to your shared space and assigning the member's initial roles, **see** "Inviting Others to Your New Space," **p.123**

THE ACCESS CONTROL FRAMEWORK

As you begin to develop your own custom applications within Groove, you'll soon discover that the three roles provided are not sufficient to satisfy all of your security requirements. Groove provides the Access Control Framework to enable Groove developers to incorporate their own defined security structure within their application. To understand the framework, we must first define a few of the elements that we'll be discussing:

- Member: A *member* is a Groove user who is a member of a shared space. This means that he has been invited and authenticated to participate in the activities of a shared space.

- Permission: A *permission* is an individual right that is granted. For example, permission to delete an image in the Sketchpad tool would be a single permission. This permission can encompass several different operations. A familiar example of permissions is shown in Figure 12.1. These are the permissions available within the Calendar tool.

- Role: A *role* is given a distinctive name that indicates the type or class of user. A role contains a set, or *collection*, of permissions. You should already be familiar with the standard set of roles available within a shared space, which includes Managers, Participants, and Guests, as shown in Figure 12.1.

Figure 12.1
The permissions provided by the Calendar tool.

- Engine: An *engine* is a general-purpose term used to describe a program that performs an essential task that other programs can use. Groove has a variety of engines, but one of the most common is the `RecordEngine` and `RecordsetEngines` that are responsible for changes to Groove's local data store.

- Operation: Traditionally, an operation is defined as a single unit of work. Within Groove, an *operation* is a method call to one of the several Groove engines. A good example would be the Delete Record operation on a recordset within the Groove database. This example, in fact, will be used later when we demonstrate how to restrict access to certain operations using the Access Control Framework.

ENGINES AND OPERATIONS

Without any type of access control in place, all changes within a shared space are instantly propagated to all other members of a shared space assuming all other members are online at the time. An engine is instructed to perform a task using an operation. It is these operations to which the Access Control Framework is used to control access. This is accomplished using constraints that we will now define.

OPERATIONS AND CONSTRAINTS

Each engine supports many different operations that allow constraints. For example, Table 12.1 lists some of the Groove engines and the operations that can be restricted using Access Control. In your script you can use the operations and methods listed to check whether a particular member has access based on their current permissions. Each returns TRUE or FALSE if the operation is permitted. Operations that take parameters are used for more specific access. For example, the `RecordSetEngine` `AddRecord` operation can take a record ID for more granular access control. Refer to Groove's API documentation for details on each engine's support operations and methods.

TABLE 12.1   ENGINES AND OPERATIONS THAT CAN BE RESTRICTED USING THE ACCESS CONTROL FRAMEWORK

Engine Name	Operations	Operation/Property Used to Test Permission	Description
DocumentShare	AddFile	CanAddFile	Add a new file to the Document Share.
	AddFolder	CanAddFolder	Add a new folder to the Document Share.
	ChangeFileContents	CanChangeFileContents	Modify the contents of a file currently in the Document Share.
	DeleteFile	CanDeleteFile	Remove a file from the Document Share.
	DeleteFolder	CanDeleteFolder	Delete a folder from the Document Share.
	RenameFile	CanRenameShareObject	Rename a file that already exists in the Document Share.
	RenameFolder	CanRenameShareObject	Rename a folder that already exists in the Document Share.
	ReplaceFile	CanReplaceFile	Replace a file currently in the Document Share defined by the attributes passed within the call.
ObjectEntryStore	AddMember	CheckOperation	Add a member to the Object Entry Store.
	AddParentRole	CheckOperation	Add a parent role to the Object Entry Store.
	Create	CheckOperation	Create a new object in the Object Entry Store.
	Delete	CheckOperation	Delete an object in the Object Entry Store.
	RemoveMember	CheckOperation	Remove a member from the Object Entry Store.
	RemoveParentRole	CheckOperation	Remove a parent role from this role.
RecordEngine	SetField	CanSetField	Set a field name in this particular record.

12

Engine Name	Operations	Operation/Property Used to Test Permission	Description
RecordSetEngine	AddRecord	CanAddRecord	Add a new record to the data store.
	RemoveRecord	CanRemoveRecord	Remove an entire record from the recordset.
	ReplaceRecord	CanReplaceRecord	Replace an existing record in the recordset with another record of the same type.
SketchTool	Modify	CanModify	Modify the current page in the Sketchpad.
TextTools	EditText	CanEditText	Edit the text contained in the text tool.

USING ACCESS CONTROL

You can get a clearer picture of how the Access Control Framework functions through a simple example using the Focus Group tool developed in Chapter 11, "Creating a Tool." At the end of Chapter 11, your tool looked like that shown in Figure 12.2. As you can see, it contains the Take Survey, Edit, and Delete buttons. Using the Access Control Framework, you can restrict access to the Delete button to members with the Manager role only in the following example.

Figure 12.2
You can restrict the capability to use the Delete button in your Focus Group tool by using the Access Control Framework.

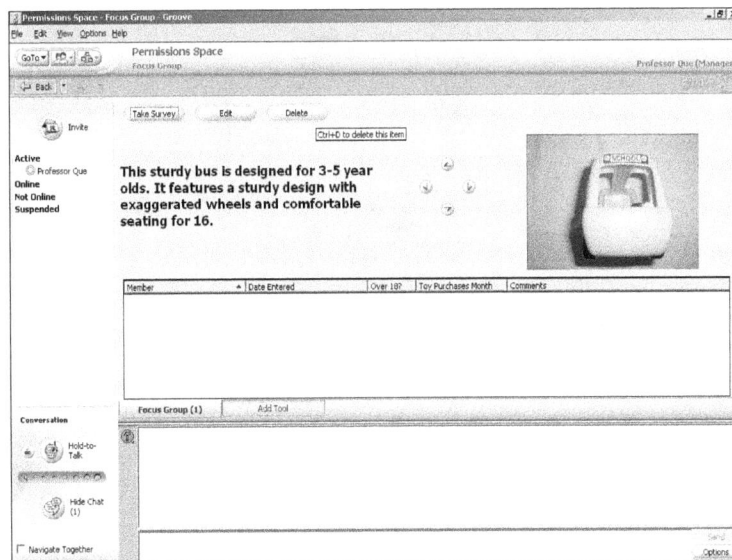

ADDING ACCESS CONTROL TO THE FOCUS GROUP TOOL

In a licensed copy of Groove, after a tool is added to a shared space, you can right-click on the tool's tab and choose Permission from the drop-down menu to see the currently assigned rights. However, this is not an option in your Focus Group tool because access control has not been defined. To enable the permission's functionality, follow these steps described in the following sections.

STEP 1: DEFINING AN ACCESS CONTROL CONTAINER   First of all, we will start by using the final Focus Group code, FocusGroup_Final.tpl, which you can download by navigating to http://www.quepublishing.com and going to this book's page by typing the ISBN (0789726777) into the Search field. For this exercise you'll need to use a text editor because defining the Access Control in a tool is not supported within the Tool Creator at this time. We'll start establishing the Access Control framework by inserting an ObjectTypes element.

Within ObjectTypes, you must assign a name to the ObjectType that you will be defining. In this case it will be $ComponentGroup. This name is used because you will be controlling access at the component group level, which is where the Edit and Delete capability resides. Finally, you must define the AccessControl container where all the Role assignments will reside. At this point, the following code should be added immediately after the ComponentGroup definition, as shown in Figure 12.3:

Figure 12.3
Add the
ObjectTypes
element within the
tool template.

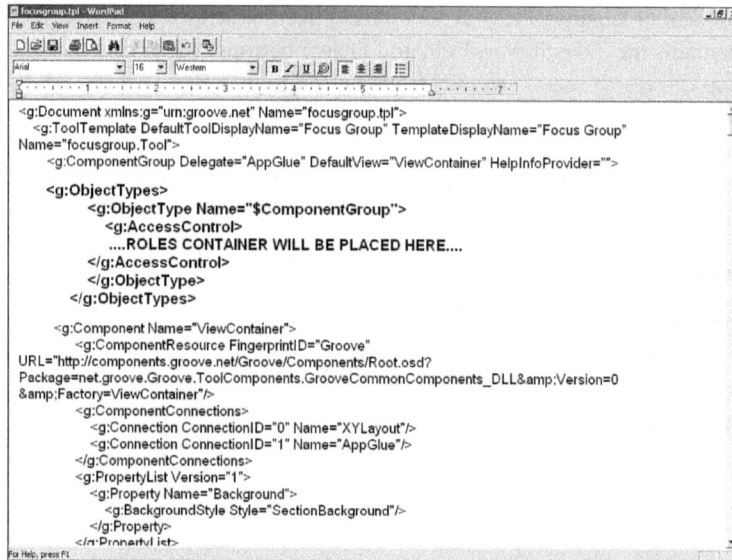

```
<g:ObjectTypes>
  <g:ObjectType Name="$ComponentGroup">
    <g:AccessControl>
    .........ROLES CONTAINER WILL BE PLACED HERE.........
    </g:AccessControl>
  </g:ObjectType>
</g:ObjectTypes>
```

STEP 2: ADDING THE ROLES CONTAINER AND THE MANAGER ROLE All of the roles you define must be contained within a `Roles` container. You need to place the code for the `Roles` container and the `role` you are defining within the `AccessControl` elements, as shown in Figure 12.4.

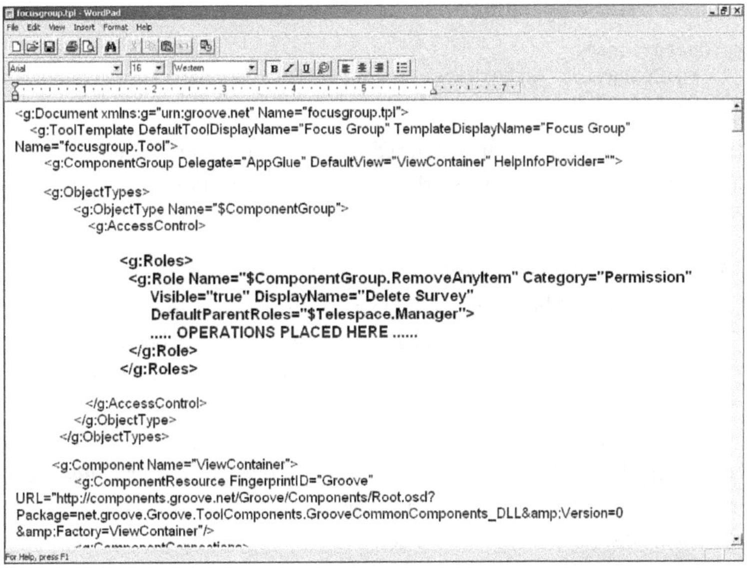

Figure 12.4
Add the `Roles` container within the `AccessControl` elements.

```
<g:Roles>
  <g:Role Name="$ComponentGroup.RemoveAnyItem" Category="Permission"
  Visible="true" DisplayName="Delete Survey"
  DefaultParentRoles="$Telespace.Manager">
  ......OPERATIONS PLACED HERE......
  </g:Role>
</g:Roles>
```

You can define the following attributes for a role:

- `Name`: A unique name for the role. This must be unique within the `Roles` element that you defined in the previous section.
- `Category`: The category of role. This can either be a Role or Permission.
- `Visible`: Whether or not this is a role or permission that is visible within Groove. When you are using inheritance of roles and permission it is possible that some roles are only meant to be part of larger, visible, roles. Using the `Visible` property can make these smaller, subordinate roles invisible to the user.
- `DisplayName`: The name that will display to the user for this Role or Permission if the `Visible` property has been set to true.
- `DefaultParentRoles`: This is used for inheritance. In this case you are using the Manager of the shared space (telespace) as the parent role. Each child inherits the operations and permissions of the parent specified here.

STEP 3: DEFINING THE OPERATIONS THE ROLE CAN PERFORM   After setting the role attributes, you now need to specify the operations that the role can perform. Each engine defines a list of operations, or tasks that can be controlled using the access control framework. In this case, with the `RecordSetEngine`, you will be controlling the capability to remove any item from the list of surveys presented in the `DataViewer` control. For this example, you'll be defining a single operation with the following code and adding it within the `Role` element:

```
<g:Operations>
    <g:Operation TargetName="RecordSetEngine" Name="RemoveRecord"/>
</g:Operations>
```

In this example, you've only defined a single operation. When the operation is defined, you need to set these attributes so that Groove understands what operation the access control pertains to:

- `Name`: The actual operation to which you want to grant access.

- `TargetName`: The name of the target of the operation in the `Name` attribute. In this case, you are specifying the `RecordSetEngine`, which has been defined in your `ComponentGroup` previously for accessing the underlying survey data records.

STEP 4: TELLING THE `RecordSetEngine` THAT THE ACCESS CONTROL FRAMEWORK IS BEING USED   In the next step, you will be using an operation on the `RecordSetEngine` to determine if the current user has permission to delete a record. To enable this, you need to tell the `RecordSetEngine` that access control is being used. This is enabled by setting the `AccessControl` property to true for your `RecordSetEngine` component definition as shown in Figure 12.5.

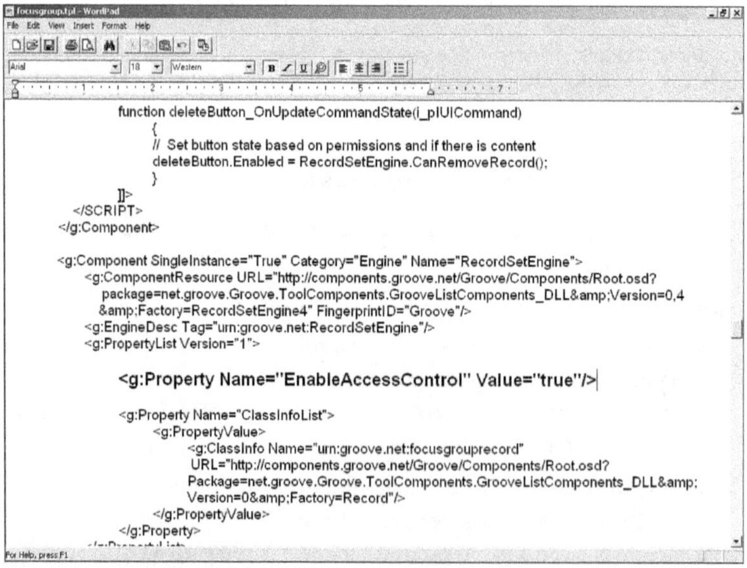

Figure 12.5
The `AccessControl` property is used to tell the `RecordSetEngine` that you will be using the Access Control Framework to control its operations.

```
function deleteButton_OnUpdateCommandState(i_pIUICommand)
{
    // Set button state based on permissions and if there is content
    deleteButton.Enabled = RecordSetEngine.CanRemoveRecord();
}
]]>
        </SCRIPT>
    </g:Component>

    <g:Component SingleInstance="True" Category="Engine" Name="RecordSetEngine">
        <g:ComponentResource URL="http://components.groove.net/Groove/Components/Root.osd?
            package=net.groove.Groove.ToolComponents.GrooveListComponents_DLL&amp;Version=0,4
            &amp;Factory=RecordSetEngine4" FingerprintID="Groove"/>
        <g:EngineDesc Tag="urn:groove.net:RecordSetEngine"/>
        <g:PropertyList Version="1">

            <g:Property Name="EnableAccessControl" Value="true"/>

            <g:Property Name="ClassInfoList">
                <g:PropertyValue>
                    <g:ClassInfo Name="urn:groove.net:focusgrouprecord"
                     URL="http://components.groove.net/Groove/Components/Root.osd?
                     Package=net.groove.Groove.ToolComponents.GrooveListComponents_DLL&amp;
                     Version=0&amp;Factory=Record"/>
                </g:PropertyValue>
            </g:Property>
```

```
<g:Property Name="EnableAccessControl" Value="true"/>
```

NOTE

> Without setting the `EnableAccessControl` to true, all operations will be permitted. The default value is false, which means that no type of access control is in place.

STEP 5: SETTING THE DELETE BUTTON STATUS   Up to this point you've defined the operation that a shared space manager is allowed to perform. However, you still need to enable and disable the Delete button depending on the current user's role. Because `OnUpdateCommandState` is called often, whenever a component's state needs refreshed, it is a good place to put your code to enable or disable the button. Adding this code to script in the `AppGlue` component sets the Delete button to enabled or disabled depending on whether the `CanRemoveRecord` operation is true:

```
function deleteButton_OnUpdateCommandState(i_pIUICommand)
    {
    // Set button state based on permissions and if there is content
    deleteButton.Enabled = RecordSetEngine.CanRemoveRecord();
    }
```

`CanRemoveRecord` returns true or false depending on the role of the current user and the operations allowed using the access control framework you defined in this example. Although you are only dealing with the `RemoveRecord` operation, there are other operations that can be defined within a similar access control framework. This function should be added to the `AppGlue` component. Refer to the GDK documentation for the operations available for all the components. You can find the complete listing of the Focus Group tool with access control enabled in the `FocusGroup_With_Access_Control.tpl` file, which you can download from the book's page by navigating to http://www.quepublishing.com and typing the ISBN (0789726777) into the Search field.

CAUTION

> The `OnUpdateCommandState` is called very frequently. If there is too much processing required for each call to the function it could drastically degrade your tool's performance. If you must use this event, be sure that your routine is efficient and exits the function as soon as possible.

TESTING THE ACCESS CONTROL YOU'VE DEFINED

If you've followed the previous series of steps correctly, you should now have enabled some limited access control in the Focus Group tool. To verify that it's working properly, follow these steps:

1. Add the `FocusGroup_With_Access_Control.tpl` file to the `/My Templates` folder that was created for rapid prototyping. Create a new shared space and add the Focus Group tool to the space.

→ If you have not enabled Rapid Prototyping at this point, **see** "The Rapid Prototyping Process" **p. 363** (Chapter 11)

2. Right-click the Focus Group tool tab and choose Permissions from the drop-down menu. You should see the permissions listing, as shown in Figure 12.6. You should now see the Delete Survey permission.

Figure 12.6
The Delete Survey permission has now been added to the list of available permissions.

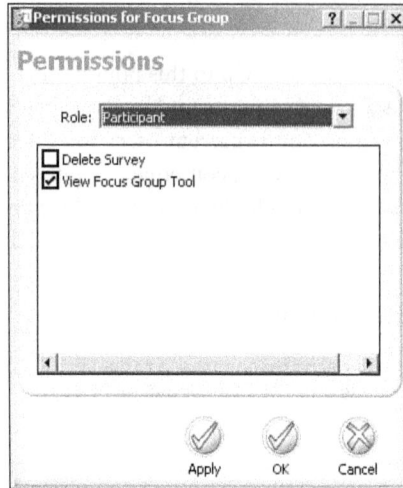

3. By default, the Manager of the shared space will have Delete permission for the Focus Group tool. This being true, the Delete button will be enabled. Now, uncheck the Delete permission for the Manager and click the Apply button. The Delete button should automatically become grayed out, as shown in Figure 12.7. By re-checking the Delete Survey permission again and clicking the Apply button, you should then see the Delete button change back to its re-enabled state.

Figure 12.7
After removing the Delete Survey permission for the Manager role, you can see that the Delete button is now grayed out.

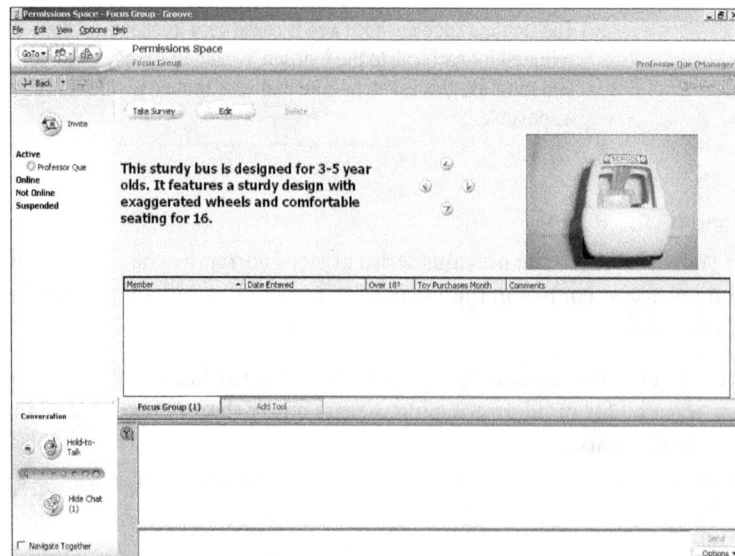

> **TIP**
>
> Even after you set the Enabled property to false for your Delete button, when the user moves the mouse pointer over the disabled button it will still display the ToolTip text. This might confuse the user into thinking that the button is still enabled when in fact it isn't. If you have this issue within your application, you might want to completely hide a button by setting the `Visible` property to false. In this way, the button itself and any associated ToolTip will not display, which eliminates the possibility of confusing the user.

After finishing the previous example, you have enabled simple access control for your tool. Although outside the scope of this simple example, it is possible to create a much more complex access control hierarchy to suit your tool needs. Although you used the default Manager role provided, you also have the ability to create new roles and inherit operations from other roles. For a more in-depth examination of the Access Control Framework refer to the GDK Documentation and the Technical Notes contained on Groove's Developer Zone at `http://www.groove.net/devzone`.

USING GROOVE SCRIPT LIBRARIES

If you created a tool using the tutorial in Chapter 11, one thing probably became very apparent: tool template files can become very large and hard to follow. This is not a problem specific to Groove, but a problem in just about every scripting language. Developers overcome this problem by making their code *modular*. This involves breaking up code into separate modules that each perform a specific function or set of functions. Groove also provides the capability to create modules using something called *Groove Script Libraries*, or GSLs. Groove Script Libraries are collections of code that are stored in files separate from the main body of code. Using these not only helps clean up your template code but also offers these additional benefits:

- Code can be shared among different templates. This offers the capability for code reuse not only within your own tool templates, but enables others to leverage your code snippets.

- It's much easier to find specific functions that may be causing problems when you are troubleshooting. You can quickly narrow down issues to a particular library that has been included.

- Although sharing code helps eliminate redundancy, using Groove Script Libraries can also make maintaining code easier because it will only need to be modified in one location.

At this time, GSLs can only contain the script that you would include within the `<SCRIPT>` tags within your application. No component definitions or layouts of any type can be contained within a GSL file.

To use GSLs in your tool template, follow these steps:

1. Create the script (without the `<SCRIPT>` tags) that you would like to include within your tool template.

2. Save this script within a text file with a .GSL extension

3. Inject this GSL file into the Groove application. In your example, you will manually inject the file in your development environment. In Chapter 13, you will learn how you can publish your tool templates and GSL files automatically.

4. Within your tool template glue code, add a SCRIPT tag that will reference the GSL in this format:

```
<SCRIPT FingerprintID="<FingerprintID>"
SRC="http://your.company.com/Consolidator/Consolidator.osd?Package=Consolidato
r.ConsolidatorM
ainView_GSL&amp;Version=0&amp;Factory=Open"/>
```

The following two attributes used within the element specify:

- FingerprintID: A fingerprint used if the component has been signed. In our example, you will turn off component signing so this field will not be set.

- SRC: The source of the GSL file. This is very similar to the component source set in Chapter 11.

5. Inject the tool template.

CAUTION

> Be sure to inject the GSL file prior to injecting the tool template itself. Otherwise, the tool injection will fail because it will not be able to find the referenced GSL file.

TIP

> You can edit the GSL file and its script without having to reinject the tool template. All changes to the GSL file will be automatically used within the tool when the GSL file is injected.

USING A GSL FILE IN THE FOCUS GROUP TOOL

If you recall in Chapter 11, you collected participant information on a subform within the tool. The income field was populated automatically using the following script in the Initialize function. You will move the code contained in the Initialize function to a GSL file:

```
function Initialize()
{
// Load the income combo box
incomeCombobox.AddItem("Less than $20,000");
incomeCombobox.AddItem("$20,000 to $29,999");
incomeCombobox.AddItem("$30,000 to $49,999");
incomeCombobox.AddItem("$50,000 to $79,999");
incomeCombobox.AddItem("$80,000 to $99,999");
incomeCombobox.AddItem("Over $100,000");
}
```

In our scenario, you'll create a new function that will no longer reside within the tool template itself but within a GSL file in the following example:

1. Create a GSL file named `incomeModule.gsl` that will contain your new function `populateIncome` (see Listing 12.1).

LISTING 12.1 THE populateIncome FUNCTION

```
function populateIncome()
    {
    // Load the income combo box
    incomeCombobox.AddItem("Less than $20,000");
    incomeCombobox.AddItem("$20,000 to $29,999");
    incomeCombobox.AddItem("$30,000 to $49,999");
    incomeCombobox.AddItem("$50,000 to $79,999");
    incomeCombobox.AddItem("$80,000 to $99,999");
    incomeCombobox.AddItem("Over $100,000");
    return null;
}
```

2. Now that the GSL file has been created, you can inject the GSL file into your Groove installation. For your purposes here, you will manually inject the GSL files using the Groove Database Navigator. Like your sample tool, the GSL file must be added to the `templates.xss` database.

3. In your glue code within the tool template, you must now reference the GSL file. With the `VoteSubformGlue` component, you can include the following code:

```
<SCRIPT FingerprintID="<FingerprintID>"
SRC="http://your.company.com/Consolidator/Consolidator.osd?Package=Consolidato
r.ConsolidatorMainView
_GSL&amp;Version=0&amp;Factory=Open"/>
```

4. Because you are replacing the `Initialize` function script with your new function, you must add the appropriate function call. The `Initialize` function will now be replaced with this new `Initialize` function:

```
function Initialize()
    {
    // Load the income combo box
    populateIncome()
}
```

In this example, you have created a simple function that does not accept any parameters and only returns a null value. Your code functions exactly as before except that the Income combo box population routine is found within its own file. The complete tool template file can be found in Listing 12.3 and the included `IncomeModule.Gsl` file can be found in Listing 12.4.

SCRIPT LIBRARIES PROVIDED WITH GROOVE

Groove provides several script libraries that contain code you can utilize within your own tool templates. The names of these Groove Script Libraries and a description of the types of functions contained within are described in Table 12.2.

12

TABLE 12.2 **USEFUL SCRIPT LIBRARIES PROVIDED WITH GROOVE THAT YOU CAN USE IN YOUR OWN TOOL GLUE CODE**

Name	Description
GrooveGlobalHelperFunctions.gsl	The set of functions provided by this script library are used in many tools because it provides a variety of useful functions for manipulating strings, accounts, and the Windows Clipboard.
GrooveTextHelperFunctions.gsl	These functions provide trim functions that are not provided in JavaScript by default. Trim functions are used to remove empty spaces from strings of text.
GrooveArrayHelperFunctions.gsl	This library provides functions that are to be used with array data types within your script. For example, functions are included that enable you to sort the elements contained within an array.
GrooveDocumentShare.gsl	This library contains functions that can be utilized when writing tools that need the ability to share documents among members within a shared space.
GrooveAccountToolContainerHelper.gsl	At this time, this library's functions are primarily used by Groove's own components to access tools using a particular account.
GrooveCalendarHelper.gsl	This library contains functions that are intended to supplement the built-in date functions provided by JavaScript. In addition to the data and time manipulation functions, there are also functions provided for working with Groove's own calendar component.
GrooveCommonToolCategoryStrings.gsl	This library contains useful variables that can be used within the tool template. Strings are provided to assist with category manipulation, common accelerator keys, and strings used for common user interface functions. There are only variable definitions here and no script functions are included in this library.

ADDING MENUS TO A TOOL

To create tools with a consistent look and feel, you should add menus that enable the user to perform many of the tasks within the tool. Although not required, these are usually the same functions that may already be serviced by a graphical element, such as a button, that is a part of the tool's user interface. Groove enables you to create the following three different types of menu items:

- Menu items that reside in the menu external to the tool that is shared by the transceiver, as shown in Figure 12.8. In this figure you can see that the New, Window and New, Event menu options are provided in the example.

Figure 12.8
The New menu item resides in the external Groove Transceiver menu, which can be modified to contain tool-specific options.

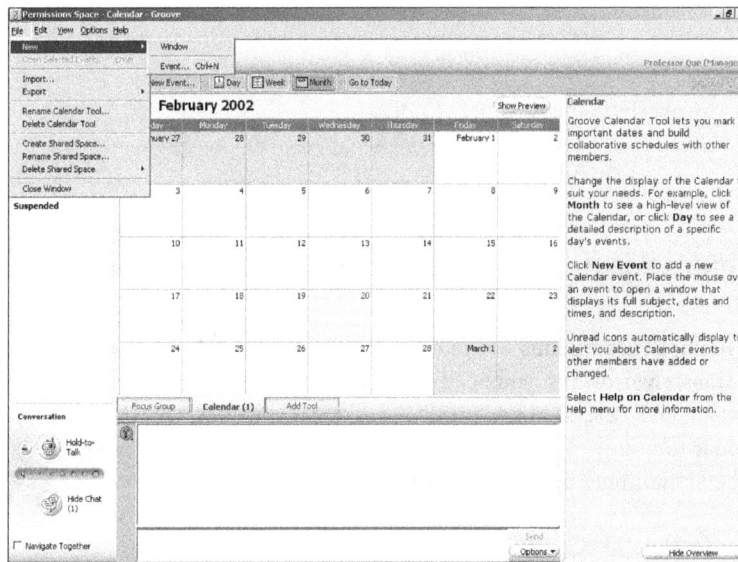

- Menu items that appear in the client area above the tool window, as shown in Figure 12.9. These are below the menu shown in #1 but outside of your normal tool window. In the Figure you can see the New Event menu is included in this area.

- Context-sensitive pop-up menus that appear in response to right-click events. These pop-up windows are standard in most Windows applications.

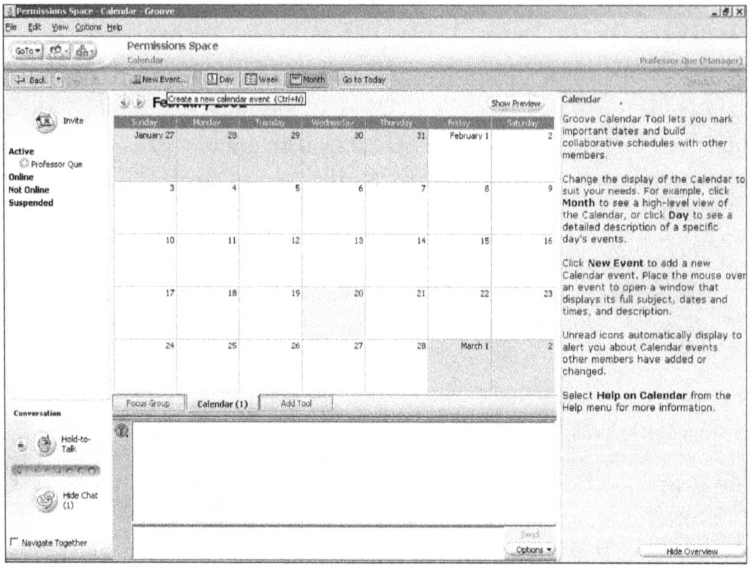

Figure 12.9
The New Event button is actually a menu item that appears in the Client Area of a tool that you can also use for your own tool-specific menus.

CREATING A MENU IN THE TOOL'S CLIENT AREA AND GROOVE'S OWN TRANSCEIVER MENU

To implement menus within a tool's Client Area and to add options to Groove's own Transceiver menus, you need to use a container explicitly designed for these options. The containers described previously are *external components* meaning that they are external to your tool itself. We have not discussed them to this point so we will give a brief overview before jumping into an example.

USING EXTERNAL COMPONENTS

In the Focus Group tool example described in Chapter 11, you used many of Groove's common components to construct your user interface and for other processing. For example, you were able to add the Button component to your form to create a Take Survey button. This component could be considered *internal* to the tool because the component and all its properties were defined in the tool template itself. However, it is possible to reference components that are *external* to your tool that reside in the Groove transceiver. This will be the case when you try to modify the menus contained within a tool Client Area. These external components are actually ToolBar components that are provided with the standard Groove user interface components. To access the menu items contained within them by accessing these external objects, there are a few things that must be taken care of within your tool:

- You must create an instance of the IGrooveUICommandListener that is used by any processes that monitor changes and actions within the user interface. In this case, you'll be adding script functions to respond to any click events on the ToolCommandContainer for "Client Area" menus events and within GlobalCommandContainer for any Transceiver menu events.

- You must explicitly add items to each `ToolBar` when your tool is activated. The process of activating, or using the tool, brings the tool into *scope*. Scope is a term usually used for variables, but in this context a tool is in scope when it has been selected within a shared space.

- As the tool goes out of scope, you must remove any items from the menu that were added. Without this, any menu item added would remain within the menu as the user navigated to different areas within Groove. This would be awkward because some menu options may only pertain to a particular tool and would have no use in other areas of Groove. For instance, a Vote menu option would likely be an invalid option when the user switches to the Sketchpad tool. Switching tools in a shared space and closing the shared space itself are two ways that a tool can go out of scope.

- External objects must be defined in the form's delegate between a set of `<g:ExternalObjectConnections>` tags. As you'll see in your menu examples this is very similar to the way that you've defined your component connections. In fact, you'll be defining the external object connections directly beneath your delegate component connections that were defined in Chapter 11.

The global Transceiver menu and the client menu each have their own specific name. The Groove Transceiver menu shell uses the `GlobalCommandContainer`. An example menu is shown in Figure 12.5. You can see the `GlobalCommandContainer` container holds the File, New, Window, and other assorted menu options.

ADDING A MENU WITHIN YOUR FOCUS GROUP TOOL'S CLIENT AREA

For a menu within the client area you need to use the `ToolCommandContainer`. A sample menu is shown in Figure 12.9. You can see the `ToolCommandContainer` container holds the New Event, Day, Week, Month, and Go To Today menu options.

In the following example, you will add a new menu to the Focus Group tool client area.

STEP 1: USE THE FOCUS GROUP TOOL

Using the code found in `FocusGroup_Final.tpl`, save the tool template file into your *Groove Installation*/Data/My Templates folder. Ensure that rapid prototyping has been enabled by running `EnableMyTemplates.reg` and restarting Groove. This will enable you to use rapid prototyping to test your tool. You can edit the file using a text editor or by loading it into the Tool Creator tool. You'll be using the Tool Creator in the following steps.

STEP 2: ADD THE EXTERNAL OBJECT CONNECTION

Because the Transceiver menu is external to the tool, you must add an external component connection to the tool template. Click the Components tab within the Tool Creator tool, highlight the `AppGlue` component, and select the Component Source tab, as shown in Figure 12.10.

Figure 12.10
Add the connection to the
`ToolCommandContainer`
external object.

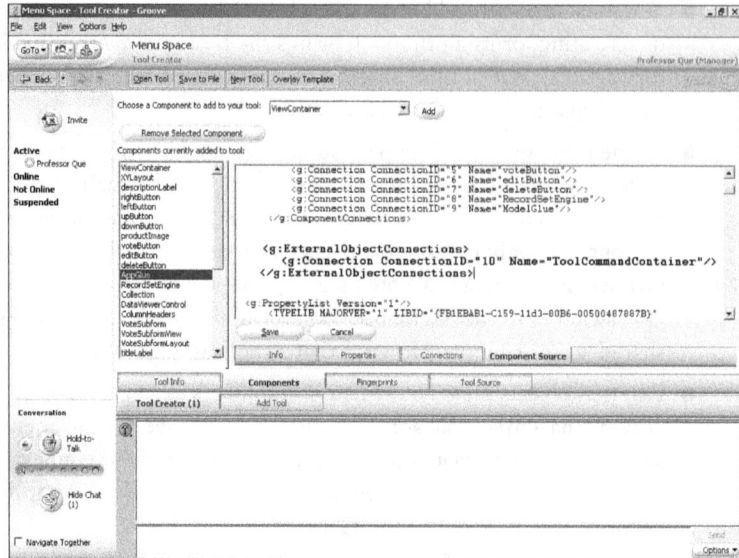

Insert the following code for the external object connection:

```
<g:ExternalObjectConnections>
  <g:Connection Name="ToolCommandContainer" ConnectionID="10"/>
</g:ExternalObjectConnections>
```

Click the Save button after you've added the code.

→ For more information about the AppGlue component that enabled you to use glue code in your tool,
see "Readying Your Tool to Accept Glue Code," **p.394**

STEP 3: ADD THE USER INTERFACE COMMAND LISTENER

Because you need to listen to commands performed on this external object, you need to
implement the user interface command listener. Within the AppGlue component you need
to add an IMPLEMENTS section:

```
<IMPLEMENTS IID="{DB821822-5C76-4215-A5B4-408D29F9C552}"
LIBID="{4253A641-5FA3-11D2-98C2-0080C7E30BA4}">
        <SCRIPT>
        <![CDATA[
            function OnCommand(i_UICommand)
                {
                ExecuteGlobalMenuCommand(i_UICommand);
                }
        ]]>
        </SCRIPT>
</IMPLEMENTS>
```

This section will fall outside the first set of SCRIPT tags but within the AppGlue component
container. Be sure to place this after the closing </SCRIPT> tag in the AppGlue component
container or else it will not work properly. Within the IMPLEMENTS tag, you need to define

the OnCommand function with a single parameter. Place this within the SCRIPT tags found within the IMPLEMENTS tags, not within the AppGlue SCRIPT tags. This will be executed when a menu item is clicked.

STEP 4: DEFINE A FUNCTION TO RESPOND TO THE EXTERNAL OBJECT CONNECTION

After adding the external object connections in step 1, you can respond to the event for the successful connection to the external ToolCommandContainer object. This is defined with the following function within the AppGlue component script:

```
function OnConnectToExternalObject(i_Object, i_ConnectionID)
    {
    }
```

Be sure that this is added within the SCRIPT tags for the AppGlue component and not within the SCRIPT tags used in Step 3 above. Your function will take two parameters. The i_Object parameter will contain a reference to the external object that was connected. The i_ConnectionID parameter will indicate which external connection was established. In this case, you'll expect to receive the connection ID of 10 that corresponds to the ToolCommandContainer object.

STEP 5: DEFINE YOUR GLOBAL VARIABLES

There are a few variables you'll need to access globally. First of all, you can create a global variable that will hold your command container. Place the following definition after the initial SCRIPT tag within the AppGlue component:

```
//Globals for tool menu
var g_toolCommandContainer;
```

Also, you need to define a variable that will hold the current state of your menu. This will be set to true when the menu is currently displayed and set to false when it is not visible. This is used to prevent the addition of multiple copies of the menu and should be placed directly after the global variable you just defined:

```
// Tool Command Container State Variables
var g_toolCommandsShown = false;
```

STEP 6: EVALUATE THE CONNECTION ID OF YOUR MENU OBJECT

Step 4 explained how the onConnectToExternalObject will receive the i_ConnectionID parameter with the connection ID of the external object. You'll evaluate this so you can take the appropriate action with the following statement, which should be added within the OnConnectToExternalObject function you defined in Step 4:

```
if (10 == i_ConnectionID)
    {
    //If TRUE we've connected to the ToolBar
    }
```

If this statement is true, you know that the ToolCommandContainer connection has been established. Following this statement you can begin initializing the menu.

12

STEP 7: ASSIGNING A REFERENCE TO THE EXTERNAL ToolBar COMPONENT

Following the statement in step 6, you can add the code in response to a TRUE evaluation of the statement. Beginning with the opening brace of the IF statement, you must first set the object passed in to your tool command container with the following statement:

```
g_toolCommandContainer = i_Object;
```

You are assigning it globally because you will need to access your object later outside the scope of the function. Add the assignment statement within the OnConnectToExternalObject function within the AppGlue component.

STEP 8: SINKING EVENTS FROM YOUR MENU

Next, you must sink events from your menu with the following code, which is placed in the same IF statement defined in Step 6:

```
ConnectObject(g_toolCommandContainer, "g_toolCommandContainer");
```

If you recall from Chapter 11, after you assign a form delegate, you can execute a function in response to an event, such as the clicking of a button, with the following code:

```
function leftButton_OnCommand(i_pIUICommand)
{
...code in response to event goes here
}
```

However, because you are dealing with an external object the events are not sunk automatically. This is the reason why the ConnectObject statement is required. There are cases other than external objects when you may need to explicitly tell Groove to sink events:

■ For objects that you want to use something other than the default interface. Many objects have a default interface that is used, you can override this interface if needed.

■ To listen to events for objects created at runtime. For example, if creating form elements dynamically (such as buttons on a form) you will need to add a ConnectObject statement for each new component created to sink these component's events.

For more information on Delegates and specifically a Form Delegate, **see** "Delegates" **p.360**

STEP 9: CHECKING THE CURRENT MENU STATE

After connecting to the command container object in the last step, you are ready to add the menu items and display the menu. However, this code must first check the global state variable to ensure the menu is not currently displayed:

```
if (!g_toolCommandsShown)
    {
```

So if the g_toolCommandsShown variable is currently set to false, it means the menu is not displayed and you can continue to build and display the menu. Once within the IF statement, you need to toggle the state to indicate that the menu is currently displayed:

```
g_toolCommandsShown = true;
```

The code should be added directly after the ConnectObject statement from step 8.

STEP 10: DETERMINE THE POSITION TO INSERT THE NEW MENU

Depending on what menus are currently available, you need to find the next position in which to insert the new menu. To do this without replacing any other menus, you need to find the last menu position and add 1 to it:

```
//Determine position to insert menu
var numMenuPosition =
g_toolCommandContainer.GetNumberOfUICommands() + 1;
```

This should be placed directly after the current code contained in the IF statement from Step 8. Adding 1 to this gives you the new empty position where the menu should be inserted.

STEP 11: ADD THE NEW COMMAND CONTAINER

Now that you have a global variable holding the tool command container, you can insert a new user interface command container. Directly after the code in step 10, enter the following code:

```
//Insert a UICommandContainer into the ToolCommandContainer
var pToolCommandContainer;
pToolCommandContainer =
g_pToolCommandContainer.InsertUICommandContainer("Menu1",
numMenuPosition);
```

The InsertUICommandContainer container accepts two parameters in this order:

1. URL: The URL or unique name to assign to the new command container.
2. Position: The position index for the new container.

This function will return a reference to the command container that you've named pToolCommandContainer in this example. You need to then grab the interface for this newly created command container:

```
// Ask the UICommandContainer we just inserted for its
UICommandContainer interface
pToolCommandContainer = pToolCommandContainer.UICommandContainer;
```

STEP 12: SET THE MENU BUTTON PROPERTIES

With the interface to the new command container, you need to set a few properties that will determine the text on the menu button, the shortcut key to the menu, and the ToolTip that will appear:

```
// Set the properties for the UICommandContainer
pToolCommandContainer.UICommand.Label = "Focus Group Menu";
pToolCommandContainer.UICommand.Tooltip = "Click this for a list of
options";
pToolCommandContainer.UICommand.Mnemonic = "Alt+M";
```

This code should be placed directly after the code in step 11.

STEP 13: ADDING THE MENU TO THE COMMAND CONTAINER

Now you are ready to begin adding the appropriate menu items. In this step, you'll be finishing the block of code you've added in the preceding steps, so add all statements after the code from step 12. Each menu item is a command within your command container. First, you'll define a variable to hold each command:

```
var pToolCommand;
```

Then you can add the first item using the InsertUICommand method on the command container:

```
//Insert the first menu item
pToolCommand = pToolCommandContainer.InsertUICommand("MenuItem1", 0);
```

The InsertUICommand method takes two parameters in this order:

- URL: A string identifying the menu item.
- Position: The new position of the menu item.

The command container index is zero-based so you will use 0 here to indicate it will be the first menu inserted. This method returns a reference to the new command itself so you can set the label that will be displayed for the menu item and the shortcut key combination (mnemonic) for the option:

```
pToolCommand.Label = "Take Survey";
pToolCommand.Mnemonic = "Alt+M+1";
```

In addition to this menu item, you'll add a few more, giving each a new unique index and label:

```
//Insert the second menu item
pToolCommand =
pToolCommandContainer.InsertUICommand("MenuItem1", 1);
pToolCommand.Label = "Edit Survey";
pToolCommand.Mnemonic = "Alt+M+2";

//Insert a separator
pToolCommandContainer.InsertSeparator("MenuSeparator1", 2);

//Insert third menu item
pToolCommand =
pToolCommandContainer.InsertUICommand("MenuItem2", 3);
pToolCommand.Label = "Delete Survey";
pToolCommand.Mnemonic = "Alt+M+3";
```

You can see what the menu looks like in Figure 12.11. The complete code for this example is in the tool_menu.tpl file, which you can download from http://www.quepublishing.com/.

Figure 12.11
The newly added
Focus Group Menu
enables users to per-
form the various tool
operations.

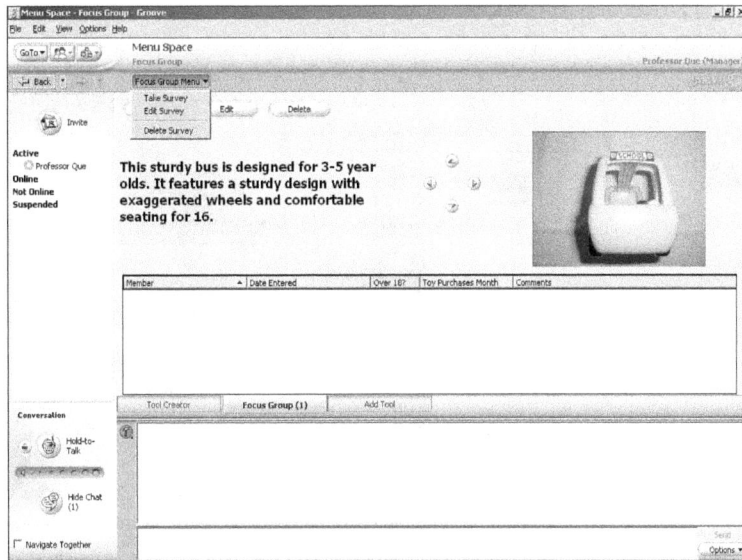

N O T E

You've also used the `InsertSeparator` method to add a gray line to separate menu items. This is useful for grouping common menu items together. It also needs an appropriate position index value although it is essentially a non-functioning element within the menu.

ADDING A TOOL MENU ITEM TO THE GROOVE TRANSCEIVER MENU

To add a new menu item to Groove's Transceiver menu, you need to use the `GlobalCommandContainer`. In the following example, you will add the Take Survey option to the Options menu.

STEP 1: USE THE FOCUS GROUP TOOL

Using the code found in the `FocusGroup_Final.tpl` file, save the tool template file into your *Groove Installation*/Data/My Templates folder. Ensure that Rapid Prototyping has been enabled by running `EnableMyTemplates.reg` and restarting Groove. This will enable you to use Rapid Prototyping to test your tool. You can edit the file using a text editor or by load-ing it into the Tool Creator tool. You'll be using the Tool Creator in the following steps.

STEP 2: ADD THE EXTERNAL OBJECT CONNECTION

Because the Transceiver menu is external to the tool, you must add an external component connection to the tool template. Click the Components tab within the Tool Creator tool, highlight the `AppGlue` component, and select the Component Source tab, as shown in Figure 12.12.

Figure 12.12
Add the connection to the
GlobalCommandContainer
external object.

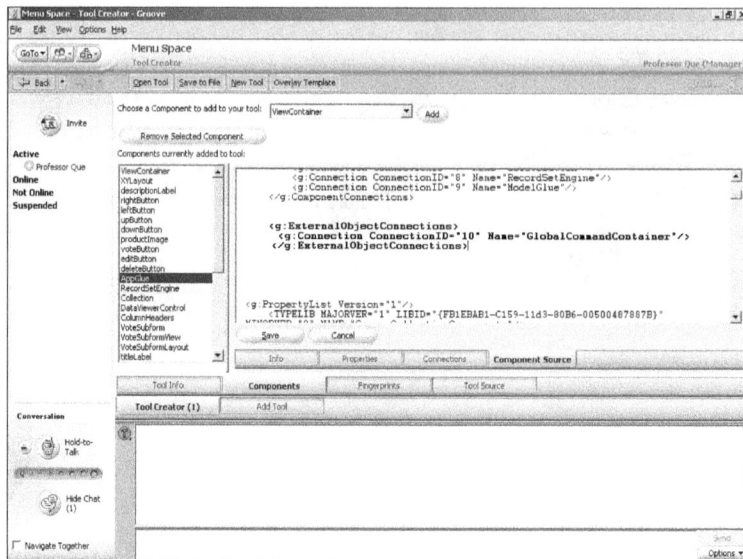

Insert this code for the external connection:

```
<g:ExternalObjectConnections>
  <g:Connection Name="GlobalCommandContainer" ConnectionID="10"/>
</g:ExternalObjectConnections>
```

Click the Save button after you've added the code.

STEP 3: ADD THE USER INTERFACE COMMAND LISTENER

Because you need to listen to commands performed on this external object, you need to implement the user interface command listener. Within the AppGlue component you need to add an IMPLEMENTS section:

```
<IMPLEMENTS IID="{DB821822-5C76-4215-A5B4-408D29F9C552}"
LIBID="{4253A641-5FA3-11D2-98C2-0080C7E30BA4}">
      <SCRIPT>
      <![CDATA[
         function OnCommand(i_UICommand)
            {
            ExecuteGlobalMenuCommand(i_UICommand);
            }
      ]]>
      </SCRIPT>
</IMPLEMENTS>
```

As shown in the figure, this section will fall outside the first set of SCRIPT tags but within the AppGlue component container. Within the IMPLEMENTS tag, you need to define the OnCommand function with a single parameter. This will be executed when the click event occurs.

Step 4: Define a Function to Respond to the External Object Connection

After adding the external object connections in step 1, you can respond to the event for the successful connection to the external `GlobalToolCommandContainer` object. This is defined with the following function within the `AppGlue` component script:

```
function OnConnectToExternalObject(i_Object, i_ConnectionID)
    {
    }
```

Make sure that you place this code within the `AppGlue` component `SCRIPT` elements and not within the `IMPLEMENTS` elements added in the last step. Your function will take two parameters. The `i_Object` parameter will contain a reference to the external object that was connected. The `i_ConnectionID` parameter will indicate which external connection was established. In this case, you'll expect to receive the connection ID of 10 that corresponds to the `GlobalCommandContainer` object.

Step 5: Define Your Global Variables

There are a few variables you'll need to access globally. First of all, you can create a global variable that will hold your command container. Add the following declaration within the `AppGlue` component `SCRIPT` elements:

```
//Globals for menu
var g_globalCommandContainer;
```

Also, you need to define a variable that will hold the current state of your menu. This will be set to true when the menu is currently displayed and set to false when it is not visible. This is used to prevent the addition of multiple copies of the menu:

```
// Global Command Container State Variables
var g_globalCommandsShown = false;
```

Step 6: Evaluate the Connection ID of Your Menu Object

Step 4 explained how `onConnectToExternalObject` will receive the `i_ConnectionID` parameter with the connection ID of the external object. You'll evaluate this so you can take the appropriate action with the following statement:

```
if (10 == i_ConnectionID)
    {
    //IF TRUE EXECUTE THIS BLOCK OF CODE
    }
```

This should be placed within the `AppGlue` component `SCRIPT` elements. If this statement is true, you know that the `GlobalCommandContainer` connection has been established.

Step 7: Assigning Out Global Tool Container Object

Following the statement in step 3, you can add the code in response to a TRUE evaluation of the statement. Beginning with the opening brace of the IF statement from Step 6, you can first set the object passed in to your global command container with the following statement:

```
g_globalCommandContainer = i_Object;
```

You are assigning it globally because you will need to access your object later outside the scope of the function. By adding this statement to the code, you are able to assign the global command container to the global variable that you created previously.

STEP 8: SINKING EVENTS FROM YOUR MENU

Next, you must sink events from your menu with the following code within the IF statement block:

```
ConnectObject(g_globalCommandContainer,
 "g_globalCommandContainer");
```

This code will enable you to respond when the user clicks an item on the menu.

If you recall in Chapter 11, you could simply add a connection to each component and you could define functions to respond to events such as the clicking of a button with the following code:

```
function leftButton_OnCommand(i_pIUICommand)
{
...code in response to event goes here
}
```

However, because you are dealing with an external object the events are not sunk automatically. This is the reason why the ConnectObject statement is required. There are cases other than external objects when you may need to explicitly tell Groove to sink events:

- For objects that you want to use something than the default interface
- To listen to events for objects created at runtime. For example, if creating form elements dynamically (such as buttons on a form) you will need to do a ConnectObject to each new component created to sink these component's events.

STEP 9: CHECKING THE CURRENT MENU STATE

After connecting to the command container object in the previous step, you are ready to add the menu items and display the menu. However, this code must first check the global state variable to ensure the menu is not currently displayed. The code in this step should be added directly after the ConnectObject code shown in the previous step:

```
if (!g_globalCommandsShown)
    {
```

So if the g_globalCommandsShown variable is currently set to false, it means the menu is not displayed and you can continue to build and display the menu. Once within the IF statement, you need to toggle the state to indicate that the menu is currently displayed:

```
g_globalCommandsShown = true;
```

Using the globalCommandsShown variable you can ensure that the menu item is not added more than once.

STEP 10: DETERMINE THE POSITION TO INSERT THE NEW MENU

Depending on what menus are currently available, you need to find the next position in which to insert the new menu. To do this without replacing any other menus, you need to find the last menu position and add 1 to it:

```
//Determine position to insert menu
var numMenuPosition =
g_globalCommandContainer.GetNumberOfUICommands() + 1;
```

Adding 1 to this gives you the new empty position where the menu should be inserted. The code should be added directly after the code added in step 9.

STEP 11: ADD THE NEW COMMAND CONTAINER

Using the global variable holding the command container, you now insert a new user interface command container using the following code, which should be placed after the code in the previous step:

```
//Insert a UICommandContainer into the ToolCommandContainer
var globalCommandContainer;

g_menuFileNewCommandContainer =
g_globalCommandContainer.OpenUICommandContainer("GUICC_Options");

globalCommandContainer =
g_menuFileNewCommandContainer.UICommandContainer.InsertUICommandContainer("Take
Survey",
numMenuPosition);
```

You can see in the code that you first had to get a reference to the proper container using the `OpenUICommandContainer` method. This method accepts a single parameter that indicates the URL of the container. In our case, we wanted to use the `GUICC_Options` container. The `InsertUICommandContainer` container accepts two parameters in this order:

1. `URL`: The URL or unique name to assign to the new command container.
2. `Position`: The position index for the new container.

12

> **NOTE**
>
> To find the valid container URLs, you can look at the source for the `standardtrans-ceiver.tpl` file. You can easily look at the file by adding the Groove Database Navigator to a shared space and expanding the templates database. Select `standardtrans-ceiver.tpl` in the list and click the View Document button to view the contents of the file. Within the file, you'll find a component called the `GlobalCommandContainer` that will contain all the valid URLs that can be used.

This function will return a reference to the command container which you've named `pIUICommandContainer` in this example. You need to then grab the interface for this newly created command container:

```
// Ask the UICommandContainer we just inserted for its
//UICommandContainer interface
globalCommandContainer = globalCommandContainer.UICommandContainer;
```

STEP 12: ADDING THE MENU TO THE COMMAND CONTAINER

Now you are ready to begin adding the appropriate menu items. Each menu item is a command within your command container. First, you'll define a variable to hold each command:

```
var pIUICommand;
```

Then you can add the first item using the `InsertUICommand` method on the command container:

```
//Insert the first menu item
pIUICommand = pIUICommandContainer.InsertUICommand("MenuItem1", 0);
```

The `InsertUICommand` method takes two parameters in this order:

1. URL: A string identifying the menu item.
2. POSITION: The new position of the menu item.

The command container index is zero-based so you will use 0 here to indicate it will be the first menu inserted. This method returns a reference to the new command itself so you can set the label that will be displayed for the menu item and the shortcut key combination (mnemonic) for the option:

```
globalCommand.Label = "Take Survey";
globalCommand.Mnemonic = "Alt+M+1";
```

The finished menu is shown in Figure 12.13. The entire code for this example can be found in the `transceiver_menu.tpl`, which you download from the book's Web page by navigating to `http://www.quepublishing.com/` and typing the ISBN (0789726777) into the Search field.

Figure 12.13
The Take Survey option now appears in the Transceiver menu.

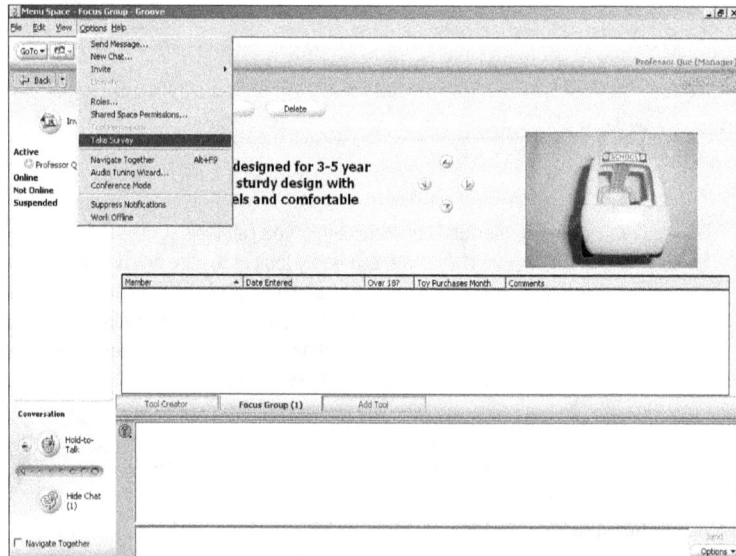

CREATING CUSTOM HELP TEXT FOR YOUR TOOL

Although the Groove tools you create should be intuitive for users, Groove provides the capability to add different types of help text that users can access. You can create three different types of help:

- Overview Help: This help will often show in the right pane of the tool window when the View Overview option is chosen in the View menu.
- Balloon Help: Appearing in a pop-up graphical balloon, this help is used to point out different features.
- ToolTips: ToolTips often appear as pop-up text when a user holds her mouse pointer over a particular object within the tool interface.

CREATING OVERVIEW HELP FOR YOUR TOOL

Groove enables you to create help overview text that will accompany your tool. The following example will demonstrate how to create a help overview for the Focus Group tool, using the code in the FocusGroup_Final.tpl file.

STEP 1: CREATE YOUR HELP TEXT

Overview help should be in standard Rich Text Format. Although you can create your help text manually, it's much easier to do it using a word processor. Most word processors support the format so you can probably use the one you already use daily. In this example, you've created the help text using Microsoft Word. In your example you've added a variety of different text formatting options including italics, bold, font size changes, colored text, and a hyperlink to the Groove Web site. After the document is entered, choose File, Save As and be sure to choose Rich Text Format in the Save as Type field as shown in Figure 12.14.

Figure 12.14
Saving your help file in Rich Text Format using Microsoft Word.

Step 2: Add the `TextView` Component

To support the RTF format, you must first include the `TextView` component. Part of Groove's text tools library, it must be added as a component within your Focus Group tool template. The component can be added within the Tool Creator tool. Load the tool template, click the Components tab, and add the `RichTextView` component from the list. Click the Properties tab. The only property that can be changed within the Tool Creator is the `ReadOnly` property. Set this to true and click the Set Value button. There are a few other properties that you can set, but you'll need to set these manually in the source code. Click the Component Source button and add the following code after the `ReadOnly` property (but still within the `PropertyList` elements):

```
<g:Property Name="BackStyle" Value="transparent"/>
<g:Property Name="MenuStyle" Value="static"/>
<g:Property Name="BorderVisible" Value="false"/>
```

Click the Save button after you've added this code. You can customize the behavior of your text entry area using these properties as follows:

- `ReadOnly`: A setting of true disables editing of the help text by the user. This is the recommended setting.

- `BackStyle`: This can be changed to determine how the background of the text entry area will appear. Opaque is the default setting.

- `MenuStyle`: This can be set to either Normal or Static. You can use the Static setting when you plan on the text within the component not changing. With this setting you won't get all the editing commands like Cut and Paste. However, if you plan on the component contents changing the "normal" setting will provide all the editing commands.

- `BorderVisible`: If this is set to true, a sunken border will be displayed around the editing area. If it's set to false, no border will be displayed.

Step 3: Add the `RTFHelpProvider` Component

Now that you've added the `TextView` component, you need to add the `RTFHelpProvider` component. This works in conjunction with the `TextView` component to provide the overview help functionality. Click on the Components tab in the Tool Creator tool and add the `RTFHelpProvider` component. The Tool Creator tool does not enable you to set any properties except by editing the component source directly. So, click the Component Source tab and add the following properties within the `PropertyList` elements:

```
<g:Property Name="ContextHelpURL"
Value="Help\yourcompany.com\Tools\HelpProvider\HelpProviderHelp.htm"/>
<g:Property Name="ContextHelpDisplayType" Value="0"/>
<g:Property Name="HelpDisplayName" Value="GDK HelpProvider Tool"/>
<g:Property Name="HeaderText" Value="GDK HelpProvider Tool"/>
<g:Property Name="Content" Value="">
   <g:PropertyValue>
   <![CDATA[
   <<<<<<HELP RTF TEXT HERE>>>>>>
```

```
]]>
    </g:PropertyValue>
</g:Property>
```

You'll note that the `Content` property is slightly different than the rest. It is followed by a `PropertyValue` element because this is where your Rich Text Format help text will be placed. The insertion point for the help text source has been noted in the code.

STEP 4: RETRIEVE THE RTF SOURCE AND INSERT INTO COMPONENT

Within the `CDATA` tag in step 3, you need to insert the RTF source code. Because Microsoft Word will automatically interpret the source, you should open the RTF file in a simple editor such as Notepad. In Figure 12.15, you've opened your sample file in Notepad. Although it looks rather cryptic, you don't need to worry about the file details. Click the Component Source tab for the `RTFHelpProvider` and paste the Rich Text Format source between the `CDATA` braces.

Figure 12.15
This is how the Rich Text Format file looks when opened in Notepad.

Although it looks intimidating, there is no need for you to understand all the RTF source details. Just be careful not to delete any of the braces when you cut and paste the RTF file.

STEP 5: ADDING THE COMPONENT CONNECTION

To use the `RTFHelpProvider` component, you must add a connection to the `RTFView` component. Select the Component Source tab and add the following to the `RTFHelpProvider` component:

```
<g:ComponentConnections>
  <g:Connection Name="RTFView" ConnectionID="13" />
</g:ComponentConnections>
```

Be sure that this is placed this within the `Component` container tags and after the closing `PropertyList` element.

Because the Help Overview itself resides outside the tool window and is a part of the Transceiver interface, you'll also note the following external object connection:

```
<g:ExternalObjectConnections>
  g:Connection Name="HelpHandler" ConnectionID="0"/>
</g:ExternalObjectConnections>
```

This connection has already been added for you so you won't have to add any code to establish this connection. When you add the `ComponentConnections`, be sure you do not override this `ExternalObjectConnections` code block.

STEP 6: VIEWING THE RESULTS

If you followed the steps correctly, you should now have help overview text added to the tool. Save the tool template source back into the `\My Templates` folder. Add the new tool to a shared space and you should have the Show Overview option in the View menu. After selecting Show Overview, your help file will be displayed on the right side of the screen as shown in Figure 12.16. You can find the complete code for this example in the `help_overview.tpl` file, which you can download by navigating to `http://www.quepublishing.com/` and typing the book's ISBN (0789726777) into the Search field.

Figure 12.16
Here you can see how the Help Overview text looks that you've added to your tool.

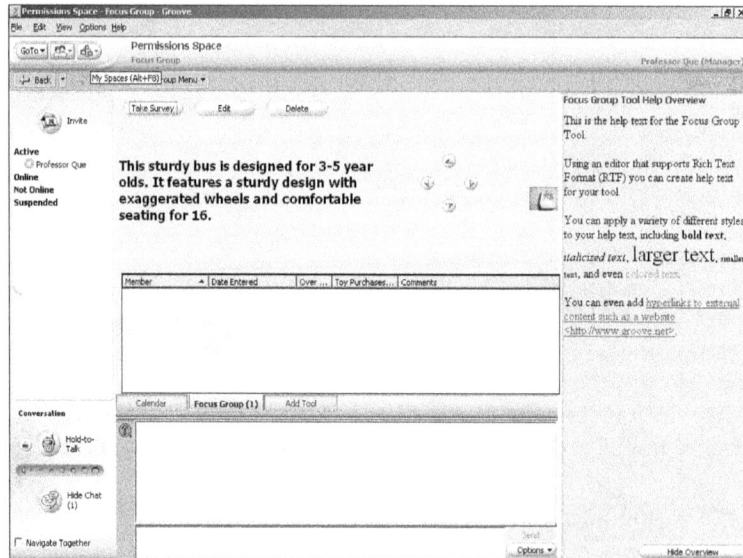

CREATING BALLOON HELP FOR YOUR TOOL

A pop-up balloon help window is very simple to implement. The following example demonstrates how to add balloon help text to your Focus Group tool to help point out the rotate buttons.

STEP 1: CREATE THE LABEL COMPONENT

The text for your balloon help will come from Groove's standard `Static` text component. Using the Tool Creator tool and the tool template from `FocusGroup_Final.tpl`, click the Components tab and add the `StaticText` component. After the component has been added, click the Info tab and change the name of the component to `balloonHelpLabel`.

STEP 2: POSITIONING THE BALLOON HELP

The `balloonHelpLabel` component must be positioned where you want it to appear on the screen. Our Focus Group tool example from Chapter 11 uses the XY Layout because it enables you to precisely position every component. So you will also used this to position your `ballonHelpLabel` component. Choose the `XYLayout` component from the Components tab, select the `Layout` property, and add the following to the layout, as shown in Figure 12.17.

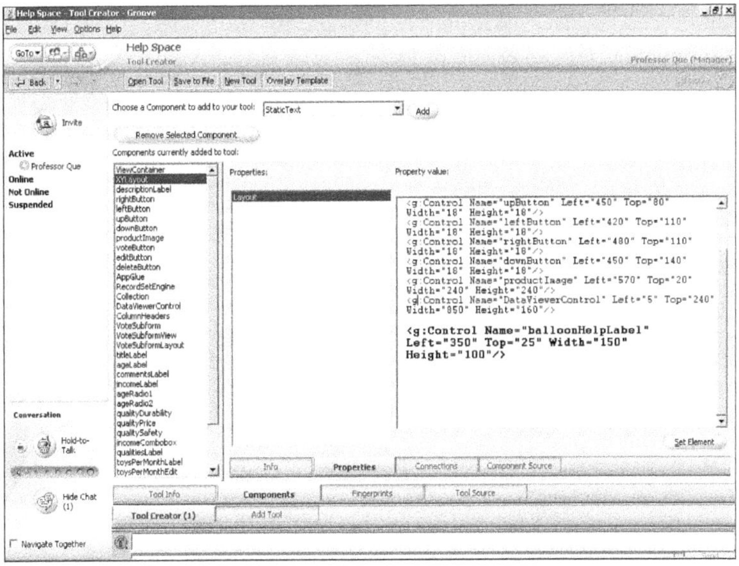

Figure 12.17
You must add an entry to properly position the Balloon help in your XYLayout.

```
<g:Control Name="balloonHelpLabel" Left="350" Top="25" Width="150" Height="100"/>
```

Click the Set Element button after you've made the addition.

STEP 3: ADDING A CONNECTION TO THE XYLayout COMPONENT

In the following step you will be referencing your XYLayout component. To do this, you must add a connection to the component in your AppGlue component. Click the Components tab and select the AppGlue component. Select the Component Source tab and add the following connection after the already defined connections:

```
<g:Connection ConnectionID="10" Name="XYLayout"/>
```

Make sure that this Connection element is added before the ComponentConnections closing element. Click the Save Source button after you've added the connection.

You must add a connection to the XYLayout component so you can access it from the glue code contained within the AppGlue component.

STEP 4: CALLING THE ROUTINE TO DISPLAY THE HELP BALLOON

The final step required is to create the function to display the balloon itself. All of this additional glue code will be added to the scripting host for your form, the AppGlue component. Because you want the help to display when the tool is opened you can add it to the OnViewContainerShow function to display the balloon when the XYLayout view container is displayed.

Within this function, you can call the DisplayControlBalloonHelp, which is a method on the view container itself. Within the Tool Creator tool, select the AppGlue component from the Components tab. Click the Properties tab and you can add the following function within the Source code text area:

```
function OnViewContainerShow()
    {
    XYLayout.DisplayControlBalloonHelp("BalloonHelpLabel", "Use the rotate buttons
to view the product at different angles", 10);

}
```

This method takes three parameters in this order:

- i_Name: The name of the Static text label created for the balloon. The positioning of this static component within the layout will be used for the position of the balloon itself.
- i_Text: The text to appear within the balloon help.
- i_Timeout: The time (in seconds) that the balloon help should be displayed. If this is set to 0 the balloon help will not be dismissed.

NOTE

This is a basic example of creating balloon help that will satisfy most requirements. However, there is additional functionality available such as monitoring balloon help events and moving balloon help once it is created. Refer to the IGrooveUIManager documentation provided for the GDK for additional information.

The complete source for the Focus Group tool with the balloon help enabled is contained in the `balloon_help.tpl file`, which you can download from `http://www.quepublishing.com/` by typing the book's ISBN (0789726777) into the Search field.

CREATING TOOLTIPS

ToolTips are extremely simple to implement. In fact, they have already been added to your Focus Group tool example. They are commonly used to display an interface component's shortcut key as you did with your Vote button with the following line:

```
<g:Property Name="Tooltip" Value="Ctrl+V to vote on this item"/>
```

Many of the common user interface components support the `Tooltip` property. You can see what this ToolTip looks like in Figure 12.18. Refer to the GDK for the list of components supporting this feature.

Figure 12.18
Here you can see the ToolTip information that is displayed when a user holds the mouse pointer over the Take Survey button.

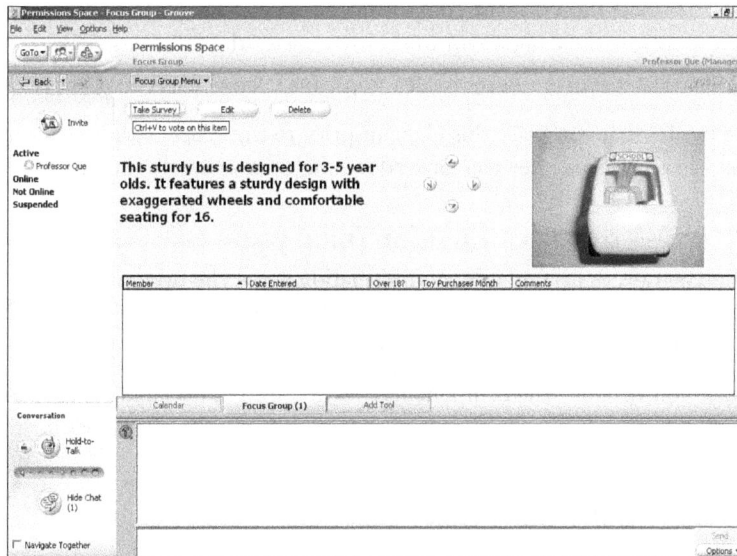

ADDING AN ACTIVEX CONTROL TO THE FOCUS GROUP TOOL

There are literally thousands of ActiveX controls available for use within your tool templates. Some must be licensed while others are offered as freeware. It's possible to use ActiveX controls with or without a graphical user interface. Groove provides the `ActiveXWrapper` component that is used to "wrap" an ActiveX component so the component can be used within a Groove tool. In the following example, you see how this is done by using the Microsoft Text to Speech component to add "spoken" descriptions to your Focus Group tool.

STEP 1: ADD THE `ActiveXWrapper` COMPONENT TO THE FOCUS GROUP TOOL

Load the Focus Group tool template code into the Tool Creator tool. Click on the Components tab and add the `ActiveXWrapper` component.

STEP 2: SET THE `ProgID` PROPERTY

The `ActiveXWrapper` control must know the `ProgID` of the ActiveX control that is going to be used. In this case, you will be using the `ProgID` of the Microsoft Text to Speech control. Click the Properties tab and highlight the `ProgID` property. In the Property Value text box enter the value `TextToSpeech.TextToSpeech.1`. Click Set Value after you've added the value.

STEP 3: ADD THE `ActiveXWrapper` CONTROL TO THE LAYOUT

Like any other user interface component, you must specify the location where the `ActiveXWrapper` component will be placed within the tool template. Click the Components tab and select the `XYLayout` component. Select the Properties tab and select the `Layout` property. Add the component to the layout with the following code:

```
<g:Control Left="5" Height="50" Top="180" Name="ActiveXWrapper" Width="90"/>
```

Be careful that you place this element prior to the `PropertyValue` closing element. Click the Set Element value after you have added the component to the layout.

STEP 4: ADD A BUTTON TO ENABLE THE PRODUCT DESCRIPTION SPEECH

If users want to hear additional information about the product being displayed they can click the Speak button. So you must add a standard button component to the tool template. Click the Components tab and add the `Button` component.

After you've added the component, click the Info button and set the Component name to `speakButton` so you can reference it later. Click the Properties tab for the `speakButton` component and set the following properties:

Autosize: False

Cancel: False

Checkbox: False

Default: False

Enabled: True

Label: Speak

LinkButton: False

Radiobutton: False

SingleLine: True

Style: StandardButton

Tooltip: Click this to hear additional product information.

STEP 5: ADD THE speakButton CONTROL TO THE LAYOUT

Like any other ActiveXWrapper component, you must specify the location where the Speak button will be placed within the tool template. Click the Components tab and select the XYLayout component. Select the Properties tab and select the Layout property. Add the component to the layout with the following code:

```
<g:Control Left="100" Height="50" Top="180" Name="speakButton" Width="90"/>
```

This should be placed after the element added in Step 3 but before the PropertyValue closing element. Click the Set Element value after you have added the component to the layout.

STEP 6: ADD THE CONNECTIONS FOR THE ActiveXWrapper AND THE speakButton

To access the speakButton and your ActiveXWrapper component from your glue code contained in the AppGlue component, you need to add the component connections. Click the Components tab and highlight the AppGlue component. Click the Component Source tab and add the following two connections:

```
<g:Connection ConnectionID="9" Name="speakButton"/>
<g:Connection ConnectionID="10" Name="ActiveXWrapper"/>
```

These should be added prior to the ComponentConnections closing element. Click the Save button after you've added these connections.

STEP 7: ADD THE FUNCTION TO RESPOND TO THE speakButton CLICK EVENT

With the appropriate connection defined in step 5, you can now add a function where you will place the code that will activate the Text to Speech ActiveX control. In the same Component Source tab used in step 5, add the following function:

```
function speakButton_OnCommand(i_pIUICommand)
   {
   //Code to activate the ActiveX component goes here
   }
```

Click the Save button after you've added the function definition.

STEP 8: ADD THE CODE TO ACTIVATE THE TEXT TO SPEECH ACTIVEX COMPONENT

Within the function defined in step 6, you are now able to add the code that will activate the Text to Speech control. Using the default component settings, you only need to make a call to the Speak method and pass in the text to be spoken as the only parameter:

```
ActiveXWrapper.Speak("This product is yellow with four wheels.");
```

Click the Save button after you've added the statement.

12

NOTE

> When developing your own applications that use ActiveX components, you will want to add additional error trapping routines. JavaScript provides the TRY - CATCH block of code that enables you to trap many errors and exit gracefully if one is found. Without proper error trapping, you can be setting yourself up for many different problems including incomplete and corrupt data stored within the local Groove databases.

STEP 9: TESTING THE ActiveXWrapper

With everything in place, you should now be able to test the ActiveXWrapper component and the Text to Speech ActiveX control. Click the Save to File button in the Tool Creator tool. When prompted for the location, save the tool template as focusgroup.tpl within the Groove Installation\Data\My Templates folder. Enter a new or existing shared space and add the Focus Group tool to a space and you should see the screen shown in Figure 12.19.

Figure 12.19
Using the ActiveXWrapper, you have successfully added the Microsoft Text to Speech ActiveX control to your Focus Group tool that was developed in Chapter 11.

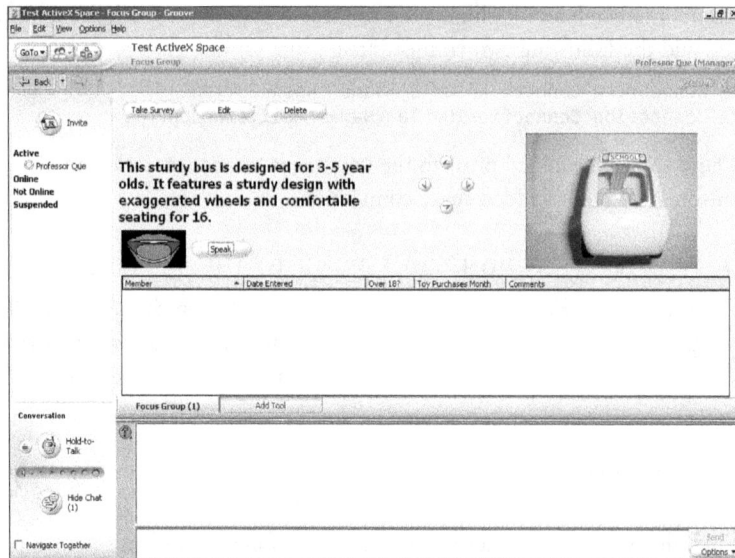

Notice the ActiveX control you placed on the form on the left of the screen. Clicking the Speak button will activate the Text to Speech ActiveX control and you will hear a sentence further describing the product. For this example, we have stuck to the default settings and used only a single sentence for the demonstration. The Microsoft Text to Speech component offers many different configuration options that you can use. Refer to the Microsoft Text to Speech control documentation for more information on the methods and properties supported.

FINDING AN ACTIVEX CONTROL'S ProgID

If you have registered an ActiveX control on your system but are unsure of the ProgID that must be used to reference it, you can find it by following the steps presented in the following example.

STEP 1: START THE REGISTRY EDITOR

Choose Start, Run in Windows and enter **regedit** into the Run field. Then click the OK button and the Registry Editor should start.

STEP 2: SEARCH FOR THE CONTROL NAME

Because you know what the control is that you want to use, you can now search the Registry to find the appropriate ProgID. Under the HKEY_LOCAL_MACHINE\SOFTWARE hive, highlight Classes. Then choose Edit, Find from the menu. Enter your search criteria, as shown in Figure 12.20, and click the Find Next button. Leave all the default search options checked as shown in the figure.

Figure 12.20
Within the Registry Editor you can select Edit–Find to access the search function that is an easy way to find an ActiveX control's entry within the Registry.

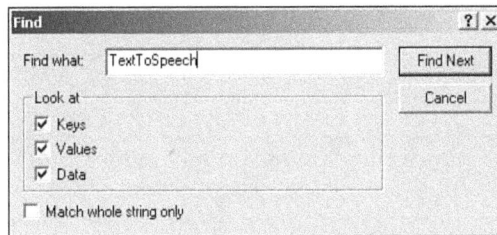

STEP 3: FINDING THE RIGHT REGISTRY ENTRY

After clicking Find Next in step 2, you may need to press F3 several times to find the next entry. You are looking for an entry that contains a ProgID folder. Within this you'll find the ActiveX control's ProgID value. In the example in Figure 12.21, you will use the ProgID of TextToSpeech.TextToSpeech.1.

For more information on how ActiveX controls work, refer to http://www.microsoft.com and search for ActiveX controls.

Figure 12.21
Using the Find function you were able to find the appropriate ProgID for the Microsoft Text to Speech ActiveX Control.

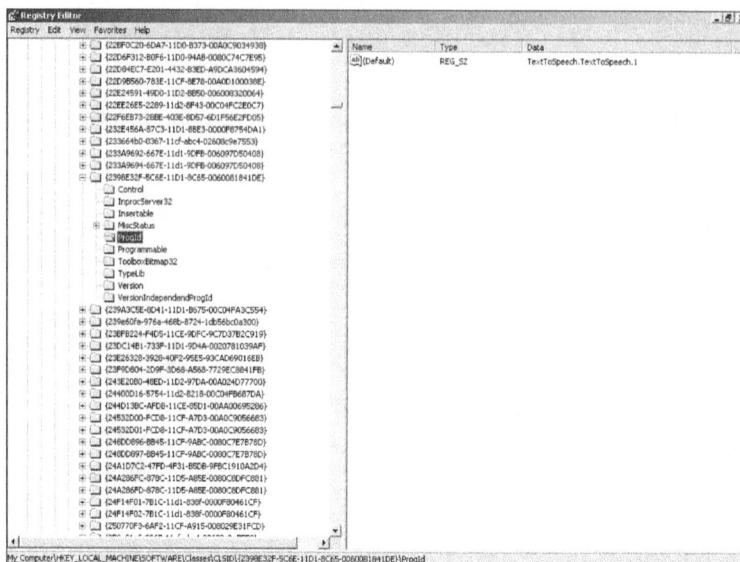

CHAPTER **13**

PUBLISHING A NEW TOOL

A BRIEF OVERVIEW OF THE TOOL PUBLISHING PROCESS

Up to this point we've demonstrated how you can begin creating your own custom tools by writing a tool template. However, you've been creating your tool locally and using the rapid prototyping feature of Groove to test your tool. Although it is still likely that you would use rapid prototyping to initially test your component in a small group, it is not practical for a large scale deployment. For this you need to publish your tool for others to download and inject. Groove uses a modified version of the OSD, or Open Software Description, to package your tool and all required components for deployment within an organization or over the Internet.

In Chapter 4, "Understanding Shared Spaces," you saw how simple it is for a user to inject a new tool into his Groove installation. Although tool injection appears to be a simple one-step process to the user, there are several steps Groove performs behind the scenes to guarantee the integrity of tool installations. When preparing to publish your tool, these steps are important to understand. In Figure 13.1, you can see what happens when a Groove user clicks the .GRV file to inject a new tool. Groove examines the .GRV file to determine where the OSD file is and retrieves the Tool Descriptor file. The Tool Descriptor is then added to the Groove user's account and a copy is stored to disk. Using the version number(s) contained in the Tool Descriptor document, Groove's Component Services can examine the Manifest to determine whether the correct versions of dependent components are present. If components are needed, Groove will download each component using the location specified in the OSD. After all the dependent components are installed, the new tool will be available when the user clicks the Add Tool button in a shared space. Although not shown in the figure, when the tool is first added to a shared space any additional, non-dependent components will be downloaded.

→ For information on injecting additional Groove tools, **see** "Finding Additional Tools," **p. 120**

Figure 13.1
A brief illustration of what typically happens when a user clicks a .GRV file to inject a Groove tool.

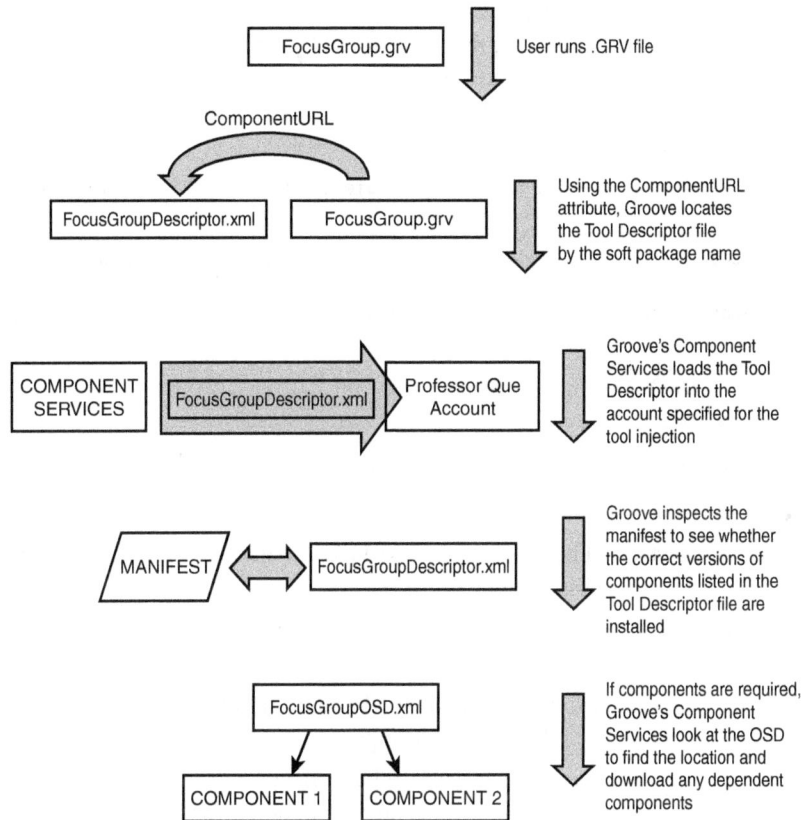

THE TOOL DESCRIPTOR DOCUMENT

The Tool Descriptor file is an XML document that describes a tool and how it will be used within a shared space. The Tool Descriptor contains basic information about the tool, but the tool descriptor's most important job is that it specifies where the Open Software Description file is located. When a user opens a .GRV file to inject a new tool, the Tool Descriptor file is the first file downloaded. Groove will compare the Tool Descriptor contents to what is currently contained in the manifest to determine if any components need downloaded. If a component is not installed, it will reference the OSD specified and download the needed components.

The Tool Publisher tool creates a Tool Descriptor file for you automatically based on the information you've entered into the fields within the Tool Descriptor tab. For most tools, the Tool Descriptor document created will suffice. If your needs are more sophisticated (for instance, if you are using the same Tool Descriptor for more than one tool) you can still use the document as a starting point and edit it manually. For example, the Tool Publisher tool automatically created this Tool Descriptor file for you after supplying some basic tool information:

```
<g:Document Name="Focus Group ProjectDescriptor.xml" xmlns:g="urn:groove.net">
    <g:TemplateDescriptorList>
        <g:TemplateDescriptor Author="Professor Que" LongName="Focus Group tool"
➥Name="FocusGroup"ResourceURL="http://home.fuse.net/groove/Focus%20Group%20Project
.
➥osd?Package=com.yourcompany.FocusGroupTool.focusgroup_tpl&amp;Version=0,0,0,0&amp
;
➥Factory=Open" Type="Tool" />
    </g:TemplateDescriptorList>
</g:Document>
```

The `TemplateDescriptor` element contains several important values, including the following:

- `Author`: The author of the tool.
- `LongName`: The longer name used to describe the tool. This will be displayed within the Add Tools list within a shared space.
- `Name`: A shorter name used to reference the tool.
- `ResourceURL`: This specifies where the OSD file can be retrieved from should Groove need to download components. Within this attribute, there are several important values specified including the following:
  - `Package`: The package to be retrieved from the OSD file. Usually this will be specified using reverse domain notation for consistency.
  - `Version`: The version of the tool. This is what Groove uses to compare against the manifest to determine whether the tool has already been installed.
  - `Factory`: The `Factory` is used to tell how Component Services will install the component. For most components, this will be the Open factory type that specifies the mode of instantiation.

Figure 13.2 shows how a typical Tool Descriptor file is structured.

13

Figure 13.2
The typical Open Software Description document structure for a Groove Workspace tool.

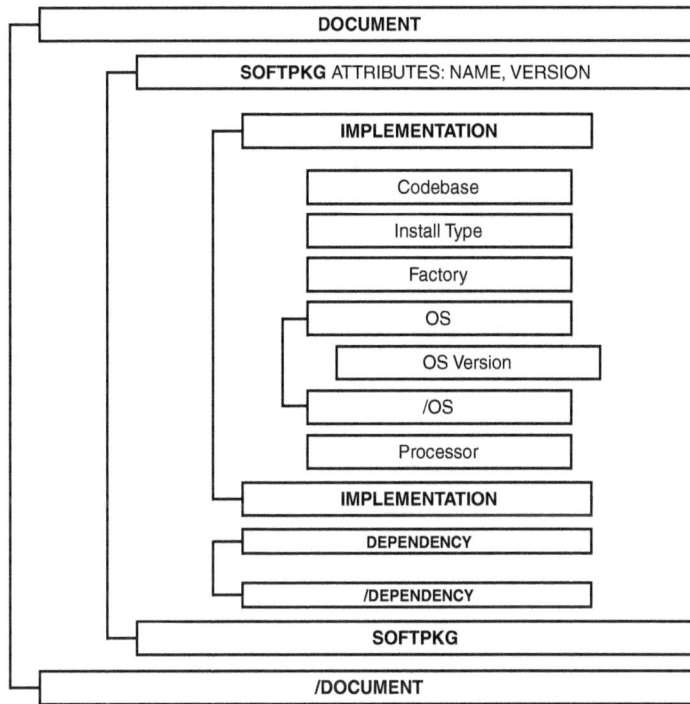

AN OVERVIEW OF THE OPEN SOFTWARE DESCRIPTION

The Internet has proven to be a great tool for deploying software. Now, no matter what the physical location, a connection to the Internet is all that's needed to receive software packages for installation. With interconnected computers the norm, developers now have the option of providing users with a "self service" mechanism so they can download and install their own components without help. However, with the growing complexity and interdependencies of software package components, there needed to be a better way to deploy software.

The Extensible Markup Language is designed to be a standard way to define documents to be transmitted over the Web. This same language was also seen as a great way to aid in software deployment. The Open Software Description is an XML term used to describe the different software components that make up an application and to define any of the dependencies between the components. Being written in XML, the OSD provides a standard way for deployment of software packages. Not only does the OSD standard enable the initial deployment of packages, but it also supports versioning that can greatly simplify the inevitable software upgrades that follow most initial releases. Introduced by Microsoft and Marimba incorporated back in 1997, the Open Software Description is still widely used today.

SUMMARY OF THE OPEN SOFTWARE DESCRIPTION ELEMENTS

An OSD file itself follows the same basic structure. The elements contained within the XML documents used with Groove Workspace tools consist of standard elements defined by the W3C and some that are extensions that Groove has created. A typical Groove OSD file contains these elements and attributes, as shown in Figure 13.2:

- SOFTPKG: The standard SOFTPKG element is used to define single or multiple software packages that might be installed. This is always the base of the OSD file structure. The two attributes you commonly see used for Groove OSD files are
  - NAME: This attribute assigns an arbitrary name to the software package. This is important to remember because it is used in the tool descriptor and the .GRV files you'll be creating later.
  - VERSION: This attribute details the version number of the software. It is in the format major, minor, custom, and sequence version.
- IMPLEMENTATION: This element is a child of the SOFTPKG element. There can be several different types of these for each software package, usually one for production, staging, test, and so on. You will commonly see these attributes and elements included in the document:
  - CODEBASE: As a standard child element, this points to where the software package is located. For example, the YourApp10 GDK sample OSD uses this:
    ```
    <CODEBASE HREF="http://components.yourcompany.com/GDK/Samples/YourApp/
    YourApp10/YourApp10ItemDetails.tpl"/>
    ```
  - INSTALL TYPE: This element is a Groove extension to the OSD and specifies the type of installation for this software package. The available options will be discussed when you use the Tool Publisher tool in the section "Setting the Install Options for Each Project File" later in this chapter.
  - FACTORY: This element is a Groove extension to the OSD and specifies how the software will be instantiated. Most Groove tools will use the Open:
    ```
    <g:Factory Name="Open" Type="XML Document" DatabaseURI="$TEMPLATESURI$"
    DocumentName="YourApp10ItemDetails.tpl"/>
    ```
  - OS and OSVERSION: These standard elements indicate the type of operating system supported and the versions of the operating system supported by the software. The version number is provided in major, minor, custom, and build version format. For example, a Groove tool that is supported on Microsoft NT version 4.0 might include
    ```
    <OS VALUE="WinNT">
        <OSVERSION VALUE="4,0,0,0"/>
    </OS>
    ```
  - PROCESSOR: This standard element indicates the processor the software will run on such as Alpha, MIPS, PPC, or x86, for example:
    ```
    <PROCESSOR VALUE="x86"/>
    ```

■ DEPENDENCY: The DEPENDENCY element can be the child of a SOFTPKG element or an IMPLEMENTATION element. It is used to indicate explicit dependencies between software distributions or different software components. For Groove tools, it is common to find dependencies to such things as record schemas for tools making database changes.

GROOVE'S EXTENSIONS TO THE OSD

So far I've mentioned a few elements that are Groove extensions to the OSD structure. These have been added to support the additional needs of Groove tool template installations. Groove needed a way to allow more granular control of installations than the Open Software Description provides. As you'll see when you publish your own tool, Groove adds the following features that are not part of the standard Open Software Description:

■ The capability to specify individual components and not just complete software packages. This allows the Open Software Description to provide support for installations at the individual component level.

■ The capability to specify the target for installation files. You will see this shortly as you package image files with your Groove installation and have them automatically copied to a specific directory so it can be referenced within your tool template.

■ The capability to specify in which of Groove's underlying databases an XML document should be placed. You will use this feature when you copy your Focus Group tool template into a Groove database.

There will undoubtedly be more extensions to the standard by Groove in the future as needs warrant them. However, this will give you a good idea of how Groove has taken an existing standard and extended it further to accommodate its application needs.

THE GROOVE MANIFEST

Groove needs a way to keep track of all components and descriptors that reside on a particular device. This is more than a list of component names stored in a list somewhere. Groove's modular design allows individual components to be replaced without requiring a total reinstallation of the Groove client. To support these types of piecemeal replacements, Groove must not only know the name of a component but also the current version installed and any other dependencies it may have with other components. This is stored in something called the Manifest, which is an important concept to understand when you begin to deploy your own tools. The Manifest itself is stored in the underlying Groove database called components.xss. Using the Database Navigator tool, you can open this database and select the Manifest.xml document. Click the View Document button after you've selected this file and you should see the document shown in Figure 13.3.

13

Figure 13.3
Use the Database
Navigator to view the
Manifest.

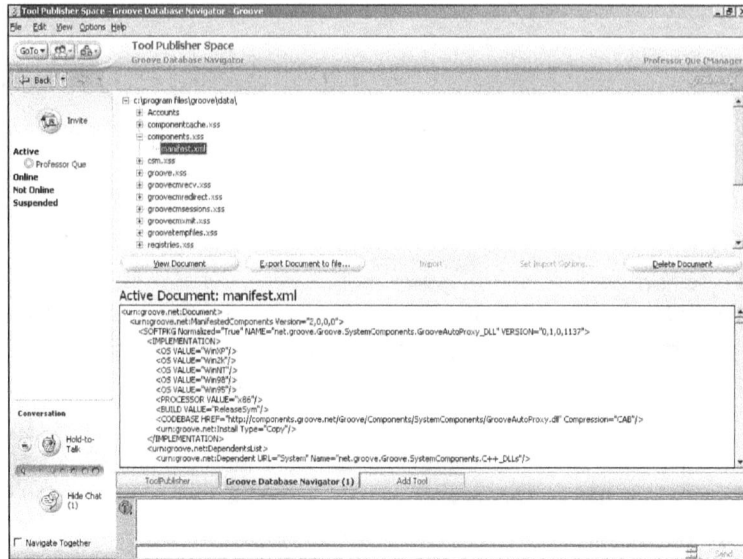

TIP

> The `manifest.xml` file can become extremely large. After clicking the View Document
> button, there may be a delay before the document is shown. You may want to select `man-
> ifest.xml` and click the Export Document to File button to save it to disk. Once saved,
> you can open it within a text editor.

ABOUT VERSIONING GROOVE COMPONENTS

It's important to understand how Groove uses versioning to ensure that published component upgrades work correctly. We touched briefly upon the numbers that make up the version in Chapter 10, "The Foundation for Development: The Groove Development Kit,"
and your brief discussion of the Tool Publisher tool, but let's look at it in more detail.

Adhering to the Open Software Description standard, Groove uses version numbers in the
major, minor, custom, sequence format. For example, a version number of 1,0,0,1397 indicates a major version number of 1, a minor version number of 0, a custom version number
of 0, and a sequence version number of 1397. You should follow these basic principles when
versioning your Groove components:

- Major Version Number: The Major version number is changed when there have been
  drastic changes to the tool. This is usually due to data model changes that make the
  new version of the tool incompatible with the old version. This number should only be
  changed if you do not intend to upgrade current users of the tool to the newer version.
  In other words, you want to avoid an upgrade because the changes would cause a compatibility problem.

TIP

> If you create a new Major version of a tool, there are certain things that you must do to ensure there is no confusion with the previous version of the tool:
>
> - Change the name of any SOFTPKGs included in the OSD so that there is no duplication of prior package names.
> - Rename your tool template (.tpl) file
> - Change the tool name in the tool descriptor file and tool template so users can easily differentiate between the versions
> - Create a new .GRV file specifying the new version
>
> Although these steps must be taken for Major version changes, most tool upgrades will be handled by incrementing the Minor version.

- Minor Version Number: For most tool upgrades, this will be the version that you will increment. When this version number is changed, most users will be prompted to upgrade to the latest version of the component. By incrementing the Minor version number you are guaranteeing that all data stored in the previous version will be compatible with the latest version of the tool. Unlike the changes for the Major version change, you should keep the tool template filename, tool name, and details in the tool descriptor the same.

- Custom Version Number: The Custom version number is an industry standard and is not used by Groove when comparing version numbers. Most Groove tool developers don't use this number because the value has no impact on component installations.

- Sequence Version Number: The Sequence version number is an industry standard and is not used by Groove when comparing version numbers. However, you will note that Groove typically includes the build number of the Groove client in this field for its own set of default tools. This is handy to use for your own customer tools to identify the build number of Groove that the tool was tested with. When a new build or release of Groove is available, you can update the version number once it has been thoroughly tested.

CAUTION

> The sequence version number can be important, especially if you use any features that are in "preview" status. Groove Workspace often comes with new and extremely useful features but mark them as "preview" to indicate they may or may not be included in future releases. By using the sequence version number, you will be better prepared to troubleshoot backward compatibility problems.

13

THE GROOVE MANIFEST CONTENTS

If you examine the Groove manifest contained in the manifest.xml file, you'll notice that it's using the same elements we just described in the Open Software Description discussion earlier. This is not coincidence because it does use the same standard. Think of the Groove manifest as a running Registry that contains entries for any component that was part of the

Groove installation on a particular device. Each entry is identified by a version number so that Groove knows when it needs to update to a newer version of a component or if it already has the latest version so no update is necessary. Let's look at the chess tool's entry in the manifest in the following example to see how component information is stored in the manifest.

STEP 1: SAVE THE `manifest.xml` FILE TO DISK

If you haven't already saved the `manifest.xml` file to disk, add the Groove Database Navigator to a shared space and open the tool. Navigate to the `component.xss` database and highlight the `manifest.xml` file. Click the Export Document to File button and save the file to disk. Open the `manifest.xml` file you just saved in a text editor such as Notepad.

STEP 2: FIND THE FIRST CHESS TEMPLATE ENTRY

If you are using Notepad, choose Edit, Find and search for "chesstemplate". This should bring you to the SOFTPKG entry for the chess tool template which looks like:

```
<SOFTPKG Normalized="True"
NAME="net.groove.Groove.Templates.Tools.ChessTemplate_TPL" VERSION="0,0,0,0">
        <IMPLEMENTATION>
            <g:Factory DatabaseURI="$TEMPLATESURI$"
DocumentName="ChessTemplate.tpl" Type="XML Document" Name="Open"/>
        </IMPLEMENTATION>
        <g:DependentsList>
            <g:Dependent URL="System" Name="net.groove.Groove.Obsolete"/>
        </g:DependentsList>
</SOFTPKG>
```

This is the first entry for the chess tool template. This uses the standard SOFTPKG element to indicate that it is a software component. Using the VERSION attribute you can see this is:

Major Version: 0

Minor Version: 0

Custom: 0

Sequence: 0

This is an early version of the component that is now obsolete. The next step will continue our search for the latest, non-obsolete, entry in the manifest for this component.

STEP 3: FIND THE NEXT CHESS TEMPLATE ENTRY

Choosing Edit, Find and finding "chesstemplate" again will bring you to the next chess tool template entry in the manifest. The SOFTPKG entry will look like this:

```
 <SOFTPKG Normalized="True"
NAME="net.groove.Groove.Tools.Personal.Games.Chess.ChessTemplate_TPL"
VERSION="0,2,0,1137">
….rest of package description is here…
</SOFTPKG>
```

This has brought you to the most recent entry for the chess tool template in the manifest. Looking at the VERSION attribute you can see it contains:

Major Version: 0

Minor Version: 2

Build: 0

Sequence: 1137

While looking at the dependencies for this component tells you that there is more going on with this entry, the versioning is the most important concept to note. This second entry has incremented the Minor Version number to indicate that this is the newest version of the component. If a user attempts to inject another version of the chess tool component, Groove will examine the version number of the component to be injected to see if it is the same, a newer version, or an older version of the latest component entered in the manifest. Subsequent versions of the tool should increment the minor version number or they will not be injected. In fact, by the time you read this, you may very well have a newer Minor Version of the component. In this case, the next version of the tool would likely use a Minor Version of 3, although it can be anything as long as it is greater than 2. The sequence number in this case is used to specify the build version of Groove that the tool was introduced with. In this case, Build 1137 is the Groove client version corresponding to this component.

PUBLISHING A CUSTOM TOOL

Now with your background of the different files used by Groove for publishing a tool, you're now ready to look at a real example. In the following example, we'll show how to take the Focus Group tool that we built in Chapter 11, "Creating a Tool," and prepare it for distribution to other Groove users. You can download the source for the Focus Group tool from the Web page for this book, which you can find by navigating to http://www.quepublishing.com and typing the ISBN for this book (0789726777) into the Search field there.

CREATING A TOOL DESCRIPTOR FILE

First you need to describe your tool and how it will be used within a shared space by creating a tool descriptor file. By using the Tool Publisher tool's graphical interface you can create a file that uses the elements outlined in the "Overview of the Tool Descriptor" section.

STEP 1: OPENING THE TOOL PUBLISHER TOOL

The Tool Publisher tool is provided with the Groove Development Kit. If you have not injected the tool, follow the directions in Chapter 10. Create a new shared space and add the Tool Publisher tool. Once added to the shared space, the Tool Publisher tool should look like Figure 13.4. By default, the Tool Publisher will open to the Project Information tab.

Figure 13.4
The Tool Publisher tool provides a graphical interface to enable you to publish your tools so others may download and install them.

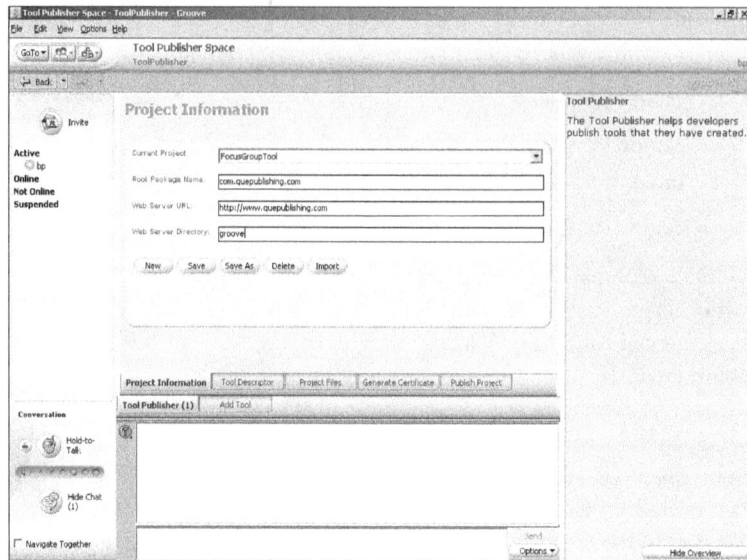

STEP 2: CREATING A NEW PROJECT

The Tool Publisher initially opens to a project named Untitled. You'll want to create a new project for this exercise. Click the New button and you will be prompted to enter a project name as shown in Figure 13.5. Enter the name **FocusGroupTool** in the space provided and click the OK button. This should return you to the Tool Publisher Project Information page with FocusGroupTool now selected in the Current Project drop-down menu.

Figure 13.5
All work in the Tool Publisher tool is identified by its project name that is entered when you click the New button.

STEP 3: ENTERING THE PROJECT INFORMATION

In the Project Information screen you can enter the information that will be used to describe the current project. A *project* can be thought of as a collection of all the files needed to successfully publish a new Groove tool. Up to this point, you've only dealt with creating the tool template in your examples in Chapter 11 and Chapter 12. However, as we explained earlier in this chapter, there are several files needed in addition to the tool template for publishing that are outlined earlier in this chapter. The Project Information page enables you to supply the following information:

- **Current Project:** The name of the project currently selected. All projects you've created using the Tool Publisher will be displayed in this drop-down list box. Selecting a project from the list makes it the active project that the Tool Publisher displays.

- **Root Package Name:** This defines a default base name for all package names within the installation. The recommended format for this name is using reverse domain notation.

  For example the root package name of `com.quepublishing.groove` would automatically be appended to all packages within the installation. In your example, the one package will be your tool template file `focusgroup.tpl`. So if this root package name was used, Groove would automatically append it to the .TPL file making it:

  `com.quepublishing.groove.focusgroup_tpl`.

  You'll note that the period in the template filename is replaced with an underscore. This is a standard replacement you'll see in Groove files so the period is not mistaken as a separator in the name.

- **Web Server URL:** This is the URL on the site that will be providing the components for download. This does not include any paths under the root directory.

- **Web Server Directory:** This is the directory where all the components will be stored. For example, if you set this field to *groove* this will be appended to the Web Server to find the files needed. Using the Web Server URL listed previously, this will translate to `http://www.quepublishing.com/groove`.

For your example, you'll be using the project information shown in Figure 13.6.

Figure 13.6
Here we show all the Tool Publisher project information for your Focus Group tool project.

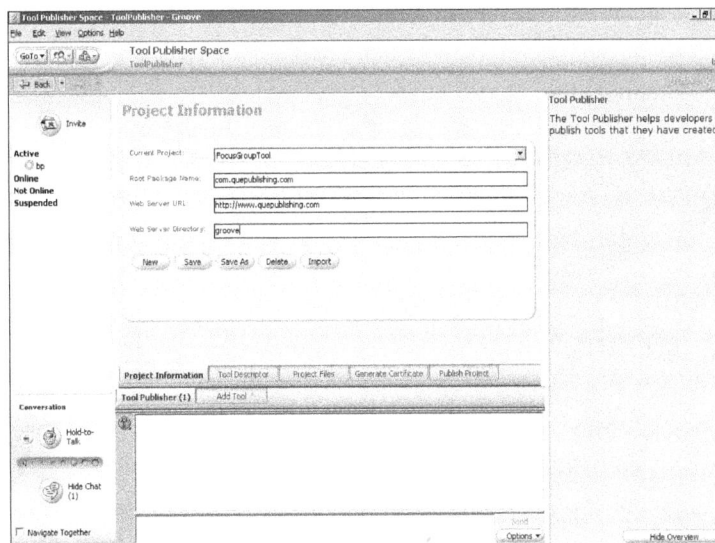

STEP 4: ADDING THE TOOL TEMPLATE TO THE TOOL DESCRIPTOR LIST

Each tool template within a project can have a description stored in a tool descriptor file. By clicking the Tool Descriptor tab you see all the descriptor files created for this project. By default, there are no files included so you'll want to include the Focus Group tool template file that you developed in Chapter 11. The tool template file `FocusGroup_final.tpl` can be downloaded from `http://www.quepublishing.com`. Click the Add Templates button as shown in Figure 13.7. Locate and select the tool template file and click the Open button.

Figure 13.7
Click the Add Templates button to add your Focus Group tool template to the project.

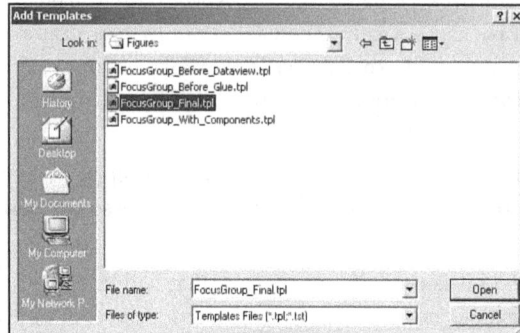

STEP 5: MODIFYING THE TOOL TEMPLATE DESCRIPTOR

After adding the `focusgroup.tpl` tool template file in step 5, you can now modify the tool descriptor properties. As shown in Figure 13.8, modify the following fields:

- Name: Contains the name for the template file.
- Long Name: Contains a longer, usually more descriptive name for the tool template.
- Description: This contains a description of the tool template.
- Author: The author of the tool template.

If you have multiple tool templates within a single project, you can modify the properties for each one by selecting the appropriate template in the list box on the left side of the screen.

NOTE

When you first select the Tool Descriptor tab, you may notice that the tool information you typed previously does not display. No information was lost, you just need to highlight the tool template on the list box again to retrieve and edit the information.

DEFINING THE PROJECT FILES

By using Rapid Prototyping you were able to create and modify only your tool template file in order to see the results. Now that you are intending to deploy the tool to other users, there is additional information required to ensure that the deployment goes smoothly. You can access the Project Files maintenance screen by clicking the Project Files tab.

Figure 13.8
By selecting the Focus Group tool template, you can specify the information that will be contained in the tool descriptor file.

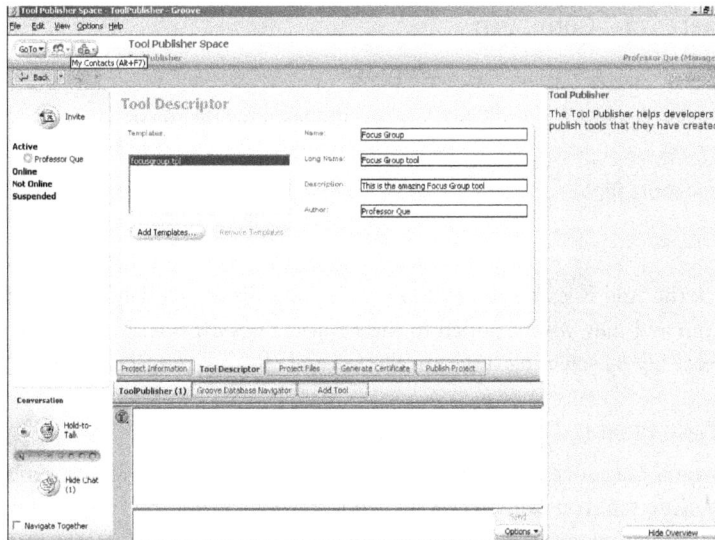

ADDING FILES TO THE PROJECT

By clicking the Info tab (opened by default) as shown in Figure 13.9, you can see all the files currently associated with the project. In the figure you can see the tool template that was added when you created the tool descriptor file along with the tool descriptor file itself. The tool descriptor file is a well-formed XML document created by the Tool Publisher and named by taking the project name and adding `Descriptor.xml` to the end of it. For your example, it has been named `FocusGroupProjectDescriptor.xml`. At this time you should add the rest of the Project files needed for your tool. For your Focus Group tool this includes all the files shown in Table 13.1.

TABLE 13.1   THE LIST OF FILES NEEDED FOR THE FOCUS GROUP TOOL

File	Purpose
`focusgroupschema.xml`	This defines the database schema you will use for the Focus Group tool's underlying data.
`product1.jpg`	An image representing one side of the product being reviewed by the focus group.
`product2.jpg`	An image representing one side of the product being reviewed by the focus group.
`product3.jpg`	An image representing one side of the product being reviewed by the focus group.
`product4.jpg`	An image representing one side of the product being reviewed by the focus group.

continues

TABLE 13.1   CONTINUED

File	Purpose
productB.jpg	An image representing the top of the product being reviewed by the focus group.
productT.jpg	An image representing the bottom of the product being reviewed by the focus group.

Click the Add Files button and select all these files from the file system. Click the Open button and they will be added to the Project Files list box. At any time you may remove a project file by selecting it within the list and clicking the Remove Files button.

SETTING PROJECT FILE PROPERTIES FROM THE INFO TAB

For each file added to the project, you must define additional properties for it. From the same Info tab, you can select a file from the list and set the following properties on the right side of the screen as shown in Figure 13.9.

Figure 13.9
After highlighting each file within a project you can edit the properties of each file.

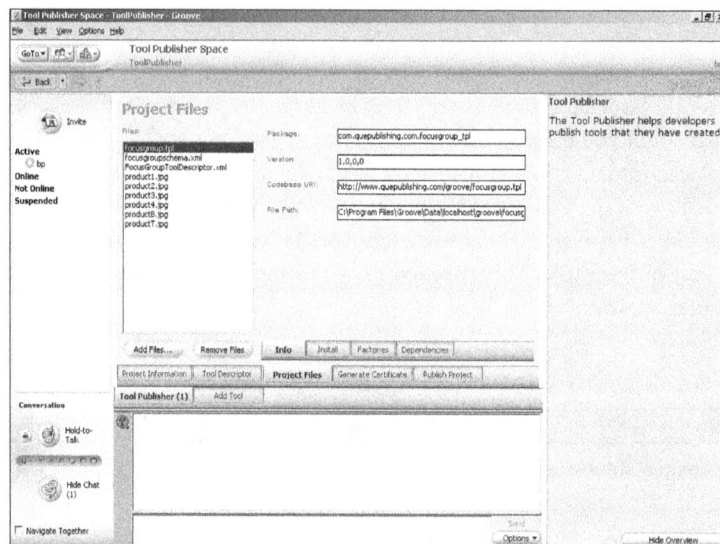

- Package: This field should have been automatically completed using the Root Package Name provided on the Project Information page. The name of the Project File will be appended to the Root Package name. For example, your tool template file focus-group.tpl will contain com.quepublishing.groove.focusgroup_tpl in this field. Note that it will use reverse domain notation and replace any periods with the underscore character.

- Version: Most of the time for custom tools, version numbers for all project files will be the same. However, it is possible to use a different version number for each project file. This will be stored in the format Major, Minor, Custom, and Sequence numbers. For your example here, you will use the Version 1,0,0,0 for all files to indicate that this is Major Version 1 and Minor Version 0 of each file.

- Codebase URI: This field will contain the actual location of the project file when the project is deployed. This will usually be a URL pointing to the resource such as this example, which uses `http://www.quepublishing.com/groove./focusgroup.tpl`.

- File Path: This is the file path where the component is stored on the local file system. This will only be used for the Tool Publisher tool to indicate where the file was originally stored.

SETTING THE INSTALL OPTIONS FOR EACH PROJECT FILE FROM THE INSTALL TAB

Using the Tool Publisher tool, you can specify the different installation options for each file, as shown in Figure 13.10, including the following:

Figure 13.10
You can set the installation options for each file within the project.

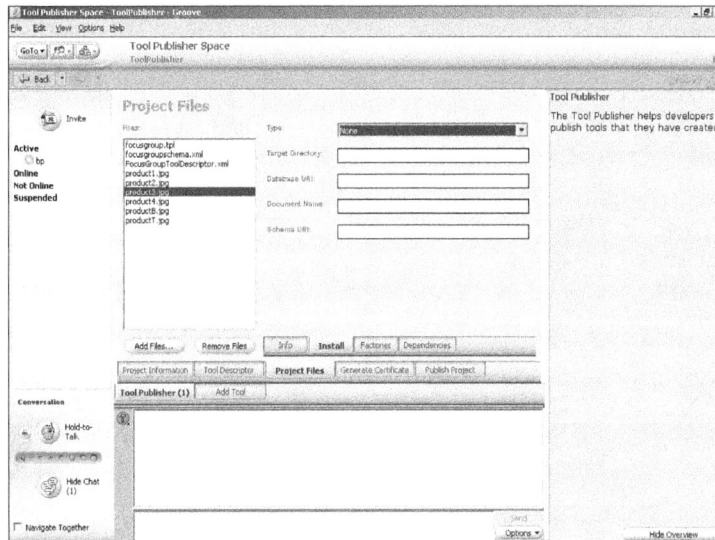

- Type—The type of installation required for this file. You can make a selection from the drop-down list provided. The different options include:

  - Import to XSS: This option is used to import the tool template (.TPL) into a Groove database (.XSS).

  - Copy: Copy is often used to copy the tool descriptor file into Groove's XML data directory. However, this can also be used to copy other files needed for your tool, including graphics files and dynamic link libraries (DLLs).

- Unpack CAB: Cabinet or CAB files are compressed archives that contain files in a particular directory structure. This is often more convenient than deploying individual files. If you are familiar with the Microsoft Windows installation and update process, you may have noticed that it uses cabinet files extensively.
- Install CAB: By reading an information file (.INF) stored within a cabinet file, Groove can install the contents of the cabinet file automatically. This not only includes copying files needed but can perform other tasks such as modifying the Registry.
- InProc Server: For components functioning as an in process server, this install type copies the DLL and registers it in the target client system.
- External: For installations with an executable file such as INSTALL.EXE or SETUP.EXE, this type will execute the program to begin the installation.

■ Target Directory—The target installation directory (if applicable).

■ Database URI—The URI to a database resource (if applicable).

■ Document Name—The name of the project file.

■ Schema URI—The URI to a schema file.

SPECIFYING INSTALL OPTIONS FOR THE TOOL TEMPLATE FILE The tool template file must be added to the Groove manifest so that Groove is aware of the tool and will list it as a tool that can be added to a shared space. Highlight the focusgroup.tpl file as shown in Figure 13.11 and set the properties to the following:

Figure 13.11
Specify these installation properties for the tool template file.

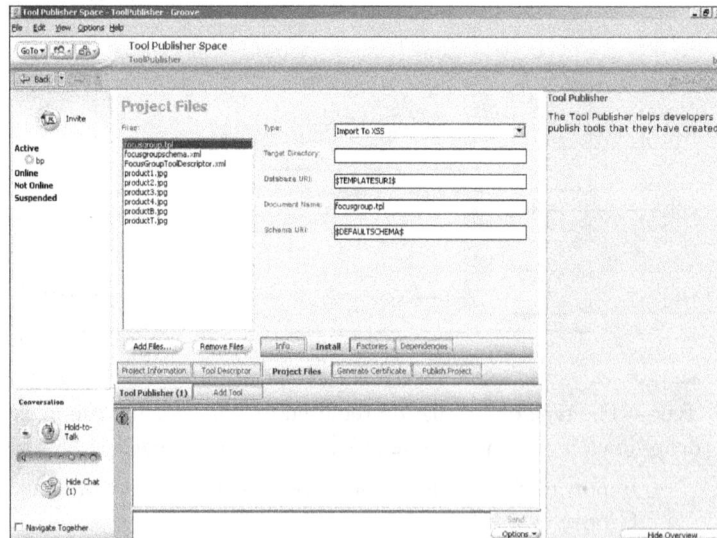

■ Type: Import to XSS

This value indicates that this file must be copied into the Groove database.

- Target Directory: <BLANK>

  Because the tool template is being copied into the database, a place on the file system does not need to be specified here.

- Database URI: $TEMPLATEURI$

  The TEMPLATEURI variable indicates that the tool template should be placed with the rest of the tool templates in the database.

- Document Name: focusgroup.tpl

  This specifies the name of the tool template file itself.

- Schema URI: $DEFAULTSCHEMA$

  Most tools use this variable to indicate that they will use the default database schema provided with Groove.

SPECIFYING INSTALL OPTIONS FOR THE TOOL DESCRIPTOR FILE   The tool descriptor file was created automatically when you set the properties on the Tool Descriptor tab. Clicking on the Install tab and selecting the FocusGroupToolDescriptor.xml file takes you to the screen shown in Figure 13.12. The Tool Publisher tool has automatically specified the Type and Target Directory fields. The field values should contain:

Figure 13.12
After clicking the tool descriptor file you can see that the installation options have automatically been configured.

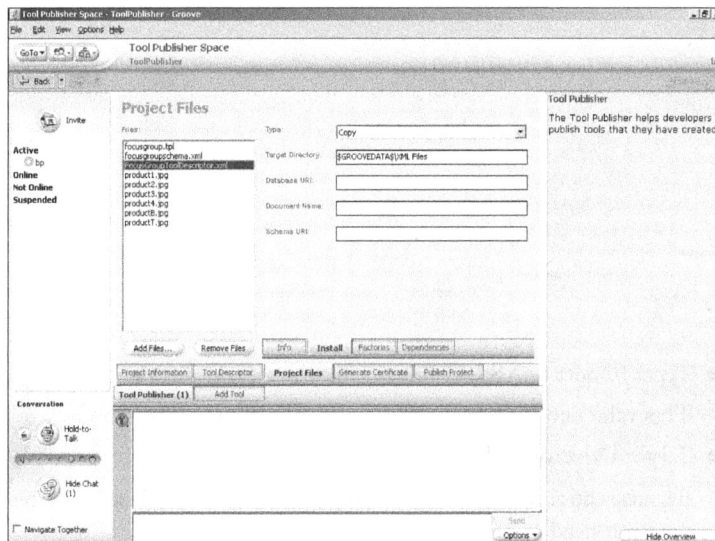

- Type: Copy

  This specifies that the XML tool descriptor file should be copied to a directory on disk. The target is specified in the Target Directory field.

- Target Directory: $GROOVEDATA$\XML Files

  This is the standard location for the XML files that Groove uses. The $GROOVEDATA$ value is a constant that represents the Data folder for this Groove installations. For most installations, this is usually the C:\Program Files\Groove\Data folder but may be different depending on the installation directory chosen.

- Database URI: <BLANK>
- Document Name: <BLANK>
- Schema URI: <BLANK>

SPECIFYING INSTALL OPTIONS FOR THE FOCUS GROUP SCHEMA FILE   You defined your Focus Group tool record schema in the focusgroupschema.xml file. Like the tool template, it must also be copied into the Groove database by specifying the correct installation options. Highlight the focusgroupschema.xml file and set the properties as shown in Figure 13.13:

Figure 13.13
The Focus Group tool record schema used must be copied into the database using these installation options.

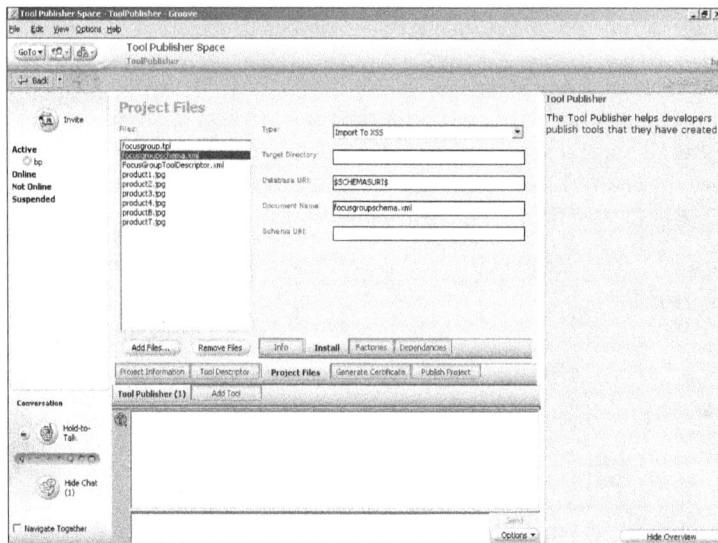

- Type: Import to XSS

  This value indicates that this file must be copied into the Groove database.

- Target Directory: <BLANK>

  Because the record schema is being copied into the database, a place on the file system does not need to be specified here.

- Database URI: $SCHEMASURI$

  The SCHEMASURI variable indicates that the record schema should be placed with the rest of the schemas in the database.

- Document Name: focusgroupschema.xml

  This specifies the name of the schema file itself.

■ Schema URI: <BLANK>

This field is left blank because the schema is located in the default schema location specified by $SCHEMASURI$ in the Database URI field.

SPECIFYING INSTALL OPTIONS FOR THE PRODUCT IMAGES   In the "Adding Glue Code for the Image Rotation Buttons" section in Chapter 11, you added the feature to the Focus Group tool that enabled users to rotate the product image. The rotation is enabled by a collection of images that represent each view of the product. For your tool to use these images, you need to copy each of the images to the user's local file system during the installation. For each of the .jpg images provided, modify the project file installation settings as shown in Figure 13.14:

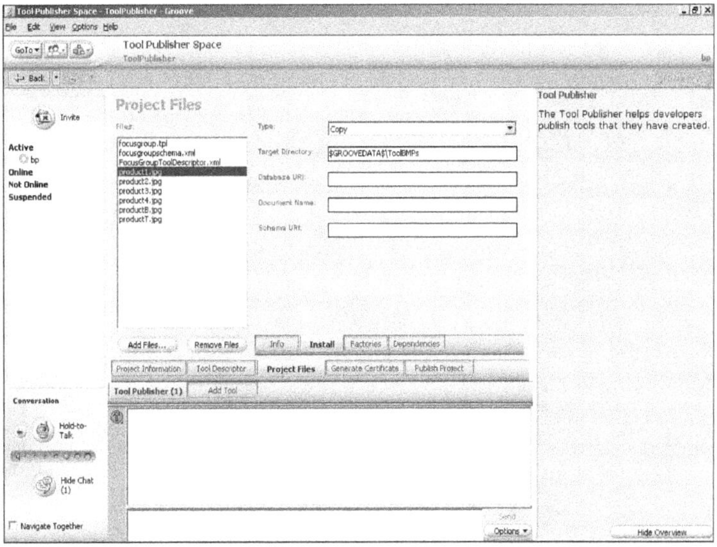

Figure 13.14
These installation options are used to copy each of the images needed for your image control to the specified directory.

■ Type: Copy
■ Target Directory: $GROOVEDATA$\ToolBMPs
■ Database URI: <BLANK>
■ Document Name: <BLANK>
■ Schema URI: <BLANK>

These settings indicate that you will copy the image file to the ToolBMPs folder located under the *Groove installation folder*/Data directory. You are using the variable $GROOVEDATA$ which automatically provides the path to the Groove installation folder.

SETTING EACH PROJECT FILE FACTORY PROPERTIES USING THE FACTORIES TAB

For some project files, you must provide additional information as to how Component Services will handle the file during installation. In your project, you will define factory settings for the tool template, record schema, and tool descriptor file. Because the product image files are simply copied to the file system you will not need any factory settings for them. Thus each of the factory types for each of these will be set to *None*. We'll describe the settings for the rest of the components in the following sections.

SETTING THE FACTORY SETTINGS FOR THE TOOL DESCRIPTOR FILE   The correct settings for your Tool Descriptor file is displayed in Figure 13.15.

Figure 13.15
These Factory settings will be used for the Tool Descriptor file.

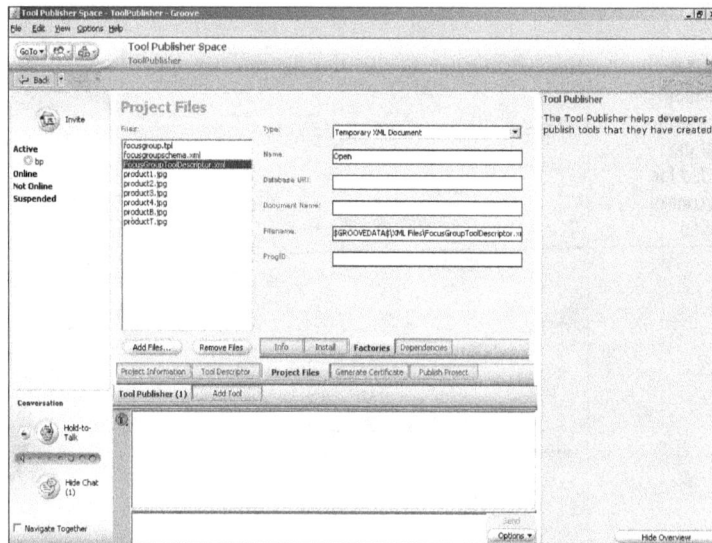

- Type: Temporary XML Document
- Name: Open
- Database URI: <BLANK>
- Document Name: <BLANK>
- Filename: $GROOVEDATA$\XML Files\Focus Group ProjectDescriptor.xml
- ProgID: <BLANK>

SETTING THE FACTORY SETTINGS FOR THE TOOL TEMPLATE FILE   The following settings are displayed in Figure 13.16:

- Type: XML Document
- Name: Open
- Database URI: $TEMPLATESURI$

- Document Name: `focusgroup.tpl`
- Filename: `<BLANK>`
- ProgID: `<BLANK>`

Figure 13.16
These factory settings will be used for your tool template file.

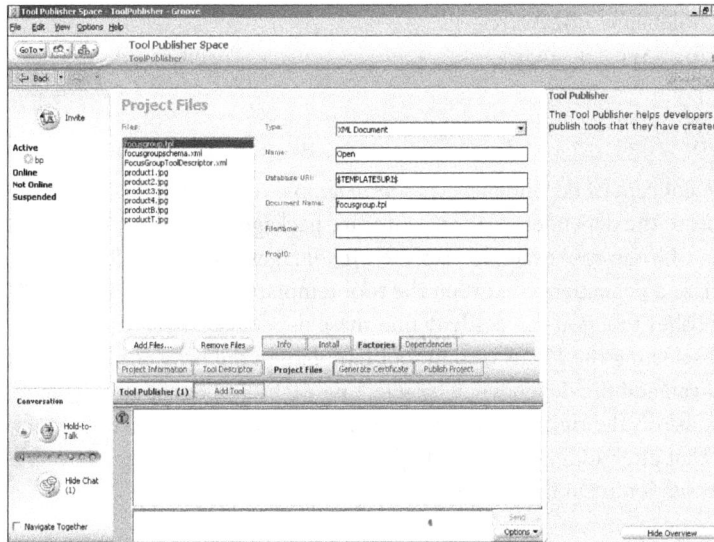

SETTING THE FACTORY SETTINGS FOR THE SCHEMA FILE   The following settings are displayed in Figure 13.17.

Figure 13.17
These factory settings will be used for your record schema file.

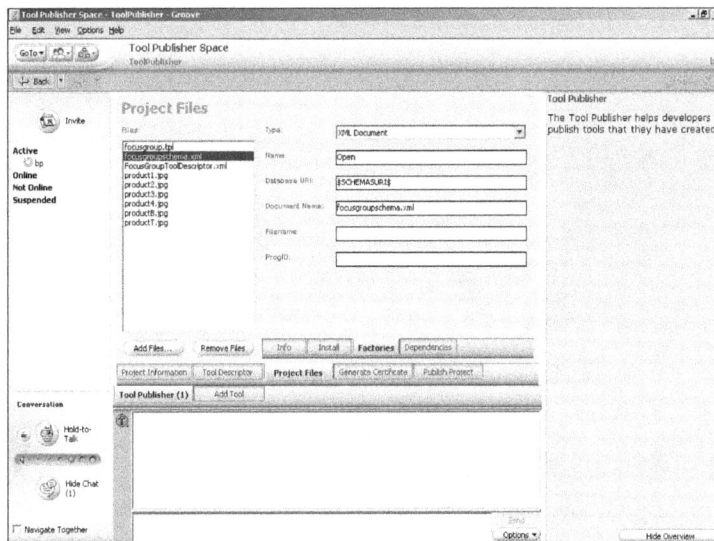

13

- Type: XML Document
- Name: Open
- Database URI: $SCHEMASURI$
- Document Name: focusgroupschema.xml
- Filename: <BLANK>
- ProgID: <BLANK>

SETTING PROJECT FILE DEPENDENCIES USING THE DEPENDENCIES TAB

The concept of dependencies is pretty simple to understand. Dependencies are defined to indicate the dependence of one software package on another file. For example, because your Focus Group tool example uses the .jpg images for the product image display, you should declare a dependency between the tool template and each of the image files. Using the Tool Publisher tool you can easily define these dependencies by clicking the Dependencies tab and selecting the Focus Group tool template in the project files list to the left of the screen. You can add the dependency by selecting each .jpg image in the Choose Dependency targets list on the right side of the screen and clicking the Add button. In Figure 13.18 you can see that after adding three of the image file dependencies they have been moved to the *Depends On* list in the center of the screen.

Figure 13.18
In this example you've established the dependencies for three of the product images to your tool template file.

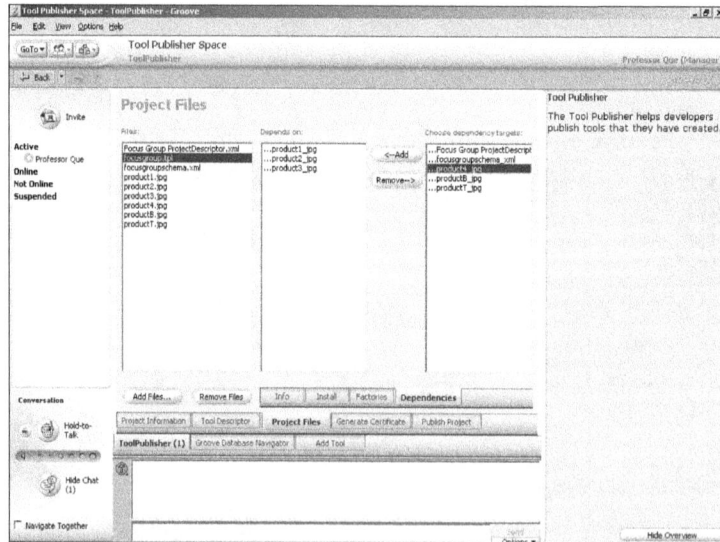

CREATING A SECURITY CERTIFICATE FOR THE PROJECT

Currently, Groove requires that all components be signed by an X.509 digital certificate. The Tool Publisher tool enables you to create such a certificate for use with your component by choosing the Generate Certificate tab as shown in Figure 13.19. This certificate will be used to digitally sign all the components within this project. There are several fields you need to complete to identify the certificate including the following:

Figure 13.19
The Generate Certificate tab enables you to digitally sign your project components.

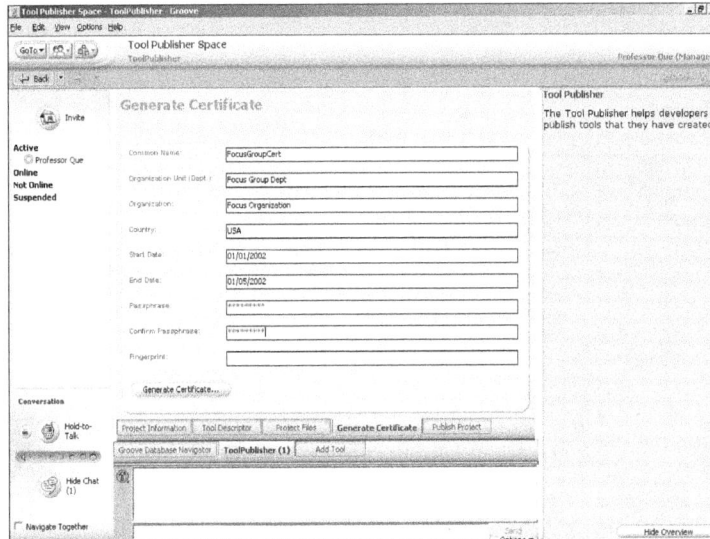

- Common Name: A unique name identifying the certificate being used. This should be uniquely identified so it is not confused with other certificates that have been created in the past.
- Organization Unit: The name of the department creating the certificate.
- Organization: The name of the organization creating the certificate.
- Country: The country of origin of the certificate creator.
- Start Date: The beginning date the certificate is value. This should be in the format MM/DD/YY.
- End Date: The last date the certificate is valid. This should be in the format MM/DD/YY.

NOTE

You should make the interval between the start and end dates as short as you can. It's considered a good practice to help eliminate a tremendous number of these developer-generated certificates from staying active. When the end date is reached, it will not prevent current installs from using the tool, it will only prevent new installs from occurring.

- Passphrase: A passphrase used to secure the certificate. For your example I've used the password spongebob.
- Confirm Passphrase: This field is just used to confirm the Passphrase entered because the Passphrase will not be displayed as you type.
- Fingerprint: This will be generated for you using an algorithm and the passphrase provided.

Click the Generate Certificate button to create the file. You'll be prompted to save the certificate XML document to disk. Choose a familiar place to save the file and click the Save button. After the certificate has been saved to disk, you'll notice that the Fingerprint field has been calculated as shown in Figure 13.20.

Figure 13.20
After completing the fields and clicking the Generate Certificate button a Fingerprint ID will be generated.

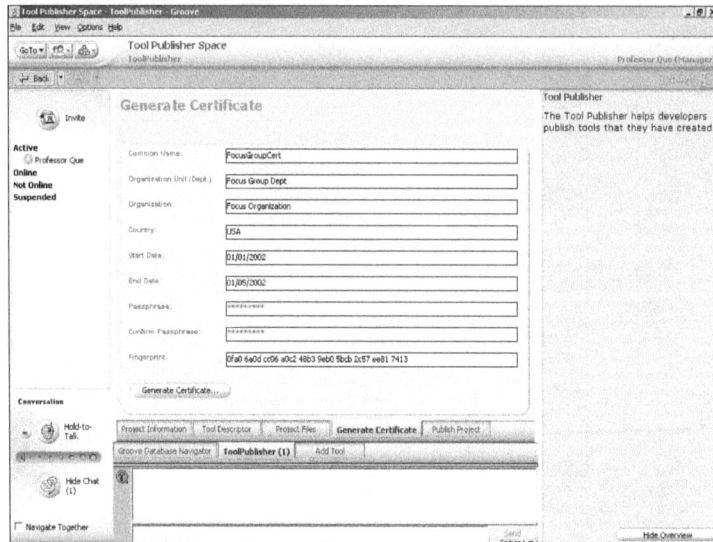

PUBLISHING YOUR PROJECT

After configuring the project and the files that make it up, you are now ready to publish the project. This is the last step in the process and will create files that can be deployed to an Internet or intranet site so others can download your tool. Clicking the Publish Project tab will display the screen shown in Figure 13.21. The screen is split into two sections. The top section is for creating the files while the bottom section is used for signing your Open Software Description file using the certificate you generated earlier. The next two sections outline the details of each section.

CREATING YOUR PROJECT FILES

At this point, the Tool Publisher tool is ready to generate the files needed for the publishing process. There are two fields at this point that need to be completed as shown in Figure 13.21:

- Tool Display Name: This is the actual name that will be displayed once a user injects the tool. It should be descriptive so the user will recognize the tool when choosing tools for addition to a shared space.

- Output Directory: This is where all the files will be placed. This has no impact on the tool injection process but simply states where the files will be outputted.

Figure 13.21
After clicking the Publish Project tab, you have the option for creating the files needed for publishing the tool and signing your OSD file.

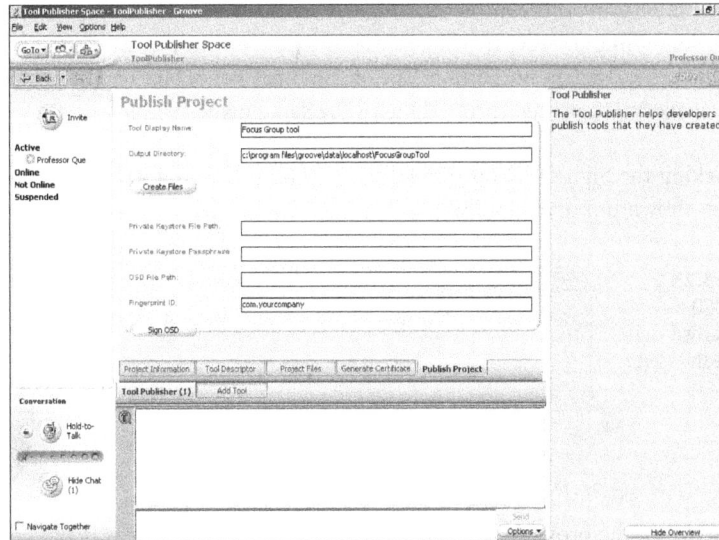

Clicking the Create Files button will output the tool descriptor, .grv file, and the .osd file. It will alert you when the files are created as shown in Figure 13.22. After the files are created, you are ready to digitally sign your project in the next step.

Figure 13.22
An alert is displayed when the tool publishing files have been created.

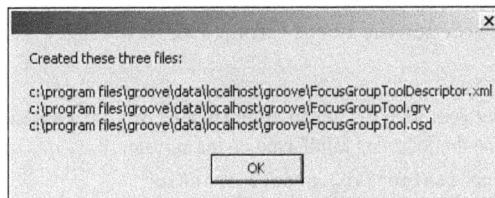

SIGNING THE OSD FILE

Earlier we showed how a temporary certificate can be created using the Tool Publisher tool. Using this certificate you can now sign the Open Software Description file by completing the following fields:

■ Private Keystore File Path: This indicates where the private keystore file is stored that was created when you created the certificate in the section "Creating a Security Certificate for the Project" section. Unless you've moved the file, the value for this field has already been filled in.

■ Private Keystore Passphrase: This is the same passphrase used to create the certificate earlier.

■ OSD File Path: This is where the OSD file should be stored. It will default to the path where the keystore file is stored. However, you can save the OSD file wherever you like.

- Fingerprint ID: This is the Fingerprint ID used to identify the Fingerprint. It should be something unique. It will automatically default to the location of your tool files using reverse domain notation. Most of the time, you won't need to change this unless you have another fingerprint ID with the same name being used elsewhere.

Clicking the Sign OSD button will notify you it has completed the signing by displaying the alert shown in Figure 13.23.

Figure 13.23
After the OSD file has been signed you will receive this alert.

> Signed the OSD File "c:\program files\groove\data\localhost\groove\FocusGroupTool.osd".
> Put the signed OSD file in the directory "c:\program files\groove\data\localhost\groove".
>
> OK

TESTING THE TOOL INSTALLATION PROCESS

Taking all the project files and copying them to a Web server is the next step of the process. Giving each user the URL for the .grv file is all you need to do to distribute the tool. In your example, you would let everyone know they can go to http://www.quepublishing.com/groove/FocusGroupTool.grv to download the tool. After the file is opened the tool injection process should take care of the rest. Not only will the tool template be copied into the Groove database, but also the supporting images, files, record schema, and tool descriptor files. After the process is completed, users adding a tool to a shared space should now see the Focus Group tool in the list.

NOTE

> In order for your Web site to understand that a .grv file is associated with Groove, you must define the following MIME type on the server:
>
> .grv: application/vnd.groove-injector
>
> Consult your Web server documentation for information on defining MIME types.

EXAMPLE: ADDING THE GROOVE INJECTOR MIME ENTRY TO IIS 5.0

To publish a tool to a Web site and have the injection process begin when the user chooses the .grv file, you must properly add the Groove injector MIME type to the Web server. The following steps outline how to add it to a Web server running Microsoft Internet Information Server 5.x.

STEP 1: OPEN UP THE IIS MANAGEMENT CONSOLE

Click Start, Control Panel to open the Microsoft Windows Control Panel. In the Control Panel, click the Administrative Services icon. Click the Internet Services Manager icon and you should be taken to the IIS management console as shown in Figure 13.24.

Figure 13.24
Using the Internet Information Server console you can add the MIME entry.

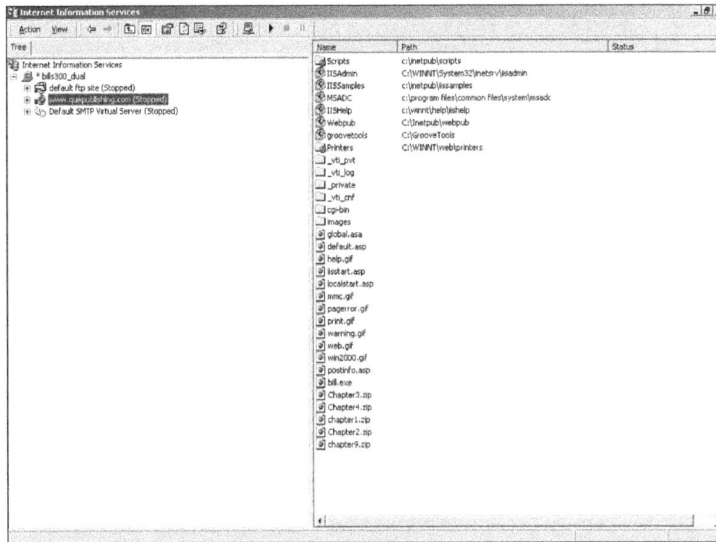

STEP 2: SELECT THE PROPERTIES OF THE SITE

Right-click the site hosting the tool and choose Properties from the drop-down menu as shown in Figure 13.25.

Figure 13.25
Right-click the Web site that will be receiving the MIME entry and choose Properties from the drop-down menu.

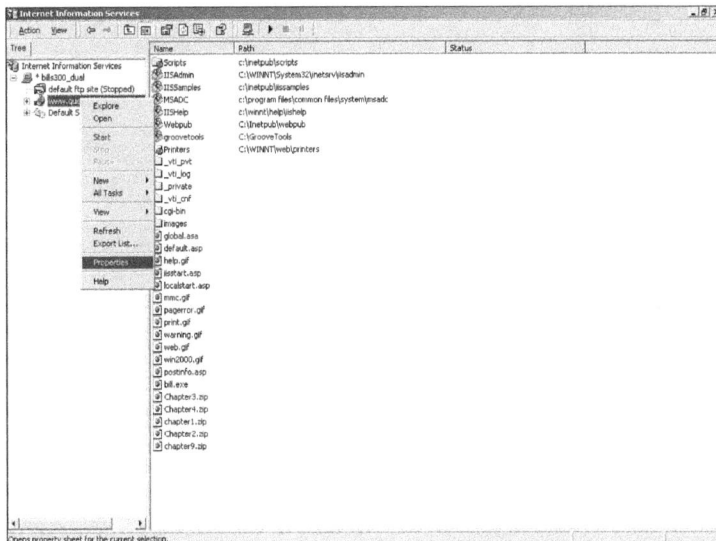

STEP 3: NAVIGATE TO THE HTTP HEADERS TAB

MIME File Types are set within the HTTP Headers tab. Click this tab and you should see the screen shown in Figure 13.26. Click the File Types button to continue.

Figure 13.26
Click the File Types
button to change the
MIME Map.

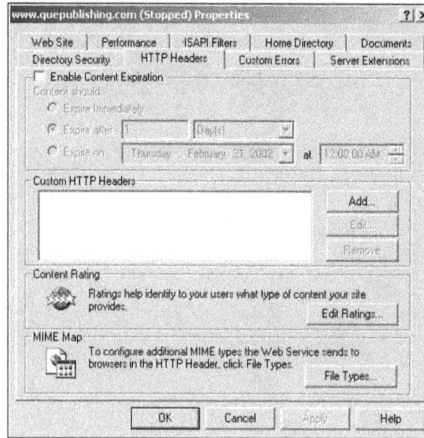

STEP 4: ADD A NEW FILE TYPE

After you clicked the File Types button in step 3, you should see the screen shown in Figure 13.27. Click the New Type button and you will be brought to File Type entry screen as shown in Figure 13.28.

Figure 13.27
After clicking the File
Types button you
should see all the file
types that are config-
ured.

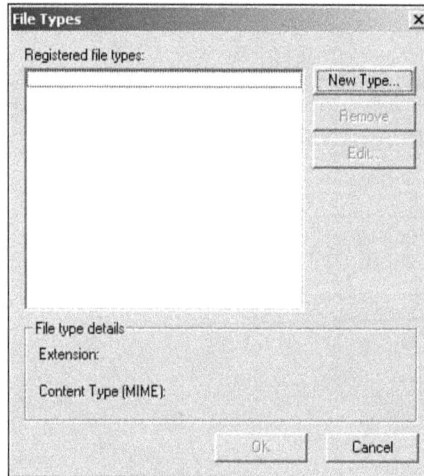

Figure 13.28
After clicking the
New Type properties
you will be prompted
for the type details.

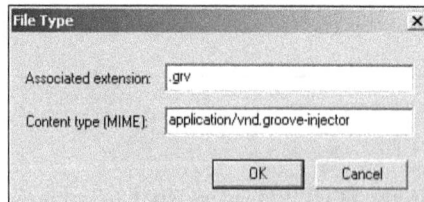

STEP 5: ENTER THE GROOVE INJECTOR PROPERTIES

In the File Type entry screen, enter the following into the fields provided:

■ Associated `extension.grv`

■ Content type (MIME): application/vnd.groove-injector

After shutting down and restarting the Web server, users clicking on any Groove `.grv` files should now have the option to open the file directly and begin the injection process.

TROUBLESHOOTING

I BROWSED TO A SITE THAT OFFERED SEVERAL GROOVE WORKSPACE TOOLS FOR DOWNLOAD. HOWEVER, WHEN I CLICK THE TOOL LINK THAT POINTS TO THE `.grv` FILE I ONLY SEE XML SOURCE CODE IN MY BROWSER. THE TOOL INJECTION NEVER SEEMS TO START.

This indicates that the MIME content type was not set up properly on the Web server. Contact the host of the Web server and have them add

■ The associated `extension.grv`

■ `application/vnd.groove-injector`

TOOL BEGINS THE INSTALLATION PROCESS BUT THE USER RECEIVED AN `Installation failed! Certificate has expired` MESSAGE.

This means the certificate used for the Open Software Description file has expired. Have the tool developer resign the OSD using a certificate with a valid expiration date and reinstall the tool.

TOOL BEGINS THE INSTALLATION PROCESS BUT THE USER RECEIVES AN INSTALLATION FAILED! URL NOT FOUND MESSAGE.

This usually means

■ The `.grv` file points to an OSD file at a URL that is not valid

■ The user is not currently connected to the Internet or intranet where the tool files are stored

FINDING MORE INFORMATION ON PEER-TO-PEER TECHNOLOGY

In this appendix

There are many different exciting peer-to-peer initiatives underway. Some have strictly commercial intent while others are academic efforts. Groove works hard in the peer-to-peer community to champion standards that will become valuable additions to its product. Here are a few resources will help you find out where peer-to-peer technology currently stands and some of the exciting prospects for the future.

PROJECT JXTA

This project (`http://www.jxta.org`), headed by the scientists at Sun Microsystems, is an effort to provide a way for developers to easily create peer-to-peer applications. This architecture is designed to be platform independent as it uses XML almost exclusively for sending messages. In this way, just about any application platform with an XML parser can interpret JXTA messages. JXTA uses a concept called "pipes," which are the conduits for communication between the peers. Initial prototypes implementing JXTA were written in Java, but they maintain that the development moving forward will be language independent.

PEERPROFITS

It's really hard to keep up with all the changes in the peer-to-peer technology arena. Just as one company goes out of business, another starts up. This site (`http://www.whimsical.net/peerprofits/`) is a great way to keep abreast of the newest changes in the industry. In addition to the latest news, you'll also find whitepapers on peer-to-peer and a directory of business contacts working in the peer-to-peer technology industry.

IBM DEVELOPERWORKS

One of the most impressive collections of information about peer-to-peer and other emerging technologies can be found at IBM's developerWorks site (`http://www-106.ibm.com/developerworks/`). Not only can you find information about the peer-to-peer standards being developed, but you can also find information about some of the latest research in areas such as wireless peer-to-peer networking and the peer-to-peer security architecture. To get started, visit the site and search the libraries for "peer-to-peer technology" and other related terms.

OPENP2P.COM

This site, sponsored by O'Reilly, contains a multitude of information about peer-to-peer technology. With a staff of regular contributors, you can find articles about many of the different facets of the technology. Topics are neatly arranged so you can quickly drill down to find original articles or links to articles from other sources. The information found here ranges from technical "how to" articles to other articles dealing with the societal and cultural impact of the technology.

INTEL'S PEER-TO-PEER INITIATIVE

Very often, it's the software companies that you see undertaking most peer-to-peer initiatives. However, when a major chip manufacturer such as Intel entered the fray, it added a new type of player into the mix. Intel's work includes new middleware aimed at enhancing the performance of peer-to-peer services. This site outlines the current work Intel is doing with peer-to-peer and where future endeavors are headed (`http://cedar.intel.com/cgi-bin/ids.dll/topic.jsp?catCode=BYM`).

PEER-TO-PEER WORKING GROUP

The Peer-to-Peer working group (`http://www.peer-to-peerwg.org/`) is a collection of companies working collectively toward a networking infrastructure standard for peer-to-peer technology. Like other groups, they've had their share of issues working with this technology that many believe has not matured yet. They believe that a non-proprietary standard must be developed by the industry before the technology will be embraced.

Appendix A

B

Sources for Learning More About the Extensible Markup Language (XML)

In this appendix

Groove adheres to open standards by using XML documents throughout the application. Whether it is a new tool template or the Open Software Description (OSD) used to publish a tool, a basic understanding of the XML syntax is required. Although many people have heard the term XML, many do not understand even the most basic details of the language. An in-depth exploration of XML syntax is beyond the scope of this book. Luckily there are different places offering assistance.

THE WORLD WIDE WEB CONSORTIUM

If you want to go straight to the source, you can access all the working drafts for the XML standard at the World Wide Web Consortium (W3C) Web site (http://www.w3c.org/XML/). It's a little daunting for beginners due to all the information presented in a sometimes not-so-friendly format, but experienced developers regularly use it as a reference site. The primary goal of this consortium is to develop standards that will enable the continued evolution of the World Wide Web. XML is only one of the common languages they are working on, but probably is the one that has evolved the most dramatically over the past few years. The current version of the XML specification is still 1.0, but by browsing this site you can see there are many different working groups actively working on different facets of the language. On the site, you can browse all working drafts that have been submitted for review by the W3C. After significant review, these drafts can become a formal recommendation by the W3C to the outside community. A very useful overview of what XML is about can be found in "XML in 10 Points" at http://www.w3c.org/XML/1999/XML-in-10-points. Even though this document was drafted back in 1999, the points it outlines still guide the design of the language and its extensions today. They are

- XML is for structuring data.
- XML looks a bit like HTML.
- XML is text, but isn't meant to be read.
- XML is verbose by design.
- XML is a family of technologies.
- XML is new, but not that new.
- XML leads HTML to XHTML.
- XML is modular.
- XML is the basis for RDF and the Semantic Web.
- XML is license-free, platform-independent, and well-supported.

THE ISSUE OF NAMESPACES

Namespaces are a rather confusing topic for many, but one that every Groove tool developer has come across (http://msdn.microsoft.com/msdnmag/issues/01/07/xml/xml0107.asp). In each XML document used within Groove, you'll find a reference to a namespace with a line like this:

```
<g:Document Name="TestTemplate.tpl" xmlns:g="urn:groove.net">
```

Review the information at this link to find a great article entitled "Understanding XML Namespaces," which gives an excellent explanation of what namespaces in XML are and how they work that uses simple-to-understand terminology.

BOOKS ON XML

There are many good books out there on XML. Some are handy as a quick reference and some are more in-depth. A few of my favorites include:

- *XML by Example* by Benoit Marchal, ISBN 0789725045

  For a beginner, it helps to have lots of examples. This book starts with a great introduction to the XML structure, which builds a strong foundation for Groove developers as they construct tool templates, XML descriptor files, and the other files used in tool development and publishing. This book's real world emphasis goes beyond the basics and explores tools you can use to construct XML documents more efficiently.

- *Charles F. Goldfarb's XML Handbook* by Charles F. Goldfarb and Paul Prescod, ISBN 0130651982

  This one has a special place in my collection just because it's written by a man who many call "The Father of XML Technology." This book is a good choice for Web developers who are familiar with HTML already. By explaining the differences between XML and HTML, it does a great job of bridging the gap from those developers who already have Web development experience.

- *Beginning XML*, by David Hunter, et al., ISBN 1861003412

  Although some of this book might be a little too technical for novices, information is presented in a manner that gently eases you into the XML language. Of special interest in this book is a great introduction to writing well-formed XML and a good introduction to the concept of namespaces.

TROLLING THE NEWSGROUPS

The Usenet newsgroups continue to be a great resource for beginners and experienced developers. There are several different groups dedicated to XML including

```
comp.text.xml
```

This is probably one of the most popular groups for discussing the implementation and development of XML.

```
comp.text.sgml
```

Because XML is a subset of SGML, there are still many XML discussions that happen here. However, many discussions here may not specifically talk about XML so it's not the best place to post XML discussions.

```
microsoft.public.xml
```

Because Microsoft has spearheaded a lot of XML initiatives, this is a great place to learn about Microsoft-specific activity in this area. However, non-Microsoft discussions abound here as well. For those interested in XML as it pertains to Microsoft's .NET strategy and other products, several newsgroups have recently been created including the following:

```
microsoft.public.dotnet.xml
```

```
microsoft.public.sqlserver.xml
```

```
microsoft.public.xml.soap
```

```
microsoft.public.xml.soapsdk
```

XML is considered an evolution of the Standard Generalized Markup Language (SGML) so good information on both topics can be found in the group `comp.text.sgml`.

INDEX

A

access control

adding to the Focus Group tool, 430-435

containers, 430

delete button status, 433

engines, 432-433

roles, 432

Roles container, 431

testing, 433-435

Access Control Framework

constraints, 427-429

documentation, 435

engines, 427-429

members, 426

operations, 427-429

permissions, 426-427

restrictions, 427-429

roles, 426

accessing Hosted Services, 264-265

Account and User Identification Subsystem (Groove Framework), 310

accounts

current account information, 80-81

deleting, 96

identities, 86-87

importing, 51-55

log in, 76

multiple computers, 48-50, 95

My Account area, 85, 87-88

online presence options, 96-97

overview, 42-47

saving account information, 48-50

viewing, 53-55

ACID, 312

action items (Meetings tool), 259-260

activating Groove, 41, 95

Active Debugging, 338-342

ActiveX (COM) component development, 353

ActiveX controls, 459-463

ActiveXWrapper component, 459-462

adding

components (tools), 323

contacts, 97-98, 181-183

devices to a domain, 282-283

files to folders listing (Files tool), 210-211

groups, 297

images to Pictures tool, 229

members to a domain, 268-275

note pages (Notepad tool), 237-238

product packages to accounts, 279-280

tools to shared spaces, 141, 163

adjusting microphone/speaker volume, 150

connections, 56-58, 396-397

connectors, 349

conserve mode, 56

constraints, 427-429

Contact Manager tool

  contacts

    adding, 181-182

    importing, 181

    reviewing edited contacts, 182-183

  functionality, 179-180

  keyboard shortcuts, 183-184

  navigating, 180-181

  permissions, 184

  troubleshooting, 184

  viewing contact information, 179-180

contacting users, 86

contacts

  adding, 97-99, 181-182

  aliases, 99

  Contact Manager, 181-183

  copying, 99

  creating, 97-98

  deleting, 98

  exporting, 99

  finding, 98

  handling conflicts, 100

  importing, 99, 181

  keyboard shortcuts, 101

  My Contacts, 97, 183

  non-Groove contacts, 99

  pasting, 99

  removing, 98

  reviewing edited contacts, 182-183

  searching, 98

  shared spaces, 163-164

  updating, 100-101

  viewing, 98

copying contacts, 99

Create Tool Wizard, 319

creating

  contacts, 97-98

  identities, 90-91

  instant messages, 102-103

cryptography, 42

custom components, 352

custom installation policies, 289-292

custom tools, publishing, 475-492

custom version number, 473

Customer Service Manager Viewer, 342-344

Customer Services Subsystem (Groove Framework), 311

cutting event entries (Calendar), 177

D

data exchange counters, 81

Data Model Delegate, 362

Data Storage and Persistence Subsystem (Groove Framework), 311-312

Database Navigator tool (Groove Development Kit), 333-336

databases

  deleting databases, 336

  deleting documents, 336

  importing documents, 335-336

  Manifest.xml, 471-472

  navigating, 334-335

  saving databases, 335

  saving documents to a file, 335

keyboard shortcuts, 224

messages

previewing, 220

reading, 219-220

permissions, 225

topics, 220-223

distributed storage, 17

DLLs, 69

Document element, 350

Document Review tool

functionality, 240

interface, 240-241

keyboard shortcuts, 247-248

permissions, 248

review sessions, 241-247

domain policies, 284-292

domains

adding members to a domain, 268-275

choosing, 266

definition, 264

deleting members from a domain, 276

devices, 282-284

exporting list of domain members, 275

finding members in a domain, 275

groups, 296-298

product packages, 277-282

usage reports, 298-301

viewing members in a domain, 267-268

Download Manager, 312

downloading

Groove Development Kit (GDK), 308

skins, 110-111

DPP (Device Presence Protocol), 10, 68

drawing with Sketchpad

drawing tools, 196-200

freehand drawing, 197

lines, 197

shapes, 197-198

text, 199-200

drop-down menus, 78-79

Dynamic Services, 311

Dynamics Manager, 311

E

edge of the network, 9

Edit component, 355

editing

co-editing, 215-218

custom installation policies, 292

documents, 240-248

event entries (Calendar), 173-174

identities, 89-90

tasks, 252

electronic business cards, 88

elements

!CDATA element, 397-398

Component element, 355

ComponentGroup element, 351-352

ComponentResource element, 355

Document element, 350

Property element, 355

PropertyList element, 355

ToolTemplate element, 350-351

email

identities, 94

shared space invitations, 131

emulation software, 31

engines

Access Control Framework, 427-429

components, 352

definition, 427

RecordsetEngine, 404-406

Files tool

co-editing, 215-218

creating folders, 209

file conflicts, 212-213

files

adding to folders listing, 210-211

creating, 211

deleting, 213

hyperlinks, 213

opening, 211

printing, 213

renaming, 213

reviewing edited files, 214

saving, 211-212

functionality, 208

hiding folders listing, 209

interface, 208

keyboard shortcuts, 214

permissions, 214-215

filtering

meeting display (Meetings tool), 261

task list list display, 253

finding

contacts, 98

members in a domain, 275

tools, 141-142

fingerprints, 326-327

firewall transparency, 23-24

firewalls, 64-65, 67-69

Focus Group tool

access control, 430-435

ActiveX controls, 459-463

capabilities, 346

components, 369-393

creating, 367-393

data collection, 402-408

data viewing, 408-413

engine, 368-369, 404-406

form delegate, 367-368

functionality, 365-366

global variables, 398

glue code, 394-400

GSL file, 436-437

initialization code, 399

install options, 484-485

layout, 367-368, 378-393

menu, 441-452

processing subform data, 420-423

saving, 390

schema, 401-413

screen layout, 366

scripting language, 367-368

source, 475

testing, 393-394, 400-401

user interface, 366

viewing, 390

voting subform, 413-423

folders (Files tool)

adding files, 210-211

creating, 209

creating files, 211

hiding folders listing, 209

opening files, 211

saving files, 211-212

Form Delegate, 361-362

form delegates (tools), 320-321

formatting

Outline entries, 189-190

Sketchpad text, 200

Fortune **magazine, 11**

freehand drawing, 197

full-duplex sound cards, 30

G

groups

adding, 297

moving users into, 297-298

uses, 296

viewing, 296

groupware, 9-10

GRV file, 347

GSLs (Groove Script Libraries)

GrooveAccountTool-ContainerHelper.gsl, 438

GrooveArrayHelper-Functions.gsl, 438

GrooveCalendarHelper.gsl, 438

GrooveCommonTool-CategoryStrings.gsl, 438

GrooveDocumentShare.gsl, 438

GrooveGlobalHelper-Functions.gsl, 438

GrooveTextHelper-Functions.gsl, 438

Focus Group tool, 436-437

uses, 435-436

guest role (shared spaces), 125

H

Hailstorm, 25

help

Help and Support area, 85

Learning Groove sessions, 64

newsgroups, 64

technical support, 64

tools, 144

help text

balloon help, 453, 457-459

overview help, 453-456

ToolTips, 453, 459

helper components, 352

hiding

folders listing (Files tool), 209

Outline entry details, 192

high-function endpoints, 9

Hosted Services

accessing, 264-265

availability, 264

devices, 282-284

digital certificates, 292-295

domain groups, 296-298

domain policies, 284-292

domains, 266-276

logging in, 264-265

product packages, 277-282

usage reports, 298-301

uses, 264

HTML layout, 356-359

hyperlinks

event entries (Calendar), 177

files (Files tool), 213

images (Pictures tool), 229-230

Outline entries, 192

tools, 142-143

I

IBM developerWorks, 498

IDE (Integrated Development Environment), 318

identities, 63

accounts, 86-87

creating, 90-91

default, 90-91

deleting from the directory, 93-94

editing, 89-90

R

RAM, 30

rapid prototyping, 363-365, 423

reading messages (Discussion tool), 219-220

recalling notifications, 83

receiving instant messages, 106-107

recording audio, 151

RecordSetEngine component, 321, 356, 404-406

redisplaying notifications, 83

referencing components, 358

Registry editor, 61

Registry Files (Groove Development Kit), 310, 337

relay services, 23-24

removing

  attached files and URLs from instant messages, 105

  identities from the directory, 93-94

renaming

  files (Files tool), 213

  tools, 139-140

Rendezvoo, 64

replying to instant messages, 107

reports on usage, 298-301

resizing

  images (Pictures tool), 229

  objects in Sketchpad, 201

resource management, 19

reviewing

  documents (Document Review tool), 240-248

  edited contacts (Contact Manager tool), 182-183

  edited rows (Outline tool), 190-191

  event entries (Calendar tool), 174-175

  file changes (Files tool), 214

  shared space changes, 162

revoking

  product packages for a specific domain members, 278-279

  product packages for all domain members, 277

RichTextView component, 454

roles

  definition, 426

  limitations, 426

  shared spaces

    assigning, 125-126

    changing, 126-127

    guest role, 125

    manager role, 124-125

    modifying, 126-127

    participant role, 125

    permissions, 127-128

    uses, 124

rollbacks, 312

rows in outline

  indenting, 189

  inserting, 188

  moving, 189

  outdenting, 189

  reviewing edited rows, 190-191

  selecting, 189

  sorting, 190

RTFHelpProvider component, 454-456

running Groove, 38-40, 75

S

view containers (tools), 319-320, 356-360

viewing

accounts, 53-55

contacts, 98

contacts (Contact Manager tool), 179-180

devices, 282-283

domain members, 267-268

event entries (Calendar), 173-174

groups, 296

images (Pictures tool), 230-231

licenses, 95

Outline entries, 190-191

presence information of tools, 143-144

product packages, 277

sketches (Sketchpad), 195

vCards, 107

views, 168-171, 352

Virtual Message Queue, 315

Visual InterDev

breakpoints, 339-342

script debugging, 338-342

VMWare, 31

volume (microphone/speakers), 150

W

W3C (World Wide Web Consortium), 27, 502

Web and real-time communications, 11

Web Browser tool

Favorites list

adding favorites, 235

creating folders, 235

opening, 234-235

uses, 234

functionality, 233

interface, 233-234

keyboard shortcuts, 236

limitations, 236

permissions, 236

RealName keywords, 234

secure Web sites, 236

visiting Web sites, 234

Web browsers, 31

Web installation, 32-36

Web Services (Groove Framework), 313

Welcome Page

Help and Support area, 85

illustration, 84

My Account area, 85, 87-88

My Contacts area, 85, 97, 101

My Spaces area, 85

purpose, 84

whiteboard. See Sketchpad tool

Win4Lin, 31

Windows 2000, 31

Windows 98, 31

Windows emulation software, 31

Windows for Workgroups, 16

Windows Me, 31

Windows NT, 31

Windows Sound Recorder, 104

Windows XP, 31

WINE, 31

wizards

Audio Tuning Wizard, 149-152

Create Tool Wizard, 319